RESEARCH
DESIGN
IN
COUNSELING

RESEARCH DESIGN IN COUNSELING
Second Edition

P. Paul Heppner
University of Missouri, Columbia

Dennis M. Kivlighan, Jr.
University of Missouri, Columbia

Bruce E. Wampold
University of Wisconsin, Madison

Brooks/Cole • Wadsworth
I(T)P® An International Thomson Publishing Company

Belmont • Albany • Bonn • Boston • Cincinnati • Detroit • Johannesburg • London
Madrid • Melbourne • Mexico City • New York • Pacific Grove • Paris
Singapore • Tokyo • Toronto • Washington

Sponsoring Editor: Eileen Murphy
Editorial Assistant: Julie Martinez
Advertising Communications: Heidi Clovis
Production Editor: Tom Novack
Manuscript Editor: Alan Titche
Permissions Editor: Elaine Jones
Interior Design: Vernon T. Boes

Cover Design: Christine Garrigan
Production Service: Penmarin Books
Composition: The Cowans
Cover Printing: Phoenix Color Corp.

For more information, contact:

WADSWORTH PUBLISHING COMPANY
10 Davis Drive
Belmont, CA 94002
USA

International Thomson Publishing Europe
Berkshire House 168-173
High Holborn
London WC1V 7AA
England

Thomas Nelson Australia
102 Dodds Street
South Melbourne, 3205
Victoria, Australia

Nelson Canada
1120 Birchmount Road
Scarborough, Ontario
Canada M1K 5G4

International Thomson Editores
Seneca 53
Col. Polanco
11560 México, D. F., México

International Thomson Publishing GmbH
Königswinterer Strasse 418
53227 Bonn
Germany

International Thomson Publishing Asia
60 Albert Street
#15-01 Albert Complex
Singapore 189969

International Thomson Publishing Japan
Hirakawacho Kyowa Building, 3F
2-2-1 Hirakawacho
Chiyoda-ku, Tokyo 102
Japan

Printed in the United States of America

10 9 8 7

Library of Congress Cataloging-in-Publication Data

Heppner, P. Paul.
    Research design in counseling / P. Paul Heppner, Dennis M.
Kivlighan, Jr., Bruce E. Wampold.—2nd ed.
        p.   cm.
    Includes bibliographical references and index.
    ISBN 0-534-34517-4
    1. Counseling—Research—Methodology.   I. Kivlighan, Dennis M.
II. Wampold, Bruce E.   III. Title.
    BF637.C6H42   1998
158'.3'0724—dc21   98-29539

WE DEDICATE THIS BOOK TO:

MARY, who continues to be my best friend and partner in life.—P.P.H.

MARY SUZANNE, MARY CLAYTON, and MARTIN,
my real research support group.—D.M.K.

MY STUDENTS, whose enthusiasm for learning is inspiring,
and to MY FAMILY, whose love is nourishing.—B.E.W.

CONTENTS

PREFACE

This second edition of *Research Design in Counseling* represents a substantial revision from the first edition. Because the first edition was well received by students and faculty, we retained its original organization and content coverage. However, each chapter has been revised and updated to reflect new information developed since the first edition was published in 1992. In addition, we have added three new chapters (10, on Qualitative Research; 16, on Outcome Research; and 18, on Program Evaluation) as well as greatly expanded others. In short, the second edition of *Research Design in Counseling* provides more breadth and depth concerning design and methodological issues in counseling research.

This book, like the first edition, was written for those learning the fundamentals of conducting research in counseling. It serves as a text in research methodology courses for master's and doctoral students in counseling psychology and counselor education programs. In particular, the book is aimed at first- and second-year graduate students in the early phases of work on research projects. Although there are numerous research design books in experimental psychology and in education, there is a notable absence of research design texts in the specialty area of counseling.

There are several problems in teaching research methods to graduate students in counseling. Often students are quite anxious about conducting research, and they view research activities (particularly their thesis or dissertation) with more than a little apprehension. Another problem is that some students lack interest in research, in part because they do not adequately understand the philosophy of science, the history of counseling research, and the current research literature. Consequently, when they read a journal article, they are confused by the methodology and procedures and cannot place the study in a broader context of research within counseling. Many times students become too focused on the limitations of research and lose sight of the benefits. Moreover, many students learn about research methods in general research methods courses in other curriculum areas, such as higher and adult education, educational psychology, school psychology, experimental psychology, and so forth. Counseling students often become bored with or confused by research methods taught abstractly (or content-free), or by methods taught with what seems like irrelevant examples from other disciplines (for instance, school psychology).

As with the first edition, a primary purpose of this book is to provide an introduction to the basics of research design that are of particular relevance to counseling. However, the book does not provide recipes for conducting research. Instead, it facilitates a conceptual understanding of research design, with an emphasis on acknowledging the strengths and weaknesses of all designs. Thus, the book does not favor one design over another per se, but rather emphasizes the need to consider the inherent strengths and weaknesses of any particular design in the context of both previous research (knowledge bases) and the particular type of information being sought.

The second edition is divided into four parts. Part One focuses on philosophical, ethical, and training issues. Basic philosophical and paradigmatic issues are introduced, as are the ethical responsibilities of the researcher. The major change from the first edition pertains to separating validity issues from those involved in choosing a particular research design. Specifically, Chapter 3, Choosing Research Designs, now is much smaller and more directly introduces a critical issue in research: drawing inferences or conclusions from data. Chapter 4 then focuses exclusively on Validity Issues in Research Design. We hope that this division of the material makes these important design issues more understandable. The chapter on ethics (Chapter 5) has been updated to include a number of changes in the ethical code from the American Psychological Association and in the fourth edition of *Publication Manual* (1994), as well as revised to introduce the notion of virtue ethics. In essence, Part One establishes the basic foundation for conducting empirical research.

Part Two of the book discusses structural aspects of major research designs: between-groups and within-subjects designs, quasi-experimental and time-series designs, single-subject designs, and quantitative descriptive designs. In these chapters we introduce the strengths and weaknesses of basic research designs and provide research examples from the counseling literature to illustrate the various designs. The most obvious change from the first edition involves expanding coverage of descriptive designs into chapters on quantitative and qualitative research. The quantitative chapter represents a major expansion. Specifically, we have added contemporary critiques of survey research, including a study that documents some of its major shortcomings. We also used Cattell's Data Box (1966) to add a discussion of six different types of factor analysis (O-, P-, Q-, R-, S-, and T-Type factor analyses) to the material on classification or data reduction research. Coverage of passive research designs has been expanded by adding a discussion of moderation and mediation in regression analysis and by providing an example of a study that examined both moderation and mediation. Likewise, Chapter 8, Single-Subject Designs, has been extensively revised to reflect a new conceptual framework for understanding within-subjects measurement. Specifically, Hilliard's (1993) three dimensions for describing intrasubject designs are used to form a typology of single-subject research. Hilliard defines three categories of single-subject designs: (a) single-case experiments, (b) single-case quantitative analyses, and

(c) case studies. In Chapter 8 we describe single-case experiments and single-case quantitative analyses designs. In addition to this new conceptual framework, we have updated the examples used to illustrate these types of studies. Chapter 10, Qualitative Research, is a totally new chapter. It contains an extensive discussion of the worldviews underlying quantitative and qualitative research. Qualitative research is then characterized by comparing it to quantitative research in terms of reality, representations of the world, domain knowledge, intellectual bases, level of inquiry, role of investigator, role of participants, generalizability, bias, validity, reliability, product, audience, control, goals, voice, and power structure. General methods for collecting data (namely, observations, interviews, and existing materials), analyzing data, and presenting data are discussed.

In Part Three we discuss some basic methodological issues in research design: designing and evaluating the independent variable; designing and choosing the dependent variable; population issues; investigator, experimenter, and participant bias; and analogue research. Chapter 12, Designing and Choosing the Dependent Variable, has been extensively revised to reflect changes in the conceptualization of reliability and validity. It describes how reliability and method variance affect the obtained relationships among observed variables. Structural equation modeling, a method for estimating the true relation between psychological constructs, is explained and illustrated. Various types of error and how these errors affect the conclusions derived from counseling research are discussed. Finally, the importance of multiple operations in research is emphasized. Chapter 13, Population Issues, has been revised to reflect the latest thinking on research with various populations. This material is important for understanding and conducting research that is applicable to traditionally underserved populations and is in line with the increased understanding of diversity issues in counseling research.

The final three chapters in Part Three mostly represent new material. Chapter 16, on outcome research, a totally new chapter for this edition, uses Kazdin's (1996) six strategies for conducting outcome research to organize outcome research in counseling. These strategies include (a) treatment package strategy, (b) dismantling strategy, (c) constructive strategy, (d) parametric strategy, (e) comparative outcome strategy, and (f) client and therapist variation strategy. In addition, we provide contemporary examples from the counseling literature of each of these strategies. The later sections of Chapter 16 focus on three important methodological issues in outcome research: (a) selecting the appropriate comparison group, (b) assessing treatment integrity, and (c) measuring change. Chapter 17 represents a major revision from the first edition; this chapter provides a general introduction and overview of counseling process research and discusses some of the complexities of the major design issues in this type of research. The last section of this chapter categorizes and provides examples of instruments used to assess different aspects of counseling process research. A unique feature of this book is its emphasis on methodological issues in counseling process and outcome research, both of which receive a great deal of attention from counseling researchers. Chapter 18, Program Evaluation, is written by Matrese Benkofske and Clyde Heppner, two psychologists who not only have formal training in program evaluation but also a wealth of experience in this area. This chapter describes what program evaluation is, how it is similar to and differs from counseling research, and how program evaluation is used within counseling settings. This chapter nicely extends the traditional parameters of "research" by incorporating a wide range of methodological and design issues into the area of program evaluation.

Part Four focuses on writing and publishing the research report. Many students (and professionals) have trouble approaching that last hurdle—writing. Chapter 19 includes material on research training, a topic that was not included in the previous edition. This material includes ways in which counselor trainers can create an environment that encourages students to conduct research and provides them the skills required to conduct research that will have important outcomes. We hope this section will provide a framework that is helpful in organizing the research report.

Beyond introducing students to basic design issues, a second purpose of this book is to introduce counseling students to the counseling literature. Thus, the text discusses and provides examples of studies not only to illustrate design issues, but also to provide background information on previous research in counseling. Although the book is not comprehensive of all the research in counseling, it provides beginning graduate students an overview of some of the findings of some of the foremost researchers in the profession.

The final purposes of the book are to demystify the research process and to attend to the typical affective reactions of beginning-level graduate students in counseling. Thus, early in the book we focus on issues relating to research training, in part to stimulate discussion among students and faculty about the issues that can arise in various research training methods. Moreover, we focus on and normalize common fears about science in general and about identifying research topics in particular. We have attempted to communicate that research is a challenging and stimulating endeavor—that research can be fun!

Many people have been very helpful in the preparation of this book. Over the past 20 years a number of graduate students in the counseling psychology programs at the University of Missouri, Columbia, the University of Oregon, and the University of Wisconsin, Madison, have contributed ideas and observations and have been a constant source of inspiration, support, and challenge—all of which have ultimately contributed to the development of this book. Moreover, students and colleagues not only at our home institutions but across the United States and abroad—such as at the University College Cork (Ireland) and National Taiwan Normal University—have provided reinforcement as well as identified a number of needed changes. We are extremely grateful for their feedback and encouragement. In addition, we are grateful to the following reviewers who provided insightful suggestions: Gerry Dizinno, St. Mary's University; Thomas Dowd, Kent State University; Joshua Gold, University of South Carolina; Chip Hunter, Barry University; and Saundra Tomlinson-Clarke, Rutgers, The State University of New Jersey.

Likewise, Deborah Harms, Terri Kennedy, and most recently Janet Kelty diligently and efficiently typed innumerable drafts of the chapters and were instrumental in managing all of our writing on the computer. They deserve our sincerest gratitude for deciphering our writing.

It continues to be a delight to work with the staff at Brooks/Cole. Eileen Murphy deserves special attention for her patience, persistence, and cheerful good humor. She and her staff helped immensely in correcting our grammar and clarifying our writing. Tom Novack at Brooks/Cole and Hal Lockwood and his staff at Penmarin Books have done a wonderful job producing the book, not only in polishing our writing but in helping us identify many details that needed our attention.

P. Paul Heppner
Dennis M. Kivlighan, Jr.
Bruce E. Wampold

PART ONE

PHILOSOPHICAL, ETHICAL, AND TRAINING ISSUES

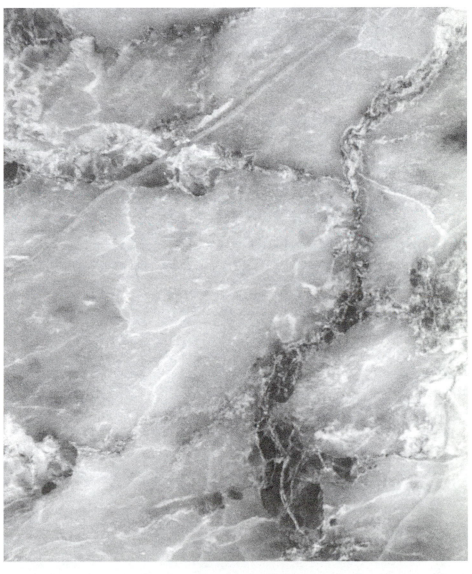

CHAPTER 1

SCIENCE AND TRAINING
IN COUNSELING

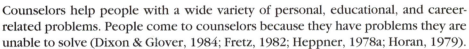

Counselors help people with a wide variety of personal, educational, and career-related problems. People come to counselors because they have problems they are unable to solve (Dixon & Glover, 1984; Fretz, 1982; Heppner, 1978a; Horan, 1979).

We as professionals assume responsibility for not only promoting the welfare of the people who seek our services, but also protecting clients from harm. Thus, as professionals we need to continually update and extend our knowledge about human nature and the field of counseling as well as evaluate our services, especially because the applied nature of our work affects the daily existence of thousands of people.

Consider the real-life example of a husband and wife who sought career planning assistance. After a thorough intake, they were assigned to a computerized career planning program. Both of them completed the program and were amazed to learn that they received exactly the same results.

> Careful checking of the program revealed that the program was reporting scores accurately for the first individual who used the program each day. The second and all subsequent users that day, however, were getting an identical printout of the first user's results. The first user's results continued to appear until the machine was turned off. In essence, every user, except the initial user each day, was receiving invalid results. For us, this resulted in many hours of calling clients to inform them that they had received invalid results. After expressing our shock to the manufacturer, we were told simply: "Oh, yes, we found that out a month ago and it has been fixed on new disks. We'll send you a new set." One wonders how many other career centers never found this error and continued to use a program that gave users blatantly invalid results. (Johnston, Buescher, & Heppner, 1988, p. 40)

This example involves a computer programming error that was not caught through careful evaluation. Many other examples could be listed in which clients receive less than desirable treatments because of outdated information, ineffective or inappropriate counselor interventions, or erroneous knowledge about human behavior and the change process.

Medical professionals also aid people, although they obviously focus primarily on medical problems. The medical profession has advanced over the centuries and has become increasingly more sophisticated. Important lessons can be learned from the trials and tribulations of the medical profession. Consider the historical lesson from the so-called thalidomide babies. In the early 1960s a drug called thalidomide was prescribed in England, Canada, the United States, and several other countries for pregnant women experiencing morning sickness. The drug was administered before adequate empirical tests had been completed. Some medical scientists in England argued that the effects of the drug should have been tested scientifically, especially in comparison with groups of women who did not receive the drug. Others, however, argued more convincingly that it was unethical to withhold (from the comparison group) a drug that was "known" to greatly ease women's problems with pregnancy. For some time after the drug was introduced, a number of medical professionals observed an increase in the number of deformed babies whose arms and legs resembled buds that precede limb development in the human embryo. Years later, after appropriate empirical tests had been completed, researchers discovered that thalidomide administered to women during the critical embryonic period caused these major deformities in the babies. Although the drug was quickly taken off the market, for thousands of infants the damage had already been done.

How do we know whether we are promoting the welfare of or actually harming those who seek our services in the counseling profession? None of us in the profession would intentionally want to harm clients. Counseling, however, can have detrimental effects on people (see Lambert, Bergin, & Collins, 1977). How do we know our interventions are effective? (This question has led to identifying what are referred to as empirically validated treatments; see Wampold et al., 1997.) What is sufficient proof that we as a profession can afford to accept? If someone proclaims that a certain intervention is effective, should we believe it? If your supervisor maintains that a certain technique is effective, is that sufficient evidence? What kind of *knowledge* must a profession be based on to succeed? The answers to these questions rest in the manner in which the profession has developed its knowledge base.

The purpose of this chapter is to examine how the counseling profession has developed its knowledge base. The first half of the chapter focuses on the role of science in the counseling profession. In the second half we introduce you to training issues related to the scientific enterprise in counseling.

THE ROLE OF SCIENCE IN COUNSELING

Science plays an essential role in developing the knowledge upon which the counseling profession is based. In this section we take a close look at science as it relates to counseling. We first discuss different ways of knowing, and particularly the scientific way of knowing. Then we discuss the scientific method as applied to human behavior and introduce you to some of the issues under debate in the philosophy of science. Finally, we discuss some issues pertaining to a philosophy of science for the counseling profession. These philosophical issues are complex and intricate; our purpose is to introduce you to the basic issues, and thus we provide only a brief overview. Nonetheless, these issues form the foundation for future research and training in the profession.

Science as a Way of Knowing

Charles Peirce, a nineteenth-century American mathematician, philosopher, and logician, stated that there are at least four ways of knowing, or of "fixing belief" (Buchler, 1955). The first method is the method of tenacity—that whatever belief one firmly adheres to is truth. These "truths" are known to be true because we have always known them to be true; Kerlinger (1986) noted that frequent repetition of these "truths" seems to enhance their validity! A second method of knowing is the method of authority. If noted authorities such as the president of the United States, a state governor, a well-known psychologist, or a clinical supervisor says it is so, then it is the truth. A third method of knowing is the a priori method, or method of intuition (see Cohen & Nagel, 1934). This method is based on the notion that what agrees with reason, what makes sense, is true. The fourth method of knowing is the scientific method, which involves empirical tests to establish objective, verifiable facts. We would add a fifth way of knowing—what is learned through one's own direct experiences in the world. Through countless experiences, each individual construes a "reality" of the world; some of his or her perceptions may match those of others with similar experiences, while other perceptions and conclusions about the world may not match those of others. Dangers exist if this method is used alone because biases can develop or information can be distorted. Moreover, the events we experience can represent a biased sample, which in turn can lead to inaccurate conclusions.

Given the overwhelming complexity of life and the vast amounts of knowledge needed even in daily living, people most likely acquire "truths" through all five of these ways of knowing. Obviously, error can be involved in any of these ways of knowing. Such error, if it affects the knowledge on which counseling is based, can be dangerous for the counseling profession and our clients. To be credible, reliable, and effective, a profession must be built on dependable facts or truths, rather than on tenacity, decrees from authority figures, or subjective opinions. Knowledge on which to base a profession that aims to facilitate growth and positive change in clients must be based as much as possible in a reality outside of professionals' personal beliefs and biases. The scientific method has been developed to create such knowledge.

Basically, the scientific method is a set of assumptions and rules about collecting and evaluating data. The explicitly stated assumptions and rules enable a standard, systematic method of investigation that is designed to reduce bias as much as possible. Central to the scientific method is the collection of data that allows investigators to put their ideas to an empirical test, outside of or apart from their personal biases. In essence, "the proof of the science is in the experiment" (Ruch & Zimbardo, 1970, p. 40). "Stripped of all its glamour, scientific inquiry is nothing more than a way of limiting false conclusions about natural events" (Ruch & Zimbardo, 1970, p. 31).

There are obvious costs to acquiring knowledge by using the scientific method. Conducting empirical investigations is costly in terms of time, energy, and resources. Putting complex and internal cognitive and affective processes to empirical test is a difficult and elusive task. Sometimes when we try to identify specific processes or variables we become mechanistic and lose the Gestalt, or whole picture. Sometimes the lack of sophistication of our research methods results in conclusions that tell us little about real-life processes.

But the risks of building a profession on nonscientific evidence are far greater. The thalidomide babies are one clear example of the risks associated with not empirically testing one's opinions. Conducting therapy based only on personal hunches and opinions is risky and might well result in harming clients (see Lambert, Bergin, & Collins, 1977, for data regarding client deterioration as evidenced by increased social maladjustment, more negative views about oneself, and decreases in overall problem-solving skills). It is important that the knowledge on which the profession is built be based on objective or verifiable information that can be put to empirical or quantifiable tests. In this way, the methods used to establish our "truths" have a built-in self-correction process; each empirical test is independent of previous findings and can either verify or disconfirm the previous knowledge. In contrast, subjective ways of knowing that do not involve empirical tests run the risk of creating myths. These myths hinder the progress of a profession.

This does not mean that the professionals' beliefs, hunches, and even biases are not useful in exploring ideas and perhaps extending the field's knowledge. We can undoubtedly learn a great deal about human behavior from the more subjective ways of knowing; it is clear that many ideas and breakthroughs regarding therapeutic orientations and techniques have initially sprung from practitioners' direct experience with people. However, it is important to note that these ideas must be empirically tested. In fact, no major orientation has been maintained in the profession without substantial empirical support. Parenthetically, even though the scientific method tends to provide data that are prone to less bias or distortion, Howard (1982) cogently recommended that we "periodically obtain evidence demonstrating the adequacy" of the various assumptions or procedures involved in the scientific method (p. 324).

In short, the knowledge on which the credibility of a profession is based must be objective and verifiable rather than subjective and untestable. Even though the scientific method has costs and is not problem-free, building a helping profession without it is too risky. Credibility is important for the counseling profession as a whole, as well as for each person in the profession.

Science as Applied to Human Behavior

In the mid-1800s there was much confusion and speculation about the nature of human behavior. John Stuart Mill suggested that "the backward state of the moral (human) sciences can be remedied by applying to them the methods of physical science, duly extended and generalized" (Mill, 1843/1953). Not only was Mill's suggestion adopted by the newly emerging social and behavioral sciences, but it has dominated research in these areas ever since (see Polkinghorne, 1983, 1984). The basic philosophy of science that has been generalized from the physical sciences has been referred to as the received view (Putman, 1962) or the standard view of science (Manicas & Secord, 1983). This outlook has drawn heavily on the logical positivism of the 1930s (Hanfling, 1981) and contains the following elements:

1. Knowledge, as opposed to mere opinion, is contained only in statements based on or linked to direct observation. The only kind of statements free from personal bias (and thus distortion) are those grounded in observation.
2. The accumulation of facts or knowledge will result in general laws of human behavior. Human nature is lawful; the goal of science is to identify the causal relationships among variables. The overall goal of science is to develop theories of human behavior, which consist of a network of knowledge statements that are grounded in observation and tied together by deductive logic.

The idea of a rigorous link among observations, hypotheses, and theory was appealing; after all, "the hard-nosed scientist," like the proverbial Missourian, wants to be "shown" the evidence (Manicas & Secord, 1983). In addition, the notion of discovering laws of human behavior based on the accumulation of objective data promised credibility as well as utility for a young profession.

In the past two or three decades, psychology has become more sophisticated in its methodologies and procedures, but the basic elements of the received view of science still predominate within science (Manicas & Secord, 1983; Polkinghorne, 1984). The received view, however, has come under attack from philosophers of science (for example, Bhaskar, 1975; Harre, 1970, 1972; Kuhn, 1970; Lakatos, 1970; Suppe, 1977; Toulmin, 1972). As a result, an alternative paradigm referred to as the realist's view of science has emerged (see Manicas & Secord, 1983, for a brief overview). Basically, this view proposes that (1) knowledge is a social and historical product and cannot be obtained only by studying the individual in isolation; (2) the experiences of an individual, whether observable or not, are appropriate topics of study; and (3) the focus of research should not be on events and finding relationships among events, but rather on examining the underlying "causal properties of structures that exist and operate in the world" (Manicas & Secord, 1983, p. 402).

The received view also has been criticized by counseling psychologists (for example, Howard, 1984; Patton, 1984; Polkinghorne, 1984). Critics have maintained that observations are not absolute but instead are filtered through the subjective, phenomenological world of the observer (see Patton, 1984; Polkinghorne, 1984). Moreover, some have contended that people's subjective internal activities, such as their plans, intentions, feelings, and thoughts, are essential domains of counseling (see, for example, Howard, 1984) and thus merit scientific examination. Finally, it also has been argued that our view of human nature is becoming increasingly more sophisticated (Polkinghorne, 1984), making it more difficult to delineate single "laws" of human behavior, which subsequently makes prediction of human behavior more complex.

The debate over the philosophy of science is exceedingly complex and inter-twined with our view of human nature, the adequacy of our research methods, the content of our research investigations, and the perceived utility of our research findings. The interested reader might explore these issues further by examining some of the following: Bhaskar (1975), Caple (1985), Dar (1987), Harre (1974, 1980), Lakatos (1970), Manicas and Secord (1983), Meehl (1978, 1987), Polkinghorne (1983), Schutz (1964), Serlin (1987), Serlin and Lapsley (1985), Toulmin (1972), as well as the special issue of the *Journal of Counseling Psychology* focusing on the topic of philosophy of science and counseling research (Borgen, 1984b; Dawis, 1984; Ford, 1984; Howard, 1984; Patton, 1984; Polkinghorne, 1984; Strong, 1984; Tyler, 1984).

A Philosophy of Science for the Counseling Profession

With regard to a philosophy of science for the counseling profession, we will dis-cuss four issues: (a) the goals of science in counseling, (b) the importance of methodological diversity, (c) the need to examine and expand our assumptions regarding human nature, and (d) our responsibility for applying research tools. All of these issues affect the quality and type of research conducted within counseling.

Goals of Science in Counseling

Science is a mode of controlled inquiry for developing an objective, effective, and credible "way of knowing." Historically, the basic functions of the scientific approach were typically considered as twofold (see, for example, Kerlinger, 1986). The first function was to advance knowledge, to make discoveries, and to learn facts in order to improve some aspect of the world. The second function was to establish relations among events and develop theories, thereby helping profes-sionals to make predictions of future events. We will now discuss philosophical issues related to each of these functions, specifically within the field of counseling.

In our view, the goal of the scientific method in counseling is indeed to advance knowledge, make discoveries, and acquire facts about counseling. However, in the realm of counseling, phenomena of interest include both observ-able events and subjective, self-reported experiences. Indeed, researchers for some time have examined a wide range of phenomenological or self-report vari-ables in counseling (for example, client satisfaction with counseling, perceived counselor expertise, client self-efficacy, supervisee self-efficacy, and client reac-tions to counselor statements). The expansion of our knowledge is often guided, in part, by pressing questions or problems that professionals in the field have con-cerning their work. For example, one pressing question has been whether client expectations about the counselor or the counseling process affect later outcomes in counseling, such as problem resolution or premature termination (see Hardin, Subich, & Holvey, 1988; Tinsley, Bowman, & Ray, 1988). Or the pressing question may result from a practitioner's dissatisfaction with her or his inability to help certain clients make effective decisions about their career plans (see Rubinton, 1980, for a study that explored the utility of different career interventions for clients with different decision-making styles). Thus, scientific research is designed, in part, to provide answers to pressing questions or problems. In this way, research in counseling can be very practical; in fact, one view is that the adequacy of our research can be evaluated by how relevant the findings are for practitioners (Krumboltz & Mitchell, 1979). Scientific research in counseling can thus increase our understanding by providing data that describe and explain counseling phenomena. In short, there is a great deal of value in the ordinary description of behavior and the human experience.

It is also important to develop knowledge bases and research perspectives that emphasize the social and historical context of the individual. People do not think, feel, or behave in isolation, but rather in the context of a rich personal and social history. Research that increases understanding of how individuals interact within a broader social and personal environmental context is crucial to the development of knowledge about counseling. For example, the role of counseling centers on university and college campuses has received considerable attention since the early 1950s. A critical issue within this line of research has involved the types of problems that are viewed by various groups (such as students, faculty, counseling center staff) as appropriate to explore in a counseling center. (This line of research is sometimes referred to as problem appropriateness research.) In reviewing the research accumulated during a 30-year span, Heppner and Neal (1983) observed that some of the findings seemed inconsistent. However, upon examining the research more closely, especially in conjunction with broader social events, they observed that historical events (such as the Vietnam War) seemed to explain some discrepancies in the research. Thus, the goal of science is to expand our knowledge not only about individuals, but also about the interactions between individual actions and a larger personal, social, and historical context.

Research, however, is guided by more than practical problems. To achieve scientific understanding, the researcher often needs to organize observations and facts into a logical framework that explains some aspect of behavior. Thus, research is often guided by theoretical issues within a line of work and seeks to establish general relations and conditional statements among events that help professionals to understand phenomena. The accumulation of facts or knowledge will not likely result in general laws or broadscale theories of human behavior as it was earlier conceived. Human behavior is multidetermined; that is, a single action can be determined by any one of several preceding events. Moreover, human actions consist of complex chains in which preceding events increase or decrease the probability that some subsequent action will occur, but behavior is not a uniform process across individuals or even within individuals over time. Meehl (1978) likewise concluded that for a variety of reasons (such as individual differences, polygenic heredity, random events, nuisance variables, and cultural factors), human psychology is difficult to scientize and that "it may be that the nature of the subject matter in most of personology and social psychology is inherently incapable of permitting theories with sufficient conceptual power" (p. 829). Thus, the range of human variability and complexity does not much lend itself to description by general principles or broad theories, and even less to prediction.

In short, we are suggesting that it is exceedingly difficult (if not futile) to develop broadscale theories aimed at predicting human behavior in general. However, skilled therapists are able to make better predictions about individual people when they combine research knowledge about specific relations among variables with a host of qualifying information, namely the biographical and social history of the individual. In this way, therapists use "the discoveries of science, but in order to bring about changes in the everyday world, also employ a great deal of knowledge that extends beyond science" (Manicas & Secord, 1983, p. 412). Thus, it is useful for counseling professionals to continue to organize facts and knowledge into theoretical frameworks that can be used as ingredients within more complex conditional models of behavior. Theoretical frameworks that consist of sets of conditional statements that can be qualified by specific information about an individual may allow both the needed specificity and complexity in explaining and predicting individuals' behavior. In sum, we believe that the second function of science is to help explain and predict human action, but in a much more complex and idiographic manner than acknowledged in the received view.

The Importance of Methodological Diversity

Inherent in the traditional view of science was the assumption that the "best" knowledge (and thus best research methodology) could be obtained from tightly controlled, experimental research that used randomization and control groups. There was an implicit hierarchy, with experimental studies at the top and correlational and descriptive studies at the bottom, seemingly based on an assumption that experimental investigations resulted in superior information. We disagree with such assumptions and maintain instead that the selection of the research method must fit both the phenomenon under investigation and the type of information sought (also see Ford, 1984; Howard, 1982, 1984; Patton, 1984; Polkinghorne, 1984). For example, we believe that far too often we attempt to do experimental, between-groups studies before we have an adequate description of some phenomenon; thus, in some cases, descriptive studies might very well yield more useful and important information than a controlled experimental investigation.

There does seem to be a growing consensus for methodological diversity within counseling. Authors such as Borgen (1984a, 1984b, 1992), Ford (1984), Gelso (1979, 1982), Goldman (1982), Harmon (1982), Hill (1982), Hill & Gronsky (1984), Hoshmand (1989), Howard (1982, 1983, 1984), Neimeyer and Resnikoff (1982), Patton (1984), and Polkinghorne (1984) have cogently argued for greater creativity and flexibility in using existing research methods to examine important questions within counseling. Howard (1982) provided a parable that underscores the notion that different methods present advantages and limitations:

> In practice, one never demonstrates that one methodological approach is always superior to another. An elaboration and extension of a parable by the astronomer Eddington might draw this point into sharp relief. Eddington tells of a scientist who wished to catalogue the fish in the sea (the research question).

He took a net of two-inch mesh (a research method) and cast it into the sea repeatedly. After carefully cataloguing his findings he concluded that there were no fish in the sea smaller than two inches. In this apocryphal example, the scientist's trust in the adequacy of his method was somewhat misplaced and led the researcher to draw an inaccurate conclusion. However, if someone had doubted the adequacy of the netting procedure and performed an investigation specifically to test its adequacy relative to some specific alternative procedure, the misinterpretation might have been recognized. For example, our researcher might have considered an alternative research method: namely damming a small inlet of the sea, draining the water, and examining the bodies of the fish left behind. In finding fish smaller than two inches, the limitations of the netting procedure would become apparent. One would not be surprised, however, to find that the largest fish obtained via the damming approach was substantially smaller than was obtained with the netting approach: another potential problem. Therefore, research testing the adequacy of research methods does not prove which technique is better but provides evidence for the potential strengths and limitations of each. From this information, researchers can determine when one of two approaches, or both, should be the method of choice. (p. 319)

Methodological diversity is essential for important advances in the field of counseling and development.

The Need to Examine and Expand Our View of Human Nature

The assumptions one makes regarding the basic qualities of human nature (that is, cognitive, affective, behavioral, and physiological processes) affect how one conceptualizes human behavior. Moreover, our view of human nature affects the research problems we examine in counseling. Our views of human nature have changed dramatically in the past century and are still evolving. Consistent with the beliefs of some of the previously mentioned writers (such as Borgen, 1984a; Howard, 1984; Patton, 1984; Polkinghorne, 1984; Strong, 1984), we believe there is a need to expand our view of how human beings operate, particularly within counseling. One increasingly accepted major change of view concerning human nature pertains to human rationality. For example, Gelatt (1989) has noted that his view of human decision making, especially within a counseling context, has changed dramatically in the last 25 years. In 1962 he stressed rational processes in decision making, whereas in 1989 he stressed intuitive processes and positive uncertainty (that is, accepting uncertainty and inconsistencies). Gelatt's 1989 perspective is consistent with those of a host of other writers who at that time emphasized nonrational and unsystematic processes within human decision making (for example, Heppner, 1989; Meehl, 1978; Strohmer & Blustein, 1990; Tversky & Kahneman, 1981). Related to unsystematic processing are chance events or luck. Meehl has cogently argued that our view of human nature should also include chance events; "luck is one of the most important contributors to individual differences in human suffering, satisfaction, illness, achievement, and so forth, an embarrassingly 'obvious' point that social scientists readily forget" (Meehl, 1978, p. 811).

A number of suggestions have been made for how we might expand our view of human beings, such as human agency (Howard, 1984), phenomenological perspectives within language (for example, Patton, 1984; Pepinsky, 1984), cognitive mediational processes (for example, Martin, 1984), and information processing (for example, Heppner & Krauskopf, 1987), particularly in nonlinear causal chains (for example, Ford, 1984; Maruyama, 1963). It is striking that all these suggestions are process-oriented, thus suggesting that it may be fruitful to examine more dynamic and microscopic processes at this point within counseling research. The major point here is that our view of human nature affects the research problems we examine in counseling. Thus, researchers must examine their assumptions about human nature and be creative in investigating human processes within counseling. In this regard, other areas of psychology (such as social psychology, developmental psychology, and cognitive psychology) provide rich sources of information for investigating basic human processes in a counseling context.

Our Responsibility for Applying Research Tools

Much of the responsibility for adequately applying the scientific method to counseling phenomena rests with researchers. Strong (1984) aptly delineated this issue:

> Scientific development in counseling psychology has not been as helpful to the pragmatic enterprise of counseling and therapy as we would like. It would be wrong to conclude that it has not been helpful, as many practices of counseling today have grown out of scientific efforts, such as behavior therapy, relationship skills, and psychological tests. There is a frustration that scientific efforts have had less pragmatic import than desired. I believe that this state of affairs is not the result of inherent limitations of the scientific enterprise, but of inadequacies in our conceptions of the objects of inquiry—human beings and the phenomenon of behavior change through interpersonal interaction. (pp. 472–473)

The methods of science are only the tools we use to obtain knowledge about phenomena. A flashlight is a good analogy. A flashlight is a useful tool, but it will shine light only where we point it. If we cannot find the object we are looking for with a flashlight, it does not necessarily follow that we should throw the flashlight away, but rather that we should change the direction of the light. Similarly, our research methods will give us information only about the content we examine. If we are dissatisfied with the results, it does not necessarily follow that we should eliminate the research methods, but rather that we should try new angles with our research methods. It is possible, however, that we may need a bigger flashlight, or perhaps a flashlight that can bend around a corner. Thus, sometimes new research methodologies may be needed to help us acquire new or different types of knowledge. Developing new methodologies or alternative ways of collecting data obviously challenges the problem-solving and creative abilities of researchers. Presently, there are many ideas that we cannot examine adequately because we do not have the appropriate methodologies or measurement instruments. Researchers must be creative and versatile not only in the methodologies they use but also in the types of data they collect in examining the phenomena that are central to counseling and human development.

The Importance of a Scientific Approach

Consider this true story of a group of faculty who were ardent believers in Freud's conception of psychoanalysis. These faculty members were relatively isolated from other professionals and had a habit of hiring only their own graduates. (They noted that since they rarely had a faculty opening and the job market was so restricted, they would feel like traitors if they hired someone else's student instead of one of their own.) These people believed that clients' paranoid fantasies could be major obstacles to uncovering unconscious psychological conflicts. Consequently, they would not allow any live recording (audio or visual) or direct observation of therapy sessions. Nor would they allow any kind of written self-report data to be collected from clients. Their primary method of knowing seemed to be the method of authority (Freud), and it included little opportunity to objectively confirm or disconfirm Freud's ideas. Moreover, they so firmly believed in their truths that they scoffed at the utility of other therapeutic techniques such as systematic desensitization, the Gestalt empty chair, and reflection. Consequently, this group of psychologists, in the absence of any objective data, discovered very little beyond Freud's early formulations of the therapeutic process. The bottom line is that this group did not advance the knowledge of their field; by today's standards (as well as students' evaluations), their therapy practices were archaic, and their training philosophies and methods totally inadequate.

This story illustrates how the lack of a scientific approach can hinder growth within a discipline, even to the point of stagnation. The counseling profession will best be advanced by methodological diversity, a broader view of human processes, and tolerance toward a broad range of inquiry systems. Polkinghorne (1984) aptly summarizes this perspective:

> When a discipline gives priority to understanding its object of inquiry over its commitment to a particular research form, and when it recognizes that all research methods—including those developed within the received view—abstract from the object of investigation only certain information, there is a strong indication that this discipline will also open itself to multiple strategies of investigation. It will train its members in the scholarly and rigorous use of the various logics of understanding, and it will support, through its publications and conventions, the sharing of knowledge gained through multiple forms of research. Finally, the discipline will participate in the further development and refinement of all of the research methods that offer understanding and information for practice in the field. (p. 428)

TRAINING IN COUNSELING

Although training within counselor education programs varies considerably, most counselor education programs incorporate science and scientific activities. In this section we discuss the dominant training model, the scientist-practitioner model of training. It is important to note, however, that even within this model there is considerable latitude for various interpretations and training activities. Thus, each of the various training programs that espouse the scientist-practitioner model has its unique interpretations and variations. We first provide a brief overview of the scientist-practitioner model and summarize some concerns about this model. Then we focus specifically on the scientific domain of training and discuss ideas needed to broaden our concept of scientific training within two areas: basic scientific thinking skills and basic research application skills. Finally, we discuss students' typical reactions to scientific activities and delineate training strategies.

The Scientist-Practitioner Model

Most graduate training programs in counseling espouse the scientist-practitioner model of training. The scientist-practitioner model has been referred to as a "living tradition"; it is "one of our oldest ideas; it remains the foundation of most training programs" (Claiborn, 1984). Basically this model consists of training in both scientific and practitioner activities. The scientific activities include courses such as statistics, research design, evaluation, counseling research literature, and philosophy of science, while the practice-oriented side includes courses such as counseling methods, counseling theories, personality, assessment, and practica.

When students enter a graduate training program in counseling, they typically have a wide range of interests along the scientist-practitioner continuum. Most students are primarily interested in being practitioners, a few are interested in being researchers, and others are interested in both research and practice. (It is crucial to note that these interests often change over time, not only during graduate training but throughout one's career as well; thus, later in this section we discuss the need for students to prepare themselves broadly to allow for career changes over time.)

The scientist-practitioner model goes back almost 50 years. The first national conferences for the training of clinical and counseling psychologists were held in Boulder, Colorado, and Ann Arbor, Michigan, in 1949 and 1950, respectively. One major purpose of the Boulder conference was to develop a broad model of training. After two weeks of meeting daily, the clinical psychologists developed what they dubbed the scientist-practitioner model of training, which is also referred to as the Boulder model (Raimy, 1950). The creators of that model stressed the philosophy that in addition to learning the skills of the practitioner, students also need to be trained to do research. The counseling psychologists affirmed this model in Ann Arbor. In addition, the field of counseling psychology has repeatedly reiterated its commitment to the scientist-practitioner model, most notably in 1951 at the Northwestern conference (Whiteley, 1984), in 1964 at the Greystone conference (Thompson & Super, 1964), and again in 1987 at the Atlanta conference (Meara et al., 1988). In the 1990s there has been "an increasingly active interest in and commitment to making the scientist-practitioner model work" (Watkins, 1994, p. 318). The scientist-practitioner model also has been incorporated into the *Standards for the Preparation of Counselors and Other Personnel Service Specialists* (1977) established by the American Association for Counseling and Development (AACD).

Meara et al. (1988) succinctly amplified on the scientist-practitioner model:

> Those at the Georgia [Atlanta] conference agreed that because psychology is a science, both the generation and application of psychological knowledge are based on scientific views of the world. Psychologists, whatever their work, are professionals and their attitude toward their work is scientific.
>
> The scientist-professional model is an integrated approach to knowledge that recognizes the interdependence of theory, research, and practice. The model emphasizes systematic and thoughtful analyses of human experiences and judicious application of the knowledge and attitudes gained from such analyses. An attitude of scholarly inquiry is critical to all the activities of those educated in the scientist-professional model.
>
> The model encompasses a variety of research methods, assessment techniques, and intervention strategies. The counseling psychologist is engaged in the pursuit and application of psychological knowledge to promote optimal development for individuals, groups, and systems (including families), and to provide remedies for the psychological difficulties that encumber them. To implement these goals, the scientist-professional psychologist adopts a scientific approach based on observation of psychological phenomena. This approach generates theoretical constructs and propositions, which are in turn tested as hypotheses (Claiborn, 1987; Pepinsky & Pepinsky, 1954). (p. 368)

Concerns with the Model

An increasing number of writers from both counseling and clinical psychology have questioned the utility of the scientist-practitioner model (for example, Albee, 1970; Gelso, 1979). In addition, several writers have questioned the value of psychological research for practitioners (for example, Goldman, 1976; Howard, 1984; Levine, 1974; Polkinghorne, 1983; Raush, 1974). They have contended that most practitioners do not use research findings in their practice, and that, in fact, research findings are often meaningless. This contention has led some writers to the conclusion that research training is not necessary for practitioners (for example, Frank, 1984; Hughes, 1952; Meehl, 1971). Others have suggested that students are not receiving adequate training in how to think scientifically, whether it be about clients or about research (for example, Anderson & Heppner, 1986; Claiborn, 1984; Goodyear & Benton, 1986). In assessing professional training issues pertaining to counseling research, Gelso (1979) noted that the "modal counseling psychologist publishes no research following the attainment of the doctoral degree" (p. 25). Carkhuff (1968) suggested a more extreme estimate: The last research project of 95% to 99% of graduates is the doctoral dissertation. These data are in contrast to the widely espoused scientist-practitioner training model as well as the research training goals established by the AACD in their *Standards for the Preparation of Counselors* (1977).

The debate regarding the utility of the scientist-practitioner model is a complex one involving multiple factors. For instance, the model itself could be unrealistic and impossible to fulfill in reality (see, for example, Albee, 1970; Gelso, 1979). Conversely, perhaps the training students receive in scientific activities is inadequate or even inappropriate (see, for example, Anderson & Heppner, 1986;

Claiborn, 1984, 1987; Gelso, 1979; Goodyear & Benton, 1986; Heppner, Gelso, & Dolliver, 1987; Magoon & Holland, 1984; Royalty et al., 1986; Wampold, 1989). Moreover, it could also be that graduate training in practitioner activities does not adequately incorporate scientific activities (see, for example, Anderson & Heppner, 1986; Claiborn, 1984, 1987; Goodyear & Benton, 1986; Heppner & Anderson, 1985). It does seem questionable whether graduate students are taught to think about applied problems and to process information as scientists (see, for example, Betz, 1986; Claiborn, 1987). Perhaps the type of research being conducted is too distant from the reality of the practitioner (see, for example, Howard, 1984; Polkinghorne, 1984), or perhaps our research methods reduce counseling phenomena to meaningless numbers (see, for example, Goldman, 1976). Or maybe our professional journals are structured in ways that make it cumbersome for practitioners to find and assimilate the information they need (see, for example, Anderson & Heppner, 1986; Gelso et al., 1988; Heppner et al., 1992). Yet another factor could be that students admitted to graduate programs have predominantly social or interpersonal interests (see, for example, Holland, 1986; Magoon & Holland, 1984) or have been selected on a very narrow range of criteria (Bernstein & Kerr, 1993).

There is no doubt that research has enhanced the practice of counseling. Even though a practitioner may not be able to cite a specific reference, his or her graduate school training was likely based on a tremendous amount of research data, all the way from personality theory to intervention strategies. The accumulation may be slow, but the data eventually advance our working knowledge of the field (Heppner & Anderson, 1985). The fact that research continues to be criticized for not being relevant, however, is noteworthy and should be cause for concern for educators (that is, the people responsible for training). Perhaps the truth occupies a middle ground: The scientific method and research have advanced the field, but they have not been as helpful as we would like them to be.

A central issue in the debate over the scientist-practitioner model is the role of scientific training in the development of a competent and professional counselor. Hans Strupp, a noted clinical psychologist with a great deal of experience in practice, research, training, and professional affairs, concluded in 1981 that inadequate training in the scientific process has been a major problem in the development of the mental health profession in general:

> Despite notable exceptions, the mental health professions have not done an impressive job of training truly first-rate clinicians and practicing therapists. These deficiencies are now coming back to haunt us in the form of demands by the government, insurance companies, and society at large for more stringent controls. I cannot do justice to these important issues in a few words, but the declining status of organized psychoanalysis may teach some lessons of what not to do, to wit, total commitment to a single theoretical and technical model; enshrinement of theoretical formulations as dogma; imperviousness to research progress in neighboring fields; rigid indoctrination of trainees; failure to inspire students to become critical and independent thinkers; failure to teach students abiding respect for empirical data and rival hypotheses; insufficient attention to clinical realities—patient selection, formulation of treat-

ment goals, bold experimentation with alternative technical approaches, systematic exploration of the limits of existing approaches, and the like. How many of our own training programs and clinical supervisors take these matters seriously? How many students are given thorough training in diverse theoretical and technical approaches? How many supervisors are intimately familiar with the frontiers of current research? The influence of research, as noted previously, must make itself felt largely through the kinds of attitudes instilled in student therapists toward clinical work. Harry Stack Sullivan once expressed amazement at how difficult it is for most people to think seriously of even one alternative hypothesis to explain clinical observations. In short, clinical training must not only be comprehensive and thorough, but it must educate students to become thinking clinicians who can effectively apply quality control in their daily practice. Unless we succeed in selecting and training clinicians who can exercise this kind of self-surveillance, who practice responsibly and effectively while being mindful of their human and professional limitations, it is predictable that governmental controls and bureaucratic rules will make a charade of professional work in this area. It may already be later than we realize. (pp. 217-218)

The scientist-practitioner model in its ideal form (that is, implicitly 50% practitioner and 50% scientist/researcher) may be just that—an ideal that is rarely found in reality. Gelso (1979) proposed that it may be more realistic to train students in both domains (in varying degrees depending on their interests) with the expectation that students will find a suitable place for themselves on the scientist-practitioner continuum. Thus, one student might prefer a 20%–80% split while another might choose a 75%–25% split. Such training goals may be more realistic and, as Gelso speculated, entail less discouragement for both faculty and students. Gelso's idea is promising. Moreover, it is important for the profession to value equally both ends of and various points along the continuum. It also seems that even if a person were trained within a scientist-practitioner model, he or she might choose not to engage in any research per se; we suggest that such a choice would not necessarily negate the model because *other training outcomes* such as scientific thinking are associated with the scientific domain of the model. For example, a psychologist can be a scientist-practitioner and not engage in any research activity. What we are suggesting is that the product of a scientist-practitioner program need not necessarily be a researcher but rather a counselor who thinks scientifically. In fact, equating science only with research activities may be the major problem with previous operationalizations of the scientist-practitioner model.

A counseling center staff member might be engaged primarily in direct client service and, say, one program evaluation project (see Chapter 18); this might be a 5%–95% science-practice split of *professional activities.* A faculty member (three-quarters time) with a quarter-time direct service appointment in the counseling center might have a 75%–25% split of professional activities. Regardless of the type of *professional activities* a counselor selects along the scientist-practitioner continuum, we nonetheless still maintain that all graduate students in counseling should receive basic training in both the scientific and practice domains.

The Need to Broaden Scientific Training

Most counselor education programs provide comprehensive training in the practice domain (for example, courses in counseling methods and counseling theory, multiple practica, and a year-long internship). The basic training most programs provide in the scientific domain, however, is deficient in at least two areas: basic scientific thinking skills and basic research application skills. We now discuss these two topics in some detail.

Training in Basic Scientific Thinking Skills

All counselors, regardless of where their professional activities fall on the scientist-practitioner continuum, need basic scientific thinking skills. Scientific thinking refers to a controlled method of inquiry and reasoning, typically to collect data of some kind for the purpose of testing a hypothesis. Clearly, it is essential to have research scientists within the counseling profession who continually expand our knowledge bases; these people obviously need training not only in basic scientific thinking skills, but also in research methods, statistics, philosophy of science, writing, and logic, and they need a multitude of opportunities to apply and extend their research skills. Moreover, a crucial characteristic of a professional counselor is the integration of "scientific thinking" into the daily activities of professional practice (see Anderson & Heppner, 1986; Berdie, 1972; Claiborn, 1984, 1987; Goodyear & Benton, 1986; Hoshmand, 1994; Pepinsky & Pepinsky, 1954). Scientific thinking can be instrumental in how counselors both process information about a specific client during counseling and evaluate the counseling process.

How a person thinks is an exceedingly complex process (see, for example, Anderson, 1983; Neisser, 1976). It is becoming increasingly clear over time that human beings often think or process information in both rational and irrational ways, in systematic and unsystematic ways, and in linear and nonlinear ways (see, for example, Fiske & Taylor, 1984; Heppner, 1989; Kanfer & Busemeyer, 1982; Gambrill, 1990; Nisbett & Ross, 1980; Strohmer & Blustein, 1990; Tversky & Kahneman, 1974). Moreover, there is reason to believe that one's cognitive processes (that is, how one thinks) interact with one's affective processes and behaviors, thereby creating a complex triadic process (Heppner & Krauskopf, 1987). The research to date clearly indicates that people do not think as "objective computers" but rather are selective or biased in the type of information to which they attend (Gambrill, 1990; Nisbett & Ross, 1980; Turk & Salovey, 1988). In particular, people often attend to information that confirms their existing beliefs or discount information that is contrary to their existing beliefs (see Lichtenberg, 1984; Slusher & Anderson, 1989). Such biases can lead to problems for professional counselors as they process information about clients and evaluate the effectiveness of their work. (For references that discuss thinking processes and biases in counseling, see Abramson, 1988; Heppner & Frazier, 1992; Ingram, 1986; Turk & Salovey, 1988.)

Carl Rogers was very aware of this danger of counselor bias; in 1955 he observed that he could "deceive himself in regard to my creatively formed subjective hunches" about a client (p. 275). He believed that the scientific method, as a way of thinking, led him to check "the subjective feelings or hunch or hypothe-sis of a person with the objective fact" (Rogers, 1955, p. 275). Rogers would often check his hunches very directly by asking the client, "Do you mean this?" or "Could it be this?" Rogers would sometimes go a step further and develop a writ-ten transcript of an interview to analyze the relationships between counselor and client statements. Years later his face would still light up with excitement about what he would learn about a particular client, or the counseling process, by step-ping back from the immediacy of an interview to analyze those transcripts (Rogers, personal communication with P. P. Heppner and L. A. Lee, January 1984).

Pepinsky and Pepinsky (1954) initially articulated a prescriptive model of counselor thinking based on the scientific method. Strohmer and Newman (1983) succinctly summarized their model:

> The counselor observes the client, makes inferences about his or her current status and the causal inferences, and then, based on these inferences, makes a tentative judgment about the client. The counselor then proceeds in an exper-imental fashion to state the judgment as a hypothesis and to test it against inde-pendent observations of the client. Through a series of such tentative judgments and tests based on these judgments, the counselor constructs a hypothetical model of the client. This model then serves as the basis for mak-ing predictions (e.g., which treatment approach is most appropriate) about the client. (p. 557)

In essence, Pepinsky and Pepinsky (1954) were suggesting that the coun-selor incorporate a scientific thinking model by (a) generating hypotheses based on (b) the data that the client presents, followed by (c) empirical testing of the hypotheses, to develop (d) a model that can be used (e) to make predictions about the client. The essence of this approach is that it is *data-based* or *empirical*, which lessens the chance of personal biases or subjectivity. Scientific thinking in this way involves a continual generation and evaluation of hypotheses based on data. Spengler, Strohmer, Dixon, and Shivy (1995) nicely extended the Pepinskys' model by integrating it with the human inference literature, which effectively operationalized scientific thinking and identified a number of inferential errors commonly made in counseling.

Training in scientific thinking may be particularly important in evaluating counseling outcomes. Goodyear and Benton (1986) have referred to a particular counselor bias in assessing counseling outcomes, a bias they call a "walk-through empiricism" mentality:

> That is, as the counselor has successes, he or she will form impressions of what techniques are proving useful. Although this walk-through empiricism can be valuable, it is also subjective and therefore unreliable if it is used as the sole source of data.
>
> An analogy might be drawn from medicine where not so long ago a fre-quent remedy was to treat people by bleeding them of "bad blood." Physicians believed a cause-effect relationship—that the bleeding caused a cure—and continued to offer this as a common treatment for many years. Yet, the treat-ment was no doubt responsible for many patient deaths that might have been avoided if the procedure had been tested empirically. (p. 291)

Thus, training in scientific thinking and methodologies can help counselors evaluate the effectiveness of counseling interventions more objectively and with less personal or subjective bias.

The empirical approach is a crucial feature that distinguishes the counselor from a nonprofessional layperson, in large part because of its self-corrective characteristics:

> Both layman and scientist tend to construct "possible worlds," but whereas the layman's attitude predisposes him to fit what he sees and hears into a preconceived set of ideas about his world, the scientist tends to look upon his assumptions as tentative and problematic and subject to change as his observations fail to confirm his theoretical expectations. (Pepinsky & Pepinsky, 1954, p. 198)

Thus, Claiborn (1987) concluded that the difference between the counselor-as-scientist and the scientist is more a matter of goals than of procedure. We believe that it would be worthwhile to pursue more thorough training in basic scientific thinking skills to reflect training outcomes associated with a more integrated scientist-practitioner model. To facilitate the development of scientific thinking, particularly with practice-oriented students, Hoshman (1994) developed a practice-oriented approach to research supervision; her experiences led her to conclude that a practice-oriented approach engages students' interest and prepares them for contributing scholarly research relevant to practice. At this point, more attention is needed on the efficacy of different approaches of scientific thinking for different types of students. "The process of critical thinking, hypothesis-testing, and other elements of the scientific method should be engendered and integrated into all aspects of training" (Belar & Perry, 1992, p. 72).

It seems important to address one final point concerning the debate over the utility of the scientist-practitioner model. This model is in fact a hypothesis: It hypothesizes that scientific thinking enhances practice skills, and that practice training positively influences scientific endeavors. It is surprising that this hypothesis has not been put to an empirical test. Research is long overdue on this fundamental hypothesis. Moreover, it is surprising that the efficacy of training methods to enhance scientific thinking skills has not been reported in the literature (see Heppner et al., 1992, for some recommendations regarding curriculum reform).

Training in Basic Research Application Skills

The counseling research literature contains a great deal of information about client populations, counseling processes and outcomes, assessment, interventions, crisis intervention, professional issues, and a variety of special topics (see reviews by Betz & Fitzgerald, 1993; Borgen, 1984a; Gelso & Fassinger, 1990; Watkins, 1994). A great deal of the counseling research literature appears in professional journals such as the *Journal of College Student Development,* the *Journal of Counseling and Development,* the *Journal of Counseling Psychology,* the *Journal of Multicultural Counseling and Development, The Counseling Psychologist,* the *Journal of Vocational Behavior,* and *Counselor Education and Supervision.* In addition, a number of other journals in other areas of psychology and education— such as the *Psychological Bulletin;* the *Journal of Personality and Social*

Psychology; the *Journal of Aging;* the *Journal of Consulting and Clinical Psychology; Professional Psychology; Research and Practice; Behavior Therapy; Sex Roles; Cognitive Therapy and Research;* the *Journal of Educational Psychology; Educational and Psychological Measurement; Developmental Psychology; American Psychologist;* and the *Journal of Clinical and Social Psychology*—contain a broad range of articles relevant for those in the counseling profession. Finally, more concentrated or condensed information is also available in several handbooks on a wide range of topics, such as *Effective Psychotherapy: A Handbook of Research* (Gurman & Razin, 1977), *Handbook of Counseling Psychology* (Brown & Lent, 1984, 1992), *Handbook of Psychotherapy and Behavior Change* (Bergin & Garfield, 1971, 1994; Garfield & Bergin, 1978, 1986), *Handbook of Racial/Ethnic Minority Counseling Research* (Ponterotto & Casas, 1991), *Handbook of Multicultural Counseling* (Ponterotto et al., 1995), *Handbook of Multicultural Assessment* (Suzuki, Meller, & Ponterotto, 1996), *Career Counseling: Process, Issues, and Techniques* (Gysbers, Heppner, & Johnston, 1998), *Handbook of Vocational Psychology* (Walsh & Osipow, 1995), *Career Counseling for Women* (Walsh & Osipow, 1994), and *Career Development and Vocational Behavior of Racial and Ethnic Minorities* (Leong, 1995). There are also many useful, specialized resource books on various counseling topics; two books that are useful in developing research projects on career planning in the school system, for example, are *Designing Careers: Counseling to Enhance the Quality of Education, Work, and Leisure* (Gysbers & Associates, 1984) and *Developing and Managing Your School Guidance Program* (Gysbers & Henderson, 1988).

In short, the counseling research literature, as well as the literature from other areas in psychology and education, contains a wealth of information about counseling and human behavior. This information is obviously essential for any person engaging in counseling research. Moreover, this information also can be an extremely useful database or tool in helping a practitioner solve particular client problems. Anderson and Heppner (1986) observed that counselors' knowledge bases can quickly become out of date. While preparing a book of readings on recent innovations in counseling, Anderson was impressed with the number of articles being published on topics that only ten years earlier were not taught to counselors in training (such as bulimia, sleep disorders, and spouse abuse). Thus, counselors in the field need to train themselves continually to work effectively with new client problems.

Gelso (1985) has also observed that reading the research literature affects his thinking about the counseling process:

> I would offer that it is important to think about research as that which helps us use our heads more clearly and less prejudicially. It helps us think about what we do and organize our ever-changing personal theory of the processes in which we are involved, be they counseling, psychotherapy, consultation, supervision, and so on. We should not expect empirical research to capture the felt essence of those processes. Only the practice of them will do that. Most of the research findings that I read are relevant to my clinical practice in the following way: they help me think in a less biased way, they help me further refine my usually private theory of my practice, and they allow me to add small pieces of new information to my conceptual system. (p. 553)

The professional research literature is a resource that can both provide a wealth of useful information about specific client problems and suggest topics for additional research. Moreover, reading the literature may affect the counselor's thinking and refine his or her conceptualizations of the counseling process. Thus, a basic activity for all graduate students in counseling is to become active consumers of research (see Goodyear & Benton, 1986).

The research literature has at times been criticized for not having much value for the practitioner for a wide variety of reasons (see, for example, Gadlin & Ingle, 1975; Goldman, 1976, 1977, 1982; Howard, 1985; Levine, 1974; Raush, 1974; Ross, 1981). Learning how to use the research literature (for example, becoming familiar with the types of articles in different journals, learning how to access information most efficiently) and making the literature a part of one's problem-solving repertoire does not simply happen, but rather typically involves specific training. The literature contains a number of suggestions for facilitating students' perusal and application of the research literature, such as (a) identifying key articles for students rather than allowing them to select what they read almost at random, (b) providing specific training in using the literature as a problem-solving tool to help solve client problems, (c) providing specific training in applying research methods to identify solutions to client or agency problems, and (d) increasing the efficiency of communicating information in the professional journals (for more detail regarding specific training strategies, see Anderson & Heppner, 1986; Claiborn, 1984; Heppner & Anderson, 1985; Wampold, 1986a). Likewise, for more information on a broad array of recommendations from the Project to Integrate Practice and Science for enhancing training in the scientist-practitioner model, see Heppner et al. (1992). In short, we suggest that the profession examine methods to train students to apply the results of scientific research to practice.

Students' Typical Reactions to Scientific Training

Typically, beginning graduate students have a number of fears associated with the training they are about to receive, although it is not uncommon for these fears to remain unexpressed. Some students doubt they can be effective counselors (Will I be able to really listen and understand my clients? Will I be able to help my clients change? What if my clients don't like me as a person? What if my clients don't return for counseling?). Other students question whether they can succeed academically (Will I get through the required courses? Dr. Groucho Knails has a reputation for being very demanding in class; can I make it through his required courses?). Many students question whether they can adequately learn the skills associated with research and science (How can I, a mere graduate student, come up with a good research idea? Can I do a thesis? A dissertation? Will I get bogged down in my research and never finish my degree? Statistics scare me—I don't like math.). These and other fears are common and even developmentally normal. For the rest of this section we focus primarily on students' typical reactions to science and the scientific enterprise and explore possible training strategies. We believe it is essential to discuss the affective components associated with scientific activities to facilitate development in this area.

Most incoming graduate students have had some experience (or even a lot) with helping other people, and consequently the benefits of counseling and other practitioner activities are abundantly clear. Moreover, for most of us, helping people is a personally rewarding experience, and students have an understanding of those rewards. Conversely, most incoming students have had considerably less experience with science (Gelso, 1979). Typically, students do not imagine themselves making contributions to the profession by publishing in our professional journals. Moreover, students do not have a long history in the profession and are unable to identify how previous research has contributed to the profession. Similarly, students do not have a clear understanding of the utility of the scientific method as a way of thinking, either about research or clients. Finally, the student typically has had relatively little experience of expanding one's understanding about clients and applied problems by engaging in research activities, reading the professional literature, and contemplating one's empirical findings. From our experience teaching research methods, we have been struck by *many* students' surprise and actual delight as they get past their initial fears and begin to apply their new knowledge about research design. We often have heard comments like, "I'm actually *enjoying* this research course"; "I never thought I would be a researcher; now I'm beginning to reconsider my career goals"; "This research stuff is contagious; I'm starting to think about research studies a lot and I want to collect data now!" In sum, the major point is that often beginning graduate students have considerably less information about research and science than about practitioner activities. Moreover, there is evidence that as students obtain more experience with scientific activities (especially if it is early in their training), their research interests increase and they place a higher value on the role of research (Gelso et al., 1983; Royalty et al., 1986).

From our experience working with students, a major issue is their affective reactions to science, and especially to research. In particular, students' performance anxiety is a central and crucial affective issue. Other educators have come to similar conclusions (see, for example, Claiborn, 1984; Gelso, 1979). Common student disclosures include: "I don't know enough to conduct any meaningful research on my own. How can I do a thesis? How can I criticize previous research?" "Any data that I could uncover using 'science' would be so basic and bland as to make it worthless." "I feel completely inadequate in even conceiving a study that comes at counseling from a unique perspective." "Although I made it through the statistics and research design courses, once I start to do some research I'll be 'found out'; it will become clear that I'm incompetent and really don't know how to do research." "What if I make a mistake and report inaccurate findings?" "I've had trouble writing before, and I'm scared that I will run into debilitating writing blocks again in my research." "I fear that my results will be statistically nonsignificant, and all of my research efforts and time will just be one big waste." "I've seen other students in the throes of a dissertation. The whole process seems overwhelming: tedious, long, anxiety-producing, confusing, and complicated." All of these feelings, and many others, are usually developmentally normal; since students have had little, if any, research experience, they have reason to question and doubt their skills and abilities. It is important to remember, however, that the reason for attending graduate school is to acquire new skills—skills the student currently does not have. If the student had enough previous experience to ease all of these doubts, he or she probably would not need to be in a training program.

In fact, some of these performance-anxiety fears are developmentally common for many postdoctoral years. This suggests to us that acquiring the necessary research and thinking skills occurs over a long period of time; it does not happen all at once. Just as it is unreasonable to expect to become an Olympic downhill skier in four years, it is also unreasonable to expect to become an expert researcher in four years of graduate education (Nancy Downing, personal communication, June 28, 1990).

Clara Hill, a creative and innovative researcher from the University of Maryland, was invited to write a personal account of her evolution as a researcher. Her account illustrates how she made decisions, how complex the process of research can be, and most importantly, how she coped with the ups and downs along the way. For example, consider her comments regarding her "crisis of faith in research":

> After this series of studies I underwent a crisis in terms of research. I had achieved tenure, had my first baby, and turned 30. I started questioning everything. Because I could see so many imperfections in my research, I was not very proud of my work. It had taken an incredible amount of time for little "hard information." I could not even remember the results of many of my studies. Further, I seemed woefully far from even describing what happens in the counseling process let alone understanding what counselor behaviors were useful in effecting change. I despaired that counseling was far too complex to be studied. I had previously had lots of doubts about my research, but it was mostly related to self-confidence in my research abilities. This crisis seemed to have more to do with whether I felt that research was a viable means to answer questions about the counseling process. (Hill, 1984, p. 105)

Hill's behind-the-scenes disclosures are illuminating as well as relieving. Her article should be required reading for all graduate students in counseling, perhaps during their first course on research methods. We have found that students resonate strongly with Hill's frustrations, jubilations, feelings of inadequacy, and doubts about the role of research. (In fact, informal data collected from a beginning-level research methods course taught by the first author suggest that some students rated Hill's article as one of the most important readings in the course.) The evolution of her confidence in studying her own ideas in her own way not only sends a useful message but also illuminates the developmental processes of a researcher.

Another major issue pertains to beginning students' understanding of science and its role in our profession for both research and practice. Most beginning students do not have much of an understanding of the role of science in our profession. One unfortunate outcome is that students sometimes fill this void with misinformation, like "science = statistics." Or "the scientific method is too intellectual, too cognitive, and unrelated to the experiences of real people." Or "the scientific method is so mechanical and reductionistic that it cannot be used adequately to study the complexities of real human behavior." Some students say to themselves, "I just want to be a therapist, not a scientist"; very simply stated, they "just want to help people."

In our view, all of these statements reflect a lack of understanding of science and the scientific method, and of the counseling process as well. A noted counselor-educator from the University of Minnesota, Ralph Berdie, discussed the role of science in training professional counselors almost two decades ago (Berdie, 1972). Berdie was discouraged with the outcomes of the typical counselor-education training:

> Counselors repeatedly ask for training that will be of more practical assistance. They want their periodicals and literature to provide them with examples of how to solve problems—recipes or cookbooks that will aid them. A survey of counselors in 1971 reported that "a majority seemed to think they would like the content of counseling journals changed to something more practical, more realistic, and less theoretical" (Bradley & Smith, 1971).
>
> The present counselor's difficulty is not that he [sic] has too much theory, but rather too little. He [sic] does not have enough ideas and concepts to understand the problems that face him or to develop approaches and solutions to these problems. He [*sic*] asks to be told what to do and how to do it, because he does not know enough to figure this out for himself. His professional preparation has failed to provide him with knowledge, theory, and concepts, and these are what he needs. (pp. 452–453)

Counseling has been characterized frequently as *either* an art *or* a science, but, as Goodyear and Benton (1986) note, this is a rather narrow view:

> This dichotomy, however, oversimplifies the situation and perhaps exists because of a misunderstanding of the scientist role. Scientists are too often confused with technicians, the people who apply the findings of science but without theoretical understanding. . . . The best scientists overlap with the best artists in their capacity for alternative ways of perceiving, in their creativity, and in their openness to new experiences. (p. 290)

There is no doubt that counseling is a very complex process, one that defies a simple description. But this complexity does not mitigate against a scientific way of thinking about that complex process. The scientific method is simply a set of tools to establish a controlled mode of inquiry about our professional activities. Those of us in the profession are in control of how we use those tools, or we can develop new ones. If we cannot "make the tools work," the fault could lie with the tools, or it could lie with the users; however, to simply throw our hands up or toss our tools away is dangerous. Similarly, after much deliberation Carl Rogers concluded that "science will never depersonalize, or manipulate, or control individuals, only people could do that" (Rogers, 1955, p. 277).

The final issue we will discuss is the idea that students' research training is often less than rewarding. Gelso (1979) offered the following proposition: "Training programs tend not to take the [students'] ambivalence toward research into account and, to a remarkable degree, lack deliberateness in their attempts to capitalize on and strengthen the positive side of the ambivalence" (p. 27). In general, the research training most graduate students receive is less sophisticated and less thorough than their practitioner training.

Consider this not-too-hypothetical example, offered by Gelso (1979):

> Harold/Hannah Helpful, our typical student, enters graduate school with much ambivalence and anxiety about the scholarly requirements of that situation, as well as the role of science in his/her career. He/she knows he/she has done quite well in school all along, but the scholarly demands of a doctoral program are a different ball game for him/her. Yet he/she is indeed ambivalent, not negative. At the same time, he/she probably endows the faculty with some degree of omniscience. What the student runs into during the first year is a bewildering array of requirements, including courses (unfortunately, sometimes even in his/her specialty) that are demanding but unexciting. Usually this includes one or two statistics courses that teach little if anything about counseling research, but seem wedded to the scientific enterprise. These courses often deepen the student's anxiety and deaden motivation. The task is to get through them.
>
> Toward the end of the first year our hypothetical student must start thinking thesis. More anxiety. Up to that point he/she has done no research, acquired no confidence, and at best has gotten through statistics unscathed. The student does not know how to generate ideas that later may be translated into scientifically answerable questions. The process goes on, through the preliminary meeting with the advisor, the thesis proposal meeting, and the thesis orals. All steps along the way are all too often filled with more threat and anxiety than pleasure of discovery. The fortunate student gets by without massive revisions of the thesis and can take a deep breath until the next major scientific hurdle, the dissertation. When assessed against the criterion of, "Is it positively reinforcing?" this unfortunately not very exaggerated description of the scientific regimen of graduate school hurdles is a dreadful failure. (p. 28)

Unfortunately, when students have little experience with research and science, one bad experience can create tremendous attitudinal and motivational damage and move a student a long way from future scientific activities. Although empirical evidence is scant on graduate-level research training, it does appear that some training programs actually decrease students' interest in research (Royalty et al., 1986). Moreover, some students report feeling "disenchanted with research" when they perceive unethical and unprofessional approaches to conducting research in their training environment (more on this in Chapter 5).

A number of ideas aimed at increasing the effectiveness of graduate-level training in science and research have been published in the past few decades (see, for example, Anderson & Heppner, 1986; Claiborn, 1984; Gelso, 1979; Gelso et al., 1988; Goodyear & Benton, 1986; Heppner, Gelso, & Dolliver, 1987; Hoshmand, 1989; Magoon & Holland, 1984; Royalty & Magoon, 1985; Seeman, 1973; Wallerstein, 1971; Wampold, 1986a). The ideas range from broader programmatic philosophies to more specific events (such as seminars and workshops) and focus on faculty, students, curricula, and environmental variables. Some of these ideas include the following:

- Encourage faculty to provide more complete self-disclosure and modeling of positive and negative aspects associated with research

- Provide more positive reinforcement to students, such as publicly acknowledging research publications
- Organize early and minimally threatening involvement in research training during students' training
- Uncouple the artificial connection between research and statistics
- Teach students to integrate their own experiences with the findings in the research literature to facilitate involvement and thinking
- Develop more social activities within the research enterprise, such as research teams
- Provide more explicit training on how science and counseling practice can be wedded
- Emphasize the suitability of multiple research methodologies for different research questions
- Train students how to conduct research in an agency
- Promote workshops aimed at increasing graduate students' awareness of and interest in professional writing
- Develop a sequence of training events to create academic environments that are conducive to learning
- Focus training specifically on emotional fears of students about research
- Emphasize the role of scientific thinking in graduate training
- Increase the amount of feedback to and supervision of students regarding the development of specific scientific-thinking and research skills
- Introduce students more systematically to the research literature and emphasize its applications to practice
- Teach students how to apply research findings as a problem-solving tool
- Teach students how to apply research methods to solve real-life problems or answer real-life questions (for example, within an agency)
- Have graduate students keep a log of their own research ideas, starting at the beginning of their graduate program
- Develop a graduated series of experiential and didactic research training courses analogous to counseling practice, including prepractica, practica, advanced practica, and internship
- Open students' proposal and defense committee meetings to other students
- Develop approaches to research supervision that emphasize clinical thinking and practice-oriented approaches to inquiry
- Link dissertations to journal publications
- Reorient research advisors to assume more of a consultative, mentoring role
- Train students to make their work environments more conducive to research activities
- Train students to seek researcher support in their work environments
- Cultivate research environments that are consistent or congruent with the personalities of the researchers
- Focus graduate training on three interrelated factors in students: their sense of efficacy as scientists, their interest in doing research, and the value they place on research during their forthcoming careers
- Create postdoctoral research opportunities for counseling psychologists

- Develop theory and conduct research on all aspects of research training
- Develop more specific accreditation standards for research training

Despite all these ideas, in some ways training students in research and scientific thinking is still an "area of inquiry in its infancy" (Gelso et al., 1988, p. 402). More attention should be given to the sequence of training activities as well as students' affective reactions to research training. In addition, it seems important to attend much more to individual differences among students. For example, one study found support for the notion that psychologists with different personalities (using Holland code high points) preferred different research environments (Royalty & Magoon, 1985). Thus, it may be helpful for students to understand more clearly their personality style and the implications for finding research endeavors more or less rewarding. "For example, investigative researchers may be more willing to conduct theoretical research, whereas social researchers may be more willing to conduct practical, applied research and may be more interested in team research. Artistic researchers may be more creative with less traditional and less restrictive methods of research (e.g., case studies)" (Royalty & Magoon, 1985, p. 461). Gelso (1979, 1993, 1997) has developed a comprehensive theory of influence in the research training environment that affects graduate students' interest in research. Some research has now provided empirical support for the theory (see Gelso, Mallinckrodt, & Judge, 1996; Kahn & Gelso, 1997; Kahn & Scott, 1997). Another promising variable is research self-efficacy, or one's confidence in being able to complete various aspects of the research process successfully (Gelso, 1993; Phillips & Russell, 1994). Research has found a positive relationship between research self-efficacy and both perceptions of the training environment (Gelso et al., 1996; Kahn & Scott, 1997; Phillips & Russell, 1994), and interest in research (Kahn & Scott, 1997). Moreover, some research suggests that the research training environment may have a more potent influence on women's (versus men's) research self-efficacy and productivity (Brown, Lent, Ryan, & McPartland, 1996). Perhaps consideration of students' affective reactions, values, and individual differences (such as research self-efficacy) and of the training environment will enhance our training endeavors.

SUMMARY AND CONCLUSIONS

The counseling profession helps people with a wide variety of personal, educational, and career-related problems. Most of all, we must be very cognizant that we are working with real people, many of whom are experiencing psychological pain of some sort and are in need of professional assistance. To be credible, reliable, and effective, the profession must be built on a dependable knowledge base, rather than on tenacity, decrees from authority figures, or subjective opinions.

Science represents a way of knowing, a way of establishing truths about the profession. There is much debate over how we might best proceed in our scientific endeavors and how students should be educated. The careers professional counselors choose will most likely demand professional activities that fall at various points along the scientist-practitioner continuum. It is important to note, however, that one's professional interests and desires often change throughout one's career. Thus, we strongly encourage students to prepare themselves broadly throughout graduate school to acquire skills within both the scientific and practice domains. From our experience, it is sad to witness students who have not acquired necessary skills within either the science or practice domains and then do not have career options available to them later in life.

We strongly believe that there can be a much greater integration between the science and practice domains, not only within counselor training but also within the professional activities of all counselors. Carl Rogers's hope for the future was that "each researcher would be a practitioner in some field and each practitioner would be doing some research (Heppner, Rogers, & Lee, 1984, p. 19). This is one type of integration; we have also suggested that scientific research training be broadened (and integrated) to include basic scientific thinking and basic research application skills. In our personal experience, our research has clearly been facilitated by observations made during many hours of counseling practice. Moreover, our experience has been that our thinking and counseling skills have been sharpened, extended, and clearly enhanced by subjecting our thinking to empirical tests as well as contemplating new ideas from the research literature. Integration might also happen on another level: between those who are primarily research-oriented and those who are practice-oriented. In some ways, the people who have the most well-developed set of observations of the counseling process are those who are heavily engaged in counseling practice; it behooves the typical researcher to develop collaborative relationships with such practitioners. In short, we suspect that both scientific and practice-oriented professional activities could be enhanced by a more complete integration of the two domains.

We have suggested in this opening chapter that a critical ingredient of counseling is the counselor's attitudes toward science and research. We have discussed some common fears that students have about scientific activities that may present obstacles and negatively affect students' attitudes. It is sad to see students not only have bad experiences with research, but also feel so angry and hurt that their attitudes about science are adversely affected. Educators must attend to students' affective experiences during training in the scientific domain and develop more effective didactic and experiential components in the training curriculum. Moreover, students must help by "educating" faculty about their experiences; we strongly encourage students to take the necessary risks to disclose, and we encourage faculty to listen.

We have also maintained that a basic issue in scientific training is scientific thinking. Those at the Atlanta conference in 1987 concluded that "an attitude of scholarly inquiry is critical to all the activities of those educated in the scientist-professional model" (Meara et al., 1988, p. 368). Such an outcome requires not only scientific skills but also scientific values. The latter are also important goals and need specific attention in training (perhaps by way of discussions about the philosophy of science, research methods, the slow but steady accumulation of knowledge, and students' own research experiences).

An attitude of scholarly inquiry goes beyond scientific thinking and involves curiosity, inquisitiveness, healthy skepticism, exploration, and a desire to learn. In a way, all counseling professionals are pioneers in extending the boundaries of their own knowledge throughout their careers, and possibly extending the knowledge bases of the profession as well. In this way, scholarly inquiry involves discovery, excitement, and even a sense of adventure. Not surprisingly, pioneers in the field of counseling and development report that they were motivated to achieve, in part, by the joys of intellectual discovery, "the thirst to know something" (Pepinsky, cited in Claiborn, 1985, p. 7).

Maintaining a pioneering attitude in professional scholarly inquiry can also be a way of life. Enos Mills was an early pioneer in the mountainous area of Colorado that is now Rocky Mountain National Park. In the following quote, Mills (1924) aptly describes the qualities of a pioneer's life. Even though he was referring to pioneering in the American West, the qualities of life he describes also apply to the pioneering attitude involved in discovering professional knowledge through scholarly inquiry:

> Those who live pioneer lives are usually the most fortunate of people. They suffer from no dull existence. Each hour is full of progressive thought, and occasions which call for action accompanied by the charm of exploration— action that makes their lives strong, sincere, and sweet. Their days are full of eagerness and repose, they work with happy hands. The lives of pioneers are rich with hope and their future has all the promise of spring. (p. 9)

We hope that your life in the counseling profession will be a good place for you to be a pioneer and that scientific thinking will enrich your life with discoveries that are exciting to you and beneficial to the various clienteles we serve.

CHAPTER 2

IDENTIFYING AND OPERATIONALIZING RESEARCH TOPICS

The purpose of this chapter is to provide an overview of the process of selecting a research topic and developing the research idea into a testable hypothesis. The chapter describes the five main components of this process: identifying research topics, specifying research questions and hypotheses, formulating operational definitions, identifying research variables, and collecting and analyzing data. For pedagogical reasons we present these activities in separate sections. However, in reality these activities are often intertwined, and the researcher often intersperses thinking and planning across all of these activities as she or he progresses from identifying the topic to developing specific research hypotheses.

IDENTIFYING RESEARCH TOPICS

A wide range of experiences can play a role in helping the researcher develop research ideas. At times, developing a research idea can involve a great deal of creativity as the researcher integrates information from diverse sources and in novel ways. It is often exciting to develop innovative ideas that may lead to important contributions of new knowledge, and it is exhilarating to think that no one has thought of this idea before (at least for a short period of time!). Various pioneers in the field of counseling have commented on the joys of discovery and learning they have experienced by engaging in research. (Interested students might read some of the interviews with early counseling pioneers that appeared in the "Pioneers in Guidance" and "Lifelines" series in the *Journal of Counseling and Development,* as well as in the "Legacies and Traditions" forum of *The Counseling Psychologist.* For example, Anne Roe, in reflecting on her career, stated simply that "nothing is as much fun as research. . . . I miss that [in retirement]" [Wrenn, 1985, p. 275].) At other times, developing a research idea can involve very little creative thought as the researcher takes a previous research idea one logical step further. But even here there is the fun of learning and discovery.

At first, developing research ideas often seems difficult for inexperienced researchers; they cringe at the thought of developing an original research idea that *no one* has *ever* had before! Typically, the experienced researcher has little difficulty in developing research ideas. In fact, often the veteran researcher has too many research ideas, and a more difficult problem is deciding which ideas to pursue.

Several ingredients differentiate the experienced researcher from the inexperienced. The experienced researcher usually has a very large knowledge base, not only about a given topic but about several other topics as well. Such a researcher can most likely process information about these topics in sophisticated ways, identifying the most important findings, combining research findings, dovetailing an idea from one topic with another, and elaborating on or extending ideas in novel ways. In addition, the experienced counseling researcher often has a considerable wealth of information from his or her applied counseling experiences that can be the source of many ideas and hypotheses. The veteran researcher also typically knows a great deal about the skills needed to conduct research, such as knowledge of research design, methodology, assessment, statistics, data collection, data analysis, and technical writing. All of these knowledge bases are important tools in facilitating the processing of large amounts of information about specific research projects in sophisticated and often novel ways. Perhaps equally important, the experienced researcher typically has confidence that he or she can effectively conduct research, and thus has the needed level of self-efficacy.

In contrast, the inexperienced researcher has far less knowledge about specific research topics and often has trouble identifying the most important or relevant information. The novice often has less applied experience in counseling, and most likely has less-developed conceptualizations of the counseling process. The inexperienced researcher has perhaps only a vague sense of the various research activities (such as recruitment of participants, data collection) and harbors doubts about his or her ability to do research well. In fact, in many counseling programs, well-articulated guidelines for conducting research are not available to students, leaving the impression that the research process is rather mystical. Drew (1980) noted that a logical place to turn for information is a college or departmental catalog, which describes a thesis or dissertation project. Typically such documents say something to the effect that the thesis "must be an original contribution to the field." When viewed literally, the word *original* can engender considerable anxiety as the trainee tries to develop a completely novel research idea. In addition, the idea must represent "a contribution to the field," which makes the task seem even more formidable. It is the rare trainee who believes at the outset that he or she can make a "real contribution" to the field; after all, we are talking about *Science!* Most often the inexperienced researcher interprets "original contribution" much too broadly and tries to develop a new topic area by creating a new assessment instrument to measure new constructs, a new research methodology to collect data previously not collected, and new statistical procedures to handle old problems. In reality, most experienced researchers would feel quite a sense of accomplishment if they did all of these things during an entire *career.* In short, the inexperienced researcher often takes on too much in trying to develop an "original contribution." Not surprisingly, our experience has been that graduate students in beginning research design courses ask questions about how to identify "good" research topics and "good" research ideas. Also not surprisingly, they often ask whether a particular idea is "enough" for a thesis.

We will make some suggestions here to help beginning researchers to identify a research topic. Essentially, the task is to identify some general topic that may (a) contribute to the profession's bases in meaningful ways, and (b) simultaneously stimulate and motivate you to explore and learn more about the topic. Most inexperienced researchers in counseling need to learn more about the body of knowledge and the directions of current research efforts. Thus, for such students we do not simply recommend sitting and thinking hard about research topics and hoping that the ideal research question will present itself, but rather a more active, information-collecting approach.

A good first step in identifying possible research topics is to start collecting information about previous research, both within and outside of counseling. Thus, read widely in the professional journals and books, such as those listed in Chapter 1. Reading widely will not only provide you with information about what is being published, but it also may help you to clarify what topics are of most interest to you. Sometimes it is useful to start with a general review of the counseling literature (see Betz & Fitzgerald, 1993; Borgen, 1984a; Gelso & Fassinger, 1990; or peruse the handbooks mentioned in Chapter 1). Another strategy is to begin by looking for more focused literature reviews on specific topics (the *Psychological Bulletin* is a journal devoted to evaluative and integrative reviews; see Dolliver, 1969, for an excellent example of an influential evaluative review of measured versus expressed vocational interest). Books on specific topics are often useful resources. For example, a student interested in conducting research with racial/ ethnic minorities would be wise to examine Ponterotto and Casas (1991). There is no substitute for this time-consuming process, although at first you might peruse the literature and read abstracts to develop a broad overview. A good beginning is to spend at least five hours a week reading and exploring the journals for six weeks or more.

In addition to regularly reading the journals, capitalize on the faculty and student resources on your campus. While this sounds simplistic, it often provides useful information. Talk with these people about their past and present research projects. What are they most excited about now? What was the most stimulating idea at a recent national, regional, or state convention they attended? What do they consider as hot or promising topics? Follow up your discussions with these people with readings they might suggest to you.

In addition to faculty in general, your advisor or research supervisor is often an invaluable resource. Typically, your advisor's role is to facilitate your work on your thesis. Thus, another strategy is to begin research training by working closely within your advisor's research interests; this approach resembles an apprenticeship model. An advantage of this strategy is that your advisor can more easily facilitate the identification of workable research ideas, methods, and procedures. Some faculty believe that master's-level students should be assigned research topics because students are typically overwhelmed with their first research project. Assigning research topics may be directive, but sometimes it is appropriate for students who have trouble getting started.

Although we said earlier that we do not recommend simply sitting and think-ing hard, we do recommend thinking and reflecting *after* you have collected a wide variety of information. What do you like and dislike about a particular line of research? Pay attention to what bothers you about a study. Was something omit-ted? How could you improve the study? Also try to bring your own observations and beliefs into your research topics. Many experienced counselors use their own observations about a topic (for example, the counselor supervision process, or counselor self-disclosure) as a source of ideas for research topics. This is riskier for the inexperienced counselor and researcher, however, because a lack of experi-ence may provide less reliable observations. To facilitate reflecting and brain-storming, sometimes it is helpful to record ideas, observations, and questions in a journal or log.

While reading and thinking about previous research in counseling, it is important to keep in mind at least four issues: your particular interests, a way to build on previous research, the role of theory, and the utility of research in answering real-life applied questions.

It is essential to continually assess which topics intrigue you most within the broad field of counseling. What are you most curious about? Are there certain top-ics that you are motivated to pursue, or perhaps feel a special commitment to investigating because of your beliefs or values? Are there any topics that you believe previous researchers have overlooked? In short, pursuing research topics that you are curious about and are motivated to pursue will likely provide the intellectual stimulation needed to sustain you through the various research tasks.

It is important to realize that a great deal of research in counseling is extend-ing the results of previous research. Typically, our research proceeds by adding one or two new pieces of information per study. Thus, a researcher might extend a previous study by adding one or two new constructs or by developing a new assessment instrument to operationalize a construct. Often a researcher uses a data collection method similar to that used in previous research, or instruments used in three or four previous studies. In short, it is essential to focus on investi-gating a few constructs only, and not to try to do too much in developing an "orig-inal contribution." Most often our knowledge bases in counseling increase in small steps by building only slightly on previous research.

A considerable amount of research within counseling applies or tests theo-ries about personality, human behavior, and the persuasion process as they apply to topics in counseling. For example, Stanley Strong (1968) initially conceptual-ized counseling as a social influence process and used research and theory on per-suasion from social psychology to develop a two-phase model of influence within counseling. Subsequently, a great deal of research has examined the persuasion or social influence process within counseling (see reviews by Corrigan et al., 1980; Heppner & Claiborn, 1989; Heppner & Dixon, 1981; Heppner & Frazier, 1992; Hoyt, 1996; Strong et al., 1992). Likewise, another theoretical perspective that is influencing counseling research is that of developmental models in counselor training (see Bernard & Goodyear, 1998; Holloway, 1987, 1992, 1995; Watkins, 1997). Sometimes a new model or theory is developed by integrating different bodies of research. For example, McCarn and Fassinger (1996) developed a model of lesbian identity formation by integrating literature on lesbian/gay identity, racial/ethnic identity, and gender issues related to identity development; subsequently, a number of research directions were proposed. Or sometimes research will test and extend either competing theories or different conceptualizations of the same phenomena. For example, in 1971 Cross published a model on black racial identity that has been modified by refinements and elaborations (see, for example, Cross, 1978; Helms, 1990; Parham, 1989; Parham & Helms, 1981, 1985b). Subsequently, a number of white racial identity models have been proposed, debated, and empirically tested (see, for example, Atkinson, Morten, & Sue, 1989; Behrens, 1996; Helms, 1984, 1990; Rowe & Atkinson, 1995; Rowe, Bennett, & Atkinson, 1994; Sue & Sue, 1990; Thompson, 1994). Similarly, sometimes theory and research from one topic can be extended to another related topic. For example, women's career development has been the focus of both theoretical models and empirical research for some time (see, for example, Betz & Fitzgerald, 1987; Farmer, 1985; Farmer, Wardrop, Anderson, & Risinger, 1995; Fassinger, 1990; Harmon, 1977; Walsh & Osipow, 1994). Models of women's career development were then integrated with empirical research on lesbians' career development to develop a minority group model of career development (Morgan & Brown, 1991). Thus, another strategy in identifying research topics is to examine any theories, whether they are found within the counseling literature or outside the counseling literature, that might be helpful to the work of counselors.

A considerable amount of research within counseling stems from questions about applied problems. Thus, another way to identify research topics is to contemplate what is unknown or unclear about the counseling process, various treatment programs (such as social skills training, marriage enrichment workshops, or men's support groups), or outreach programs (for example, rape prevention or alcohol awareness programs). Most important, are there some real-life questions that an agency director or some other personnel would like some information about? Perhaps a counseling center director would like to know how clients would react to a detailed, computer-assisted intake like CASPER (see McCullough & Farrell, 1983; McCullough, Farrell, & Longabaugh, 1986). Or a therapist might have questions about effective interventions for treating sexually abused children. Child sexual abuse has been the topic of a great deal of attention (even debate) and has stimulated research on the efficacy of a number of psychosocial interventions (see Enns et al., 1995). Many times unresolved problems or questions about applied aspects of counseling are a rich source of research topics.

In summary, ideas for research projects can come from a wide range of sources. It is often useful for students to use a combination of strategies as they enter the world of research.

SPECIFYING RESEARCH QUESTIONS AND HYPOTHESES

Typically, the purpose of research is to answer questions, solve problems, or develop theories of interest to counseling, and ultimately to add to the existing knowledge in the field. It is one thing to identify a *topic* you want to research (such as client thoughts-not-said in group therapy or the effects of art therapy). It is a significant step to move beyond the research topic to an unresolved problem or specific research question or hypothesis that can guide your research. In fact, developing testable research questions is often quite troublesome for inexperienced researchers.

After identifying a possible research topic (for example, counselor supervision), it is important that you become knowledgeable about the previous research on that topic, perhaps even by writing a formal review paper. There is no substitute for becoming thoroughly knowledgeable about a topic by identifying current research findings, previous research obstacles, and previous researchers' suggestions for future research. As we indicated earlier, many times developing a specific research idea means extending a line of research one logical step further. Thus, examining key studies or incisive reviews is essential. Pay particular attention to the discussion section in those studies. Often there is explicit discussion of future research needs or of the next logical step. The authors often identify these needs by phrases such as "future research should" or "additional research might examine." These suggestions could be the basis of your research idea.

Conversely, sometimes previous research is based on certain assumptions, procedures, and ways of thinking that blinded the researchers to the obvious or critical constructs for a particular topic. Thus, a researcher can be at an advantage by coming at a research topic with a new or fresh perspective, untainted by the assumptions of previous researchers.

At this point, begin to attend more closely to the constructs that have been used in the previous research. What psychological processes are interesting and important to researchers in the field? Stated simply, *research questions* explore the relations among or between constructs. For example, "Does the client's level of dysfunction affect the working alliance formed in counseling?" is a research question. In contrast, a *research hypothesis* is more specific in that it states the expected relationship between the constructs, as in "More-dysfunctional clients will form poorer alliances in counseling than will less-dysfunctional clients." Often, distinctions are not made between questions and hypotheses. However, it should be kept in mind that hypotheses specifically state the expected relationship.

From our experience, students have difficulty developing research questions and hypotheses for several reasons. Perhaps most frequently, students may lack a theoretical structure for their investigation and thus cannot conceptualize relevant research hypotheses that will empirically test or extend previous research. Research hypotheses are often deduced from theory (Wampold, Davis, & Good, 1990). At other times students select constructs they have no way of measuring or testing. For example, one doctoral student was stymied because he could not clearly assess what he meant by counselor personal power and autonomy. Sometimes students have not thought in depth beyond the research topic and have not asked themselves what specific constructs they are most interested in examining. Thus, they may be unable to be more specific than being interested in "something about computerized career information services." At other times students are reluctant to decide on specific constructs, choosing instead to delay or procrastinate for an array of conscious and unconscious reasons. All these diffi-

culties in developing research questions and hypotheses are not atypical for inexperienced researchers. Most important, such difficulties suggest that additional
reading and thinking are necessary. Researchers can make serious errors by proceeding to select participants and assessment instruments without ever clarifying
their research questions or hypotheses and exactly what they are looking for in
their research.

Drew (1980) has identified three useful, general categories of research questions (or hypotheses): descriptive, difference, and relationship. *Descriptive questions* essentially ask what some phenomena or events are like. In these studies,
experimental manipulations typically are not used, but instead information is collected on inventories, surveys, or interviews. Sometimes we have questions about
counseling events or phenomena that are best answered by collecting information
to describe events, such as the types of events that trigger counselor anger
(Fremont & Anderson, 1986) or the themes in AIDS support groups for gay men
(Stewart & Gregory, 1996). Likewise, if we wanted to identify the professional
needs and experiences of ethnic and racial minority psychologists, a survey might
be a useful strategy to collect information, which was precisely the approach chosen by Constantine, Quintana, Leung, and Phelps (1995). At other times we use
statistical procedures such as factor analysis (see Tinsley & Tinsley, 1987) or cluster analysis (see Borgen & Barnett, 1987) to describe how people or events might
be categorized. For example, one group of researchers used cluster analysis to
describe different types of career indecision in students (Larson, Heppner, Ham,
& Dugan, 1988). Descriptive research is discussed more fully in Chapters 9 and 10.

Difference questions ask if there are differences between groups of people,
or even within individual participants. The key feature in this type of question is
a comparison of some sort. Such research questions tend to focus on groups of
individuals; the groups may differ on some dimension or may receive different
treatments. For example, a study by Mallinckrodt and Helms (1986) examined a
difference question in determining whether physically disabled counselors' disabilities give them certain therapeutic advantages relative to able-bodied counselors. Likewise, Tracey, Leong, and Glidden (1986) compared help seeking and
problem perception in Asian-American and white clients. Similarly, Kelly and
Achter (1995) examined differences between high self-concealers (people who
keep secrets) and low self-concealers on attitudes toward counseling; they found
that high self-concealers had more negative views about counseling when they
were told that counseling involves revealing highly personal information. Difference questions are often examined in between-group and within-group designs
(see Chapter 6).

Relationship questions explore the degree to which two or more constructs
are related or vary together. Such questions tend to use correlational statistics or
more complex regression analyses. For example, a study by Marx and Gelso (1987)
examined a relationship question by studying the relationship between client satisfaction with termination and five client variables suggesting loss in the termination process. Likewise, Good et al. (1995) examined the correlations between
gender role conflict and several other inventories (for example, attitudes about
masculinity, fear of intimacy, social desirability) to provide estimates of construct

validity for the Gender Role Conflict Scale (O'Neil, Helms, Gable, David, & Wrightsman, 1986). Cournoyer and Mahalik (1995) extended this line of research by using canonical analysis, a multivariate approach to examining relations among multiple variables. Relationship research questions are discussed more fully in Chapters 9 and 10.

What constitutes a testable research question? According to Kerlinger (1986), a research question (a) asks a question about (b) the relationships between two or more constructs that can be (c) measured in some way. First, the question should be worded clearly and unambiguously in question form. Second, the research question should inquire into a relationship between two or more constructs, asking whether Construct A is related to Construct B. (If a particular relationship is stated, the research question becomes a hypothesis.) This second criterion pertains mostly to difference and relationship questions, while descriptive questions often seek to collect or categorize information. Finally, not only is a relationship between constructs examined, but somehow this relationship also must be measurable.

For example, consider a research question like, "Is supervision effective?" One might immediately ask, "Effective at what?" Is the researcher interested in the effectiveness of supervision to lower a trainee's stress level to conceptualize clients, or to intervene with clients? In short, such a question lacks specificity. Now consider the research questions developed by Wiley and Ray (1986), who were interested in the topic of the changing nature of supervision over the course of training. In particular, they were interested in testing Stoltenberg's (1981) counselor complexity model concerning developmental levels of counselor trainees. (Stoltenberg proposed that counselor trainees develop in a predictable way over the course of graduate training, and that counseling supervision environments should be adapted in ways that match the needs of the trainee.) Wiley and Ray developed three specific research questions, each of which inquired about relationships between two or more constructs and was amenable to being measured or tested in some way. For example, one of their questions was: To what extent do supervision dyads with a more congruent person-environment match on developmental level report higher satisfaction and learning than those with a less congruent match? The construct of the congruent person-environment match was concretely operationalized via the use of an assessment instrument called the Supervision Level Scale. Likewise, satisfaction and learning were operationalized in terms of a brief outcome instrument. Parenthetically, while Wiley and Ray obtained results that provided some support for conceptualizing supervisees and supervision environments developmentally, mean satisfaction and learning ratings did not differ by person-environment congruency.

Thus, the function of a testable research question or hypothesis is to provide direction for experimental inquiry. The testable research question or hypothesis not only identifies the topic but also identifies specific constructs of interest within that topic. After a researcher has developed a specific research question or hypothesis, he or she can then proceed to determine how data can be collected, what participants to use, what instruments to use, and so on. Many of these methodological decisions are directly dependent on the investigator's specific question or hypothesis.

Although the research question provides direction for designing a study, it is important to note that in the formative stages—as an investigator continues to develop the design and methodology of a particular study—it is not uncommon to revise or change the original research question. The investigator may encounter measurement or participant availability problems, which may dictate a slightly different research question. Or the researcher may find new data that suggest additional complexity in the topic and thus require revision of the research question. In short, any of a number of events may lead the researcher to process more information and subsequently to revise or sharpen the research questions in the formative stages of study design.

Sometimes graduate students get discouraged about their false starts and begin to feel a sense of inadequacy because they "couldn't get it right the first time." There often is an assumption that a "real researcher" proceeds through a logical series of ordered steps, starting first of all with a brilliant, incisive research question. Our experience has been that effective researchers generally examine a wide range of design issues when developing a research question, such as choosing instruments and participants or examining external validity issues. In short, revision of research questions is typical during the formative design stages, and often it is desirable. Of course, once data collection has begun, revision of the research question is no longer functional or appropriate.

FORMULATING OPERATIONAL DEFINITIONS

After the initial development of the research question or hypothesis, it is crucial that all terms or constructs in the question be defined concretely so that the research idea can be empirically tested. More specifically, each construct must be operationally defined, which means specifying the activities or operations necessary to measure it in this particular experiment. Kerlinger (1986) referred to operational definitions as "a sort of manual of instructions" that spells out what the investigator must do to measure or manipulate the variables during the procedures of the study.

For example, considerable interest has been shown concerning developmental models of supervision, which in essence postulate that trainees' skills and supervisory needs change over time as trainees attain different developmental levels (see Ellis et al., 1996; Holloway, 1987, 1992, 1995). A critical issue is how one operationally defines developmental level. Some of the initial investigations operationally defined developmental level as the training level of the student, such as beginning practicum student, advanced practicum student, and doctoral-level intern (see, for example, Heppner & Roehlke, 1984; Reising & Daniels, 1983; Worthington, 1984). Thus, developmental level was concretely or operationally defined in terms of training level.

The primary function of an operational definition is to define the constructs involved in a particular study. In a way, the operational definition provides a working definition of the phenomenon (Kazdin, 1980). Thus, the operational definition allows the researcher to move from general ideas and constructs to more specific and measurable events.

A problem arises when researchers investigate a given construct but develop different operational definitions for it. Consider again the example of developmental levels of counseling trainees. Whereas developmental level was initially defined as trainee level (see, for example, Reising & Daniels, 1983), Wiley and Ray (1986) defined developmental level in terms of supervisors' ratings on an instrument (the Supervision Level Scale) that assesses the trainee developmental level along five dimensions. Wiley and Ray's definition is more specific and is based on Stoltenberg's (1981) theoretical model. Interestingly, Wiley and Ray (1986) found that these two definitions of developmental level result in quite different categorizations of trainees.

This example aptly depicts the problem of different operational definitions for the same construct. As research information accrues over several investigations, it becomes difficult to summarize information on supervisees' developmental level because of the different operational definitions. More important, different operational definitions sometimes lead to very different results. This is a crucial point for the inexperienced researcher to comprehend, because it implies that the results from a particular study must be qualified or restricted according to the operational definitions used in the study. It is also important to note that as research within a topic progresses and becomes more complex, operational definitions often undergo revision as knowledge accumulates and researchers become more sophisticated, as in the supervision literature.

IDENTIFYING RESEARCH VARIABLES

Up to this point we have referred to variables rather generally. Often there is confusion and debate about the terms used to describe or designate the variables in a research study. We hope to alleviate some of this confusion by using specific terms throughout this book to describe the various types or classes of variables found in research designs. Specifically, the terms *independent variable* and *dependent variable* have been used in both experimental and descriptive research to define different types of variables.

In classical or "true" experiments, the researcher attempts to examine causality by systematically varying or altering one variable or set of variables and examining the resultant changes in or consequences for another variable or set of variables. In such experiments, the variable that is varied or altered is called the independent variable. More specifically, the independent variable is the variable that is manipulated or controlled in a study. Usually an experiment involves two or more levels of the independent variable (for example, treatment and no treatment), sometimes referred to as conditions. For example, in a study that compares cognitive versus interpersonal treatments for depression, the type of treatment (cognitive vs. interpersonal) would be the independent variable.

To examine the effects of the manipulation of the independent variable, concomitant changes in another variable, the dependent variable, are observed. In an experimental study, changes in the dependent variable are supposed to depend on or be influenced by changes or variations in the independent variable. In the previous example, the comparison is made by measuring some dependent variable. One example of a dependent variable is the depression scores on a standardized test (for example, the MMPI-D scale). In classical or "true" experiments we infer that a change (if one exists) in the dependent variable was caused by the manipulation of the independent variable. Thus, the terms *independent variable* and *dependent variable* have causal implications.

These terms are sometimes used to describe the variables in nonexperimental studies as well. For instance, the predictor variables in a regression equation are sometimes referred to as independent variables, and the criterion variable is sometimes referred to as a dependent variable. This can be confusing because of the notions of causality implied in the terms. To alleviate this type of confusion, we will primarily utilize the terms *independent variable* and *dependent variable* to describe variables in experimental studies, although some exceptions will have to be made. Independent and dependent variables are discussed further in Chapters 11 and 12.

COLLECTING AND ANALYZING DATA

Once the constructs referenced in the research question or hypothesis have been operationally defined and the design of the study determined, the researcher collects data. The actual process of data collection depends, of course, on the design of the experiment.

The design of the study must be determined—and that is the primary focus of the remaining chapters of this book. The final step of collecting and analyzing data, which is most appropriately discussed in various statistical books, will be briefly addressed in several statistical issues presented throughout the book.

Once the data are collected, sense must be made of them. Data usually consist of numbers that index characteristics of the participants. The data are summarized and analyzed with the express purpose of testing the research question or hypothesis. Specifically, the data are examined to determine whether or not the hypothesized relationship indeed exists.

When you are imbedded in the intricacies of data collection and analysis, it is often difficult to remember that the goal is to answer a question or test a hypothesis. Inevitably, decisions need to be made during the course of a study. At these times, always think about how various alternative methods will affect your ability to shed light on the original problem. Will a course of action obscure or clarify the original research question?

SUMMARY AND CONCLUSIONS

The purpose of this chapter is to provide an overview of the process of selecting a research topic and developing the research idea into a testable hypothesis. A number of activities are involved in narrowing a general topic to a series of specific, testable research hypotheses, such as developing research questions or hypotheses, identifying specific variables, and operationalizing variables. Typically, researchers intersperse thinking and planning into all of these activities as they proceed in reading relevant research literature and developing a particular topic. The outcome should be a specific, well-defined, clearly articulated research hypothesis.

We want to emphasize that it is normal, and even expected, for inexperienced researchers to make false starts and to modify aspects of their research project as they hone the final research question and hypothesis. Sometimes students get the impression that once they have had courses in research methods, statistics, and counseling theory, they ought to be able to produce research questions that have all the bugs worked out. They fear that if they do not perform flawlessly, their competence as a researcher will not only be questioned, but it will be clear that they do not have "the right stuff" to complete the program or have a research career. Regardless of how many courses a student has taken, there is no reason to expect a graduate student to be an expert researcher. Rather, it may be useful for students to regard their initial research attempts as training projects.

It is also important to note, especially for beginning researchers, that all research studies have limitations of one kind or another (such as lack of experimental control or concerns regarding generalizability). Gelso (1979) referred to this phenomenon as the Bubble Hypothesis and suggested that all research studies have some type of flaw or weakness. Sometimes inexperienced researchers create problems for themselves by trying to develop the perfect study or dissertation. In truth, these entities do not exist. Thus, it is essential for the inexperienced researcher to keep in mind the goal of developing a study that provides the profession with another piece of information, not the definitive study. Most often our knowledge bases in counseling are increased by adding one or two more pieces of information per study, with each study building on the previous research in some relatively small way. Over time, these small pieces accumulate and our knowledge about a particular topic is substantially increased.

C H A P T E R 3

CHOOSING RESEARCH DESIGNS

The purpose of this chapter is to provide an overview of some of the issues and trade-offs related to what is commonly referred to as research design. We begin by defining research design as a central component of scientific inquiry. Here we briefly introduce a key concept in research,: drawing inferences or conclusions from our data. Next we discuss the "research design myth," which is the conclusion that one design, a priori, is "better" than others. The third and major section of the chapter introduces one way of classifying research designs; the central theme is the balance between experimental control and generalizability of the research findings. The final section revisits the goal of choosing the best research design for a particular study, in which we suggest that it is inappropriate to focus only on the merits of any specific design without consideration of other factors, especially the match between the prior research knowledge, one's resources, and the type of research questions being examined.

SCIENTIFIC INQUIRY AND RESEARCH DESIGN

In Chapter 1 we identified the role of science as extending the profession's knowledge bases and theoretical underpinnings. Moreover, we maintained that the best way to establish credible knowledge bases (ways of knowing) was through a systematic and controlled method of inquiry, known as the scientific method. In this chapter, as well as the next, we will focus more on what we mean by *systematic* and *controlled.*

The basic task of the experimenter is to design research in such a way as to identify relationships between constructs and while ruling out as many plausible rival hypotheses or explanations as possible. The goal, put simply, is to determine if there is a relationship between two constructs, A and B, even though many sources of bias and confounding variables might distort the relationship between A and B. Perhaps an analogy might help. Ever since human beings began harvesting grains, there has been a need to separate the grain itself (the wheat) from its protective shield (the chaff), a dry, coarse, inedible material. In a way, the chaff gets in the way of digesting the wheat. In a similar way, the researcher wants to isolate the constructs of interest to his or her research question (the wheat) and remove as much as possible any other constructs (the chaff) that might contaminate, confound, bias, or distort the constructs of interest. Although the analogy of separating the wheat from the chaff is an oversimplification, it does highlight the essential task of the scientific method: *isolating the constructs of interest and trying to draw conclusions about the relationships among those constructs.* Any particular experiment can never completely eliminate all the explanations; some types of explanations will be left untested. This is a very crucial point to understand about research design; we will elaborate on this point throughout the chapter.

How does the researcher separate the "wheat" from the "chaff"? The basic tool of the researcher is what we call research design. Research design involves developing a plan or structure for an investigation, a way of conducting or executing the study that reduces bias, distortion, and random error. Different research designs have different strengths and weaknesses, and each will minimize different types of bias. Sometimes bias is also referred to as error, error variance, or noise. One of the most critical decisions in research is selecting a research design whose strengths and weaknesses help the researcher to examine specific research questions in a valid, systematic, and objective manner by reducing as many rival hypotheses or explanations as possible while isolating the relevant variables of interest. Research design, then, is a set of plans and procedures that researchers use within scientific inquiry to obtain empirical evidence (data) about isolated variables of interest. From the evidence, or data, the researcher then draws inferences about the constructs in his or her research question. We say "inferences" because the researcher can never rule out all of the rival hypotheses between, say, two constructs, A and B.

WHAT IS THE BEST DESIGN?

In the past, researchers have examined questions like: Does counseling/therapy work? What is the best type of counseling? Which clients benefit the most from therapy? The common thread among these three questions, and many like them, is their assumption of what Kiesler (1966) labels a uniformity myth. Simply stated, we have oversimplified counseling to assume that psychotherapeutic treatments are a standard (uniform) set of techniques, applied in a consistent (uniform) manner, by a standard (uniform) therapist, to a homogeneous (uniform) group of clients. Kiesler believed that these myths have greatly hampered progress in unraveling and understanding psychotherapy research; subsequently, he advocated research that addresses the question of what the best types of treatments are for particular types of clients across different settings.

No doubt, the uniformity myth has and continues to hamper research within counseling. We believe that counseling researchers often operate under an equally pervasive, often subtle, and definitely hindering uniformity myth about research design; we call this the "research design myth." The "research design myth" is not that all research designs are alike, but rather that one design is a priori "better" than others. Sometimes students will ask, "What is the best research design?" Often students and, unfortunately, experienced researchers believe that there is one right or best type of research design, apart from the type of research question they are examining. Research design is like a tool to help researchers examine specific research questions. But just as a carpenter has many different kinds of tools (for example, hammers, pliers, and screwdrivers), each with different functions, different research designs have different types of functions. For example, if a carpenter wanted to pound a large nail into an oak plank, a hammer would likely be the best tool to choose, but this does not mean that using a hammer every time the carpenter needed a tool would be a wise strategy—it would take a long time for the carpenter to remove a screw from the oak plank with a hammer. In short, it is an oversimplification to assume that there is one best type of research design. Rather, it is more appropriate to consider what knowledge is already known in a particular topic, and what type of research question is now being examined. Thus, we maintain that the more helpful question is, "What is the best research design for this particular problem at this time?"

A CLASSIFICATION OF RESEARCH DESIGNS

Historically, several broad categorizations of research designs have been described. Campbell and Stanley (1963) discussed design in terms of preexperimental designs, experimental designs, and quasi-experimental designs. Kazdin (1980) referred to experimental designs, quasi-experimental designs, and correlational designs. We will describe and discuss these major types of designs later in the book. Here we note that the different types of research designs may present particular strengths or weaknesses with regard to internal and external validity. In short, researchers must consider various trade-offs.

Two major issues affecting the inferences that researchers might make are experimental control and generalizability. It is an oversimplification to conceptualize research design in terms of these two issues alone; in Chapter 4 we will discuss these two issues in considerable depth, and we will also introduce two more issues affecting valid inferences. At this point, however, we want to highlight experimental control and generalizability in terms of the tension or trade-offs between these two issues in selecting a particular research design. Note that our discussion follows a positivistic and post-positivistic mode of thinking; see Chapter 10 for alternative ways of knowing that focus on qualitative designs.

Briefly, on one side of this trade-off the experimenter might use a particular research design to exercise as much experimental control as possible to ensure an accurate investigation of his or her research question. Kerlinger (1986) described this process as the "MAXMINCON" principle. He observed that the researcher first of all tries to *max*imize the variance of the variable or variables pertaining to the research questions. Second, the researcher tries to *min*imize the error variance of random variables, particularly due to errors of measurement or individual differences of participants. Third, the experimenter tries to *con*trol the variance of extraneous or unwanted variables that might affect or bias the variables in question.

Whereas the "MAXMINCON" principle applies most directly to traditional experimental research (between-group or within-group designs), the essence of Kerlinger's principle applies to all research designs: Control the experiment so as to obtain the most accurate investigation of the research question. Experimental control allows researchers to make more inferences about causal relationships between variables, which is referred to as the internal validity of the study (internal validity is discussed in greater depth in Chapter 4). Studies that are high in control typically use random selection of participants, random assignment of treatments, and manipulation of an independent variable or variables to permit the researcher to make inferences about causality. Studies that are low in control lack either or both random assignment to treatments (quasi-experimental studies) or manipulation of an independent variable (descriptive studies and ex post facto designs). In low-control studies, researchers can make inferences about relationships but not about causality.

At the same time, it is important to emphasize that counseling is first and foremost an applied specialty. It is therefore important to ascertain that the phenomenon one wishes to examine has some relevance to counseling. Whereas experimental control is a central ingredient of research design, a second key issue is generalizability of the results to applied settings, which is referred to as external validity (for more details regarding external validity, see Chapter 4). Our research knowledge must be grounded in and responsive to applications of counseling. For example, some studies use participants from the population of interest in a naturally occurring form, such as real clients seeing experienced therapists, or students who are truly undecided about a major or career choice. Inferences from these studies tend to more generalizable to actual counseling applications.

It is important to note that in an applied field such as counseling, experimental control is often difficult and sometimes unethical. For example, it is often difficult to minimize error variance due to individual differences across clients, and there may be ethical dilemmas associated with particular treatment interventions or experimental manipulations. In short, within an applied context that involves the lives of real people who are struggling and need psychological assistance, experimental control often presents obstacles for the researcher. Moreover, the more steps a researcher takes to maximize control, the more simplified (or even artificial) the research context can become. Again we encounter a major research design issue for the counseling researcher: the balance and trade-offs between experimental control and generalizability.

Gelso (1979) used the concepts of external and internal validity to create a typology of research designs that we find helpful. Gelso essentially proposed that we can organize counseling research along two dimensions, that research can be either high or low in control (internal validity) and conducted in either a field or a laboratory setting (external validity). Gelso acknowledged that although these categories were inevitably simplifications, they were nonetheless useful in understanding the strengths and limitations of types of research designs.

Figure 3-1 is a representation of the different types of research using Gelso's (1979) two (high and low internal validity) by two (high and low external validity) matrix. We have made changes in two aspects of Gelso's classification system to

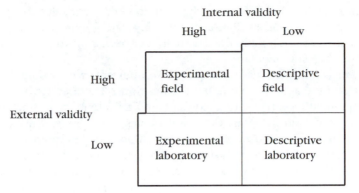

FIGURE 3-1
Types of research designs classified by levels of external and internal validity.

reflect a broader set of operations. The most significant change involves the shape of the matrix. In our figure, the box that represents high internal and high external validity is smaller than the other three boxes due to the nonindependence of the internal and external validity dimensions. Since internal and external validity are not independent, it is difficult to have an experimental field study with internal validity as high as that of an experimental laboratory study, or with external validity as high as that of a descriptive field study. A second change involves using the label *descriptive* instead of Gelso's label *correlational* to describe studies low in internal validity. The term *correlational* seemed to unnecessarily limit our thinking about the nature of studies low in internal validity; *descriptive,* in contrast, does not imply the restriction of these designs to one statistical operation (correlation).

Descriptive Laboratory Studies

Descriptive laboratory studies have low external and low internal validity. These studies are characterized by investigations that do not exercise experimental controls (such as randomization or manipulation of independent variables) and that are conducted in a laboratory setting of some kind. A descriptive laboratory study is low in external validity because it uses a setting that in some ways can only simulate a real-life setting. For instance, a study of some aspect of the counseling process could use undergraduate students as clients and trainees as counselors. Such "counseling" may or may not be like that which takes place between real clients and experienced counselors. In other words, there would certainly be questions about the extent of generalizability of findings from this type of study.

A descriptive laboratory study is low in internal validity because it lacks experimental control in the sense of manipulation of an independent variable or randomization of participants. Rather, the descriptive laboratory study involves describing in detail some aspect of counseling, by identifying, labeling, or categorizing data, as well as obtaining basic descriptive statistics such as means, standard deviations, and correlations among variables. Returning to the counseling example, a researcher may want to determine the likelihood of client self-exploration given certain counselor responses. Rather than manipulating counselor responses, the researcher may want to study their natural occurrence. In this way, the study is descriptive, not experimental.

If internal and external validity are so important, why would a researcher conduct a study that is low along both dimensions? There are two main reasons for conducting these types of studies. First, a laboratory setting allows the researcher some control over extraneous variables, even though the experimenter may choose not to manipulate some of them. Data can be more easily collected, the researcher need not worry as much about experimental variables adversely affecting the therapeutic assistance a client receives, and the researcher can expect and encourage more involvement from the participants. A second reason for conducting descriptive laboratory studies is that it is impossible to study some phenomena in a field or real-life setting. The data collection procedures may be so extensive and/or intensive that the very presence of these procedures alters the process under examination to the extent that it is no longer natural or real.

Elliott's (1985) study of helpful and nonhelpful events in counseling interviews is a good example of a descriptive laboratory study. He had counselor trainees conduct an interview with a recruited client. After the interview, the client reviewed the tape and rated each counselor statement on a nine-point helpfulness scale. Most and least helpful counselor statements from each counseling dyad were then given to judges who sorted the statements into categories. Cluster analysis was then used to put the statements into categories. In this manner, Elliott was able to develop a taxonomy of helpful and nonhelpful events in early counseling interviews.

This study is low in internal validity because no manipulation of counselor statements occurred. Rather, statements were classified as helpful or nonhelpful on the basis of an a posteriori (after the fact) rating of helpfulness. The study is low in external validity because counselor trainees and recruited clients served as the participants, and because the video-recall procedure probably altered aspects of the counseling. This study does, however, provide important information about the counseling process that certainly advances our understanding of an important concept—perceived helpfulness to clients of counselor statements.

For the researcher considering a descriptive laboratory study, Chapter 15 contains information about the conduct of analog research, with special emphasis on the issue of generalizability of laboratory studies. In addition, Chapters 9 (on descriptive research) and 10 (on qualitative research) contain information on different types of descriptive designs.

Descriptive Field Studies

Descriptive field studies have high external and low internal validity. These studies are characterized by investigations that do not exercise experimental controls (randomization, manipulation of variables) and are conducted in a real-life setting. A descriptive field study is often high in external validity because a sample of participants can be taken directly from a population of interest. In counseling research, for example, this would mean the study of real clients seeing actual therapists. A descriptive field study is low in internal validity because variables are studied as they occur naturally rather than being manipulated.

For a study to be truly high in external validity, the data-gathering procedures must not have sufficient impact on the participants to disrupt their normal set of actions. The two most common examples of this type of study are retrospective studies that use data routinely collected as part of an agency policy, and single-subject studies of individual counseling. A classic study representing descriptive field research is the Menninger project (Wallenstein, 1989), a very large study conducted over a 35-year period that examined the effectiveness of counseling (thus, an outcome study) with patients who received more than 1000 hours of analysis. Client-therapist pairs were selected for this study only after counseling had formally ended. As Wallenstein (1989) states, clients and therapists were totally unaware during treatment of which cases would be analyzed. In addition, the study used only data that were routinely collected during treatment. Because of the lack of experimental control in this study, a number of problems regarding internal validity are raised, such as threats from history and selection (terms that will be explained more fully in Chapter 4). The real-life nature of this study makes it intriguing because it has high external validity and applicability, even though the findings are only suggestive at best.

A study by Liddle (1996) demonstrates some of the advantages and disadvantages of descriptive field studies. The author was interested in examining whether gay and lesbian clients would benefit from choosing a gay or lesbian therapist, as well as relating specific therapist practices to therapy outcomes. Participants were 392 lesbian and gay men obtained from 29 states and three Canadian provinces. The results revealed that gay, lesbian, and bisexual therapists of both genders, and heterosexual female therapists were all rated as more helpful than heterosexual male therapists. In a second analysis, Liddle (1996) examined the relations between 13 therapist practices (nine negative and four positive) and (a) client ratings of a therapist as unhelpful, and (b) termination of therapy after one session. (One example of a negative therapist practice was some indication by the therapist of the assumption that the client was heterosexual before the client indicated his/her sexual orientation.) Eight of the nine negative therapist practices were significantly associated with both outcome variables. The three negative therapist practices that had the strongest association with the outcome variables were the therapist blaming the client's problems on the client's sexual orientation, the therapist's refusal to see the client after the client disclosed his/her sexual orientation, and the therapist's indication that he or she believed that a gay or lesbian identity is bad, sick, or inferior. Conversely, all four of the positive therapist practices (for example, the therapist's willingness to deal with the client's sexual orientation when it was relevant) were inversely related to the counseling outcomes.

These findings have some important practical implications. "The therapists whom these clients find helpful tend to be those who have educated themselves about issues of concern to gay and lesbian clients (including societal prejudice, internalized homophobia, relationship issues, and community resources) and those who help their clients work toward a positive gay or lesbian identity" (Liddle, 1999, p. 399). This study is high on external validity because of its large number of participants and because the sample was obtained across the United States and Canada. Conversely, it is not known how many people were asked but declined to participate, or whether the methods of recruiting participants resulted in any systematic biases in the sample. The study is low on internal validity, as no variables were manipulated. Thus it is not possible to make causal statements concerning the effects of therapist practices on therapeutic outcomes. In addition, any of a number of other counselor behaviors may have affected the counseling process and outcome. The study used an open-ended (free recall) format with an unspecified time (for example, one or five years ago), which might have resulted in some distortion.

For researchers interested in conducting descriptive field studies, Chapter 8 (on single-subject designs) and Chapter 17 (on process research) provide guidance for the conduct of this type of research, with an emphasis on therapeutic counseling. Chapters 9 and 10, on descriptive designs, provide an overview of some common descriptive designs, whereas Chapter 7 covers ex post facto designs.

Experimental Laboratory Studies

Experimental laboratory studies have low external and high internal validity. These studies are characterized by manipulation of independent variables and are conducted in a laboratory setting. An experimental laboratory study is low in external validity because instead of using participants directly sampled from a population of interest, the experimenter sets up a situation to resemble a naturally occurring one. This research is often high in internal validity because the experimenter can randomly assign participants to treatments and manipulate one or more independent variables. Because these studies are high in internal validity, the researcher can and does make inferences about causality. The extent to which these inferences about causality can be generalized to the populations and settings of interest is the critical question about experimental laboratory studies.

A study by Worthington and Atkinson (1996) typifies some of the advantages and limitations of experimental laboratory studies. The researchers were interested in examining the effects of a counselor's attributions or beliefs about the specific causal agents that are antecedents to physical or psychological distress. Forty undergraduate students volunteered to serve as clients for three sessions of counseling role plays with 11 graduate-student counselors. The students were then told of the counselor's attributions of the cause of their problems, which were manipulated to either agree or disagree with the student's own attributions. The results revealed that clients whose attributions agreed with the counselor's rated their counselor as more credible sources of help.

These findings suggest that client-counselor attributional similarity is beneficial to some counseling outcomes. Because of the experimental controls used, the authors could conclude with a high degree of certainty that the similarity or dissimilarity of the client-counselor attributions affects client ratings of counselor credibility. Thus, the study has a high degree of internal validity. However, the study is low in external validity, and it is unclear whether these results would generalize to real counseling interviews involving real clients presenting real problems.

For readers interested in using an experimental laboratory design, Chapter 15 details issues in the conduct of analog research. Chapter 6 describes between-groups and within-subjects designs, which are what many authors refer to as "true" experiments.

Experimental Field Studies

Experimental field studies have moderate external and internal validity. These studies are characterized by investigations that manipulate independent variables and are conducted in a real-life setting. An experimental field study attempts to examine causality through random assignment of treatments and control of independent variables. Such experimental control moves the study away from the examination of naturally occurring counseling. At best, the researcher has a study moderately high in external validity. Even though an experimental field study attempts to examine causality in a naturally occurring setting, the researcher can never exercise the same control in the field as in the laboratory. Hence, an experimental field study can be at best only moderately high in internal validity. An experimental field study allows for the best combination of inferences about cause and generalizability that is attainable within a single study. Typically, though, an experimental field study can obtain neither the same level of certainty about causality as is possible in an experimental laboratory study nor the same level of certainty about generalizability as in a descriptive field study.

Hogg and Deffenbacher (1988) offer an example of an experimental field study. These authors were interested in comparing an interpersonal and a cognitive approach in the group treatment of depression. They also included a no-treatment control condition in the design. External validity was emphasized by using clients seeking help at a university counseling center and experienced group therapists. However, threats to external validity existed because of the use of pretesting and possible reactions to experimental procedures (tape recordings). Internal validity was emphasized by random assignment of clients to interpersonal and cognitive groups and by standardized treatment for the two conditions. Internal validity was threatened by the nonrandom assignment of clients to the control condition (clients who came to treatment late in the semester were used to form the control group). This study is a good example of the sacrifices that researchers must often make in external and internal validity considerations in order to conduct an experimental field study. Researchers wanting to do experimental field studies should read Chapter 5 describing between-groups and within-subjects designs, and Chapter 7 on quasi-experimental designs.

ON CHOOSING A RESEARCH DESIGN

We now return to the question of choosing the best research design. If, as we have argued, there is no a priori best design, then one might conclude that the choice of design does not matter; all designs are equally good and bad. This, of course, would be true only if research were conducted in a vacuum. It might be true that there is no one best design for research within the counseling profession as a whole, *but at any particular time in the history of a topic area there may be more or less useful ways to approach a specific research question.* We propose that the usefulness of a particular research design for examining a specific research question is a function of (a) the existing knowledge bases pertaining to the specific research question, (b) the types of research designs used and inferences made to develop the existing knowledge bases, (c) the resources available to the researcher, (d) the specific threats to the validity of the particular design being considered, and (e) the match or fit between previous research knowledge (factors a and b), the design being considered (factor d), and one's resources (factor c). Moreover, we believe that it is essential to be aware of Gelso's (1979) Bubble Hypothesis (the idea that all experiments will be flawed somehow), and thus we maintain that both paradigmatic diversity and programmatic research are also basic considerations in selecting a design.

Typically, research on a particular question is conducted within an existing body of knowledge. Thus, it is imperative for the researcher to ascertain both what the previous research suggests about a particular topic area and the kinds of questions that remain unanswered. As a researcher forms a particular research question, it is important to ask what kind of knowledge will add to the existing literature. At the same time, the researcher must evaluate what type of research design will provide the kind of knowledge that is needed. Perhaps a descriptive study would add the most useful knowledge or basic normative information about a topic. Or perhaps an experimental study that isolates the interactive effects of two independent variables would help explain previous contradictory findings. Thus, the utility of a research design needs to be evaluated in the context of the existing research knowledge in a given area.

Equally important is the type of research design used and the inferences drawn to develop the existing knowledge bases. The types of research designs used affect the types of inferences made in developing a knowledge base. Thus, if a particular topic has been predominantly researched in laboratory settings, then perhaps research focused on field settings will now add the most useful knowledge in that area. Or if a topic has been investigated through tightly controlled experimental studies, then perhaps descriptive studies might now add some useful information. Any type of design can be overused in a particular area, a condition that can produce an unbalanced and subsequently weak knowledge base. (In Chapter 15 we present a brief overview of the social influence literature in counseling, and we provide details of an example of this problem of overusing any particular design.)

Many times inexperienced researchers do not read the method sections of research reports. One of this book's authors admits (sheepishly) to committing this sin during much of his early graduate studies. Instead, students usually read the introduction and then skip to the discussion. While this might suffice for obtaining content knowledge in an area, it misses the important aspect of learning about how the studies were conducted. We suggest a simple technique that inexperienced researchers can use in examining a body of literature. Make a copy of Figure 3-1, and as you read the method sections of various studies within a topic area, place the study into the appropriate cell. It should quickly become apparent which designs have been used and perhaps overused.

It is also important to note that different designs require different resources and have different costs. For instance, a researcher might decide that a descriptive field study was needed to examine the relationship between counselor techniques and a client's perception of the working alliance. But should she do a correlational study or use an intensive single-subject design? The answer to this question should be obtained, in part, by examining the resources available. To do the correlational study, the researcher would probably need to find 30 to 50 client-counselor dyads. It may take a great deal of work to find these dyads, but the data analyses may be fairly easy and painless. On the other hand, for an intensive single-subject study the researcher may have an easy time finding one dyad willing to participate. However, a rather involved, intensive process of analyzing the data will likely ensue. Thus, a researcher must not only examine the resources available but also must look at the costs of choosing a particular design.

In choosing a research design, it is also of utmost importance to remember that each experiment has strengths and weaknesses, and moreover that each experiment is typically flawed in some way. Gelso (1979) understood this idea as he offered the Bubble Hypothesis, which suggests that doing research is similar to trying to apply a sticker to a car windshield. When an air bubble forms between the sticker and the windshield, the owner presses the bubble in an attempt to eliminate it. No matter how hard he tries, however, the bubble reappears somewhere else. The only way to get rid of the bubble is to throw the sticker away, but then the owner is left without a sticker. In a similar manner, every piece of research and every research design is flawed (has a bubble). The different research designs will have different limitations and strengths (the different designs may change the location of the bubble), but no single design can entirely eliminate the bubble. The researcher can either stop doing research (throw the sticker away) or can be cognizant of the size and location of the bubble for any given design.

The Bubble Hypothesis clearly points out that if only one type of research design is advocated by a discipline, then the bubble will always be in a similar place on the sticker—all the research will contain similar flaws or blind spots. On the other hand, if multiple research designs are advocated, each with different "bubble" locations, then the cumulative effect will be a clearer, more accurate picture of the research problem. Viewed in this manner, the usefulness of a particular design at a particular time is determined by the locations of the "bubbles" in the studies that have previously addressed this question. This type of reasoning led Gelso (1979) to suggest that all types of research designs are useful and that knowledge can be advanced only when the same problem is examined using multiple design strategies. He thus argued for paradigmatic diversity. In fact, there is a growing consensus within (and outside) the field of counseling that the discipline is strengthened when alternative designs are used (see, for example, Gelso, 1979; Harmon, 1982; Kazdin, 1978; Polkinghorne, 1984).

The Bubble Hypothesis and the need for paradigmatic diversity underscore the importance of programmatic research on a particular topic. Put another way, a series of investigations, conducted by the same or different researchers, that successively extends our knowledge bases along a particular line of research on a particular topic is highly desirable for the profession. The reason is that a series of related investigations that build on each other tends to accumulate more useful knowledge bases than does a series of isolated investigations. Consider the following examples and notice how the researchers used different research methods for different purposes.

Hill and her colleagues (Hill, Helms, Spiegel, & Tichenor, 1988) used a descriptive laboratory study as the first step in developing a client reactions system. Recruited clients seen by counselors-in-training used a preliminary version of the reactions system to record their reactions to interviews. Based on client feedback and item analysis, a revised reactions list was formulated and then used in a descriptive field setting. Thus, Hill's group initially used a descriptive laboratory strategy to develop a measure and then followed it up with a descriptive field design that evaluated both the utility of the measure and the implications of the findings. In short, once appropriate measures have been found or developed, it is then important to examine how these variables operate in real-life settings.

A study by Marx and Gelso (1987) also illustrates programmatic research. Because little research had been done on the termination of individual counseling, these authors sought to describe the termination process using a descriptive field study. They did this in two ways: by using content analyzing termination sessions and by examining variables that correlated with client satisfaction concerning termination. One variable that related to satisfaction with termination was the amount of time spent talking about termination. This finding could serve as a springboard for the next step in a program of research, perhaps an experimental field study. One might wonder if there is a causal relationship between the amount of time the counselor spends talking about termination and client satisfaction with termination. Actual clients and counselors could be used to examine this question. For instance, dyads could be randomly assigned to a high or a low termination-discussion condition. Subsequently, more refined questions could be asked, such as how soon (for example, in a middle session or the next-to-last session) the counselor should begin to address termination.

SUMMARY AND CONCLUSIONS

In this chapter we have extended our discussion of science and the scientific method to basic research design considerations. We have maintained that the basic task of the experimenter is to design research in such a way as to simultaneously identify relationships between constructs and eliminate as many rival hypotheses as possible. Kerlinger (1986) has labeled this the "MAXMINCON" principle. Research design involves developing both a plan or structure for an investigation and a way of executing the study that simultaneously reduces certain kinds of error and helps the researcher obtain empirical evidence (data) about isolated variables of interest.

We have further maintained that two central issues in research design are experimental control and generalizability, and that different types of research designs represent different trade-offs between these two central issues. While it can be debated which of these issues is of greater importance, or which issue should take priority in beginning a line of research (see Campbell & Stanley, 1963;

Gelso, 1979; Stone, 1984), we believe that in an applied specialty such as counseling, both issues are essential. While internal validity may be the sine qua non (Campbell & Stanley, 1963), the applied nature of our work in counseling cannot be ignored (and indeed must be emphasized). Although we have maintained that internal and external validity are not independent, they also are not incompatible, especially across multiple investigations. Thus, we need programmatic research that is designed to maximize the benefits of both internal and external validity across investigations. Moreover, within such an investigative blend there is a useful place for laboratory research in extending theoretical issues. As Stone (1984) has argued, "a preoccupation with immediate application can lead us to dismiss important research" (p. 108) that extends our theoretical understanding. In essence, we are underscoring the need for balance in our research; we suggest that investigative styles that prohibit certain types of research (such as naturalistic research) are dangerous because they reduce the possibility of gaining certain types of knowledge.

We have also suggested that the goodness of a particular design hinges not only on the threats to validity it allows, but also on the context provided by previous research and existing knowledge bases. Thus, in addition to evaluating the threats to validity, the researcher needs to consider (a) the existing research content, (b) the type of research designs used, and (c) the resources available. The researcher must choose a research design with strengths and weaknesses that match the needs of the research question, a design that will provide the type of knowledge needed at this particular time in history. In this way, a series of research studies, each with different strengths and weaknesses, may add the greatest breadth to our knowledge bases. Thus, we strongly encourage using programmatic research that emphasizes paradigmatic diversity to build broad knowledge bases for the counseling profession.

CHAPTER 4

VALIDITY ISSUES IN RESEARCH DESIGN

The challenge for the researcher is to select a design that allows the most useful and uncontaminated investigation in order to draw valid conclusions about research questions. Whereas we discussed the trade-off between internal and external validity in Chapter 3, this chapter provides a more detailed analysis of four major inferences made by researchers in evaluating the validity of a particular research design. Specifically, the purpose of this chapter is to define and discuss threats to (a) statistical conclusion validity, (b) internal validity, (c) construct validity of putative cause and effect, and (d) external validity.

FOUR TYPES OF VALIDITY AND THE THREATS TO EACH

Chapter 2 presented an overview of the research process. Based on theory, clinical practice, or observation, the researcher states one or a set of research hypotheses. Recall that a research hypothesis is a conjecture about the relationship between or among constructs. The next step is to operationalize the constructs so that they can be measured. In a true experimental design, the independent variable is manipulated by the researcher to assess the effect of the manipulation on a dependent variable. Statistical methods are often (although certainly not always) used to help the researcher decide whether or not the manipulation had the hypothesized effect.

As an illustration, consider the following example. Suppose that a researcher suspects that cognitive treatments of social anxiety have had only limited success because the interventions do not generalize to behavioral situations. The researcher hypothesizes that in vivo behavioral exercises added to cognitive therapy will improve the efficacy of the therapy. In vivo behavioral exercises are operationalized carefully by designing homework that involves a progressive set of situations in which clients first smile at a stranger, later engage strangers in a short conversation, and finally arrange a social encounter. Social anxiety is operationalized by having the participants report on the (fictitious) ABC Anxiety Test the anxiety that they experienced after talking with a stranger that the researcher arranged for them to meet (called a confederate). The independent variable is manipulated by randomly assigning the participants to one of two conditions: cognitive therapy alone or cognitive therapy plus behavioral exercises. Further suppose that 40 participants are randomly chosen from people who (a) answered an advertisement for a program to treat social anxiety and (b) were assessed by the researcher in a clinical interview to be socially anxious. After the ten-week program, anxiety is assessed using the confederate and the ABC Test; a statistical test indicates that there is a reliable difference between the groups in the hypothesized direction. That is, the mean level of anxiety, as indicated on the ABC Test, is lower for the group that received the exercises, and this difference has a low probability of occurring by chance.

Pleased with these results, the researcher concludes that (a) a true relation exists between the independent variable and the dependent variable (that is, participants who receive exercises in addition to cognitive therapy have lower scores on the ABC Test than participants who receive cognitive therapy only), (b) the manipulation of the independent variable was indeed the cause of the difference in scores (that is, the exercises were the cause of the lower anxiety scores), (c) behavioral exercises increase the effectiveness of the cognitive treatment of social anxiety, and (d) the results are applicable to socially anxious participants generally (and not just to the participants in this particular study). These conclusions, or more specifically inferences, seem reasonable in this case; however, there are always flaws in any research, and it is appropriate to keep in mind that one or more of these inferences may be incorrect.

The degree to which inferences reflect the actual state of affairs is referred to as validity. If in vivo exercises in fact reduce anxiety, then the inferences made by the researcher in our example are valid. The purpose of this section is to discuss the principles of validity so that researchers and consumers of counseling research can evaluate the probable validity of the inferences made in a particular study. Although there are many ways to look at the validity of research, the framework presented by Cook and Campbell (1979) is a generally accepted and particularly useful model. Cook and Campbell have created a taxonomy that classifies validity into four types: statistical conclusion validity, internal validity, construct validity of putative causes and effects, and external validity. This typology was derived from Campbell and Stanley's (1963) original conception of internal and external validity. Other discussions of validity are presented by Bracht and Glass (1968) and by Wampold, Davis, and Good (1990).

In this chapter we present an overview of the four types of validity identified by Cook and Campbell, and examine threats to each of these types of validity. Many of the subsequent chapters in this book focus on these types of validity in more detail.

Overview of the Types of Validity

We will approach Cook and Campbell's four categories by examining the four major inferences made by the researcher in the anxiety example. The first question was whether or not there was a relationship between the in vivo exercises used in this study and scores on the ABC Test. In our example, there was a statistically significant relationship between the independent and dependent variables. One of the major inferences made in interpreting research concerns the existence of a relationship between (or among) the variables in the study. The researcher may conclude that there is a relationship or that there is no relationship. *Statistical conclusion validity* refers to the degree to which the researcher has come to the correct conclusion about this relationship.

The second major inference to be made in interpreting research is an answer to the following question: Given that there is a relationship between the variables, is it a causal relationship? In our anxiety example, the researcher concluded that the statistically significant differences between the anxiety levels for the two groups was due to (caused by) the addition of the exercises. *Internal validity* refers to the degree of certainty with which such statements can be made about the existence of a causal relationship between variables.

The third major type of inference is *construct validity of putative causes and effects.* Construct validity concerns how well the variables chosen to represent a hypothetical construct actually capture the essence of the hypothetical construct. One of the major issues with construct validity involves confounding—the possibility that what one researcher interprets as a causal relationship between constructs A and B, another researcher might interpret as a causal relationship between A and C, or between D and B. In our example it was presumed that the ABC Anxiety Test used in a contrived situation with a confederate was a suitable measure of the social anxiety of the participant, and that the particular exercises used in this study were truly in vivo exercises appropriate for social interactions. If the operationalizations of the constructs of this study were adequate, then the causality attributed to the independent and dependent variables justifies statements about the causality of the constructs used in the research hypotheses. Thus, construct validity of putative causes and effects refers to the degree to which the measured variables used in the study represent the hypothesized constructs. In our example, in vivo exercises (in conjunction with cognitive therapy) were the putative cause, and anxiety was the putative effect.

To be of any value to researchers and practitioners, the causal relationship between the hypothesized constructs must be generalizable to persons other than those in the particular study. In the context of our fictitious example, to what extent can we generalize the use of in vivo behavioral exercises to other socially anxious people? *External validity* refers to the degree to which the causal relationship is generalizable across persons, settings, and times.

The question arises of how these types of validity can be assessed. This is a difficult process because one can never be totally certain of what is true, but the basic procedure is to establish estimates of validity by ruling out as many threats to validity, sometimes called sources of invalidity or rival explanations, as possible. For each of the four types of validity, we will discuss here several threats or sources of invalidity. Each threat represents a possible explanation that would invalidate the inference made in the study.

Researchers strive to conduct research that rules out as many threats to validity as possible. It is crucial to understand that no study will adequately eliminate all threats to validity. Moreover, different research designs place different emphases on the importance of these four types of inference (validity). Ideally, a researcher should be able to choose a design that will enable him or her to be fairly certain about all four types of inference. Unfortunately, these types of inferences are not independent. Designs that increase the certainty of both causal inferences (internal validity) and statistical conclusion validity often do so at the expense of decreasing the certainty of either inferences from samples to populations (external validity) or the meaning of the operations (construct validity). Likewise, designs that increase the certainty of inferences from samples to populations or about constructs do so at the expense of decreasing the certainty of inferences about the extent of relationships or causality. The point is that there are trade-offs with different types of research designs, not only with regard to these four types of inferences, but with respect to other factors as well.

A study that has reasonable levels of validity will be useful scientifically because the conclusions reached can be tentatively accepted. Additional studies should be designed that will rule out threats that were plausible in the original study. Through the accumulation of studies, threats to a research hypothesis can be ruled out and a strong conclusion can be reached. For example, no single study of smoking and health has unequivocally established a causal relationship between smoking and disease; however, the accumulation of many studies (and there have been thousands) rules out, with almost absolute certainty, any threats to this conclusion. (The Tobacco Institute's statement that no *one* study has ever scientifically established an unequivocal causal relationship between smoking and health is true, as far as it goes.)

We will now discuss specific threats to the four major types of validity. Cook and Campbell (1979) indicated, and we concur, that the boundaries between threats are not rigid. Rather than debate whether one aspect of a study represents one threat or another, we think it is more important that you understand the major concepts so that you can make a reasonable assessment of the validity of studies you review or design.

Threats to Statistical Conclusion Validity

In this section we define statistical conclusion validity and delineate seven threats to this type of validity. First, however, we need to examine the role of statistics in counseling research. Although most students study statistics outside the context of design, it is necessary to realize that statistical analysis is just one of many parts of the research process. Typically, a statistical test is used to examine whether there is indeed a relation between the variables in a study. In the anxiety example, most likely a two-group independent *t* test would be performed.

Traditional statistical tests are employed to test two competing hypotheses: the null hypothesis and an alternative hypothesis. The null hypothesis predicts that there is no relationship between the variables in the study. The alternative hypothesis states that there is some true relationship between the variables (which is typically the relationship that the authors have reason to believe might exist). In the anxiety example, the null hypothesis would be that the mean scores on the ABC

Anxiety Test for those who receive in vivo exercises would be equal to the mean scores for those who do not receive the exercises. The alternative hypothesis would be that the mean anxiety scores for those who receive the in vivo exercises would be lower than for those who do not receive this treatment. Rejection of the null hypothesis and acceptance of the alternative hypothesis lends credence to the hypothesis that in vivo experiences add to the efficacy of cognitive therapy.

Now, a crucial point. Statistical hypotheses are stated in terms of what is true for a *population.* When we speak of a true relationship between variables, we mean that generally the relationship exists across all persons in a population, although certainly there will be variability among individuals. The behavioral exercises might be generally helpful, even though perhaps slightly less helpful for some persons than for others or may even be a hindrance for a few. Thus, when we conduct a study on a sample drawn from a population, it may be possible that the results of the analysis for the sample are not indicative of the true relationship between the variables. For our example, it is possible that the participants selected to be in the study were unusual in some way and that the results obtained are not indicative of the true relationship.

Statistical tests, which are based in probability theory, are used to indicate whether one should reject the null hypothesis—that there is no relationship—and accept the alternative that there is a relationship. A statistically significant t test in the anxiety example (say with the p value set at $p < .05$) would indicate that one could comfortably believe that a true relationship exists between the independent and dependent variables. However, it is possible that this conclusion is in error. That is, the null hypothesis of no relationship may be true, even though a statistically significant result was obtained due to, say, sampling error. The significance level of 0.05 indicates, however, that the chances of incorrectly concluding that a true relationship exists are fewer than 5 in 100. Incorrectly concluding that a true relationship exists is called a *Type I error.* Type I errors are pernicious because they result in claims that something is going on when it is not; for example, a Type I error in the anxiety study would perpetuate the belief that in vivo exercises were helpful when they were not.

Another type of error can be made: One can incorrectly conclude that there is no relationship. Suppose the t test in the anxiety example was not statistically significant; in this case, the researcher could not conclude that the independent variable was related to the dependent variable. Nevertheless, there might have been a true relationship between these two variables even though for any of a variety of reasons the researcher did not find it. This type of error is called a *Type II error.* One of the major reasons for Type II errors is that variability in the participants' responses tends to obscure true relationships. This variability, often called error variance, can be thought of as static on a radio receiver that obscures the true signal. Even if the true signal is strong, an electrical storm can generate sufficient static that one cannot hear a favorite program. Conditions that create error variance lead to threats to statistical conclusion validity (more on this later).

It is important to realize that one is never totally certain that a statistically significant result indicates that a true relationship exists. Similarly, a nonsignificant result does not absolutely indicate that no relationship exists. Nevertheless, various factors or threats can decrease the confidence with which we conclude either that there is or is not a true relationship between variables. These threats are discussed next. Although some of these topics are more appropriately discussed in statistics or measurement courses, discussion of them here will, we hope, facilitate an understanding of statistical conclusion validity.

Low Statistical Power

Power refers to the probability of correctly deciding that there is a true relationship, if indeed a true relationship exists. Clearly, if there is a true relationship, we want to design a study that is able to detect this relationship. Studies with low power often result in the conclusion that no relationship exists when in fact a true relationship exists. Insufficient power most often results from using too few participants. For example, in a study with fewer than ten participants, the probability of obtaining a statistically significant result (that is, concluding that there is a relationship) will likely be very small, even when the relationship between the variables is strong. Power will be discussed in more detail in Chapter 13; here we need only note that inadequate statistical power is a threat to statistical conclusion validity.

small n

Violated Assumptions of Statistical Tests

All statistical tests rely on various assumptions (for example, traditional parametric tests typically rely on the assumption that scores are normally distributed). When the assumptions are violated, the researcher and consumer may be misled about the probabilities of making Type I and Type II errors. For example, if the p level of a statistical test is set at 0.05 and the test is statistically significant (that is, $p < .05$), one commonly believes that the likelihood of incorrectly concluding that there is a true relationship is less than 5%. However, if the assumptions of the test are violated, this probability may be much higher. Thus, the statistical conclusion validity is reduced because there is more chance for making Type I and II errors. The pernicious aspect of violated assumptions is that it is difficult to determine whether or not there are violations, and, if so, the degree to which the violations affect the results. We advise you to be aware of the importance of assumptions when using statistical tests; we leave the details of violated assumptions to statistics texts and courses.

"Fishing" and Error-Rate Problems

As previously discussed, when a researcher employs any one statistical analysis there is a chance of incorrectly concluding that a relationship in fact exists. The probability of making this error is given by the significance level for the test (for example, $p < .05$, or 5 chances in 100). However, the probability of this error escalates dramatically when more than one test is conducted. For example, if ten statistical tests are conducted, the probability of making at least one Type I error (incorrectly concluding that a relationship exists) is at least 0.40 (see Hays, 1988, for a discussion and calculations of experimentwide error rates). The point is this: When a researcher conducts many statistical tests, some are likely to be statistically significant by chance and thus lead to false interpretations, sources of statistical conclusion invalidity. Sometimes researchers engage in "fishing," which is simply conducting many statistical tests on a data set without sating specific hypotheses. This procedure inappropriately capitalizes on chance events and increases the probability of a Type 1 error occurring. Matching the statistical test to the research hypothesis is preferable (Wampold, Davis, & Good, 1990).

Unreliability of Measures

Unreliable measures introduce error variance and obscure the true state of affairs, and thus such measures cannot be expected to be related to other measures. For example, think of a bathroom scale that yields a dramatically different weight each time you get on it (that is, the readings are random). It is unlikely that scores obtained from this scale will be related to any other scores (such as caloric intake) in any systematic way. Thus, the unreliability of measures provides another threat to statistical conclusion validity. Reliability and its effects on research outcomes are discussed further in Chapter 12.

Unreliability of Treatment Implementation

Although a researcher might have carefully developed a particular treatment intervention, it is still possible for treatments to be delivered or implemented in a variety of ways. For example, the in vivo homework exercises in our fictitious study may have been assigned in a variety of ways. One of the group therapists may have given the exercises to the clients in written form at the end of the session with no explanations, while another therapist may have explained them and their rationale in detail. These variations tend to lead to uncontrolled variability that obscures the true relationship between the independent and dependent variables. Thus, unreliability of treatment implementation is another threat to statistical conclusion validity. Standardization of treatments is desirable and is discussed in more detail in Chapter 11.

Random Irrelevancies in the Experimental Setting

Any aspect of the experimental setting that leads to variability in responding will increase the error variance and obscure a true relationship. In the fictitious anxiety study, the situations in which the exercises were practiced were not controlled. Some participants may have completed their exercises in a singles bar, others at work, and still others in the grocery store. The differences in these situations would likely lead to variability in responding, which again increases the error variance and threatens statistical conclusion validity.

Random Heterogeneity of Respondents

Differences in participants can often lead to variability in responding. For example, in our anxiety study, physically attractive participants may have had more success in the exercises than less attractive participants. Thus, differences in attractiveness would have led to variability in responding, adding to the error variance (and again obscuring any true relationship). From this point of view, homogeneous samples (for example, all participants having equal attractiveness) are preferable to heterogeneous samples (participants having various levels of attractiveness). However, the results from homogeneous samples can be appropriately generalized only to populations with similar characteristics (see Chapter 13). To some degree, statistical procedures (such as the analysis of covariance) or some design characteristic (such as matching) can be used to remove variance due to some nuisance factor, such as personal attractiveness in heterogeneous populations (see Porter & Raudenbush, 1987; Wampold & Drew, 1990). The essential point is that random heterogeneity of respondents increases the variability of responses and is thus a threat to statistical conclusion validity.

Threats to Internal Validity

Internal validity refers to the confidence one can have in inferring a causal relationship among variables while simultaneously eliminating rival hypotheses. Internal validity is concerned with the most basic aspect of research, the relationships among the variables of interest (typically the independent and dependent variables). Thus, internal validity in an experimental study focuses on whether or not the manipulation of the independent variable was responsible for the differences observed in the dependent variable. In our example, was it the in vivo behavioral exercises that caused the lower anxiety scores in the treatment group, or is there some other explanation for the results? Since one can never know the true state of affairs, internal validity is assessed by the extent that alternative explanations for the results can be ruled out. The more alternative explanations that can be ruled out, the higher the internal validity. As will become evident, internal validity is directly related to experimental control, such as that achieved through random selection of participants, random assignment to groups or treatments, manipulation of the independent variable, and determination of measurement times. Our discussion of internal validity begins by examining three very basic research designs. We will then discuss in considerable detail 13 specific threats to internal validity.

To illustrate internal validity, consider the three designs diagrammed in Figure 4-1. The subscripts for the observations (for example, O_1) are used to indicate the order of different observations. The first design, called a one-shot pretest/posttest design (Campbell & Stanley, 1963), involves observing a sample of participants (O_1), administering some treatment (X), and then observing the participants afterward (O_2). Consider a study designed to test the efficacy of a psychoeducational intervention to teach fifth graders about sexual abuse. Suppose that the pretest is a 30-item knowledge test related to sexual abuse (for example, "What should you do if a stranger asks to touch you under your bathing suit?"). The psychoeducational intervention, which consists of puppet shows, plays, discussions, and workbooks, lasts throughout the school year. At the end of the school year the knowledge test is readministered. We would expect that the posttest scores would be higher than the pretest scores (that is, $O_2 > O_1$).

Design 1: One-shot pretest/posttest design O_1 X O_2

Design 2: Non-equivalent group posttest-only   X O_1
          design   - .
                                                                             O_2

Design 3: Randomized posttest-only design   R   X O_1

                                                                             O_2

FIGURE 4-1
Three possible research designs, where O = observation, X = treatment, and R = random assignment.

Suppose that this relationship is observed; generally the participants score higher after the psychoeducational program than before it. The question is this: Was the psychoeducational program the cause of the increase in scores on the knowledge test? (Take a few minutes and think of alternative explanations for this increase.) There are actually many alternative explanations. Perhaps over the course of the school year the participants learned about sexual abuse from their parents, friends, or television. Or perhaps they scored better at the second administration of the test because they had taken the test before and were more comfortable with the format of the questions. Or perhaps their reading ability had improved during the year and they scored better because they understood the questions better. Clearly, there are a number of problems with attributing causality in this example.

      One of the problems with the first design is that the performance of the participants who receive the treatment is not compared to the performance of participants who do not receive the treatment. In Design 2 in Figure 4-1, there are two groups of participants; one group receives the treatment and one does not. After the treatment, observations are made. Let's say the psychoeducational program is implemented in Chris Jones's class but not in Dale Wong's class. If the psychoeducational program increased knowledge, then we would expect the scores in Chris's class (O_1) to be higher than those in Dale's class (that is, $O_1 > O_2$). Again, assuming that this is the case, was the psychoeducational program the cause of this difference? Possibly, but again there are strong alternative explanations for the difference. The most problematic is that it is possible that Chris's class already knew more about sexual abuse before the intervention began. The students may have been placed in Chris's class because it was the accelerated track, or the students may have been placed in Dale's class because they had behavioral/emotional problems. Basically, the problem here is that there is no way of knowing or inferring that the students in the classrooms were comparable before the intervention.

(There are other problems as well—for example, Chris may have discussed sexual abuse with his students.)

The best way to make groups comparable is to randomly assign participants to the groups. Although random assignment will be discussed in more detail in subsequent chapters, the principle is that each participant has the same likelihood of being assigned to one group as to the other group. Or, said another way, participants are not assigned in any systematic way that might bias the composition of the groups. (Keep in mind that random assignment most likely will result in some small initial differences between groups. This is sampling error and is accounted for in statistical tests.) Design 3 in Figure 4-1 involves two groups containing participants who were randomly assigned. For example, students were randomly assigned either to a treatment group (they receive the psychoeducational program) or to a group that does not receive treatment (called a no-treatment control group; in this case they might have a study period during the time the other group receives the psychoeducational program). Now, if the expected pattern of scores is obtained ($O_1 > O_2$), it is more difficult to find alternative explanations to the conclusion that the psychoeducational program was responsible for the higher scores. However, there are still some alternative explanations. Perhaps a student in the treatment group had been abused, and this led to a very emotional discussion during the treatment; this event and the ensuing discussion, rather than the content of the psychoeducational program, may well have caused the higher scores for the treatment group.

The anxiety study described at the start of this section is an example of Design 3, which is called a randomized posttest-only design. In this context, one group receives cognitive therapy plus the in vivo behavioral exercises, whereas the other receives only the cognitive therapy. In this way, statistically significant differences can be causally attributed to the addition of the exercises (although there are still some threats to this attribution).

We now discuss 13 threats to internal validity (also see Cook & Campbell, 1979). Keep in mind that each of these threats is basically an alternative explanation for causal attributions.

History

History refers to an event that transpires during the time when the treatment is administered and may affect the observations. Thus, history refers to any events in the participants' school, work, or home life (for instance, a television program, a newspaper article, a term paper, or the death of a family member). In our example, history is a threat in Design 1 because a television special on sexual abuse may have been aired while the intervention was being administered. There is no way to determine whether it was the television special or the psychoeducational program that resulted in the increase in knowledge.

The primary way to control history is to use two groups (as in Designs 2 and 3) so that the event affects both groups equally (or nearly equally). In our example, the participants in the treatment and control groups would have equal access to the television special, equalizing this threat. (Note that in Design 2, students in one class might stay up later, possibly due to increased homework or some other reason unique to that group, making late night specials more accessible to them than to the other class.) Still, try as the researcher might, it is possible that an event would occur that would affect only one of the groups. The threat that occurs from an event that affects only one of the groups is called local history.

Threats due to history can be reduced in a number of other ways. First, observations on the groups should be made at the same time. For example, in Design 3, O_1 and O_2 should occur at the same time. Delaying observations for one group leaves open the possibility that some important event may occur after one group is tested but before the other is tested, creating a threat due to local history. Second, the shorter the treatment, the less opportunity there is that an event will occur. Third, the participants can be isolated during the treatment, thereby reducing the likelihood that an extraneous event will affect them. This is similar to sequestering a jury; however, this is extremely difficult to accomplish with human participants in naturalistic settings.

Maturation

Maturation refers to normal developmental changes in participants between the pretest and the posttest that might affect the results. Obviously, studies of physical and mental abilities will be affected by maturation. Design 1 is an example of a study that is particularly vulnerable to the threat of maturation, especially if the time span between O_1 and O_2 is long. For example, if the treatment in a study is a one-year program to increase the physical strength of third graders, gains in strength (that is, $O_2 > O_1$) could be due to maturation instead of to treatment.

Design 3 controls for maturation provided that O_1 and O_2 take place at the same time. The participants in this study design were randomly assigned to groups that therefore were most likely comparable before the study began. It can be expected that participants in each group will mature at the same rate.

Testing

Testing refers to changes in scores on a test due to taking the test more than once. Participants' scores often improve due to familiarization with the test, recall of items and previous responses, and so forth. For example, participants might be asked to perform anagram tasks both before and after a problem-solving intervention. However, the practice performed on the first anagram task might account for improved performance on the posttest, apart from the effect due to treatment. Testing is a threat in Design 1 because improvement in scores from the pretest to posttest could be due to taking the test a second time. Effects of testing should always be considered when pretests are given. Testing is not a threat in Designs 2 and 3 because the participants are tested only once in these designs.

Instrumentation

Instrumentation refers to changes in the measuring device or procedure over the course of a study. One might think that a "test is a test," that its properties cannot change from, say, pretest to posttest. Realize that scores are often obtained from assessments that do not involve tests—for example, observations, interviews, electronic and/or mechanical devices, and so forth. Observations by "objective" coders are known to change or "drift" systematically during the course of a study (Kazdin, 1982). Often raters may change or refine definitions as a result of increased experience with the rating process, thereby changing their rating behavior over time. Electronic devices are subject to changes in weather. Even paper-and-pencil tests are subject to the threat of instrumentation; scoring of the tests may differ systematically from pretest to posttest, especially if the tests are subjectively scored.

Statistical Regression

Statistical regression refers to changes in scores due to the fact that generally, participants who score low on the pretest will score higher on the posttest, and participants who score high on the pretest will score lower on the posttest. (For this reason, statistical regression often is referred to as regression toward the mean.) As an example, consider a batting champion in baseball. Obviously, he obtained this title because he is a good hitter. Still, his batting average for a given year is also due in part to serendipity. Perhaps there was a warm spell in his home city in the spring, the player next in the lineup had a good year (and so the opposing team could not pitch around him), he was injury-free, he had more than his share of luck as several balls just eluded the outstretched gloves of fielders, his personal life was stable, and so on. It is unlikely that all these factors will be favorable the next year, and so it is logical to predict that although he likely will have another good year, he will not be the batting champion again. (Indeed, batting champions rarely repeat.)

Similarly, someone who scores low initially is likely to score higher the next time around. Consider the example of a state bar examination. The examinee who scores the lowest during an exam administration is obviously deficient in his or her knowledge. However, because the examination does not perfectly measure knowledge of the law, this score is also due to other factors. The examinee may have been late to the examination (and therefore more anxious), may have misunderstood some questions, may have missed all questions on which he or she guessed, and so forth. On reexamination, all of these factors are unlikely to be in operation and he or she will do better, although still below average. (Interestingly, the examinee might attribute the gain to better study habits!)

Statistical regression is a problem especially when an experimenter chooses research participants because of their extreme standing on some variables (such as high levels of depression). If participants are selected based on their extremely low scores, then as a group they can be expected to score higher on the posttest, *regardless of whether or not they have received any treatment.* Again, consider Design 1 in Figure 4-1. Suppose that participants were selected for a study because they fell above a certain cutoff score on a paper-and-pencil test of depression (higher scores indicate greater depression). Upon subsequent testing (that is, at posttest), these participants generally will score lower (less depressed) than they did previously. Therefore, a statistically significant difference from pretest to posttest (that is, $O_1 > O_2$) may be due entirely to statistical regression. Design 3 controls for regression because the participants are randomly assigned (that is, have comparable scores), and thus the regression toward the mean for both groups will be about the same.

Selection

Selection refers to differences between groups that exist before implementation of the treatment. Selection is often a threat when participants are initially chosen for a study based on some group membership—that is, when participants are assigned to a particular treatment or control group because they are part of an existing group. Design 2 is subject to the threat of selection. Recall that in our example, the students in Chris's class may be very different from the students in Dale's class, and therefore observed differences (for example, $O_2 > O_1$) could well be due to these initial differences rather than to the treatment. In the absence of random assignment of participants to groups, selection is always a potentially serious threat to the internal validity of a study.

Attrition (or Mortality)

Attrition or mortality refers to the effect of participants dropping out of a study. (Cook and Campbell, 1979, use the term *mortality;* we prefer *attrition* because it is free of epidemiological connotations.) Attrition can be a particularly pernicious threat because it can affect all designs and because its severity is difficult to assess. When participants drop out of a study, the scores that remain at posttest may not be representative. For example, consider Design 1 with participants who are depressed. If the most depressed participants drop out, then the observations at posttest will tend to indicate less depression because the most extreme scores are no longer considered. Therefore, the fact that $O_1 > O_2$ could very well be due to the fact that the scores that remain at posttest are unrepresentative. (In this instance, the pretest scores for those who drop out would not be analyzed either, but the discussion illustrates the problems of attrition that ensue.)

When more than one group is involved and the attrition across the groups is not comparable, *differential attrition* is said to exist. Design 3, which has been immune to most of the threats to internal validity so far discussed, is subject to differential attrition. We will consider a few applications of Design 3 to indicate how differential attrition may work. First, consider the psychoeducational example in which the participants were randomly assigned to either a treatment group or a control group. Suppose that five of the participants in the treatment group moved out of the school district, whereas none of the control participants dropped out of the study. If the five participants were representative of the other participants, then their removal would have no effect on the outcome (other than to reduce power, and possibly to make the tests more sensitive to violations of assumptions).

Now consider Design 3 for our fictitious anxiety study. Recall that one group received cognitive therapy plus in vivo exercises, whereas the second group received only cognitive therapy. Because the exercises are anxiety-provoking in their own right, it may well be that the most anxious participants will drop out of the cognitive therapy plus exercises group (treatment group) rather than complete the exercises (a not-uncommon avoidance reaction). Because the participants who drop out of the first group are the most anxious, their attrition will tend to decrease the anxiety scores in this group (that is, decrease O_1) and could be responsible for a significant difference between the groups (that is, $O_1 < O_2$) in favor of the treatment group.

A third application of Design 3 will demonstrate how differential attrition can act against ascertaining that a treatment is effective. Consider a treatment for depression that is effective and provides an immediate palliative effect. Again suppose that the participants are randomly assigned to the treatment condition and to a waiting-list control group (the participants in this group will receive the treatment after the study ends, if it is found to be effective). Because depression is a particularly distressing disorder, the most depressed participants in the control group might be most inclined to drop out of the study and seek treatment elsewhere. If this does in fact occur, the control group scores will reflect a drop in depression because the highest scores have been removed. If this drop due to differential attrition is about the same as the effect of the treatment, then the posttest scores will be about equal (that is, $O_1 = O_2$), even though the treatment was effective!

In short, attrition can serve as a threat to internal validity. To some extent the effects of differential attrition often can be assessed by administering a pretest. This topic will be discussed in Chapter 6.

Interactions with Selection

Many of the threats to internal validity discussed so far can work in concert with selection to affect the results of a study. Consider Design 2 in the psychoeducational example. Suppose that even though the participants were not randomly assigned to Chris's and Dale's classes, they were roughly equivalent on all relevant characteristics (intelligence, previous knowledge, motivation, socioeconomic status, and so forth). Suppose as well that a local television station ran a series about sexual abuse on the late-night news. It would appear that selection is not a threat because of the comparability of the groups, and that history is not a threat because the television series aired when both groups of participants could watch it (assuming that O_1 and O_2 occurred at the same time). However, selection and history could interact; perhaps Dale assigned a great deal of homework and children stayed up late to complete it, and therefore they were awake at the time when this series aired. In this example, the scores in the control group could be improved by the interaction of selection and history, obviating treatment effects. It could also work in the opposite direction: If for some reason Chris's class were the students who stayed up late and watched the series, then it would be difficult to know whether an observed effect for the treatment group was due to the psychoeducational treatment or to the television series.

When designing or reading research, keep in mind that selection can exacerbate problems with the other threats to validity. Although we illustrated a selection/history interaction, it is important to remember that all of the afore-mentioned threats can interact with selection.

Ambiguity About the Direction of the Causal Influence

In the previous examples, the independent variable was manipulated to determine its effect on the dependent variable. Even if the threats to the internal validity of the studies can be ruled out, it would appear that the manipulation of the independent variable caused the concomitant change in the dependent variable, and not vice versa. However, the direction is not as clear in designs in which the independent variable is not manipulated. Consider studies in counseling that examine counselor empathy and therapeutic gains in clients; several studies have found a positive relation between these two variables (Mitchell, Bozarth, & Kraft, 1977). Does the empathy of the counselor cause client progress, or does client progress cause the counselor to be more empathic? Unless the temporal order is known, the directionality of causality in correlational or passive designs is difficult to determine.

Diffusion or Imitation of Treatments

Occasionally the treatment delivered to one group is unwittingly allowed to spread to other groups. This is particularly likely when the treatment is primarily informational and of much interest. Suppose a study is being conducted on sexual abuse. Because of the relevance of this topic, students in the treatment group may discuss it with students in the control group, thereby effectively delivering the treatment to both groups. Diffusion of treatments makes it difficult to find differences among or between groups even when the treatment is effective.

Compensatory Equalization of Treatments

Most counselors are naturally reluctant to withhold programs from participants in control groups. When personnel directly or indirectly involved in a study provide some type of service to participants in a control group to compensate for their assignment to a group that does not receive treatment, compensatory equalization of treatments is said to exist and might pose a threat to internal validity. In counseling, participants in the control group will often seek services elsewhere (clergy, other counseling services, and so forth). In school settings, administrators, feeling bad for the control group, may provide extraordinary experiences, such as field trips, movies, and so forth. These experiences may well affect the scores for these participants, especially if the dependent variable is nonspecific (for example, self-concept).

Compensatory Rivalry by Participants Receiving Less Desirable Treatments

Compensatory rivalry refers to efforts by participants in the control group to out-perform participants in the treatment group to prove that they are "just as good, if not better." This threat to validity occurs most often when the participants' performance will be publicized and there are consequences of not performing well. To illustrate this threat, suppose that counselors in a mental health center are randomly assigned to a treatment group or a control group. The treatment consists of refresher courses on assessment, diagnosis, and service delivery. Because the counselors find such courses remedial and demeaning, they are determined to demonstrate that they do not need the courses. Therefore, the participants in the control group work extra hard to demonstrate that they are competent in these areas.

Resentful Demoralization of Participants Receiving Less Desirable Treatments

Resentful demoralization is, in some ways, the opposite of compensatory rivalry. Rather than working extra hard to perform, participants in the less desirable treatment group (or in a control group) will often become demoralized, which tends to decrease performance. For example, participants in a study of depression, even if informed that they might be assigned to a control group, might feel more depressed than usual when actually assigned to the control group. Their sense of having little control over the reinforcers in their world is reiterated. The demoralization of the participants in the control group adds to the level of depression of these participants, and therefore differences between scores on the posttest (that is, $O_1 < O_2$) may be due to the demoralization of the control participants rather than to the effectiveness of the treatment.

Threats to Construct Validity of Putative Causes and Effects

Construct validity refers to how well the independent and dependent variables represent the constructs they were intended to measure. When there is ambiguity about the constructs, a confound is said to exist. More technically, a confound is an alternate construct that cannot be logically or statistically differentiated from a hypothesized construct. Suppose that a researcher hypothesizes that male clients with personal problems prefer female counselors, and male clients are randomly assigned to one of two groups. One group reads a description of a counselor who has a female name and views a photograph of a female counselor; the other group reads the same description, but with a male name and a male photograph. After receiving the materials, each participant indicates his willingness to see the counselor for a personal problem. Suppose that the results indicate that the clients prefer, as predicted, the female counselor (and further suppose that the statistical conclusion validity and the internal validity are adequate). A logical conclusion is that male clients prefer female counselors for personal problems. However, there is an alternative explanation: It may well be that the female in the photograph is more physically attractive than the male counselor. As a result, the willingness to see the female counselor may be due to personal attractiveness rather than to gender. In this example, the two constructs (physical attractiveness and gender) have been confounded.

    Construct validity is relevant to both the independent variable and the dependent variable. With regard to the independent variable, the groups should vary along the dimension of interest but should not systematically vary on any other dimension. If the independent variable is meant to operationalize gender (as in our previous example), then the groups should differ on this dimension (which was the case) but should not differ on any other dimensions (such as physical attractiveness). Likewise, the dependent variable or variables should measure what they are intended to measure and should not measure irrelevant factors. Issues related to independent and dependent variables are discussed in more detail in Chapters 11 and 12, respectively.

Cook and Campbell (1979) identified ten threats to construct validity. We briefly review these threats, following their nomenclature. Keep in mind that these threats are discussed in more detail in subsequent chapters. These threats were seen to cluster into two main groups: construct underrepresentation and surplus construct irrelevancies. Construct underrepresentation happens when we fail to incorporate all of the important aspects of the construct. On the other hand, surplus construct irrelevancies happens when we include irrelevant aspects as part of the construct. Consider an analogy: If we use a fishing net with holes that are too big, some of the fish that we want to catch will get away (construct underrepresentation). If we use a net with holes that are too small, we will catch a lot of smaller fish that we do not want (surplus construct irrelevancies). In many ways the search for construct validity is like trying to find a net with holes that are just right for catching our target fish.

Inadequate Preoperational Explication of Constructs

To make a construct operational, one must first have a careful, rational analysis of the construct's important or essential components. A threat to construct validity from inadequate preoperational explication of constructs occurs when such an analysis has not taken place. To adequately operationalize a construct, it should be defined clearly. When a construct is referenced by a name but not discussed in detail, it is often difficult to ascertain exactly what is intended. *Spouse abuse* may refer to physical acts with the intent to harm, to any physical acts, to physical and verbal attacks, and so forth. Decisions about the nature of a construct should not be arbitrary; proper definitions are needed so that the research hypotheses follow from theories and so that they can be properly operationalized.

Mono-Operation Bias

Mono-operation refers to single exemplars of the levels of the independent variable or single measures of the dependent variable. Mono-operations are problematic because frequently the essence of a construct cannot be captured by a single exemplar or a single measure. Most likely, mono-operations underrepresent the construct and contain irrelevancies.

Mono-operations of the independent variable result when only one exemplar of each treatment is used. For example, in the gender study mentioned earlier, all of the participants in the female-counselor group read the same name and description of the counselor and viewed the same photograph. That is, a single exemplar of a female counselor was used; similarly, a single exemplar of a male counselor was used. Clearly, this operationalization of gender is narrow and the results are restricted to this particular operationalization, thereby creating a threat to the larger construct of gender. It would have been preferable to have several descriptions, male and female names, and photographs. Including variations of exemplars raises the issue of whether the variations have an effect on the dependent variable; if this is of concern, the experiment can be designed to test the effect of the variations (see Chapter 6).

With regard to the dependent variable, a single measure often will not reflect the construct adequately. The ABC Anxiety Test may reflect social anxiety to some extent, but it will fail to do so perfectly. By adding other measures of social anxiety, the construct is operationalized more completely. The technical bases for the use of multiple dependent measures to operationalize a construct are found in statistics and measurement; these bases are discussed conceptually in Chapter 12. The essential point here is that mono-operation bias presents a threat to construct validity, typically by underrepresenting a construct.

Mono-Method Bias

As mentioned previously, multiple measures are important in capturing the essence of a construct. However, if all the dependent measures use the same method, there may well be a bias introduced by the method. For example, self-report measures often share a common respondent bias. If a participant responds in a socially desirable way to all self-report instruments, then consistent bias is introduced by this method. If two constructs are measured in the same way (for instance, self-report), the correlation between variables may result from method variance rather than any true correlation between constructs. Another example of mono-method bias pertains to the measurement of depression. Instead of using only self-report measures, a more valid method of operationalizing the construct of depression would be to use a client self-report measure coupled with a therapist and observer measure of depression.

Mono-method bias can also apply to independent variables. Presenting written descriptions, names, and photographs (even multiple exemplars of each) operationalizes gender using one method. The question remains: Would the results be similar if gender were operationalized using a different method (such as videotapes of the counselor)? In short, mono-method bias introduces threats to construct validity.

Hypothesis Guessing Within Experimental Conditions

Hypothesis guessing occurs when experimental participants try to figure out what the researcher wants (that is, his or her hypothesis) and then attempt either to comply or rebel against these presumed expectations. One of the most problematic things about hypothesis guessing is that it is very difficult to determine when it occurs, how often it occurs, and the direction and magnitude of its effect. For example, if the participants in the gender study guess that the hypothesis is actually related to their willingness to see a counselor of a specific gender, then they may respond in a certain way to please the researcher, to show that they are open-minded and nonsexist, and so forth. Ethical principles dictate that the purpose of research be explained to participants before their consent to participate; how-ever, frequently it is desirable to make the specific research hypothesis difficult to guess (see Chapter 5 for a discussion of these ethical issues). In short, hypothesis guessing can obscure or diminish true treatment effects and is thus a threat to con-struct validity.

Evaluation Apprehension

Participants often are apprehensive about being evaluated, especially by experts, and will respond in ways that make them appear better adjusted or healthier than is actually the case. (This is related to mono-method bias because self-report mea-sures most readily reflect the effects of evaluation apprehension.) When appre-hension about being evaluated affects the responses of participants, the dependent measure is confounded with this bias, thereby producing a threat to construct validity.

Experimenter Expectancies

Although experimenters are portrayed as objective scientists, there is evidence that this is not the case. They are often eager to find particular results, and this bias is often communicated to participants in subtle (and sometimes not-so-subtle) ways. For example, if the experimenter is also the counselor in a treatment study, he or she may be overly eager to help the clients to show the effectiveness of his or her valued treatment. When this happens, it is unclear whether the causal ele-ment is the treatment or the expectations; such uncertainty threatens the con-struct validity of the study. Experimenter expectancies are discussed in detail in Chapter 12.

Confounding Constructs and Levels of Constructs

Frequently, constructs that are continuous are operationalized with discrete exem-plars. For example, the experience level of the counselor is often an independent variable in treatment studies. Experience is a continuous variable with a wide range. If the experience levels chosen are either at the low end of the continuum (for example, novice counselors, those with one practicum course, and those with a master's degree) or at the high end of the continuum (doctoral-level counselors with 10, 15, and 20 years of experience), then it might be concluded that experi-ence does not affect counseling outcomes. A very different result might be obtained with experience levels that span the continuum. When restricted levels of the con-struct are chosen, the construct is confounded with levels of the construct.

Interaction of Different Treatments

When participants receive more than one treatment, it is difficult to determine whether an effect is due to a single treatment or to the latest treatment in the context of the previous treatments. Suppose that it was found that the psychoeducational program for sexual abuse was not effective, and that subsequently a computer-assisted instruction program was tested with the same participants and found to be effective. Would the computer-assisted instruction program have been effective had it not followed the psychoeducational program? In this example, the question is unanswerable. Thus, the interaction of different treatments provides a confound and is a threat to construct validity of the treatment. This problem is inherent in within-subjects designs (see Chapter 6).

Interaction of Testing and Treatment

Occasionally the pretest can sensitize participants to the treatment such that their performance on the posttest is due in part to some combination of the effects of the treatment and the pretest. That is, the treatment would not have been effective (or as effective) had the pretest not been given. Ways to control this threat are discussed in Chapter 6.

Restricted Generalizability Across Constructs

Any treatment can have an effect on multiple constructs. For example, a treatment may have a positive effect on some outcome variables, a negative effect on others, and no effect on still others. Restricted generalizability across constructs occurs when an overly narrow range of outcome variables is examined. Establishing the relationship between two constructs restricts conclusions to those variables. Often, other important constructs are not investigated and the research can be criticized because these other constructs might be the most interesting piece of the psychological puzzle. There have been numerous investigations of minority group preference for types of counselors (Coleman, Wampold, & Casali, 1995); however, missing from most of this research are constructs related to counseling outcomes. Does the fact that an Asian-American client *prefers* an Asian-American counselor imply that an Asian American would produce the most desirable outcome in this context? Thus, restriction of the constructs used in a study is a threat to the construct validity of the study.

Threats to External Validity

External validity refers to the generalizability of a study's results. To what group of persons, settings, and times do the results of the study apply? Traditionally, external validity has been approached by examining samples from populations. First, a population is defined; second, a random sample is drawn from that population. Based on the results of the research with the sample, conclusions are made about the population. Unfortunately, truly or even approximately random sampling is possible only infrequently. Consider the study with socially anxious participants. It is impossible to randomly sample from the population of all socially anxious individuals in the United States. The concepts of sampling and the inferences that can be drawn in the absence of random sampling are discussed in Chapter 13.

Cook and Campbell (1979) broadened the concept of external validity to include generalization *to* the population and generalization *across* populations. Random sampling from a well-defined population refers to the generalizability *to* the population; however, since true random sampling is infrequently conducted, generalization to the population is difficult. Of greater practical importance is the generalizability of results *across* different populations. Consider the social anxiety example and suppose that the study finds that cognitive therapy plus exercises is significantly more effective than cognitive therapy alone in reducing social anxiety (assume that the statistical conclusion validity, internal validity, and construct validity are adequate to draw valid inferences). Across which populations are these results generalizable? Do they apply equally to all socially anxious participants? To males and females? To adolescents and adults? To various minority groups? And do the results also apply to participants in various settings (social gatherings, public places), to people of different ages than the participants, and so forth?

Generalizability across populations is of particular interest to counseling researchers. Paul (1967) admonished researchers to determine which treatments work with which types of clients in which settings. The intricacies of testing for generalizability across persons, settings, and times are discussed in detail in Chapter 13. As indicated there, generalizability across populations is determined by examining possible interactions between the treatment and various population characteristics. For example, if a statistical interaction occurs between a treatment variable and gender, then the treatment is not equally effective with males and females.

Generalization across various kinds of persons, settings, and times is tested by examining statistical interactions between the treatment (or the independent variable) and persons, settings, or times. We will briefly discuss three threats to external validity that serve to limit the generalizability of research results.

Interaction of Selection and Treatment

Interaction of selection and treatment refers to generalizability across persons. Person variables relevant to counseling research include gender, racial or ethnic background, experience level, degree of dysfunction, intelligence, cognitive style, personality, level of acculturation, and sexual orientation, among others. Clearly, there are many choices for populations to be studied; some considerations in choosing populations are discussed in Chapter 13. In short, the external validity of a study is strengthened when the research examines the relationship between the independent and dependent variables across different categories of persons.

Interaction of Setting and Treatment

Interaction of setting and treatment refers to generalizability across settings. How generalizable are results obtained in a university counseling center to a community mental health setting, a hospital setting, or private practice? There are obvious differences between these settings, and there is little reason to believe that results necessarily generalize across these settings. Much research is conducted at counseling centers, perhaps because staff members are motivated, interested, and proactive; however, there are factors that may differentiate this setting from others. Thus, the external validity of a study is strengthened when the relationship between the independent and dependent variables is examined across different settings.

Interaction of History and Treatment

Interaction of history and treatment refers to generalizability across time. Counseling approaches valued in the 1960s may no longer be valued in the twenty-first century. Epidemiological studies of anxiety in Cuba during the Cuban Missile Crisis may not apply to anxiety levels during *glasnost* in the Soviet Union or to "ethnic cleansing" in the Balkans. To be of much use, research results should be applicable to the future, but obviously one cannot sample from future populations. Generalizability across time is often achieved through replications at different times or by analyzing prior research across time periods (for an example of the latter, see Heppner & Neal, 1983). In short, establishing external validity across time periods is more difficult and often requires retrospective analyses or replications after the passage of time.

SUMMARY AND CONCLUSION

In this chapter we discussed four types of validity in considerable detail. Statistical conclusion validity refers to the degree to which a researcher has arrived at the correct conclusion about the relationships among the variables in a research question. Internal validity refers to the degree to which statements can be made about the existence of a causal relationship among the variables. Construct validity of putative causes and effect refers to the degree to which the variables measured in the study represent the intended constructs. Finally, external validity refers to the degree to which the relationship among the variables is generalizable beyond the study to other people, settings, and times. Although one can never establish each of the four types of validity with total certainty, researchers establish estimates of validity by ruling out as many threats to the validity as possible. Most importantly, different types of designs typically represent trade-offs with regard to the four types of validity.

A wide range of different threats to each of the four types of validity exist. How does one assess the severity of a threat? In some instances, statistical tests can be used to determine whether or not a threat is problematic. For example, if pretests are administered, differences among participants who drop out of a study can be compared statistically to those among remaining participants. Or external validity can be assessed by examining the statistical interaction between the independent variable and some person, setting, or time variable.

A second way to assess validity is to logically examine the likelihood of a threat's occurrence. In some instances, it is very unlikely that a particular threat is problematic, even in the absence of direct evidence. For example, although maturation may be a threat in some designs, if the treatment lasts only one hour, participants are very unlikely to mature much during that time. Or if the pretest is a commonly used test and the treatment is lengthy, interaction of testing and treatment probably will have little effect on the results. Diffusion of treatments will be impossible if participants are strangers and do not have the opportunity to meet.

It is also possible to reduce threats to validity by building into the study some aspects that control for the threat. Consider the example of the study in which photographs of counselors of both genders were presented to the participants. Recall that personal attractiveness was a potential confound in that study. To control for the confound, the researchers could have judges rate the personal attractiveness of various photographs and then match them so that the personal attractiveness of the photographs was constant across the groups.

In sum, our discussion of validity provides a framework for assessing the types of inferences made in research and the subsequent validity of a study. The fact that many threats were presented indicates that many things can weaken or strengthen any particular study. Keep in mind that no research can be designed that is not subject to threats to validity to some degree, which is in essence the thesis of Gelso's (1979) Bubble Hypothesis. The objective is to design and conduct research in such a way as to minimize the threats and maintain the possibility of obtaining interpretable findings. In this respect, programmatic research is needed because studies can build on each other, and a threat to one study can be ruled out in a future study. In fact, programmatic research on a given topic that examines similar variables over time is essential to creating useful knowledge bases within scientific inquiry in the counseling profession.

CHAPTER 5

ETHICAL ISSUES IN COUNSELING RESEARCH

Ethics are not simply proper etiquette, but rather "they are expressions of our values and a guide for achieving them" (Diener & Crandall, 1978, p. 14). In essence, "ethics is a generic term for various ways of understanding and examining the moral life" (Beauchamp & Childress, 1994, p. 4). Ethical principles help researchers achieve their goals while avoiding strategies that compromise their values, and ethics helps them make decisions when their values are in conflict (Diener & Crandall, 1978). We believe that ethics are nothing less than central to the conduct of research. Just as morality is a part of everyday living, ethics is a way of living that permeates the research enterprise. Because of the centrality of ethics in research, this chapter is placed toward the beginning of the book so that ethical reasoning can be integrated into basic design considerations not as an afterthought, but as an intrinsic feature of the research endeavor. Indeed, research suggests that students in counseling training programs regard ethical training as essential for their professional roles (Wilson & Ranft, 1993). To assume that being a counseling researcher involves technical research design skills alone is to have a very incomplete picture. We maintain that it is essential for researchers to be aware of their ethical responsibilities to research participants, co-workers, the profession, and society as a whole.

In this chapter we focus on the investigator's responsibility in two general categories: ethical issues related to scholarly work and ethical issues related to participants. In today's complex world these topics take on a complexity not even imagined several decades ago. It is important to underscore at the outset that ethical issues in research are rarely cut-and-dried, and sometimes one ethical principle will conflict with another to create a tangled and murky dilemma. Our main goals in this chapter are to (a) introduce and sensitize the reader to the ethical issues involved in counseling research, (b) underscore the complexity of real-life ethical dilemmas, which sometimes do not have clear answers, and (c) discuss common strategies and the reasoning process for designing research with ethical rigor.

The first section of this chapter discusses fundamental ethical principles as well as virtue ethics that form the core of our professional values. Specifically, we will discuss the fundamental ethical principles of nonmaleficence, beneficence, autonomy, justice, and fidelity. In addition, we will introduce ethical guidelines that have been suggested by the American Psychological Association and the American Counseling Association (formerly the American Association for Counseling and Development). Next we introduce the notion of virtue ethics and specifically highlight prudence, integrity, respectfulness, and benevolence. In the second section of the chapter we discuss ethical issues related to scholarly work, specifically (a) execution of the research study, (b) reporting the results, (c) duplicate and piecemeal publication, (d) publication credit, and (e) plagiarism. In the final section we discuss ethical issues pertaining to participants: (a) risks and benefits, (b) informed consent, (c) deception and debriefing, (d) confidentiality and privacy, and (e) special considerations for treatment issues. We end with a brief section on responding to ethical dilemmas.

FUNDAMENTAL ETHICAL PRINCIPLES

To facilitate professionals' decision making with regard to ethics, both the American Counseling Association (ACA) and the American Psychological Association (APA) have developed a set of ethical principles or guidelines: *Ethical Standards,* referred to hereafter as *ES* (AACD, 1988), and *Ethical Principles of Psychologists,* referred to hereafter as *EPP* (APA, 1992). These principles are presented in Appendixes A and B and will be referred to in the discussion of ethical issues throughout the chapter. Implicit in these professional codes of ethics are more general and fundamental ethical principles. "Because ethical codes may be too broad in some cases and too narrow in others, [the more fundamental] ethical principles both provide a more consistent framework within which cases may be considered and constitute a rationale for the choice of items in the code itself" (Kitchener, 1984, p. 46). In this chapter we focus on five fundamental ethical principles: nonmaleficence, beneficence, autonomy, justice, and fidelity. In essence, these fundamental ethical principles are central but implied building blocks for the professional codes of ACA and APA. We briefly discuss these general principles to clarify the essence of ethical issues and facilitate an understanding of professional ethical codes. Readers interested in a fuller discussion of such fundamental ethical principles are directed to Beauchamp and Childress (1979); Diener and Crandall (1978); Drane (1982); Kitchener (1984); and Lindsey (1984).

Nonmaleficence

Diener and Crandall, in their book *Ethics in Social and Behavioral Research* (1978), succinctly concluded that "the most basic guideline for social scientists is that subjects not be harmed by participating in research" (p. 17). This central principle has been referred to as the principle of nonmaleficence (above all do no harm; Beauchamp & Childress, 1979). This includes not inflicting intentional harm and avoiding the risk of harming others. Thus, it is the responsibility of the investigator to plan and act thoughtfully and carefully in designing and executing research projects, because harm can occur intentionally or unintentionally. Kitchener (1984) noted that a number of ethicists and psychologists have argued that nonmaleficence should be the paramount ethical principle in applied psychology (Beauchamp & Childress, 1979; Brown, 1982; Frankena, 1963; Rosenbaum, 1982; Ross, 1930). Thus, these professionals have argued that if we must choose between harming someone and perhaps helping another person, the strongest obligation would be to avoid harm. Diener and Crandall (1978) have argued that nonmaleficence can be superseded only if volunteers knowingly participate and the benefits are of great import.

Beneficence

Beauchamp and Childress (1979) concluded that acting ethically not only involves preventing harm but also contributes to the health and welfare of others. Doing good for others is beneficence. This central ethical principle is the essence of the goal of counseling—to help people resolve problems that they have been unable to resolve on their own. Moreover, beneficence constitutes the core of the ethical principles advocated by APA and ACA. In the Preamble to *Ethical Principles of Psychologists* (APA), the Ethics Code "has as its primary goal the welfare and protection of . . . individuals and groups." Likewise, the first sentence in the Preamble to "Ethical Standards" (AACD, 1988) proclaims that "members are dedicated to the enhancement of each individual and thus to the service of society."

Inherent in beneficence is competence. If our value is to help others, particularly those in need who come to rely on our services, then we have an obligation to help others as competently as possible. Such reasoning has a number of implications for service delivery, professional training, and research. With regard to the research, Lindsey (1984) noted that the beneficence principle mandates the profession to do effective and significant research to maximally promote the welfare of our constituents. Likewise, White and White (1981) argued that it is our responsibility as a profession to provide all the knowledge and skill we can marshall to benefit our clients.

Another interpretation of beneficence is not only contributing to the welfare of others, but also having an active, altruistic, group/community-oriented approach that "gives back" to the research participants and the community. In fact, the ethical codes have been criticized for emphasizing the prevention of harm rather than the provision of benefits (Casas, Ponterotto, & Gutierrez, 1986; Ponterotto & Casas, 1991). Ponterotto and Casas (1991) pointed out the need for more tangible actions that result not only in positive research outcomes, but also benefits for racial/ethnic minority communities. Such a goal might be achieved by systematically investigating psychosocial problems (for example, substance abuse) as well as psychocultural strengths in minority individuals and communities. In short, an important aspect of beneficence is for researchers to take an active, altruistic approach "to ensure that their efforts result in tangible, direct, indirect, short-term, and long-term benefits to the targeted racial/ethnic minority community" (Ponterotto & Casas, 1991).

Autonomy

The principle of autonomy centers around the liberty to choose one's own course of action, including freedom of action and freedom of choice (Kitchener, 1984). The principle of autonomy is woven into American political institutions, law, and culture. Not surprisingly, Rokeach (1973) found that Americans ranked individual freedom as one of their most esteemed values. In many ways, autonomy is the cornerstone of subjects' rights to voluntarily participate in psychological research, or conversely to decline to participate. Since the Nuremberg trials after World War II, the principle of autonomy has received increased attention in research. At the center of this attention is the notion of informed consent, or educating potential subjects about a particular research project so that they can make informed decisions about participation.

Justice

The principle of justice implies fairness (Benn, 1967). Because the quantity of services and goods in any society is limited, there are conflicts between people. Thus, a vast array of laws have developed as part of our judicial system for deciding what is fair. In essence, the principle of justice is based on the assumption that people are equals. Thus, as initially suggested by Aristotle, equals should be treated as equals, and unequals should be treated unequally only in proportion to their relevant differences (Beauchamp & Childress, 1979; Benn, 1967). Gender and race are not relevant characteristics for deciding access to mental health services, but this is not to suggest that gender and race might not be relevant considerations concerning different treatments. The concept of justice also implies just rewards for one's labor, and ownership of the fruits of one's labor.

Fidelity

The principle of fidelity implies faithfulness, keeping promises or agreements, and loyalty (Ramsey, 1970). This principle applies directly to voluntary interpersonal relationships, including counselor-client, student-teacher, and researcher-participant. Not fulfilling a contract (by, for example, engaging in deception or breaching confidentiality) is a violation that infringes upon the other individual's choice to enter into a mutually agreed-upon relationship. Issues of fidelity and trustworthiness are central to the helping professions such as counseling. The principle of fidelity is important for the reputation of the profession as well as for individual professionals in their work as counselors, supervisors, consultants, educators, and researchers.

VIRTUE ETHICS

Within the past decade there has been increased attention to virtue ethics (see, for example, Beauchamp & Childress, 1994; Meara, Schmidt, & Day, 1996). The previous section on ethical principles focused on fundamental principles, or what some may refer to as obligations (Meara et al., 1996). By contrast, virtue ethics focuses on ethical ideals to which professionals aspire. In fact, the 1992 APA ethical code has been criticized for not being idealistic enough (see, for example, Bersoff, 1994; Keith-Spiegel, 1994; Payton, 1994; Vasquez, 1994). But to which ethical ideals should our profession aspire?

Meara et al. (1996) identified four major virtues: prudence, integrity, respectfulness, and benevolence. Prudence reflects foresight, appropriate caution, and good judgment. They suggested that prudence is the cornerstone virtue for professional psychology and is required for fulfilling the spirit of many of the basic ethical principles. Moreover, Meara et al. (1996) maintained that particularly in a multicultural milieu, prudence is especially relevant because "a prudent individual is aware that another's definition of the situation is not necessarily one's own" (p. 40). Integrity refers to a "coherent integration of reasonably stable, justifiable moral values, together with active fidelity to those values in judgment and in action" (Beauchamp & Childress, 1994, p. 473). Thus, integrity is a virtue that involves adherence to a set of values over time. Respectfulness refers to holding another in high esteem, not interfering with another, and in essence regarding individuals or communities in terms they themselves define (Meara et al., 1996). Such a virtue is, again, especially important in a multicultural society. Benevolence refers to "wanting to do good" and "contributing to the common good" (Meara et al., 1996, p. 45).

Clearly, virtue ethics pertains to a wide range of ethical issues involving scholarly research and its participants. Virtue ethics are at the heart of our character as helping professionals. Although they do not prescribe specific behaviors for solving ethical dilemmas, virtue ethics constitute the cornerstones underlying our ethical decisions.

ETHICAL ISSUES RELATED TO SCHOLARLY WORK

The study of human behavior is constantly changing and progressing. This evolution reflects a commitment to continually "work to develop a valid and reliable body of scientific knowledge based on research" (*EPP*, Preamble). One of the basic purposes of scientific endeavors in counseling is to increase our knowledge about topics of value to the counseling profession. This broad and vital goal reflects the fundamental ethical principle of beneficence. In a very simple way, the counseling researcher has a responsibility to provide accurate information about counseling-related phenomena "to improve the condition of both the individual and society" (*EPP*, Preamble) and for the "enhancement of the worth, dignity, potential, and uniqueness of each individual and thus to the service of society" (*ES*, Preamble). It can be argued that accurate information promotes the profession's knowledge bases, and that inaccurate and misleading information may distort or even falsify the profession's knowledge bases. In short, given the role of science within the profession, scientists have the responsibility "to under-take their efforts in a totally honest fashion" (Drew, 1980, pp. 58–59). Although any of a number of factors may tax the typical researcher (for instance, publica-tion pressure or fatigue), it is imperative that the researcher keep in focus the ulti-mate aim of the scientist—to extend our knowledge bases with accurate, reliable, and thus usable information. If the researcher loses sight of this essential goal, then in our opinion she or he has no business conducting research and may only hinder the profession and the people we try to help.

It is important to note that the goal of providing "accurate information" and extending the profession's "knowledge bases" can sometimes be at odds with pro-moting the welfare of others and society. Even though it can be argued that research that led to the atomic bomb extended existing knowledge bases and was instrumental for the Allied victory in World War II, it can also be argued that this research did not promote the welfare of many people, as it resulted in the deaths of thousands of people. Seeman (1969) aptly concluded: "The existence of Hiroshima in man's history demonstrates that knowledge alone is not enough, and that the question 'knowledge for what?' must still be asked. If knowledge in psychology is won at the cost of some essential humanness in one person's relationship to another, perhaps the cost is too high" (p. 1028). Likewise, Jensen (1969, 1985) pub-lished research (and there is considerable controversy about whether the data were biased) that has been interpreted as showing that African Americans are intellectu-ally inferior. Clearly, it can be argued that Jensen's writing did not promote the wel-fare of African Americans. In short, the essential point is that more information does not necessarily promote human welfare. At a minimum, expanding our knowledge bases raises deeper moral issues about right and wrong (K. S. Kitchener, personal communication, January 2, 1990). Thus, it is imperative to note the complexity, and sometimes the contradictions, in the seemingly straightforward goals of extending knowledge bases and promoting human welfare.

Next we will discuss the implications of the researcher's responsibility to provide accurate information concerning five matters: execution of the research study, reporting the results, duplicate and piecemeal publication, publication credit, and plagiarism.

Execution of the Research Study

A study must be properly executed if it is to establish valid knowledge bases and adhere to the fundamental ethical principle of beneficence. The researcher has a responsibility for accurately and reliably planning and conducting the research investigation (*EPP,* 6.06; *ES,* D.3, D.8). The researcher also has the responsibility for evaluating its ethical acceptability, weighing scientific values and rights of par-ticipants, and then conducting all aspects of the study in a careful, deliberate man-ner "that minimizes the possibility that results will be misleading" (*ES,* D.8). Moreover, it is especially important that in developing a study "psychologists con-sult those with expertise concerning any special population under investigation or most likely to be affected" (*EPP,* 6.07). Thus, to reduce methological biases and errors, it is essential that researchers have an accurate and sensitive understanding of the target population. Moreover, to enhance both the validity and pragmatic value of the research, consulting with community leaders and agencies is encouraged (Ponterotto & Casas, 1991).

Conducting research typically involves multiple tasks and requires a lot of attention to many details. Typical procedural tasks include contacting participants, arranging experimental conditions, randomly assigning participants to conditions, locating and assembling assessment instruments, administering instruments, coding data, entering the data into a computer, and analyzing the data. Within these major tasks are a myriad of steps and processes, such as collating questionnaires, checking the accuracy of the coded data against the original data set, and checking for data entry errors. In short, many, many tasks confront the researcher in a typical research project, and the researcher is responsible for the accuracy and reliability of carrying out all of them.

Problems can occur if the investigator becomes lax during any phase of executing a study. For example, differential participant biases may be created if participants are not solicited according to a standardized recruitment procedure (see Chapter 14 for a detailed discussion of such biases). Or distortion can occur if the researcher does not impress upon all assistants the need for accuracy in matching participants to all of their questionnaire data. Research assistants can be invaluable resources, but they typically need close supervision. Moreover, sometimes it is difficult for research assistants to maintain high levels of performance in extremely difficult or boring tasks, and especially when they do not understand the purpose of the task (or study) or the need for great precision. Drew (1980) noted incidents in which research assistants actually recorded fictitious data rather than conscientiously performing the needed task. Investigators are responsible for the competence of assistants working with them (*EPP*, 6.07), as well as for the ethical treatment of the research assistants themselves. In short, the researcher needs to maintain constant vigilance over all phases of executing a study to ensure the collection of accurate and reliable data.

Reporting the Results

Reporting the results of a study, although seemingly a straightforward task, entails responsibilities and often complexities. The fundamental ethical principles involved are beneficence and nonmaleficence. The investigator has a responsibility to report accurately and prevent misuse of research results (*EPP*, 6.21; *ES*, D.7, D.8). This implies that the researcher must honestly report findings and present them in a way that is clear and understandable to readers.

The investigator's task is to present the facts of what happened in the study. Sometimes researchers believe that their data will have greater value if they confirm their hypotheses or support a well-known researcher's theory. It is probably true that most published research reports statistically significant findings. However, it is imperative to note that the researcher is not responsible for whether the data do or do not support a particular theory; perhaps the theory is incorrect. As

Carl Rogers once said, "The facts are always friendly," implying that one should not feel bad about data that does not support a given hypothesis (personal communication to P. P. Heppner and L. A. Lee, January 1983). Thus, the job of the investigator is to report the results honestly, regardless of any preconceived notions, predictions, or personal desires.

The researcher also has a responsibility to present proper interpretations of findings. This is especially important when the data may have multiple interpretations (as in qualitative research), or when data were collected with a special population with possibly unique cultural patterns. For example, Ponterotto and Casas (1991) recommended that other researchers verify their interpretations of the findings by involving racial/ethnic minority individuals who have more knowledge of the phenomena under study. Likewise, researchers can ask participants in a qualitative study to verify the accuracy of patterns and conclusions that were drawn from the data (see Chapter 10).

Investigators have a responsibility to discuss the limitations of their data and to qualify their conclusions accordingly. Discussion of limitations is especially important when the research might be "construed to the detriment of persons in groups of specific age, disability, race/ethnicity, gender, national origin, religion, sexual orientation, social class, or other vulnerable groups." Moreover, it is important to explicitly mention "all variables and conditions known to the investigator" that might have affected the results of the study (*ES,* D.7). Sometimes researchers believe that if limitations are discussed, their results will be weakened, perhaps so much as to prevent their publication in a professional journal. It is important to remember that the goal of the researcher is to provide the most accurate information possible about the phenomenon of interest. Specifying the limitations is helpful to the profession, and often to future researchers as well. In our view, if a study's limitations are such that they in fact substantially reduce the probability of publishing the results, then the long-term interests of the profession are probably best served if the results are not published. It is antithetical to the long-term goals of a scientist to publish information that is misleading or to suppress disconfirming data.

The investigator also has a responsibility, after research results are in the public domain, to make original data available to other qualified researchers who may want to inspect them and verify claims (*EPP,* 6.16; *ES,* D.9). This necessitates storage of raw data for some time after a study is published, typically for five years (*EPP,* 6.25).

Perhaps one of the most serious problems is the intentional fabrication of data. It is clearly unethical to produce fraudulent data (*EPP,* 6.21). There are at least three basic varieties of concocting fraudulent data: (a) inventing findings without any actual data collection, (b) tampering with or doctoring actual findings to more closely resemble the desired outcome, and (c) trimming actual findings to delete unwanted or discrepant information (Keith-Spiegel & Koocher, 1985). Tampering of the findings can also include presenting post hoc findings as if they were planned; such fabrication obviously provides misinformation to the profession and serves only to increase confusion and misunderstanding. Unfortunately, numerous instances of fraudulent research have been reported in the scientific community in the past decade (see Keith-Spiegel & Koocher, 1985, pp. 363–364),

attracting attention in the general media and even provoking congressional investigations (Broad & Wade, 1982).

Perhaps the most publicized report of fabricating data involves Sir Cyril Burt,
a noted British psychologist whose research on identical twins was read and cited
internationally. Burt was a well-known scientist who was knighted in 1946 in
recognition of his work (Drew, 1980). Burt has been exposed posthumously for
publishing implausible and fictitious data that supported his own theory of inher-
ited intelligence. Not only did such fabrications mislead the psychological profession for many years, they also became a major source of embarrassment to the
profession.

Clearly, the fabrication of data represents a loss of "scientific responsibility"
(Keith-Spiegel & Koocher, 1985, p. 364) and does little to promote human welfare.
The goals of science are then trampled in the pursuit of personal rewards and short-
term gain. Although a quest for personal recognition and the pressure to publish
(the academic publish-or-perish dilemma) may distort a researcher's motivations,
probably the most significant inducement pertains to securing grant funds.
Researchers who make startling discoveries often are awarded grant funds; grant
renewals are contingent upon continued research performance and the breaking
of new ground. But sometimes in this pursuit the basic aim of science—extending
the knowledge bases of a profession—is lost. Fabrication of data results in especially negative consequences for the counseling profession because most of our
research is also aimed at improving psychological services to people in need.
Thus, fabrication of data does more than create confusion; it can also reduce the
effectiveness of the counseling profession, which affects the lives of real people.
The federal government has promulgated rules that define fabrication, falsification, or plagiarism as *misconduct*. Furthermore, the rules require institutions to
have procedures for investigating and sanctioning the misconduct of scientists
they employ (see the Department of Health and Human Services, 1989).

Duplicate and Piecemeal Publication

Another issue relates to the duplicate publication of data. Obviously, publishing
the same data in different journal articles creates some problems. Duplicate publication may give the impression that there is more information in our knowledge
base on a particular topic than is warranted. Suppose that a journal article reports
a relationship between a new relaxation training technique and stress management, and that shortly thereafter another article appears in a different journal
reporting the same finding—the same relaxation training technique is helpful in
reducing stress. The second article appears to replicate the first study, and thus
creates the impression that the effect of this new relaxation training technique on
stress management is a robust finding. In reality, however, these two articles only
represent one data set, and the perception of replication is inaccurate. Moreover,
duplicate publications waste valuable resources, including journal space and
reviewers' and editors' time. In short, "psychologists do not publish, as original
data, data that have been previously published" (*EPP*, 6.24).

A related issue pertains to what is referred to as piecemeal publication. Piecemeal, or fragmented, publication involves publication of several and perhaps slightly different studies from the same data set. Piecemeal publication is not necessarily synonymous with duplicate publication, although it can be. For example, it is possible in piecemeal publication to have one study reporting findings on relationships among depression, hopelessness, and suicidal ideation, while a second study from the same data set reports on relationships among depression, hopelessness, suicidal ideation, and irrational beliefs.

The prohibition of piecemeal publication does not include reanalysis of published data to test a new theory or methodology, although the new article needs to be clearly labeled as such (American Psychological Association, 1994). Likewise, there are times when multiple reports from large longitudinal studies are warranted, especially when the time lag across data collection is significant. Similarly, sometimes multiple reports from a large data set are warranted if the studies are theoretically or conceptually distinct, and thus the data cannot be meaningfully combined into one article. Parsimoniously presenting research is desirable, however, and should be done whenever possible.

It is strongly recommended that authors clearly identify instances of multiple publication from the same data set. Moreover, authors should inform editors of the possibility of multiple publication and preferably provide the relevant articles so that editors can make informed decisions regarding fragmented publication. When in doubt, consult the APA *Publication Manual* (American Psychological Association, 1994), journal editors, and colleagues.

Publication Credit

Researchers have a responsibility to adequately and accurately assign credit for contributions to a project (*EPP*, 6.23; *ES*, D.12). The issues involved with publication credit primarily relate to the fundamental ethical principle of justice. On the one hand, assigning publication credit seems like a straightforward and simple process. People who made minor contributions are acknowledged in a footnote, while those making major contributions are given authorship and listed in order of how much they contributed. In reality, these decisions can be complicated and emotional, primarily because of ambiguity surrounding the term *contribution.* What constitutes minor and major contributions? Some contend that the person who contributed the most time to a project deserves to be first author, while others argue that expertise, or even seniority, should determine author order. At other times it is reasoned that the one who conceived the idea for the study should be the principal or first author. Determining the author order often becomes difficult when the authors were primarily engaged in separate activities, such as writing the manuscript, analyzing the results, collecting the data, designing the study, and supervising the conduct of the study. Assigning publication credit becomes complicated as researchers debate whether all of these contributions are equally important, or whether some contributions should be assigned greater weight than others.

Accurately assigning publication credit is important for several reasons. First and foremost, it is important to publicly acknowledge the contributions of all the people involved in the study—to give credit where credit is due (*EPP*, 6.23; *ES*, D.12). In addition, publication credit is often important in one's professional career, helping one gain entrance into graduate school, obtain professional employment, and earn professional promotion. Moreover, public acknowledgment of one's professional contributions can serve as a "psychic reward" to compensate for the low monetary rewards associated with writing for scholarly outlets (Keith-Spiegel & Koocher, 1985). Sometimes the order of authorship on a publication is important, as the first author is accorded more credit (and responsibility) for the scholarly work than are the other authors. For example, only the first author will receive recognition in citational indices such as the Social Science Citation Index. Clearly, then, determining the order of authorship is relevant to career-related issues.

Ethical Principles of Psychologists and *Ethical Standards* are ambiguous in addressing most of these issues. The *Publication Manual of the American Psychological Association* (1994) provides more direction; major contributions typically include writing the manuscript, formulating the research question or hypotheses, designing the study, organizing and conducting the statistical analysis, and interpreting or writing the results. It is often suggested that "minor contributions" to publications be credited in footnotes. Typically, such "minor" professional contributions include such activities as giving editorial feedback, consulting on design or statistical questions, serving as raters or judges, administering an intervention, collecting or entering data, providing extensive clerical services, and generating conceptual ideas relevant to the study (for example, directions for future research). Paid research assistants are remunerated for their contribution. Thus, a common introductory footnote (usually found at the bottom of the first page of a journal article) reads something like: "The authors would like to thank Josephine Computer for statistical assistance and Helen Grammar and Chris Critical for helpful editorial comments." Usually, these contributors went out of their way to help the authors in minor but significant ways. Thus, it is important to publicly recognize these minor contributions. However, the author should receive permission from contributors before thanking them in a footnote. Another type of footnote is a public acknowledgment of a funding source that sponsored the research. A footnote might acknowledge, "This research was supported by a grant received by the first author from the National Institute of Mental Health" (complete with reference to the grant number).

How to distinguish between a minor contributor and a major contributor (an author) and how to determine the order of multiple authors are not clearly specified in *EPP* and *ES*. *EPP* does state that "principal authorship and other publication credits accurately reflect the relative scientific or professional contributions of the individuals involved, regardless of their professional status" (6.23). Spiegel and Keith-Spiegel (1970) surveyed over 700 professionals to examine their opinions about determining authorship. They found modal trends, but not a firm consensus, for the following criteria, in their respective order: (a) generation of hypotheses and design, (b) writing the manuscript, (c) establishing the procedure and collecting the data, and (d) analyzing the data. Contributions tend to be valued according to their scholarly importance, as opposed to the amount of time they required. Moreover, respondents in two studies did not rate professional status as a determining variable

(Bridgewater, Bornstein, & Walkenbach, 1981; Spiegel & Keith-Spiegel, 1970), which suggests that merit rather than degrees or status is typically a stronger determinant of professional contribution. In short, the list of authors should include those individuals who made a major scholarly contribution to the study in the ways just listed.

The order of authorship (in the case of multiple authorship) typically reflects differential amounts of scholarly contributions. That is, the person who made the greatest scholarly contribution to a project should be the principal or first author, with the others listed in order of their relative contributions. The process of determining authors and order of authorship is very important, perhaps as important as the outcome. Because a great deal of ambiguity enters into deciding authorship, authors may have different opinions about author order. The potential for authors to feel slighted or cheated is greater when author order is autocratically decided by one person, such as the first author. Thus, from our experience, a mutual decision-making process is most desirable, and preferably a consensus model in which those involved discuss these issues.

Sometimes the order of authorship is decided at the conclusion of a study (a post hoc strategy) and just prior to the submission of a manuscript for editorial review to a journal or to a professional convention. The advantage of assigning authorship at this time is that it is possible to assess how much each person actually contributed. The disadvantage is after-the-fact disappointments: A person might have wanted or expected to be first author but was unaware of either how the order was to be decided or other members' contributions. Or a worse scenario: A person might have thought that his scholarly contribution was sufficient to qualify him as an author, but then learned after the study that his contribution was deemed minor and that he would be acknowledged only in a footnote. Another strategy (the a priori strategy) is to assign authorship before implementing a study. The advantage here is that as a result of the opportunity to discuss and clarify the relevant issues beforehand, informed decisions and agreements can be made by all participants. The disadvantages to this strategy are that a person might contribute considerably more or less than he or she initially agreed to, or an inexperienced researcher might want to be first or second author without clearly understanding the implications of such an assignment in terms of the tasks and skills needed.

A third strategy is to combine both the post hoc and a priori strategies, discussing author-related issues before the study is conducted, perhaps developing a tentative author order, and then evaluating the accuracy of that initial order after all the tasks have been completed. This strategy offers the benefits of both of the other strategies and minimizes the disadvantages and disappointments.

A final strategy is to assign the order of authorship by chance (for example, by drawing straws). This strategy is sometimes used when it truly seems that each author contributed equally, and it is literally impossible to differentiate among their contributions. It may also seem that any author order would misrepresent the contributions of both the first and last authors. In these situations, authors may use some arbitrary method of assigning the order of authorship. If this strategy is used, an introductory footnote should acknowledge that the author order was determined by chance. Parenthetically, assigning author order by alphabetizing names is not a random process (ask people with names like Zimmer or Zytowski). If chance is to be used as the method of assignment, then drawing straws, pulling numbers from a hat, drawing cards from a deck, or some other random means of assigning order is more desirable.

Winston (1985) has developed a system for analyzing contributions to data-based articles that can facilitate decisions about author order. The system delineates eleven activities common to a research project: (a) conceptualizing and refining research ideas, (b) searching the literature, (c) developing a research design, (d) selecting the instrument, (e) constructing the instrument or designing a question-naire, (f) selecting statistical analyses, (g) collecting and preparing data, (h) per-forming statistical analyses, (i) interpreting statistical analyses, (j) drafting manuscripts (first draft, second draft, and so on), and (k) editing the manuscript. Winston suggested that the people involved in the project, as a group and through consensus, assign points for each task. Because some tasks require more or less skill and time than others and vary in importance, the assigned points will be different for different activities; the interested reader might compare his or her assignment of points to those initially specified by Winston. The next step, again through group consensus, is to assign points to each person for each of the eleven activities. Points are then totaled, and the order of authorship is based on the point distribution. This system appears promising not only because it provides more specific criteria for determining author order but also because it could facilitate communication and make explicit the decision-making process within the research group.

One final note. A very complicated issue pertaining to publication credit involves graduate students' theses and dissertations. Often graduate students feel that because they have contributed a great deal of time, effort, and sometimes money, they have contributed the most to their project. Faculty advisor input might include providing encouragement and technical assistance in designing the study, developing major interpretative contributions, providing funding and other support, and writing major parts of the manuscript. However, it is unclear how much of the faculty advisor's contribution is a part of her or his teaching and train-ing role within the university. There is a real potential for exploiting graduate stu-dents if a faculty member has them perform most (if not all) of the research tasks and then claims publication credit, particularly first authorship. *EPP* indicates that "a student is usually listed as principal author on any multiple-authored article that is substantially based on the student's dissertation or thesis" (6.23). Keith-Spiegel and Koocher (1985) noted that the number of ethical complaints about this issue has resulted in a policy statement issued by the APA Ethics Committee (1983), which provides detailed guidelines. Whereas the Ethics Committee wrote specifi-cally about dissertations, their guidelines pertain equally well to theses. The guide-lines are as follows:

1. Only second authorship is acceptable for the dissertation supervisor.
2. Second authorship may be considered *obligatory* if the supervisor des-ignates the primary variables, makes major interpretative contributions, or provides the database.

3. Second authorship is a courtesy if the supervisor designates the general area of concern or is substantially involved in the development of the design and measurement procedures or substantially contributes to the write-up of the published report.
4. Second authorship is *not* acceptable if the supervisor provides only encouragement, physical facilities, financial support, critiques, or editorial contributions.
5. In all instances, agreements should be reviewed before the writing for publication is undertaken and at the time of submission. If disagreements arise, they should be resolved by a third party using these guidelines.

Plagiarism

Researchers have a responsibility to acknowledge the original contributions of other writers and to clearly distinguish their own original scholarly insights from the work of others (*EPP*, 6.22; *ES*, D.11). Again, these issues revolve primarily around the fundamental ethical principle of justice. Plagiarism can occur in the direct, verbatim copying of another's work, or less explicitly, as in duplicating ideas from others' work without proper citation. Quotation marks and proper citation form should be used when quoting a passage verbatim from another article; paraphrasing sentences from other articles should include a citation to the original work. In both cases of plagiarism, the original author does not receive proper acknowledgment or credit for his or her work. Keith-Spiegel and Koocher (1985) nicely depicted this issue:

> Copying the original work of others without proper permission or citation attribution is often experienced as "psychic robbery" by the victims, producing the same kind of rage expressed by those who arrive home to find the TV set and stereo missing. When plagiarizers reap financial rewards or recognition from passing someone else's words off as their own, the insult is still greater. Readers are also misled and, in a sense, defrauded. Plagiarism and unfair use of previously published material are among the more serious ethical infractions a psychologist can commit. (p. 356)

Plagiarism can occur on several levels. A researcher might omit necessary citations through inattention, perhaps by not being sufficiently careful or conscientious. The plagiarism in such cases is unintentional and due more to oversight. Another level involves the difficulty sometimes encountered in determining what is original in a researcher's ideas. For example, after a researcher has read and written in an area for 20 years, ideas from a variety of sources often blend together in a complex knowledge base. The researcher may one day conceive of what seems like a new insight, and publish it. However, in reality the "insight" had already been published years ago; the researcher simply did not remember the original source. Or, as researchers work together and not only share ideas but also build upon each other's ideas, the ownership of ideas becomes unclear. Sometimes researchers working in slightly different areas may duplicate each other's ideas without being aware of their common work. These types of plagiarism are difficult to control; one needs to be as conscientious as possible while acknowledging that memory lapses can create less-than-ideal conditions.

Another level of plagiarism involves the conscious or intentional exclusion of another person's writing because of petty jealousies or interpersonal competition. Thus, a writer might intentionally fail to cite the relevant work of a particular researcher in part because the writer does not want to publicly acknowledge the researcher's work, but also because the writer would like to have sole credit for an idea or contribution. A final level of plagiarism involves the verbatim copying of another's writing or the duplicating of ideas with the motive of presenting one-self as the original contributor, all the while knowing full well that this is not the case. In these situations the plagiarist has control and has made some deliberate choices.

The point is that acknowledging the contributions of others is basically a matter of fairness and integrity—in essence, of giving credit where credit is due. Not citing the original author may seem like a rather small issue, but it is really quite important. Imagine that you have worked very hard for two or three years, creating and building a new conceptual model. Naturally, you are very proud of this accomplishment. Then someone publishes a similar model and this person receives the credit for developing this innovative model. Being cited is often meaningful to authors and serves as an important psychic reward. In addition to fairness and integrity, there is also the matter of saluting (in a small way) previous researchers for their accomplishments. From a historical perspective, it is impor-tant not only to recognize the authors whose work preceded one's own, but also to recognize where one's work fits into the bigger picture. It is a sad comment on the profession when petty jealousies prevent mutual recognition or even collabo-ration that might result in important contributions. Keep in mind as well that the federal government considers plagiarism to be misconduct in science, and that employing institutions are required to investigate all cases of suspected plagiarism and provide sanctions where appropriate.

Although not appropriately recognizing an author's contributions is prob-lematic, overcrediting an author can also be an issue, most notably when citing one's own research. For example, overly laudatory reference to one's own "semi-nal, ground-breaking research that will revolutionize the entire field in the next sev-eral years" is inappropriate. It is best to leave these types of judgments to others.

ETHICAL ISSUES RELATED TO PARTICIPANTS

A central issue in all psychological and educational research is the dignity and wel-fare of the people who participate in the study. The goal of the ethical researcher is to develop a fair, clear, and explicit agreement with participants so that their deci-sion to participate in an experiment is made voluntarily, knowingly, and intelligently (Keith-Spiegel & Koocher, 1985). In this manner, participants are not coerced and make informed decisions about the benefits and risks associated with taking part in a particular experiment. The most fundamental ethical principles implied in the treatment of participants involve nonmaleficence, autonomy, and fidelity.

Historically, the dignity and welfare of those participating in research have not always been of foremost concern. Probably the most notorious example of abuse of participants occurred in the experiments conducted during World War II in Nazi prison camps, where many prisoners died from lethal doses of chemicals and various levels of physical abuse. Physicians conducted research on such topics as effective ways of treating severe frostbite (which involved subjecting individuals to freezing temperatures), infected wounds, and deadly diseases such as malaria and typhus (which involved subjecting individuals to infectious germs) (Stricker, 1982). Fortunately, the Nuremberg trials at the end of World War II, which tried 23 physicians for these research atrocities, served as an initial impetus for guidelines of ethical treatment of research participants. In fact, the Nuremberg Code has been the basis for subsequent ethical principles regarding human subjects in research (Keith-Spiegel & Koocher, 1985). Unfortunately, yet other research tragedies stimulated additional concern and the need for additional regulation. In 1962, the thalidomide scandal (see Chapter 1) came to public attention because of innumerable gross neonatal deformities. Consequently, the U.S. Food and Drug Administration introduced much stricter regulations for tightly controlled experimentation on drugs and other products (Stricker, 1982). Not long afterward, public attention became focused on a program conducted by a hospital in Brooklyn, where 22 chronically ill patients were injected with cancer cells as part of a study to examine the body's capacity to reject foreign cells. The patients were not informed of their participation. This, and other studies involving excessive shock treatment conditions and subjecting participants to diseases such as syphilis, served to raise public awareness of ethical issues related to informed consent of research participants. Subsequently the issue of informed consent crystallized, and obligations to research participants were made clearer (Stricker, 1982).

Diener and Crandall (1978) discussed a number of research studies that have raised concern about ethical issues in research (for example, inducing extreme levels of fear in participants, suppressing disconfirming data, jeopardizing continued employment of participants). As awareness of and sensitivity to the rights of both human and animal participants in psychological and educational research have increased, there have been major changes in the regulation of research.

One of the major changes has been development of the Code of Federal Regulations (rev. March 3, 1983), which implemented Public Law 93-348 (July 12, 1974) establishing institutional review boards (IRBs) and an ethics guidance program to protect human participants in biomedical and behavioral research.

All research projects with human participants are subject to federal regulations governing research. Initially, IRBs were established as five-person panels to preview research proposals and weigh potential risks and benefits for all research that sought funding from the Department of Health, Education, and Welfare (now the Department of Health and Human Services, hereafter referred to as DHHS). Although IRBs still serve this function, most institutions now routinely have all research proposals reviewed by an IRB committee of peers at their institution. In essence, the typical IRB certifies that projects comply with the regulations and policies set forth by the DHHS regarding the health, welfare, safety, rights, and privileges of human participants. The general procedure is for the investigator to complete and submit to the IRB a form that summarizes basic information about the research (see Exhibit A at the end of this chapter for an example of one such form). Key issues in evaluating the ethicality of any research project are the risks and benefits involved to the participants, and whether participants have been fully informed about the study so they can make an informed decision to voluntarily participate (informed consent). Given the increased sensitivity to informed consent, documentation of the participant's consent is now required unless specifically waived. General requirements have been developed for documenting informed consent (see *Federal Register,* Volume 46, Number 16, January 26, 1981).

In this section of the chapter we discuss a number of complexities and complications related to using human participants that often arise for the psychological researcher in general, and for the counseling researcher in particular. Assessing potential harm or risk is a difficult and sometimes imprecise process. Because there is some level of risk (even if it is minuscule) in every experiment, how much risk or harm is too much? In some research, deception is needed to adequately investigate a particular construct, and if the full truth were known to a participant, the validity of the experiment might be significantly reduced. Thus, without deception, knowledge of some aspects of human behavior may be inaccessible. But deception conflicts with informed consent and the fundamental principles of autonomy and fidelity. This section focuses on these issues in greater detail as we discuss the issues involved in protecting the dignity and welfare of the people who participate in research investigations. Specifically, we will discuss issues pertaining to risks and benefits, consent, deception and debriefing, confidentiality and privacy, and treatment issues.

Risks and Benefits

The ethical researcher's goal is to conduct an investigation that creates new knowledge (the beneficence principle) while preserving the dignity and welfare of the participants (the nonmaleficence and autonomy principles). It almost goes without saying that one would not want to harm participants in any way. Particularly for the counseling researcher, the goal is usually to alleviate human suffering; thus harm is antithetical to the immediate and long-term goals of the professional counselor. But harm can be manifested in many ways. The most obvious way involves physical harm, or even death, as in the Nazi "research" during World War II. However, harm can also consist of embarrassment, irritation, anger, physical and emotional distress, loss of self-esteem, exacerbation of stress, delay of treatment, sleep deprivation, loss of respect from others, negative labeling, invasion of privacy, damage to personal dignity, loss of employment, and civil or criminal liabilities. Part of the difficulty in predicting harm is that different people may react to the same experimental condition in very different ways. For example, most clients may feel very comfortable rating their expectations for the counseling they are about to receive; some clients might even enjoy this reflection. However, a few clients might experience distress or embarrassment, or even guilt, by participating in this exercise. Sometimes cross-cultural differences contribute to unintended reactions, which underscores the complexity of this issue. Researchers need to assess harm not only in a general sense, but also with regard to the intended participants' worldview and cultural background.

It is the researcher's responsibility to identify potential sources of risk and eliminate or minimize them to protect potential participants (*EPP*, 6.06; *ES*, D.4). The professional codes of ethics suggest that the researcher should carefully assess the potential risks of involvement for participants and take precautions to protect participants from physical and mental discomfort, harm, and danger that might occur in a study (*EPP*, II.C.5; *ES*, D.4). Implied in these statements is that it is the responsibility of the investigator to reduce risk and prevent harm by detecting and removing any negative consequences associated with a study, to the extent possible.

One of the problems inherent in assessing risk potential is that the task is often subjective, ambiguous, and involves an estimation of probabilities. Typically one does not have prior, empirical, objective data about whether the experimental condition is stressful (and to collect such data would require administering the experiment to participants). Moreover, the type and level of stress that would be harmful is ambiguous and likely varies across cultures and individuals. That is, what is perceived as harmful in one culture may not be perceived as such in another culture. Thus, assessing harm may also involve cross-cultural sensitivity. In short, assessing risk is difficult, if not impossible, to quantify.

Acknowledging the difficulty, ambiguity, and imperfectness of the task, there are at least two main strategies for obtaining approval to conduct a study, typically from an institutional review board. The first strategy involves making a best estimate of the risk/benefit ratio of the study. That is, a comparison should be made of the potential benefits that might accrue from the study relative to the potential risks to participants. This involves a three-step process: (a) assessing risks, (b) assessing benefits, and (c) comparing risks and benefits. For example, a study might be considered ethically acceptable if the potential benefits greatly outweighed the potential risks, or if failure to use the experimental procedures might expose participants to greater harm. Assessing the benefits derived from a particular study, however, is also a difficult and ambiguous task. This assessment is complicated by the question of "benefit for whom?" That is, should participants be the ones to receive the benefit directly, or could it be a larger group, as when a profession's knowledge base is increased. Some may argue that benefits from any single study may be minimal, but that over time programmatic research does increase the profession's knowledge base. Still, balancing individual costs against societal benefits is a difficult task. Moreover, it can be argued that the investigator is at a disadvantage to judge the cost/benefit ratio accurately because he or she may be overly biased regarding the benefit of the study (Diener & Crandall, 1978). In short, in principle the risk/benefit ratio is appealing, but in practice it is difficult to apply. Nonetheless, the risk/benefit ratio is one useful strategy for assessing the ethical issues associated with a particular study.

The second strategy involves several procedures to minimize risk or reduce the probability of harm. Whenever the potential for substantial risk is present, the investigator should search for other possible designs or procedures. The researcher needs to exhaust other possibilities for obtaining the same or similar knowledge by using a slightly different design. A common practice is to consult

with colleagues not only to obtain ideas regarding alternative designs or procedures, but also to obtain alternative perspectives in assessing risks and benefits.
Consultation with colleagues is particularly important in planning socially sensitive research or research in which cross-cultural issues and investigator bias may
be a factor. Researchers have a duty to consult with those knowledgeable about
the individuals or groups most likely to be affected (*EPP,* 6.07). Often the
researcher's problem solving with regard to ethical issues can be greatly stimulated
and facilitated by successively conferring with a wide variety of colleagues. The
process of consulting with colleagues has now been formalized at many institutions
and agencies, as we indicated earlier, into institutional review boards (IRBs) or
human subject review committees. From our experience, the IRBs serve the
extremely valuable function of providing additional perspectives in assessing risk
and suggesting possible alternative designs that are not always immediately apparent to the researcher. Even if not technically required to do so, researchers are
encouraged to solicit feedback from such committees.

The researcher can also engage in other strategies to minimize risk. We indicated earlier that one of the problems in assessing risks and benefits is the lack of
empirical data on which to make informed decisions. Thus, another strategy is to
collect some data through safer channels, such as using pilot participants and role
playing, to facilitate a more accurate assessment of risks and benefits. For example, the researcher and his or her assistants might role-play the experimental procedures in question (which is often a good idea in general), and perhaps explore
alternative procedures. Perhaps colleagues could also be asked to serve as participants to review the procedures and provide feedback on potential risks.
Colleagues often can provide very useful feedback because they can discuss their
experience as a participant in light of their knowledge of ethical and design issues.
Depending on the outcome of such role plays (that is, if the risks do not appear
to be substantial), the researcher might take another step by conducting a very
small-scale pilot study with two to five participants. In such a pilot, the researcher
should not only monitor the experimental procedures very carefully, but also
interview participants at length about their experiences and solicit suggestions for
alternative procedures. Pilot feedback can be extremely valuable, and its utility
should not be downplayed. Likewise, any frequency data from previous studies
employing the same procedures may be very useful in assessing the degree of risk;
for example, researchers might use a postexperimental evaluation to ask subjects
whether they experienced any harm. In short, role plays and pilot projects provide the researcher at least minimal data from which to assess risks and benefits.
Additional data can also be obtained by carefully monitoring the actual experiment and even interviewing randomly selected participants both immediately
after the experiment and several days later. The researcher should not stop evaluating the potential risks of a study once the study is approved by an IRB committee, but rather should remain vigilant by constantly evaluating the risks and
benefits as more data about the participants' experiences become available.

Another strategy to minimize risk is to screen participants for a particular
study and then select only those participants who have certain characteristics that
make them more resistant to the risks involved (or dismiss participants that might
be particularly at risk in the study) (Diener & Crandall, 1978). For example,

depressed participants with very low self-esteem might be at increased risk if they participated in a protracted study that involved a great deal of interpersonal feed-back from other students. In this regard, special populations (such as children, patients from a psychiatric hospital, or prisoners in solitary confinement) merit careful consideration as a group.

In summary, the ethical researcher's goal is to conduct an investigation that creates new knowledge while preserving the dignity and welfare of the partici-pants. A central issue in preserving participants' dignity and welfare is preventing harm. Thus, a major task for the researcher is to carefully assess potential risks and make every attempt to eliminate or minimize such risks. Two strategies were dis-cussed for obtaining approval to conduct a study: (a) attempting to assess and weigh the risk/benefit ratio of the study and (b) using a variety of procedures to evaluate, minimize, or eliminate potential risks. Both strategies should be used in any study involving more than minimal risk. It is important to note, however, that a great deal of ambiguity often enters assessments of costs and risks, particularly in cross-cultural situations; the researcher may often experience conflict and struggle with the imperfection of this important task. Consultation is strongly encouraged.

Consent

A critical issue in conducting studies involving risk pertains to informed consent. After a researcher has carefully evaluated potential harm and developed the best design to answer his or her question while preserving the participant's dignity and welfare, the researcher is then ready to approach participants with a fair, clear, and explicit agreement about the experiment in question (informed consent). The issue of informed consent revolves around the fundamental ethical principles of autonomy and fidelity. Consent refers to the process of giving participants the opportunity to decide whether or not to participate in a particular research study. This might appear to be a rather simple matter: Simply ask the participant if he or she would like to participate. But a number of factors make obtaining consent a rather complicated process, and a considerable amount of attention has been given to this topic in the past 20 years (see Keith-Spiegel & Koocher, 1985; Schmidt & Meara, 1984).

The professional codes of ethics clearly indicate that the investigator has a responsibility to obtain informed consent from participants (*EPP*, 6.11; *ES*, D.5, D.6). The investigator seeks to develop a specific type of relationship with poten-tial participants and thus is ethically bound to establish a clear and fair agreement that clarifies obligations, risks, and responsibilities prior to the study.

Turnbull (1977) discussed consent in this special relationship in terms of three key elements: capacity, information, and voluntariness. *Capacity* refers to a participant's ability to process information and involves two issues: a legal age qualification and ability standards. Minors, people under the age of 18, are not considered to be legally able to make some decisions and thus do not have the needed capacity in these instances. The principle of autonomy creates difficult issues when applied to using children in research (*EPP*, I.C.2). Ramsey (1970) has argued that since children have a reduced or limited capacity, it is impossible to obtain a fully rational consent from them. Moreover, the child's parent or legal guardian cannot know whether the child, if fully rational, would choose to participate or not. He argued that children should not be used in any research except research from which they would benefit directly. Ramsey's position has been regarded as too extreme (see Cooke, 1982; Powell, 1984), and parents or legal guardians are allowed to give consent. However, federal regulations indicate that a child's assent (defined as an affirmative agreement to participate) is required whenever in the judgment of an IRB the child is capable of providing assent, taking into account age, maturity, and psychological state. We encourage counseling researchers to explain to children (and to their parents or guardians), in language they can understand, what they will be asked to do in the course of the research and to secure whenever possible their agreement to participate.

Ability typically refers to mental competence and thereby protects individuals who may be at risk because of diminished mental capacities. Autonomy is again an issue. If a researcher uses institutionalized adults, then consent must be obtained from parents or legal guardians. We also suggest obtaining assent from adults with diminished capacity if at all possible. In short, a critical element of consent involves the capacity to process information about the merits and drawbacks of participating in a particular study.

The second key element of informed consent pertains to the type of *information* that potential participants are given about a study (*EPP,* 6.11; *ES,* D.5). Participants must be given all of the relevant information about a study so that they can make an informed decision about the merits and liabilities of participating. Turnbull (1977) noted the importance of two issues: the kind of information provided and the process of providing it. Thus, the information given must be complete and presented in understandable, jargon-free language. Drew (1980) referred to these issues as fullness and effectiveness. To satisfy the requirement of fullness, the information presented should contain a description of what the investigation is about and what the participant will be asked to do (such as complete two questionnaires about study habits). This should include a discussion of any type of electronic recording or filming (*EPP,* 6.13). Moreover, the explanation should include a discussion of possible risks or potential harm involved in the study, as well as a discussion of potential benefits that might accrue from participation. Failure to make full disclosures, as in the case of deception, requires additional safeguards that we will discuss later. Moreover, the information must be understandable to participants given their particular worldview.

The third element of consent is *voluntariness:* assent must be given without any element of explicit or implicit coercion, pressure, or undue enticement (*EPP,* 6.14; *ES,* D.6). Examples of coercion include requiring students to participate in a study because they are enrolled in a class, living in an institution, part of a therapy group, or seeking individual therapy; publicly humiliating participants if they choose not to participate; paying excessive amounts of money or giving other financial rewards as an inducement to participate; repeatedly contacting clients and soliciting participation; and creating undue social pressure by indicating that all of the other clients have agreed to participate. University courses (such as large introductory psychology classes) sometimes offer bonus credits for or require participation in research studies; in such situations it is essential to offer students viable alternatives to participating in research studies in order to protect their autonomy. Voluntariness can also be a complex issue in a counseling context. For example, situations in which therapists ask their clients to participate may contain elements of undue influence (for example, the therapist is very likable, or the client is vulnerable and wants to be a "good client"). In short, a key aspect of consent is that participants can voluntarily decide on participating free from blatant or subtle extraneous factors that may compel them to participate.

The notion of voluntariness does not end when a potential participant decides to participate in a study; it continues throughout the duration of a study. Thus, participants are typically informed prior to the commencement of a study that they have the right to withdraw from the experiment at any time, and that their initial agreement to participate is not binding. Keith-Spiegel and Koocher (1985) astutely observed that the wise investigator will be alert to signs of discomfort or anxiousness that might influence participants to withdraw, and rather than coerce continued involvement be concerned about the usefulness and validity of data collected under stressful conditions. Moreover, it is useful to contact participants "within a reasonable time period following participation should stress, harm, or related questions or concerns arise" (*EPP*, I.C.12).

In short, an important ethical consideration in recruiting participants in counseling research involves their informed consent. It is important that potential participants have the capacity to process information about the study, have received complete and effective information about the content and procedures of the study, and can decide on the merits of participating voluntarily, without extraneous compelling factors.

As we indicated earlier, documentation of the participant's consent is now common practice. There are a few exceptions; several categories of research are typically considered exempt from these requirements, such as observation of public behavior, the study of anonymous archival data, and certain types of survey and interview procedures. Participants are asked to sign a formal consent form indicating their informed agreement to participate if there is more than what is referred to as a minimal risk (that is, more risk to the participant than he or she would encounter in daily life). Even in studies involving minimal risk to participants, obtaining a signed consent form is advisable to avoid misunderstandings and for the researcher's own protection. It is important to note that cross-cultural issues can also create confusion or misunderstandings that may be relevant during the process of obtaining informed consent, which again reinforces the need for sensitivity to these matters while obtaining consent.

Specifically, the following elements are to be incorporated into a written consent form:

- Name, phone number, and address of the person(s) conducting the study, and whom to contact for additional information or questions; name, phone number, and address of faculty member if the investigator is a student; whom to contact in the event of a research-related injury to the participant.

- A statement that the study involves research, along with the title, purpose, and general description of the study.
- A description of the procedures, including amount of time involved and any plans for contacting participants at a later time.
- A description of any reasonably foreseeable risks or discomforts to the participant.
- A description of the benefits to the participant, or to others, that can reasonably be expected.
- In cases involving treatment or therapy, a statement of appropriate alternative procedures or courses of treatment, if any, that might be advantageous to the participant.
- A statement describing the extent to which confidentiality will be maintained.
- A statement that the results of the study may be published or reported to government or funding agencies.
- A statement indicating that participation is voluntary, and that the participant may discontinue participation at any time without any penalty.
- For research involving more than minimal risk, an explanation of whether compensation or medical treatments are available if injury occurs.

A sample of a typical consent form for adults is provided as Exhibit B, and a sample of a typical consent form for children (note the appropriate language level) is provided as Exhibit C.

Deception and Debriefing

Deception is a topic that has received considerable attention and been the subject of much debate (*EPP,* 6.15; *ES,* D.5). Deception in psychological research refers to misinforming or withholding information from potential participants about the nature of the experiment or the procedures involved in the study. Thus, deception refers to misrepresenting the facts pertaining to a study, either through acts of omission or commission. For instance, an investigator might omit or withhold some information about a study and thus disguise the true nature of the study in some way; or the researcher might purposefully provide false or misleading information, an act of commission, to deceive the participant in some way. Either way, the thorny issues of deception revolve around the fundamental ethical principles of autonomy, fidelity, and, to some extent, nonmaleficence.

It is important to note that there are many types or levels of deception. Perhaps at the simplest and most benign level, the experimenter may accurately describe the study but not disclose all the facts about it, largely because of the tremendous amount of detail involved. Or the experimenter might accurately disclose the nature of the experiment but not reveal the hypotheses so as to not bias the participants. These acts of omission usually do not bother participants. It is typically recognized that an experimenter cannot be completely forthcoming about all aspects of a study (including the researcher's hypothesis or complete descriptions of all experimental conditions); in fact, revealing such information can bias

or confound the results of a study (see Chapter 14). Other types of deception, however, mislead the participants in major ways and often lead them to feel "duped" or
"had." For example, participants might be told that they failed a problem-solving
test (that their score was in the fifth percentile) in order to examine their behavior
following failure. In reality, participants probably did not perform so poorly on the
test but were merely given bogus feedback. For the most part, the major controversy surrounding deception pertains to those situations in which participants are
entirely misled. It is on these instances of deception that we will focus here.

Obviously, the use of deception is antithetical to fully informing potential subjects about the essence of a particular study. The use of deception in psychological
research is quite a controversial topic. Schmidt and Meara (1984) reported that in
revising the APA Ethical Principles in 1981, a substantial minority of psychologists
agreed to forbid the use of any deception. The majority, however, thought that
although deception should generally be avoided, important research would be
impossible to conduct (and would never be conducted) if deception of all kinds
were unethical. For example, sometimes deception is necessary in psychological
research to adequately examine certain phenomena, like the process of persuasion. Specifically, in a study of the social influence process in counseling, some
participants might very well be predisposed not to change a particular belief or
attitude if they were told beforehand that the study was investigating variables
related to changing their beliefs. In this case, not using deception would result in
a study that did not have much generalizability or resemblance to the attitude
change process in counseling.

Schmidt and Meara (1984) noted, however, that deception may have especially troublesome consequences for counseling researchers. A core ingredient of
the counseling relationship is perceived counselor trustworthiness; deception
would most likely destroy client perceptions of trustworthiness and the working
alliance. Thus, because of therapeutic considerations, researchers examining
real-life counseling processes must address additional considerations and consequences involving deception.

Our view is that researchers should avoid deception whenever possible. In
particular, participants should not be deceived about "aspects that would affect
their willingness to participate, such as physical risk, discomfort, or unpleasant
emotional experiences" (EPP, 6.15). Moreover, the use of certain types of deception with oppressed groups is very questionable. Still, we believe there are exceptions in which deception may be allowed. Specifically, when there is little or
minimal risk and the benefits from the research are socially significant or directly
benefit the participant, deception may be allowed. However, we agree with
Lindsey (1984) that "if the risk is significant and subjects are deceived, it is a fundamental violation of the principle of autonomy" (p. 85). In addition, before conducting a study using deception, it is the responsibility of the investigator to (a)
"determine whether the use of deceptive techniques is justified by the study's
prospective scientific, educational, or applied value," and (b) determine whether
"alternative procedures that do not use deception are feasible" (EPP, 6.15). Kazdin
(1980) noted two other considerations. First, the aversiveness of the deception
itself is an important factor to consider, as there are many types of deception with

varying consequences. Some deception does not result in any harm to a participant, whereas other types of deception might result in considerable harm. Second, the researcher must weigh the potential and magnitude of the harmful effects caused by the deception. Thus, the extent or magnitude of the harm is an important consideration. In short, if an investigator decides to use deception, additional responsibilities and safeguards are required to protect the welfare and dignity of research participants, and the researcher must carefully assess the potential consequences and risks to participants. Finally, given the nature of the counseling relationship, deception in real-life counseling with actual clients would rarely seem justifiable.

If deception is justified, the investigator is responsible for informing participants about the nature of the study and removing any misconceptions as soon as is possible within the experiment (*EPP,* 6.15; *ES,* D.5). Providing a sufficient explanation is commonly referred to as debriefing. Moreover, in educational settings, if students are serving as participants to earn research credits and learn about psychological research, then debriefing also should emphasize educational issues. Exhibit D provides examples of both oral and written debriefings for an analogue study that examined variables affecting laypersons' perceptions of grief reactions. Because this study was conducted with undergraduates who earned extra credit, the debriefing nicely emphasizes educational components. Moreover, the example explains the need for the minimal level of deception used in the analogue study.

It is important to note that the effectiveness of debriefing is unclear and probably varies with each study or experimenter. Moreover, in some cases debriefing can itself create stress or harm. For example, if the researcher preselected two groups of participants who had very high or very low self-concepts, communicating this information may not be well received by some participants. In this regard, Baumrind (1976) identified debriefing as "inflicted insight." In other situations participants may feel angry because they were misled or "duped." Thus, sometimes debriefing adds additional complications and results in delicate situations with which the investigator must contend.

Confidentiality and Privacy

Investigators ask participants for a wide array of information, often of such a very personal nature that it could be harmful if publicly released. Often experimenters promise confidentiality to increase the likelihood of honest responses from participants. If a participant agrees to participate confidentially in an experiment, the principles of fidelity, autonomy, and to some extent nonmaleficence suggest that any information that the participant discloses should be protected to safeguard the welfare of the client. The professional codes of ethics clearly indicate that care should be taken to protect the privacy of participants (*EPP,* 5.07; *ES,* D.10).

Maintaining the anonymity or confidentiality of participants is now standard in counseling research. Anonymity exists when there are no identifiers whatsoever on project materials that can link data with individual participants; often researchers assign participants coded designations that appear on their respective questionnaires in lieu of their names. Thus, the participants' responses are anonymous, and even the investigator cannot identify the participants. At other times, investigators collect data and ask for participants' names. Researchers have an obligation to maintain the confidentiality of information obtained in such research. If names are used, typically code numbers will be assigned to participants when the data are transferred to coding sheets, and the original questionnaires containing participants' names will be destroyed. If someone other than the experimenter will have access to data (for example, a research assistant), this should be explained to the participants (and usually is stated in the consent form) along with plans for maintaining confidentiality. In field settings, researchers also should be alert to minimizing the invasiveness of data collection so as to protect the participants' privacy within a social milieu (*EPP*, II.C.7).

Schmidt and Meara (1984) indicated that because confidentiality is central to the counseling relationship, counseling researchers often need to be especially sensitive to maintaining confidentiality, particularly with regard to research conducted in an agency such as a university counseling center. For example, researchers must be sensitive to releasing demographic information that might identify participants in a small therapy group (for example, an eating disorder group or a consciousness-raising group for men over 30); on small college campuses, demographic information about the group composition can easily identify clients. Likewise, research using an intensive single-subject design or an intrasubject design with only a few participants also demands sensitivity to identifying characteristics; typically it is advisable to provide fictitious descriptive information that is similar to the truth if it is necessary to describe a particular client in detail, and to explicitly indicate this in whatever written or oral report is made. Sometimes investigators also communicate to participants how the data will be used (*EPP*, I.C.14). They may also obtain feedback and written approval from clients on written descriptions of the study's results to further reduce any breaches of confidentiality.

Another confidentiality issue arises if researchers want to investigate some aspect of a particular treatment procedure *after* clients have already begun treatment at an agency. Suppose there is an active relaxation training program at a university counseling center, in which students, staff, and faculty are encouraged to participate. Clients enter this program with the usual assurance of confidentiality. Let's say a researcher from the counseling department (outside the agency) is interested in evaluating some aspect of the treatment program and examining the effects of certain individual difference variables (such as coping style) on the relaxation training. Given that the clients have been assured of confidentiality at the outset, it would be a breach of confidentiality at this point to reveal client names to a researcher outside the agency. Some clients might also feel their privacy has been invaded if they were identified to a researcher *in the agency,* as they did not consent to having that person know of their seeking such services. Likewise, if an investigator should conduct a study with a sample of counseling center clients that gave their consent to participate in a study with certain specified procedures, the investigator is limited to accessing only the information or data that the clients consented to disclosing or providing, as opposed to any information in the clients' agency files (see Keith-Spiegel & Koocher, 1985). In short, counseling researchers sometimes have dual responsibilities; they need to be sensitive to confidentiality issues pertaining to research endeavors as well as to confidentiality issues inherent in therapeutic relationships in general.

Confidentiality and privacy issues in research settings can also intersect with a psychologist's duty to protect the welfare of participants and other individuals, thereby creating an ethical dilemma for the researcher. The most notable examples involve participants with homicidal and suicidal intentions that become evident during the course of a research investigation. For example, counseling researchers routinely assess the psychological adjustment of participants in various ways, such as by using the Beck Depression Inventory (BDI) (Beck et al., 1961). In this case, the difficult question concerns what to do when the investigator finds that a participant scored very high on the BDI. Or suppose the researcher is investigating suicidal intentions and in administering the Scale for Suicide Ideators (SSI; Schotte & Clum, 1982) learns that one or more participants scored very high on the SSI. Another ethical dilemma can arise when a participant reveals some information such that the participant or others will be liable for a violation of the law. In short, sometimes the counseling researcher obtains information about participants that either creates considerable concern for the general well-being of particular participants, or other individuals, or brings up criminal or civil liabilities.

Concern for the well-being of a particular participant must also be considered in light of the individual's right to privacy. In approaching one participant who had a very high BDI score after a particular investigation, the investigator was curtly informed that the participant "consented to participate in a psychological experiment, not psychotherapy." Some participants may feel embarrassed if attention is called to them within a group setting; obviously, care must be taken to avoid breaching confidentiality to other participants and to being sensitive to the effects of isolating particular individuals.

Concern for the well-being of a particular participant must also be considered relative to the amount of information an investigator has about the participant. Whereas one researcher might only have one data point (a BDI score) that is causing some concern, another researcher might have a much broader array of information (for example, questionnaire data, interview data, information about environmental stressors, knowledge about past suicide attempts) that more strongly suggests considerable reason for concern.

Clearly, the counseling researcher has ethical obligations beyond the research. Moreover, each situation presents a slightly different context and calls for slightly different interventions. The researcher faces a complex decision as he or she weighs the strength of the evidence, the individual's right to privacy, the consequences of approaching a participant with the topic, and the obligation to promote human welfare. Some IRBs now require investigators to include in the consent form a statement that indicates that if the participant reveals information that signals danger to the participant or another person, confidentiality may need to be broken. Another strategy is for researchers who collect data of a psychologically sensitive nature to routinely attach to the research questionnaire a statement communicating that it asks questions of a personal nature, and that participants are strongly encouraged to discuss the feelings reflected in the questionnaire, if they so choose. Applicable resources should then be listed, such as the address and phone number of the university counseling center or local mental health center. In addition, verbal announcements can also be made before administering the questionnaire. The following paragraph, developed as part of an introduction to the Scale of Suicide Ideation, is an example of a statement designed to facilitate such an exchange.

> The following questionnaire inquires about a variety of thoughts, feelings, attitudes, and behaviors that are sometimes related to suicide. We are interested in how frequently college students think about suicide. We realize that this is not a rare occurrence. In fact, by some estimates, up to 70 of the population at one time or another contemplate suicide. However, we want you to be aware that counseling services are available to you should your thoughts about suicide cause you some distress. To inquire about counseling, you can contact the Counseling Center [address and phone], or the Psychological Clinic [address and phone]. In the event that your score on this inventory indicates that you are seriously contemplating suicide we will contact you to express our concern and urge you to seek counseling. (Dixon, 1989, p. 42)

Treatment Issues

In the past a common strategy among researchers was to use a between-groups design to compare two or more groups of participants; one group received a particular treatment, whereas instead of the treatment one of the other groups received a placebo or had treatment delayed. Although such designs offer methodological rigor, they can present ethical problems related to withholding treatment from people in need. Clients in a waiting-list or placebo group could be at risk as they continue to struggle under duress. Thus, researchers who are interested in examining questions about comparative treatments often must examine additional ethical issues.

One of the essential issues pertains to the necessity of withholding treatment. In general, if there are treatments that are known to be effective, then withholding them from participants raises serious ethical concerns. However, there is less concern about withholding an intervention of unknown effectiveness. The researcher might examine the need to compare a particular treatment against a no-treatment group. The researcher might also consider alternatives, such as comparing the treatment of interest against a well-known treatment. Or the researcher might examine treatment comparisons in an alternative design, such as a within-subjects design. In short, as with the standards for using deception, researchers must assess potential risk and consider alternative designs to answer treatment questions.

Another consideration is the type of participants involved in the experiment. Kazdin (1980) suggested that volunteer clients solicited from a community setting may be more appropriate for a waiting-list group than are clients from a crisis intervention center. Assessing the risk potential not only involves an assessment of the setting from which participants are drawn but also consideration of a type and severity of a participant's presenting problem (for instance, depression versus assertiveness).

Kazdin (1980) also suggested that assigning participants to delayed-treatment groups might be more ethically appropriate if the participants initially came from a waiting list, which is in essence delayed treatment. For example, many agencies have waiting lists because service demands are heavier than can be met by the staff. Thus, a treatment study might be conducted by randomly assigning clients from the waiting list to the experimental conditions (treatment and delayed treatment). In such a case, some clients would actually receive treatment earlier than if they had stayed on the agency's waiting list.

Other ethical considerations that merit attention in delayed-treatment conditions include informed consent and ultimately providing treatment. Ethically, participants should be informed before an investigation if there is a possibility that they may be placed in a delayed-treatment group; they then may or may not decide to participate in the study. Moreover, participants in a delayed-treatment group are entitled to treatment after the experiment has concluded, and these participants deserve the same quality of treatment as the experimental group.

In short, counseling researchers who contemplate using placebo or delayed-treatment conditions must carefully examine additional ethical issues. As with the standards for the use of deception, we suggest that researchers assess the potential risks and consider alternative designs as ways of minimizing risks.

RESPONDING TO ETHICAL DILEMMAS

It is important to note that researchers are not likely to be entirely ethical all of the time. In fact, almost all researchers will unknowingly engage in some aspect of research that might infringe upon one of the ethical principles at some time or another. Sometimes an ethical problem may not be foreseen or may be inadequately anticipated, or the researcher may be inexperienced and have an incomplete understanding of the ethical codes. Or because there can be ambiguity in the ethical codes, inexperienced researchers may make questionable decisions. This is not to condone infringements, but rather to acknowledge that oversights and mistakes happen.

Most often, infringements occur due to a lack of sensitivity, knowledge, or experience. We can all help each other by consistently educating each other in our endeavors to conduct our research ethically and to uphold our professional responsibilities. Thus, it is important to talk with each other about ethical issues and dilemmas, particularly when we witness events that make us uncomfortable. From our experience, inexperienced professionals (for example, students, assistant professors) may become paralyzed when they witness what appears to be an ethical infraction and withdraw from the situation. Similarly, people are typically reluctant to raise ethical issues with people in authority positions. Such reservations can be very valid in some situations, but sometimes they are not justified at all. Informal peer monitoring of ethical issues is a powerful mechanism not only to monitor the appropriateness of our behavior, but also to increase our sensitivity and knowledge about ethical issues. We strongly encourage readers to confront ethical dilemmas, and whenever possible, engage in informal peer monitoring. Typically, it is recommended that concerned individuals review ethical codes, evaluate the evidence (facts versus hearsay), examine their motivations, consult with knowledgeable colleagues, and then discuss the issue with the person or people involved (see Keith-Spiegel & Koocher, 1985 for more details). Another strategy for dealing with people in authority positions is to involve other professionals in authority positions through consultation and problem solving. For more serious or repeated ethical violations, sanctions may be sought from local, state, or national ethics committees (such as state licensing boards or professional organizations such as ACA or APA), or even the judicial system. The interested reader should consult Keith-Spiegel and Koocher (1985), who provide excellent guidelines for a range of options (and sanctions) in responding to ethical situations. We encourage readers to not only examine the EPP and ES codes in the appendices, but also the *Publication Manual of the American Psychological Association* (1994). When in doubt, consult with trusted, knowledgeable colleagues and faculty.

SUMMARY AND CONCLUSIONS

We have suggested that ethics are central to the conduct of research and, in fact, permeate the entire research enterprise. Broadly speaking, ethics are a "set of guidelines that provide directions for conduct" (Keith-Spiegel & Koocher, 1985, p. xiii). For counselors, research ethics provide direction for interacting with the larger profession, other professionals, and those people who participate in our research. Moreover, how we design and conduct our research reflects our basic values, such as autonomy, fairness, promoting the welfare of others, fidelity, and above all, avoiding harm to others. Sometimes it seems that the business of life overshadows our basic values, as we cut corners to save time. It is essential to keep in mind, however, that the health and longevity of our counseling profession rest on such basic values as honesty and fairness. These values need to be emphasized throughout graduate training in a wide range of situations, and particularly with regard to research. Our values may communicate more about who we are and what we do in our research than any other aspect of our behavior. In essence, "ethical rigor needs to find as central a place of prominence in research as does methodological rigor" (Lindsey, 1984, p. 85). We not only need to "do the right thing," but also to "aspire toward ideals and to develop virtues or traits" (Meara et al., 1996, p. 24) that enable our profession to achieve our moral ideals.

• • • • • • • • • • • • • • • • •

EXHIBIT A

Protocol Review Number _____

University of Oregon
HUMAN SUBJECTS ACTIVITY REVIEW FORM[1]

I. PROJECT INFORMATION:

Investigator name: _____ Date _____

Unit (see appendix in Manual for list of units) _____ ext. _____

Project title: _____

II. PROJECT SUPPORT:

Funded _____   If funded, indicate source: unit _____

Unfunded _____   UO biomed grant _____

                                                          other UO source _____ specify: _____

    If grant proposal: pending _____ approved _____   non-UO source _____ specify: _____

III. INVESTIGATOR STATUS (check one)

Student _____   Faculty _____   Administrator _____   Other _____
(to IV.)   (to V.)   (to V.)   (to V.)

IV. FACULTY SUPERVISOR REVIEW: My signature verifies that 1) I will supervise this student's research project and 2) it complies with federal and University policies regarding protection of human subjects.

Approval _____

Date _____ (to V.)

V. UNIT REVIEW: Signature verifies that the project 1) has been reviewed by the unit and 2) complies with federal and University regulations for research with human subjects.

Approval _____

Date _____ (to VI.)

VI. OFFICE OF RESEARCH & SPONSORED PROGRAMS/REVIEW CATEGORIES:

EXEMPT	EXPEDITED REVIEW	FULL REVIEW
	Dates:	Dates:
	Assigned _____ / _____	Assigned _____ / _____
	Cond. approval _____ / _____	Cond. approval _____ / _____
Category no. _____	Approval _____ / _____	Approval _____ / _____
Approval _____	Refer to IRB _____ / _____	Disapproval _____ / _____
Date _____		
(to VIII.)	(to VIII. if approved; to VII. if not approved)	(to VII.)

VII. INSTITUTIONAL REVIEW BOARD (IRB)

Meeting date _____

Conditional approval _____

Approval _____

Disapproval _____ (to VIII.)

VIII.

Signature of IRB Chair _____ Date _____

Submit Human Subjects Activity Review form, sample informed consent form(s), and other pertinent information such as sample of survey instrument or questionnaire, grant proposal, etc., in triplicate to Office of Research and Sponsored Programs, 120 Chapman Hall (ext. 5131) following unit review and approval. Consult the Investigator's Manual on Research with Human Subjects for additional detail.

Please provide answers to all of the following questions (attach additional pages as needed). Forward in triplicate, along with the signed cover page and accompanying informed consent form(s), and proposal if available, to Office of Research and Sponsored Programs (ORSP), 120 Chapman Hall, for review and approval by the Committee for the Protection of Human Subjects/Institutional Review Board (CPHS/IRB). References are found in the Investagator's Manual on Research with Human Subjects, available from ORSP.

I.   PURPOSE AND OBJECTIVES OF THE RESEARCH

II.   DESCRIPTION OF PARTICIPANT POPULATION(S)

   1.   Who are the participant groups and how are they being recruited?

   2.   Approximate number of participants in each group to be used: _____

   3.   If advertising for participants, include a copy of the proposed advertisement. (Refer to section V in the Manual)

   4.   What are the criteria for selection and/or exclusion of participants? (Refer to sections V and VIII in the Manual)

   5.   If special populations are being used, please justify. (Refer to section X in the Manual)

III.   ACTIVITIES INVOLVING HUMAN PARTICIPANTS

1.   Describe the activities involving each participant group described in #II.1. Include the expected amount of time participants will be involved in each activity and where the activities will be conducted.

2.   How will the data be collected (check):
____ questionnaires? (submit a copy)
____ interviews? (submit sample of questions)
____ observations? (briefly describe)
____ standardized tests? (If yes, list names)
____ other (describe)

IV.   DATA

1.   How will the data be recorded (notes, tapes, computer files, completed questionnaires or tests, etc.)?

2.   Who will have access to the gathered data and how will confidentiality be maintained during the study, after the study, and in reporting of results?

3.   What are the plans for the data after completion of this study and how and when will data be maintained or destroyed? (Refer to section VIII in the manual)

V.   BENEFITS, RISKS, COSTS

    1.   What are the potential benefits to humanity?

    2.   What are the potential benefits to the participants?

    3.   What compensation, if any, will be offered to the participants and how will payment be scheduled throughout the study? (Refer to sections V and VIII in the Manual)

    4.a.   What risks to the participants are most likely to be encountered, and at what level? (Refer to section VIII in the Manual) (check):

	None	Minimal	More than minimal	Not sure
physical	____	____	____	____
psychological (emotional, behavioral, etc.)	____	____	____	____
sociological (employability, financial, reputation, etc.)	____	____	____	____
loss of confidentiality	____	____	____	____
criminal or civil liability	____	____	____	____
description	____	____	____	____
other (explain)	____	____	____	____

    4.b.   Describe any risks identified above in 4.a.

    5.   What safeguards will you use to eliminate or minimize these risks? If participants experience adverse reactions, how will they be managed?

6. What are the costs, if any, to the participants (monetary, time, etc.)?

VI. OTHER COMPLIANCE ISSUES

1. If this project may be subject to other regulations, such as state or local laws protecting special populations or the use of a new drug or device, please identify and discuss.

2. If this project involves any of the following activities, requiring consideration by another review committee, please check.
_____ animal use and care
_____ radiation safety (including use of x-rays, microwaves)
_____ biological safety (including recombinant DNA, biohazards)
_____ chemical safety (including hazardous waste materials, chemical carcinogens, flammables, lab safety)

VII. INFORMED CONSENT

1. How will the study be explained to the participants and by whom?

2. Attach informed consent form(s) you will use in the study (Refer to section IX in the Manual).

3. Indicate rationale for any special conditions relating to informed consent (e.g., request for approval to obtain oral consent or waiver of documentation). (Refer to section IX in the Manual).

CERTIFICATION:

In submitting this proposed project and signing below, I certify that: I have read and understand the Investigator's Manual on Research with Human Participants; I will conduct the research involving human participants as presented in the protocol and approved by the unit, faculty supervisor (if a student project), and IRB; I will meet all responsibilities of the research investigator as outlined in the Manual, including obtaining and documenting informed consent and providing a copy of the consent form to each participant; I will present any proposed modifications in the research to the IRB for review prior to implementation; and I will report to the IRB any problems or injuries to participants.

Signed: _____ Date: _____

8/89

•   •   •   •   •   •   •   •   •   •   •   •   •   •   •   •

EXHIBIT B
Consent to Serve as a Participant in Research[2]

I consent to participate in the research project entitled "Gender Role Conflict," conducted by Mark Sharpe under the sponsorship of P. Paul Heppner, Ph.D., and the Psychology Department at the University of Missouri-Columbia.

I understand that the only requirement of the study will be to complete four questionnaires in this one session, which will take approximately forty-five minutes.

I understand that results of this research will be coded in such a manner that my identity will not be attached physically to the data I contribute. The key listing my identity and subject code number will be kept separate from the data in a locked file accessible only to the project director. This key listing subjects' identities will be physically destroyed at the conclusion of the project in approximately one year. In addition, I realize the purpose of this project is to examine the performance of groups of individuals, not to evaluate the performance of a particular individual.

This research project is expected to provide further information on gender role conflict, which increases our understanding of the psychological effects of traditional gender roles.

I understand that the results of this research may be published or otherwise reported to scientific bodies, but that I will not be identified in any such publication or report.

I understand that my participation is voluntary, that there is no penalty for refusal to participate, and that I am free to withdraw my consent and discontinue participation at any time.

I understand that this project is not expected to involve any risks of harm any greater than those ordinarily encountered in daily life. I also understand that it is not possible to identify all potential risks in such research, but that all reasonable safeguards will be taken to minimize the potential risks.

If at any time I have questions about any procedure in this project, I understand that I may contact the investigator at 882-4351.

Signature   _____

Date   _____

•   •   •   •   •   •   •   •   •   •   •   •   •   •   •   •

•   •   •   •   •   •   •   •   •   •   •   •   •   •   •   •

EXHIBIT C
Sample Informed Consent (Children)[3]

Child's name: _____

We are interested in what attention is, so that one day we can try to help people who find it hard to concentrate on things, and we'd like you to help us. We'd like you to play a kind of game on a computer. All you'll have to do is press a button when some lights come on. It will take about an hour, but you can rest as much as you'd like, and you can stop the game whenever you want.

If you want to rest or stop completely, just tell us—you won't get into any trouble! In fact, if you don't want to play the game at all, you don't have to. Just say so. Also, if you have any questions about what you'll be doing, or if you can't decide whether to do it or not, just ask us if there is anything you'd like us to explain.

If you do want to try it, please sign your name on the line below. Your parent(s) have already told us that it is alright with them if you want to play the game. Remember, you don't have to, and once you start you can rest or stop whenever you like.

Signed: _____   Date: _____

• • • • • • • • • • • • • • •

• • • • • • • • • • • • • • •

E X H I B I T D
Oral Debriefing[4]

That concludes your participation in the study. Thanks so much for your help. Now that you have finished giving your opinion, I can explain more to you about the whole purpose of the study. I could not do so before now without biasing your responses. First, the study is concerned with more than "interviewing styles." We are more interested in impressions of college students about bereaved and depressed persons. Specifically, we wanted to find out both about your personal reactions to someone who is bereaved and also your attitudes about what is normal or pathological grief. We didn't want people to know exactly what we were looking for in advance, because it could have influenced who signed up for the experiment or the answers they gave. We regret that we could not more fully inform you before you participated. We strongly hope you will respect our need to withhold this information and will not discuss this experiment with your fellow classmates.

Some of you received instructions that you were listening to a tape of a middle-aged widow; some were told that she had become widowed three weeks ago and some were told she became widowed two years ago. If you received these instructions, you were in one of the experimental groups. Others received instructions that you were listening to a tape of someone who had lost a job. You were in a control group. In addition, some subjects hear a depressed woman on tape and others hear a nondepressed woman. We will be looking for differences in the answers of these various conditions depending on whether the subjects are male or female.

I want to tell you now that none of you will come back to participate in a further part of the experiment. When you leave today, your participation will end. It was important that you think you might come back, so we could get your reaction about whether you were willing to meet the woman you heard on the tape.

Next, let me explain that this is an analogue experiment. That means that the people you heard on tape were playing parts that were written for them in advance. The purpose of this is so each time a new group hears a particular conversation, it is done exactly the same as the last time a group heard that conversation. This allows for better control of the experiment and helps to eliminate unknown influences on the answers you gave.

I want to thank you for your participation today. Again, it is very important that you do not talk about this experiment with anyone once you leave this room. If people who participate later in the study are aware of its purpose or procedures, their answers may be biased. This would cause us to report misleading results. As we hope our research may some day assist actual bereaved persons, this is a serious problem. Please give others the chance to fairly contribute as you have today.

Does anyone have any questions? [Pause for questions.] I will sign your research cards and you are free to leave. I will stay for a moment in case you have other questions.

If you're having any difficulty dealing with either bereavement or depression, I have the telephone numbers of our University Psychology Clinic and of the Counseling Service, and I will be glad to give them to you when you have finished.

Written Debriefing[5]

This sheet will further explain the purpose of this research project beyond the oral explanation you have already heard. It will outline the independent and dependent variables and research hypotheses. It is crucial that you do not discuss the information on this sheet with any of your friends (who might inadvertently communicate with future participants) or with the experimenter who is present today. She must remain blind (uninformed) concerning the hypotheses in order to avoid influencing the experiment. You may direct any questions to Carol Atwood at 484-7276 (leave a message if no answer). Please sign this sheet as soon as you finish reading it, place it back in the envelope provided, and seal the gummed flap. Thank you very much for your help.

1. Nature of the project: This project would best relate to the major research area of social psychology—attitudes and social perception.
2. Findings of related studies: There is little previous research concerning the layperson's views of what is a healthy versus an unhealthy grief reaction, and whether or not laypersons reject or avoid the bereaved. Vernon (1970) asked participants how they would respond to a recently bereaved person that they knew. Only one-fourth of participants indicated they would spontaneously mention the death; another one-fourth preferred that neither side mention the death at all. Other researchers, such as Lopata (1973) and Glick, Weiss, and Parkes (1974), have indirectly addressed the question by interviewing widows themselves, who frequently reported experiencing strained relationships or the breakup of friendships after the deaths of their husbands.
3. Independent variables: These are the variables in the experiment that the investigator manipulates or controls. There are three independent variables in this project. The first is gender of the participants. We will look for differences in the responses of male and female subjects. Second is the depression condition (whether the woman heard on the tape is depressed or nondepressed). Third is the "bereavement (or widowhood) status"; that is, the woman on the tape is either recently widowed, long-term widowed, or not widowed (loss of a job is mentioned), depending on which written instructions you received.
4. Dependent variables: Used to measure the effects of manipulation of the independent variables. In this project, the dependent variables consisted of the written questionnaire you completed. We want to find out how much you would reject the woman heard on the tape, what your social perceptions of her were, and how pathological you found her to be.
5. Hypotheses: The research questions to be examined in the project. Please do not share this information with today's experimenter.

A. How do college students' judgments of emotional disturbance compare, based on whether the woman on the tape is recently bereaved, long-term bereaved, or nonbereaved? How do ratings of disturbance differ, depending on whether the woman on the tape sounded depressed or not depressed?

B. Do college students reject a bereaved person or a nonbereaved person more, and is this rejection affected by whether the woman sounds depressed or not depressed?

C. How does the gender of the participant (male or female) affect participants' responses?

6. Control procedures: Procedures to reduce error or unwanted variance. In this study, random assignment of participants to experimental conditions was used, except that it was not possible to randomly assign participants based on participant gender. Other control procedures used include keeping the experimenter blind to the study hypotheses, not informing participants before the experiment about the true purpose, use of an analogue procedure in which actors were used on the tapes, and use of a control group of participants who listen to the tape of a woman who is neither a widow nor depressed.

I have read the above information concerning the nature of the study, Reactions to Stressful Life Experiences. I agree not to disclose this information either to potential future participants or to the experimenter present today.

Name (Print) _____

Signature _____

Date _____

•   •   •   •   •   •   •   •   •   •   •   •   •   •   •

NOTES

1. An earlier version of this form was developed by the Committee for the Protection of Human Subjects/Institutional Review Board at the University of Oregon.

2. An earlier version of this consent form was written by Mark Sharpe. At the time this chapter was written for the first edition of the book, Mark was a doctoral student in counseling psychology at the University of Missouri-Columbia.

3. An earlier version of this form was developed by the Committee for the Protection of Human Subjects/Institutional Review Board at the University of Oregon.

4. An earlier version of this oral debriefing was written by Carol Atwood. At the time this chapter was written for the first edition of the book, Carol was a doctoral student in clinical psychology at the University of Missouri-Columbia.

5. An earlier version of this written debriefing was written by Carol Atwood. At the time this chapter was written for the first edition of the book, Carol was a doctoral student in clinical psychology at the University of Missouri-Columbia.

PART TWO

MAJOR RESEARCH
DESIGNS

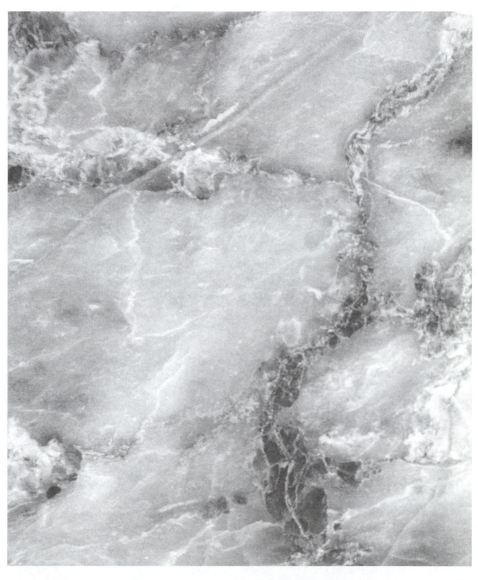

CHAPTER 6

BETWEEN-GROUPS AND
WITHIN-SUBJECTS DESIGNS

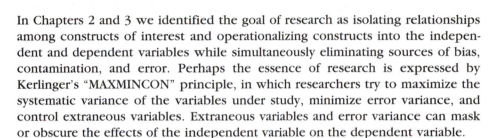

In Chapters 2 and 3 we identified the goal of research as isolating relationships among constructs of interest and operationalizing constructs into the independent and dependent variables while simultaneously eliminating sources of bias, contamination, and error. Perhaps the essence of research is expressed by Kerlinger's "MAXMINCON" principle, in which researchers try to maximize the systematic variance of the variables under study, minimize error variance, and control extraneous variables. Extraneous variables and error variance can mask or obscure the effects of the independent variable on the dependent variable.

In this chapter we will discuss two designs that often adhere to the "MAXMINCON" principle and are often referred to as true experimental designs because of their emphasis on experimental control and internal validity. Even though students sometimes feel intimidated or confused about true experimental designs because of the heavy, ominous meaning that the words sometimes convey, the designs are actually quite straightforward; the label is more ominous than the actual design. The two true experimental designs are commonly labeled between-groups design and within-subjects design.

The between-groups design often adheres to the "MAXMINCON" principle. Differences between treatments can be maximized by making the treatment (independent variable) stronger or even exaggerated. Thus, researchers will often examine the effects of extreme treatments, such as five counselor disclosures in 50 minutes, or three counselor influence attempts in 15 minutes. Moreover, the between-groups design can be arranged to control extraneous variables and minimize error variance through randomization and experimental control.

The essential feature of between-groups design is the comparison of variables across two or more groups under tightly controlled experimental conditions. In early counseling research, a common comparison group was some type of control group, a group that did not receive one of the active treatments in the study. More recently, differences between experimental treatments have been compared. To adequately make comparisons across groups necessitates that the groups do not differ in important ways before the experiment. Thus, initial differences between groups in terms of individual difference variables, demographics, and situational variables must be minimized prior to experimental manipulations to reduce threats to internal validity. Because of the emphasis on comparison and equivalent groups, assignment of participants to groups is a critical consideration in between-groups design. In fact, one of the major identifying features of between-groups design is the random assignment of participants. This design is a powerful investigative tool, and often the most strongly favored design (Campbell & Stanley, 1963; Cook & Campbell, 1979; Kerlinger, 1986).

The hallmark of the within-subjects design is that it attempts to minimize error variance due to individual variation by having each participant serve as his or her own control as all participants are exposed to all of the treatment conditions. This design, like the between-groups design, is often called a true experimental design because of the random assignment of treatments and manipulation of the independent variable. The random assignment that occurs in the within-subjects design is assignment to a time period in which the treatments are delivered. For example, suppose an experimenter wants to make a comparison between two treatments, X_1 and X_2. One group of participants could get treatment X_1 before X_2, whereas the other group would receive the opposite sequence, X_2 before X_1. In within-subjects design, each participant is assigned to either sequence randomly, as a matter of chance. Hence, the comparison in a within-subjects design is between different time periods in which separate treatment conditions are in effect.

BETWEEN-GROUPS DESIGNS

In this section we discuss some of the historical events affecting the emergence and development of the between-groups design. We then proceed to a discussion of the strengths and weaknesses of three specific between-groups designs. Because our discussion of these designs focuses on simple between-groups designs that contain one independent variable and control groups, the next section explicitly discusses issues pertaining to control groups. Subsequently we discuss more complex designs that contain two or more independent variables, which are called factorial designs. Finally, we examine a central issue of between-groups design—randomization and participant assignment. The strength of the between-groups design is based on group equivalence before the experimental manipulation, which underscores the importance of participant assignment. After our discussion of participant assignment and group equivalence, we discuss related issues of matching and dependent samples designs.

Historical Perspective

The origins of the group-comparison approach have been related to the discovery and measurement of individual differences and to the development of inferential statistics (Barlow & Hersen, 1984). Adolphe Quetelet, a Belgian astronomer, initially discovered in the nineteenth century that human traits (for example, chest expansion of Scottish soldiers) followed a normal distribution (Gleitman, 1986). Rather than interpreting his findings as indicating that some traits are normally distributed in nature, Quetelet inferred that nature was actually striving to create the "average" person, the ideal. But nature obviously failed, which resulted in errors, or variances, in traits that grouped around the mean in orderly ways. Quetelet found that the traits of the "average" person could be estimated by applying statistical techniques to the errors or differences from the mean. The study of individual differences mushroomed in the early to mid-1900s, notably through the work of F. Galton, E. S. Pearson, A. Binet, and R. B. Cattell.

Once traits were being identified and measured, the next logical step was to compare one group of people to another. Various descriptive statistics facilitated such comparisons, although R. A. Fisher's work on inferential statistics in the 1930s was one of the most influential statistical advances. Fisher's work not only provided statistical techniques, but it also made an important contribution in the realm of making inferences from samples, of generalizing the results. As an agronomist, Fisher was interested in generalizing the results obtained from a particular plot of land to many plots of land. Thus, Fisher developed statistical techniques that made it possible to estimate the relevance of data from one small group, or plot, with certain characteristics to the universe having these characteristics. Such developments in sampling theory (that is, making inferences from a sample to a larger population) greatly facilitated the group-comparisons approach within basic psychological research. By the 1950s, the *zeitgeist* in psychological research was group comparison and statistical estimation (Hersen & Barlow, 1976). In research conducted in counseling during the 1950s and 1960s, the between-groups design was used, for example, to examine differences in adjustment changes between students receiving counseling versus a control group (Williams, 1962) and in the effects of time limits (limited or unlimited) on adjustment changes (Shlien, Mosak, & Dreikurs, 1962). The group-comparison approach has been and remains extremely popular in counseling.

Three Common Experimental Between-Groups Designs

We now discuss the three most commonly identified experimental between-groups designs. To do so, we again use the symbolic representation used by Campbell and Stanley (1963) to depict each of the designs. R indicates random assignment of participants to each of the groups; O indicates an "observation" or point where data is collected as a dependent variable; and X indicates the exposure of a group to an experimental variable, often a treatment intervention of some kind. The purpose of O, in essence, is to measure the effects of X. The subscripts following O and X indicate the sequence of occurrence: O_1 is the first observation, O_2 is the second, and so on.

After describing each of these three designs, we then discuss advantages and disadvantages of each, referring particularly to validity issues. It is important to note that these three designs are most easily conceptualized as using one independent variable. For example, the independent variable may represent treatments and contain two levels—treatment and no treatment (that is, control group). After our initial discussion of the three commonly used between-groups designs, we discuss the use of two or more independent variables in what is known as factorial designs.

Posttest-Only Control Group Design

Notationally, the posttest-only control group design is conceptualized as

$$
\begin{array}{ccc}
R & X & O_1 \\
R & & O_2
\end{array}
$$

In its most basic form, this design involves the random assignment of participants to two groups; one of the groups receives exposure to a treatment while the other group serves as a control group and thus receives no treatment. Both groups receive a posttest, but neither group receives a pretest. The basic purpose of the design is to test the effect of X, the independent variable, on the dependent variable vis-à-vis O_1.

STRENGTHS.   The posttest-only control group design controls for most of the threats to internal validity and thus is a powerful experimental design. For example, history would have affected each group equally because O_1 and O_2 occurred at the same time. Likewise, maturation, instrumentation, testing effects, and regression are controlled in that they are expected to be equally manifested in both the experimental and control groups. For example, if extreme scores were used, the control group would be expected to regress as much as the experimental group. Both selection and selection-maturation effects are controlled for in that randomization would most likely make the groups comparable on these dimensions before the study. Attrition rates can be examined to determine if differential losses may have occurred across groups, although again randomization would decrease the probability of differential attrition due to preexisting differences in participants.

In many ways the posttest-only control group design is the prototypical experimental design and most closely reflects the characteristics needed to attribute a causal relationship from the independent variable to the dependent variable (Cook & Campbell, 1979). The difference between O_1 and O_2 reflects the degree to which treated participants are different from untreated participants at the end of the treatment period. Of course, the observed difference needs to be statistically significant (have statistical conclusion validity) to justify a claim that the treatment indeed is effective.

In spite of the simplicity of the posttest-only design, many researchers are reluctant to embrace this design. Their primary concern is that because the dependent variable is examined only at the end of treatment, statements about actual change cannot be made; put another way, there is no evidence to show that the treatment group improved vis-à-vis their level of functioning prior to treatment. But the crux of the matter is the comparison of the level of functioning of treated individuals (at O_1) with their level of functioning had they not been treated (O_2), not the change from before treatment to after treatment. The logic of experimentation does not require that pretreatment levels of functioning be assessed; thus, a pretest is not used.

One of the strengths of the posttest-only control group design, therefore, is that a pretest is unnecessary. Practically speaking, sometimes the repeated testing of participants is bothersome to the participants and expensive to the researcher in terms of time and effort. Furthermore, the absence of pretests obviates the need to collate the pretest and posttest scores, and hence it may be possible to have participants respond anonymously, thereby protecting the confidentiality of responses. Another advantage of the posttest-only control group design is that it eliminates pretest sensitization (which is discussed more fully as a disadvantage to the pretest-posttest control group design).

WEAKNESSES.   The absence of a pretest in this design can present problems, some of which cannot be known before the research is conducted. The arguments for pretests are presented in the discussion of the pretest-posttest control group design.

Although the posttest-only control group design is generally an internally valid experimental design, there are issues pertaining to external validity, namely the interaction of selection and treatment (Campbell & Stanley, 1963). From an internal validity perspective, selection of participants is not a threat because participants are randomly assigned across groups. However, from an external validity perspective, the generalizability of the results of the study to another population is unknown. For example, it is possible that a treatment (for example, a career-planning workshop) is effective but only for the particular sample (for example, returning adults who have a broader set of work experiences). It may very well be that the career-planning workshop is not at all effective for the typical 18-year-old freshman, or it may be that different samples of returning adults (for instance, from a community college versus a four-year university) might also respond very differently to the career-planning workshop. In short, the interaction between the selection of a particular sample and the treatment is an issue that must be tested empirically and considered and acknowledged by the researcher.

Closely related is another threat to external validity: reactivity to the experimental situation. That is, participants may react differently, perhaps in biased or socially desirable ways, because they are in an experiment, and again threatening the generalizability of the findings. Because counseling is an applied field, we are especially concerned with external validity, and these and other threats to external validity merit serious consideration.

Finally, a practical issue pertaining to this design is that of timing. To adequately control for history effects, the investigator must conduct the experimental and control sessions simultaneously. Sometimes this requirement places excessive time and energy constraints on the experimenter. Nonetheless, history effects may not be controlled for if the experimenter conducts the two sessions, say, one month apart. The greater the time differential between group administrations, the greater the likelihood of confounding history effects.

AN EXAMPLE.   A study examining stress management with math anxiety depicts the unique advantages of the posttest-only design. Sime, Ansorge, Olson, Parker, and Lukin (1987) were interested in examining whether combining cognitive and relaxation techniques would be an effective intervention for math anxiety and might ultimately improve academic performance on an introductory statistics examination. The authors chose to conduct their research with students in a real-life testing situation; thus, participants were 56 students enrolled in an under-graduate statistics course. The authors randomly assigned the students to one of two groups, the treatment group and the control group. Dependent measures included anxiety measured both before and after the exam, and actual perfor-mance on the statistics examination. Training for the experimental group con-sisted of three 15-minute training sessions that focused on both relaxation and cognitive interventions. The other group did not receive any intervention and thus served as a no-treatment control group. The results indicated that the treat-ment intervention lowered participants' ratings of anxiety both before and after the exam, but it did not affect students' actual performance on the examination.

In this study, pretesting the participants on the anxiety measures before the training sessions and giving an actual classroom examination would have demanded considerably more time of both participants and researchers, but prob-ably would not have added relevant information. Thus, the advantages of not administering a pretest allowed the researchers to add other features to their design, such as reversing the treatment conditions before the next examination. In addition, the study avoided the pretest sensitization threat to external validity.

Pretest-Posttest Control Group Design

Notationally, the pretest-posttest control group design is conceptualized as

$$R \quad O_1 \quad X \quad O_2$$
$$R \quad O_3 \quad \quad O_4$$

This design involves the random assignment of participants to two (or more) groups, with one group receiving treatment while the other group receives no treatment and thus serves as a control group. Both groups receive a pretest and a posttest. The purpose of the design is to test the effect of the independent vari-able, X, which is reflected in the differences between O_2 and O_4.

STRENGTHS.   This design controls for most of the threats to internal validity dis-cussed by Campbell and Stanley (1963), and in that way it is similar to the posttest-only control group design. The unique strength of this design pertains to the use of the pretest, which allows the researcher to perform various analyses that may be helpful in making valid inferences.

One of the most important reasons for giving a pretest is that pretest scores can be used to reduce variability in the dependent variable, thereby creating a more powerful statistical test. In essence, such a strategy attempts to minimize error variance, in line with the "MAXMINCON" principle. Much of the variance in any dependent variable is due to individual differences among the participants. Knowledge of the pretest level of functioning allows the researcher to use statistical methods, such as the analysis of covariance, that remove the variance found in the pretest from the variance in the posttests. Such procedures can reduce drastically the number of participants needed to achieve a desired level of statistical power (Porter & Raudenbush, 1987). Of course, the pretest in this case need not be the same measure as the posttest; however, it must be linearly related to the posttest to allow use of an ordinary analysis of covariance. For example, in a study of covert desensitization, a measure of the degree to which participants can produce imagery could be measured before treatment and used as a covariate.

Another important reason to give a pretest is that it can be used to help eliminate post hoc threats to internal validity. In this regard, one strategic use of pretests is to compare participants who drop out to those who remain. If more participants drop out of the treatment group than out of the control group, then differential attrition is a particularly troublesome threat; however, if pretest scores indicate that those participants who dropped out did not differ significantly from those who remained, then concern about differential attrition is reduced.

Pretests often are used to select or deselect participants. For example, in a study on depression, the researchers may wish to select only those participants who are in the moderately depressed range. Although selection is a primary reason to use a pretest in this example, it is advisable to determine whether or not the depression pretest should be used as a covariate.

Pretest scores can also be used to describe a study's participants. For example, it would be important to describe the level of anxiety of undergraduate participants in a study of test anxiety to determine whether or not the participants were representative of those disabled by test anxiety.

Finally, the pretest-posttest scores allow the researcher to examine the individual performance of specific participants. Kazdin (1980) suggests that in this way, researchers might examine participants who benefited the most versus those who benefited the least from the treatment intervention. Identifying participants in such a fashion, combined with anecdotal information the researcher has, may suggest hypotheses for future research. In short, the pretest provides additional information for researchers, and perhaps some clues for future research directions.

Two often-stated advantages of pretests are controversial. The first pertains to comparing posttest scores to pretest scores to determine the degree to which the treatment was beneficial. The problems with making inferences from pretest measures to posttest measures are illustrated by the three possible patterns of results in Figure 6-1 on page 128. The graphs depict three scenarios in which the treatment group is statistically different at posttest from the control group. In Graph 1, the treated participants scored higher than the control participants on the posttest; treated participants appear to have improved from the pretest, whereas the controls have remained the same. In Graph 2, the treatment group was also superior on the posttest, but it appears that the treated participants did not improve vis-à-vis the pretest. In the third pattern of results (Graph 3), the treatment group was superior to the control group at posttest, and both groups' scores

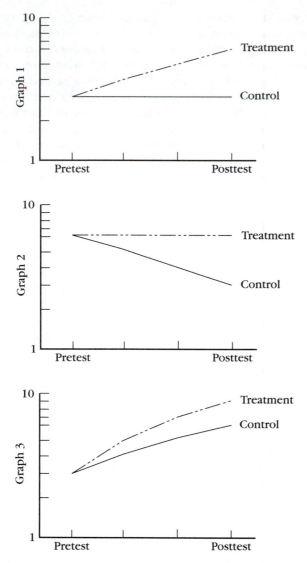

FIGURE 6-1
Three possible patterns of results for the pretest-posttest control group design.

were higher at posttest than at pretest. It would appear that Graph 1 represents the clearest outcome, but this may be illusory due to several threats to internal validity that interfere with comparing pretest scores with posttest scores. The apparent improvement in Graph 1 for the treated participants may be due to regression toward the mean, whereas the apparent lack of change of the control participants actually may be a deterioration that was masked by regression toward the mean. In Graph 2, it appears that the treatment did result in improvement, but actually there was no change from pretest to posttest. If the participants were deteriorating, as would be the case with a progressive dysfunction such as some anxiety disorders, then the control group shows the natural progression while the treatment successfully maintained the treated participants' current level of functioning. However, this interpretation of Graph 2 cannot be made unambiguously because the pattern may also be due to a historical event such as the announcement of mobilization for war, which would exacerbate anxiety disorders. The results for Graph 3 could be due to regression toward the mean, maturation, or spontaneous remission.

The point is that there are too many rival hypotheses to infer the degree to which treatment was effective by comparing pretest scores to posttest scores. For this reason, "gain scores" (differences from pretest to posttest) are typically not recommended for statistical analyses. Instead, it is better for researchers to restrict themselves to making inferences only about differences at the posttest, because fewer threats are involved. Parenthetically, statisticians typically recommend using the pretest as a covariate in analyzing the posttest scores (see Huck & McLean, 1975). These techniques adjust or reduce error variance across individuals.

We turn now to the second controversial use of pretest scores. Recall that random assignment was a means of making the groups comparable. Clearly, the groups will not be exactly the same in all aspects; random error typically characterizes the process, so there are some differences between groups. Often there is a tendency to check whether or not random assignment succeeded—that is, to see whether or not the groups were indeed comparable. Accordingly, one often examines preliminary analyses of pretest scores to ascertain whether or not there are significant differences between the groups before treatment. However appealing this process is, there are some problems associated with it (Wampold & Drew, 1990). First, how big a difference is necessary to decide whether random assignment failed? For small sample sizes, statistically significant differences between pretest scores are unlikely to be obtained; however, this is exactly the instance sampling error is most pernicious. Second, pretest scores only represent possible differences on the particular characteristics measured; what about differences in age, gender, intelligence, education, and a host of other factors? Third, if a large number of factors are compared before treatment, by chance some differences will be found, and it is unlikely that the researcher will ever conclude that random assignment succeeded. Finally, it should be remembered that statistical tests indicate the degree to which the results may have occurred by chance (the significance level), and, therefore, checking on sampling error is unnecessary. In short, it is important to note that however appealing it is to check whether or not random assignment succeeded, some problems and controversy are associated with this procedure.

Parenthetically, if one wants to ensure that a nuisance factor is evenly distributed across the groups, another alternative is to use a matching procedure. For instance, to equate groups based on intelligence, participants in the treatment and control groups should be matched on intelligence. This process, and its advantages and disadvantages, are discussed in the section on dependent samples designs.

WEAKNESSES.   It is perhaps ironic that the unique strength of the pretest-posttest control group design, namely the pretest, is also the main weakness. It is often assumed that pretesting will not sensitize participants to a particular treatment. In the two-group pretest-posttest control group design, the effect of repeatedly administering a test to the treatment group (O_1 to O_2) is the same for the control group (O_3 to O_4). Therefore, the effect of repeated testing is not a threat to internal validity.

However, the pretest may have a potential sensitizing effect pertaining to external validity, to generalizing the results from the study to other samples. It is unclear whether any changes found at posttest might be due to the groups' being sensitized by the pretest. That is, it is unclear if the same effect of X on O_2 would be found again without the sensitizing effect of O_1. For example, a pretest questionnaire on attitudes about rape might cue participants not only to reflect on this topic, but also to process information differently in the ensuing treatment, say, an awareness-enhancing workshop about date rape. Although the treatment may or may not have an effect by itself, the interactive effects of the pretest may result in substantially greater changes at posttest. A real problem could result if practitioners implemented the workshop but without the pretest, and thus had a much weaker treatment effect than they thought they would have. When researchers use the pretest-posttest control group design, they need to be cautious in generalizing the results of the study, and they must discuss this sensitization issue explicity.

AN EXAMPLE.   A study by Nezu (1986) nicely illustrates the pretest-posttest control group design. In the mid-1980s, research was consistently finding relationships between problem solving and depression, as well as psychological health in general. However, very little outcome research had been conducted to systematically evaluate the efficacy of a problem-solving approach for the treatment of depression (for more background, see D'Zurilla, 1986; Nezu, Nezu, & Perri, 1989). In Nezu's study, 26 individuals diagnosed as experiencing nonpsychotic, unipolar depression were randomly assigned to one of three conditions: problem-solving therapy (PST), problem-focused therapy (PFT), and a waiting list control group (WLC). The design can be depicted as follows:

$$R \quad O_1 \quad X_{PST} \quad O_2 \quad O_3$$
$$R \quad O_4 \quad X_{PFT} \quad O_5 \quad O_6$$
$$R \quad O_7 \quad X_{WLC} \quad O_8 \quad O_9$$

Note that Nezu used two treatment groups in addition to the control group; such a variation of the pretest-posttest control group design allowed Nezu to not only compare the treatment groups to the control group, but also to compare the treatment groups to each other. Also note that Nezu used a follow-up procedure to assess the effect of the training over time (O_3, O_6, O_9). Follow-up data can be extremely valuable but often difficult to obtain, because it can be difficult to locate participants or because the participants may not be motivated to respond to the assessments. The PST treatment was based on a systematic model of social problem solving emphasizing five components: problem orientation, problem definition and formulation, generation of alternatives, decision making, and solution implementation and verification. The PFT treatment was conceptualized as a traditional group therapy approach. Participants were administered the Beck Depression Inventory (BDI; Beck et al., 1961), the Problem Solving Inventory (PSI; Heppner & Petersen, 1982), the Depression scale of the Minnesota Multiphasic Personality Inventory (MMPI-D; Hathaway & McKinley, 1967), and the Internal-External Locus of Control Scale (I-E; Rotter, 1966). These instruments were administered at both pretest and posttest. Because questions have been raised about the long-term effects of problem-solving training, Nezu extended the design by including a six-month follow-up in which he administered the same instruments again. Treatment was conducted over eight weeks, with hour-and-a-half weekly sessions. Nezu did check on whether random assignment succeeded by doing preliminary analyses on the pretest scores (O_1 versus O_4 versus O_7). In these preliminary analyses, Nezu found that the groups did not differ on any of the dependent variables at the pretest. Thus, at least with regard to these variables, random assignment was successful. The results indicated that PST participants had significantly lower posttreatment depression scores than either the PFT or WLC groups (O_2 versus O_5 versus O_8). This improvement was found to have been maintained at the six-month follow-up. Parenthetically, Nezu also found that decreases in depression covaried with concurrent increases in perceived problem-solving effectiveness and the adoption of an internal-locus-of-control orientation.

The results of this study provided very useful information about problem-solving training. The pretest-posttest control group design was useful in checking the adequacy of the random assignment of clients (but only with regard to the dependent variables) as well as changes in the dependent variables. Nezu varied the basic design by adding another treatment group, which then allowed him to compare the efficacy of the treatment groups as well. Comparisons with existing treatments (such as traditional group therapy) provide a kind of benchmark that often helps evaluate the usefulness of a new treatment program. The six-month follow-up added an extremely useful piece of information about more long-term benefits of training; such follow-up data are typically difficult to obtain but often provide very useful data.

To examine other examples of the pretest-posttest control group design, see Deffenbacher, Lynch, Oetting, and Kemper (1996) who employed this design to examine the utility of two different interventions in reducing anger in early adolescence; the results suggested that although both the cognitive-relaxation coping skills and the social skills training interventions were effective in reducing anger in adolescents, the former was more effective in reducing anxiety, depression, shyness, and school-related deviant behavior. Likewise, Schechtman, Gilat, Fos, and Flasher (1996) examined the effects of group therapy (versus a control group) with low-achieving elementary school children; the results indicated the addition of group therapy resulted in significant gains in academic achievement, self-concept, social acceptance, and locus of control.

Solomon Four-Group Design

When there is a desire to use a pretest but some concern exists about the effect the pretest may have on the participants (such as test-by-treatment interaction), the Solomon four-group design is appropriate. Notationally, this design is conceptualized as follows:

$$R \quad O_1 \quad X \quad O_2$$
$$R \quad O_3 \quad \quad O_4$$
$$R \quad \quad X \quad O_5$$
$$R \quad \quad \quad O_6$$

This design is a combination of the pretest-posttest control group design (first two groups in the diagram) and the posttest-only control group design (last two groups). The main purpose of this design is to examine potential effects of the pretest, which is one of the main weaknesses or unknowns of the pretest-posttest control group design.

STRENGTHS.   In terms of internal validity, this design controls for most threats to internal validity. The Solomon four-group design contains the strengths of both the pretest-posttest control group and the posttest-only control group designs. The unique strength of the Solomon four-group design is that it explicitly examines the potential sensitizing effect of the pretest as it might interact with the treatment, X. The researcher can easily test for pretest sensitization by comparing O_2 to O_5, the only difference between these observations being the pretest prior to the treatment for O_2. Thus, this design is useful if the investigator not only wants to test the effect of some treatment, X, but also wants to examine whether the pretest sensitizes participants to the treatment.

Another strength of this design is that it inherently includes a replication test of the treatment intervention. That is, if a significant treatment effect is found when comparing O_2 to O_4, this design allows the researcher to examine whether this treatment effect will be replicated by comparing O_5 versus O_6. If the researcher finds a treatment effect in both cases, the results of the study will be considerably stronger because the treatment has been found to be effective across two trials. In this way, the replication results will enhance the generalizability of the treatment and thus the external validity of the study.

WEAKNESSES.   The major drawback to using this design is that it costs the investigator a great deal in terms of time, energy, and resources. In essence, the Solomon four-group design contains the two previous designs (pretest-posttest control group and posttest-only control group), which means that the experimenter is almost conducting two investigations. The Solomon four-group design is especially costly if the treatment is a long and rather complex intervention. Such treatments often require considerable effort, such as training therapists (perhaps before each treatment session), preparing training materials, and obtaining financial compensation for therapists. Many times ethical considerations are involved in the intervention, particularly with regard to the control group; an example is withholding treatment from the control group during part or all of the research study. A common option is to offer treatment to control participants after the experiment is over; it is important to plan on this additional cost (that is, additional service delivery for two more groups of participants).

AN EXAMPLE.   Our examination of the professional journals revealed that the Solomon four-group design is used infrequently in counseling research. A study by Dixon, Heppner, Petersen, and Ronning (1979) illustrates most of the major elements of the Solomon four-group design. In the mid-1970s the utility of training clients in some sort of problem-solving method was unclear, and there were many unanswered research questions. The investigators wanted to assess the effects of problem-solving training in general, but they also wanted to test the effects of pretesting. Because of costs involved, the Solomon design was modified and participants were assigned to one of three groups: a pretest-posttest treatment group, a pretest-posttest control group, and a posttest-only control group. Treatment consisted of didactic presentations, group discussions, and directed practice in five hour-and-a-half sessions that were designed for systematic training in five stages of problem solving (problem definition, goal selection, strategy selection, strategy implementation, and evaluation). The investigators used the generation of alternatives, decision-making skill, and participants' perceptions of their problem-solving skills as dependent variables. The results indicated that training did influence the quality of responses, but it did not necessarily increase the number of alternatives. However, it was also found that the treatment group differed from the posttest-only control group only; it did not differ from the pretest-posttest control group. These results suggested a practice effect; simply taking the dependent measure twice resulted in the same outcome as the treatment. Participants participating in the workshop also reported using fewer impulsive behaviors during the problem-solving process than the control participants reported.

The value of the Solomon design in this particular study is rather compelling. By using two control groups, the authors were able to isolate the effects of training as well as the practice effects. Erroneous conclusions might well have been drawn if only a posttest-only control group design or a pretest-posttest control group design had been used.

Use of Control Groups

To this point, the designs discussed have included a control group. The expressed purpose of this arrangement is to compare treated participants with nontreated participants. In this way, the effect of the treatment vis-à-vis no treatment can be determined. However, the use of control groups is oftentimes precluded. For instance, it is unethical to withhold treatment from participants who are in need of treatment and who have a condition for which a treatment is known to work. For example, it would be unethical to have a control group of suicidal clients in a study of a new crisis-intervention technique. Furthermore, the research question may not refer to the absence of a treatment. For example, a study by Malkiewich and Merluzzi (1980) examined within conceptual-level theory the relative effectiveness of matching client conceptual level with treatments (desensitization and rational restructuring) differing in structure. To examine this matching question, a control group is not needed; inclusion of a control group, however, would answer the additional question of whether either of these two treatments is more effective than no treatment.

Although some research questions do not call for control groups, the logic of much research dictates the use of a control group. *Control group* refers generically to a class of groups that do not receive any of the active treatments in the study. A *no-treatment control group* receives no treatment. It should be realized that even though this implies that the researchers do not provide any treatment, participants in such groups often seek treatment elsewhere (for example, Frank, 1961; Gurin, Veroff, & Feld, 1960).

Often it is practically and ethically difficult to have a group that does not receive any treatment. However, a viable control condition can be obtained by using a *waiting-list control group.* Typically, participants are randomly assigned to either the treatment condition or the waiting-list control group; at the end of the treatment phase and the posttests, the treatment is made available to the participants in the waiting-list control group. (If more than two treatments were studied, the participants might be given the choice of the available treatments, or the one that proved most effective.) In either the pretest-posttest control group design or the posttest-only control group design, the treatment given to the waiting-list participants is not part of the design but may be analyzed anyway to strengthen the results (Kazdin, 1980) or to rule out threats to validity of quasiexperimental designs (Cook & Campbell, 1979). One disadvantage of the waiting-list control group is that long-term follow-up of the control participants is precluded (because they have by then received treatment). Another disadvantage is that although ultimately the participants in the waiting-list control group receive treatment, the treatment is withheld for some time (for more details on this topic, see Chapter 16).

Another type of control group is the *placebo control group.* Participants in a placebo control group are led to believe that they are receiving a viable treatment, even though the services rendered them are nonspecific and supposedly ineffective. For example, in a group counseling outcome study, participants in the placebo condition may be in a discussion group with no active group counseling. The rationale for including a placebo control is that it enables separating out the specific effects of a treatment from effects due to client expectations, attention, and other nonspecific aspects. Some investigators contend that the major effects of the counseling process are due to nonspecific factors (see, for example, Frank, 1961); inclusion of a placebo control group allows determination of whether the effects of a treatment are greater than those obtained under conditions that appear to clients to be viable but do not contain the major aspects of the active treatments. One commonly used placebo is the subconscious reconditioning placebo (SRP). Participants are told that the SRP reconditions the subconscious by using subliminal messages, when actually nonsense syllables are presented. Participants believe they are receiving a viable treatment; in fact, SRP has been found to be as effective as other treatments in the areas of smoking cessation (Sipich, Russell, & Tobias, 1974), test anxiety (Russell & Lent, 1982), and speech anxiety (Lent, Russell, & Zamostny, 1981). Of course, inclusion of a no-treatment or a waiting-list control group with a placebo control group strengthens the design considerably because differences between the placebo and no-treatment control groups gives an estimate of the strength of effect of nonspecific factors.

A final type of control group is the *matched control group.* Participants in a matched control group are paired in some way with participants in the treatment group. Although the primary purpose of this type of design is to reduce variance due to a matching factor (and will be discussed later in this chapter under dependent group designs), one application of this design is worth mentioning here. Length of counseling is often a troublesome variable in outcome studies. If the length of treatment is constrained to a given length of time, the treatment may not adequately represent the real way in which the treatment is delivered, reducing the construct validity of the independent variable. However, if the treatment is allowed to vary from one client to another as determined on a case-by-case basis, the timing of the posttest for the control participants is problematic: If the treatment lasts from 7 to 20 weeks and the posttest is administered immediately following termination, when should the posttest be administered to the control participants? The matched control group design solves this problem by administering the posttest to a control participant at the same time the posttest is administered to his or her paired participant in the treatment group, thereby holding time of treatment constant over the treatment and control groups.

Factorial Designs

Factorial designs are used when two or more independent variables are employed simultaneously to study their independent and interactive effects on a dependent variable. It is cumbersome initially to relate factorial designs to the three between-group designs previously discussed; basically, factorial designs are extensions of these earlier designs, namely by the addition of independent variables. Whereas previously we used the notation of Campbell and Stanley, with factorial designs it is more useful to visualize the design by diagramming the levels of the independent variables into cells. For example, if a study were examining three levels of an independent variable, there would be three cells, diagrammed like this:

The scores on the dependent variables are conceptualized as being placed in each of the cells. If there were 30 participants (10 participants per cell), there would be 10 scores for each dependent variable in each cell.

In the Nezu (1986) study previously discussed, the design was a pretest-posttest control group design with three levels of the independent variable, problem-solving treatment. This design could also be diagrammed as follows:

$$X_{PST} \qquad X_{PFT} \qquad X_{WLC}$$

Let's suppose that Nezu was curious about how the gender of participants might affect their reactions to the treatments. Perhaps he had observed some female participants reacting more favorably, or had had some other experiences that led him to hypothesize that females might respond more favorably to the treatments than males. Here we have a situation in which there are two independent variables of interest, the problem-solving treatments and the gender of participants. The dependent variables could be the same as before: BDI, MMPI-D, PSI, and I-E. Participants could be randomly assigned to the treatment conditions (a manipulated variable) but obviously not to the gender conditions (an attribute variable). Participant assignment therefore must be altered slightly, perhaps by first assigning females at random to the treatment/control cells, and then randomly assigning males to the treatment/control cells. The cells for these two independent variables would be diagrammed like this:

Treatments

		PST	PFT	Control
	Males			
Gender	Females			

This design is verbally described as a 2 (gender: males versus females) × 3 (treatment: PST, PFT, and control group) design, which results in six cells. (Alternatively, if there were two independent variables that each had three levels, the design would be a 3 × 3 design and have nine cells.) It is important to note that this 2 × 3 hypothetical study is essentially a pretest-posttest control group design, but now we have two independent variables.

STRENGTHS.   The unique strength or advantage of the factorial design is that it tests the effects of two or more independent variables, and of their interaction with each other, on the dependent variable. The factorial design provides more information than the single-independent-variable designs because it simultaneously tests two or more variables. In our hypothetical study, the researcher could examine whether the levels of problem-solving training have an effect on the dependent variables, as well as whether a participant's gender has an effect on the dependent variables. (The effect of an independent variable on a dependent variable is often referred to as a main effect.) Because of the efficiency of such simultaneous tests in factorial designs, it is not uncommon for researchers to test two, three, or even four independent variables in one study. Usually these added independent variables are person (personality) variables. For example, Kivlighan, Hageseth, Tipton, and McGovern (1981) examined how Holland type (Holland, 1985a, 1987) interacted with treatments that varied in terms of the amount of interpersonal involvement. More important, factorial designs allow the investigator to examine the interaction of the independent variables. An interaction means that the effect of one of the independent variables depends on the levels of one or more other independent variables. In our hypothetical example, the investigator could examine whether the effects of gender interact with the effects of treatment. The researcher might find that one of the treatments does not have the same effect on all participants, but instead results in more favorable responses among female participants than among male participants. Thus, factorial designs not only result in more information because they examine the effects of more than one independent variable; factorial designs also result in more complex information about the combined effects of the independent variables.

Another advantage of factorial designs is that if the independent variable added to the design is related to the dependent variable as expected, then the unexplained variance in the dependent variable is reduced. Reducing unexplained variance is again related to Kerlinger's "MAXMINCON," which in essence increases the power of the statistical test for analyzing factorial design (for example, in the analysis of variance, the denominator of the F ratio is reduced).

In a way, our fictitious example indicates how the factorial design can provide important qualifications about relationships between variables. The factorial design provides some answers about the conditions under which a treatment may operate, such as the gender of participants, the type of therapist, the age of clients, or the problem-solving style of clients. Whereas the single-variable study most often investigates whether a variable (most notably some treatment) has any effect, the factorial design examines more complex questions that approximate the complexity of real life.

WEAKNESSES.   While at first one might think the more information, the better, it is important to realize the costs involved as more variables are added to designs. With the addition of variables, the results of the study become more complex. In a 2×2 design, the researcher would typically examine the main effects of variable A, the main effects of variable B, and the interaction of A with B. In a 2 (A) $\times$ 2 (B) $\times$ 3 (C) design, the investigator would typically examine the main effects of variables A, B, and C; the two-way interactions of A with B and B with C; and the three-way interaction among A, B, and C. Complex interactions between three, four, or more independent variables typically are difficult to interpret, and the results of the study may be unclear. Researchers should not add independent variables just to have more than one independent variable; instead, independent variables should be carefully selected on theoretical and empirical grounds after thought is given to the research questions of interest.

Another disadvantage of the factorial design is the flip side of an advantage: If additional independent variables are added to the design and these variables turn out to be unrelated to the dependent variable, then the power of the statistical test may be reduced rather than increased. There are also complications regarding the conclusions that can be drawn when the independent variable is a status variable (for example, counselor gender) and is not manipulated (for more details see the discussion in Chapter 13).

AN EXAMPLE.   A study by Stein and Stone (1978) is a frequently cited investigation that used a factorial design. These researchers were interested in assessing the utility of a conceptual-level (CL) matching model in the initial phase of counseling. Conceptual level has been described in terms of personality development and related to both cognitive complexity and interpersonal maturity (Harvey, Hunt, & Schroder, 1961). In general, the CL matching model generally predicts an inverse relation between CL and degree of structure preferred. Thus, low CL people profit more from a highly structured environment, whereas high CL people benefit more from a less structured environment. In essence, Stein and Stone sought to determine whether these relationships between CL and structure would occur in counseling. They used a 2 (client conceptual level: high versus low) × 2 (counselor-offered structure: high versus low) × 2 (interviewers: A versus B) design to compare the effects of matching in a 40-minute counseling interview. They predicted that matched persons (low CL, high structure; high CL, low structure) would respond better than mismatched persons (low CL, low structure; high CL, high structure). No differences were expected across interviewers, and none were found; still, the authors tested the effects of this variable to identify any systematic bias due to the interviewers themselves. Dependent measures included client participation, client self-disclosure, client satisfaction, and perceived counselor helpfulness and under-standing. Although the results did not totally support their hypotheses, their results clearly suggested that CL did interact with counselor-offered structure to produce some of the predictable effects of client verbal behavior, perceptions of the coun-selor, and satisfaction with counseling. The authors interpreted their results as sug-gesting that it may be important for counselors to alter their interviewing style to capitalize on the apparent strengths or preferences of each client. In sum, this study nicely illustrates one advantage of a factorial design—namely, testing the interaction between two variables. In this study the interaction between CL and counselor-offered structure was predicted and, in general, supported.

Participant Assignment

Because the basic purpose of the between-groups design is to make comparisons between participants from different groups, it is critical that the people in the groups do not differ in important ways before the experiment or measurement begins. Participant assignment is also predicated on participant selection, which pertains to external validity. That is, a researcher might satisfactorily assign under-graduate students to one of four group conditions (participant assignment), but the results might not be generalizable to counseling center clients (a participant selection issue).

The intended outcome of assigning people to groups is to eliminate system-atic differences across groups before the experiment, so that if any changes are detected in one or more of the groups after the experiment, the change can be attributed to the independent variable. Participants therefore need to be assigned to groups in an unbiased fashion and free from extraneous variables.

The most effective way of ensuring comparable groups is to assign partici-pants to groups in such a way that each participant has the same probability of being assigned to each group. Such assignment tends to equalize both known and unknown sources of participant variation across groups, so that extraneous variables will not bias the study.

A number of procedures exist for randomly assigning participants to groups: The most common method is to use a table of random numbers, or a computer program that generates random numbers, to determine the order of assigning participants to groups. For example, if a researcher had four groups, participants could be randomly assigned by the order that the numbers 1, 2, 3, and 4 appear consecutively in the random list of numbers (for example, 4, 1, 4, 2, 2, 3, 1, and so on). Numbers other than 1 through 4 would be ignored. In this instance, the first participant would be assigned to group 4, the next to group 1, the third to group 4, and so on. In short, such a procedure reduces the probability of systematic biases or variations in participants between groups.

Note that random assignment would most likely result in unequal numbers of participants in each of the four groups. For statistical purposes it is better to have equal numbers across groups. To deal with this issue, Kazdin (1980) suggested assigning participants in blocks, or in the preceding example, in blocks of four participants. Within each block of four participants, the experimenter would simply randomly assign one participant to each of the four groups. This procedure is particularly useful when participants begin the experiment periodically, or at different times.

In counseling research, a researcher will often have a total sample identified and available at the beginning of an investigation. For example, a researcher might have 20 people who are available and have expressed an interest in some kind of treatment group, such as assertiveness training or group therapy. In this situation, the investigator knows the total number of participants, their names, and their general characteristics such as age and gender. Underwood (1966) has labeled this type of participant pool as captive. In this situation, random assignment is easily accomplished at one time via a random table, or even by drawing names from a hat. Quite often in counseling research, however, we do not have the entire sample at the outset, but rather must engage in sequential assignment (Underwood, 1966). For example, imagine that a researcher is investigating the effect of two types of precounseling information on client expectations of therapy. Most counseling centers have only a few clients beginning therapy each day, which would necessitate randomly assigning clients to the two types of precounseling information each day. In this case, clients can be assigned to either treatment as they enter counseling via some sort of randomization process.

Does randomization *always* result in equivalent groups? Simply put, no. Random assignment refers to a method of assigning participants in a bias-free manner; the method should be considered distinctly different from the outcome or results. Randomization distributes participants, and thus extraneous variables, by chance across the researcher's groups. Because randomization distributes by chance, it is possible that by chance some extraneous variable will not be distributed equally across groups.

Consider a study conducted on ways to enhance the problem-solving effectiveness of college students (Heppner, Baumgardner, Larson, & Petty, 1988). Participants were randomly assigned to two groups, a treatment group and a delayed-treatment group. Four instruments were used as pretest-posttest measures: the Problem Solving Inventory (PSI; Heppner & Petersen, 1982), the Level of Problem Solving Skills Estimate Form (LPSSEF; Heppner, 1979), the Ways of Coping Scale (WCS; Folkman & Lazarus, 1980), and the Mooney Problem Checklist (MPC; Mooney & Gordon, 1950). Statistical analyses of the pretest measures revealed no significant differences on the PSI, LPSSEF, and WCS; however, the delayed treatment group had significantly lower scores on the MPC. Thus, sampling error can exist even when one uses randomization. Randomization simply ensures that differences in groups are due to sampling error, not to systematic error.

Dependent Samples Designs

One of the concerns raised in this chapter related to whether or not random assignment equated groups adequately on some factor, such as intelligence or pretest level of psychological functioning. Implicit in this concern is the assumption that the factors identified are important factors in the study—that is, that intelligence or level of psychological functioning are important variables in the study. Importance in this context can be defined in two ways.

First, the factor may be theoretically important to understanding the phenomenon under investigation. In this case, the factor should be examined for its own sake. For example, if intelligence is thought to be an important variable theoretically, then it should be included as an independent variable in a factorial design. In this way the effects of intelligence, as well as the effects of the interaction of intelligence with the treatments (or with other independent variables), can be determined.

Second, if the factor is not interesting for its own sake, it is labeled a nuisance factor. Although a nuisance factor is not examined explicitly (that is, by inclusion as an independent variable in a factorial design), it remains an important consideration in the design of an experiment. For example, pretest level of functioning may not be interesting to the researcher in the sense that the effectiveness of treatment for clients at different levels of psychological functioning is not a burning research question. Nevertheless, it is desirable to have the treatment and control groups comparable on psychological functioning. A particularly useful way to accomplish this goal is to match participants on the basis of their pretest scores and then randomly assign one of the matched participants to the treatment group and the remaining participant to the control group, as illustrated in Table 6-1. As a result, the two samples are dependent. In this way, the researcher can be relatively certain that levels of psychological functioning are comparable across the two groups. More important, if the nuisance factor is related to the dependent variable as expected, then the variance in the nuisance variable can be removed from the variance in the outcome variable, resulting in a more powerful statistical test (Wampold & Drew, 1990). The typical statistical test for this type of design is the dependent samples t test (sometimes called the paired t test or correlated t test).

Essentially, the dependent samples t test accomplishes the same purpose as the analysis of covariance—it reduces unexplained variance and yields a more

TABLE 6-1
Assignment of Participants to Treatment and Control Groups in a
Dependent Samples Design

Pairs of participants	Treatment		Control
1	S_{11}	is matched with	S_{12}
2	S_{21}	is matched with	S_{22}
3	S_{31}	is matched with	S_{32}
–	–		–
–	–		–
–	–		–
N	S_{n1}	is matched with	S_{n2}

NOTE: Paired participants have comparable scores on pretest.

powerful test. The analysis of covariance does not require that participants be matched, and the reduction in unexplained variance is accomplished statistically, by the design of the experiment. The dependent samples design reduces uncertainty by matching comparable participants. Two participants who have high pretest scores are also likely to have high posttest scores; differences in posttest scores for these two matched participants are due presumably to the treatment (and other uncontrolled factors).

Dependent samples can be accomplished in other ways as well. Often natural pairs, such as monozygotic twins, are used. Because monozygotic twins have identical genetic material, using such pairs holds all hereditary factors constant. Other natural pairs include litter mates (not often applicable to counseling researchers), marital partners, siblings, and so forth.

Another means of creating dependent samples is to measure the participant in more than one condition, even though this is difficult to accomplish in the treatment and control conditions. Consider two treatments—say, treatments for increasing the degree to which participants use a computerized career exploration programs. Each participant would be exposed to one of the treatments (for example, token reinforcement for use of the system), and then use of the system would be assessed; then the participant would receive the other treatment (for example, social reinforcement for use of the system), and use of the system is again assessed. Of course, the order of the treatments would need to be randomized. In this way, all nuisance factors are controlled because each participant serves as his or her own control. Such a design, called a repeated measures design, contains many of the aspects of the within-subjects design discussed in the next section.

The idea of two dependent samples can be expanded to include more than two groups (for example, two treatment groups and a control group). Typically, the dependency is created by matching or by repeated measures (it is a bit difficult to find enough monozygotic triplets for such a study!). For example, Haupt (1990) was interested in counseling students on religious issues; he had reason to believe that the type of counselor responses to a client's religious statements would affect how the client perceived the counselor's expertness, attractiveness, and trustworthiness. Haupt believed that participants' beliefs about Christianity would most likely affect how participants would react to the counselor responses. In considering assigning participants to one of three group conditions, Haupt decided to ensure group equivalency on this attitudinal variable. Consequently, as he assigned participants to one of the three groups, he first identified three participants who had identical scores on a scale measuring beliefs about Christianity, and then randomly assigned each of these participants to a different group. As a result, participants had identical scores on their beliefs about Christianity across each of the three groups. When more than two participants are matched and assigned to conditions, the design is called a randomized block design. Each group of matched participants is called a block, and the participants within blocks are randomly assigned to conditions. The randomized block design is typically analyzed with a mixed model analysis of variance (see Wampold & Drew, 1990).

In sum, matching is a way to control for a nuisance factor that is believed or known to have an effect on the dependent variable. Dependent sample designs are powerful tools for increasing the power of statistical tests. Properly used, these designs can enable the researcher to accomplish the same purpose with far fewer participants. Unfortunately, dependent sample designs are underused in counseling research.

One final note: Many times in counseling research, randomly assigning participants to groups is not possible. For example, ethical problems would arise if a researcher tried to randomly assign clients to therapists with different levels of counseling experience, such as beginning practicum, advanced practicum, doctoral-level interns, and senior staff psychologists. It is quite likely that a client with complex psychological problems would be assigned to an inexperienced therapist who is ill-equipped to work therapeutically with such a client. In such applied situations, randomization may well introduce more practical problems than it solves experimentally. Sometimes researchers will attempt to show that clients are equivalent (matched) on several dimensions such as age, gender, presenting problem, and personality variables. Matching in this type of post hoc fashion can rule out some dimensions in comparing clients, but it is important to realize that many variables, known or unknown, are simply left uncontrolled. Thus, a weakness of such field designs is that unknown variables may confound the relationships among the variables being investigated.

WITHIN-SUBJECTS DESIGNS

The remainder of this chapter examines within-subjects designs. Remember that the hallmark of the within-subjects design is that it attempts to minimize error variance due to individual variation by having each participant serve as his or her own control. Similar to the between-groups design, participants are randomly assigned to groups or treatments, and independent variables are manipulated. The unique feature of the within-participants design is that all participants are exposed to all of the treatment conditions; random assignment involves assigning people to different sequences of treatment. In this section we first provide an overview of two types of within-participants designs: crossovers and Latin Square designs. We then discuss the strengths and limitations of the traditional within-participants design.

Crossover Designs

Suppose a researcher wanted to compare the effects of two treatments—test interpretation of the Strong Interest Inventory (SII) and work genograms—on a dependent variable, vocational clients' career maturity. The researcher could use the following within-participants design:

$$O_1 \quad X_1 \quad O_2 \quad X_2 \quad O_3$$

O_1, O_2, and O_3 represent different observations—in this case, administration of a career maturity inventory (say, the Career Maturity Inventory; Crites, 1978). X_1 represents the test interpretation treatment, and X_2 represents the genogram treatment. This is called a crossover design; all participants are switched (that is, crossed over) to another experimental condition, usually halfway through the study. Suppose the researcher conducted this study with 20 vocationally undecided adults as diagrammed. Suppose the researcher found a significantly greater change in career maturity between O_2 and O_3 than between O_1 and O_2 ($p < .01$); could he or she conclude that genograms are better at promoting career maturity than test interpretation? This conclusion would be quite tenuous because of the threats to internal validity embedded in this design, such as history (events may have happened to the participants between the administrations), maturation (normal development may have occurred), order effects (that is, perhaps genogram treatments are more effective if they are presented as a second treatment), or sequence effects (that is, perhaps the genogram treatment is effective only if it follows and perhaps adds to a SII test interpretation). In point of fact, a major difficulty in the within-subjects design is the possibility of confounding order or sequence effects. Order effects refers to the possibility that the order (that is, the ordinal position, such as first or third) in which treatments were delivered, rather than the treatment per se, might account for any changes in the development variable. Sequence effects refer to the interaction of the treatments (or experimental conditions) due to their sequential order; that is, treatment X_1 may have a different effect when it follows treatment X_2 than when it precedes treatment X_2.

How might the researcher control these threats to internal validity? One of the primary mechanisms used to control such threats is counterbalancing, which involves "balancing" the order of the conditions. The following is a diagram of a counterbalanced crossover design:

$$\begin{array}{cccccc} R & O_1 & X_1 & O_2 & X_2 & O_3 \\ R & O_4 & X_2 & O_5 & X_1 & O_6 \end{array}$$

The R's in the design indicate that participants are randomly assigned to two groups. X_1 and X_2 in the diagram represent the two treatments again, the O's represent the different observation periods. O_1 and O_4 designate a pretesting assessment, O_2 and O_5 represent an assessment at the crossover point, and O_3 and O_6 indicate testing at the end of the experiment. Thus, the groups differ only in the order in which they receive the treatments. In this case, counterbalancing also controls for sequence effects: X_1 precedes X_2 once, and X_2 precedes X_1 once.

It is important to be aware of two issues with regard to counterbalancing. First, the researcher can now use some simple statistical procedures to determine whether the order of the treatment conditions made any difference vis-à-vis the dependent variables. For example, a simple t test can be conducted on O_2 versus O_6 to determine whether treatment X_1 resulted in differential effects depending on whether the treatment was administered first or second. A similar t test can be conducted on O_3 versus O_5 for treatment X_2. These analyses are important not only for the present research, but also so that future researchers can know about order or sequence effects. A second issue is that even if there is an order effect, it can be argued that these effects are "balanced" or equal for both treatments (given the preceding example), and that order effects are therefore controlled.

Stiles, Shapiro, and Firth-Cozens (1988) used a counterbalanced crossover design to examine differences in session evaluation and client postsession mood for an interpersonal-psychodynamic treatment and a cognitive-behavioral treatment. Of the 40 clients studied, 19 were randomly assigned to receive eight sessions of interpersonal-psychodynamic treatment followed by eight sessions of cognitive-behavioral treatment. The remaining 21 clients first received eight sessions of cognitive-behavioral treatment followed by eight sessions of interpersonal-psychodynamic treatment. Session evaluation and postsession mood (both client and counselor ratings) were assessed by having the client, counselor, and external raters fill out a Session Evaluation Questionnaire (Stiles, 1980) for each session. Results showed that counselors and external raters saw interpersonal-psychodynamic sessions as significantly more powerful (that is, deep) and more uncomfortable (that is, rough) than cognitive-behavioral sessions. Likewise, clients rated the interpersonal-psychodynamic sessions as significantly more uncomfortable (that is, rough), and their postsession mood was significantly more positive following cognitive-behavioral sessions. Finally, external raters saw counselors' moods as more positive following cognitive-behavioral sessions. It is also important to note that Stiles and colleagues (1988) found no evidence for carry-over effects (that is, for one treatment affecting the rating of another treatment).

Latin Square Designs

A second type of within-subject design is the Latin Square design. As the number of treatments being compared increases, the counterbalancing of treatment order and sequence becomes increasingly complex. The critical issue is ensuring that all treatments are "balanced" or presented in the same ordinal position (that is, first, second, or third) with the same frequency (for example, three times). How should the researcher decide on the order of treatments? Suppose a researcher wanted to compare three treatments (X_1, X_2, and X_3) using a within- subject design. He or she could randomly assign the order of treatments for each participant. The problem with random assignment is that with a large number of participants, the treatment order normally balances out—that is, an equal number of participants receive the X_1 treatment first, second, and third (likewise for X_2 and X_3). But with a small number of participants, there can be large discrepancies in the distribution of treatments. For example, with 12 participants, suppose that 8 of these participants are randomly assigned to receive treatment X_1 at the first point in the sequence and 4 receive X_2 first, but that no one receives X_3 first. Thus, X_2 and X_3 would not be presented first with the same frequency as X_1. This is critical because a number of studies have shown that treatments given first are more effective (Morrison & Shapiro, 1987).

The researcher can guard against such an imbalance by predetermining a set sequence of treatments that is balanced for order and then randomly assigning clients to a particular order of treatments. A Latin Square is a way of predetermining the order of treatments. The major characteristic of a Latin Square is that each treatment appears in each ordinal position. The following is an example of a Latin Square design for three treatments, X_1, X_2, and X_3.

Group	Order of treatment		
	1st	2nd	3rd
1	X_1	X_2	X_3
2	X_3	X_1	X_2
3	X_2	X_3	X_1

The one problem with the Latin Square design is that the particular sequence of treatments cannot be controlled (or assessed statistically). In the preceding design, for instance, treatment X_1 never directly follows treatment X_2. Because all possible sequences are not represented in the Latin Square, it is not possible to entirely rule out this type of sequence effect as a rival hypothesis. This problem is usually considered minor, however, compared to order effects.

Hermansson, Webster, and McFarland (1988) used a Latin Square design to examine the effects of deliberate counselor postural lean on levels of communicated empathy, respect, and intensity. They manipulated three levels of the independent variable, postural lean (forward, backward, and counselor's choice). Each counselor conducted three consecutive sessions with a different client. For the first 9 minutes of an 18-minute session, the counselor was seated upright, then for the next 9 minutes each counselor leaned forward, backward, or counselor's choice. The particular order of forward, backward, or choice was determined by the Latin Square. Each counselor was randomly assigned to a particular sequence. The results of this study suggested a compensatory process between deliberate counselor lean and verbal communication. Specifically, a required forward lean was associated with decreased levels of intensity and empathy, whereas a required backward lean showed a significant increase in the levels of intensity and empathy. There were no significant effects for the choice condition.

Strengths and Limitations

At least six factors specific to the design itself can affect the appropriateness of a within-subjects design for a particular research question. These six factors are (a) experimental control, (b) statistical power, (c) time, (d) order and sequence effects, (e) measurement considerations, and (f) restriction of certain independent variables.

Experimental Control

The traditional within-subjects design is potentially a powerful design because of its reliance on random assignment of treatments and manipulation of independent variables. The experimenter can often obtain a great deal of experimental control with this design, and the threats to internal validity tend to be low with a counterbalance crossover design. Moreover, the within-subjects design tends to minimize error variance due to normal individual variability by using each participant as his or her own control. The reduction of individual error variance is a noteworthy advantage of the within-subjects design, which merits consideration when the researcher is especially concerned about such error.

Statistical Power

Because each participant receives all levels of the independent variable, some advantages from a statistical perspective result. In general, a researcher can use half the number of participants in a counterbalanced crossover design and still retain the same statistical power as in the between-subjects design (see Kerlinger, 1986 for a more complete statistical discussion of this matter).

Time

Although a within-subjects design can use fewer participants to obtain statistical power similar to a between-groups design, the trade-off is that the within-subjects design takes longer to conduct. Consider the researcher who wants to compare interpersonal and cognitive-behavioral approaches to the treatment of depression. Suppose he or she recruits 24 depressed clients. If the experimenter chooses to use a between-groups design, he or she can randomly assign 12 participants to 12 sessions of interpersonal treatment, and the remaining participants to 12 sessions of cognitive-behavioral treatment. In this design, at the end of 12 weeks the researcher has conducted the study and has collected the data. If the researcher instead uses a within-subjects design with only 12 clients—randomly assigning 6 clients to receive 12 sessions of interpersonal therapy followed by 12 sessions of cognitive therapy, and assigning the remaining 6 participants to receive treatment in the reverse order—the researcher would need 12 more weeks than in the between-groups design to collect the data. Thus, an important consideration is the trade-off between the number of participants and the time required. Because of dissertation deadlines or pressure to publish, it may often seem that time is a more valuable resource than participants. We would encourage researchers, however, not to be too quick to overlook within-subjects designs only because of the time factor.

Order and Sequence Effects

As we indicated earlier, a special problem of within-subjects design is the effects of order and sequence. Order effects can be seen as threats to internal validity.

Even when order effects are controlled, as in the counterbalance crossover and Latin Square designs, it is still important to check whether the order of the treatments affected the dependent variable. It can be argued that because counterbalancing equalizes any effects due to order, the researcher can ignore such order effects. This strategy, however, does not provide any information about the basic question: Were there any order effects in a particular study? Such information can be useful to future researchers as they design their investigations on a similar topic. Likewise, practitioners may be interested in knowing if the order of treatments makes any difference as they plan to maximize their interventions.

Sequence effects can also create threats to internal validity. In a counterbalanced crossover design, this sequence, or carryover effect, can be statistically examined because all possible sequences are represented in the study. Recall that Stiles and colleagues (1988) examined for and found no sequence effects. However, in the Latin Square design all possible sequences are not represented. Thus, the Latin Square design typically has less internal validity because sequence effects are more difficult to eliminate.

Measurement Considerations

There are two measurement issues that merit attention when one is considering a within-subject design: (a) ceiling and floor effects, and (b) equivalency of scale points. *Ceiling and floor effects* refers to problems associated with the upper or lower limits of dependent measures. In essence, the upper or lower limit of a dependent variable may limit the amount of change that can be demonstrated on that variable. Although this can be a problem for any research design, it can be a particular problem for within-subjects designs because they rely on multiple testing, which examines continued increases or decreases in the dependent variable. Consider Stiles, Shapiro, and Firth-Cozens (1988) again, the design of which is diagrammed as follows:

$$R \quad O_1 \ X_1 \ O_2 \ X_2 \ O_3$$
$$R \quad O_4 \ X_2 \ O_5 \ X_1 \ O_6$$

Suppose that in that study the effect of the two treatments, interpersonal psychodynamic treatment and cognitive-behavioral treatment, on client depression was also assessed. Further suppose that at pretest (O_1 and O_4) all clients had a pretest score 21 on the Beck Depression Inventory (BDI), and that after the first treatment for both groups of participants, the crossover testing (O_2 and O_5) revealed that all clients had a BDI mean score of 2. Since the BDI score cannot be lower than 0, there is little or no room for the second treatment to show improvement.

There is a related measurement problem in within-subjects designs that involves the equivalency of scale points. For example, is a change in the mean BDI score from 15 to 10 equivalent to a change from 10 to 5? Again, this problem is not atypical of between-groups designs, but these problems are exacerbated by the within-subjects designs. For example, variables involving instructions or participant expectancies may be difficult to reverse at the crossover point.

Restriction of Variables

A final consideration in the use of within-subjects designs involves the restriction of certain independent variables. It may not be possible to use certain independent variables in a within-subjects design. It is impossible, for example, to induce both the expectation that a given treatment will be effective and then the subsequent expectation that it will not be effective. Or two treatments may be too incompatible with each other. Kazdin (1980) offered the conflicting approaches of systematic desensitization and flooding. It is important for the researcher considering a within-subjects design to closely examine the effects that multiple treatments may have on one another. Given that each participant receives all treatments, the experimenter must assess whether the combination of multiple treatments can be administered realistically and fairly. Finally, variables that involve some personality, demographic, and physical characteristics may not vary within the same participant in a given experiment (Kazdin, 1980). For example, a participant cannot be both a male and female participant, or be a participant from both a rural and an urban community.

One final note: It also seems important that one does not limit research by concluding too quickly that particular treatments are incompatible. Kazdin (1980) suggested that "behavioral and psychodynamic therapy could not easily be compared within a particular set of participants." However, Stiles and co-workers (1988) did use, quite successfully, a within-subjects design comparing eight sessions each of exploratory (interpersonal-psychodynamic) and prescriptive (cognitive-behavior) therapy. Although worries about treatment contamination may be present or even pervasive among counseling researchers, this study challenges us to fairly evaluate the crossover effect and to be creative in our thinking about within-subjects designs.

SUMMARY AND CONCLUSIONS

There are two types of true experiments: between-groups and within-subjects designs. These are true experiments because in both cases there is random assignment of treatments and manipulation of an independent variable. In between-groups designs, the random assignment allots participants to treatment conditions to create experimental and control groups. In contrast, in within-subjects designs, all participants are exposed to all treatment conditions. Thus, the overall goal of the within-subjects design is to compare the effects of different treatments on each participant. Both designs lend themselves to Kerlinger's "MAXMINCON" principle.

In terms of between-groups designs, we discuss the posttest-only control group design, the pretest-posttest control group design, and the Solomon four-group design. These experimental designs are clearly powerful designs, as they can rule out many rival hypotheses. Each design controls for all the common threats to internal validity. A key feature of these designs is the random assignment of participants; randomly assigning participants to groups is a major source of control with regard to internal validity. Kerlinger (1986) concluded that between-groups designs "are the best all-around designs, perhaps the first to be considered when planning the design of a research study" (p. 327). Likewise, Campbell and Stanley (1963) indicate that these designs are "most strongly recommended" (p. 13). Because control groups are commonly used in these designs, we discussed issues pertaining to different types of control groups, such as no-treatment groups, waiting-list control groups, placebo groups, and matched control groups. Because randomization of participants is a defining characteristic of between-groups design, we also discussed participant assignment, group equivalence, and dependent samples designs.

We also described two traditional within-subjects designs, the crossover and Latin Square designs. Both of these designs make comparisons between two or more groups of participants, but in a different way from the between-groups design. In the crossover design, all participants are switched to another experimental condition, usually halfway through the study. Counterbalancing was introduced within this design as a way of reducing bias due to order effects. The Latin Square design was introduced as a design suitable for research questions that examine more than two levels of the independent variable. We suggested that at least six factors specific to the traditional within-subjects design can affect its utility for examining a particular research question, namely (a) experimental control (particularly with regard to individual participant variation), (b) statistical power, (c) time, (d) order and sequence effects, (e) measurement considerations, and (f) restriction of certain independent variables. In particular, we encouraged researchers to be creative in the application of traditional within-subjects designs. In short, within-subjects designs offer a powerful means of identifying causal relationships. The advantage of these designs concerns their ability to reduce both error variance (by using each participant as his or her own control) and the number of participants needed in a particular study.

Within-subjects designs have been underused in counseling research. In developing this chapter, we scanned several counseling journals in search of research examples that used a within-subjects design; we were struck by the less frequent use of this design relative to the between-groups design. For example, the 1988 and 1997 volumes of the *Journal of Counseling Psychology* contained reports of 22 true experimental designs (within-subjects and between groups). Of these, 19 (86%) were between-groups designs and 3 (14%) were within-subjects designs. These percentages would probably be similar if other years or other counseling-related journals were examined. In addition, within-subjects designs have not been used to examine a particular content area or population in counseling research. Although these numbers may suggest that the between-groups design may be better suited for research questions in counseling, we suspect that this is not the case. The within-subjects design has a number of strengths, most notably the reduction of participant variability, that ideally suit it for research in counseling.

Clearly, the between-groups and within-subjects designs are useful designs for examining research questions of interest to those in the counseling profession. These designs are flexible and can be made applicable to a wide variety of research problems; in fact, the factorial design is widely used in counseling research. However, it is important for the researcher in counseling to evaluate the strengths and limitations of these designs relative to the type of research question being asked and type of participants needed. Given the applied nature of many of our research questions in counseling, the researcher needs to consider carefully a broad range of issues pertaining to external validity to evaluate the utility of the true experimental designs in providing the most-needed information. In addition, many times the random assignment of participants to groups cannot be done because of ethical constraints, such as in a study of the effects of different levels of sexual harassment. We think it is erroneous for students to be taught that the between-groups design is simply "the best"; instead, students should be encouraged to consider the strengths and weaknesses of various designs in relation to different research questions. In other words, the utility of the design needs to be evaluated in the context of the research question, the existing knowledge bases, and internal and external validity issues.

CHAPTER 7

QUASI-EXPERIMENTAL AND TIME-SERIES DESIGNS

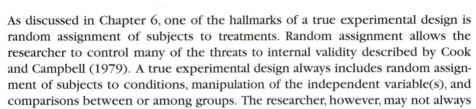

As discussed in Chapter 6, one of the hallmarks of a true experimental design is random assignment of subjects to treatments. Random assignment allows the researcher to control many of the threats to internal validity described by Cook and Campbell (1979). A true experimental design always includes random assignment of subjects to conditions, manipulation of the independent variable(s), and comparisons between or among groups. The researcher, however, may not always be able to use a true experimental design.

According to Cook and Campbell (1979), the most compelling reasons to deviate from a true experimental design is the cost. (Still, in some instances it may be impossible to use a true experimental design even when cost is not a constraint.) Conducting a true experiment is typically quite expensive in terms of time and resources. It is a lot less expensive to evaluate naturally occurring differences in treatment settings. In addition, true experiments usually involve the comparison of two, or more rarely three, treatments; it is critical in these situations that the treatments compared are very likely to be successful and conceptually important. To conduct a true experiment with treatments that are not well conceived and lack empirical support is both a waste of time and resources and ethically questionable. Quasi-experimental and time-series designs can be especially useful in providing preliminary empirical evidence for verifying potentially effective treatments or for explaining phenomena.

The researcher may not be in a position to randomly assign subjects to conditions. For example, in many clinical settings, clients may have to be assigned to a treatment based on their availability or some other situational variable, or it may be unethical to withhold treatment. When the researcher encounters a situation in which it is not practical or feasible to randomly assign subjects to conditions, he or she can use a quasi-experimental design. Like a true experiment, the quasi-experiment involves the manipulation of one or more independent variables, but there is no random assignment of subjects to conditions. Thus, a major identifying characteristic of a quasi-experimental design is the lack of random assignment of subjects to conditions.

In other circumstances, a researcher may want to investigate the effects of an intervention or treatment when no appropriate control or comparison group is available. In this situation, the researcher can infer whether the intervention or treatment had an effect by comparing observations made before and after the onset of the intervention. Such a design, referred to as a time-series design, requires multiple observations over time and the introduction of a treatment at a specified point in time. In other words, in a time-series design the researcher can and does manipulate one or more independent variables, but there is no random assignment to groups or between-group comparisons.

Because the researcher has less control in quasi-experimental and time-series designs than in an experimental design, the interpretation of the results of these studies has less certainty. In terms of the "MAXMINCON" principle, the researcher using a quasi-experimental design can both maximize differences in the independent variable(s) and minimize error variance due to measurement issues, just as with true experimental designs. However, because there is no random assignment of subjects to treatments, he or she cannot control all of the various threats to internal validity. Many research design texts cover quasi-experimental and time-series designs in a superficial manner, emphasizing the increased certainty that accrues when interpreting the results of a true experiment. The emphasis on true experiments may be appropriate for the more laboratory-oriented specialties within psychology, but for many counseling researchers the controls of the laboratory are not available, or may even be undesirable (because of reduced external validity), in the applied setting. Given the applied nature of counseling research, this chapter focuses on delineating quasi-experimental and time-series designs that can be useful for the counseling researcher.

The first half of the chapter focuses on quasi-experimental designs. There are two major classes of quasi-experimental designs: nonequivalent-groups designs and cohort designs. In nonequivalent-groups designs, comparisons are made between or among subjects in nonrandomly formed groups. We initially discuss three types of uninterpretable and four types of interpretable nonequivalent-groups designs. We then discuss cohort designs, a special case of nonequivalent-groups designs. Cohorts are groups of subjects that are assumed to be similar because they temporally follow each other through a formal or informal institution. The second half of the chapter focuses on time-series designs. The defining characteristic of a time-series design is multiple observations over time (Cook & Campbell, 1979). These observations can involve the same object—for instance, the client's level of perceptual processing for each statement during a counseling session—or different but similar objects, such as monthly totals of clients requesting service at a counseling center.

QUASI-EXPERIMENTAL DESIGNS

In many clinical situations the experimenter cannot randomly assign subjects to treatments because of institutional, practical, or ethical constraints. In such cases the experimenter may have to work with preestablished groups. For

instance, an investigator may want to examine the effect of a group session summary (a therapist's written summary of a group session that is mailed to each
group member prior to the next session) on session quality and group-member
involvement (Yalom, 1985). Group leaders may not agree to randomly assigning
clients to groups, because many leaders believe that selecting members to form
a compatible mixture is one of the most important decisions a leader makes.
The investigator may consequently be restricted to preformed groups. In this
case, he or she could use summaries in two preformed groups and not use summaries in two other preformed groups. The researcher could then compare ratings of session quality and member involvement in the groups that did and did
not receive the summaries. This design would be a quasi-experimental design
because there is manipulation of an independent variable (summary versus no
summary) and a between-conditions comparison, but no random assignment of
subjects to conditions.

This example also nicely illustrates some of the drawbacks of quasi-
experimental designs. In this case, the members were selected and the groups
composed for a reason (perceived compatibility). If the investigator indeed finds
a difference between the groups, one possible explanation is the effect of the independent variable (group summaries), but another equally plausible explanation is
selection differences. Perhaps the group leaders who led the groups that received
the summaries were more effective at composing counseling groups. In that case,
the differences between the two conditions may reflect differences in clients, not
in the experimental manipulation. In short, whenever an investigator uses previously established groups (classes in schools, wards in a hospital, or therapy
groups), he or she must always be aware that these groups were probably established for some reason, and that differences found between them may have more
to do with the selection process than with the experimental manipulation.

Selection may also have a more indirect effect by interacting with other variables (Kazdin, 1980). A selection-by-threat interaction effect occurs when the
threats to internal validity operate differently across the treatment conditions. For
example, in our group summary example, the group leaders may have used very
different selection criteria in establishing their groups. The group leaders in the
treatment (receiving summaries) condition may have selected only passive-
dependent clients for the group (believing that these clients get the most from a
group treatment), whereas the leaders in the control condition may have selected
clients with various interpersonal styles (believing that a heterogeneous group
leads to a better outcome). If passive-dependent clients mature at a faster rate than
do clients with other interpersonal styles, then a selection-maturation interaction
might account for any observed differences across conditions. Likewise, history,
testing, regression, mortality, or other factors may interact with selection to produce differences across conditions (see Chapter 3).

The preceding examples illustrate that selection is a key variable in examining the adequacy and usefulness of a quasi-experimental design. We will suggest in
this chapter that the usefulness of quasi-experimental designs for advancing
knowledge is directly related to how thoroughly the investigator examines and
controls for the selection criteria used in forming the initial groupings.

Historical Perspective and Overview

One of the most important and confusing questions that psychotherapy and counseling researchers have grappled with concerns the effects of counseling: Does
counseling work? To answer this question we need to compare a group of clients
who have received counseling to a group of clients who have not. The most rigorous (in terms of internal validity) test of the effects of counseling would involve
the random assignment of clients to treatment (receiving counseling) and no-
treatment conditions. The random assignment of clients to a no-treatment condition would in effect constitute the withholding of service, which can, of course,
raise ethical issues for the researcher. To avoid this type of ethical dilemma, early
counseling researchers attempted to find other groups of subjects with which to
compare the effects of counseling.

Many of the classic outcome studies in counseling used quasi-experimental
designs. For example, Klingelhofer (1954) was interested in examining the effects
of academic advisement on the scholastic performance (grade point average) of
students placed on academic probation. He compared three groups of students in
this study, all of whom were on academic probation. One group received four one-
hour counseling sessions, a second group received one one-hour counseling session, and the third group received no counseling interviews. The students who
received one or four hours of counseling were randomly assigned to groups. The
students in the uncounseled group were drawn from students who had been on
academic probation during the preceding year. In essence, Klingelhofer's study
had elements of both experimental and quasi-experimental designs.

The comparison between the students receiving one or four hours of counseling was a true experiment because there were random assignment of subjects
to treatments, manipulation of the treatment variable, and a between-groups comparison. The comparison between the students who did and did not receive counseling was a quasi-experimental design because the students were not randomly
assigned to conditions. This particular type of quasi-experimental design is called
a cohort design. The students who had been on probation the year before the
study formed one cohort, and the students on probation during the experimental
year formed a second cohort. Klingelhofer assumed that the students in the two
cohorts were similar because the same rules were used to place students on academic probation both years.

The results of this study did not reveal any differences in subsequent grade
point average for students counseled for either one or four sessions. There was, however, a significant difference in grade point average between students who had and
had not received counseling. Nonetheless, this result must be interpreted with some
caution because pretreatment differences between the students in the two cohorts
may have existed due either to some unknown selection factor or to different historical events during their year on probation. Despite these possible limitations,
Klingelhofer's study of the effectiveness of one widely used counseling intervention
represents a typical quasi-experimental study of counseling in the 1950s and 1960s.

In the following sections we examine the two major classes of quasi-
experimental designs: nonequivalent-groups designs and cohort designs. In
nonequivalent-groups designs, comparisons are made between or among sub-

jects in nonrandomly formed groups. For example, a researcher may want to examine the effects of a videotape that provides precounseling information on subsequent counseling dropout rates. He or she may be able to find a counseling agency that uses such a tape and compare the agency's dropout rate with the dropout rate for an agency that does not use this type of tape. Obviously, because the clients at the two agencies may be different on a number of variables that relate to dropout rate (for example, ethnicity), the clients in the two agencies represent nonequivalent groups. As we will discuss subsequently, the usefulness of a nonequivalent-groups design is related to how much the researcher knows about possible pretreatment differences among subjects in the nonequivalent groups.

Cohort designs are a special case of nonequivalent-groups designs. According to Cook and Campbell (1979), cohort designs are "particularly useful for drawing causal inferences [because] a 'quasi-compatibility' can often be assumed between [adjacent] cohorts that do and do not receive a treatment." However, the compatibility in a cohort design will never be as high as in an experiment with random assignment. Nonetheless, cohort designs have a relative advantage over other types of nonequivalent-groups designs.

Nonequivalent-Groups Designs

In the following examples we diagram the nonequivalent-groups quasi-experimental designs. The symbol Non R represents the nonrandom assignment of subjects to groups. As in the previous chapters, X indicates the independent variable or treatment, and O indicates observations of the dependent variable.

We begin our discussion of nonequivalent-groups designs with three designs that are virtually uninterpretable because of multiple threats to internal validity. We describe these designs so that you can be aware of their shortcomings and have a basis for their comparison with the more-interpretable nonequivalent-groups designs.

Uninterpretable Nonequivalent-Groups Designs

The one-group posttest-only design can be diagrammed as follows:

$$X_1 \quad O_1$$

In this design, observations are made of the dependent variable only after subjects have undergone some type of treatment. This design is impossible to interpret because there is no way to infer that any type of change has taken place. In addition, the lack of a control group makes it impossible to investigate the presence of maturational or historical processes.

A posttest-only nonequivalent design can be diagrammed as follows:

$$\text{Non R} \quad X \quad O_1$$
$$\text{Non R} \quad \quad O_2$$

In this design, the two groups are formed in a nonrandom manner. The subjects in the first group receive the experimental treatment (X) while the subjects in the second group do not receive any treatment. Change is measured by comparing the posttests (O_1 and O_2).

The posttest-only nonequivalent design need not compare a treatment with a control group. Two or more active treatments can be compared using this type of design. The following is a diagram of a posttest-only nonequivalent design comparing three active treatments:

$$
\begin{array}{lll}
\text{Non R} & X_1 & O_1 \\
\text{Non R} & X_2 & O_2 \\
\text{Non R} & X_3 & O_3 \\
\end{array}
$$

Once again, the groups are formed on a nonrandom basis. Treatments (X_1, X_2, and X_3) are administered to the subjects in the three groups, and then posttests (O_1, O_2, and O_3) are used to assess changes.

Posttest-only quasi-experimental designs are especially weak because of the difficulty in attributing results to the intervention. The lack of random assignment of subjects to groups allows the possibility that the groups may differ in some important manner prior to treatment. Typically, students are assigned to classes, patients to wards, clients to groups, and residents to living groups based on some rationale, which suggests that the natural groupings we encounter will differ prior to treatment on a few, or in some cases many, dimensions. Thus, one of the problems with the posttest-only nonequivalent design is that it does not allow for an assessment of any of the possible differences that exist before treatment.

Consider the following example. Suppose an investigator wants to examine the usefulness of an in-class program in alleviating depression in children. He or she might select two classes of sixth graders in a school and then provide one class with the intervention. After one month he or she assesses the students' level of depression. Suppose further that after treatment, the students who received the intervention show less depression. This result may indicate an effect of the treatment, or it may reflect differences between the two classes in their levels of depression before the intervention. Perhaps the principal decided to assign students to classes on the basis of their social skills levels. Research has documented the relationship between social skills and depression (see, for example, Lewinsohn et al., 1980). Because there was no pretest, the possible differences in the initial levels of depression could not be assessed.

Another uninterpretable design is the one-group pretest-posttest design. This design is diagrammed as follows:

$$
O_1 \quad X \quad O_2
$$

In this design, pretest observations (O_1) are recorded, a treatment is administered, and posttest observations are made. This design is better than the one-group posttest-only design because by comparing pretest-posttest observations, we can determine if a change occurred. However, the possible cause of this change is still quite ambiguous. For example, the treatment might be responsible for any observed change, but history (the occurrence of other events between pretest and posttest) might also account for the change. Alternatively, if the intervention or treatment was initiated because of a particular problem (for example, academic probation, as in the Klingelhofer study), then the posttest scores might improve because of statistical regression toward the mean. Another possible explanation for changes in the posttest score is maturation, in which case the change may have nothing to do with the treatment and instead reflects simple growth and development. Without a comparison group, it is impossible to rule out these and other threats to internal validity.

Interpretable Nonequivalent-Groups Designs

A more useful nonequivalent-groups design is the pretest-posttest design:

$$\text{Non R} \quad O_1 \quad X \quad O_2$$
$$\text{Non R} \quad O_3 \quad \quad O_4$$

In this design, subjects are nonrandomly assigned to groups and then pretested on the dependent variable. One group then receives the experimental treatment while the other does not. It is important to note that this design need not involve a treatment-control group comparison; it may involve the comparison of two or more active treatments.

The pretest-posttest nonequivalent-groups design is a stronger, and therefore more interpretable, design than the posttest-only nonequivalent design because it allows for an examination of some of the inevitable pretreatment differences. The investigator using a pretest-posttest nonequivalent-groups design can assess similarity of subjects on the dependent variable(s) of interest and on other variables that may be related to the dependent variable. It is important for the researcher to remember, however, that pretest equivalence on the dependent variable(s) and on other assessed variables does not mean that the groups are comparable on all dimensions that are important to behavior change. A demonstration of pretest equivalence, however, does increase one's confidence in attributing any observed posttest differences between groups to the experimental manipulation rather than to some selection difference. It is also important to note that usually O_1 and O_3 are not exactly equal. In instances when $O_1 \neq O_3$, the researcher must decide what is "close enough." One way to decide whether or not the two groups were equivalent at pretesting is to decide beforehand on a difference that is "too large," such as when $O_1 - O_3$ exceeds one standard deviation of O in a normative population. The researcher can then use a statistical test to see whether $O_1 - O_3$ is greater than this number. If it is not, then the researcher can conclude that the two groups were equivalent (on this one particular measure) at pretesting.

In the pretest-posttest nonequivalent design, it is unlikely that observed differences between groups can be attributed to factors such as history, maturation, or testing. However, there can be a selection-by-threat interaction that can pose a threat to internal validity. In other words, an event might affect subjects in only one group, or it might affect them differently from subjects in the other group(s). For example, because of some selection bias, the subjects in one group may mature faster (selection × maturation) or be more likely to encounter some historical event (selection × history) than those in the other group.

Like its experimental equivalent, the pretest-posttest nonequivalent-groups design may have problems with external validity because subjects in the different groups might react to the intervention(s) based on a sensitizing effect of the pretest. Also, subjects in one group may react differently to the pretest than subjects in the other group(s). Still, Kazdin (1980) argued, and we agree, that the possible problem of pretest sensitization is minor compared to the problems of trying to interpret the results of a nonequivalent-groups design when there has been no check on pretreatment equivalence.

Sometimes the researcher may not want or be able to pretest the subjects in the groups in a nonequivalent-groups design. This may happen when he or she is worried about the possible effects of pretest sensitization, or when he or she is working with archival data and no pretest was given. In this case, the researcher may choose to use a nonequivalent-groups design with a proxy pretest measure (a proxy pretest involves a similar but nonidentical variable). This design is diagrammed as follows:

$$\text{Non R} \quad O_{A1} \quad X \quad O_{B2}$$
$$\text{Non R} \quad O_{A1} \quad \quad O_{B2}$$

The $_A$ and $_B$ in this design represent two forms of a test or tests designed to measure similar constructs. In this design, groups are formed nonrandomly and a proxy pretest (O_{A1}) is administered to both groups. Later, one group gets the experimental treatment (X), and then both groups are retested with a different posttest (O_{B2}). The viability of this design depends on the ability of the researcher to find a pretest measure (O_{A1}) that relates conceptually and empirically to the posttest (O_{B2}).

For example, a researcher may want to examine a new method of counselor training. He or she finds two training programs willing to participate and institutes the new method in one program. At the end of the first year the researcher administers a paper-and-pencil counseling skills test to all students in the two programs and finds that the students in the treatment program scored higher on this test. However, the researcher is worried about possible pretreatment differences in counseling skill level. Suppose the researcher finds that Graduate Record Exam (GRE) scores are correlated ($r = .80$) with scores on the paper-and-pencil counseling skills test. In this case, the researcher can use the pretreatment GRE score (O_{A1}) to examine possible pretreatment differences between students in the two programs.

The pretest-posttest nonequivalent-groups design can be strengthened by the use of an additional pretest. This design is diagrammed as follows:

$$\text{Non R} \quad O_1 \quad O_2 \quad X \quad O_3$$
$$\text{Non R} \quad O_1 \quad O_2 \quad \quad O_3$$

This design is similar to the pretest-posttest nonequivalent-groups design except for the addition of a second pretesting to enhance the interpretability of the design. One of the main threats to the internal validity of a pretest-posttest non-equivalent-groups design involves a selection-by-maturation interaction. In other words, the subjects in the two groups may be maturing at different rates because of some selection characteristic. The addition of a second pretest allows the researcher to examine this possibility. The difference between O_1 and O_2 for the treatment and control groups can be examined to see if the groups are maturing at different rates.

The addition of a second pretest significantly enhances the interpretability of a nonequivalent-groups design. A review of the counseling literature, however, suggests that two pretests are rarely, if ever, used. We strongly recommend that researchers contemplating the use of a nonequivalent-groups design consider the addition of a second pretest.

Although the reversed-treatment pretest-posttest nonequivalent-groups design is also rarely used in counseling research, we include a discussion of this design here because it is one of the stronger nonequivalent-groups designs. We hope that an understanding of the strengths of this design will encourage its use in counseling research. The design is diagrammed as follows:

$$\text{Non R} \quad O_1 \quad X+ \quad O_2$$
$$\text{Non R} \quad O_1 \quad X- \quad O_2$$

In this design, X+ represents a treatment that is expected to influence the posttest (O_2) in one direction, and X– represents a treatment that is expected to influence the posttest in the opposite direction.

For example, a researcher may want to test the hypothesis that structure is related to productive group development. Certain schools of therapy contend that ambiguity enhances therapy because lack of structure increases anxiety, and anxiety is necessary for productive work to occur. Other schools contend that anxiety interferes with group work and that structure should be used to lessen the amount of anxiety that group members experience. To test this hypothesis, the researcher could obtain pretest and posttest measures of the quality of group interactions from two groups of clients. One group of clients could be given explicit information about group procedures, and the other group could be given more ambiguous information. Posttest scores could be examined to see if the levels of quality of group interactions moved in opposite directions.

This design renders a selection $\times$ maturation threat to internal validity improbable. It is hard to imagine that two groups of subjects would spontaneously mature in different directions. The usual pattern of differences in maturation between two groups is in the rate, not the direction, of maturation.

The reversed-treatment design is also stronger in terms of construct validity. As Cook and Campbell (1979) point out, the "theoretically causal" variable must be rigorously specified if a test depends on one version of the cause affecting one group one way and another group the other way. The main problem with a reversed-treatment design is an ethical one. For example, it is usually unethical to administer a treatment that would cause subjects to become more depressed. The researcher wanting to use the reversed treatment design must, therefore, display a good deal of thought and creativity.

Cook and Campbell (1979) discuss several other nonequivalent-groups designs (for example, repeated treatments). Because these designs are so rarely used in counseling research, we believe that a discussion of them is not warranted here. The interested reader is referred to Cook and Campbell (1979) for a discussion of the less common designs. In addition, Cook and Campbell provide an excellent summary of the statistical analysis of nonequivalent-groups designs.

AN EXAMPLE OF A NONEQUIVALENT-GROUPS DESIGN FROM COUNSELING RESEARCH.   Taussig (1987) used a nonequivalent-groups design with a proxy pretest to examine the effects of client-counselor ethnicity matching and the time of goal setting on the number of kept, canceled, and broken appointments. In addition, she analyzed possible interactions between these variables and client ethnic status and gender. In this study, client-counselor ethnicity match and the time of goal setting were used to form nonequivalent groups. In other words, clients were not randomly assigned to counselors, and the time of goal setting was not randomly specified.

Taussig hypothesized that client-counselor pairs mismatched on ethnic status would share fewer cultural expectations about counseling and thus would have fewer kept and more canceled and broken appointments than client counselor pairs matched on ethnic status. She also hypothesized that early goal setting with Mexican-American clients would lead to fewer kept and more canceled and broken appointments than early goal setting with Anglo-American clients. Taussig reasoned that relationship building would take longer with Mexican-American clients and predicted that early goal setting would disrupt this relationship-building process.

The data for this study were obtained from the archival client records of 70 Mexican-American and 72 Anglo-American clients seen at a community mental health center. The independent variables were client ethnicity (Anglo-American, Mexican-American), counselor ethnicity (Anglo-American, Mexican-American, other Spanish-speaking), and timing of goal-setting (setting goals within 14, 21, or 28 days, or not at all). Client-counselor match was examined by noting the ethnicity of clients across types of counselor ethnicity.

Four pretest proxy variables were used in the design: annual income of the client, client age, client employment status, and goal resetting (number of times goals were set for the client). Each of the variables was related to one or more of the dependent variables: kept, canceled, and broken appointments. Specifically, these pretest variables were used as covariates in an analysis-of-variance design. In this manner the author hoped to control several pretreatment differences that could have affected the analysis of counselor-client match and/or duration of goal setting. The results of the analysis of covariance showed that none of the dependent variables were related to duration of goal setting. However, in terms of the counselor-client ethnicity match, when Mexican-American clients were matched with other Spanish speaking counselors, more kept appointments resulted. Counselor-client ethnicity match was not related to appointments kept for the Anglo-American clients.

The Taussig study is a good example of the use of a nonequivalent-groups design. It was certainly less expensive (in time and money) for Taussig to access client records than to go into an agency, randomly assign clients to counselors, and randomly determine duration of goal setting within a particular client-counselor dyad. Her finding that ethnic matching was related to kept appointments but probably not to goal-setting duration provided preliminary information for future research, and she avoided wasting time and effort in a more-costly true experimental design. Another strength of the study was the use of proxy pretest variables to look for possible selection differences. The major weakness of the Taussig study involves the possibility of selection effects. We do not know, for instance, why clients were assigned to particular therapists, or why goals were set with some clients within 14 days and never set with other clients. In other words, the conditions examined in the study (client-counselor ethnicity match and duration of goal setting) were formed on some unknown basis that could have affected the results of the study.

Cohort Designs

Cohort designs are typically stronger than nonequivalent-groups designs because cohorts are more likely to be similar to each other; their environment is the same except for the treatment variable. For example, the sixth-grade class at a particular school one year is likely to be similar to the sixth-grade class the following year. However, this would not be the case if, for example, school district lines were redrawn between the two years. It is therefore important for the researcher to have as much knowledge as possible about conditions that could affect the cohorts. Cohort designs are strengthened when the researcher can argue conceptually and empirically that the two cohorts did in fact share similar environments, except of course for the treatment. Three types of cohort designs have been used in counseling research. We will use the notations suggested by Cook and Campbell (1979) to diagram these designs. The first design, a posttest-only cohort design, is diagrammed as follows:

$$O_1$$
$$----$$
$$X \quad O_2$$

In this design, the broken line indicates that the two groups are successive cohorts and not nonequivalent groups. The O_1 represents a posttest administered to one cohort, whereas the O_2 represents the same posttest administered to the second cohort. It is important to note that these testings occur at different times because the cohorts follow each other through the system; however, the posttesting does occur at a similar point in each cohort's progression through the institution.

Slate and Jones (1989) used a posttest-only cohort design to test the effect of a new training method for teaching students to score the Wechsler Intelligence Scale for Children-Revised (WISC-R). One cohort of students took the intelligence testing course during the fall semester, the other cohort during the spring semester. The fall cohort received a standard scoring training procedure, whereas the spring cohort received the new training method. Given the results that students in the spring cohort made fewer scoring errors on the WISC-R than did students in the fall cohort, Slate and Jones (1989) concluded that the new training method was effective. These authors assumed that the students in the fall and spring cohorts were similar prior to training, and buttressed this assumption by examining several possible sources of pretreatment differences. For example, they found that the gender composition was similar across the two cohorts and that the students in the two cohorts had similar GRE scores and grade point averages.

In a second type of cohort design, posttest-only cohort designs are strengthened by partitioning the treatment, which involves giving different amounts of the treatment to different groups of subjects within a cohort. A posttest-only cohort design with partitioned treatments is diagrammed as follows:

$$O_1$$
$$- - - - - -$$
$$X_1 \quad O_{2a}$$
$$X_2 \quad O_{2a}$$

where O_1 is the posttest given to the first cohort, X_1 represents the first level of treatment, X_2 represents the second level of treatment, and O_{2b} is a posttest measure given to all members of the second cohort regardless of level of treatment administered.

In the Slate and Jones (1989) study, suppose that some of the students in the second cohort practiced the new scoring procedure for two hours and that the other students in the cohort practiced it for four hours. Slate and Jones could have analyzed the results separately for these two groups of students. If the students who had practiced for four hours (O_3) committed significantly fewer scoring errors than the students who practiced for two hours (O_2), and if the treatment cohort committed fewer errors than the no-treatment cohort, then the assertion that the treatment was effective would be strengthened, particularly with regard to the amount of training needed.

In short, the posttest-only cohort design can be useful, particularly relative to the posttest-only nonequivalent-groups design. Because clients experience various aspects of counseling treatments in different amounts, we urge researchers to use partitioning as a way of strengthening the internal validity of the posttest-only cohort design in counseling research. The disadvantage of this design, however, is the ambiguous inference when cetain results occur. If, for example, $O_1 < O_{2a}, O_1 < O_{2b}$, but $O_{2a} = O_{2b}$, then both treatments are superior to the no treatment condition, but there are no differences between the two treatments.

The third (and final) cohort design that we will discuss is the pretreatment-posttreatment cohort design, diagrammed as follows:

$$O_1 \quad O_2$$
$$- - - - - - - - -$$
$$O_3 \quad X \quad O_4$$

As in the previous design, the broken line represents the use of cohorts. The first cohort is pretested (O_1) and posttested (O_2), and then the second cohort is pretested (O_3), treated (X), and posttested (O_4).

The main advantage of the pretest-posttest cohort design over the posttest-only cohort design is the increased assurance the pretest provides for asserting that the two cohorts were similar prior to the treatment. In addition, the use of the pretest as a covariate in an analysis of covariance provides a stronger statistical test. The main disadvantage of this design is that the pretest can constitute a threat to external validity because of pretest sensitization. We believe that in most cases the advantages of a pretest to examine pretreatment compatibility across groups outweigh the threat to construct validity.

AN EXAMPLE OF A COHORT DESIGN FROM COUNSELING RESEARCH.   Hogg and Deffenbacher (1988) used both an experimental design and a quasi-experimental cohort design in comparing cognitive and interpersonal-process group therapies for treating depression. Depressed students seeking treatment at a university counseling center were screened in an intake interview for (a) presence of nonpsychotic, unipolar depression, (b) absence of major psychopathology, and (c) absence of high suicide lethality. Additionally, prospective subjects had to receive a score of 14 or greater on the Beck Depression Inventory (BDI; Beck et al., 1979). Clients meeting these criteria were randomly assigned to cognitive or interpersonal group treatments. A control cohort was formed by selecting clients who met the same screening criteria but who came to the counseling center too late in the fall semester to be assigned to any type of treatment. In essence, the authors used the Christmas break to form a cohort, assuming that students who came to the counseling center before versus after the break were similar. The subjects in the control group received no formal treatment during the break. The comparison of the treatment subjects and the control subjects constituted the cohort part of the design.

Subjects in the treatment and control groups were administered the BDI, the Minnesota Multiphasic Personality Inventory-Depression scale (MMPI-D; Hathaway & McKinley, 1942), the Automatic Thoughts Questionnaire (ATQ; Hollon & Kendall, 1980), and the Self-Esteem Inventory-Adult Form (SEI; Coopersmith, 1981). Treatment subjects were assessed at pretreatment, midtreatment (4 weeks), posttreatment (8 weeks), and follow-up (12–14 weeks). Control subjects were assessed before the semester break and 8 weeks later, which was equivalent to the pretest-posttest assessment period for the treatment group. The comparison of the treatment and control groups constituted a pretest-posttest cohort design.

Hogg and Deffenbacher performed initial analyses to assess equivalence across groups prior to treatment. They found no pretreatment differences across groups on the BDI, MMPI-D, ATQ, or SEI scales. A repeated measures (pretesting, posttesting) MANOVA (BDI, MMPI-D, ATQ, and SEI) was used to compare treatment and control groups. The treatment versus control comparison and the treatment-control by time (pretest-posttest) interaction were not significant. However, a significant change was found for both groups from pretest to posttest; such differences over time are sometimes referred to as time effects. The findings indicated that subjects in both the treatment and control groups significantly decreased depression and distorted cognitions, and increased self-esteem. This time effect is ambiguous because it is open to alternative explanations (for example, regression to the mean, maturation, test sensitization, and so on).

Hogg and Deffenbacher highlighted one of the problems inherent in cohort designs in their discussion of the lack of difference between the experimental and control groups. Even though no significant differences were found between those who received active treatments and members of the waiting-list control group, using Christmas vacation as a naturalistic waiting list period may have produced a significant temporal confound. Students who are depressed at the end of a semester may differ significantly from those seeking counseling services at the beginning of a semester. Additionally, interview data indicated that many waiting-list students felt considerable relief from depression over the holiday, changes made apparent by dramatic differences in posttest scores. The evidence of symptom transiency and wide client variability is in sharp contrast to other studies (see, for example, Fuchs & Rehm, 1977; Shaw, 1977) that have reported little improvement for depressed subjects in waiting-list groups, although these studies did not coincide with a holiday break. The potential temporal and subject-selection confounds made the validity of the apparent equivalence between the waiting-list and treatment cohorts highly questionable. For future research, the use of vacation periods as a naturalistic waiting-list condition is not recommended as a solution to the "rigorous methodology versus professional ethics" dilemma inherent in depression research (Hogg & Deffenbacher, 1988, p. 309).

In sum, the Hogg and Deffenbacher (1988) study was well conceived and executed. The authors used the semester break to form a cohort to use as a comparison in addition to the comparison of the two active treatments. They also comprehensively addressed the issue of pretreatment equivalence by comparing treatment and control groups across multiple measures. Interestingly, Hogg and Deffenbacher used the limitations (selection, temporal confound) inherent in the cohort design to argue against accepting the null hypothesis. One could possibly argue that, in fact, the treatments actually had no effect beyond the passage of time. Alternatively, Hogg and Deffenbacher could have used an additional control group. For instance, they could have recruited nonclients (through a subject pool) who had BDI scores greater than 14 and who met the criteria for nonpsychotic unipolar depression. These subjects could have been tested during the same time frame as the treatment subjects. This type of control could rule out the temporal (Christmas holiday) confound in examining the results.

TIME-SERIES DESIGNS

The defining characteristic of a time-series design is multiple observations over time (Cook & Campbell, 1979). These observations can involve the same subject (for instance, the client's level of perceptual process for each statement during a counseling session) or different but similar subjects (for example, monthly totals of clients requesting services at a counseling center). In an interrupted time-series design, a treatment is administered at some point in the series of observations. (The point at which the treatment takes place is called an interruption of the series.) To use an interrupted time-series design, a researcher must know the specific point in the series of observations when the treatment occurred. The logic of the interrupted time-series design involves comparing the observations before and after the treatment or interruption. If the treatment has an effect, there should be a difference in the observations before and after the interruption.

Although the logic of comparing pre- and postinterruption observations for evidence of difference is simple and straightforward, the statistical analysis can be complex. The reader who is interested in the relevant statistical analysis is referred to Cook and Campbell (1979). In this section we concentrate on the logical analysis of interrupted time-series designs. (Chapter 8 discusses time series as applied in single-subject designs.)

Although we could not find an example of a time-series design in the counseling journals, we believe that these designs can be profitably used in counseling research. In the next section we describe two time-series designs with the hope of stimulating counseling researchers to consider these designs in planning their research.

Simple Interrupted Time Series

The most basic time-series design is the simple interrupted time series, diagrammed as follows:

$$O_1 \quad O_2 \quad O_3 \quad O_4 \quad O_5 \quad O_6 \quad X \quad O_7 \quad O_8 \quad O_9 \quad O_{10} \quad O_{11} \quad O_{12}$$

Multiple observations occur both before (O_1-O_6) and after (O_7-O_{12}) the treatment (X) is initiated. The diagram shows an equal number of observations before and after the treatment, but this is not a requirement for the design.

The interrupted time-series design has two advantages over the quasi-experimental designs previously described. First, the time-series design allows the researcher to detect maturational changes that may occur prior to treatment initiation. The researcher does this by looking for changes in the pretreatment observations. If found, these maturational changes can be controlled for in a statistical analysis, allowing a more powerful test of the effect of the treatment. The second advantage of the time-series design is that it also allows for the analysis of seasonal trends. Many data examined by counseling researchers vary systematically over time. For example, more clients seek counseling around holiday periods. It is obviously important to account for this type of systematic variation if a researcher is interested in testing an intervention that affects clients' use of counseling services. The statistical analysis of time-series designs can also control for these types of systematic variations.

Unfortunately, the statistical analysis of interrupted time-series can be quite complicated and require considerable expertise (Crosbie, 1993). One of the main problems in analyzing time-series data is dealing with the problem of autocorrelation. Autocorrelation occurs when each score in a series of scores is more similar to the preceding score than it is to the mean score for the series. When scores are autocorrelated, error variance is deflated and a t test comparing scores from before and after the interruption is artificially inflated. Therefore, researchers have developed sophisticated statistics to deal with the problems of autocorrelation. Crosbie (1993) generically refers to these statistical techniques as interrupted time-series analysis (ITSA).

According to Crosbie (1993), ITSA conceptually involves five steps. Although the statistical operations are beyond the focus of this text, we provide the following brief overview of the steps: (a) estimating the model, which involves identifying and describing the pattern of autocorrelations that exist in a series of observations; (b) removing from the series of observations any slope, which is the systematic rise or decline in the magnitude of observations before or after the interruption in the series; (c) determining the estimates for the autoregressive function, which involves calculating a model that describes the particular pattern of autocorrelation present in the series of observations; (d) subtracting this autoregressive function from the original scores in the time series, in essence controlling for the effects of autocorrelation; and (e) using the general linear model to compare observations (now uncorrelated) from before the interruption to observations after the interruption.

In one example of a simple interrupted time-series design, a researcher might want to assess the effects of a counseling center's adoption of a time-limited model of counseling. The center could initiate the time-limited model in September of one year. The researcher could examine the number of clients on the waiting list each month for the preceding three years and the number of clients on the waiting list during the current year. The analysis of this design would require a comparison of the number of clients on the waiting list prior and subsequent to the initiation of the time-limited model.

One of the main threats to the internal validity of a simple interrupted time-series design is history. In other words, something other than treatment could affect the researcher's observations. One way to reduce such a threat is to add a second dependent variable. This second time-series design is called an interrupted time-series design with nonequivalent dependent variables. This design is diagrammed as follows:

$$O_{A1} \quad O_{A2} \quad O_{A3} \quad O_{A4} \quad X \quad O_{A5} \quad O_{A6} \quad O_{A7} \quad O_{A8}$$
$$O_{B1} \quad O_{B2} \quad O_{B3} \quad O_{B4} \quad X \quad O_{B5} \quad O_{B6} \quad O_{B7} \quad O_{B8}$$

In this design, O_A represents one dependent variable and O_B represents a second. Otherwise, the design is identical to the simple interrupted time-series design. If the O_A series shows an interruption at the time of treatment and the O_B series does not, then the internal validity of the treatment effect is enhanced. In other words, it is unlikely (although possible) that history would have an effect on one conceptually related dependent variable but not the other. The trick in using this design is to select dependent variable B such that theoretically the treatment will have no effect.

In the simple interrupted time-series design previously described, the researcher could add a second set of observations—for example, the number of clients requesting services each month. If the number of clients on the waiting list (O_A) shows an interruption at the time that the time-limited model was introduced

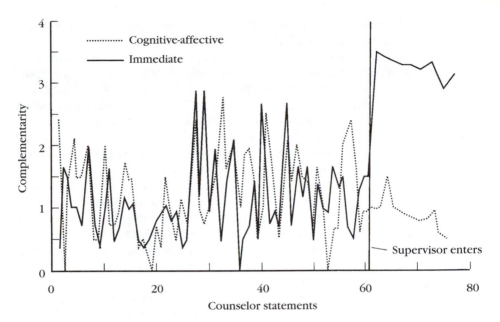

FIGURE 7-1
Counselor complementarity before and after "live supervisions."

but the number of clients requesting services (O_B) does not show a similar inter-ruption, then the researcher can conclude that the initiation of the time-limited model caused a reduction in the waiting list. It is unlikely that history could cause this effect because history would likely also affect the number of clients request-ing services.

Kivlighan (1990) used this type of interrupted time-series analysis to study the effects of live supervision in counselor training. Beginning counselor trainees saw a recruited client for four 50-minute counseling interviews. Advanced coun-seling doctoral students provided live supervision for the counselor trainees. This supervision involved viewing the counseling interview from behind a one-way mirror, entering the session at some point, commenting on the counseling process, and providing direction for the counselor. The observations in this study con-sisted of ratings of each of the counselor statements. Trained judges rated each counselor statement on both a cognitive-affective dimension and an immediacy dimension (statements about the client-counselor relationship versus statements outside of the counseling experience). Based on the training model used, Kivlighan predicted that after the interruption (the supervisor entering the room), the coun-selor's statements would be less cognitive and more immediate.

Figure 7-1 shows ratings of statements taken from one counselor-client-supervisor triad during the interview. The supervisor intervened between the 60th and 61st counselor statements. A visual inspection of these graphs suggests that the counselor's statements became more immediate and less cognitive after the supervisor's intervention. Based on a statistical analysis of this time series was performed with the SPSS-X Box-Jenkins procedure, Kivlighan concluded that the live supervision interventions influenced the novice counselor to use more affective and immediate statements with clients.

This study illustrates the usefulness of interrupted time-series analysis in studying counseling processes. By using two dependent variables, Kivlighan strengthened his confidence in the assertion that the observed changes were not due to a history confound. The study could have been further strengthened by replicating this analysis with other counselor-client-supervisor triads, which could enhance the generalizability of the results.

There are two major problems for researchers contemplating using an interrupted time-series design. First, as noted above, ITSA takes considerable expertise because of the complicated statistical models involved in the analysis. Second, because seasonal trends and autoregressive functions must be assessed, long series of observations (perhaps 50 to 100 observations on each side of the interruption) are necessary. Recent advances in ITSA procedures have addressed these two problems. Specifically, Crosbie (1993) developed ITSACORR, a relatively simple procedure that can be used with data from short time series (as few as five observations pre- and postinterruption).

ITSACORR uses the estimated autocorrelation to model the autocorrelation parameter. The effects of autocorrelation are controlled by using this autocorrelation parameter as an independent term (a linear constraint) in a general linear model. Rather than removing slope from the series of observations, ITSACORR estimates and then statistically compares the slopes for the pre- and postinterruption observations. ITSACORR produces an overall F test and two t tests. The overall F tests whether there is any overall difference between pre- and postinterruption observations (that is, F is an omnibus test of the mean and slope parameters). One of the t tests is associated with the intercepts; this tests whether or not the mean levels of observations are different pre- and postinterventions. The other t test is associated with the slopes; this tests whether or not the direction and/or the rate of change in the observations differs for pre- and postintervention periods.

Daus (1995) used an interrupted time-series design and the ITSACORR program to examine the effects of case presentations on counselor self-efficacy. Case presentation is an integral part of most practicum training experiences, and trainees have identified it as the most meaningful practicum activity (Ravets, 1993). Despite its widespread use and perceived effectiveness, case presentations have not been shown to change either trainees' counseling skills or their perceptions of their counseling skills.

To examine the effects of case presentation on counselor self-efficacy, Daus (1995) had counselor trainees, enrolled in an individual counseling practicum class, fill out the Counseling Self-Estimate Inventory (COSE; Larson et al., 1992) after each class period. These COSE scores were the repeated observations in the time-series analysis. The case presentation served as the interruption in this series of observations. Because the counselor trainees had several case presentations during the semester, each series of observations had several interruptions. Daus (1995) used the ITSACORR program to see if the intercepts and the slopes of counselor self-efficacy changed from pre- to postinterruption (i.e., the case presentation).

The data from "Trainee 3" in Figure 7-2 is illustrative of the ITSACORR analy-

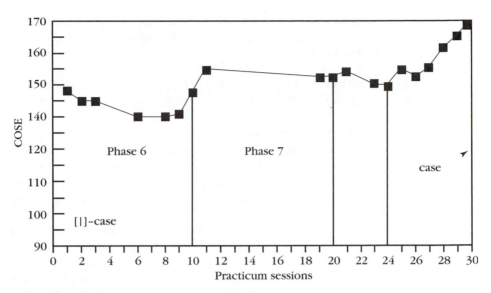

FIGURE 7-2
Group supervision time series for "Trainee 3."

sis in the Daus (1995) study. As seen in this figure, COSE scores are plotted along the y-axis and praticum sessions are plotted along the x-axis. "Trainee 3" had her first case presentation during the tenth practicum session. There were six COSE observations (practicum sessions 1, 2, 3, 6, 8, and 9) before this case presentation (interruption) and seven observations (practicum sessions 10, 11, 19, 20, 21, 23, and 24) after the case presentation. The overall omnibus F test for this data was significant (F (2, 10) = 8.30, $p < .01$). This significant F test showed that there was an overall change in COSE scores from pre- to postinterruption. In addition, both t tests were significant: (a) for intercept, t (11) = 3.64, $p < .01$, and (b) for slope, t (11) = -2.40, $p < .05$. The significant t test for the intercept showed that the average level of counselor self-efficacy was higher after the case presentation than before it. The significant t test for the slope showed that the rate of change for counselor self-efficacy was different after the case presentation than before it. This change in slope is evident in Figure 7-2. Before the case presentation there was a downward trend in self-efficacy scores, but after the case presentation the scores leveled off. These results suggested that, at least for this one trainee, the case presentation resulted in an overall increase in self-efficacy and also halted a pattern of declining self-efficacy. For a more extended discussion of counselor self-efficacy, see Larson (1998) and Larson and Daniels (1998).

Analysis of Concomitance in Time Series

At times, counseling researchers are interested not in examining the effect of a treatment in a time series, but whether changes in one variable in the time series cause subsequent changes in another variable in the series. For instance, do changes in the counselor's level of self-disclosure affect the client's level of self-disclosure? This type of analysis, referred to as an analysis of concomitance in time series, is diagrammed as follows:

$$O_{A1} \quad O_{A2} \quad O_{A3} \quad O_{A4} \quad O_{A5} \quad O_{A6} \quad O_{A7} \quad O_{A8}$$
$$O_{B1} \quad O_{B2} \quad O_{B3} \quad O_{B4} \quad O_{B5} \quad O_{B6} \quad O_{B7} \quad O_{B8}$$

In essence, the researcher observes two dependent variables over time. In the example just given, the researcher checks to see whether the counselor's level of self-disclosure adds predictability to the client's level of self-disclosure over and above the predictability obtained from patterns in the client's level of self-disclosure. An introduction to the statistical analysis of concomitance in time series can be found in Cook and Campbell (1979).

According to Gottman and Markman (1978), the related questions "How does a particular therapist's behavior affect the client?" and "How does a particular client's behavior affect the therapist?" can be answered through an analysis of concomitance. Bivariate time-series analysis and spectral analysis are two sophisticated methods for answering questions about concomitance. Unfortunately, only rarely have time-series analyses been applied to counseling/psychotherapy research. According to Jones, Ghannam, Nigg, and Dyer (1993), in time-series analysis the researcher attempts to infer a causal relationship between observations constituting one series of data points (for example, counselor self-disclosure) and observations of a second series (for example, expressions of client resistance). In other words, the researcher asks whether series A (counselor self-disclosure) can predict series B (level of client resistance).

Although describing time-series analysis can quickly become very technical, we will provide here a very brief overview of the conceptual issues. In the terminology of time-series analysis, the relationship between two series is the cross-correlation function. However, spuriously large cross-correlation coefficients can be found when two time series have large autocorrelations (correlations of a time series with itself). Therefore, time-series analysis involves two steps. In the first step, each individual time-series is examined for the presence of nonstationary trends, partial autocorrelations, and correlated error. This examination involves plotting and examining the autocorrelation (ACF) and partial autocorrelation (PACF) functions. If the ACF or PACF plots indicate significant autocorrelations or partial autocorrelation functions for an individual time series, then the series is made stationary by transforming the series (for example, differencing is one technique used to control for nonstationary trends in the data). Once the identified series are made "well behaved" (that is, any nonstationary trends, partial autocorrelations, and correlated error are removed from the data), these transformed series are then cross-correlated at various lags. The cross-correlation coefficients from this second step are examined for the presence of significant lead/lag relationships. If a significant lead/lag relationship is identified, the leading variable is interpreted as a potential "cause" of the lagging variable. If the only significant cross-correlation coefficient is for zero lag, then no presumption about the causal direction of the relationships is possible.

AN EXAMPLE OF A TIME-SERIES DESIGN IN COUNSELING RESEARCH.   As stated, time-series designs have not been used often in counseling research. Recently, however, Kivlighan, Multon, and Patton (1996) used time-series analysis to examine the predictive validity of the Missouri Addressing Resistance Scale (MARS). Twelve adult outpatient clients who completed 20 sessions of planned short-term psychoanalytic counseling provided data for the analysis. One series of observations (series A) consisted of weekly ratings, by trained observers, of the counselor's manner of dealing with client resistances on the Exploring and Working Through Resistance scales of the MARS. The second series of observations (series B) consisted of weekly ratings, by trained observers, of the level of client resistance using the Resistance Scale (Schuller, Crits-Christoph, & Connoly, 1991).

Kivlighan and colleagues (1996) computed the mean cross-correlation coefficients (CCC) for the Exploring and Working Through Resistance scale of the MARS and the Resistance Scale composite resistance score for the sample as a whole. In interpreting a CCC, a positive lag meant that the Exploring and Working Through Resistance score from the MARS led the Resistance Scale resistance composite, whereas a negative lag meant that the Resistance Scale resistance composite led the MARS Exploring and Working Through Resistance Scale. Also, just like a correlation coefficient, the sign of the CCC denoted the direction of the relationship while the absolute value of the CCC indicated the magnitude of the relationship.

The time-series analysis revealed that for Exploring and Working Through Resistance there was a significant reduction of resistance at lags 1 and 2. Specifically, there were significant negative relationships (that is, negative CCCs) between the Exploring and Working Through Resistance scores and the composite level of client resistance (at lag 1, $r = -.67, p < .05$; at lag 2, $r = -.59, p < .05$). These results showed that increases in the therapists' attempts to explore and work through the client's resistance in one session result in fewer manifestations of client resistance in the two subsequent sessions.

SUMMARY AND CONCLUSIONS

We believe that quasi-experimental and time-series designs have a place in contemporary counseling research. They are especially useful in examining relationships in applied settings. It is critically important that counseling psychologists and counselors conduct their research with real clients, workers, and students. Experimental designs are often impossible in these settings for a variety of logistical, methodological, and ethical reasons. Especially for findings from studies that do not use real clinical populations or settings, it is important to have replications in a more applied, real-life setting. Studies using quasi-experimental or time-series designs in real settings could be the final point in a series of investigations.

Because there are inherent problems with the interpretation of the results of quasi-experimental and time-series designs, however, researchers must exercise caution. We strongly recommend against the use of posttest-only nonequivalent-groups designs in counseling research. As previously discussed, the absence of any way to assess pretreatment equivalence renders the results from a posttest-only nonequivalent-groups design virtually uninterpretable. In addition, when using a pretest-posttest nonequivalent design, we recommend that the researcher attend carefully to how the naturally occurring groups were formed; in applied settings, there is usually some basis on which groupings are made. The more the researcher understands the basis on which the naturally occurring groupings were formed, the better he or she can examine or control for preexisting differences. This can be accomplished by using the selection variable as a covariate in the analysis.

When using the pretest-posttest nonequivalent-groups or cohort designs, we recommend that researchers consider using multiple pretest measures or multiple pretesting times to examine pretreatment equivalence. Using multiple measures or measurement periods strengthens the assertion of equivalence of conditions prior to intervention. Also, when using a cohort design the researcher must be vigilant in looking for any differences (other than the experimental manipulation) in what is occurring for subjects during the different time periods.

Finally, we believe that counseling researchers have underused time-series designs. These designs can be especially useful in the evaluation of new and innovative programs. Because time-series designs are often used with a single sample from a population, questions concerning their external validity exist. Therefore, researchers should consider replication when they plan their research.

CHAPTER 8

SINGLE-SUBJECT DESIGNS

The focus of counseling is on helping people cope more effectively with their environment; thus, most often counseling professionals are concerned with the welfare of individuals. However, methodological issues have plagued the development of a scientific analysis of individuals to the point where single-subject research designs have sometimes been regarded as unscientific. Error variance, extraneous variables, and numerous sources of bias—major threats to Kerlinger's "MAXMINCON" principle—have beset researchers using single-subjects. The purpose of this chapter is to discuss issues pertaining to experimental designs that use a single-subject, counselor-client dyad, group, or organization. The central thesis of this chapter is that single-subject designs, like other experimental designs, can play an important role in the pursuit of knowledge within the counseling profession. However, certain methodological considerations must be addressed within Kerlinger's "MAXMINCON" principle. Thus, this chapter will present a variety of approaches that can be considered single-subject designs. However, important distinctions must be made concerning different types of studies that use a single-subject, and concerning the varying amounts of experimental control that are used. Moreover, the researcher must be aware of the strengths and weaknesses of this particular design and qualify his or her conclusions accordingly (which is also the case with the other designs as well).

According to Hilliard (1993), counseling research typically examines either between-subject variation (intersubject research) or within-subject variation (intrasubject research). Hilliard classifies single-subject research as intrasubject research. In intersubject research, the researcher usually examines differences between or across subjects cross-sectionally. In intrasubject research, the variables of interest are assumed to vary within the subject over time. Therefore, intrasubject research involves a longitudinal perspective achieved by repeated measurements of the variable(s). As defined by Hilliard (1993), intrasubject research "refers to research that focuses on the temporal unfolding of variables within individual [subject]s" (p. 374). Hilliard argued that counseling researchers have either ignored intrasubject variability or attempted to assess it indirectly through intrasubject correlations. As pointed out by Gottman and Markman (1978, p. 28), "the question 'How does a particular therapist's behavior affect the client?' is a within-dyad question," not an intersubject question. Accordingly, intrasubject research addresses many of the questions that interest counseling researchers.

Hilliard (1993) describes three dimensions that can be used to describe types of intrasubject designs. The first is the type of data analyzed. Quantitative data can be categorical, ordinal, interval, or ratio. Qualitative data, in contrast, takes the form of text. The second dimension involves the operation of the independent variable; it can either be manipulated or simply observed. When the independent variable is manipulated, the study is considered experimental (Hilliard, 1993); the study is considered passive-observational when the independent variable is not manipulated by the researcher. The third dimension involves the focus of the research. As described by Hilliard, research can focus on either testing or generating hypotheses. Research that tests hypotheses has been referred to as the context of justification; research designed to generate hypotheses has been referred to as the context of discovery.

Hilliard (1993) used these three dimensions to define three categories of single-subject (intrasubject) designs: (a) single-case experiments, (b) single-case quantitative analyses, and (c) case studies. Even though both the single-case experiments and the single-case quantitative analyses use quantitative data, the major difference between these two designs is the treatment of the independent variable: In single-case experiments, the independent variable is manipulated, whereas in single-case quantitative analysis, the independent variable is observed. Only single-case experiments and single-case quantitative analyses are discussed in this chapter. (Case studies are examined in Chapter 10 on qualitative research.) Within the behavioral tradition, single-case experiments have been conducted almost exclusively. Many similarities exist between single-case experiments and single-case quantitative analyses, although the former are usually distinguished by comparisons between baselines and different treatment phases. Actually, the theoretical orientation (behavioral or nonbehavioral) need not be restricted to the type of single-subject design.

As a preface to both of these types of designs, the first section of this chapter provides a brief historical picture of designs using a single subject, in psychology as well as in counseling. Then we discuss the single-case quantitative designs, making a distinction between the traditional uncontrolled case study and the single-case quantitative design. We then focus on the single-case experimental designs, which are sometimes referred to as either behavioral intrasubject designs (Kazdin, 1980) or time-series designs (Drew, 1980). We discuss several defining features of these behaviorally oriented time-series designs, and then describe and illustrate two different types of designs: AB time series and multiple baseline. In the final section we discuss advantages and limitations of single-subject designs.

A HISTORICAL PERSPECTIVE OF SINGLE-SUBJECT DESIGNS

The study of individual subjects not only has a long history in psychology, but also has played a prominent role in the development of the applied professions. Perhaps the most extensive chronology of the historical sequence of events affecting the development of the single-subject design is to be found in Barlow and Hersen (1984); the interested reader is directed to that source for a more detailed account.

When psychology was initially developing into a science, the first experiments were performed on individual subjects. For example, during an autopsy of a man who had been unable to speak intelligibly, Broca discovered a lesion in the third frontal convolution of the cerebral cortex. The discovery that this area was the speech center of the brain led to the systematic examination of various destroyed brain parts and their relationship to behavior (Barlow & Hersen, 1984). Likewise, Wundt made pioneering advances in perception and sensation by examining the specific individuals' introspective experience of light and sound. Ebbinghaus, using a series of repeated measurements, made important advances in learning and memory by examining retention in specific individuals. Both Pavlov's and Skinner's conclusions were gleaned from experiments on single organisms, which subsequently were repeatedly replicated with other organisms. In short, important findings and advances in psychology with wide generalizability have been made from systematic observations of individuals.

At the beginning of the twentieth century, a number of advances facilitating the examination and comparison of groups of subjects were made. The invention of descriptive and inferential statistics not only facilitated group comparisons but also emphasized a philosophy of comparing the averages of groups rather than studying individuals. Barlow and Hersen (1984) noted that the pioneering work and philosophy of Fisher on inferential statistics was most likely influenced by the fact that Fisher was an agronomist. He was concerned with the farm plots that on average yielded better crops given certain fertilizers, growing conditions, and so forth; individual plants per se were not the focus. In short, as psychology developed in the middle of the twentieth century, the methods of inquiry were primarily influenced by statistical techniques such as the analysis of variance.

Meanwhile, in the early 1900s the primary, if not sole, methodology for investigating emotional and behavioral problems within the applied fields of psychiatry, counseling, and clinical psychology was the individual case study. Thus, cases such as Breuer's treatment of Anna O. and Freud's Frau Emmy formed the basis of "scientific" observations, which gradually grew into theories of personality and psychotherapy. These studies of therapeutically successful and unsuccessful cases were not tightly controlled investigations from a methodological standpoint. In addition, the typical practitioner was not well trained in the scientific method of critical thinking, and such practitioners extrapolated from the early case studies in fundamentally erroneous ways. Consequently, outlandish therapeutic conclusions were often reached; for example, Max (1935) concluded on the basis of uncontrolled case studies that electrical aversion therapy resulted in "95 percent relief" from the compulsions of homosexuality.

However, as the fields of counseling and clinical psychology developed in the 1940s and 1950s, more and more clinicians became aware of the inadequacies of the uncontrolled case study (Barlow & Hersen, 1984). Greater methodological sophistication led the applied psychologists to operationalize variables, to adopt the model of between-groups comparisons, and to adopt Fisher's methods of statistical analysis. Armed with these new methodological tools, researchers attempted to document the effectiveness of a wide range of therapeutic techniques, as well as the efficacy of therapy itself. These efforts were most likely fueled by the writing of Hans Eysenck, who repeatedly claimed that the profession did not have very compelling evidence for the effectiveness of therapy (Eysenck, 1952, 1961, 1965). In fact, Eysenck claimed that a client's chance of improving was about the same whether he or she entered therapy or was placed on a waiting list (Eysenck, 1952). Eysenck's charges concerning the lack of empirical support for therapy's effectiveness challenged the very existence of the therapeutic professions.

Although it has taken considerable time, researchers have begun to unravel the evidence concerning the efficiency of therapy. Paul (1967) noted that a global measurement of therapeutic effectiveness was inappropriate because of the overwhelming complexity and number of confounding variables. He suggested that investigators instead examine the question, "What treatment, by whom, is most effective for this individual with that specific problem, and under which set of circumstances?" (p. 111). Others noted that clients were erroneously conceptualized as being similar to each other (the uniformity myth; Kiesler, 1966) rather than as individuals with differences that clearly interact with counseling outcomes. Still other investigators noted that the group comparisons masked important variations across clients, specifically that some clients improved but others actually got worse (Truax & Carkhuff, 1967; Truax & Wargo, 1966). In short, although group comparison methods and inferential statistics substantially facilitated research on the effects of psychotherapy, researchers quickly encountered a number of confounding variables that underscored the complexity of the therapeutic experience.

In response to the confusion about and the complexity within the therapeutic process, other methodologies have been subsequently proposed and explored, such as naturalistic studies (Kiesler, 1971a), process research (Hoch & Zubin, 1964), and a more intensive, experimental single-subject design (Bergin & Strupp, 1970). On the surface it might seem that the applied professions have come full circle, returning to the study of the individual. This is true only in part, because there is considerably more methodological sophistication in scientifically studying an individual subject today than there was during the early part of the twentieth century.

SINGLE-CASE QUANTITATIVE DESIGNS

Perhaps the prototypical single-case quantitative design is the uncontrolled case study. "Case study" here refers to a study that simply consists of observations of an individual client, dyad, or group made under unsystematic and uncontrolled conditions, often in retrospect. Observations may be unplanned and may consist of "recollections" or intermittent records of statements or behaviors that seem to support a particular hypothesis. The lack of experimental control means that it is difficult to exclude many rival hypotheses that might be plausible in explaining the client's behavior, and thus this type of study provides ambiguous information that is difficult to interpret clearly.

A good example of the traditional case study is provided by Daniels (1976) in his investigation of the effects of thought stopping in treating obsessional thinking. He reported that he found the sequential use of several techniques to be beneficial with clients who wished to control depressing thoughts, obsessive thinking, constant negative rumination, or acute anxiety attacks. The sequential techniques used consisted of thought stopping (Wolpe, 1969), counting from 10 to 1 (Campbell, 1973), cue-controlled relaxation (Russell & Sipich, 1973), and a modification of covert information. Training consisted of three one-hour sessions to teach the client the various techniques. Daniels reported that these procedures were successful, and that clients responded positively to a "sense of control and immediate success" (p. 131). Although this report may be a useful source of ideas for generating hypotheses for future research, the lack of experimental control makes it difficult to interpret the results unambiguously. Clients may have felt compelled in some way to report success, or perhaps the successful effects were temporary and short-lived, or maybe techniques other than thought stopping were responsible for any client changes.

More recently, investigators have used single subjects in counseling research by examining variables much more intensively and rigorously. An intensive single-subject design is defined here as the systematic, repeated, and multiple observation of a client, dyad, or group to identify and compare relationships among variables. More specifically, observations regarding a clearly identifiable variable are made in a systematic manner and are typically are planned before the beginning of data collection. Many times these observations are made repeatedly to allow a comparison over time. Observations are often made from multiple sources, allowing a multimodal assessment, including, for instance, (a) cognitive, behavioral, and affective variables, and (b) process and outcome data. The data or observations are collected in such a way as to provide information about the relationships among certain variables or comparisons of variables within the same subject (especially pre-to-post). When comparisons are made within the same subject, the subject serves as his or her own control. In short, the intensive single-subject design is quantitative and is characterized by multiple observations over time that closely scrutinize some variables of interest within a client. The single-subject design involves comparisons of some sort, which is essential for establishing scientific evidence (Campbell & Stanley, 1963). The comparisons can be on the same variable across time, or across different variables.

Hill, Carter, and O'Farrell (1983) provide an example of an intensive single-subject design. They observed one client and one therapist over 12 sessions of insight-oriented therapy; measurements consisted of both process and outcome data obtained through subjective and objective means. More specifically, process measures were used to assess verbal behavior, anxiety, and verbal activity level (rated by judges) for both the client (college student) and counselor. In addition, both the client and counselor gave subjective impressions of session effectiveness and significant events for each session. The client and her mother, who was in close contact with the client, also made summary evaluative statements following treatment. Outcome measures, which consisted of the Hopkins Symptom Check-list, Tennessee Self-Concept Scale, Target Complaints, and satisfaction and improvement ratings, were collected immediately after the completion of coun-seling and at two-month and seven-month follow-ups. The first goal of the study was to describe the process and outcome of the therapeutic treatment; the second was to explore the mechanisms of change within the counseling process. With regard to the second goal, (a) comparisons were made between the best and worst sessions, (b) positive and negative events in each session for both client and coun-selor were analyzed, and (c) the immediate effects of counselor verbal behavior on client verbal responses were analyzed statistically through sequential analysis.

Outcome measures indicated that treatment was generally positive and resulted in improvement after the 12 sessions. Even though this improvement was maintained at the two-month follow-up, the client seemed to have relapsed at the seven-month follow-up. The process measures suggested that interpretations, direct feedback, Gestalt exercises, and examination of the therapeutic relationship (all within the context of good rapport and support) seemed to be important mechanisms of change. More recently, Wampold and Kim (1989) conducted more sophisticated sequential analyses on the process data and found that the coun-selor's minimal encourager responses reinforced description responses (story-telling) by the client, and that confrontation did not lead to opening up or greater client experiencing.

The study by Hill and colleagues (1983) nicely illustrates an intensive exam-ination of a single subject within a therapeutic context. A great deal of data were systematically collected from multiple sources (client, counselor, mother, judges) and across time. For example, over 11,000 responses were categorized in examin-ing client and counselor response modes. In addition, the objective and subjective data collected from various perspectives allowed comparisons to be made and subsequent conclusions to be drawn based on the convergence of a wide range of information, rather than on a single data point. It is important to note that the gen-eralizability of the conclusions obtained from this single case is unclear, and that replications are needed. Subsequent research by Hill and her colleagues has resulted in important replications as well as extensions (see Hill, Helms, Spiegel, & Tichenor, 1988; Hill, Helms, Tichenor, Spiegel, O'Grady, & Perry, 1988; Hill & O'Grady, 1985; O'Farrell, Hill, & Patton, 1986).

Martin, Goodyear, and Newton (1987) provide another good example of an intensive single-subject design with their study of a supervisory dyad during the course of an academic semester; their strategy merits attention. The authors employed an intensive single-subject design to compare the "best" and "worst" supervisory sessions as a means of increasing scientific knowledge about the supervisory process. Similar to Hill, Carter, and O'Farrell (1983), this study used multiple measures of process and outcome variables from multiple perspectives (trainee, supervisor, judges). Specifically, information from the supervisor and trainee perspective was obtained by assessing perceptions of themselves, each other, and the supervisory process. Each person (a) evaluated the quality of each session in terms of depth, smoothness, positivity, and arousal; (b) reported expectations about supervision in terms of interpersonal attraction, interpersonal sensitivity, and task orientation; (c) identified and discussed the occurrence of critical incidents within supervision; and (d) maintained a personal log of their reactions within and to supervision on a weekly basis. Two other measures, activity level and the categorization of interactions, were used to allow inferences about the supervisory process by objective judges. All these data were examined by comparing the "best" and "worst" sessions.

Conclusions from this study were based on the convergence of data from the multiple sources and made relative to findings from previous counseling and supervision research. For example, multiple sources of data suggested that the "best" session focused around clarifying the supervisory relationship very early in the semester (second session), a finding that substantiated and extended an earlier conclusion reached by Rabinowitz, Heppner, and Roehlke (1986). Another conclusion was that substantial differences in activity levels differentiated the "best" from the "worst" session, which is consistent with a pattern noted by Hill, Carter, and O'Farrell (1983), as well as by Friedlander, Thibodeau, and Ward (1985). Methodologically, the important point here is that conclusions and hypotheses that can direct future research were obtained by examining the convergence of data from multiple sources over time from an intensive single-subject design. Webb et al. (1965) called this convergence from multiple sources and multiple observations "triangulation." They maintained that multiple independent measures can provide a form of cross-validation.

Recently there has been a renewed interest in using single-subject designs in counseling research. For example, the *Journal of Consulting and Clinical Psychology* devoted a special section to articles illustrating single-case (subject) research (Jones, 1993); several of the articles used the single-case quantitative design. In general, these articles are noteworthy for their statistical sophistication in addressing questions of intrasubject variation. For example, Spence, Dahl, and Jones (1993) were interested in investigating associative freedom, an important concept in psychoanalytic theory. Specifically, they wanted to know whether counselor behavior influenced the degree of associative freedom in a client's speech. Free association is at the heart of psychoanalytic practice, because it is through this process that the client and counselor come to understand the client's unconscious processes. Spence, Dahl, and Jones (1993) operationalized associative freedom as the co-occurance rate (COR) for highly associated pairs of pronouns. Specifically, the COR for 14 pronoun pairs (for example, his/hers) were examined. COR was the number of times the first word (in this instance, his) was followed by the second word (hers) within a predetermined space of text (that is, everything the client said between two therapist interventions) divided by the total number of words spoken by the client in that space of text. Spence and colleagues (1993) also counted the number of counselor interventions per hour and rated 18 specific counselor interventions.

As hypothesized, associative freedom (measured as the COR of the 14 pronoun pairs) increased over the course of the counseling. In addition, the number of counselor interventions was positively correlated with associative freedom (COR). The major analysis in this study involved examining the relationship between the characteristics of the counselor's intervention and the client's level of associative freedom. This analysis was carried out by examining cross-correlations between the type of therapist interventions and the amount of client associative freedom.

Cross-correlations examine the time-lagged relationship between two variables, in this case type of counselor intervention and client associative freedom (COR). In time-series terminology Spence et al. (1993) predicted that the type of counselor intervention would lead to (be associated with) client associative freedom. The time-series analysis is a sophisticated method for answering this type of intrasubject (within-subject) question. In the terminology of time-series analysis, the relationship between two series (that is, counselor intervention and COR) is the cross-correlation function. The cross-correlation coefficients from Spence et al. (1993) were examined for the presence of significant lead/lag relationships.

SINGLE-CASE EXPERIMENTAL DESIGNS

Single-case experimental designs also examine the relationship between two or more variables, typically within one or a few subjects. Clearly, the largest single influence in the development of this design has come from researchers operating within an operant conditioning paradigm, using specific target behaviors and clearly identifiable treatment phases, although the utility of the intrasubject design need not be restricted to that theoretical orientation. Moreover, these designs revolve around multiple or continuous measurements of a dependent variable. Comparisons are made on the dependent variable across specific treatment phases, which makes these intrasubject designs a special type of within-subjects designs (see Chapter 6). The multiple measurements are often referred to as time-series designs, which have been used in economics for almost half a century (Davis, 1941). A considerable amount of writing has been done on the single-case experimental design, most notably in the past 20 years. Readers interested in this topic might examine Baer, Wolf, and Risley, 1968; Barlow and Hersen, 1984; Kazdin, 1978; Kratochwill, 1978; and Levin and Kratochwill, 1992.

In this section we first discuss several common features of intrasubject designs (Drew, 1980; Kazdin, 1980). Then we describe and illustrate two different types of intrasubject designs: AB time series and multiple baseline.

Common Features of Single-Case Experimental Designs

The first common characteristic of single-case experimental designs involves the specification of treatment goals. Because intrasubject designs grew out of an operant conditioning paradigm, most studies have specified behavioral goals, often referred to as "targets" or "target behaviors." In essence, target behaviors are the dependent variables of the investigation. The treatment goal can consist of cognitions, affective reactions, behaviors, physiological responses, or personality characteristics. If systems (groups, families, organizations) are used as the subject of the design, then system characteristics (communication patterns, cohesion, involvement) can be designated as treatment goals.

The second defining feature of intrasubject designs is the repeated measurement of the dependent variables over time. The measurement might occur on a weekly basis, or daily, or even several times a day. Many times this assessment process starts before the initiation of treatment, in which case it is referred to as a baseline assessment. Because this assessment process is continuous (or nearly continuous), the researcher can examine the patterns in the dependent variable over time. The independent variable is typically a treatment intervention, often referred to as the intervention. The multiple measurement of the intrasubject design is in stark contrast to other research designs that might collect a single data point before and after an intervention.

The third characteristic of single-case experimental designs is the inclusion of different treatment phases, each representing a different experimental condition. One method of phase specification is to designate a baseline and a treatment phase. Baseline data are collected before treatment initiation and are used both to describe the current state of functioning and make predictions about subsequent performance. The second method of defining time periods involves the random assignment of different treatments to different time periods (days, sessions). The basic purpose of changing from one phase to another is to demonstrate change due to the onset of the independent variable or intervention.

The stability of baseline data is an important feature of most intrasubject designs. Change cannot be detected after the onset of an intervention if the baseline data are unstable—that is, are either increasing, decreasing, or lack consistency. Thus, before the researcher can ascribe causality to an intervention, he or she must obtain an accurate and stable assessment of the dependent variable before the introduction of the intervention. This is especially the case when a baseline-versus-treatment-intervention-phase comparison is used. This is not true, however, in designs that randomly assign treatments to phases.

AB Time-Series Designs

There are many variations on the AB time-series design. Here we discuss three specific designs: AB, ABAB, and randomized AB.

The AB Design

The AB design is basically a two-phase experiment; the A phase is a baseline period, and the B phase is an intervention phase. Typically, multiple measurements or observations are taken during each phase. For example, each phase might be six weeks long, with two observations each week. These multiple observations enable the researcher to ascertain first of all if the baseline period is stable, which allows a suitable assessment of the subject before the intervention. If the baseline period is unstable (that is, measurements are accelerating or decelerating), it is often difficult to draw inferences about the effects of the intervention. Multiple observations after the intervention enable a thorough assessment of the effects of the intervention over time. If only one observation per phase were collected, the study would basically be a one-group pretest-posttest design (see Chapter 6), which typically has a number of threats to internal validity. The multiple measurements within an AB design, referred to as a time-series format, provide greater stability over time. The AB design, like the traditional within-subjects design previously discussed, has the subject serve as his or her own control or comparison. Thus, the basic comparison is between the A phase (baseline) and the B phase (intervention) within the same subject. If a researcher measured only the B phase, he or she would have no basis for comparison and would find it impossible to infer any effects due to the intervention.

Wampold and Freund (1991) noted that the use of statistical methods to analyze the data generated by single-subject designs is controversial. Rather than employing statistical techniques, researchers plot the raw data and make inferences from the graph. Such a visual analysis, however, is imprecise and can be unreliable and systematically biased (for example, see DeProspero & Cohen, 1979; Furlong & Wampold, 1982; Wampold & Furlong, 1981a). Consequently, a variety of statistical tests have been proposed for single-subject designs (see Kazdin, 1980; Wampold & Freund, 1991). The interested reader might examine statistical procedures such as the two standard deviation rule (Gottman, McFall, & Barnett, 1969), the relative frequency procedure (Jayaratne & Levy, 1979), lag analysis (Gottman, 1973, 1979), Markov chain analysis (Lichtenberg & Hummel, 1976; Tracey, 1985), time-series analysis (see, for example, Glass, Willson, & Gottman, 1974), randomization tests (see, for example, Edgington, 1980, 1982, 1987; Wampold & Worsham, 1986), the split middle technique (White, 1974), and the binomial test (Kazdin, 1980).

In sum, the AB design is a two-phase experiment with a single-subject (or group, or family) that typically involves multiple observations over time. The basic comparison is between phases A and B; each subject thus serves as his or her own control or comparison.

Consider the following example. Yalom (1985) has suggested that an agenda-go-round (in which the therapist asks each member at the beginning of the session to set an agenda for himself or herself for that session) can be used to improve group cohesion and member involvement. A researcher might examine this suggestion by using an AB design. This could be done by identifying a therapy group, and for the first ten group sessions measuring the level of cohesion and member involvement in each session. This would be the A phase, or baseline. For the next ten sessions the researcher could have the group leader use Yalom's agenda-go-round technique and once again measure cohesion and member involvement for each session. This would be the B phase, or intervention. The researcher could compare cohesion and member involvement during the A and B phases to see if the agenda-go-round intervention had an effect. A graph of this design is shown in Figure 8-1; it seems apparent that the agenda-go-round intervention did have an effect. This type of obvious difference is not always apparent in graphic analyses.

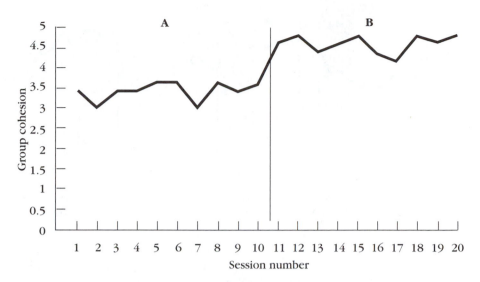

F I G U R E 8-1
AB design examining group cohesion (measured on a five-point Likert, with 1 = low cohesion, 5 = high cohesion) by session number (the agenda-go-round exercise was instituted at session 11).

A problem with this simple AB design is that the researcher cannot rule out threats to internal validity from history and maturation as possible explanations for the results. (For instance, most groups increase in cohesion over time.) Thus, although the multiple measurements strengthen this study over the one-group pretest-posttest design, this particular time-series design contains some threats to internal validity. Expansions of the AB design, including the ABAB design, were developed to circumvent some of these weaknesses.

The ABAB Design

Whereas the AB design is basically a two-phase experiment, the ABAB is a four-phase experiment, frequently referred to as a reversal design. In essence, the ABAB examines the effect of a treatment (or independent variable) by either presenting or withdrawing the variable during different phases in an attempt to provide unambiguous evidence of the causal effect of the independent variable. The ABAB design starts with a period of baseline data gathering (A_1) and a treatment phase (B_1), and then it returns to a baseline period (A_2) where the intervention is withdrawn and then a second treatment phase (B_2).

The assumption underlying this reversal is that if the independent variable caused the change in the dependent variable in the B_1 phase, then a removal of the independent variable should return the subject to a level similar to the baseline phase. Moreover, if the reversal in fact results in a return to the baseline, then readministering the independent variable at B_2 will serve as a replication, further strengthening the inferred causal relationship. If the behavior at A_2 does not revert to the baseline levels, then a causal relationship cannot be inferred between the independent and dependent variable because other (unknown) variables may

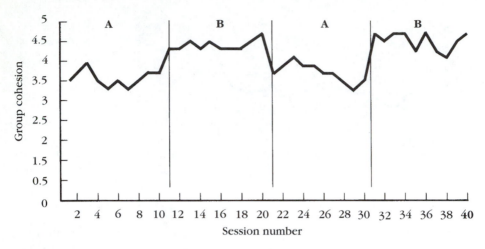

FIGURE 8-2

ABAB design examining group cohesion by session number (the agenda-go-round exercise was instituted at session 11, withdrawn at session 21, and reinstituted at session 31).

account for the change. Thus, in the agenda-setting example given earlier, an ABAB design would be as follows: Ten group sessions in which the researcher collected the baseline cohesion and member involvement data (A_1) would be followed by ten sessions in which the group leader implemented the agenda-go-round intervention, with continued data collection (B_1), followed by another ten group sessions of data collection only (A_2), and then a final ten sessions with the agenda-go-round intervention reinstituted (B_2). Figure 8-2 presents a graph of data collected from this ABAB design. Because group cohesion increased in both B phases, we can infer that the agenda-go-round exercise caused an improvement in group cohesion.

Patterson and Forgatch (1985) used an ABAB design to examine the relationship between therapist behavior and client resistance. (This study is also a good illustration of programmatic research that uses both descriptive and experimental designs to study a phenomenon.) First, using a descriptive research strategy, Patterson and Forgatch examined the likelihood of client resistance following various types of counselor behavior (for example, supportive or teaching responses). In essence, they found that client resistance following therapist teaching responses was significantly higher than the clients' baseline resistance. Because this first study was only descriptive, the authors could not infer that therapist teaching caused client resistance. To examine this causal hypothesis, the researchers used an ABAB design. Six counselors met with their clients for videotaped sessions. The counselors started with a baseline phase (A_1) in which they interacted with their clients without using teaching interventions; this was followed by a treatment phase (B_1) in which the counselors increased their use of teaching responses. Then a second baseline phase followed in which the counselors returned to interacting without the teaching responses (A_2); and then there was a final treatment phase (B_2) in which the counselors once again increased their use of teaching responses. The results of this ABAB study showed that the counselors did give significantly more teaching responses during the two treatment phases, indicating that the experimental manipulation was successful (such a procedural check is referred to as a manipulation check). More important, the clients were more resistant during the treatment phases (B_1 and B_2). These data more strongly suggests that therapist teaching behavior caused client resistance.

There are three problems with the ABAB design. The first problem is a statistical one. Most authors and editors want to report some statistical test that describes the amount of difference between the two phases (A and B; see previous references regarding statistical issues for these designs). When reported, this test is usually a t test or an F test. Both t and F tests, however, assume independent observations, and this is not the case in the ABAB design (Wampold & Freund, 1991). A second problem with the ABAB design is the possible presence of carryover effects (that is, effects from the manipulation at phase B_1 that affect A_2 or B_2). It could be that the effects of the B_1 intervention are irreversible and cannot be withdrawn. For example, if the dependent variable involves learning or skill acquisition (for example, study skills such as test-wiseness), it is difficult to reverse these treatments and return the subject to the A_1 level. Obviously, there are many interventions for which treatments are reversible and carryover effects are not present. However, in some ABAB designs, the interventions are not reversible and carryover effects present problems in drawing inferences and in isolating causal relationships. Finally, there are therapeutic situations in which it is undesirable or unethical to reverse the treatment phase, and both the client and counselor may be reluctant to withdraw an effective treatment. These concerns, among others, have led authors (see Edgington, 1987) to call for the use of randomized single-subject experiments or randomized AB designs.

Randomized AB Designs

There are many tests of randomization for intrasubject designs (see Edgington, 1980, 1987; Wampold & Furlong, 1981b; Wampold & Worsham, 1986). Even though these statistical tests are beyond the scope of this book, we present one example to introduce you to the design possibilities within randomized AB designs.

The randomized AB design involves two phases that are repeated in a randomized fashion such that the presence of an A or B phase at any point in time is dependent on random assignment. For example, the randomized AB design for examining the effects of an agenda-go-round exercise on group cohesion and member involvement might look like this:

$$
\begin{array}{cccccccccccccccccccc}
A & A & B & A & B & A & B & B & B & A & B & A & A & B & B & A & B & A & B & A \\
\end{array}
$$
Session 1 2 3 4 5 6 7 8 9 10 11 12 13 14 15 16 17 18 19 20

In this example, A represents sessions in which the agenda-go-round is not used, and B represents sessions in which this exercise is used. Because the occurrence of A and B phases is random, randomization tests or traditional parametric tests can be used (Edgington, 1980) to compare cohesion and involvement scores for the A and B sessions.

This design has a second advantage: It enables the researcher to analyze carryover effects by setting up the following simple 2×2 factorial design.

Phase	Preceded by phase A	Preceded by phase B
A	(1) Data from sessions 2, 13	(2) Data from sessions 4, 6, 10, 12, 16, 18, 20
B	(3) Data from sessions 3, 5, 7, 11, 14, 17, 19	(4) Data from sessions 8, 9, 15

Data are assigned to cells based on whether they come from phase A or B and on which phase preceded the phase in question. For example, the first cell in the table contains the data from all phase-A sessions (all sessions without the agenda-go-round) that were preceded by a phase-A session (session without the agenda-go-round). In a like manner, the second cell of the table contains all data from phase-A sessions (without agenda-go-round) that were preceded by a phase-B session (with agenda-go-round). A factorial ANOVA using this setup would provide a main effect for phase A versus B, a main effect for preceding phase (preceding A versus preceding B), and an interaction effect for phase × preceding phase. The interaction analysis directly tests for carryover effects.

Jauquet (1987) actually used this randomized AB design to examine the effects of an agenda-go-round on group cohesion and member involvement. The leader of a training group for graduate students either did (B) or did not (A) begin group sessions with an agenda-go-round exercise, based on a random AB schedule. Because research by Kivlighan and Jauquet (1990) had shown that agenda quality was related to cohesion, cohesion at each meeting was measured by member ratings on the Engaged and Avoiding scales of the Group Climate Questionnaire (MacKenzie, 1983). Involvement was rated by objective observers who viewed videotapes of the session, unaware of the purpose of the study. A 2 (with agenda-go-round, without agenda-go-round) × 2 (preceded by an agenda go-round, not preceded by an agenda-go-round) ANOVA revealed no main or interaction effects for observer-rated involvement. Likewise, a similar 2×2 ANOVA revealed no main effects for phases or preceding phases on the Engaged and Avoiding scales. There was, however, a significant interaction effect on the Engaged and Avoiding scales. An examination of the means showed that sessions without agenda-go-round that followed agenda-go-round sessions were rated by the group members as more engaged and less avoidant than any of the other combinations. This finding suggests that a periodic use of the agenda-go-round intervention may enhance members' perception of cohesion in groups.

Not only is Jauquet's study important in demonstrating the usefulness of a randomized AB design from a statistical analysis standpoint, it also demonstrates the usefulness of examining for carryover effects. A simple *t* test comparing the results during the A and B phases would have suggested that the agenda-go-round intervention did not have an effect on the dependent variable. The factorial analysis suggested that the simple question of whether or not to use an agenda-go-round is misleading. Instead, Jauquet's study suggested that the more appropriate question is when and how much to use the agenda-go-round. In a nonrandomized ABAB design, the researcher would never have been alerted to this possible interaction effect.

Some final comments about the AB time-series designs seem warranted. First, although we have discussed and illustrated AB designs as having only two (A and B) phases, this need not be the case. A design could contain three (A, B, and C) or more phases. A three-phase design could compare a baseline phase to two different treatments, or it could compare three different levels of an independent variable. The basic logic of the AB design remains the same no matter how many phases are involved; the researcher is attempting to isolate the effects of the independent variable by examining different levels (or trends) across different phases.

Many times AB designs are not considered because of possible ethical concerns. For instance, one may question whether it is appropriate to withdraw a treatment that seems to be having a positive effect on a client. Although this is an excellent question, it is important to note this is the same dilemma faced by members of the medical profession in the early 1960s in prescribing thalidomide for morning sickness; unfortunately, they decided not to withhold treatment because of the perceived effectiveness of the drug. In short, it is important to adequately test the efficacy of our counseling interventions empirically before assuming their effectiveness. But suppose for a moment that we do have strong empirical support for a particular treatment. Even though withholding treatment is a valid concern if the researcher is faced with a question of treatment or no treatment for a client, the time series AB designs can be modified to compare treatments, as in an ABC design. This situation probably more accurately reflects the reality of the practitioner, for rarely must a clinician decide between a single intervention and no treatment at all, but rather among alternative interventions. Modified AB time-series designs that still allow basic comparisons between phases can be particularly helpful in this situation.

Another concern with AB designs is related to carryover effects of an intervention and the perceived unsuitability of some variables for some theoretical orientations. For example, Gelso (1979) reasoned that one cannot reverse a client's insight (the theoretical effect of an appropriate interpretation), and thus the AB designs would not be well suited for such content. We believe that the AB designs can be successfully applied to a wider range of topics than is typically acknowledged, although the researcher may need to be creative in adapting the AB designs. For instance, we believe that the interpretation-insight link is not a one-time event, but rather that multiple interpretations lead to increasing client insight. One current debate in analytic psychotherapy concerns the relative importance of here-and-now versus there-and-then interpretations. This could be studied in a randomized AB design by randomly altering the focus of a counselor's interpretations across sessions. In the then-and-there condition, the counselor's interpretations might focus on how the relationship the client is talking about is similar to past relationships. Conversely, in the here-and-now condition, the interpretations might focus on how those events (or feelings or thoughts) apply to the counseling relationship. The point is that AB designs are not only appropriate for behavioral researchers, but can be fruitfully employed within other theoretical orientations as well.

Multiple-Baseline Designs

The second type of intrasubject design is the multiple-baseline design. The essential feature of this design is that data are recorded on more than one dependent variable, or target behavior, simultaneously. Like the AB designs there is continual collection of data, but in multiple-baseline designs there are two or more data collection baselines on different dependent measures. The intervention being examined is applied to the different dependent measures at different times. If the intervention is truly the causal agent, there should be change on the dependent variable that was targeted by the intervention, but not on the nontargeted dependent variables. Thus, whereas the ABAB design attempts to identify causal relationships by withdrawing the intervention and reversing the change, the multiple-baseline design attempts to determine causality by identifying changes in some but not all of the multiple dependent measures. In short, the basic assumption is that with several dependent measures, one or more of these variables can serve as controls while the intervention is simultaneously applied to one of the dependent measures. One of the problems with the multiple-baseline approach is the possible nonindependence of the dependent variables; thus, when the intervention is targeted at one of the dependent variables but all of the dependent variables change, the cause of the change is unclear (more on this later).

There are three different versions of the multiple-baseline design. The first variation involves collecting data on two or more dependent variables in the same individual. For example, a researcher may want to examine the effects of therapeutic homework assignments on the amount of family communication. To use a multiple-baseline design, he or she would have to identify at least two behaviors to measure family communication, perhaps (a) the amount of time after dinner the husband and wife spend talking and (b) the amount of time after dinner the parents spend talking with the children. Like the AB designs, the multiple-baseline design starts with a period of baseline assessment. In our example, this would involve daily recordings of interaction time between (a) spouses and (b) parents and children. Next, the intervention is targeted at one of these dependent variables; a homework assignment is initiated that is designed to increase interspousal communication. The basic assumption in this example is that the second behavior (amount of communication between parents and children) serves as a control for the first behavior (amount of communication between spouses). If the intervention is causally related to interspousal communication, there should be a change in the amount of time the husband and wife spend communicating but not in the amount of time the parents spend communicating with the children. As with AB designs, data are collected on these two behaviors for a specified period of time—say, one week. Finally, a homework assignment can be designed to increase parent-child communication. A change in the amount of time spent in parent-child communication would be expected to occur only after the introduction of this intervention. Sometimes three to five different behaviors are identified and targeted over successive time periods to assess the effects of a particular intervention. Continuation of a stable baseline in the behaviors not targeted for intervention (that is, the controls) indicates the absence of coincidental influences other than the experimental intervention.

The second variation of the multiple-baseline design is to identify the same response across different subjects. Returning to our previous example about agenda setting, a researcher may want to test Yalom's (1985) hypothesis concerning the relationship between the quality of group member agendas and their subsequent involvement in the group. Specifically, Yalom stated that group members will initiate more high-level interactions when the agendas for the group are realistic, interpersonal, and here-and-now oriented. The researcher could begin by making a baseline assessment of each group member's interactions over the first five group sessions. He or she could then begin to train individual group members to set realistic, interpersonal, and here-and-now agendas. Only one group member would be trained at a time, and the initiation of the training with the individual group members would be staggered; the researcher might train a different member every fifth group session. A change in any individual's quality of group participation would be expected to occur contingent on his or her receiving the agenda training, whereas no change would be expected in those not trained. The basic assumption in this example is that individuals can serve as controls when they have not received the intervention. Data collection is continuous, and only those individuals who have received the intervention are expected to change on the dependent measure. A possible source of contamination in this example is that subjects who have not received training might learn how to set effective agendas by observing their peers who have received training.

The third variation of the multiple-baseline design is to identify a given response for one subject but across different situations. As in all illustrations of the multiple-baseline design, a subject can refer to an individual, a group, a classroom, or a larger unit. Suppose a researcher wants to examine the effects of token reinforcement (the independent variables) on a child interacting with peers (the dependent variable). The amount of interaction with peers could be observed both before and after school on the playground, during a baseline period. The researcher could then begin token reinforcement of prosocial interactions only before school. The researcher would then expect to find a change in the amount of interaction with peers in the morning but not in the afternoon. Later the token reinforcement could be done in the afternoon also, and a consequent change in this baseline would then be expected.

Because the logic of the multiple-baseline design requires that the researcher show changes in one assessed behavior while another assessed behavior remains constant, one of the main concerns in using this type of design is the independence of the dependent variables. If there is a relationship between two or more of the behaviors, then a change in one behavior may well lead to a change in the other. If two behaviors show simultaneous change but only one received the independent variable, then it is impossible to rule out threats to internal validity such as history and maturation. Such unintended changes in baselines seriously jeopardize the strength of the multiple-baseline design and typically produce a study with uninterpretable results.

One way to guard against this complication is to carefully assess the independence of the behaviors, perhaps by correlating the baseline behaviors (Christensen, 1980). Another possible solution is the use of several dependent variables; Kazdin and Kopel (1975) recommended using four or more variables. By increasing the number of baselines, the researcher can guard against the possibil-ity that two of the baselines are dependent on each other.

A final comment about multiple-baseline designs seems warranted. In review-ing articles from major counseling journals for inclusion as examples in this sec-tion, the authors were not able to find any recent studies using multiple-baseline designs. This absence is in stark contrast to journals in clinical psychology, and especially the behaviorally oriented journals (for example, *Behavior Therapy, Behavioral Assessment,* and *Journal of Applied Behavior Analysis*). This suggests that this design is being used infrequently in counseling research.

ADVANTAGES AND LIMITATIONS OF SINGLE-SUBJECT DESIGNS

Single-subject designs have a number of advantages and limitations, which we will initially discuss in a rather simple and absolute sense. In weighing these advan-tages and limitations, it is imperative to distinguish between the uncontrolled case study on the one hand, and the intensive single-subject design and single-case experimental design on the other. In our view, much less can be learned from the uncontrolled case study because of the multitude of rival hypotheses. Conversely, the comparisons and control in the intensive single-subject design and single-case experimental design provide stronger empirical support and thus lend greater util-ity to the research design. It is also important to note that the advantages and lim-itations need to be considered relative to two variables: the existing scientific knowledge pertaining to a specific question and the previous research method-ologies employed in examining that particular research question.

Advantages

Single-subject designs are versatile. Here we discuss five uses: as a means of col-lecting information and ideas, and generating hypotheses about the therapeutic process; as a means of testing therapeutic techniques; as a means of testing new methodologies; as a means of studying individuals and rare phenomena; and as a means of providing exemplars and counterinstances.

A Means of Collecting Information and Ideas, and Generating Hypotheses about the Therapeutic Process

Although the traditional between-groups design has been useful in examining out-comes in psychotherapy, a prominent difficulty has been the obscuring of individ-ual variations in group averages. The therapeutic process is complex and highly variable. Clients differ from each other in significant ways; they are not uniform (Kiesler, 1966). Rather, clients process information about themselves, their experi-ential worlds, and counseling in idiographic ways, and even differently from one time to the next. The same can be said of counselors; therapists not only differ in important ways from each other, they also are different from one time to another.

The counselor-client relationship is equally complex and idiographic. Thus, in the context of the complex and detailed process of therapy, intensive single-subject methodologies in particular are ideally suited for microscopic analyses and for expanding scientific knowledge. In fact, some 30 years ago Bergin and Strupp (1970) maintained that the intensive single-subject design would be one of the primary strategies to clarify the mechanisms of change within the therapeutic process. More recently, intensive single-subject designs have also been recommended for obtaining an in-depth analysis of the therapeutic process (Bergin & Lambert, 1978; Gelso, 1979; Hill, Carter, & O'Farrell, 1983; Resnikoff, 1978).

Both the intensive single-subject design and the single-case experimental design offer unique opportunities to carefully scrutinize aspects of the therapeutic process in depth. Methodologies that use very time-consuming procedures such as interpersonal process recall (Kagan, 1975) or assessing cognitive structures by using an associative network (Martin, 1985) are often impossible when large numbers of subjects are involved. However, these procedures are more feasible when only one or a few clients are involved. In a way, the single-subject design can allow for a more complete description of what happens in counseling and the mechanisms involved in change. The studies mentioned earlier by Hill, Carter, and O'Farrell (1983) and Martin, Goodyear, and Newton (1987) provide good examples of microscopic analyses of variables involved in the change process. These studies provide important in-depth information that contributes to our scientific knowledge base about counseling and supervision. More specifically, Hill and colleagues (1983) noted that intensive single-subject designs (a) permit a more adequate description of what actually happens between a counselor and client, (b) facilitate more integration of process data with positive or negative outcomes, (c) allow a close examination of the change process in the therapeutic relationship, and (d) allow outcome measures to be tailored to an individual client's problems.

Tracey (1986) provides a good example of using a single-subject design to initially examine a relatively new counseling variable, topic determination, followed by a larger study using a between-groups design. Topic determination pertains to reaching agreement between the counselor and client on what is to be discussed and how it is to be discussed. In his first study, Tracey (1986) compared four continuing counseling dyads (two dyads were determined to be successful while two dyads were identified as unsuccessful) and two dyads that had terminated prematurely. All dyads involved nonpsychotic clients seen at a university counseling center using a time-limited therapy format. Consistent with his hypothesis, the premature termination dyads had lower levels of topic determination than the continuing dyads. Tracey then conducted a second study in which he examined 18 dyads (6 who terminated prematurely, and 12 who were continuing). The results from his between-groups analysis confirmed his first study in identifying a significant relationship between premature termination and topic determination.

The single-subject design also provides a rich source of data that can spark ideas or hypotheses. For example, a case study approach, even though it typically is uncontrolled, can offer suggestive data about some aspect of counseling. Suppose a therapist has developed a special interest in counseling clients who have an especially difficult time with grieving the loss of a significant other. As the therapist's skills are honed over time, she begins to detect certain patterns in the grief victims she works with in therapy, such as overdependence and problems with intimacy. The therapist then collects some objective test data with the next client to check her hunches, which are verified. Thus, the case study approach, first informally with individual clients and later with more objective test data, can be a rich source of ideas and hypotheses for more systematic research. It is important for the therapist to be cognizant, however, that such observations and ideas are subject to information processing biases and subjective inference processes (see Turk & Salovey, 1988). Although such observations obviously do not provide rigorous scientific data, nonetheless important information can be obtained from single-subject studies of some aspect of counseling, even from a relatively uncontrolled case study.

It is important to qualify our comments regarding the use of single-subject designs in generating ideas. Historically, individual cases not only have been the source of ideas, but also have been influential in the formulation of personality and psychotherapy theories. For example, Freud's psychoanalytic theory depended heavily on his observations of individual clients. Cases such as those of Ann O., Frau Emmy von N., and Fraulein Elizabeth von R. greatly affected the development of Freud's ideas regarding catharsis, repression, and free association (Monte, 1980). Thus, the core of Freud's psychoanalytic theory was based largely on observations from case studies. Still, generalizing from uncontrolled case studies to the development of entire theoretical models is extremely suspect and generally ill advised. The process of collecting suggestive information and generating hypotheses is only a small part of a broader process of developing theories.

A Means of Testing Therapeutic Techniques

Single-subject designs provide a useful means to test the effects of specific therapeutic techniques. The testing of techniques might happen at several levels: (a) the discovery of a new technique, (b) an intentional examination of a relatively new technique, (c) the application of an established technique to a new population or treatment situation, and (d) an in-depth examination of well-established technique.

Occasionally therapists will discover new techniques through a trial-and-error process with individual clients. Breuer's work with Anna O. resulted in the discovery of a "talking cure" or catharsis. In essence, Breuer found through trial and error that some of Anna's symptoms were relieved or disappeared simply by talking about them (Breuer & Freud, 1955). George Kelley, in part out of boredom with the Freudian interpretations, began fabricating "insights" and "preposterous interpretations," and discovered that often clients could change their lives in important ways if they believed these "alternative constructions of the world" (Monte, 1980, p. 434). Likewise, Rogers abandoned the traditional directive and diagnostically oriented therapeutic style after a dismal therapeutic failure in which a client reentered and redirected therapy by initiating a discussion of her troubled marriage. Rogers discovered that "it is the client who knows what hurts, what direction to go, what problems are crucial, and what experiences have been deeply buried" (Rogers, 1961, pp. 11–12). In short, therapists often stumble onto or create new techniques through their therapeutic work with individual clients. The intentional and consistent examination of new techniques within the informal case study, as well as the more formal single-subject design, can yield useful information about the counseling process. Thus, new observations by the therapist might be informally or formally tested with additional clients to further determine the effectiveness and generalizability of the technique.

The single-subject design can also be used effectively to test the application of an established technique with a new problem or a new population. Kazdin (1980) noted that the extension of a given technique to a new problem is really quite common in the literature. For example, systematic desensitization has been found to be applicable to a wide range of phobias or fears, such as fear of heart attacks (Furst & Cooper, 1970) and fear of sharks (Krop & Krause, 1976).

Finally, the single-subject design also lends itself well to an in-depth examination of the effectiveness of a certain technique. For example, a great deal of information could be collected about how a client is processing or reacting to repeated use of a certain technique, such as the Gestalt empty-chair technique, counselor touch, or counselor self-disclosure. Thus, in-depth information could be collected on the use of a specific technique over time.

A Means of Testing New Methodologies

The single-subject design is especially well suited to testing new research methodologies. This design allows the investigator to "experiment" in a way with a new methodology or procedure. The investigator can determine whether a new methodology provides new or more useful information, or whether some aspect of counseling is better understood in some way.

Several investigations by Jack Martin provide excellent examples of testing new methodologies by using single-subject designs. Martin has conceptualized counseling through a cognitive mediational paradigm (Martin, 1984), in which he maintained the necessity of examining the cognitive processes of clients. Martin suggested that the information contained in a client's cognitive structures, and the organization of that information, would have considerable appeal to researchers of counseling outcomes. Using an information-processing perspective, Martin tested a methodology to assess a client's cognitive structures (Martin, 1985). At the end of each session with a client, fictitiously called Carla, he would ask her to relax and then give the first associations to the following words: problem, Bill (fictitious name for her husband), and Carla. As the client mentioned specific word associations, Martin wrote each on a small square. After Carla had responded to the three memory probes, she was asked to arrange the labels on a laminated board using distance and drawing lines to symbolically depict relationships among the words. Martin found that this procedure produced "an incredible amount of data" (p. 558). The pre-to postcounseling diagrams revealed that Carla had acquired important knowledge about battering (the presenting problem) and her options concerning this particular problem (for example, take advantage of a Women Center's program). Carla's outcomes also reflected important changes in her affective processes, from passive, reactive emotions (such as guilt or shame) to more active emotions (such as hope or anger). Martin (1985) thus concluded that this particular method of assessing a client's cognitive structures provided very useful data that nicely captured some of the richness and subjective nature of the change process in counseling. Thus, this particular single-subject study provided important information about a new methodological procedure. Given the idiosyncratic nature of the data from this new method, group data would initially be quite overwhelming and not lend itself well to "averaging" across clients. The important point is that the results of Martin's initial study provided empirical support for additional examination of this new methodology.

A Means of Studying Individuals and Rare Phenomena

A major difficulty noted by many applied researchers and practitioners is the obscuring of individual variations and outcomes when subjects are examined in groups and their data are simply "averaged." In fact, trying to think about the "average" or "typical" client is generally not very useful when developing interventions. Clients are seldom homogeneous or "uniform."

By contrast, the single-subject design is particularly well suited to describing the idiosyncracies of individual clients, because of its intensive and often microscopic analyses. Thus, the single-subject design can be considered a useful tool for examining change within a single individual. In fact, Bergin and Strupp (1970) proposed that the single-subject design be used as the primary methodology to isolate specific mechanisms of change. The case study approach can provide some information as well, but most often it lacks experimental control, which confounds even tentative conclusions.

The single-subject design also lends itself to more qualitative approaches in studying individuals (see Neimeyer & Resnikoff, 1982; Polkinghorne, 1984). In this way, the single-subject design can be used to collect data about the "thinking frameworks" of individuals (Edgington, 1987; Neimeyer & Resnikoff, 1982) or higher mental processes (Wundt, 1916). Polkinghorne (1984) aptly suggested that human action and decision making, which are central to the therapeutic and counseling processes, appear to be related to a "means-end rationality" or mode of processing information. Heppner and Krauskopf (1987) noted similar thinking processes by using an information-processing model to describe client problem solving in a counseling context. The single-subject design may be particularly well suited for gathering information about (a) how clients process information, (b) the thinking steps or means involved in reaching some end or goal (logically or illogically), (c) an individual's plans and intentions (Heppner & Krauskopf, 1987; Howard, 1985), and (d) how such plans affect the processing of information and subsequent behavior. The complexity of such information processing may be examined more feasibly via a single-subject design, at least initially. In short, single-subject designs are useful to study individuals, particularly as counselors use some of the more qualitative approaches in examining higher mental processes.

The single-subject design is particularly useful in studying rare phenomena, such as multiple personality. Kazdin (1980) illustrates this particular advantage of single-subject designs in a discussion of the well-publicized report of the "three faces of Eve" (Thigpen & Cleckley, 1954, 1957). Eve represented a rare personality and offered a unique opportunity to study this phenomenon.

In addition to rare phenomena, the single-subject design can also be used to study relatively low-frequency occurrences, such as male anorexics and international college students under situational stress (for example, Iranian students during the Iran Hostage Crisis of 1980, and aborted grief reactions; see Corazzini, 1980). Although a typical university counseling center usually has a very broad range of clients, it is often difficult to study infrequent occurrences in a group comparison format. It is not usually feasible, or ethical, to withhold treatment until enough of these low-occurrence clients seek counseling to enable random assignment of clients to groups, and so forth. Thus, the single-subject design is useful to investigate various idiosyncracies or commonalities across clients with similar presenting problems, such as clients with aborted grief reactions.

A Means of Providing Exemplars and Counterinstances

The single-subject design can be used to provide exemplars to highlight findings, particularly if these findings run counter to existing beliefs or theories (in which case exemplars become counterinstances). Given that the intensive and single-case experimental designs generally provide stronger experimental control, these findings obviously lend themselves better to such highlighting.

More specifically, the findings from a single-subject design can be used to provide data in support of a particular point, argument, or theory. For example, Strupp (1980a, 1980b, 1980c) conducted a series of single-subject studies comparing therapists each with a successful and unsuccessful case in brief psychodynamic therapy. A wide variety of process and outcome measures were used to examine events related to therapeutic effectiveness. Negative outcomes were related to client characterological problems (as compared to neurotic problems) or counseling countertransference issues. Positive outcomes were related to the client's ability to take advantage of the therapeutic relationship and to work within the therapist's framework. Strupp then used these results to propose that patient variables were more powerful events in assessing therapeutic outcomes, even to the point of overshadowing therapists' attitudes and technical skill.

Kazdin (1980) addressed the problem of symptom substitution stemming primarily from psychoanalytic thinking. The general assumption was that treatment of overt, problematic behavior, rather than teatment of the underlying cause, may result in symptom substitution. However, research on specific problematic behaviors such as phobias or bed wetting did not result in the appearance of substitute symptoms (see, for example, Jones, 1956; Meyer, 1957; Yates, 1958). Thus, this early research using primarily uncontrolled case studies cast doubt on the unqualified notion of symptom substitution, suggesting that this phenomenon may be more complex than previously assumed.

Caution obviously must be used when employing findings from single-subject designs as exemplars or counterinstances. As mentioned previously, in early research relatively uncontrolled case studies were not just overused as exemplars but were used as the primary database in the construction of personality theories.

Although the generalizability of the findings from single-subject designs must always be questioned, the results can highlight a particular point or cast doubt on previously held beliefs, suggesting that, at a minimum, there are exceptions to the rule or that the rule is somehow incorrect. However, exemplars should not become the only or even primary database relating to a particular phenomenon. Thus, it is imperative to consider both the need for additional empirical evidence and the advantages and limitations of single-subject designs in giving such findings persuasive value.

Limitations

As traditionally conceived and conducted, the individual case study almost completely lacks experimental control. Many of Cook and Campbell's (1979) threats to internal validity are present, such as history, maturation, testing, selection, and mortality. In addition, many times "data" are collected in unsystematic and even retrospective ways. After working with a particular client for some time, the therapist may reflect back (sometimes months later) to collect his or her "observations" about the case. Such retrospective analyses most likely involve multiple sources of bias and distortion (for example, memory loss, memory distortion, subjective impressions, or selective attention) and blur any temporal succession pertaining to causal relationships. Sometimes the "data" also consist of verbal client self-reports collected by the counselor. If the client believes he or she is doing the counselor a favor by completing a questionnaire, data obtained in such a manner may very well be contaminated or biased, most likely by demand characteristics inherent in the situation. Likewise, data may be collected from the client with instruments of unknown reliability or validity, thereby calling into question the adequacy of the data. In short, any of a number of biases of uncontrolled variables can obscure the relationship between the variables under examination and thus obscure interpretation of the findings. While it *may* be true that variable x affected variable y in some way, it also may be the case that many other variables created the effect on variable y. The upshot of the uncontrolled case study is that there may be several plausible explanations for the observed effect on variable y, thus limiting the scientific value of the study. The uncontrolled case study is a weak source of "data" and at best is suggestive.

By contrast, the intensive single-subject design and the single-case experimental design typically involve more systematic observations and experimental control. For example, the study by Hill and colleagues (1983) involved combining subjective and objective data from multiple sources (client, counselor, judges, the client's mother). In addition, the study made comparisons within the data collected, specifically between the "best" and "worst" sessions. Such comparisons serve to identify relationships among variables within the same subject. When comparisons are made within the same individual (and thus the subject serves as his or her own control), some of the threats to internal validity are controlled for. These well-controlled investigations typically provide stronger empirical evidence, allowing fewer rival hypotheses and subsequently more definitive conclusions. A disadvantage of the intensive single-subject design is that experimenters may find what they expected to find and overlook information that is contrary to their expectations. For example, subsequent analyses of data from Hill and colleagues (1983) revealed several facets of the interaction between the counselor and client that were undetected by those researchers' analysis (Wampold & Kim, 1989).

A major issue in using single-subject designs is the generalizability of the findings to other individuals or situations. Even if one isolates specific relationships among variables, it is unclear whether the results would generalize to other clients with similar concerns or diagnosis (client generality) or whether a particular technique would work in a different setting (setting generality) (Barlow & Hersen, 1984). In short, the generalizability issue has been a major limitation of the single-subject design.

Generalizability is also a major concern for studies comparing groups. Neimeyer and Resnikoff (1982) persuasively argued that inferences derived from *any* sampling procedure must be tentatively ventured and carefully restricted. They note that quantitatively oriented studies deal with the representativeness issue primarily by using statistical sampling. Qualitatively oriented approaches rely more on theoretical sampling, generalizing only to people with characteristics similar to those of the individuals studied.

Tracey and Ray (1984) provide an example of replicating single-subject designs. They conducted a study that focused on the interactional stage differences between successful ($n = 3$) and unsuccessful ($n = 3$) time-limited counseling by examining six counseling dyads; data from each dyad were examined individually, which meant that Tracey and Ray conducted six single-subject studies. They hypothesized that the successful (but not the unsuccessful) dyads would be characterized by three fairly distinct stages of high, low, and again high levels of complementarity. To examine complementarity, Tracey and Ray examined who determined the topic of discussion in the counseling session. Specifically, the sequence of topic-following/topic-initiation was used as an index of complementarity and was analyzed using a Markov chain model to test for differences in the sequence of topic responses over time. Analyses of each dyad revealed support for their hypothesis for each successful and unsuccessful dyad. Specifically, topic determination was found to change significantly over time for successful dyads but to remain constant for unsuccessful dyads. Thus, replicating the pattern of results across six dyads adds considerable strength to the external validity of this study. Parenthetically, Tracy and Ray (1984) also found that the differences between unsuccessful and successful dyads disappeared when the data were combined or aggregated across dyads, which underscores the potential loss of information when averaging across individuals.

SUMMARY AND CONCLUSIONS

The common goal of all counseling research methods is to facilitate an understanding of human behavior. Different methodologies provide different types of data and information about human behavior. Single-subject designs permit an

examination of an individual person, dyad, or group. It can be argued that a practitioner counseling a specific client is less concerned with group averages than
with the individual's behavior. It is not sufficient to rely on normative data that suggest a particular intervention strategy works with, say, three out of four clients and
thus simply to rely on probabilities. Single-subject designs, particularly those of an
intensive, systematic, or time-series nature, can provide information about the
uniqueness of client responses and counselor interventions. However, researchers
must be particularly sensitive to various sources of bias and extraneous variables,
and must make every attempt to control such variables when considering
Kerlinger's "MAXMINCON" principle.

More specifically, we discussed two main types of single-subject design, the
single-case quantitative design and the single-case experimental design. Within the
former, we discussed the uncontrolled case study as well as the more recent intensive single-subject design. A case study refers to a study that consists simply of
observations of an individual, dyad, or group that are made under unsystematic and
uncontrolled conditions. The intensive single-subject design typically involves
more experimental control and consists of systematic, repeated, and multiple
observations of an individual, dyad, or group under experimental conditions
designed to identify and compare relationships among variables. In our view, the
comparisons and control in the intensive single-subject design provide stronger
empirical support and thus give it more utility than the case study.

The single-case experimental designs also examine the relationship between
two or more variables, typically within one or a few subjects, and involve considerable levels of experimental control. These designs are characterized by specific
treatment goals, numerous and repeated measurements of the dependent variable,
and the inclusion of different phases or periods of time (each representing a different experimental condition such as a baseline phase or an intervention phase).
The basic purpose of changing from one phase to another is to demonstrate
change, presumably due to the onset of the independent variable or intervention.
Two major types of intrasubject designs were discussed: AB time-series designs
(AB, ABAB, randomized AB) and multiple-baseline designs. We maintain that the
time-series designs are not only appropriate for behavioral researchers, but can be
fruitfully employed within other theoretical orientations as well.

The uncontrolled case study currently appears infrequently, if at all, in the
major counseling journals. The intensive single-subject design has begun to
appear in the counseling journals, particularly since the appearance of Hill et al.
(1983). It is extremely rare for any counseling journal to contain a report of a study
using an intrasubject design.

We strongly believe that the intensive single-subject design can be a powerful
methodology to increase understanding of counseling and the counseling process.
The single-subject design can be used for (a) collecting information and ideas, and
generating hypotheses about the therapeutic process, (b) testing therapeutic techniques, (c) testing new methodologies, (d) studying individuals and rare phenomena, and (e) providing exemplars and counterinstances. However, limitations
imposed by threats to both internal and external validity must be clearly examined
and considered. Bergin and Strupp (1970) initially predicted that the single-

subject design would be one of the primary strategies used to clarify the process of counseling; this remains to be demonstrated. Nonetheless, because we strongly believe in the potential of this methodology, our first recommendation is to use the single-subject design more frequently in counseling research. Intensive single-subject designs that use both quantitative and qualitative data can be especially rich in providing more holistic data of both a content and process nature. Moreover, we believe that it is erroneous to relegate the single-subject design to merely "exploratory" research, in which any "findings" must subsequently be subjected to the "real" methods of science (Neimeyer & Resnikoff, 1982).

A number of the examples cited in this chapter were intentionally drawn from group counseling. One of the main obstacles in group counseling research is sample size. Many times in group counseling research, the variable of interest is a group-level variable such as cohesion. Often, however, researchers use individual scores, such as each subject's attraction to the group, so they can increase the size of the groups in a between-groups design. Researchers could circumvent this sample-size problem by using more intrasubject time-series designs.

Accordingly, our second recommendation is an increased use of intrasubject designs in group (and family) research. This recommendation could also help address a second problem in group research—that most group counseling studies use analogue groups of very short duration. Time-series designs allow the researcher to study the group as an entity and to use real client groups without having to line up a prohibitively large number of subjects.

Our third recommendation is the increased use of randomized designs in AB time-series research. Randomized designs offer additional complexity and flexibility, and enable the researcher to examine for the presence of carryover effects between treatments. In addition, randomized designs permit the use of powerful parametric statistical analyses. Editors are often reluctant to publish studies that do not have statistical comparisons, and readers rely on these statistical comparisons as a way of comparing studies for AB time-series designs; parametric statistical tests can only be performed appropriately when A and B phases are randomly assigned.

A final methodological consideration in discussing the use of the single-subject methodology is the type of data or knowledge currently available on a particular research question. For example, a considerable number of studies have investigated the therapeutic technique of thought stopping. In 1978, Heppner reviewed the published investigations to determine the clinical efficacy of thought stopping. This body of literature consisted of 22 studies, 20 of which were case studies that lacked experimental control (Heppner, 1978b). Thus, this body of "knowledge" concerning the clinical efficacy of thought stopping was based largely on data collected from a single methodological perspective, a phenomenon that has been called paradigm fixation (Gelso, 1979). The point is that merely ascertaining the advantages and limitations of the single-subject design is not enough; researchers must also weigh these advantages and limitations relative to the applicable existing scientific knowledge base and the types of designs used in past research.

CHAPTER 9

QUANTITATIVE DESCRIPTIVE DESIGNS

Descriptive designs are research strategies that enable the investigator to describe the occurrence of variables, the underlying dimensions in a set of variables, or the relationship between or among variables. Basically, descriptive designs help to define the existence and delineate characteristics of a particular phenomenon. For example, a descriptive study might present information that establishes the frequency of date rape, problems faced by college students, or vocational undecidedness in entering freshman students. Observation is at the core of the descriptive process; the utility of a descriptive study is directly dependent on the quality of observations—or more commonly in counseling, the quality of the instruments or assessments. Moreover, it is impossible to observe all instances of a phenomenon, so instead the researcher carefully studies the phenomenon in a sample drawn from the population of interest. Thus, the reliability and validity of the observations and the generalizability of the sample are two critical issues in descriptive research.

Unfortunately, many texts on research design devote little attention to descriptive designs. This lack of attention stems partially from what we call the "pure science myth," which holds up the experimental design paradigm a priori as the "correct" or "best" mode of scientific investigation.

Moreover, the received view of science tends to emphasize the testing and verification of theories, as well as comparisons among competing theories. Consequently, research in counseling has largely become a science of verification, and less a science of description and discovery. Greenberg (1986a) argued that counseling psychology should place greater emphasis on discovery paradigms. He believes that the empiricist tradition, with its emphasis on the controlled between-groups experiment, has been overvalued by counseling researchers. We strongly agree. Consequently, a great deal of research in counseling is based on poorly described phenomena that likely are poorly understood. Too often researchers attempt to manipulate and control variables before enough is known about those variables.

Physical scientists, by contrast, spend a great deal of time observing, describing, and classifying events. Tests of competing theories are relatively infrequent in the physical sciences. This order of things has seemingly been reversed in counseling research. Inadequately described phenomena are often subjected to rigid verification, with disappointing results. Before one can test the adequacy of a theory in explaining a phenomenon, one needs a reliable and detailed description of the phenomenon. A central thesis of this chapter is that descriptive designs do have an important role in the scientific process, and that one should strongly consider using these designs to address certain research questions. We see considerable value in descriptive research in counseling.

At first glance, the "MAXMINCON" principle that we hve emphasized seems antithetical to descriptive research. For example, by exercising experimental control, it might seem that the experimenter would interfere with or change the natural phenomenon he or she was attempting to describe. On the one hand, many variables are left uncontrolled in descriptive research, and thus cause-and-effect statements are inappropriate. On the other hand, the investigator can exercise considerable care in making observations so as to minimize measurement errors, which can create considerable error variance. Thus, the quality of the observations is the heart of descriptive design. Likewise, the researcher can exercise experimental control to reduce bias and extraneous variables by using random sampling. Accordingly, in this chapter we emphasize measurement, observation, and sampling as we review the different types of descriptive designs.

In this chapter we discuss three major types of quantitative descriptive research: (a) survey or epidemiological research, (b) classification or data reduction research, and (c) passive research designs. Briefly, research strategies designed to characterize the occurrence of behaviors are commonly known as epidemiological or survey designs. Classification research uses factor and cluster analysis as strategies for categorizing and reducing data, primarily by identifying underlying dimensions or groupings in a set of variables. Research strategies that examine the relationship among or between variables are referred to as correlational designs. This type of design includes studies that use correlational or regression analyses.

SURVEY OR EPIDEMIOLOGICAL RESEARCH DESIGNS

Hackett (1981) observed that survey research is one of the oldest and most widely used research methods in the social sciences. The use of surveys have been traced to ancient Egypt, and surveys were conducted to assess social conditions in England in the eighteenth century (Glock, 1967). Today surveys are commonplace, particularly as public opinion polls and political surveys. Surveys are also widely employed by counseling researchers. For example, 27 of the 57 data-based articles submitted to a counseling-related journal, *Counselor Education and Supervision,* during July 1991 through June 1992 were survey studies (Fong & Malone, 1994).

The basic aim of survey research is to document the nature or frequency of a particular variable (for instance, the incidence of rape) within a certain population (for example, American college students). Surveys typically use self-reports to identify facts, opinions, attitudes, and behaviors, as well as the relationships among these aspects; data are often collected through questionnaires, mailed surveys, telephone interviews, or personal interviews. The functions of survey research are to describe, explain, or explore phenomena (Babbie, 1979). Descriptive research provides basic information about a variable or phenomenon (for example, the frequency of rape on college campuses). Explanatory research attempts to identify variables (such as beliefs about women, or beliefs about the acceptability of physical aggression) that might explain the occurrence of a phenomenon (such as rape on college campuses). Exploratory research is often conducted when the researcher wants to learn about a poorly understood phenomenon (for instance, how rapists rationalize rape).

Often it is useful for counselors to carefully observe or describe the occurrence of a variable; consequently, survey research has made important contributions to the counseling profession. For example, early researchers (see Brotemarkle, 1927; Schneidler & Berdie, 1942) documented the frequency and types of problems that college students experienced. Many studies have been conducted to assess college students' problems and needs (such studies are therefore called needs assessments; see, for example, Blos, 1946; Carney & Barak, 1976; DeSena, 1966; Koile & Bird, 1956; McKinney, 1945; Rust & Davie, 1961). As college populations have changed over time, needs assessments have been used both to document changes in students' needs (Heppner & Neal, 1983) and to identify needs within specific populations (for example, adult students; Warchal & Southern, 1986). Such documentation has had both theoretical and practical significance. On a theoretical level, description of the types of problems encountered by college students has facilitated the formulation and testing of student development theory (see, for example, Chickering, 1969); on a practical level, this information has helped the staffs of college counseling centers to design programs and deliver services appropriate to the needs of students. Parenthetically, this line of research has led to a number of studies that have examined not only the typical problems experienced by students, but also the appropriateness of services delivered by counseling centers (as viewed by students, faculty, and counseling center staff), and ultimately larger issues such as the role and functions of university counseling centers (see the review by Heppner & Neal, 1983). Other examples of survey research include studies examining the level of distress in psychologists (see, for example, Thoreson, Miller, & Krauskopf, 1989), alcoholism among psychologists (see, for example, Thoreson, Budd, & Krauskopf, 1986), job analysis of psychology internships in counseling center settings (Ross & Altmaier, 1990), and career development of college women (Harmon, 1981, 1989) and college men (Super, 1957).

A common strategy using survey designs is to compare information across two or more groups. For instance, Koplik and DeVito (1986) compared the problems identified by members of the college classes of 1976 and 1986; this is known as a survey cross-sectional design. Other times a researcher might use a survey longitudinal design and compare, say, students' responses when they were freshmen versus their responses when they were sophomores. Several authors have also examined gender differences in, for example, students' perceptions and reporting of problems (see, for example, Koplik & DeVito, 1986; Nagelberg, Pillsbury, & Balzor, 1983) and in academic careers (Thoreson et al. 1990). Comparisons have also been made based on race, year in school, educational level, time of year, type of academic program, and type of service requested. The accumulation of this type of research, particularly for a college population, enables counselors to describe with a high degree of confidence both the types of problems encountered on college campuses and their differential distribution across segments of the student population. In addition, the accumulation of these descriptive findings is instrumental in the process of theory building. For instance, one consistent finding in this body of research is the difference between males and females in the number and types of problems recorded. This finding has led to theoretical speculation about gender differences in problem perception.

Survey research is not limited to documenting the existence of problems within a population. In fact, a wide range of other types of behavior or variables can be described using this type of approach. For example, Hill and O'Grady (1985) were interested in counselor intentions, which they described as the "why" of a counseling intervention. They analyzed the responses of 42 experienced therapists and documented the relative frequency of use of 19 theoretically derived intentions. In addition, they examined the differential use rates of the various intentions as a function of the therapist's theoretical orientation. From these descriptive analyses, Hill and O'Grady were able to construct a profile of intention use for experienced counselors and to identify intentions that characterized various theoretical positions.

In sum, the aim of epidemiological/survey research is to describe, explain, or explore the occurrence of a variable. This design is most useful in describing a phenomenon about which we lack information, in terms of either frequency or categorization of occurrence.

Despite—or maybe because of—the popularity of survey research, commentators have been critical of this type of research design. For example, Fong (1992, p. 194), in an editorial in *Counselor Education and Supervision,* said, "... I have become aware of the large number of survey studies being conducted that are so casually designed that they are invalid and unpublishable." She went on to identify two critical problems with many survey studies:

> Too often, I have reviewed manuscripts that report surveys of a sample that is convenient, not representative, or that represents only a subgroup of the intended population under study. Likewise, I regularly find that the survey instrument was not developed by careful selection of relevant variables or was solely developed by the researcher without any pilot or reliability studies. (Fong, 1992, p. 195)

In a follow-up to her editorial, Fong and Malone (1994) reported on the design and data analysis errors found in survey studies submitted to *Counselor Education and Supervision* from July 1991 through June 1992. Among the 27 survey studies submitted to the journal during this time, Fong and Malone described four types of research design errors as follows:

> (a) absent of or unclear research question to guide data collection and analysis; (b) sample errors such as failure to obtain a sample appropriate to the research questions, inadequate sample, or non-representative sample; (c) instruments, frequently author-made, lacking reliability or inappropriate for the variables

being studied; and (d) other methodological problems that prohibited generalization of results, for example, data collection procedures (Fong & Malone,
1994, pp. 357–358)

In addition, these authors identified two types of data analysis errors: "(a) inappropriate method of data analysis (for example, simple tests when data [are] multivariate)" and (b) piecemeal analysis, "which occurs when the study data is divided
so the analysis presented in the manuscript is only a piece of the research" (Fong
& Malone, 1994, p. 358). Fifty-nine percent of the 27 survey studies had absent or
unclear research questions. Sample and instrumentation errors each occurred in
48% of the studies, whereas 29% of the studies contained errors that made generalization impossible. Data analysis errors were less common in the reviewed surveys. Only 8% of the reviewed studies had problems due to piecemeal publication,
whereas the wrong statistic was used in 33% of the studies.

Fong's (1992; Fong & Malone, 1994) writings make a clear statement about
the problems associated with survey designs. Researchers considering a survey
study should pay particular attention to the issues she raised. Although a well-
designed survey can add substantially to our knowledge in a particular area, a
poorly designed survey is little more than a waste of time for the researchers and
the potential participants.

Design Issues in Surveys

At least four major activities are included in the conduct of survey research: (a)
matching the survey design to the researcher's questions, (b) defining the sample,
(c) selecting and developing a data collection method, and (d) analyzing the data.
(These activities are generic; they apply to all forms of research. We discuss matching the survey design to the researcher's question in Chapters 2 and 3, deriving the
sample in Chapter 13, and selecting and developing the data collection method in
Chapter 12.)

The actual design of a survey study is fairly straightforward. Unlike for true
or quasi-experimental designs, the researcher does not form the actual groups a
priori. Although groups may be formed for comparison's sake (for example, males
versus females), the survey is often given to the entire identified sample. Even
when the researcher decides ahead of time to compare, for example, males and
females, he or she often finds these participants as they occur in the population.
Some surveys purposefully sample from two groups—for example, interns versus
practicum students, or clinical psychology programs versus counseling psychology
programs. Even when this type of purposeful sampling does occur, the researcher
cannot assign participants to be in one group or another as can occur in true
experimental or quasi-experimental research. Specifically, in survey designs the
researcher does not manipulate an independent variable, and so is not concerned
with manipulation checks.

Perhaps the most frequent way of collecting data in survey research is
through self-report questionnaires, and particularly mailed questionnaires. The primary advantage of mail surveys is the ease of data collection, particularly when the

sample covers a wide geographical area (in which case it would be difficult to collect on-site data). One of the biggest potential disadvantages is the difficulty of getting participants to return mailed questionnaires. Often the return rate from the first mailing is only 30%, which raises questions about the external validity of the results. Was there some reason why the majority of the participants did not respond? Would their responses be different from those of the 30% who responded? It is doubtful that one could safely generalize from a 30% return rate (of a sample) to the target population. Because the return rate is such a critical issue in mail surveys, researchers usually try to make it easy both to complete the questionnaire (by keeping it short) and to return it (by including a stamped, addressed return envelope). Two sets of reminder letters or postcards are also usually sent. Babbie (1979) suggested that a follow-up letter be sent about two or three weeks after the initial mailing, and subsequently two or three weeks later as a final follow-up. Researchers commonly report obtaining around a 30% to 40% return rate from an initial mailing, and approximately 20% and 10% returns from the two successive follow-ups. There is no concensus concerning an "acceptable" return rate. Although some published survey research is based on less than a 40% return rate, some researchers recommend at least a 50% return rate as an "adequate" basis for findings (Baddie, 1979); others recommend at least 80% to 90% (Kerlinger, 1986).

Whatever method the researcher uses to collect data, the final step entails data analysis. A critical starting point for data analysis is checking the adequacy of the sample. This involves checking how closely the sample resembles the general population along a number of important dimensions. For instance, is the proportion of male and female (or black and white, or young and old) respondents in the sample similar to the proportions in the general population? Another especially important type of check when using mail questionnaires is a comparison of respondents and nonrespondents. For example, when using a college population, do respondents and nonrespondents differ in sex, year in school, major, grade point average, and such? Only after this type of sample adequacy checking has been done should the data be analyzed and interpreted.

Survey research with diverse populations can present some unique challenges. Ponterotto and Casas (1991) discussed three issues that counseling researchers should consider when using a survey design with culturally, linguistically, and/or economically diverse groups. The first issue concerns how to tailor the survey to the particular group under study: Do the respondents understand the questions in the way that the researchers intended? Are any items offensive to people in the group the researcher wants to survey? Do potential respondents understand how to respond to the format? According to Ponterotto and Casas, these questions can be addressed by examining the language and format of potential questions in a pretest conducted on a pilot sample that is representative of the target population. These authors suggest that the survey be pilot-tested on a sample that represents about 5% of the target sample. When the pilot test is administered, the respondents should be interviewed to make sure that the questions asked were meaningful, clear, and appropriate for the purpose of the survey.

The second issue raised by Ponterotto and Casas (1991) involves research with participants who do not speak standard English. In this case the researcher must translate potential questions into the participants' native language. Unfortunately, this translation process is neither straightforward nor simple. The processes involved in successful translation are back translation and decentering. In back translation, a bilingual person first translates the original questions into the new language; once this translation is complete, then another bilingual person translates the translated questions back into English. Any discrepancies between the original and the back-translated versions of the questions are identified and corrected. The process of translation and back translation is then repeated until the back-translated version matches the original version. However, that the words of a question can be correctly translated and back translated does not mean that the words' meanings are the same in both languages. Decentering attempts to address the issue of comparable meaning across language and cultural groups. In decentering, the researcher attempts to ensure that no specific language is the "center" of attention. This decentering is accomplished by having bilingual judges examine both versions of the survey and compare the meanings of the questions.

The third issue to be addressed involves the distribution and collection of the survey. As noted by Ponterotto and Casas (1991), some socioeconomic and/or cultural groups may not trust researchers who are connected with the "White middle-class establishment" (p. 103). This suggests that response rate may present a larger problem with these groups of participants. According to Ponterotto and Casas (1991), it is important to be able to ascertain the reason for a low response rate. These authors recommend that the researcher attempt to interview a random subsample of respondents and nonrespondents. In particular, the researcher should attempt to determine the characteristics that distinguish the respondent and non-respondent groups.

An Example of Survey Research

Good, Thoreson, and Shaughnessy (1995) were interested in documenting the incidence of professional impairment for counseling psychologists. Their specific research questions were as follows:

> (a) What is the prevalence of past and current substance use reported by counseling psychologists? (b) Are counseling psychologists aware of colleagues with substance abuse problems? If yes, are they complying with APA ethical principles by taking appropriate action? and (c) What is the psychological functioning (i.e., personal and professional life satisfaction, work-related stress, and psychological distress) of counseling psychologists? p. 707)

The first two questions called for an examination of the occurrence or frequency of these specified events and were measured with two author-constructed scales. To address the third research question, the authors chose three constructs based on their review of the current literature. The three constructs were measured with validated inventories, including: (a) the Satisfaction with Life Scale (Diener et al., 1985), (b) the Work Related Strain Inventory (Revicki, May, & Whitley, 1990), and (c) the Brief Symptom Inventory (Derogatis, 1992).

The authors wanted to generalize their results to the population of counseling psychologists. Accordingly, a sample of counseling psychologists was obtained by randomly selecting 1000 (500 men and 500 women) members of Division 17 (the Division of Counseling Psychology) of the American Psychological Association. These 1000 potential participants were sent the "Division 17 Health Practices Survey" via the United States Postal Service. In an attempt to increase the response rate to the survey, Good et al. (1995) sent a second copy of the survey to potential participants two weeks after the initial mailing, and then sent a reminder postcard to each potential participant one week after the second mailing.

Of the 405 surveys returned, 12 were incomplete or unusable. This represented a 39% return rate. The final sample, based on returned surveys, was 55% female and 45% male, with an average age of 48.2 years. The sample consisted of predominantly married respondents (71%), with single (14%), divorced (13%), and widows/widowers (3%) making up the rest of the sample. In addition, the sample was predominantly white (94%); the remainder of the sample was Black/African American, 2%; Asian/Asian American, 2%; Hispanic/Hispanic American, 1%; and other, 1%.

One of the strongest aspects of Good, Thoreson, and Shaughnessy's study was their attempt to check the representativeness of their sample. They accomplished this check by comparing selected demographic characteristics of their sample's participants to those same demographic characteristics for members of Division 17 as a whole. For example, there was a similar percentage of degree type in the sample (Ph.D., 82%; Ed.D., 14%; and master's degree, 3%) and in the membership of Division 17 (Ph.D., 78%; Ed.D., 17%; and master's degree, 5%). Good and colleagues suggested that their sample was representative of Division 17 because the demographic characteristics of the sample closely matched those of Division 17.

As to the first research question—What is the prevalence of past and current substance use reported by counseling psychologists?—the authors' results revealed that 19.7% of the sample reported "almost daily/daily" previous use of alcohol, while 16.4% of the counseling psychologists surveyed indicated "almost daily/daily" current use of alcohol. Usage rates were also reported for cigarettes, marijuana, tranquilizers, hallucinogens, stimulants, opiates, cocaine, and sedatives. In response to the second research question—Are counseling psychologists aware of colleagues with substance abuse problems?—the researchers found that 40% of the sample knew at least one female psychologist and 62% of the respondents knew at least one male psychologist who had substance abuse problems in the past. However, only 19% of the respondents reported that they had confronted a colleague about his or her substance problem. The most frequently cited reasons for not confronting the colleague about her/his substance abuse problem were: (a) knew of subtle changes but lacked tangible evidence of negative impact (53%), (b) did not see it as detrimental to their job performance (42%), and (c) thought it would do no good (39%).

To determine the relationship between substance use and psychological functioning (the third research question), the authors initially created an index of substance use by summing the reported levels of use. This substance use composite was correlated with the measures of psychological functioning. Good and colleagues used a Bonferroni correction to guard against the increased risk of Type I error that results from examining multiple correlations (28 correlation coefficients were obtained in this analysis). The Bonferroni correction was obtained by dividing the study-wide alpha level (p = .05) by the number of pair-wise correlations (28). This resulted in an adjusted alpha level of p = .001. Using this alpha level, none of the correlations between current levels of substance use and the measures of psychological functioning (personal satisfaction, professional satisfaction, work-related strain, and the Global Severity Index of the Brief Symptom Inventory) were significant.

The study by Good et al. (1995) is exemplary in many ways. The authors carefully defined the research questions and used the existing research literature to select measures of the central constructs. The use of their tailor-made questionnaires in conjunction with previously constructed questionnaires having known psychometric characteristics strengthened the design. In addition, the authors examined the internal consistency of the previous and current substance use scale calculated from their author-constructed measure. They were also cognizant of possible problems with statistical conclusion validity. To assure that fishing/error rate problems did not contaminate the relationship between substance use and psychological functioning, they used the Bonferroni method to adjust the study-wide alpha level to account for the multiple correlations they examined. Whereas it is important to be concerned with the study-wide alpha level, readers should note that the Bonferroni method is an extremely conservative approach for dealing with this issue; it drastically reduces the power to detect an effect. Finally, the authors used multiple measures to assess psychological functioning, thereby increasing the construct validity of putative causes and effects. An additional strength of the study involves the sampling procedure. Whereas the response rate was relatively low (only 39%), the comparison of the sample's demographic characteristics to those of Division 17 members strengthened the contention that the sample was indeed representative of the target population. Weaknesses of the study include the relatively low return rate and the relatively low internal consistency estimates for the previous and current substance use scales. Nonetheless, the data from this descriptive study are important because substance use among counseling psychologists and the confrontation of impaired colleagues are phenomena about which we know relatively little. These findings have immediate implications for professional training of counseling professionals.

CLASSIFICATION OR DATA REDUCTION RESEARCH DESIGNS

Often in counseling research it is necessary to reduce or simplify a data set to only a few variables by developing categories, subgroups, or factors—in general, some sort of classification system. Frequently, a taxonomic system simplifies a data set and has important theoretical implications as well. In chemistry, for example, the periodic table provides a means of classifying elements and also describes underlying dimensions of atomic structure (protons, electrons, and neutrons). The establishment of reliable and valid categorical and dimensional systems likewise can advance the counseling profession.

Greenberg (1986b), in writing about psychotherapy research, contended that there is a "dearth of conceptually clarifying classification schemes" (p. 712). He believes that comprehensive classification schemes are a critical base for counseling research and that there is a need for more research with such a focus. In fact, all sciences start from commonly accepted bases of description and classification.

Two commonly used classification strategies are factor analysis and cluster analysis. Both of these procedures describe data sets by reducing or categorizing the data into simpler underlying structures or subgroups. Specifically, factor and cluster analyses assume that these are a small number of "latent variables" or constructs that account for the relationships among the many variables examined. Next we define and discuss these two techniques, provide an overview of the steps involved in using them, and examine illustrations from contemporary counseling research.

Factor Analysis

Factor analysis is a class of multivariate statistical methods whose primary purpose is data reduction and summarization (Hair, Anderson, & Tatham, 1987). Factor analysis examines the interrelationships among a large number of variables and condenses (summarizes) that information into a smaller set of common underlying dimensions or factors. These dimensions or factors presumably correspond to underlying psychological constructs. Thus, the fundamental aim of factor analysis is to search for underlying psychological constructs seen in the common dimensions that underlie the original variables (Hair et al., 1987). This statistical technique is often used in developing and validating assessment inventories.

There are two major types of factor analysis: exploratory and confirmatory. In exploratory factor analysis, the most commonly used type, the researcher examines a set of data to determine underlying dimensions, without any a priori specification of the number or content of these constructs. In confirmatory factor analysis, the researcher first identifies (either theoretically or through previous research) the number of dimensions he or she expects to find and the items or scales in the data set that will correlate with (or "load on") each construct; this is called the model. The researcher then examines how well the model fits the actual relationships observed in the data. The analysis can either confirm (hence the name) or disconfirm the researcher's model. Because the researcher can specify a model, confirmatory factor analysis allows researchers to test theoretical propositions.

As an example of exploratory factor analysis, suppose a researcher has observed over a ten-year period that for some adult clients, changing careers is a difficult process. The researcher begins to wonder what distinguishes the people who have difficulty from those who do not. After considerable reflection, more observation, and a review of the professional literature, she develops a 100-item questionnaire that assesses barriers associated with changing careers. Such an instrument has not existed before, for little is known about barriers to changing careers. But answering a 100-item questionnaire is time consuming, and the questionnaire does not group together or identify common barriers; the researcher can only compute a total score of barriers, or look at individual barrier items. Factor analysis could condense these 100 items by aligning them with factors that characterize the data set. For example, the researcher might conclude through factor analysis that there are three main types of career barriers, reflecting (a) career myths, (b) self-efficacy, and (c) attributional styles. The researcher could then summarize a client's career barriers into these three types and provide scores for each of these factors. A client might score exceptionally high on career myths, which would suggest that interventions are especially needed on this dimension. Moreover, the three factors provide theoretical extensions of the topic of career barriers or of the career planning process in general. In sum, factor analysis analyzes a large number of variables and condenses or summarizes them into common or underlying dimensions. Parenthetically, interested readers could follow up on this not-so-hypothetical example by reading M. Heppner, Multon, and Johnston (1994).

Factor analysis has been used frequently in the counseling literature to identify common dimensions relating to a wide array of topics. For example, this technique has been used to describe dimensions of vocational interest (Fouad, Cudeck, & Hansen, 1984), supervisory styles (Worthington & Stern, 1985), expectancies about counseling (Tinsley, Workman, & Kass, 1980), and perception of counselors (Barak & LaCrosse, 1975). Tinsley et al. (1980) found four factors that account for a large portion of the variance in clients' expectations about counseling: personal commitment, facilitative conditions, counselor expertise, and nurturance. Likewise, Phillips et al. (1985) described three dimensions of decision-making styles: rational, intuitive, and dependent.

Although factor analysis is frequently used, most counseling researchers seem to be unaware that there are in fact several different kinds of factor analyses. To understand these different types of factor analyses, the counseling researcher first needs to be aware of Cattell's (1966) description of types of data. As described in Cattell's Data Box (1966), data can vary along three dimensions: persons, variables, and occasions. Combinations of these three dimensions create six different types of factor analysis. In any one type of factor analysis (or principal components analysis), one of these dimensions is held constant, one dimension is randomly sampled, and the final dimension is examined for the presence of latent factors (Tinsley, 1992). Cattell designated the factor or principal components analysis of each of the six possible combinations of these three data dimensions with a letter ranging from O to T (Table 9-1).

O-Type and P-Type factor analyses are used with single cases, because in both of these types of factor analysis the person dimension is held constant. Researchers using O-Type factor analysis are looking for dimensions within occasions (or types of occasions) by sampling across variables. For example, a number of counseling theories describe stages across counseling sessions. Stage models presume that the counseling sessions within a particular stage are similar to each other and different from sessions drawn from another stage of counseling. As far as we can tell, no counseling researcher hs empirically identified stages of counseling. Rather, sessions have been arbitrarily divided into stages (that is, first third, middle third, last third). O-Type factor analysis could be used to empirically examine the existence of stages. To do this, the counseling researcher would first decide on a large number of variables to examine. For example, Jones's (Jones, 1985; Jones et al., 1993) Psychotherapy Process Q-Sort would be an ideal choice because it contains 100 independent items. Each session would be rated with the Psychotherapy Process

TABLE 9-1
Types of Factor Analysis as Described by Cattell's (1966) Data Box

Type of factor analysis	Data dimension held constant	Data dimension sampled	Data dimension examined for factors
O-Type	Persons	Variables	Occasions
P-Type	Persons	Occasions	Variables
Q-Type	Occasions	Variables	Persons
R-Type	Occasions	Persons	Variables
S-Type	Variables	Occasions	Persons
T-Type	Variables	Persons	Occasions

SOURCE: Adapted from Tinsley, 1992.

Q-Sort, and then sessions would be factor analyzed across the 100 Psychotherapy Process Q-Sort items. The number of factors derived from this analysis would tell the researcher how many different types of sessions there were in the data.

Counseling researchers using P-Type factor analysis are looking for dimensions within variables by sampling across occasions. In other words, P-technique factor analysis attempts to discover latent dimensions in variables across a sample of occasions. Examining how variables go together (relate) is a common use of factor analysis. However, using occasions as the sampled variable is far less common than using persons. According to Tinsley (1992), "P correlations [and factor analyses] are ideal for examining issues pertaining to developmental processes, including developments occurring within the counseling process" (p. 66). Although P-Type factor analysis is ideographic, by focusing the examination of relationships at the level of the single individual it is possible to obtain more normative information by chaining together observations (data) from several individuals.

As early as 1950, Cattell and Luborsky used P-Type analysis to describe the dimensions of psychotherapy change from a 54-session psychotherapy of a client with school adjustment difficulties and a peptic ulcer. Despite this early successful study, P-Type factor analysis has rarely been used in counseling or therapy research. The *Journal of Consulting and Clinical Psychology* devoted a special section to research using P-Type factor analysis (Russell, 1995); one study within this special section attempted to describe patterns of verbal interactions within treatments (Stiles & Shapiro, 1995). Stiles (1988) has suggested that the process-outcome correlation strategy cannot identify variables that contribute to therapeutic efficacy. He suggests that researchers instead focus on the interactions patterns between clients and counselors. Stiles and Shapiro (1995) used P-Type factor analysis to identify and describe these patterns of client-counselor interaction in two types of treatment: psychodynamic-interpersonal and cognitive-behavioral. All counselor and client responses were coded into one of eight Verbal Response Modes Categories (Stiles, 1992): (a) disclosure, (b) edification, (c) question, (d) acknowledgment, (e) advisement, (f) confirmation, (g) interpretation, and (h) reflection. The dimensions of client-counselor interaction were quite similar across the two types of treatment. Each treatment had a revealing, storytelling, explaining, and inquiring dimension. The psychodynamic-interpersonal treatment also had interpreting and exploring dimensions, whereas the cognitive-behavioral treatment had prescribing and reframing dimensions. Each of these dimensions contained a specific pattern of client and counselor verbal response modes. For example, the client's acknowledgment verbal response mode and the counselor's edification, disclosure, and question response modes loaded on the explaining factor. Stiles and Shapiro (1995) concluded that verbal exchange patterns of clients and counselors involved joint participation, with each participant (client and counselor) engaging in a specific role. The verbal exchange patterns identified through P-Type factor analysis appeared to consist of one participant actively contributing to and the other participant attentively facilitating the exchange.

Tinsley (1992) labeled Q-Type and R-Type factor analyses "static designs" because occasions are held constant. In Q-Type factor analysis, the counseling researcher tries to identify types of persons by seeing how people go together across variables sampled. There has been an ongoing interest among counseling researchers in identifying types of people. Usually, however, cluster analysis (see later in this chapter) was used in studies describing typologies of people. Q-Type factor analysis offers an alternative methodology for forming typologies of people. As in O-Type factor analysis, the researcher would begin by identifying a large number of items to administer to the research participants. Q-sorts are ideal for this type of analysis because they are constructed to have independent items. Once administered to a group of participants, the participants are factor-analyzed, and typologies are formed from the resulting factor loading matrix.

Counseling researchers are typically familiar with R-Type factor analysis. The vast majority of studies in psychology in general, and in counseling psychology specifically, have used R-Type factor analysis; this is the type of analysis used in most test construction. In R-Type factor analysis, the researcher attempts to identify latent dimensions that explain the relationship among the variables examined. The counseling researcher identifies a substantial number of participants and then administers the variables to them. In the case of test construction, the variables would be test items. The variables are factor-analyzed to identify the dimensions that explain the covariance among the items.

S-Type and T-Type factor analyses are labeled "monovariate designs" by Tinsley (1992) because only one variable is examined. In T-Type factor analysis, the researcher attempts to describe types of occasions. The purpose is similar to O-Type factor analysis. An S-Type factor analysis could also be used to empirically examine the stage models postulated by some counseling theorists (Egan, 1994). The researcher would identify one variable that theoretically should change across stages of counseling. For example, several theorists (see, for example, Gelso & Carter, 1994) believe that working alliance follows a high-low-high pattern across three phases of counseling. To test this hypothesis, the Working Alliance Inventory (Horvath & Greenberg, 1989) could be administered every session to a number of clients. If Gelso and Carter's hypothesis is correct, the S-Type factor analysis of counseling sessions (occasions) should identify two factors that describe counseling sessions: a "high working alliance" factor with loadings from early and late sessions, and a "low working alliance" factor with loadings from middle sessions.

As in Q-Type factor analysis, S-Type factor analysis is used to identify types of persons. As in T-Type factor analysis, however, only one variable is examined. For example, depression could be measured in a group of participants on a weekly basis for a year. Once the data were obtained, persons would be factor-analyzed across the 52 weeks. The resulting dimensions would define how many types of depressed people existed. For instance, some people may remain constantly "depressed," whereas others may show a great deal of variation in their level of depression over time. These different types of depressed people may need different types of counseling interventions.

Conducting a Factor Analysis

Factor analysis is a multivariate statistical method that involves a number of decision points, which sometimes entail rather complex procedures with specialized vocabulary. Many of these decision points are beyond the scope of this text; a wide variety of more detailed resources are available for further consultation to aid decisions about which variables will serve as the basic data. Often the researcher will develop his or her own questionnaire, the items of which constitute the variables. A great deal of time, planning, and reflection are needed to develop quality items (see Chapter 10); for one example, see Wade (1998). Factor analysis (and cluster analysis as well) lack independent and dependent variables as we defined those terms in Chapter 2. Sometimes a researcher might factor-analyze an existing instrument, or factor-analyze all of the items from two or three instruments to identify common factors across instruments.

After the variables have been selected or developed, the sample is defined, and then the data are collected and entered into a computer. The researcher then factor-analyzes the data. Computers and statistical software programs have greatly facilitated this process, although several major decision points still exist for the researcher.

The purpose of factor analysis is to identify common dimensions of a set of variables. The researcher also wants to see which items go together to make up a factor. In a previous example, the researcher wanted to know which factors account for the types of career-change barriers that people experience, and which of the 100 items make up each factor. While much of the actual factor analysis procedure is technical and beyond the scope of this chapter, you should be aware of four critical decision points that the researcher encounters in performing a factor analysis.

First, the researcher must decide what type of factor analysis to use in analyzing the data. The choice of factor analysis type involves assumptions about the treatment of item variance. For example, principal factors factor analysis only analyzes the common variance among the items to be factor-analyzed. Principal components factor analysis, by contrast, analyzes all of the item variance (common and unique). Typically, because of the difference in item variance analyzed, a principal factors factor analysis will identify fewer underlying constructs than will a principal components factor analysis.

Second, the researcher must decide how many factors exist in a set of data. The actual factor analysis procedure produces a range of possible factor solutions. While specific criteria can be used to suggest how many factors may exist, many times deciding on the number of factors is not a clear-cut process. Two researchers looking at the same data might decide that a different number of factors exist. You should be aware of this situation when you read the report of a factor analysis. One of the major advantages of confirmatory factor analysis is that the researcher decides on number of dimensions beforehand and tests whether the data confirm or disconfirm his or her expectations.

A third decision point involves the method of rotation. The solution from a factor analysis must be rotated to enable the researcher to interpret the meaning of the underlying constructs. In a factor analysis solution that, for example, contains two constructs, the rotation would involve rotating the x-axis and y-axis so that the items "loaded" on only one of the two constructs. If the two underlying constructs are uncorrelated, the x-axis and the y-axis are at a 90° angle. A rotation where the constructs are uncorrelated is called an orthogonal rotation. If, however, the two underlying constructs are correlated, the x-axis and the y-axis are at an angle less than 90°. A rotation where the constructs are correlated is called an oblique rotation. The choice of rotation method has important implications for the interpretation of the underlying constructs.

Naming the derived factors is the fourth important decision that the researcher makes. To do this, he or she examines all of the items that make up a factor and attempts to choose a name that captures the conceptual meaning inherent in the items. Obviously, this naming process is subjective, and researchers examining the same set of items may propose different names for the same factor. You should also be aware of the subjective nature of the factor naming process when examining the report of a factor analysis.

Examples of Factor Analysis

R-Type Factor Analysis.   Tinsley, Roth, and Lease (1989) used both confirmatory and exploratory factor analysis to examine the dimensions that define group leadership. The main purpose of this study was to attempt to confirm a four-factor model of group leadership originally described by Lieberman, Yalom, and Miles (1973). In a classic study of group leadership, Lieberman and colleagues found that leader, member, and observer ratings of leadership converged on a four-factor structure of leadership. They labeled these factors emotional stimulation, caring, meaning attribution, and executive functioning. The researchers wanted to determine whether group leaders' self-ratings, obtained from a large number of these leaders, would confirm this four-factor structure.

The study used both survey and factor analysis methods. These authors randomly selected 500 members of the Association for Specialists in Group Work and mailed them survey questionnaires. Usable responses were returned by 200 of the 500 identified group leaders. The survey instrument contained 130 items, five items measuring each of the 26 leader characteristics studied by Lieberman et al.

Twenty-six scale scores (one score for each of the 26 leader characteristics) were calculated for each participant. These scale scores were used as the data for the factor analysis. Tinsley et al. first used confirmatory factor analysis to ascertain if the 26 scales would result in the four factors described by Lieberman et al. They found that only 8 of the 26 scales loaded on (or scored highest on) the factor that they theoretically should have loaded on. Tinsley et al. concluded that their analysis failed to confirm the factor model proposed by Lieberman et al.

Because of this failure to confirm, Tinsley et al. then used exploratory factor analysis to determine how many and what dimensions accounted for self-rating of leadership. The authors examined eight-, nine-, and ten-factor solutions before adopting an eight-factor solution that they believed best explained the data. Next, Tinsley et al. examined the scales that correlated with each factor and determined a name for the underlying construct that these items represented. For example, the scales managing/limit setting, mirroring command stimulation, cognizing, charismatic leader, and model all loaded on (were a part of) the first factor. Tinsley et al. named the underlying construct "cognitive direction." In a similar manner they examined the scales that loaded on the other factors and derived names for the underlying constructs. The constructs they named were affective direction, nurturant attractiveness, group functioning, verbal stimulation, charismatic expert, individual functioning, and nonverbal exercises.

Tinsley et al. concluded that the four factors identified by Lieberman et al. could not adequately account for the self-rating of leadership obtained in their sample. In fact, eight factors were used to account for the obtained self-ratings. Tinsley et al. concluded that group leadership is more complicated and multifaceted than the Lieberman et al. model would suggest.

The Tinsley et al. study is an excellent example of the use of factor analysis. It is exemplary because they explicitly delineated for readers the basis for their choice of the number of factors and for naming the factors. In this way readers are invited to make their own judgments about the critical choices made by the researchers.

P-TYPE FACTOR ANALYSIS.   Patton, Kivlighan, and Multon (1997) used P-Type factor analysis to describe the salient dimensions of the counseling process across 20 sessions of time-limited psychoanalytic counseling. Even though P-Type factor analysis is ideographic in that it focuses the examination of relationships at the level of the single individual it can obtain more normative information by chaining together observations (data) from several individuals. Patton et al. used chained P-Type analysis to discover the latent dimensions in the counseling process in our client-therapist sample.

Patton et al. described the latent dimensions underlying 16 process variables collected from clients (Working Alliance Inventory), counselors (Working Alli-ance Inventory; ratings of Positive and Negative Transference from the Missouri Identifying Transference Scale) and independent observers (Counselor Empathy, Collaboration, Abrupt/Shifting, Oppositional, Flat/Halting, and Vague/ Doubting Resistances from the Resistance Scale; Highlighting/Interpreting Resistance and Exploring and Working Through Resistance scales from the Missouri Addressing Resistance Scale; and Psychodynamic Interviewing Style and Time-Limited Dynamic Psychotherapy Specific Strategies scales from the Vanderbilt Therapeutic Strategies Scale) using P-Type principal components analysis. Ratings from each counseling session for each counselor-client dyad were subjected to an exploratory factor analysis (iterative principal-components extraction).

Four factors met the Kaiser-Guttman retention criterion of eigen values greater than 1.0, and Cattell's scree test also suggested a four-factor solution. Patton et al. therefore retained the four-factor solution. Their four factors explained 67.1% of the total variance. Patton et al. labeled the factors (a) Client Resistance, (b) Client Transference, (c) Psychoanalytic Technique, and (d) Working Alliance. Once these dimensions of the counseling process were identified, Patton et al. examined both the interrelation of the dimensions in a time-series analysis and how these dimensions were related to counseling outcome.

The Patton et al. (1997) study provides a good example of how P-Type factor analysis can help counseling process researchers describe parsimoniously the dimensions of counseling process. By chaining together the data from several counselor-client dyads, Patton et al. maximized the data from their relatively small client-counselor sample.

O-TYPE FACTOR ANALYSIS.   O-Type factor analyses are rare in counseling research. Group counseling theorists seem to agree that groups develop through a series of successive stages, each of which is described as having a predominant interactional quality. Despite the widespread "clinical" agreement about the nature of group development, there has been little objective empirical evidence for the existence of group stages. Tschuschke and MacKenzie (1989) used O-Type factor analysis to empirically examine the stages in two in-patient psychotherapy groups. One of these groups was more successful, and the other less successful, in terms of leader-rated member outcome, and group attendance and drop out.

The two in-patient groups were analyzed separately, creating a situation in which persons (in this case, the group was the "person") were held constant. The variables examined in this study were derived from the Gottschalk-Gleser (1969) system of verbal content analysis. Specifically, ratings were made on (a) death anxiety, (b) mutilation anxiety, (c) separation anxiety, (d) guilt anxiety, (e) shame anxiety, (f) diffuse or nonspecific anxiety, (g) overtly outward-directed hostility, (h) covertly outward-directed hostility, (i) inward-directed hostility, and (j) ambivalent hostility. For the more successful group, 19 sessions were analyzed; for the less successful group, 17 sessions were analyzed—both with the Gottschalk-Gleser (1969) system.

The O-Type factor analysis yielded four factors in the more-successful and five factors in the less-successful group. Sessions were assigned to factors based on their highest factor loading score. In the more-successful group the four factors occurred sequentially, as would be predicted by group development theory. For example, the first four sessions analyzed in the more-successful group all loaded on one factor. The less-successful group, however, showed no sequential patterning of factors across the sessions examined. Different types of sessions seemed to occur almost randomly. For example, the first session examined loaded on factor 2, the second on factor 1, the third on factor 4, and the fourth on factor 3. Tschuschke and MacKenzie (1989) concluded that following a sequential pattern of stage development was characteristic of the successful counseling process.

Cluster Analysis

Often in counseling we would like to be able to identify natural groupings or sub-types of clients, counseling responses, or counselors. Cluster analysis is a class of multivariate statistical method, the primary purpose of which is to reduce data by identifying and then classifying similar entities into subgroups (Hair, Anderson, and Tatham, 1987). This statistical technique classifies objects, variables, or persons so that each object is very similar to others in its cluster. Thus, within each cluster, objects, variables, or persons are homogeneous, but there is considerable heterogeneity among clusters (Hair et al., 1987). According to Borgen and Barnett (1987), cluster analysis can be used to categorize objects (counselor statements), people (counseling center clients), or variables (items on a test).

Cluster analysis is frequently used to put people into subgroups, which is quite functional for examining individual differences in counseling research. Consider the previous example about career barriers. Suppose the researcher was interested not in identifying underlying dimensions of career barriers, but rather in identifying subgroups of clients, each of whom experienced various barriers in changing careers. The researcher then might assess 100 clients by administering five or six instruments that she thought would measure some aspect of career barriers (for example, self-esteem, motivation to change, or risk-taking propensity). After collecting and entering the data into a computer, she might use cluster analysis procedures to identify, say, four subgroups of clients: (a) a low self-esteem group, (b) a low motivation group, (c) a group lacking career information, and (d) a low risk-taking group. These results might suggest that different career planning interventions should be designed for these subgroups of clients. In sum, cluster analysis condenses or summarizes a large number of variables by placing objects (such as people) or variables into categories or subgroups.

Unlike factor analysis, cluster analysis has been used infrequently in the counseling literature until recently. In terms of identifying types of people, Megargee and Bohn (1979) used cluster analysis to develop a typology of criminal offenders based on MMPI profiles, whereas Rojewski (1994) used the Career Decision Scale (Osipow et al., 1976) to identify three types of career indecisive adolescents. Hill and O'Grady (1985) used cluster analysis of variables to develop a classification of counselor intentions. Their 19 therapist intentions were collapsed into four categories: assessment, therapeutic work, nonspecific factors, and problems. Using a similar analysis, Hill, Helms, Spiegel, and Tichenor (1988) found five clusters of client reactions. As an example of clustering other objects, Wampold and White (1985) used cluster analysis to analyze research themes in counseling psychology. Examining common citations among 27 articles published during 1982, they concluded that the social influence model was a common underlying theme in the 27 articles.

Performing a Cluster Analysis

As with factor analysis, many of the processes involved in cluster analysis are beyond the scope of this text. Interested readers should consult the following references for more details: Aldenderfer and Blashfield, 1984; Blashfield, 1984; Borgen and Barnett, 1987; Borgen and Weiss, 1971; Hair et al., 1987; and Lorr, 1983.

Similar to factor analysis, the researcher must determine the appropriateness of the design to the research question. Borgen and Barnett (1987) noted that the purposes of cluster analysis are exploration (to find a certain structure or set of groupings), confirmation (to test an existing classification, perhaps based on theory), and simplification (to reduce a complex data set into a simpler structure). The researcher must also define a sample and select the appropriate instruments. The latter assumes added importance in cluster analysis, because the instruments are the tools for measuring the similarity between objects. To use the flashlight analogy again, a flashlight will provide light only in the direction in which it is pointed. Likewise, objects can be determined to be similar only in the ways they are measured. After data are collected, the researcher proceeds to the statistical procedures involved in cluster analysis.

The two major decision points in cluster analysis are similar to those involved in factor analysis. Like factor analysis, the cluster analysis procedure produces a number of possible cluster solutions. The researcher must decide on the best solution for the data set. Fewer guidelines are available in cluster analysis than in factor analysis for making this decision, so the number of clusters retained is a subjective decision. Once this decision has been made, the researcher attempts to name the clusters. To do this, he or she examines the items or individuals that make up a cluster and tries to identify an underlying commonality or construct. Obvi-ously, this naming process is subjective, and disagreement about the meaning of the cluster can occur.

In sum, cluster analysis can be a very powerful data reduction technique, although its application is not as well developed as that of factor analysis. Different measures and categorizing techniques often result in different clusters, and thus the researcher must often be cautious and tentative.

Two Examples of Cluster Analysis

The first example of cluster analysis involves the categorization of people, specifi-cally counseling center clients. Heppner et al. (1994) were interested in using pre-senting problems to describe the types of clients seeking help at a university counseling center. As these authors noted, counseling researchers have tradition-ally been interested in describing the types of problems that confront college stu-dents. Such research, however, has generally tabulated only the frequency of occurrence for various types of problems. Heppner et al. wanted to move beyond the general description of presenting problems to developing an empirically derived classification system of college students' presenting problems at a univer-sity counseling center. Because clients present with multiple problems, simple fre-quency counts do not adequately describe their concerns. Heppner et al. (1994) therefore derived the following eight problem categories from the CASPER (McCullough & Farrell, 1983) program: (a) global distress rating, (b) chemical prob-lems, (c) suicide problems, (d) thought problems, (e) physical problems, (f) interpersonal problems, (g) mood problems, and (h) leisure activities. These eight problem categories were used as clustering variables in a cluster analysis.

Heppner et al. used the Ward method of cluster analysis to analyze the data. The error term (semipartial R^2 values) was used to determine the appropriate number of clusters to examine. Based on this information, Heppner et al. chose to evaluate a 12-cluster solution. It is important to note that the clients within a cluster had similar profiles on the CASPER dimensions examined. Subsequently, three clusters were dropped because they contained fewer than eight clients, leaving a nine-cluster solution. Heppner et al. examined the mean problems ratings when naming the clusters. For example, the clients in Cluster 6 reported the highest number of days experiencing physical problems, while the other seven problem categories were all in the low to moderate reporting range. Because these clients were almost exclusively reporting physical concerns, Heppner et al. named this cluster of clients Severe Somatic Concerns. The names for the other eight client clusters were (a) Severe General Distress, (b) High General Distress, (c) Interpersonal Concerns, Moderate Distress, (d) Interpersonal Concerns, Low Distress, (e) Moderate Physical, Mood, Interpersonal Concerns, (f) Moderate Somatic Concerns, (g) Chemical Concerns, Moderate Distress, and (h) Situational Adjustment, Unassessed Concerns.

The stability of the identified cluster solution was assessed by randomly dividing the sample into two groups and rerunning the cluster analysis. The nine-cluster solution was replicated in the two subsamples. To validate the cluster solution, Heppner et al. used demographic variables that were external to the clustering process; specifically, they examined how the clusters of clients differed in terms of client (a) age, (b) gender, (c) race, (d) use of medication, (e) relatives with alcohol problems, and (f) relatives with mental illness. For example, the clients in the Severe Somatic Concerns Cluster had greater medication use than did the clients in the other clusters. In addition, minority clients were over represented in the High General Distress Cluster.

The Heppner et al. (1994) study provides a good example of clustering people, for several reasons. First, they used a reliable and valid problem identification system to obtain the clustering variables. Both the participants-to-variable ratio and the participants-to-cluster ratio were large, suggesting that the obtained clusters were not a function of chance findings. Heppner et al. replicated the cluster solution through a split sample procedure. Finally, the authors used a relatively large number of variables not used in the clustering procedure to validate the cluster solution. Several weaknesses were also apparent in this study. First, the CASPER problem list may not have represented the scope of problems encountered at a university counseling. For example, career and academic concerns were not represented among the problems assessed in CASPER. Second, several researchers have attempted to validate their cluster solutions by analyzing their data with a different clustering method. Heppner et al. could have further examined the stability of their cluster solution by using an alternate clustering method (i.e., average link clustering).

Elliot (1985) provides an example of a study using cluster analysis to categorize objects. Surprisingly, before 1985 there was no system for classifying helpful and nonhelpful therapeutic events. Such a system can both help process researchers describe the counseling process with greater consistency and facilitate training. Elliott (1985) set out to derive a taxonomy of helpful and nonhelpful events in brief counseling by using a three-step process. First, clients were asked to describe the most helpful and least helpful events in a counseling session. Next, judges sorted the descriptions of events into categories. Finally, these sorts were combined and cluster-analyzed.

Twenty-four student clients identified 86 helpful and 70 nonhelpful counselor responses. Their descriptions of these responses were then given to 34 judges, who were instructed to create 3 to 12 categories for classifying these descriptions. Similarity was calculated by tabulating the number of judges who put each pair of events into the same category.

Elliott used two clustering methods (average linkage and maximum linkage) to cluster the data. These methods yielded high levels of agreement. The analysis identified eight kinds of helpful events, which were grouped into two higher-order superclusters (note the hierarchial outcome). One supercluster, the task supercluster, contained four categories: perspective, problem solution, problem clarification, and focusing awareness. The other supercluster, the interpersonal supercluster, contained another four clusters: understanding, client involvement, reassurance, and personal contact. The six clusters of nonhelpful events were misperception, negative counselor reaction, unwanted responsibility, repetition, misdirection, and unwanted thoughts.

This study is a good example of the process recommended by Borgen and Barnett (1987). Especially noteworthy is the use of two methods of cluster analysis (average and maximum linkage) to examine the stability of the derived clusters. The use of two methods of clustering was a type of within-sample replication in that two different methods resulted in similar solutions. Elliott also validated the derived clusters by examining their relationship to counselor response modes. For example, Elliott found that paraphrases were usually followed by focusing awareness but not by unwanted thoughts. Moreover, he found that particular sets of following responses were nicely described by the derived categories. The major weakness of Elliott's study involves the sampling procedure: Because he used undergraduates recruited from a psychology class in the research, it is unclear whether their responses are generalizable to a client population. This study could have been strengthened by replicating the cluster structure with a more clinical population. Despite this weakness in sample selection, Elliott's study is a good example of a carefully designed cluster analysis study. If replicated, the clusters he found could add greatly to research in the counseling process.

PASSIVE RESEARCH DESIGNS

What is the relationship between interest/job congruence and satisfaction with one's job (see, for example, Gottfredson & Holland, 1990)? Can we predict a student's acquisition of counseling skills by knowing his or her MMPI score? What is the relationship between a person's self-efficacy expectations and his or her choice of career options (Betz & Hackett, 1981, 1987; Lapan, Boggs, & Morrill, 1989)? These are questions that can be addressed by passive designs. Cook and

Campbell (1979) refer to these designs as passive because the researcher neither actively forms groups or conditions through random or nonrandom assignment, nor actively manipulates an independent variable.

Passive designs are used to examine the relationship between or among variables. A simple passive design examines the relationship between two variables (for instance, depression and social skills); more complex designs examine the collective contribution of two or more variables to the variation in a third variable.

In a simple passive study, the investigator collects data on two variables (x and y) and then uses a statistical analysis (typically a Pearson product moment correlation) to describe their relationship. The correlation coefficient, or r, provides an index of the degree of linear relationship between the variables. Suppose that as x increases, so do the scores on y; then x and y vary together, or covary, and have a "strong positive relationship." If x scores do not vary with y scores, we typically say there is no relationship between x and y. The correlation coefficient between two scores can range from +1.00 (a positive relation) to –1.00 (a negative relation). The amount of variance that is shared between two variables is the square of the correlation. Thus, the correlation between x and y might be +0.5, which means that the amount of variance shared between these two variables is 25% (0.5^2).

For example, Hoffman and Weiss (1987) were interested in the relationship between individual psychological separation and healthy adjustment. They developed an inventory of common problems to reflect healthy adjustment, and correlated this measure with scores from another inventory that measured four aspects of psychological separation. Two hundred sixty-seven white college students completed the two self-report inventories. Hoffman and Weiss found that students with greater conflictual dependence on their mothers or fathers reported more problems (r = 0.43 and 0.42, respectively). Because the results are correlational, however, the direction of the relationship between conflictual dependence and reported problems cannot be determined; conflictual dependence may cause more emotional problems, or having more problems may lead to greater conflictual dependence on parents, or a third variable may cause both conflictual dependence and emotional problems. In short, the passive design Hoffman and Weiss used allowed them to describe the degree of relationship between two variables— individual psychological separation and psychological adjustment.

Although passive designs have been used throughout the history of counseling research, this design has not been linked to a particular type of question or to a specific content. Rather, studies employing a correlational design have been used to describe relationships among a wide variety of variables of interest to counseling researchers.

A study by Nocita and Stiles (1986) is a particularly noteworthy example of the use of a simple passive design. These authors wanted to assess the relationship between a client's level of introversion and his or her perception of counseling sessions. The client's level of introversion was assessed by the Social Introversion scale of the MMPI. At the conclusion of each counseling session, clients also filled out a Session Evaluation Questionnaire (Stiles, 1980), which assessed the client's perception of session depth and smoothness and his or her feelings of positivity and arousal. Nocita and Stiles correlated the client's social introversion score with each of his or her scores on the four Session Evaluation Questionnaire scales.

Introverted clients saw the counseling session as less smooth and felt less positive after the session than the more extraverted clients. The noteworthy and unusual aspect of this study is that the correlational results were replicated with two different client samples. This type of replication is unfortunately all too uncommon in the counseling literature.

We also want to mention a more sophisticated development in the use of correlational designs. Cole, Lazarick, and Howard (1987) argued that most of the passive (as well as the experimental) research in counseling has underestimated the relationships among the variables examined because researchers tend to examine only manifest variables—derived scores, usually from an inventory, that are presumed to reflect a person's standing on a construct or latent variable. However, because manifest variables (for example, the score on the Beck Depression Inventory) contain measurement error, the relationship between two manifest variables is a function of their relationship and the reliability of the measures. Cole et al. described a method for determining the relationship between the constructs that the manifest variables are presumed to measure.

Cole et al. proposed that confirmatory factor analysis be used to examine the relationship between constructs or latent variables. To use confirmatory factor analysis, the constructs of interest must be assessed by multiple methods. For example, Cole et al. were interested in assessing the relationship between depression and social skills. The authors assessed each of the constructs from four perspectives: self-report (Beck Depression Inventory and Survey of Heterosexual Interactions), behavioral ratings (Nonverbal Cue for Depression and Social Anxiety and Skill Index), interview (Feeling and Concerns Checklist and Interpersonal Adjective Checklist), and significant other (Depression Behavior Rating Scale and a modified version of the Survey of Heterosexual Interactions). Cole et al. (1987) found an average cross-trait correlation of –0.25 across the four measures of depression and social skills. When confirmatory factor analysis was used to estimate the relationship between the constructs of depression and social skills, a –0.85 correlation was found. Rather than accounting for only 6% of the variance in depression using a Pearson product moment correlation (-0.25^2), social skills accounted for approximately 72% (-0.85^2) of this variance using confirmatory factor analysis.

The procedure described by Cole et al. is an important statistical and conceptual advance in the analysis of correlational designs. Counseling researchers are often interested in the relationship between psychological constructs, although we usually examine the relationship between manifest variables only. As with all passive designs, however, this type of analysis does not allow for causal explanation. A causal relationship between social skills and depression can only be established using an experimental design.

Ex Post Facto Designs

Many independent variables of interest to counseling researchers cannot be manipulated. For instance, gender, personality type, treatment success (versus failure), and race are important and interesting variables, but they cannot be manipulated. Designs that use these types of variables are also passive designs and are called ex post facto designs. The name literally means "after the fact." In other words, the investigation or research takes place after the groups or conditions have been formed.

In many ways, ex post facto designs resemble the posttest-only quasi-experimental design described in Chapter 7. The experimenter selects an appropriate independent variable (male versus female) and then observes differences in a dependent variable (counseling skills). For instance, do male and female therapists differ in client-perceived empathy? Ex post facto designs can have multiple levels, or be factorial; for instance, an investigator can simultaneously examine the effect of counselor race and gender on client-perceived empathy. These more complicated designs, however, share the same strengths and limitations as the simpler two-level designs.

The most obvious difference between the ex post facto design and a true experiment involves the manipulation of the independent variable. In addition, the designs also differ in the lack of random assignment in the ex post facto design—for instance, therapy continuers and dropouts are not randomly assigned to the continuer or dropout condition. Kerlinger (1986) warned about a self-selection of participants into conditions, and this is clearly the case with dropouts. This self-selection implies that there is some basis for the selection. In an ex post facto design, this selection basis—and not the variable of interest—may account for any observed differences across conditions.

Like quasi-experimental designs, ex post facto designs present a number of problems in interpreting results. One of these problems is the role of chance in the findings. Especially if the researcher examines a large number of variables, it is likely that he or she will find some significant results by chance. For instance, a researcher who seeks to distinguish between continuing clients and those clients who do not continue in therapy may give a number of instruments (50 variables in all) to clients as they come to an agency and then subsequently compare the continuers and noncontinuers on these 50 variables. Suppose the researcher finds differences between continuing and noncontinuing clients on five variables: How important are these findings? Are they a reflection of real differences or chance? Ex post facto designs can capitalize on chance, and the researcher may be misled into erroneous conclusions based on chance findings.

An Example of an Ex Post Facto Design

A study by Gade, Fuqua, and Hurlburt (1988) is an illustration of an ex post facto design because they examined both Holland type and gender. The researchers were interested in the relationship between Holland personality type and satisfaction with the educational setting in high schools that represented three different models of education (residential schools, provincially controlled schools that were predominantly Native American, and tribally controlled schools). Students were classified (not assigned) as a particular Holland type by results on the Self-Directed Search (Holland, 1985b). Satisfaction with the educational environment was measured by the Teacher Approval and Educational Acceptance scales of the Survey of Study Habits and Attitudes (Brown & Holtzman, 1967).

Two 6 (Holland code) × 2 (gender) ANOVAS were used to examine differences in teacher approval and educational acceptance. Gade et al. found significant main effects for Holland code on teacher approval and educational acceptance, and for gender on educational acceptance. There were no Holland code by gender interactions for either satisfaction variable. In terms of specific Holland codes, investigative and social students had higher school satisfaction than realistic students.

This study is a good example of ex post facto research for at least two reasons. First, the variables examined were theoretically derived. The authors did not ask if students with different Holland types would have different school satisfaction. Rather, they hypothesized (based on Holland's notion of congruence) that there would be a specific difference in school satisfaction for different Holland types, and then tested this hypothesis. A second strength was the care the authors took in selecting students from different types of schools. Because of sample heterogeneity, it is unlikely that the obtained results were caused by some characteristic of students in one particular sample.

This study also illustrates some of the weaknesses of ex post facto research. The examination of gender differences in school satisfaction seemed more empirical than theoretical. The authors never offered a theoretical explanation for why males and females might differ in school satisfaction, or why this was an important variable to address. Also, there was no theoretical discussion of possible Holland code by gender interactions. In keeping with this lack of theoretical discussion of gender differences, the authors noted only in passing the significant gender difference found on the Educational Acceptance scale. This lack of discussion seems appropriate given the lack of theoretical attention to gender differences.

In sum, passive designs are extremely important, especially in early stages of investigating phenomena. With these designs, in contrast to experimental designs, a researcher can quickly and relatively easily describe possible relationships among variables. Passive studies can rule out the existence of causal relationships—if no correlation exists between variables, there can be no causal relationship—and can suggest possible causal connections among variables that can be examined in a subsequent experimental design. One of the main weaknesses of most passive studies in counseling is the lack of attention to sample selection. When convenience samples are used, the generalizability or external validity of the results is limited.

We would like to offer three suggestions for counseling researchers considering a passive design. First, passive research should be undertaken from a strong theoretical grounding. Researchers would do well to avoid questions such as, How do these sets of variables relate? How do these groups differ? Rather, theory should be used to inform the research in the determination of the variables examined.

Second, passive designs are strengthened when they contain differential predictions. For example, theory may indicate that a variable (realistic Holland code) might be positively related to one variable (lack of accidents), not related to another (weight), and negatively related to a third (school satisfaction). A study is strengthened when these patterns of relationships are predicted and assessed. Specifically, we recommend that researchers consider examining multiple relationships, especially ones that are predicted to show results in opposite directions.

Our third recommendation is that researchers pay particular attention to sample characteristics. For instance, Gade et al. (1988) purposefully selected a varied sample in an attempt to eliminate any chance results based on sample characteristics. Researchers may want to select samples in which various demographic or psychological characteristics are held constant. For example, researchers wanting to compare "good" versus "poor" counseling sessions in terms of type of therapist response used may want to select only sessions that are temporally close. This type of selection would lessen the chance that the results were influenced by the stage of therapy.

Multiple Regression

Whereas a correlation identifies the relationship between two variables, most often researchers are interested in describing the relationships among more than two variables. For example, one might ask: If we know the correlation between x and y, would it not be more powerful to include variables a, b, and c (along with x) to study y? In many cases it is, and thus multivariate analysis or multiple regression has become increasingly popular. We will briefly focus on multiple regression here as a way of increasing our ability to describe the relationships among multiple variables. (For more details, see Cohen & Cohen, 1983; Hair, Anderson, & Tatham, 1987; Pedhazur, 1982; and Wampold & Freund, 1987.)

Multiple regression is a statistical method for studying the separate and collective contributions of one or more predictor variables to the variation of a dependent variable (Wampold & Freund, 1987). Multiple regression can be used with a passive design to describe how multiple predictor variables are related to a single "dependent" (criterion) variable. Thus, researchers frequently refer to predicting the criterion variable and discuss the extent to which they can accurately predict the criterion. Like simple correlation, multiple regression has been used with a wide variety of variables and research questions. The relationship between a "dependent" variable and a set of multiple "independent" variables is expressed as the multiple correlation coefficient R, which is a measure of how well the predicted scores correspond to the actual scores of dependent variables. The square of the multiple correlation coefficient (R^2) is the proportion of variance in the dependent variable explained by the independent variables. The word *explained* here does not necessarily imply a causal relationship, but rather an association of the dependent variable with variability in the predictor variables (Wampold & Freund, 1987).

There are three basic methods for entering predictor variables in regression equations: simultaneous, stepwise, and hierarchical regression. Because each method serves slightly different purposes and outcomes, it is important for the researcher to be familar with the strengths and weaknesses of each method (see Wampold & Freund, 1987, for an overview). In *simultaneous regression,* all of the predictor variables are entered concurrently (simultaneously) into the regression equation. Simultaneous regression is most often used for the purpose of prediction, and when there is no basis for entering any particular predictor variable before any other predictor variable. For instance, Parham and Helms (1985b) examined the relationship between racial identity attitude and self-esteem. Four racial identity attitudes were simultaneously entered in a regression equation predicting self-esteem. Parham and Helms found a multiple R of 0.36 for the analysis. Thus, racial identity accounted for about 13% of the variance (0.36^2) in the black participant's self-esteem. Examination of the specific racial identity attitudes revealed that students in the preencounter stage of racial identity formation had lower self-esteem than students in the immersion stage of identity formation.

In *stepwise regression,* predictor variables are entered into the regression equation in an order based on a specified criterion. For example, the regression model first enters the variable with the highest correlation with the "criterion" variable. The next variable that is entered is the one that results in the largest increase in R^2. This procedure is repeated until adding variables does not result in a statistically significant increase in R^2. Thus, a stepwise procedure identifies which variables contribute the most unique variance in the equation, and in what order. Cohen and Cohen (1983) recommended that stepwise regression be used only when the research goal is primarily predictive, because stepwise methods are subject to biases in the sample and thus are subject to spurious results. Kivlighan and Shapiro (1987) used a stepwise regression to predict who would benefit from a self-help career counseling program. This type of prediction was important because previous studies had shown that self-help and counselor-directed career interventions had equivalent effects (Krivatsky & Magoon, 1976). Scores for the six Holland types (realistic, investigative, artistic, social, enterprising, and conventional) were used as predictor variables. The criterion variable was change in vocational identity (Holland, Daiger, & Power, 1980). The conventional and investigative scores entered the stepwise regression as statistically significant predictors. Participant scores on the two variables accounted for 25% (adjusted R^2) of the variance in outcome. Adjusted R^2, sometimes referred to as the adjustment for shrinkage, is calculated in relation to the study's sample size; it is an estimate of what the R^2 would be if the study were replicated with several different samples. Kivlighan and Shapiro's study is also noteworthy because they used an analysis of covariance to remove the variance in the dependent variable attributable to pretest scores. The pretreatment vocational identity scores were regressed on the posttreatment vocational identity scores. The residuals (the variance in the posttreatment scores that could not be accounted for by the pretreatment scores) from this regression were used as the dependent variable in the stepwise regression. In this manner, the researchers were able to examine how much the Holland scores could accurately predict *change* in vocational identity from a pretest period to a posttest period.

In *hierarchical regression,* the researcher specifies the order of entry of the predictor variables based on some rationale (for example, research relevance, causal priority, or theoretical grounds). Lent, Brown, and Lankin (1987) were interested in examining the relationships among self-efficacy, interest congruence, consequential thinking, and various career and academic behaviors. One behavior of interest was academic grade point average. In the first step of the regression analysis, a measure of composite ability (high school rank, Preliminary Scholastic Aptitude Test) was entered first to control for the effects of previous academic performance. Next, the three theoretically derived variables (self-efficacy, interest congruence, and consequential thinking) were entered in a stepwise manner. In predicting career indecision, the multiple R for composite ability was 0.34. When interest congruence was added, the multiple R increased to 0.44 ($F = 9.62, p >$ .01). This result indicated that interest congruence added additional predictive variance beyond that accounted for by composite ability. By using a hierarchical model in which composite ability was entered first, Lent and colleagues were able to perform a more stringent test of the relationship between interest congruence and career indecision.

In evaluating the usefulness of multiple regression, it is always important to remember that the results of these types of analyses are based on correlational data. Even though regression research uses terminology from experimental designs (*dependent variable* and *independent variables;* we prefer the terms *criterion* and *predictor*), the results obtained are relational, not causal. The choice of a criterion variable and of predictor variables is always arbitrary. In other words, prediction is not causality, and thus causal statements are not appropriate with these designs. Multiple regression is suited to describing and predicting the relationship between two or more variables and is especially useful in examining the incremental as well as total explanatory power of many variables (Hair, Anderson, & Tatham, 1987). Perhaps the main caveats for researchers pertain to inadequate sample sizes (see Wampold & Freund, 1987) and spurious results due to methodological procedures.

Testing for Moderation and Mediation

Using multiple regression, counseling researchers can address a number of important theoretical questions, two of the more important of which concern the presence of *moderating* or *mediating* variables. As pointed out by Baron and Kenney (1986), however, mediation and moderation are often confused by psychological researchers, and it is important to distinguish between them. As defined by Baron and Kenney (1986), a *moderator* is a variable that affects the direction and/or strength of the relationship between a predictor (independent variable) and a criterion (dependent variable). In other words, a moderator changes the relationship between the predictor and criterion variable, and in essence it is an interaction between the predictor and moderator variable to predict the criterion. In contrast, a *mediator* is a variable that accounts for or explains the relationship between a predictor variable and a criterion variable. "Whereas moderator variables specify when certain effects will hold, mediators speak to how or why such effects occur" (Baron & Kenny, 1986, p. 1176).

A classic example of a moderator relationship is the stress buffering hypothesis that has been prominent in social support research. According to this model, social support is predicted to moderate the relationship between negative life events (for example, death of a spouse) and depression. Specifically, negative life events are theoretically related to depression. However, social support changes this relationship. When social support is low, there should be a significant positive relationship between negative life events and depression. With low levels of social support, the more negative life events a person experiences, the higher her/his levels of depression. When social support is greater, however, the relationship between negative life events and depression is attenuated; when a person has more social support, negative life events do not necessarily result in higher levels of depression. Thus, there is an interaction between negative life events and social support in predicting levels of depression.

According to Baron and Kenny (1986), moderators can be either categorical (for example, sex) or continuous (for example, amount of social support). The appropriate statistical analysis for testing for moderating effects depends on the level of measure (categorical versus continuous) of both the moderator variable and the predictor variable. Baron and Kenny (1986) describe four types of statistical analyses derived from crossing the level of measurement for the predictor and the mediator variables (for example, the moderator variable is categorical and the predictor variable is continuous). Their article should be consulted for a more in-depth discussion of the statistical issues involved in testing for moderation effects.

As an example of these analytic procedures, we describe here the statistical approach used when both the mediator and criterion variables are continuous. When both variables are continuous, the potential moderator effect is tested in a hierarchical regression. In the first step of the regression, both the predictor and moderator variables are entered into the regression equation predicting the criterion variable. This first step produces an R^2 representing the amount of variance in the criterion variable that is explained by the predictor and moderator variables in combination. In the second step of the regression, the multiplicative product or interaction (predictor $\times$ moderator) is entered into the regression equation. After this second step, a new R^2 is obtained; it represents the amount of variance in the criterion variable that is explained by the combination of the predictor variable, the moderator variable, and their product. The difference between the R^2 obtained in the first step of the regression and the R^2 obtained in the second step is the amount of variance in the criterion variable that is uniquely predicted by the interaction (product) of the moderator and mediator variables. If the difference between the R^2 values from the first and second steps of the regression is significant, then there is a moderation effect.

Often, psychological processes are hypothesized to mediate the relationship between environmental events and behavioral consequences. Ellis's (1962) ABC paradigm is a classic example of a mediational model. In this paradigm, A stands for the activating event, B stands for the individuals belief, and C denotes the consequence, usually a behavioral or emotional response. Ellis argues that the belief explains the relationship between the event and the consequence.

Figure 9-1 is a modified representation of the path model for mediation presented in Baron and Kenny (1986). This path model depicts three paths or "causal" relationships between the three variables. Path a depicts the relationship between the predictor variable and the mediator variable; path b represents the relationship between the mediator variable and the criterion variable; and path c depicts the relationship between the predictor variable and the criterion variable. In order to demonstrate that a variable is a mediator, three conditions must be met: (a) path a, the relationship between the predictor variable and the criterion variable, must be

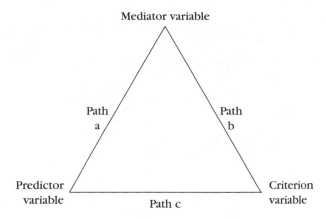

FIGURE 9-1
A mediational model (modified from Baron and Kenny, 1986).

statistically significant; (b) path b, the relationship between the mediator variable and the criterion variable, must be statistically significant; and (c) when paths a and b are controlled or accounted for, path c (the relationship between the predictor variable and the criterion variable that was significant previously), is no longer statistically significant. According to Baron and Kenny, the strongest demonstration of mediation occurs when in the third step, path c becomes zero. In most research, however, mediation is shown when path c is significantly reduced when paths a and b are controlled.

To test for mediation, Baron and Kenny (1986) recommend that a series of regression models be estimated. Specifically, the following three regression equations are run: First, run a regression model where the "mediator variable" in Figure 9-1 is the criterion variable and the "predictor variable" in Figure 9-1 is the predictor variable; second, run a regression model where the "criterion variable" in Figure 9-1 is the criterion variable and the "predictor variable" in Figure 9-1 is the predictor variable; and third, run a regression model where the "criterion variable" in Figure 9-1 is the criterion variable and the "predictor" and "mediator" variables in Figure 9-1 are both predictor variables. If the effect of the "predictor variable" on the "criterion" variable is less in the third step than it was in the second step, then mediation has been demonstrated.

Brown et al. (1996) provide an example of a study that tested both mediational and moderation hypotheses. Specifically, these authors reanalyzed data from a study by Phillips and Russell (1994). Phillips and Russell contended that both the graduate students' self-efficacy for research and their programs' research training environment impacted the scholarly productivity of counseling psychology graduate students. Brown et al. (1996, p. 536) argued that the model tested by Phillips and Russell did not "fully illuminate the nature of these two factors' [self-efficacy and research training environment] contribution to students' research productivity." According to Brown et al., social cognitive theory suggests that self-efficacy beliefs mediate the relationship between experiences gained in the research training environment and the students' subsequent research productivity. In Baron and Kenny's

T A B L E 9-2
Regression Results for the Mediational Model for Research Self-Efficacy

Variable	R	R^2	R^2 Change	F Change
Sex	.04	.00	.00	.06
Research training				
Self-efficacy	.52	.27	.27	8.21**
Sex × research training	.52	.27	.00	.37
Sex × self-efficacy	.61	.37	.10	6.57*
Sex × research training × self-efficacy	.61	.37	.00	.22

*p < .01
**p < .001

SOURCE: From Brown, Lent, Ryan and McPartland, *The Consulting Psychologist, 25*(1), pp. 535–544. Copyright © 1997 by the Division of Counseling Psychology of the American Psychology Association. Reprinted by permission of Sage Publications, Inc.

terms, the research training environment is the predictor variable, the students' research productivity is the criterion variable, and the students' self-efficacy for research is the presumed mediator. Brown et al. also believed that the sex of the graduate student may have moderated the relationships among the research training environment, the students' self-efficacy for research, and their research productivity. In other words, sex was hypothesized to be a moderating variable.

The sample consisted of 69 counseling psychology graduate students (22 men and 47 women) who completed the: (a) Research Training Environment Scale (Gelso, Mallinckrodt, & Royalty, 1991), (b) the Self-Efficacy in Research Measure (Phillips & Russell, 1994), and (c) a Demographic and Productivity Questionnaire (Phillips & Russell, 1994).

Initially, Brown et al. (1996) tested the proposed mediational model for the sample as a whole. This test involved the three conditions (steps) described by Baron and Kenny (1986). In these steps Brown et al. examined the β (beta) weights for the predictor variables. The β weight is a measure of the unique contribution of a predictor variable on a criterion variable. The authors reported three findings: (a) the hypothesized mediator variable—students' research self-efficacy—was significantly related to the criterion variable, research productivity ($\beta = .50, p < .001$); (b) the hypothesized predictor variable—students' perceptions of their training environment—was significantly related to the criterion variable, research productivity ($\beta = .29, p < .05$); and (c) the relationship between the predictor—students' perceptions of their training environment—and the criterion variable, research productivity was substantially reduced when the students' research self-efficacy was controlled ($\beta = .05, p < .50$). This reduction can be seen by examining the βs from the second and third steps of the analysis. When only the research training environment was in the regression model, β was 0.29, but when both the research training environment and the students' research self-efficacy were in the regression model, the β was reduced to 0.05. This reduction in β (to almost zero) was a strong demonstration of mediation.

Brown et al. (1996) also believed that the students' sex might moderate the relationships among the research training environment, the students' research self-efficacy, and research productivity. To test this moderation hypothesis, Brown et al.

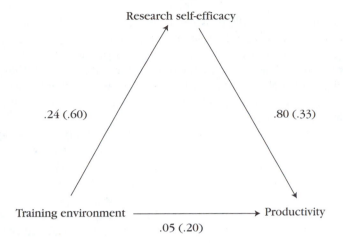

FIGURE 9-2
Path coefficients for males (outside parentheses) and females (inside parentheses) for the mediating effects of research self-efficacy for graduate students. From Brown, Lent, Ryan and McPartland, *The Consulting Psychologist, 25*(1), pp. 535-544. Copyright © 1997 by the Division of Counseling Psychology of the American Psychology Association. Reprinted by permission of Sage Publications, Inc.

(1996) added three interaction terms to the regression model. These three interaction terms were created by multiplying sex (dummy coded men = 1, women =2) times the research training environment score, times the students' self-efficacy for research, and times both the research training environment score and the students' self-efficacy for research (this is an example of a three-way interaction). Table 9-2, a reproduction of Brown et al.'s (1996) regression analysis predicting research productivity, shows that sex did not have a unique effect in predicting research productivity. However, the sex by research self-efficacy interaction term representing the moderation effect of sex on research self-efficacy was statistically significant. This result showed that the sex by research self-efficacy interaction contributed additional variance to the prediction of research self-efficacy.

Because sex was a moderator for research self-efficacy, Brown et al. then reexamined the mediation model separately for each sex. Figure 9-2, a presentation of the results from this new mediational analysis, shows that research self-efficacy is a stronger predictor of research productivity for male graduate students than it is for female graduate students (β = 0.80 for men, β = 0.33 for women). Conversely, research training environment is a stronger predictor of research productivity for female graduate students than it is for male graduate students (β = 0.24 for men, = 0.60 for women). When examining research self-efficacy as a possible mediator, the mediation effect was stronger for men (β = 0.05 after controlling for research self-efficacy) than it was for women (β = 0.20 after controlling for research self-efficacy). Brown et al. concluded that for men, the effect of the research training was indirect, being almost completely mediated by their research self-efficacy. For women, however, the research environment has a unique independent effect in addition to a mediated effect through their research self-efficacy.

Brown et al.'s (1996) study provides an excellent example of how mediation and moderation hypotheses can be tested within a multiple regression framework. The significant results from the mediation analysis provide support for a social cognitive formulation of academic behavior (see, for example, Betz, 1986). In addition, the moderation analyses suggest ways that social cognitive theory may need to be modified. For example, research productivity may come about in a different manner for men and women.

The principles described by Baron and Kenny (1986) can be applied to larger data sets to examine complex relationships among several variables. These complex models are examined by controlling the order in which predictor variables enter the regression equation. Mallinckrodt (1996) provides an excellent example of how regression analyses can be used to test complex models. Mallinckrodt was interested in how changes in working alliance and in social support affected changes in client symptoms. Specifically, he predicted that changes in working alliance would have their effect through changes in social support.

To test this model, Mallinckrodt administered to clients some social support and symptom measures, both after their intake interview and again upon completing counseling. Clients also completed working alliance measures after the third counseling session and upon the completion of counseling. To examine how changes in working alliance were related to changes in social support, Mallinckrodt used a three-step hierarchical regression. In the first regression, post-treatment social support was the criterion variable. The order of predictor variable entry was (a) social support pretreatment, (b) working alliance at the third session, and (c) working alliance at post-treatment. The partial r of 0.28, $p < .05$, from the third step of the regression represented the "path coefficient" for the relationship between changes in working alliances and changes in social support. The relationship between changes in social support and changes in clients' symptoms was tested in a similar manner. In that case, however, a five-step hierarchical regression was used. In this second regression, posttreatment symptomatology was the criterion variable. The order of predictor variable entry was (a) psychological symptoms at pretreatment, (b) working alliance at the third session, (c) working alliance at posttreatment, (d) social support at pretreatment, and (e) social support at posttreatment. The partial r of 0.28, $p < .05$, from the fifth step of the regression represented the "path coefficient" for the relationship between changes in social support and changes in client symptoms, controlling for changes in working alliance.

By running several of these hierarchical regressions, Mallinckrodt was able to test his hypothetical model of relationships among changes in working alliance, social support, and clients' symptoms. Specifically, he found, as hypothesized, that changes in working alliance affected changes in clients' symptoms only through their impact on changes in social support.

SUMMARY AND CONCLUSIONS

If, as Greenberg (1986a) asserts, the goal of a science is to describe, explain, and predict, then the descriptive designs play an important role in describing the existence and establishing the characteristics of a particular phenomenon. As we maintained in Chapter 1, the value of a design is not inherent to the design; rather, the value of a design depends on the state of knowledge in a particular area and the specific questions being addressed. Descriptive designs play a unique and important function in the process of scientific exploration.

This chapter has illustrated a number of descriptive designs, all of which describe variables by making systematic observations, summarizing information, reducing or categorizing information, or providing information about basic relationships among variables. Throughout the chapter we have emphasized that both the reliability and validity of the variables examined are critical issues in descriptive research and directly affect the internal and external validity of the research.

Survey designs allow the researcher to describe the occurrence and frequency of variables of interest. In these designs the researcher is interested in quantitatively describing the occurrence of a variable in a population. The usefulness of the research results depends to a large extent on the measurements used and the adequacy of the sampling techniques. Researchers should make efforts to use or develop psychometrically sound instruments, choose appropriate sampling techniques, maximize return rates, and include checks both between returners and nonreturners and between characteristics of the sample and parameters of the population.

Classification is also an important descriptive step in the scientific endeavor. Factor analysis and cluster analysis are statistical methodologies that can aid in this process. The factors derived from factor analysis, as well as the clusters found in cluster analysis, depend on the instruments used and the characteristics of the sample. Therefore, instrument selection and sampling are again important considerations in using these techniques. Factor and cluster solutions should be replicated on disparate samples to assure validity. It is also important to validate clusters and factors by linking them with other variables. Finally, we should remember that both of these procedures involve many decision points, and experts often disagree on criteria for decision making. Thus, the particular methodology or analysis used often affects the results, which suggests the need for further validation.

In passive designs, the researcher can examine the relationships between two or more variables. The adequacy of these designs is greatly influenced by the reliability of the measures used in operationalizing the variables of interest. Also, the size of the relationship obtained depends to some extent on the sample size; thus, many multiple regression studies include an adjustment for shrinkage to control for sample size. We hope that more researchers will use the strategy advocated by Cole et al. to account for method and error variances when assessing relationships between variables. As for other descriptive designs, sampling considerations and methodological strategies are extremely important in interpreting the results of multiple regression studies. We encourage researchers to use random sampling and/or to replicate their results when using passive designs.

Passive designs can be used to examine complex relations among variables. Regression analyses allow researchers to examine the effect of multiple predictor variables on a criterion variable. As explained in the chapter, regression analyses can be used to examine questions concerning moderation and mediation.

Increasingly, counseling researchers are using moderation and mediation analyses to examine complex theoretical models. The same cautions that apply to simple passive designs also apply to the more complex designs.

The designs described in this chapter can be important building blocks in the scientific process. Based on a careful analysis of the current state of knowledge in a given area, the researcher can choose a design that will lead to a progressively better understanding of the content area. When chosen wisely, the descriptive designs can serve the important function of describing phenomena of interest in counseling research.

CHAPTER 10

QUALITATIVE RESEARCH

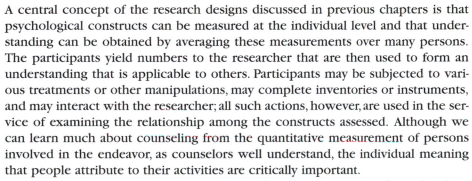

A central concept of the research designs discussed in previous chapters is that psychological constructs can be measured at the individual level and that understanding can be obtained by averaging these measurements over many persons. The participants yield numbers to the researcher that are then used to form an understanding that is applicable to others. Participants may be subjected to various treatments or other manipulations, may complete inventories or instruments, and may interact with the researcher; all such actions, however, are used in the service of examining the relationship among the constructs assessed. Although we can learn much about counseling from the quantitative measurement of persons involved in the endeavor, as counselors well understand, the individual meaning that people attribute to their activities are critically important.

Qualitative research involves understanding the complexity of people's lives by examining individual perspectives in context. The basis of this definition will become clearer as we describe qualitative research in this chapter. At this point, be assured that qualitative research is not simply a variation of a theme already discussed; rather, it is a radically different way to approach knowing and understanding.

In this chapter we explore the philosophical foundations of qualitative research, which vary greatly from those of traditional quantitative research. Four philosophical foundations, or worldviews, will be discussed. Two of them, positivism and postpositivism, are aligned with quantitative research, whereas two others, constructivism and critical theory, are aligned with qualitative research. Understanding the worldviews that underlie research is crucial to a sophisticated use of any method, qualitative or quantitative.

The next section of this chapter examines 17 aspects of research to contrast quantitative and qualitative research. This contrast will highlight the critical differences in these two research approaches and give an appreciation of qualitative inquiries.

It should be noted that qualitative research subsumes many types, each with a different purpose and with different methods. Nevertheless, various generic methods span the types of qualitative research. In the final section we discuss means of gathering data and present ways of reporting the results.

WORLDVIEWS OF RESEARCH

Worldviews are the philosophical foundations that guide understanding of the world and how inquiries are made to further that understanding. In this section we consider four worldviews of research: positivism, postpositivism, constructivism, and critical theory.

Positivism

Positivism is the paradigm that is best represented by the "scientific method" as traditionally taught in the physical sciences. According to this paradigm, the nature of the universe can be known, and the scientist's goal is to discover the natural laws that govern each and every object in the universe, and their relationship to each other. Physical laws that describe gravitation, magnetism, and electricity are examples of positivistic statements about the universe that are universal in terms of both time and context. A key principle is that "truth" exists, and given enough time, brilliant scientists, and sophisticated methods, discoveries will be made that illuminate the "truth."

In the positivistic realm, the scientist is objective; that is, the scientist neither affects the world that is studied nor is affected by it. Scientists are interchangeable in that a given experiment should lead to the same outcome and conclusion, regardless of who conducts it. Surely, some scientists are more insightful and creative than others, but in the end, experiments yield results that are self-evident to the scientific community. Confidence in results derive from the scientific method, not from the scientist; the operations of the experiment produce the results while the scientist observes objectively from the sidelines.

The scientific method involves well-defined steps. First, the scientist makes a conjecture about the nature of the universe. Second, the scientist designs an experiment such that its results will either confirm or disconfirm the conjecture. If the data conform to the prediction, the conjecture is verified. On the other hand, if the data do not conform to the prediction, the scientist concludes that the phenomenon being studied does not follow the conjecture, which is then abandoned as an explanation of truth. The hypothetico-deductive (that is, deductions made from testing hypotheses) nature of this process is characteristic of positivism. Several classic experiments provide vivid examples of positivism: Galileo dropping balls from the Tower of Pisa; the bending of light to prove Einstein's theory of relativity; Madame Curie's observations of radioactivity; and changing pressure and volume related to the gas laws.

There are other important characteristics of positivistic research. First, relations typically are expressed in terms of causality—X causes Y. Second, theories are reductionistic in that complex processes are understood by breaking them down into simpler subprocesses, which can be studied more easily. Third, laws are usually expressed mathematically, measurements are quantitative, and conclusions dichotomous (either the data conform to prediction, or they do not), resulting in the conclusion that the law is true or not.

Clearly, the description of positivistic research calls to mind the type of science conducted in the physical sciences, such as chemistry or physics, or perhaps that in the biological sciences, but certainly not research in the social sciences (except maybe psychophysics or perception). The positivistic tradition has evolved into the postpositivism paradigm that recognizes the impossibility of making dichotomous conclusions when systems are complex and the behavior of organisms has multiple determinants.

Postpositivism

Postpositivism shares with positivism the belief in a "real" reality and in the goal of discovering "truth." However, postpositivists recognize that truth cannot be fully known, and that consequently at best we make probabilistic statements rather than absolute statements about truth. The statistical models that underlie research in the social sciences are saturated with this probabilistic interpretation. The values of p associated with statistical tests are probabilities of obtaining the data, given the assumption that the null hypothesis is true. Statistical tests assert that there is truth, but that we can never conclude with certainty that our results can differentiate among competing hypotheses. When we reject the null hypothesis (that is, obtain a statistically significant result), we decide to accept the alternate hypothesis knowing that there is a small probability that we made the wrong conclusion.

Although the probabilistic nature of statistics exemplifies the postpositivistic nature of most research in the social sciences, it is only one aspect of the research process that diverges from a strict positivistic methodology. Because of the ambiguities related to recognizing that the "truth" cannot be known for certain, the logic of the positivistic scientific method is altered. In the postpositivistic paradigm, theories lead to conjectures, and the statements about truth are altered to recognize that the inferences are probabilistic. If the data are consistent with the conjecture, then confidence in the theory as an accurate description of "truth" is increased. Often the word *corroborated* is used to indicate that a study produced results consistent with prediction and that the conjecture has thus survived another test. On the other hand, if the data are inconsistent with theoretically derived conjectures, and the study is valid, then the theory has failed to be corroborated. In the postpositivist realm, it would be difficult to give up belief in a theory based on one experiment. However, a succession of studies that fail to conform to prediction would constitute evidence that the theory should be revised or abandoned. The goal in postpositivistic research is to produce, through a succession of experiments, descriptions that are closer approximations to the truth. For example, to prove that smoking causes disease, multiple experiments of various types (for example, passive designs, experimental designs using lab animals) were needed to come to the conclusion that smoking in fact leads to various detrimental health outcomes.

An examination of research methods demonstrates the degree to which post-positivism permeates what we do. Classical test theory rests on the proposition of "true scores," which is the true amount of a characteristic that a person possesses; however, any measurement is actually an obtained score that contains error (that is, obtained score = true score + error). The mere mention of reliability and valid-ity implies that constructs exist, but that random error renders our assessments of these constructs imperfect. In statistics, population parameters are "truths" about which we collect data for the purpose of estimation or hypothesis testing.

Postpositivism also recognizes that there is bias in the scientific process, and that the conclusions researchers make are influenced by the person of the researcher. Truths are not self-evident but must be arbitrated by the scientific com-munity. The process of peer review is an admission that the validity of a conclusion is open to interpretation, and that it is scientists' opinions about the veracity of a claim that dictate whether or not a result adds to the cumulative knowledge of a field. Clearly, there are canons that must be followed (that is, the study must be valid, as described in Chapter 4) if a study is to be conclusive, but it is scientists, rather than some algorithm, who determine whether the conclusions add to knowledge.

Whereas positivism and postpositivism share the view that certain truths exist and that research can shed light on these truths, constructivism and critical theory, two worldviews on the opposite end of the worldview continuum, have a very different conceptualization of reality. We discuss these two views next.

Constructivism

In the constructivism paradigm, notions of "truth" and "reality" are abandoned in favor of the notion that ideas about the world, especially the social world, are con-structed in the minds of individuals. These constructions, based on the experi-ences of individuals as they interact with the physical and social environment, are shaped by culture and may be idiosyncratic. Constructions exist and can be described, but they are not representations of truth. Constructions can be simple or complex, naive or sophisticated, uninformed or informed, but they cannot be proven true or false. An individual's constructions may change over time—as a result of education, increased experience with the environment, or maturation.

Constructivists believe that reality is created by the participants of any sys-tem. It is true that some event occurs, but it is the meaning attributed to that event that is important socially. Suppose that one is a resident of a community that under-went a natural disaster, such as a flood. Constructivists recognize the reality of the natural event, but then claim that it is the meaning that is attributed to that event that is important in determining social relations and behavior. One community might believe that the disaster occurred because the community had been immoral, and that they should therefore rebuild their community to be a better place to live in the future. These people are empowered to rebuild quickly and work energetically toward progress. Another community might feel that the flood is a very infrequent, random event and that the entire country should share their burden. This is what happens in the United States—expectations are that the government will rebuild their communities and that there is little need to structure their physical or social environment differently. Often the community rebuilds without changing the way they live; their houses remain in the floodplain because they just don't want to move.

Of course, multiple constructions of an event are possible. One group believes one way and another group believes another way. We are all familiar with groups with irreconcilable views on an issue. The important point is that constructivists believe it is the meaning that is attributed to an event, rather than the event itself, that is the important aspect for understanding behavior and social relations.

Because constructions do not represent universal truths, the investigator and the object under investigation cannot be conceived of separately. Social constructions are developed through interactions with the environment and involve mental representations and interpretations of those interactions. The investigator and the person investigated are linked, and through the investigation process the constructions of the participants become accessible to the investigator. Because the construction of a participant is internal, it is only through the interaction of the investigator and the participant, or the interaction of the investigator and the world of the participant, that the constructions of an individual can be understood. Moreover, the constructions of the investigator cannot be separated from his or her understanding of the participant's constructions.

The general methods of understanding in a constructivist world involve both *hermeneutics* and *dialectics. Hermeneutics* refers to the activity of interpretation, whether the data to be interpreted are language, behavior, text, artifacts, or other aspects of human behavior or thought. The constructivist must use these data to develop an interpretation, which, in a sense, is a description of the constructions of the participants. *Dialectics* refers to the interaction between the participant and the investigator. At the most benign level, the interaction is a conversation in which words are exchanged and interpretations of the language lead to an understanding of constructions. At the next level, the exchange involves discussing these constructions, as when an investigator shares his or her interpretations with the participant. At the most extreme level, dialectics involves changing constructions in the process of interpretation. This last level of dialectics (and some would say the essence of dialectics) is more characteristic of critical theory (see the next section) than of constructivism.

In the constructivist paradigm, there are no truths to be discovered; therefore, there can be no conjectures (that is, predictions based on hypothesized truths) or tests of conjectures. Thus, data are not collected with the aim of determining whether or not observations are consistent with conjecture. Rather, data lead to interpretations that then lead the investigator in directions that may not have been anticipated, causing the investigator to reinterpret already collected data or to collect additional data, often in ways unimaginable when the investigation began. Positivistic and postpositivistic methods are linear, whereas constructivist (and critical theory) methods are recursive (that is, the results and method influence each other).

Critical Theory

Critical theory posits that people's social constructions are shaped by the social, political, cultural, and economic forces in the environment, particularly forces created by powerful individuals. Over time, the constructions take on the appearance of reality; that is, the social reality, which has in fact grown out of the social context, is assumed to be truth. Because the constructions are so deeply embedded in society (including in the researchers themselves), it is extremely difficult to comprehend that these constructions were spawned in the societal context and are not truths. For example (and any examples chosen are necessarily controversial), the belief that the monogamous union of one male and one female for the purpose of reproduction (that is, heterosexual marriage) is natural is a socially derived position. Critical theorists would concede that it could be argued that marriage is necessary and important for the social order (as we know it), but they would contend that marriage, as an institution, was generated by the social system; that there are alternatives (homosexual unions, polygamous marriages); and that the "truth" of any "natural" propensity to marry is specious.

In critical theory, the investigator and the participant form a relationship, and the values of the investigator are vital to the activity. Inquiry, in critical theory, involves the level of dialectism that changes constructions. That is, the investigation involves a dialogue between investigator and other in such a way that the other comes to realize that his or her understanding of the world is derived from the precepts of the social order, and that these precepts can (and should) be altered. In other words, the goal of critical theory is to have the participants view structures for what they are—socially constructed beliefs—rather than as unchangeable truths. Moreover, the dialectic should lead to the participants' understanding that social action is needed to change the social order.

Feminist theory falls into the critical theoretical realm in that it contends that traditional roles for women have been socially determined, that the power in society has been allocated to males, and that these social realities can be altered. Feminism seeks to "raise the consciousness" of women so that they do not consider their place in society to be fixed as truth, but instead understand both the historical context that led to the current social situation and that the first step in change is to reject the traditional roles. Many critical theorists would contend that this worldview involves more than social action, which tends to change society at the margins, and instead necessitates radical change that dramatically replaces current social structures with others (for example, Marxism).

Perspectives on Worldviews

We have contrasted four worldviews that bear on the research process, albeit overly simplistically. Philosophers, since the beginning of humankind, have wrestled with ideas about knowledge and knowing. To understand the philosophy of science fully would consume one's intellectual energy completely, and no research would be accomplished. Even though it is vital to understand the philosophical bases of our methods of inquiry, our emphasis here is on research methods rather than on philosophy.

It is impossible to "prove" that one of these paradigms is correct, more appropriate, better, or more useful than another. They are different systems for understanding the world, but no method, either logical or empirical, can establish the superiority of any given view. Nevertheless, understanding the paradigms is important so that our methods match our belief systems, and so that the research approach is appropriate for answering research questions within the context of existing knowledge.

Some researchers (see, for example, Patton, 1987) believe that research should be nonparadigmatic, that research can be fruitfully conducted without orthodox adherence to a philosophical tradition. While this view might appear to free us from the constraints of philosophy of science, it also creates ambiguity about the purposes of research.

Because the emphasis in this book has been on quantitative research, in the next section we discuss characteristics of qualitative research by comparing it to quantitative research in several respects. Specifically, to contrast qualitative and quantitative research we examine the following aspects: reality, representation of the world, domain knowledge and theory, intellectual bases, level of inquiry, role of the investigator, the role of subjects/participants, generalizability, bias, validity, reliability, product, audience, control, goals of study, researcher's voice, and power structure. It is important to keep in mind that even though qualitative research is an endeavor that can be defined and described without reference to or comparison with quantitative research, we believe that this comparison helps students understand the principles of qualitative research.

ASPECTS OF QUALITATIVE RESEARCH

Given our presentation of worldviews, it is tempting to call the positivistic and postpositivistic worldviews "quantitative" and the constructivist and critical theory views "qualitative. "Such broad characterizations, however, can be misleading. For example, Highlen and Finely (1996) claim that the grounded theory method, a traditional qualitative method, is postpositivistic. Nevertheless, the categories quantitative and qualitative are often used and offer a useful distinction, as long as we understand that such dichotomies cannot capture the complexity of the topic. Table 10-1 presents a useful way of distinguishing qualitative from quantitative research. We next discuss each of these distinguishing features to further define qualitative research and to distinguish it from quantitative research.

Reality

Quantitative social science researchers assume that human actions are governed by rules, and that research can be profitably used to understand these rules better.

T A B L E 10-1
Quantitative versus Qualitative Research

Aspect	Quantitative	Qualitative
Reality	Truth exists; behavior is governed by rules and laws and is discoverable	Reality is a social construction; there are no truths to be discovered.
Representation of the world	Mathematical or verbal description of quantitative results	Linguistic; symbolic
Domain knowledge and theory	Used to construct hypotheses; theory-driven; deductive	Data-driven; previous knowledge can bias results; inductive.
Intellectual bases	Mathematics, statistics, logic, physical sciences	Linguistics, philosophy, anthropology, literature
Level of inquiry	Reductionistic, atomistic	Holistic
Role of investigator	Objective, dualistic	Subjective, interactive
Role of subjects/ participants	Subjects: naive to experimental hypotheses and are acted upon; deception is an ethical issue	Participants: involved in research, are fully informed, and can be involved in analysis and results
Generalizability	A sample is used to generalize to population; deductive	Applicability is more important than generalizability; inductive
Bias	Problematic; must be reduced	Accepted and acknowledged
Validity	Involves minimizing alternative explanations	Involves effect on audience and social utility; uses triangulation
Reliability	Involves measurements without error; seeks quantitative results that reflect true scores	Not relevant
Product	Research report in scientific journal; contains mathematical or statistical results, a verbal description of quantitative results, and domain-specific language (jargon)	Results written in everyday language or presented in other media; accessible to audience regardless of domain-specific knowledge; may or may not be published in scientific outlets; available, understandable, and relevant to participants
Audience	Academic community; policy implications for others are made by academics	Academic and nonacademic audiences; policy implications are integral to the product
Control	Involves controlling extraneous influences, manipulating variables, and detecting causal relationships	Involves understanding complex relationships among various factors
Goals of study	To discover truth; to explain and predict; to confirm conjectures; to extend knowledge	To describe, interpret, critique, revise, and change
Researcher's voice	That of detached, objective scientist	That of involved investigator, participant, and transformative expert
Power structure	The dominant view in the academic community in terms of publication, funding, promotion, and tenure	Is acquiring recognition; recognition from outside the scientific community is important

The general rules that govern action represent reality. To understand the status of reality in quantitative research, consider Bischoff and Tracey's (1995) study of how therapist behaviors lead to client resistance. They examined ten therapy sessions, coded each therapist and client speaking turn, and found, through a sequential analysis, that therapist directive behaviors increased the probability that the client would respond defensively. Even though the sample was small and the analysis intensive, their conclusion was general: "The present study suggests that the occurrence of client resistance is not random or independent of relationship events but rather is predicted, to a modest degree, by the antecedent behavior" (p. 492). Because, in a postpositivistic stance, the authors recognized that the results were not conclusive, they cited other consistent research in order to make a strong statement about a truth in counseling: "Thus we can say with some confidence that resistance is, least in part, a response to the therapist's previous directive behavior" (p. 492). Although this conclusion may not be universal (for example, Asian Americans' reactions to directiveness may be different; Sue & Sue, 1995), the point is that the purpose of this research was to make a general statement about how resistance is affected by therapist responses in the session.

In qualitative research, the goal is to understand the social constructions of the participants. Frontman and Kunkel's (1994) examination of successful initial sessions is illustrative of understanding social constructs. Although quantitative research has investigated the topic of successful sessions in counseling from multiple perspectives (for example, from client and counselor), Frontman and Kunkel's study was different. Instead of using coding systems developed by the researchers, they had the participating therapists respond to the general probe, "As if you were making a personal journal entry, write what you felt was successful about the session," and then let themes emerge from the data. The goal of the study was to understand how counselors construe success in the initial session rather than to test some conjecture about the nature of a successful experience.

Representation of the World

Any quantitative research that involves traditional parametric methods makes the assumption that there is some important feature of the world that can be modeled mathematically. For example, when one tests whether a treatment is superior to no treatment, the typical null hypothesis ($\mu_{TX} = \mu_{control}$) is a mathematical statement about the efficacy of treatment. Statements such as "the treatment group displayed less pathology than the control group" are verbal descriptions of a quantitative result (namely, $\mu_{TX} < \mu_{control}$).

In qualitative research, representations of the world are typically linguistic. For example, the representation may be a description of a person's construction of an event. Of course, a linguistic representation is longer and may be richer than a mathematical representation. For example, consider a portion of Worthen and McNeill's (1996) description of successful supervision:

> The therapeutic process is viewed [by trainees] on a continuum from some dis-illusionment to a fundamental sense of efficacy. With these elements in place,

the supervisee experiences a disruption in the "usual" self-as-profession operation, with the concurrent feeling of anxiety-induced emotional arousal and an
often opaquely perceived "needing." . . . [This is] addressed with a discernibly
nonjudgmental, empathizing, supporting and validating supervisory stance that
acts to normalize the struggle. As a result, the supervisee feels a "freeing" that
facilitates reduced self-protectiveness and increased receptivity to supervisory
input. (p. 28)

Occasionally, representations of the world can be expressed symbolically, as is the
case for movies, artistic renderings, music, and so forth. Poignant photographs of
the civil rights movement provided a more dramatic representation of the violent
resistance to civil rights in the South than quantified representations (such as, frequencies of assaults) or even verbal representations (such as, narratives) ever
could.

Domain Knowledge and Theory

As anyone who has had to write a literature review or defend a proposal for a
quantitative study knows, we must review existing knowledge before developing
a hypothesis to answer an important, cutting-edge question, which is then tested
in the proposed study. This is a deductive process in that theory is used to make
a specific prediction.

Qualitative research, on the other hand, typically is approached from the
opposite direction (that is, inductively). Essentially, the data are allowed "to speak
for themselves." Although the philosophy underlying the method and general
questions guide the qualitative research, conclusions emanate from the data. In
fact, a researcher's knowledge on a given topic may well bias conclusions, and such
"preconceived notions" must be acknowledged by the researcher and disclosed to
the consumer of the qualitative study.

In the constructivist frame, the goal of the research is to understand the
social constructions of the participants. Whatever the area of inquiry, the investigator will have in mind some construction, and the concern is that this social construction will bias understanding of the participants' constructions. Consequently,
investigators must be cognizant that their lens will affect their understanding of
the participants' words and actions, and must consider their conclusions in this
light. In the qualitative paradigm, the participants' words and actions are used to
construct a representation of the world, with recognition that the investigator's
knowledge will bias how those words and actions are interpreted. In Rennie's
(1994) qualitative analysis of deference in psychotherapy, he stated that "my familiarity with deference was limited to the knowledge of the common meaning of the
term" (p. 428); he then went on to briefly describe previous anthropological and
sociological investigations of deference, even though these investigations were not
used to shape the way in which he collected and analyzed the data.

Here, as in all the distinctions between quantitative and qualitative research,
a dichotomy has been formed that will not be truthful to the methods. Some pro-
ponents of grounded theory, an often-used qualitative method, allow domain-

specific knowledge and theory to guide the qualitative endeavor, although this issue is controversial (see Glaser, 1992, and Strauss & Corbin, 1990, 1994, for discussions). Wampold et al. (1995) provide an example of using domain-specific knowledge to guide qualitative inquiry. They used the fact that various Holland types have different profiles of social skills to focus a qualitative study on how investigative types (who deemphasize encoding and decoding emotion) handle conflict, an emotion-laden task.

Intellectual Bases

The methodological traditions of quantitative research lie in the realms of mathematics, statistics, logic, and the scientific method of the physical sciences. The deductive process from theory to hypothesis testing is syllogistic: If theory X is true, then result Y will be present, and if result Y is not present, then theory X is not true. Although the probabilistic nature of postpositivism complicates the logic of the scientific method, the basis of the method remains formal logic (for example, either the null hypothesis is true, or the alternative is true). The legacy of this tradition includes John Stuart Mill, Auguste Comte, Galileo Galilei, Francis Bacon, René Descartes, Thomas Hobbes, John Locke, Issac Newton, David Hume, Ludwig Wittgenstein, Bertrand Russell, Alfred North Whitehead, and Herman Helmholtz. Behaviorism is the branch of psychology that is directly descendent from the hypothetico-deductive tradition.

The intellectual bases of qualitative research are found in the disciplines that focus their inquiry on the mind and on attributions of meaning, including anthropology, linguistics, philosophy, and literature. In each of these fields, the intellectual founders of qualitative research, including Immanuel Kant, Wilhelm Wundt, Edmund Husserl, Max Weber, Freidrich Engels, Margaret Mead, and William James, rejected the idea that humans respond deterministically to sensory inputs and instead placed emphasis on the active mind that gives meaning to actions.

Level of Inquiry

Reductionism is the process of understanding a phenomena by examining component processes of some larger process. Electricity can be understood at the level of circuits, voltage, resistance, and so forth; reductionism occurs when these concepts are explored at the level of the electron. Knowing that a treatment is effective is one level of knowledge; understanding the exact mechanisms of change is a reductionistic attempt to explain the effectiveness at a more detailed level. Atomism is the process of breaking a complex phenomenon into component parts and then studying each part separately. Laboratory experiments are designed to control all factors other than those manipulated by the experimenter, based on the idea that the results will provide information about one aspect of human functioning, which can then be combined with knowledge about other aspects to understand humans in the complex world.

Qualitative researchers believe that human behavior cannot be understood outside of its context. Because humans ascribe meaning to the context, removing a person from the context of interest to the context of the laboratory will lead that person to attribute meaning to being a participant in an experiment, and the person will react in ways that do not represent their behavior in the real world. Consequently, qualitative researchers want to study behavior in context and might even go so far as to contend that it is the interpretation of the context that is the essential process to be studied. When Wampold et al. (1995) investigated the social behavior of chemists, they understood that asking these scientists to interact in an artificial situation would present a distorted picture of their sociability. In the context of the chemistry laboratory, where the participants felt comfortable and where the topic of conversation could often be their science, the scientists were affable, engaging, and interacted often. Importantly, because the chemists had relative deficits in some social skills (for example, decoding emotion), the chemists constructed a social environment that did not place demands on those particular social skills. Had the chemists been placed in a social environment in which these social skills were expected (for example, in interaction with social types), they likely would have conformed to the stereotype of the scientist—socially unskilled and socially uninvolved.

Role of the Investigator

In quantitative research, the researcher is separate from the phenomenon being studied. This separation of investigator from the truths being studied is called dualism. The researcher is conceptualized as an unbiased observer and, as previously mentioned, researchers are interchangeable in that the conclusions from the data should be self-evident. Postpositivism recognizes that researchers are biased or interpret data idiosyncratically, so that attempts are made to reduce these sources of error to the extent possible (see Chapter 14). Calculating inter-rater agreement is a recognition that part of the ratings are idiosyncratic. Quantitative research reports are traditionally written in the third person, passive voice—for example, "the researchers concluded . . . ," or "it was concluded that . . . ". Increasingly, the first person is used, but in a way that maintains the dualist perspective.

Qualitative researchers are trained to understand how their values and beliefs affect their investigations, and to make these effects known. In their qualitative study of sustaining engagement in family therapy, Friedlander, Heatherington, Johnson, and Skowron (1994) devoted four paragraphs to contextualizing their biases, of which a part is quoted here:

> Because researchers are actually the instruments used to analyze their data (Steier, 1988), and are expected to be an empathic observer of the data (Stiles, 1993), it is generally recognized that their own personal experience of the phenomenon in question and their theoretical biases should be presented for consideration. Both Myrna L. Friedlander and Laurie Heatherington have conducted couples and family therapy in inpatient, agency, and/or private practice settings for over 12 years. While both are most familiar with the structural

approach to family treatment [the approach studied] their training in family therapy and their current orientations are more eclectic.... During the development of the present model, both authors were closely following, as well as researching, the constructivist perspective on psychotherapy (e.g., McNamee & Gergen, 1992; White & Epston, 1990). (p. 440)

Friedlander et al. then went on to discuss their particular assumptions about family therapy. To quantitative researchers who consider themselves separate from the study, this personal material seems quite odd. It is important to realize that in qualitative research stating one's biases and assumptions is secondary to understanding how it affects interpretations of the data.

Role of Subjects/Participants

Although it is now required that all people that are studied be called *participants* (APA, 1994), the manner in which participants in a study are treated differentiates quantitative research from qualitative research. Traditionally, participants in quantitative research were called *subjects* because they were subjected to an experimental condition. As explained in Chapter 11, experimental conditions differ in some crucial way, but subjects are not informed of what those conditions are—or, in many cases, that there even are differences between the conditions. Often, knowledge of the hypotheses or of other details of the study are thought to influence participants' behavior, and consequently researchers tell the participants in traditional experiments as little as possible.

In qualitative research, the participants are fully informed of the research and are considered to be involved in the process. Often, a relationship is built between investigator and participant, as in participant observation; in other cases, such as interviewing, the relationship is necessary for the participant to share his or her construction in an honest manner. Qualitative researchers often share their interpretations or descriptions with participants as a way of verifying authenticity. Some forms of qualitative research seek to alter the cognitive constructions of the participants through dialectic discourse.

The qualitative research in counseling has made limited use of participants' involvement in the research process (Polkinghorne, 1994). Even though sharing descriptions and interpretations with participants is an important part of the qualitative endeavor, a perusal of the qualitative research in counseling reveals few instances in which participants are involved in the study subsequent to the point at which they provided data.

Generalizability

Because the goal of quantitative research is to discover general laws, generalizability is intrinsic to the endeavor (that is, external validity is crucial to the acceptability of a study). The results of a particular study are interesting only to the extent that they apply to people *other than those in the study.* For example, consider the typical outcome study in which two treatments are compared, and suppose that Treatment A is found to be superior to Treatment B. These results are useful primarily to the extent that the researcher can legitimately claim that Treatment A is the preferred treatment for clients in general.

In qualitative research, the *applicability* of findings is more important than generalizability. Applicability refers to the quality of the researcher's interpretations in the context in which the qualitative investigation took place. Quantitative researchers tend either to ignore context or to quantify it (as, for example, in the search for moderating variables), whereas qualitative researchers realize that context is intrinsic to the investigation, and that results have no meaning stripped of their context. Consequently, the results of a qualitative study cannot be generalized to another context. However, the results of any qualitative research can, and should, have importance to others. First, because qualitative research is inseparable from the lives of the participants, the research will have important implications for their actions. One of the authors of this text has students in his class conduct a qualitative study of their own experience as graduate students in counseling. The students interview each other and construct a model that represents their experience. These results always have (a) some aspects that appear to be related to the way we modally train counselors (that is, they represent a construction shared by counselor educators in their development and implementation of counseling training); (b) some aspects specific to the training program in which they find themselves; and (c) some aspects unique to their own experience. Each of these levels has immense implications for students and for the program.

A second way that the results are applicable is that consumers of the research will have a vicarious experience that informs them about the phenomena. Historical novels, for instance, can give those who never lived in a period an understanding of the meaning given to events. Of course, the vicarious experience is shaped by the constructions of the reader; nevertheless, this vicarious experience will shape understanding in a way that quantitative data cannot.

Finally, qualitative findings can have profound effects on policy. Policymakers are often concerned with local situations and are less interested in results from random samples, in spite of those results' relevance to their local situation. Qualitative findings are grounded in the context, give a rich description of the situation, and have (it is hoped) tapped the many voices of the participants. These characteristics are particularly useful when decision makers must sort through complicated issues and generate novel solutions that bring communities together.

Bias

Bias is anathema to the quantitative researcher, and consequently care is taken to reduce it. Positivism relies on an objective stance by the researcher, so that the results can reveal truths about the world, rather than something about the researcher. The most extreme bias is introduced when results are fabricated; such cases shake the scientific world to its roots, for nothing is so threatening as the possibility that previously valued truths are simply researchers' concoctions. Although scientific fraud is relatively rare, unconscious actions can also bias results and are probably more insidious than are the few known intentional frauds. Whatever the source of the bias, from a quantitative perspective it obscures the truth. Chapter 14 discusses the biases that can detract from quantitative studies.

In contrast, qualitative researchers recognize that their constructions will necessarily influence their understanding of participants' experiences. Skilled qualitative researchers will reflect upon their constructions and use these reflections to guide their research. Counselors are particularly suited to the task of qualitative research because through their own training and practice, skilled practitioners are able to reflect on and understand how their own psychological processes affect the counseling process. Similarly, the skilled qualitative researcher reflects upon the research process to provide a richer and better understanding of the participants' constructions of the world.

Validity

As was discussed in Chapter 4, the validity of quantitative research is established by the lack of plausible alternative hypotheses. Much planning and thinking in the design of a study is devoted to limiting the number of alternative hypotheses. Although some decisions must be made during the research, essentially the validity of the study is established when the study is designed (that is, before it is conducted). Although some designs (for example, experimental) are intrinsically more valid than others (for example, quasi-experimental), validity of quantitative studies emerges from methodological rigor.

Although the term *validity* is not often applied to qualitative research, qualitative researchers are concerned about the concept of quality. The quality of qualitative research is grounded in the results themselves. Quality can be assessed by its impact on the consumers of research, on the participants, and on the investigators (Stiles, 1993). Consumers of research are interested in the coherence of the qualitative product; that is, whether it is conceptually understandable. Readers should find the descriptions reasonable, informative, and sensible. The description should be grounded in the everyday experience of the audience while at the same time providing new insights into the world being investigated. Finally, the product of qualitative research should have social utility to the consumers: How will the understanding provided by the descriptions change the social conditions of the community?

The quality of Friedlander et al.'s (1994) study of change events in family therapy was supported by the following sources:

> (a) the testimony of the clinic staff as to the accuracy and clinical meaningfulness of the event selection criteria, (b) the verification checks by the two reviewers who independently rated the videotapes, (c) the consistency of the findings with the available literature, and (d) the internal coherence and clinical relevance of the conceptual model that resulted from our analyses (cf. Stiles, 1993). (p. 443)

Although at first glance these observations seem relatively benign, the act of using participants' testimony and examining its clinical relevance departs radically from how validity is constructed and conceptualized in quantitative studies. In quantitative studies, validity is attached to the design; if the study is valid, then its results may have implications for clinical practice. But Friedlander et al. are citing the clinical relevance of the results as evidence of validity, a very different notion.

Another aspect of validity involves the degree to which the participants change as a result of the study. Participation in the study may provide participants opportunities to tell their story and be heard, new ways to understand their experiences, and the power to change, grow, or act. Evidence for the validity of an interpretation is obtained to the extent that the participants benefit from their experience in the research. Empowerment of participants is particularly vital to the integrity of critical theory investigations, in which participants come to understand that their assumptions about reality are instead constructions derived from the current social order.

A final method for increasing the validity of a qualitative study is through triangulation (see Denzin, 1978; Patton, 1987, 1990). As navigators fully understand, a single bearing is insufficient to establish a position, two bearings can establish a position but with unknown error, and three bearings both establish a position and give an idea of the accuracy of the position (within a triangular area). Similarly, multiple views of a problem provide both a better description and some indication of the veracity of the description.

Denzin (1978) discussed four types of triangulation: data triangulation, investigator triangulation, theory triangulation, and methodological triangulation. Data triangulation refers to the use of several sources of data, such as interviews, observations, and materials (which are discussed later in this chapter). Having additional sources of data resolves ambiguities, reveals sources of bias (for example, interview questions that lead respondents to a certain conclusion), and provides richness to the understanding of the phenomenon.

Investigator triangulation involves using several researchers, usually in a team, to come to a common understanding; interpretations made by one member of the team are challenged by other members. In qualitative research, teams members should examine how each member's personal constructions influence the interpretation of the constructions of the participants. For example, in qualitative psychotherapy research, team members should be asked, "How does your own understanding of psychotherapy and your own understanding (or misunderstanding) of yourself affect the way you interpret the statements of the participants?" Hill, Thompson, and Williams (1997) have developed a process to faciliate investigator triangulation, which is described later. Triangulation can also be achieved by comparing participants' perspectives with the descriptions prepared by the investigators.

Theory triangulation uses various perspectives to interpret a single set of data. It is easy to imagine that psychotherapy researchers from different perspectives (for example, cognitive versus experiential) will provide different interpretations of the same case. Bowers and Esmond (1996) used psychological, sociological, and health provision perspectives to understand how multidisciplinary teams deliver health care to the elderly.

Methodological triangulation uses multiple methods to form an understanding. The methods could be variations of qualitative methods. Although some qualitative researchers resist using methods that span the worldview continuum, Patton

(1987) takes a nonparadigmatic stance, recommending the combination of quantitative and qualitative methods. Wampold et al. (1995) used quantitative hypothetico-deductive methods and qualitative methods (observations and interviews) to obtain an understanding of social interactions in chemistry work groups.

Reliability

In quantitative research, reliability and validity are separate, albeit related, concepts. Reliability refers to the variance in measurements that are due to true scores. In qualitative research, there is no "real" truth, and therefore the qualitative analogue of reliability does not exist. Instead, qualitative researchers discuss *the importance of findings* rather than some correspondence to "reality." It is tempting to draw parallels between qualitative and quantitative agreement by stating that consensus in a research team vis-à-vis an interpretation is similar to inter-rater agreement of observers, but such parallels ignore important differences. First, agreement among team members is not simply consensus; it also involves an interactive process among team members and between team members and the data. Second, agreement among team members is secondary to the importance of the emerging results. A team is not prohibited from presenting two alternative interpretations of data if both offer a unique understanding of a phenomenon; a similar process in quantitative research would be considered flawed because one result would deviate from reality. Third, in quantitative research, inter-rater agreement does not necessarily imply that the measurements are reliable (that is, are due to true score variation; see Chapter 12).

Product

The quantitative product is a research report written in a scientific journal. Such a report is written in the language of the discipline (that is, jargon) and presents mathematical or statistical results as well as verbal descriptions of these results. The conclusions of the report will put the results in the context of previous results to show the current representation of reality. This product is accessible, for the most part, only to those trained in the discipline.

The qualitative product is an interpretation written in everyday language or presented in some other medium (for example, film) and is accessible to an audience regardless of training in the discipline. This product may not necessarily be published in scientific outlets. Finally, the product is to be available, comprehensible, and relevant to the participants.

Audience

The audience of quantitative research is primarily the academic community. Products with the highest reputations are published in peer-reviewed journals. The quality of books are established by scholarly judgments (that is, book reviews by respected scholars) rather than by sales or popular acclaim. In fact, acceptance of a book by the general population might be denigrated because the author is viewed as pandering to public opinion. Moreover, objective research is driven by the desire to find "truth," no matter where it leads, and thus any research conducted with the intent of affecting policy would necessarily contain researcher bias. Of course, this is mostly a quantitative research ideal, because many academicians are intimately involved in public policy and collect data with implicit or explicit policy goals.

Although academicians may be interested in the products of qualitative research, the audience of qualitative research extends far beyond the confines of professional journals and books. Because the concept of change is interwoven into qualitative research, the thought of restricting the dissemination of results to other researchers is antithetical to the qualitative endeavor. Implications for change in some local context typically are imbedded in the results of qualitative research. In the critical theory context, the audience could actually be defined as the participants, who, as a result of their participation, would find themselves with a different perspective of the social order.

Control

Control is the cornerstone of positivistic research. Some research is focused on understanding the relationship between two or more constructs, and often one of the constructs is manipulated so that its effect on another construct can be assessed. The effect of all the influences in the system on this relationship is noise that must, through experimental methods, be reduced to the extent possible. As previously discussed, understanding the complex world is accomplished by understanding the simple relationships among constructs and then aggregating these findings to approximate the real world.

Behavior does not have meaning outside of its context, and understanding the meaning of behavior in context is the essence of qualitative research. According to this view, an understanding of how people behave and the meaning that they give to their experience can never be understood by isolating some small aspect and examining it alone. All acts (a) have multiple determinants acting in a complex, nonlinear way; (b) involve both overt behavior and the meaning given to these behaviors by persons; and (c) cannot be understood by reductionistic and atomistic attempts to isolate and study linear causality.

Goals of Study

The goals of quantitative research are to discover truth, explain and predict, confirm conjecture, and extend knowledge. If truth is thought of as a jigsaw puzzle, quantitative studies add pieces of the puzzle one at a time. Through repeated studies, the entire puzzle is assembled and the picture is revealed. Each study supplies one piece and accumulated knowledge is paramount. After the puzzle is finished, we have a thorough understanding of the phenomenon and can explain particular instances of behavior based on this understanding.

In qualitative research, description and interpretation are desired. Each inquiry produces a picture of a particular context. Moreover, the goal is understanding this context. These results are not applied to predict behavior generally (that is, without consideration of the context), but would be used to foster change locally. A reader of the qualitative product (assuming it is in written form) should achieve an understanding of the complexity of the context.

Researcher's Voice

The researcher's voice in quantitative research is that of the detached, objective, unbiased scientist. The goal is the advancement of knowledge, and ideally the scientist has no interest in the results other than to contribute to that goal. In contrast, qualitative researchers are involved, and their empathic relationship with participants is crucial to the research endeavor. Moreover, because the goal of the research can be to promote change in systems and participants, the qualitative researcher can become an expert in transforming knowledge and fostering change.

Power Structure

Currently, quantitative research is the most common view in most academic environments. The academic community is generally well versed in the quantitative method. Typically, quantitative researchers need not justify their mode of inquiry during publication, funding, promotion, and tenure decisions. Although qualitative research is acquiring recognition, researchers often find it necessary to justify the qualitative paradigm. Qualitative research is often judged from a quantitative perspective (for example, "This is an interesting study, but it's limited because the results are not generalizable"). In qualitative research, recognition from outside the scientific community is important, for knowledge is seen as intrinsic to change.

PRIMARY TASKS IN QUALITATIVE RESEARCH

To this point we have discussed the worldviews that form the philosophical bases of quantitative and qualitative research as well as 17 aspects of research in which qualitative research can be distinguished from quantitative research. However, there are numerous types of qualitative research, each with a different purpose and different methods. Figure 10-1, borrowed from Tesch (1990), provides a schematic for various types of research depending on the research interest. The primary categories in this hierarchy, which are based on the interest of the research, focus on (a) the characteristics of language, (b) the discovery of regularities, (c) the comprehension of the meaning of text or action, or (d) reflection. The various types

The research interest is in . . .

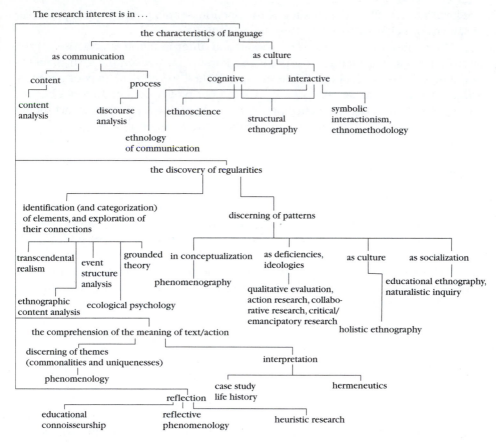

F I G U R E 10-1
An overview of qualitative research types. (Reprinted from Tesch, 1990, by permission.)

are mentioned to provide a flavor of the variations possible; readers interested in a particular approach will need to explore the specific methodological literature for that type.

Regardless of the type, the researcher must (a) gather data, and (b) analyze and present the data, two topics we explore in depth next.

GATHERING DATA

Although there are many ways to collect data in qualitative research, we discuss three primary sources here: observations, interviews, and existing materials. Wolcott (1992) refers to these sources in the active voice as *experiencing, enquiring,* and *examining,* respectively, which provides a glimpse of the state of mind of the qualitative researcher in these three activities.

Making Observations

THE NATURE OF OBSERVATIONS.   Observations are obtained by a trained observer who is present and involved in the phenomenon of interest and who makes reports of his or her observations. There are several advantages of observations in qualitative research. First, because observers can experience firsthand the transactions among persons in the field, they need not rely on retrospective reports of the participants, which could be clouded by the participants' involvement in the situation. In the vernacular, observations take place "where the action is." Second, by being close to the phenomenon, observers can feel, as well as understand, the situation. The emotion present in any situation is likely to be attenuated as time passes; the oft-spoken expression "You had to be there [to understand]" aptly summarizes this advantage of observations. Moreover, informants may not be willing or able to talk about sensitive material, may not be aware of important events, or may consider important transactions to be routine. Third, deep involvement in the process over time will allow researchers to develop conceptualizations that can be examined subsequently. In contrast to quantitative research, investigators will not have a conjecture a priori that will be confirmed or disconfirmed; qualitative researchers may, over the course of the study, come to identify themes based on the observations of the participants and to relate those themes to each other, but such themes and their relations grow out of observation. This inductive process is the basis of some methods of qualitative research, such as grounded theory (Strauss & Corbin, 1990).

Qualitative observers traditionally have followed the dictum of nonintervention (Adler & Adler, 1994), which holds that the observer does not influence the phenomenon, but acts as a recorder of events. The observer neither asks the participants questions, nor poses problems to be solved, nor suggests solutions to dilemmas. The stream of life goes on in exactly the way that it would had the observer not been present, although qualitative researchers are aware that observers can have an effect on the observed.

DEGREE OF INVOLVEMENT OF OBSERVERS.   Observers can be described by their degree of involvement in the context being observed. Traditionally, the involvement of the observer has been described as ranging from complete observer, to observer-as-participant, to participant-as-observer, to complete participant (Gold, 1958). The complete observer is entirely outside the context and would most likely be undetected by the participants. Observation of public behavior in a park by an observer seated on a bench would fit this category. The observer-as-participant is known to the participants, but is clearly identified as a researcher and does not cross over to membership in the group being observed or to friendship. In his observations of chemistry laboratories, Wampold et al. (1995) were observers-as-participants. Their presence in the laboratories during work hours was clearly recognized by the chemists, but the observers did not interact with the chemists during these periods.

Either of these two observational stances (namely, complete observer or observer-as-participant) could be used in quantitative research; the data would be transformed to numbers that indicate the degree of presence of some construct. For example, observations in a park might be used to quantify parental engagement, which could be defined as minutes spent by parent and child in face-to-face interaction. In psychotherapy research, behavior often is classified into one of many codes, with the goal of relating the degree to which the coded behaviors occurred with some other construct. As we will discuss further, even when the observer in qualitative research is not involved with the participants, the observations are not used to quantify some preconceived construct, but instead are used to gain a better understanding of the naturalistic context.

In modern conceptualizations of qualitative research, the unique contribution of participants-as-observers is their insider perspective: As participants-as-observers they can experience what the other participants are experiencing, gaining an understanding of the context in ways that nonparticipant observers cannot. Participants-as-observers sometimes fill roles within the group, although "without fully committing themselves to members' values and goals" (Adler & Adler, 1994, p. 380). Many studies of schools have involved participants-as-observers who in roles such as teachers or coaches (see, for example, Adler & Adler, 1991) become important people in the lives of the participants.

The final observational role is the complete participant, in which the investigator is a full-fledged member of the group before the research begins. Memoirs are examples of qualitative products created by complete participants in an activity. In an example from psychotherapy, Freud took the role of complete participant in his description of his cases. The degree to which one becomes a participant obviously depends on the phenomenon being studied. As Patton (1987) noted, one cannot become chemically addicted in order to become a participant in drug treatment programs, although one could be involved in such programs in ancillary ways (for example, as a staff member).

Whatever the role of the observer, the "challenge is to combine participation and observation so as to become capable of understanding the experience as an insider while describing the experience for outsiders" (Patton, 1987, p. 75). The tension between participant and observer is ever present and again emphasizes the necessity of research teams, which can process this tension and use it to produce an informative product.

METHODS OF OBSERVATIONS.   Obtaining data through observations involves several steps. In the first step, the observer must select the phenomenon and its setting. In a sense, this is the sample of qualitative research, and care must be taken in making this selection. At times this selection will be made opportunistically—because the setting is available and accessible. At other times the researcher may be invited to observe because the group values or desires a consultation by the researcher, which is the case in qualitative program evaluation. It is important that the setting be appropriate given the goals of the investigation. In quantitative research, the important consideration is the representativeness of the sample, whereas in qualitative research, greater emphasis is put on selecting settings strategically so that the data are meaningful. For example, instead of choosing a representative (that is, average) therapist to study intensively, a qualitative researcher may be more interested in studying therapists identified as successful, powerful, charismatic, or even unsuccessful. Patton (1990) provides a useful typology of sampling, including the purpose of various procedures.

The second step involves training investigators to be skilled and careful observers. Observers must be trained to attend to detail, to separate the mundane from the important, to write highly descriptive field notes, to be sufficiently knowledgeable to make sense of the context, and to be open to reconciling observations with those of other research team members. Consider a study of instructional skill in a complex context, such as sailing. In a local sailing school, the conclusion that some instructors were less skilled than others was based on how often the students capsized the boats. An interview with the instructors or the students will likely not be too informative, as the students would lack sufficient knowledge to understand the reason for mistakes and the instructors would likely attribute causality to the skill level of the students. However, an observer trained in observing interpersonal behavior and who understands the principles of sailing would be able to sort out how instruction and student actions interact and result in capsized boats.

The third step is to gain access to the context being studied. Gaining access, of course, varies greatly, depending on the people being studied. Observing public behavior involves no special arrangements other than finding a suitable vantage point, but studying secret societies, especially those engaged in illegal or undesirable behavior, will be nearly impossible because these groups are unlikely to give their informed consent to participate in a study. Fortunately, most foci of qualitative research in counseling involve groups that are amenable to being observed. Often, trust is the key to gaining entrée to a group. If its formal leader is trusted, then his or her support can be sufficient for acceptance and cooperation from the group. However, if the leader's personal influence is tenuous and relations strained, then the recommendation to accept the researcher may be counterproductive and the observations undermined.

The fourth step involves deciding the time and duration of observations. At the outset, the observations are relatively unfocused and the researcher is getting the "lay of the land," and thus the duration of observation is as important as the time of the observation. Generally, observations should be taken at various times so as not to miss something particular to a certain time. For example, a study of work climate should involve observations from all shifts and during various days of the week. Clearly, the focus of the study should guide the researcher; for example, a researcher interested in how people from various disciplines negotiate their roles in multidisciplinary settings will want to observe instances in which the disciplines work together (for example, in staff meetings or multidisciplinary work groups). As the research progresses, the data will suggest ways that the observers can focus their attention. In the study of chemistry groups, Wampold et al. (1995) found that instances of conflict demonstrated how the array of chemists' social skills guided their actions, and consequently observations were arranged during times when conflicts were more likely (for example, during transitions of one research team to another on an expensive apparatus).

The fifth and final step is to collect the data. Most frequently observational data are the researcher's field notes taken during or immediately after the observations.

Field notes are descriptions of everything relevant to understanding the phenomenon. Because relevance is not always clear in the beginning, initially field notes are likely to contain everything that happened. The novice observer will feel overwhelmed, but it should be recognized that most anything missed will be repeated over and over again. As the observations become more focused, so will the field notes. For example, if it is observed that one discipline is superior in multidisciplinary work, the observations may be focused on how this hierarchy is established as new members join the group; the field notes would similarly be focused on the process of transmitting power to incoming persons.

Field notes should contain basic descriptions of the setting—time, physical setting, persons present, the purpose of activity, and so forth—as well as complete descriptions of the interactions among the participants. Patton (1987) provides a good contrast between vague, generalized notes and detailed, concrete notes (p. 93):

> Vague: The new client was uneasy waiting for her intake interview.

> Detailed: At first the client sat very stiffly on the chair next to the receptionist's desk. She picked up a magazine and let the pages flutter through her fingers very quickly without really looking at any of the pages. She set the magazine down, looked at her watch, pulled her skirt down, and picked up the magazine again. This time she didn't look at the magazine. She set it back down, took out a cigarette and began smoking. She would watch the receptionist out of the corner of her eye, and then look down at the magazine, and back up at the two or three other people waiting in the room. Her eyes moved from people to the magazine to the cigarette to the people to the magazine in rapid succession. She avoided eye contact. When her name was finally called she jumped like she was startled.

The latter description is more complete and involves little inference on the part of the observer, whereas the vague description both involves the inference that the client was uneasy and lacks data to enable confirmation of this inference at a later time. People's conversations should be recorded as close to verbatim as possible. Audiotapes can be used to supplement field notes if they are compatible with the context.

Field notes should contain the observer's interpretations of events, but these interpretations should be so labeled to distinguish them from descriptions. Field notes might also contain working hypotheses, suggestions for interviewers, and so forth.

Undoubtedly, observations and field notes are influenced by the personal constructions of the observers. Multiple observers cross-checking their descriptions and their interpretations are vital for the integrity of observations, for trained observers may see a situation very differently. Acknowledging and honoring these perspectives is part and parcel of qualitative research.

Conducting Interviews

TYPES OF INTERVIEWS.   Qualitative researchers are interested in using interviews to make sense of people's actions in naturalistic settings. The language used by respondents is a powerful means to accomplish this goal. Basically, the interview is a face-to-face or indirect (for example, telephone) interaction between the investigator and one or more participants in which the investigator asks the respondents questions in order to obtain information.

Interviews can be classified into three types: structured interviews, unstructured interviews, and group interviews (Fontana & Frey, 1994). In a structured interview, the questions and the order in which they are asked are determined a priori. Moreover, responses are classified into categories or are quantified according to some protocol that also is developed a priori. The interviewer develops rapport with the respondent but takes a neutral stance in that he or she does not show either approval or disapproval of responses and does not follow-up on unusual, interesting, or uninformative responses. The advantages of structured interviews is that they are standardized across respondents and minimize errors. However, they have limited usefulness in qualitative research because they (a) shape data to conform to structures that emanated from the investigator's previously held beliefs about the phenomenon, (b) use a standard language across respondents (rather than questions customized to the language of particular respondents), and (c) restrict affective components of responses (Fontana & Frey, 1994). Although technically not an interview, the questions can be printed and administered to subjects, which is similar to a questionnaire except that the responses are not constrained in any way.

On the other end of the continuum, unstructured interviews provide latitude to explore the responses of participants and to adapt question for respondents, and they do not quantify or categorize these responses. Respondents are encouraged to use their own language to describe their experiences, and the interviewer asks probing questions to get a more complete description. Because the questions are not determined a priori, the interviewer has great latitude but must take care not to shape the responses by covertly reinforcing certain types of responses (for example, following up only on responses that are critical of an organization). The type of question asked in qualitative research is shaped by the type of research conducted; thus, ethnographers approach this endeavor differently from grounded theorists, for example.

Interviews, which are the most widely used means to obtain qualitative data in counseling research, span the structured/unstructured continuum. Researchers have often used some stimulus to provide richer responses. For an example of a relatively unstructured interview, consider Rennie's (1994) study of client's deference in psychotherapy, in which clients viewed a videotape of a recent counseling session (a variation of Interpersonal Process Recall; Kagan, 1975) and stopped the tape when they were experiencing something interesting or significant. The interviewer then "conducted a nondirective inquiry into the recalled experience" (p. 429), creating a description of the client's perceptions of the therapy in the client's own language without imposing predetermined categories for understanding these descriptions. As an example of a more structured approach, Frontman and Kunkel (1994), who also wanted to access clients' reactions to therapy, asked clients immediately after a session (rather than being stimulated by a videotape) to respond to the following probe: "As if you were making a personal journal entry, write what you felt was successful about the session" (p. 493). Because this probe was responded to in writing, no follow-up questions were used. Although the probe for this study was standardized, no preconceived categories were used to make sense of the responses, so that the conclusions were grounded in the data and not structured by the investigators' prior understanding of the phenomenon.

A third type of interview is the group interview, in which more than one person is interviewed simultaneously. The economy of using group interviews is self-evident, but a less obvious advantage of the group format is the interaction among the respondents, which can provide richer information as various members of the group provide more details, disagree on points, and reconcile differences of opinions. However, the skilled interviewer needs to ensure that minority opinions are allowed expression, given the natural tendency for such opinions to be suppressed. Particularly exciting possibilities exist for *focus groups,* a modality that evolved from marketing research related to reactions to products, advertisements, and services (Merton, Fiske, & Kendall, 1956). Typically, the participants in a focus group are relatively homogeneous and are asked to reflect on a particular issue. Having participants respond in a social context is thought to provide honest and responsible comments. The goal of a focus group is to obtain the participants' opinions, not to reach a consensus or reconcile opposing views; the expression of different opinions is informative. In market research, the members of a focus group are strangers, but applications to qualitative research suggest possibilities for using intact groups, such as the staff of a mental health clinic.

METHODS OF INTERVIEWING.   Counselors are well trained in the art of asking questions, and there are many similarities between the counseling interview and the qualitative research interview. (Note, however, that the purpose of the counseling interview is unique in that the client has come with the purpose of seeking help, and all actions are taken with that goal in mind.) Although the goals of qualitative interviewing will depend on the type of qualitative research conducted, a generic goal is to understand the experience of the participant; therapeutic actions should be avoided. Table 10-2, a typology of questions suitable for qualitative research, provides some examples of questions aimed at gaining understanding at various levels.

We now briefly examine the various steps in conducting qualitative interviews, adapted from Fontana and Frey (1994). The first step is to gain entrée to the setting in a way similar to gaining entrée for observations. Wampold et al. (1995) were able to gain access to two chemistry groups by first obtaining the support of the laboratory leader. Although all the members subsequently agreed to be observed, several declined to be interviewed because of the time it took away from their work.

The second step involves preparing to understand the language and the culture of the interviewees. In qualitative interviews, the investigator strives to have participants express their experiences in their own language. To achieve that goal, the questions should be understandable to participants and consistent with their values. For example, if one were interviewing elderly African Americans who were accustomed to calling themselves "colored," an interviewer who phrased questions using the term "African American" might meet confusion, resistance, or

T A B L E 10-2
Types of Qualitative Interview Questions

Type	Examples
Background	Tell me about your background.
	How long have you been with the agency?
Behavioral	If I had been with you during a typical day, what would I observe you doing?
	What do you usually do when this situation happens?
Opinion or belief	What is your opinion about the recent decision to use untrained assistants?
	What do you believe is the best way to provide service to these clients?
Feeling questions	How do you feel about the decision to reduce the number of counselors in the agency?
Knowledge questions	How do you know when to terminate?
	How do clients get assigned to counselors?
Sensory questions	Describe for me the waiting room at your counselor's office.
	When you go to the principal's office after being tardy, what do you see?
Experiential	What is it like to be a counselor at this agency?
	Describe for me your experience of being in counseling for the first time.

SOURCE: Adapted from Patton, 1987.

suspicion. In addition, the interviewer must instantly understand what the interviewee means by various idioms and expressions so that appropriate follow-up questions can be asked. This knowledge is acquired from previous experience and preparation and is accumulated over the course of the interviews. Moreover, knowledge of language and culture is needed to make sense of the interviews in the data analysis phase, which is described in the next section.

The third step is to make a decision about self-presentation. Whereas quantitative researchers are objective scientists and present themselves as such, qualitative researchers can choose among various self-presentations. For example, a researcher might present herself to abused women as a feminist as well as a researcher. Basically, the issue here is the degree to which the researchers should share of themselves; they must balance the comfort inherent in familiarity with the suspicion generated by attempts to appear to be similar to respondents.

The fourth step is to identify the interviewees. The central concept in this step is *key informants,* people whose perceptions are particularly important for understanding the context being studied. Of course, the key informants will likely be unknown to the investigator initially, but as knowledge is gained their identity will emerge. Key informants are often those who have a different experience than the norm, who are willing to divulge sensitive information, who are formal or natural leaders, and so forth. Moreover, key informants may not be directly involved in the phenomenon being studied. For example, the support staff in a mental health clinic could provide important information relative to counseling at the agency, even though they neither deliver nor receive treatment. In quantitative research the emphasis is on representative samples, but in qualitative research the goal is to obtain a depth of understanding, and thus the choice of interviewees is an emergent process.

The fifth step is to establish rapport with each interviewee, a process that is beneficial for two reasons. First, rapport leads to trust, which in turn leads to honest and descriptive responses. Second, an empathic stance enables the interviewer to better understand the interviewee's responses. Interviewers must take care, however, that the natural affinity that goes hand-in-hand with empathy does not cloud their assessment of the situation.

The sixth and final step is to decide how the interview data will be collected. If done unintrusively, interviews should be recorded and subsequently transcribed for analysis. In any case, field notes should be taken. Important information is contained in the nonverbal responses of the interviewees, and in the setting and its surroundings. (Note that the comments regarding field notes for observations apply here as well.)

Because interviewing is the predominant mode of obtaining data in qualitative research in counseling psychology, the neophyte qualitative researcher is encouraged to hone his or her skill in this area. Kvale (1996) and Douglas (1985) discuss qualitative interviewing in depth.

Using Existing Materials

Existing materials are written text and artifacts, which can often inform qualitative research in ways that observations and interviews cannot; such materials are essential to any historical study for which observations are impossible. As always, the goal is to use this material to provide a richer understanding of the phenomena being examined.

Written documents are of two types, official records and personal documents (Lincoln & Guba, 1985). Official documents include marriage certificates, licenses, contracts, records of transactions, and so forth. Personal documents include diaries, letters, E-mail, literature, field notes, and so forth. Artifacts include material and electronic traces, such as buildings, garbage, art, nontextual computer files—essentially any disturbance of the natural environment created by people.

Of the three sources of qualitative data discussed in this chapter (observations, interviews, and existing materials), existing materials present the most issues, even though such materials can be particularly valuable. Hodder (1994) gives several examples of discrepancies between material traces and people's reports of their activities (for example, report of alcohol use versus number of beer bottles found in garbage). However, the difficulty with existing materials involves the interpretation of the text or artifacts.

As an example of the ambiguity of such materials, consider the case of the historical understanding of the shape of the Earth. If one were to read many nineteenth-century texts and most current history textbooks (that is, interpreted textual material), one would conclude that fifteenth-century scholars believed that the Earth was flat and that the various explorers (most conspicuously Christopher

Columbus) thought that they were taking enormous risks by sailing westward from Europe. Indeed, the belief that Columbus proved that the Earth was round has persisted, as a perusal of most history texts will show. However, examination of fifteenth-century documents shows that, with a few exceptions, scholars and explorers firmly believed that the Earth *was* round and put faith in the relatively accurate calculations of Earth's sphericity that dated back to the Greek philosophers at around 400 B.C. (again, a conclusion based on textual material). Why does the erroneous belief that medieval scholars thought the Earth was flat persist? Russell (1991) contends that the flat-Earth error appeared in the nineteenth century and was fostered by scholars, emboldened by positivism and "at war" with religious constructions of the world, who sought to show that medieval thought was clouded by religion. The point here is that written text (as well as artifacts) must be interpreted within the context in which they were created. Literal readings can lead one astray, as illustrated by nineteenth-century writings about the flat Earth. Russell's (1991) attempts to understand the flat-Earth error led him to examine ancient Greek documents, medieval documents, nineteenth-century documents, and current textbooks. Clearly, Russell's only source for studying a phenomenon (the flat-Earth error) that could not be investigated via interviews or observations was existing materials.

One existing material has assumed primacy in qualitative research in counseling: the counseling interview (see, for example, Elliott et al., 1994; Friedlander et al., 1994; Thompson & Jenal, 1994), either represented as a verbal record (that is, a tape recording) or as text (that is, a transcript). In such studies, interpretations are made of the records of counseling. For example, Friedlander et al. (1994) examined family therapy sessions to understand how sustaining engagement was important to change.

Analyzing and Presenting Data

As is the case for the collection of data, the analysis and presentation of qualitative data depend on the particular qualitative methodology used. Here we discuss three generic means to analyze data and present results: thick description, themes and relationships, and interpretation. For more detail, see Wolcott (1994), who presented a thorough discussion of these methods, including lengthy examples.

Thick Description

Thick description is the most basic means of presenting qualitative data. Essentially, a thick description is an unadulterated and thorough presentation of the data. The researcher may write some introductory and transitory material, but principally the presentation consists of lengthy excerpts from interviews, field notes, and existing materials (text and/or descriptions of artifacts).

The consumers of thick descriptions have the raw data, which for the most part has not been altered by the investigator. In this way, "the data speak for themselves" and provide a rich account of what happened. Of course, the process of observing, interviewing, collecting materials, and deciding what to describe filters what is available to consumers. Still, even though the understanding achieved by readers of a thick description is affected by the research process, thick descriptions are closer to the phenomenon being studied than are any other means, qualitative or quantitative.

Despite the primary advantage that the data are minimally filtered, there are numerous disadvantages. True descriptions are too lengthy for journal articles, and many important thick descriptions languish as lengthy dissertations or unpublished reports. Another disadvantage is that the thick descriptions may be unfocused and uninteresting:"Readers are likely to get the idea that the researcher has been unable to sort out (or unwilling to throw away) data and has simply passed the task along. . . . [D]ata that do not 'speak' to the person who gathered and reported them are not likely to strike up a conversation with subsequent readers either" (Wolcott, 1994). It is hoped that the story, as told by the participants or as observed by the investigator, will be fascinating enough to hold the interest of readers.

Rarely are qualitative investigators able to present all data verbatim in a thick description, and thus they must use one of two strategies to present a condensed but still relatively complete description. They can either sift and identify the most important material to present, or they can summarize thick description. Either way, the investigator has the critical task of deciding what must go, and there are few guidelines. As has been emphasized throughout this chapter, crucial decisions about data should be made within a research team through a process that acknowledges the investigators' suppositions. Moreover, the process involved in examining these suppositions and making sense of the data in the context of these suppositions should be a prominent part of the presentation so that readers can understand how the descriptions were distilled to a reasonable length. Wolcott (1994) warns against presenting all descriptions at the same level and recommends using a "zoom lens" to zoom in and pull back to present a richer picture of context and detail.

Themes and Relationships

Themes are recurrent patterns in data that represent a concept, whereas relationships are the interconnections among the themes. Through development of themes and relationships, the essence of a phenomenon is revealed. Extracting themes and establishing relationships are the essence of grounded theory (Strauss & Corbin, 1990), a popular form of qualitative research. Essentially, the relationships of themes constitutes the theory, which is grounded in (is inductively developed from) the data.

The first step in this process is to generate codes for various themes that are intrinsic to the phenomenon being studied. Often tentative codes are first generated from initial observations or field notes on a word-by-word, sentence-by-sentence, or paragraph-by-paragraph reading of the text, and are then written directly on the transcripts. These codes name various patterns. For example, in a study of psychotherapy, Watson and Rennie (1994) developed the code "reflective self-examination" to describe clients' observations of themselves that were "spurred by the questions they posed about their behavior, their feelings, and their interactions with the world" (p. 503).

As the investigator progresses through the data, the explanatory power of the various codes becomes apparent. The codes are revised and refined until a clear theme is developed. When the theme is relatively robust, the investigator reexamines the data to understand how the theme functions with the phenomenon. What are the causal conditions? What is the context needed to give rise to the phenomenon? What are the intervening conditions? What are the consequences? In the Watson and Rennie (1994) study, the authors answered these questions by presenting the complex relationship among themes:

> The analysis of clients' subjective experiences during the exploration of problematic reactions provided access to the internal operations that clients engaged in to effect changes in their behavior. The model of the clients' experiences during the event highlights two important foci of clients' attention and activity during the session: client operations and session momentum. When engaged in the former, clients alternated between two primary activities: symbolic representation of their experience and reflective self-examination. . . . These two processes, together with therapists' operations, are related to clients' making new realizations and engaging in activities to alter their behavior. (p. 506)

Hill, Thompson, and Williams (1997) have recently developed guidelines for what they labeled Consensual Qualitative Research (CQR) for the purpose of identifying themes in data. They suggest that team members first look over the data separately before the team meets and discusses it. After hearing individual viewpoints, they then jointly develop constructions of the data. Another person not associated with the team, an auditor, examines the constructs along with the raw data; the auditor challenges any constructions that do not seem to fit the data. The team then reexamines their constructions and decides whether the evidence suggests revisions. In essence, the CQR approach combines the flexibility of qualitative methods with some of the rigor and replicability of quantitative methods (Tinsely, 1997).

The model of themes and their relationships provides an emerging grounded theory. As the model is developed, the investigator returns to existing data or collects additional data to test crucial aspects of the model. In their study of chemistry groups, Wampold et al. (1995) had a tentative model that described the chemists' avoidance of social interaction involving encoding and decoding emotion. Given that strong affect is intrinsic to conflictual situations, they returned to observe the chemists during conflict in order to understand more fully the interplay between the chemists' expression and understanding of emotion and their social interactions. The point is that the themes and relationships model should always be considered emergent and should guide further collection of data.

Interpretation

Interpretation, as described by Wolcott (1994), is aimed at extracting meaning and identifying context. Rather than providing a theory of a specific phenomenon by relating themes, interpretation addresses more global issues, such as "What is the role of race and ethnicity in American society?" and "How do cultural factors affect conceptions of mental health and treatment?" Wolcott noted that "at the interpretive extreme, a researcher-as-writer may seem merely to swoop down into the field for a descriptive morsel or two and then retreat once again to the lofty heights of theory or speculation" (p. 11) and that interpretation "is well suited to mark a threshold in thinking and writing at which the researcher transcends factual data and cautious analyses and begins to probe into what is to be made of them" (p. 36). Clearly, interpretation is open water in which the novice should not venture.

SUMMARY AND CONCLUSIONS

Qualitative research is based on philosophical foundations that differ from those of quantitative research. Typically, qualitative approaches entail a worldview that recognizes that the mind actively ascribes meaning to events and behavior, and that understanding these mental constructions is the purpose of scientific inquiry. The worldviews aligned with this belief are constructivism and critical theory. In this chapter we described qualitative research by contrasting it with quantitative research. However, this approach is pedagogical only; we do not intend to imply that either approach to research is superior or that one can be understood only by comparison with the other.

This chapter has only scratched the surface of qualitative research. Volumes have been written about this subject, and one could devote all of one's energy to learning about only one particular type of qualitative research. We have sought to provide the reader an appreciation of qualitative research, an overview of the general methods, and references for those who want to pursue the topic in greater depth. We recommend that students seek out ongoing qualitative research teams and volunteer to participate.

Occasionally, we have encountered students who have undertaken qualitative research under the misguided notion that qualitative research is easier or less technical than quantitative research. Rigorous qualitative research certainly is different from quantitative research, but selecting this approach will lead to disappointment if the primary motivation is the avoidance of work or numbers. Qualitative research is time consuming and thought provoking. Be prepared to stay up late, thinking about the meaning of field notes or transcripts, attempting to make sense of intrinsically ambiguous data, and writing, writing, writing.

Qualitative research in counseling is here to stay.

PART THREE

METHODOLOGICAL ISSUES

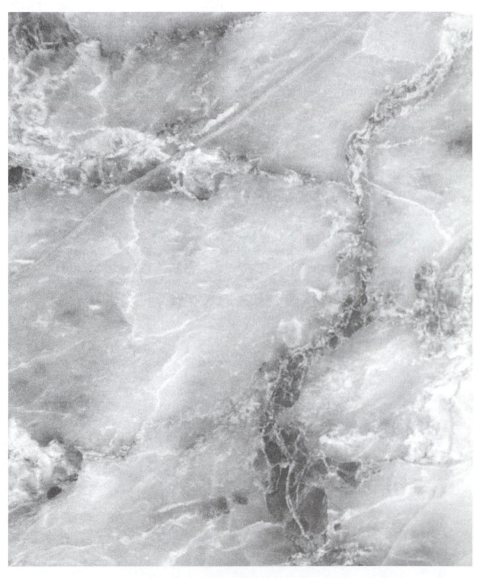

C H A P T E R 11

DESIGNING AND EVALUATING
THE INDEPENDENT VARIABLE

One of the primary goals of the research endeavor is to establish a causal relationship between the independent and dependent variables. After a researcher has identified a research question, he or she takes the critical step of selecting or designing these variables. This chapter focuses on issues pertaining to independent variables, while Chapter 12 focuses on dependent variables.

Selection, design, and evaluation of the independent variable are crucial in establishing and interpreting causal relations in a study. If the independent variable is poorly designed, the researcher's effort will be unrewarding—either the expected effect will not be found, or the results will be ambiguous or meaningless. Poorly designed independent variables create unwanted bias and extraneous variables, which are clear threats to Kerlinger's "MAXMINCON" principle.

This chapter discusses four issues related to the development and selection of independent variables. The first section discusses operationalizing the independent variable. But even when a researcher has carefully designed an independent variable, there is no assurance that the experimental manipulation will achieve its purpose, and thus the second section describes methods to check or verify the manipulation of the independent variable, often called manipulation checks. The third section focuses on interpreting the results of a study, whether the manipulation of the independent variable was successful or unsuccessful. Thus, the first section focuses on issues pertaining to the independent variable that are relevant before an experiment begins, the second section on issues during an experiment, and the third section on issues after an experiment has been conducted. In the final section of the chapter we discuss independent variables that are not amenable to manipulation, which we define as status variables.

OPERATIONALIZING THE INDEPENDENT VARIABLE

Before an experiment begins, four concerns with regard to operationalizing the independent variable are particularly important to the researcher: (a) determining the conditions or levels of the independent variable, (b) adequately reflecting the constructs designated as the cause in the research question, (c) limiting differences between conditions, and (d) establishing salience of differences in conditions.

Determining Conditions

In counseling research, the typical independent variable consists of several conditions. In the between-groups designs discussed in Chapter 6, the emphasis is on independent variables with two conditions: treatment and no treatment (that is, a control group). However, an independent variable can contain any number of conditions. A treatment study can examine three treatments as well as a no-treatment condition (that is, four conditions in all). Or a treatment group may be contrasted with a placebo control group and a no-treatment control group (that is, a total of three conditions). Of course, the independent variable is not restricted to psychological treatments; in a study of preferences for counselors, European-American or Mexican-American counselors (two conditions) would constitute an appropriate independent variable (see, for example, Ponce & Atkinson, 1989). In this chapter, independent variables are discussed generally; Chapter 16 contains a presentation of treatment outcome designs in which the independent variable is used to establish the efficacy of treatments (that is, at least one of the conditions is a treatment).

Two notes need to be made about our discussion of conditions. First, we use the term *conditions* to indicate the groups that constitute the independent variable. However, *levels of the independent variable, groups, categories,* and *treatments* are other, interchangeable terms that are used in the discussion of research design. In this context, *treatments* refers generically to conditions, and not to psychological interventions. Second, we have conceptualized the independent variable as a categorical variable—that is, each discrete category (level, condition, group, or treatment) is different. The independent variable need not be restricted to categories. Classical regression designs involve quantitative independent variables; in that case, the conditions reflect different amounts of something (see Wampold & Drew, 1990). For instance, in a drug study, the independent variable could consist of different dosage levels (for example, no drug, 2 cc, 4 cc, and 6 cc). Because true quantitative independent variables are used infrequently in counseling research, they will not be emphasized here. However, later in this chapter we discuss status variables, and these variables are often quantitative.

The most important point is that the nature of the conditions of the independent variable is determined by the researcher. This determination is often referred to as the experimental manipulation, because the researcher essentially manipulates the independent variable to determine what effect it has on the dependent variable. In this way, the independent variable is related to the cause, and the dependent variable is related to the effect.

Adequately Reflecting the Constructs of Interest

It is important that the independent variable be designed to reflect the construct or constructs designated as the cause in the research question. That is to say, the independent variable should be adequately defined or operationalized (see Chapter 2). If the causal construct is inadequately operationalized, alternative explanations for the results can be offered; these alternatives are potential confounds. In this chapter we indicate how problems associated with potential confounds can be minimized or eliminated.

To illustrate the importance of adequately reflecting the construct designated as causal, consider a study conducted by Malkiewich and Merluzzi (1980) to test the client-treatment matching model. The research hypothesis stipulated that high conceptual level thinkers would benefit from relatively unstructured counseling, whereas low conceptual level thinkers would benefit from relatively structured counseling. In this study, the structure of the counseling was one of the independent variables, and it was operationalized by including three conditions of the independent variable: a desensitization condition, a rational restructuring condition, and a control group. The desensitization group represented high structure, and the rational restructuring group, low structure. In this study, the expected interaction effect was not detected; one primary explanation for this null result was that the independent variable did not provide good exemplars of structured and unstructured counseling. It is unclear whether these two groups adequately represented differing structures, as both interventions seem rather structured. To provide a better test of the independent variable (structure of counseling), it might have been useful to provide a type of counseling that is more clearly unstructured. For example, client-centered counseling (which is often characterized as unstructured) could have been used to represent low structure, which would have provided a greater range of counseling structure.

Limiting Differences Between Conditions

The conditions selected for the independent variable should differ only along the dimension of interest. If the conditions are allowed to differ on other dimensions, the additional dimensions become confounds. To illustrate this principle, consider a study of perceived credibility of European-American and Mexican-American counselors as a function of counseling style and acculturation (Ponce & Atkinson, 1989). Although several independent variables were considered in a factorial design in this study, we focus here on the independent variable related to ethnicity of the counselor. Although there are many possible ways to operationalize ethnicity of the counselor, in this study ethnicity was manipulated by showing the participants photographs of the counselor and by using written introductions. In one condition, participants saw a photograph of a Mexican-American counselor, and the introduction used surnames and birthplaces that reflected Mexican-American ethnicity (for example, *Chavez* and *Mexico*, respectively). In the other condition, participants saw a photograph of a European-American counselor, and the introduction used surnames and birthplaces that reflected European-American ethnicity (for example, *Sanders* and *Canada,* respectively). Clearly, this arrangement operationalizes ethnicity of the counselor; the question is whether the two conditions differed on any other dimension. Because Ponce and Atkinson chose to use photographs, there exists the possibility that the Mexican-American and European-American counselors in the photographs also differed in personal attractiveness, which would provide an alternative explanation for the results pertaining to this independent variable. That is, higher ratings given to Mexican-American counselors by the Mexican-American participants may be due to either the counselor's ethnicity or personal attractiveness. Fortunately, Ponce and Atkinson were aware of this potential confound and controlled for it by ensuring that the counselors in the photographs were comparable with regard to personal attractiveness (and with regard to age, another possible confound).

Before the research is conducted, potential confounds should be considered. It is not always possible to eliminate confounds, but identifying them before the study begins can enable the researcher to add features that minimize such confounds (for example, manipulation checks, which are discussed later in this chapter). It is distressing to discover a major confound after the data are collected when some prior thought could have led to a modification of the study that ruled it out.

Often a researcher finds it necessary to argue logically that a confound has a low probability of occurring. Personal attractiveness seems to be an important variable in the counselor credibility literature (see Corrigan et al., 1980), so taking steps to rule it out was important in the Ponce and Atkinson study. However, Ponce and Atkinson did not rule out the possibility that the results of the study were due to anti-Canadian sentiment due to the then-current difficulty of negotiating a trade agreement between Canada and the United States. Although this explanation cannot be ruled out by the design of the experiment, there is no evidence that political relations with the mother country of a counselor either affects or does not affect credibility. Still, even though this confound appears to be trivial, caution must be used when ruling out confounds based on common sense or logic; after all, the research endeavor is aimed at discovering new knowledge (including, perhaps, contradicting what we believe to be true).

Some troublesome confounds are unique to treatment studies; one of them is the counselor. Ruling out counselor confounds could be accomplished by holding the counselors constant across treatments; that is, the same counselors would administer all treatments. However, some counselors may be more skilled with one treatment than with another, or counselors may have some allegiance to one treatment or the other, and so forth. Hence, the superiority of a treatment may not be due to the treatment at all, but instead to the skill or allegiance of the counselor. One alternative is to have experts in a particular treatment administer it, but this strategy introduces possible confounds related to experience, training, and so forth. Another possibility is to select relatively untrained counselors (for example, graduate students in counseling), randomly assign them to treatments, and then give them equal training in their respective treatments. Of course, this reduces the external validity of the study because the results are then generalizable only to treatments administered by inexperienced therapists. Once again, Gelso's (1979) bubble appears—there is no perfect solution to the counselor confound problem.

Establishing Salience of Differences in Conditions

The difference between the conditions on the desired dimension should be salient—that is, noticeable—to the participants. For example, Ponce and Atkinson (1989) could have used only the surname and birthplace of the counselor to operationalize ethnicity, which would have eliminated the personal attractiveness confound and made the research simpler. However, they included the photograph to increase the salience of ethnicity because without it, it would have been easy for the participants to read the half-page introduction (which focused more on the client) without attending to the counselor's surname and birthplace.

Sharkin, Mahalik, and Claiborn (1989) conducted a study of clients' motivation to pursue additional counseling that included a manipulation that may not have been salient to the participants. Participants were undergraduates who volunteered to participate in a 30-minute counseling session aimed at exploring their communication skills. Depending on whether or not they had completed a list of communication skills, half of the participants were told near the end of the session either that "by completing the brief list of your communication skills, it shows that you are motivated" or that "by signing up for this study, it shows that you are motivated." No mention of motivation was made to the other half of the participants. It may well be that given the full range of the 30-minute social interaction, participants in the motivation condition did not attend to the lone statement about motivation. This conclusion is mitigated to some degree by the fact that differences in one dependent variable were detected for the motivation versus no-motivation independent variable, although interpretation of salience based on the outcome of a study is problematic, as we will see later in this chapter.

Although it appears that salience on the important dimension of the independent variable is vital to a study's validity, there are dangers when the salience is too great. If the participants can infer the research hypothesis from the study's procedures then there is the possibility that responses will be biased. This is an aspect of hypothesis guessing, a threat to construct validity mentioned in Chapter 4. Often the inference about the hypothesis is based on the research's stated (to the participant) purpose and various procedures, as well as on the salience of the experimental manipulation. Presumably, participants who guess the research hypothesis tend to respond in ways that please the researcher and thus confirm the research hypothesis. This phenomenon often is referred to as the Hawthorne effect, after the studies in the Hawthorne industrial plant that found that workers in all experimental conditions attempted to comply with what they perceived to be the experimenters' expectations—in this case, that the workers would increase productivity.

Hypothesis guessing is a potential threat in the counselor credibility study as well (Ponce & Atkinson, 1989). Two Mexican-American researchers asked for Mexican-American volunteers from college classes. Because of these arrangements and because the salience of differences in ethnicity was increased by including photographs, the participants in the condition in which the counselor was Mexican-American may have guessed that the hypothesis involved ethnicity of the counselor and therefore raised (subconsciously) their credibility ratings to please the Mexican-American researchers. Ponce and Atkinson attempted to minimize this by disguising the exact purpose of the research, although generally there are constraints on the degree to which deception can be used in research, as we discussed in Chapter 5.

In sum, the conclusion to be reached about independent variables is that the conditions should vary on the intended dimension but not on other dimensions, and that the intended dimension should reflect the research question of interest. Furthermore, differences between experimental conditions on the intended dimension should be salient, but not transparent; participants within a condition should be aware of the critical component of the condition but should not be able to infer the research hypothesis. Of course, making decisions between salience and transparency is difficult and is one of the skills that experienced researchers acquire.

MANIPULATION CHECKS

Even when great care has been taken to define and operationalize the independent variable, there is no assurance that the experimental manipulation will achieve its purpose. It is possible for the researcher to misjudge the salience of the independent variable. To verify that a manipulation has been adequately designed, it is often advisable to check the characteristics of the manipulation. The goal of manipulation checks is to show one or more of the following: (a) that conditions vary on the intended dimension, (b) that conditions do not vary on other dimensions, and (c) that treatments are implemented in the intended fashion.

To determine whether the conditions vary on the intended dimension, judgments of characteristics related to the dimension should differ across conditions. This determination can be made in a number of ways. First, inquiries can be made of the participants themselves. For example, Jones and Gelso (1988), in a study of the effects of the style of interpretation, manipulated style by having participants listen to audiotapes of a counseling session. In one condition, the counselor's interpretations were tentatively phrased and ended with a question, and in the other condition the counselor's interpretations were decisively phrased. The manipulation check was accomplished by having the participants rate on a seven-point scale whether the counselor's comments were phrased tentatively or decisively, and whether they were in the form of questions or statements. As anticipated, there were significant differences between the conditions on both of the seven-point scales, providing evidence that the manipulation was indeed salient to the participants.

Another means to assess differences on the intended dimension is to have independent raters (persons other than the participants or the experimenters) judge the experimental materials. These independent raters could be either naive individuals (those untrained in counseling) or experts. In the ethnicity-of-counselor study discussed previously, Ponce and Atkinson (1989) also varied counselor style (directive versus nondirective). Graduate students in counseling psychology rated the dialogue of the sessions, and the intended differences in directiveness were found, lending support for the adequacy of the independent variable.

Independent raters and the participants can also be used to establish that the conditions do not vary on dimensions other than the intended one. Recall that Ponce and Atkinson's use of photographs of the counselors introduced a possible confound related to the counselors' personal attractiveness. To control for this threat, undergraduates rated the attractiveness of several European-Americans and Mexican-Americans in photographs, and the photographs used in the study were matched on the dimension of personal attractiveness. Parr and Neimeyer (1994), in a study of vocational differentiation, manipulated the relevance of occupations by having the participants circle either 12 relevant occupations, 12 irrelevant occupations, or 6 relevant and 6 irrelevant occupations, and subsequently giving them information about the 12 occupations they had circled. Later, the participants rated the occupations, and these ratings were used to check whether relevant occupations received more positive ratings than did irrelevant occupations, which they did.

Credibility of treatment is a potential confound in treatment studies. Thus, demonstrating empirically that credibility does not differ across conditions improves the validity of a treatment study. Deffenbacher, Thwaites, Wallace, and Oetting (1994), in a study of anger reduction, compared three treatments: inductive social skills training, skill assembly social skills training, and cognitive-relaxation coping skills. To test for treatment integrity, the subjects in each of the treatment groups completed a therapist evaluation questionnaire and a treatment evaluation questionnaire (Deffenbacher & Stark, 1992; Hazaleus & Deffenbacher, 1986); the researchers found that these ratings were comparable across the three treatments. In treatment studies it is important that the treatments be delivered to participants in the intended fashion. Issues related to manipulation checks are discussed further in Chapter 16.

Manipulation checks can be a very important aspect of a study. When the saliency of a manipulation is in doubt, checks provide a means of verifying the researcher's claim that the conditions differ on the intended dimension only. Whether or not manipulation checks are worth the extra time and effort required to implement them is a determination that can be made only in the context of a particular research study.

INTERPRETING RESULTS

The logic of experimental designs involves establishing a causal relationship between the independent and dependent variables. Thus far we have discussed topics related to design of the independent variable and to checking on the manipulation. Equally important is interpreting the results of an experiment, which provide much of the information upon which inferences are based. In this section we discuss various problems in interpreting statistically significant and statistically nonsignificant results with regard to the independent variable.

Statistically Significant Results

Statistical significance indicates that the results for each of the conditions are sufficiently different, and consequently the null hypothesis of no differences is rejected. That is to say, there appears to be a true difference among conditions. For example, in a comparative treatment study, a statistically significant result indicates that some treatments were more effective than others, and thus the omnibus null hypothesis of no differences among treatments is rejected.

Although it might appear that statistically significant results are easy to interpret, there is much room for confusion. As we discussed earlier, the results may be due to a confound; that is, there may be another explanation for the results other than the intended one. In a treatment study, the experience of the therapist may be a confound. Even though the researcher attempts to design independent variables in such a way that there are few plausible confounds, no experiment is perfect, and several confounds may remain. Manipulation checks can be used to rule out remaining alternatives, but manipulation checks can introduce confusion as well.

One of the most confusing instances occurs when the manipulation check fails to indicate that the conditions varied on the intended dimension, yet statistically significant differences on the dependent variable were found. This outcome is ambiguous because there are at least three explanations for the results. First, the results of the check may have been misleading; the failure to find that the conditions varied may be due to Type II error, inadequate measures, or poor procedures. A second explanation for a failed manipulation check but observed differences on the dependent variable may be related to the presence of a confound: The manipulation check was accurate (that is, the conditions did not vary on the intended dimension), but the conditions varied on some other dimension. Even if the researcher checked other dimensions and found no differences, it is not possible to check all confounds. A third possibility is that the statistically significant results were in error (that is, Type I error). Clearly, statistically significant results in the presence of failed manipulation checks are difficult to interpret.

It would seem that the best situation is when the results are statistically significant and the manipulation check showed that the conditions differed on the desired dimension. But even here ambiguities may exist. A manipulation check can be reactive, and the results may be due to the check and not to the independent variable. Asking the participants about the experimental manipulation may have sensitized them to many aspects of the study, and their responses on the dependent measures may have been due to this sensitization. For example, asking participants whether the counselor's comments were phrased tentatively or decisively (see, for example, Jones & Gelso, 1988) might cause the participants to review the preceding session critically and retrospectively change their opinion of the counselor. To minimize reactivity, the researcher should consider administering the check after the dependent measure (of course, then the check may be influenced by the dependent measure), making the check indirect rather than transparent, embedding the check in filler material, and using unobtrusive measures (see Chapter 12).

It is worth repeating that successfully checking the manipulation to determine that the conditions varied on the intended dimension does not rule out confounds, for it is entirely possible that the conditions varied on other dimensions as well. Nevertheless, interpretation is least ambiguous when the check was successful and the expected differences among conditions were found.

Statistically Nonsignificant Results

From a philosophy of science perspective, null results are very informative. Nevertheless, nonsignificant results can be due to a number of factors other than the lack of a true effect, including inadequate statistical power, insensitive instruments, violated assumptions of statistical tests, careless procedures, and bias. We can also include poorly designed independent variables to this list. As discussed earlier, Malkiewich and Merluzzi's (1980) failure to detect the expected interaction in the client-treatment matching model may have been due to an inadequately designed independent variable. Showing that the experimental manipulation successfully differentiated the conditions increases the importance of nonsignificant findings; that is, if the conditions were indeed found to be distinct as expected but the results did not produce the expected pattern, then evidence begins to accumulate that the hypothesized causal relationship is not present. Jones and Gelso's (1988) study of interpretations in counseling did not produce the expected interaction between client type and interpretation style; without the manipulation check it would have been easy to attribute the null results to lack of salience of differences in conditions (different interpretation styles). Although Jones and Gelso discussed many possible explanations for their nonsignificant findings, the manipulation check strengthened the possibility that counseling outcomes are not dependent on the interaction of client type and interpretation style, as had been thought.

Nonsignificant findings can also accompany unsuccessful manipulation checks, as occurs when the check indicates that the conditions did not differ on the intended dimension, and the expected differences on the dependent variable are not found. This circumstance suggests the distinct possibility that poor design of the independent variable was responsible for the nonsignificant findings; consequently, the importance of the null findings for the field of counseling is mitigated to a large degree.

One of the problems with omitting a check on the manipulation is that the importance of any given manipulation check is unknown before the data are collected. Consider again the study by Sharkin et al. (1989), which manipulated motivation (half the participants in a 30-minute interview were told that they were motivated because of an action they had taken). Even though the results for one dependent variable were significant, this finding does not indicate whether or not the manipulation was salient because, as we have seen, it is possible that significant results can occur even if the manipulation was not salient. Furthermore, the results for another independent variable were not significant. In this study, it is possible that the salience was sufficient to achieve a threshold for one dependent variable and not for the other. Because there was no manipulation check, the degree to which the manipulation was salient is unknown, and interpretation of the results is problematic.

STATUS VARIABLES

In this chapter we have emphasized the fact that the nature of the independent variable is determined by the researcher. By designing the independent variable in some particular way, the researcher attempts to examine its effect on the dependent variable. We have used the word *manipulation* to characterize this deliberate process. As mentioned previously, a study may contain more than one independent variable, in which case the effects of the independent variables are typically examined in a factorial design, as discussed in Chapter 6. For example, Ponce and Atkinson (1989) manipulated both counselor ethnicity (European-American or Mexican-American) and counselor style (directive and nondirective) in a 2 × 2 factorial design.

Counseling researchers are often interested in variables that are not amenable to manipulation, either due to ethical constraints or to logical impossibilities. It is not ethically permissible to assign participants to a spouse abuse condition, nor is it possible to assign participants to a gender condition. We define all participant-related variables that cannot be assigned as *status variables.* Examples include personality variables (for example, locus of control), socioeconomic variables (such as education), gender, and ethnicity. Although many researchers label these variables as independent variables, the distinction between status variables and independent variables is critical to understanding the types of conclusions that can be drawn from these two types of variables.

Independent variables are manipulated and the effect on the dependent variable is subsequently assessed; if everything goes well, a *causal relationship* is established. In contrast, status variables cannot be manipulated, and statistical tests involving them detect *associations.* For example, Vredenburg, O'Brien, and Krames (1988) classified college students as either depressed or nondepressed; depressed students vis-à-vis nondepressed students were less assertive, had less control over their depressions, had lower degrees of instrumentality and persistence, and had a higher degree of dysfunctional attitudes. Because Vredenburg et al. were not able to randomly assign participants to levels of depression (for example, manipulate the independent variable), it would not be proper to assert that depression caused any of the personality variables. The causal relation could be in the opposite direction; for example, dysfunctional attitudes may be the cause of depression for college students. Or a third variable (for example, some biochemical imbalance) could be the cause of both depression and the personality variables.

An important point must be made about the statistical analysis of status variables: Even though the analysis of status variables often is identical to that of independent variables, it is more difficult to make causal inferences because status variables are not manipulated (Cook & Campbell, 1979). It is the design, not the analysis, that determines the inferential status of the study (Cohen, 1968; Wampold & Freund, 1987). For example, Vredenburg et al. conducted analyses of variance with two groups (depressed and nondepressed); because depression was not manipulated, it cannot be said that depression was the cause of differences in the dependent variables. Parenthetically, note that depression scores in the Vredenburg et al. study were converted into a categorical variable (that is, depressed versus nondepressed). If the status variable is a continuous variable (for example, depression scores), the statistical power of the study is typically increased by using an analysis that accommodates this continuity (for example, a regression analysis), as opposed to creating a categorical variable and using an analysis of variance (see Cohen & Cohen, 1983; Wampold & Freund, 1987).

It is not unusual to include both independent variables and status variables in the same study. Ponce and Atkinson (1989) included acculturation level (a status variable) in addition to two independent variables (counseling style and counselor ethnicity). Frequently, research hypotheses are directed toward an interaction of an independent variable with a status variable; studies that address the question of which treatments work best with which clients are of this type. Two studies discussed in this chapter are examples: Malkiewich and Merluzzi (1980) examined the interaction of the conceptual level of the client (a status variable) with the structure of the counseling (an independent variable), and Jones and Gelso (1988) predicted an interaction between client type (a status variable) and counselor style (an independent variable). When interpreting the results of studies with multiple variables, one needs to keep clearly in mind the distinction between independent and status variables, particularly with reference to causal inferences.

We do not make the distinction between independent variables and status variables so that one type can be considered first class and the other inferior. The important point is that independent variables are manipulated so that causal inferences can be made directly. This is not to say that causality can never be attributed to some status variables. However, inferences in this case are made in a much different (and more difficult) manner. Consider the research on smoking and health. Smoking behavior cannot be ethically manipulated; for example, participants cannot be assigned to smoking and nonsmoking conditions. Even though there is little ambiguity about the fact that smoking is the cause of a number of diseases (P. W. Holland, 1986), this causal relationship was established by animal studies, epidemiological surveys, cross-cultural studies, retrospective comparisons, and the like. Because smoking cannot be an independent variable, the American Tobacco Institute is correct when it states that there has not been *one* study that has established scientifically that smoking is the cause of any disease; however, the causal relation has been firmly established over *many* studies. The first step in this process was to establish that a relationship exists between smoking and disease; then, alternative explanations were ruled out. Cook and Campbell (1979) provide a good discussion of the problems with attributing causality in field settings. We return to status variables in the context of sampling in Chapter 13.

Finally, it should be noted that some argue that any variable that cannot logically be manipulated cannot be the cause of any effect (P. W. Holland, 1986). For example, because it is not possible to assign gender to participants, gender cannot be a cause. According to this position, differences in rates of depression for men and women are not caused by gender; rather, differences in depression are associated with gender. Cultural or biological factors may be potential causes of this difference because, at least logically, they can be manipulated (even though it may not be practical to make such manipulations).

Confusing interpretations of studies are sometimes made because independent and status variables are not differentiated. A perusal of research articles in counseling demonstrates that status variables are often called independent variables. Nomenclature is not the issue here; there is little harm when the term *independent variable* is used inclusively. However, attributing causality without justification is an error that should be avoided assiduously. Causality is the strongest claim that can be made about relations between constructs, and one should always carefully examine the basis of causal attributions.

SUMMARY AND CONCLUSIONS

If causal attributions about the relation between constructs in counseling research are to be correctly made, the independent variable must be adequately designed. As we discussed in Chapters 2 and 3, the first step in this process is to state the research question clearly so that the manipulation of the independent variable can adequately operationalize the cause of an effect. Once the critical dimension has been identified, the researcher must design the independent variable such that the conditions vary on the intended dimension, but not on other dimensions. When the conditions vary on a dimension other than the intended dimension, a confound is said to exist, and it is not possible to ascertain whether the purported construct or the confound is the cause of an effect. Furthermore, the intended differences among the conditions of the independent variable must be salient, so that they have an effect on participants, but not so vivid as to become transparent to participants, in which case their responses may be affected. If the independent variable does indeed vary on the intended dimension and is salient to the participants, then between-group variance is *max*imized. Furthermore, avoiding confounds gives the researcher more *con*trol. Clearly, the independent variable is a critical component of Kerlinger's "MAXMINCON" principle.

To demonstrate that the experimental manipulation accomplishes what the researcher intended, it is often advisable to check the manipulation. The goal of manipulation checks is to show that the conditions vary on the intended dimension, that the conditions do not vary on other dimensions, and/or that treatments are implemented in the intended fashion. Manipulation checks typically are made by having either participants in the experiment or independent raters judge various aspects of the conditions of the independent variable. However, even when manipulation checks are used, the results of an experiment can be confusing. For example, ambiguity results when statistically significant differences are found among groups on the dependent variable but the manipulation check reveals that the conditions did not vary on the intended dimension. When the manipulation check is successful and there are statistically significant differences on the dependent variable, causal attributions are most plausible, although the researcher needs to make sure that the manipulation check was not reactive.

In many counseling studies, status variables are included in the design and analysis. Status variables are variables that cannot be manipulated by the researcher, such as personality variables, socioeconomic variables, gender, and ethnicity. Although the analysis of status variables may be identical to the analysis of true independent variables, the inferences that can be made are much different. When status variables are used, statistical tests detect associations rather than causal relations.

Clearly, design of the independent variable is a critical step in research. It is not unusual for researchers to have confidence in their manipulations only to discover after the data have been collected that a threatening confound was present. It is best always to be one's own greatest critic, and attempt to think of every possible problem with the independent variable before a study is conducted.

CHAPTER 12

DESIGNING OR CHOOSING
THE DEPENDENT VARIABLE

The basic purpose of the dependent variable (sometimes called the dependent measure) is to measure the construct that is hypothesized to be the effect (referred to as the effect construct; see Chapter 4). Thus, selecting or designing dependent variables and the methods of data collection vis-à-vis the dependent variables are critical activities for the researcher.

Typically, one subsection of the methods section of a journal article is entitled "Dependent Variables" or "Dependent Measures" and contains a brief description of and some psychometric information about the dependent variables used in the study. Only infrequently, however, is a rationale given for the choice of dependent variables: Why were these particular variables included and others excluded? Extreme caution must be exercised in this process because the choice of dependent variables can be critical to the merits of the research. For example, a mother's report may be used to assess her children's behavior, but her ratings of her children's behavior may be affected more by her own psychopathology than by the children's actual behavior (Webster-Stratton, 1988). Likewise, the reported outcome of psychotherapy and counseling differs depending on whether the effects are judged by clients, therapists, or independent raters (Orlinsky, Grawe, & Parks, 1994). Investigations with poorly chosen or poorly designed dependent variables will at best be uninformative or uninterpretable and at worst will be erroneous and misleading. Conversely, creatively designing a set of dependent variables might reveal new information that adds greatly to the knowledge base in a particular area.

In the first half of this chapter we discuss considerations in choosing or designing dependent variables. The essential issue is selecting dependent variables that are adequate operationalizations of the effect constructs in the research question of interest. In the second half of the chapter we discuss methods of data collection vis-à-vis dependent variables. In that section we classify and discuss seven nonexclusive methods of data collection that are useful in counseling research. The essential point is that because each method of data collection has different advantages and disadvantages, the task of the informed researcher is to collect data with a method that provides the type of information that is most relevant to the research question.

OPERATIONALIZING THE DEPENDENT VARIABLE

Choosing or designing dependent variables that are adequate operationalizations of the effect constructs in the research question is a critical step in research. The dependent variables must be designed or chosen to reflect the constructs embodied in the research question. This section focuses on three issues related to the design and/or selection of dependent variables. First we examine the psychometric properties of the variables; we discuss reliability and validity as considerations in understanding the degree to which a construct is properly operationalized. Second, because the researcher must take care to ensure that the dependent variables do not react with the treatment in some way, we briefly discuss the role of reactivity of the dependent variable within the experimental context. Third, we discuss several procedural issues that can potentially affect participants' responses to the dependent variable, such as total administration time of dependent variables, order of presentation, and the reading level of the instruments.

A clear research question is critical to the proper choice or design of a dependent variable, as we emphasized in Chapter 2. It is important that the dependent variables be designed to reflect the construct designated as the effect or outcome of the independent variable. For example, in a treatment study of anxiety, it should be mentioned whether the treatment is expected to affect state anxiety, trait anxiety, or both (see, for example, Smith & Nye, 1989). If the target construct is not easily differentiated from related constructs, the research question (and related discussion) should explicitly indicate how it differs. Once the relations among constructs are hypothesized and the constructs differentiated from each other, the researcher's task is to choose or design dependent variables that appropriately operationalize the construct that is expected to change as a function of manipulation of the independent variable.

Psychometric Issues

One important question about the operationalization of a construct involves the psychometric properties of the dependent variable. Researchers need to know to what extent the dependent variables they select to operationalize a construct are reliable and valid. If the estimates of reliability and validity are poor, then the operationalization of the construct is likely to be inadequate. Although entire volumes have been devoted to psychometrics, we will review the rudiments nontechnically here because they are critical to understanding the degree to which a construct is properly operationalized, and how this affects the validity of research. The skilled researcher needs to have a strong background in psychometrics and broad knowledge of the psychometric properties of the dependent variables used in a study.

Reliability

To be informative, scores on the dependent measure need to vary among a study's participants. If everyone obtained the same score on a measure, nothing can be learned about the individuals; however, when participants' scores are different, we begin to learn something about how the participants differ. It is hoped that differences between two scores are due to true differences in the level of the characteristic of interest; that is, variance in scores should reflect variance in the respondents. Unfortunately, the variance among scores may also be due to various types of error. To understand reliability, we must understand that the variances in scores obtained in any context are due to several factors.

The first vital factor accounting for variance in scores is related to the central construct being measured. In test theory, we say that for each individual a true score exists that reflects the actual level of the construct of interest. The degree to which obtained scores reflect the true scores for individuals is the reliability of the scores. More technically, reliability is the variance in scores that is due to true differences among the individuals. If an instrument produces generally reliable scores, then participants who possess more of a given construct will obtain higher scores on the variable (or lower, depending on how the variable is scaled). For example, on a scale designed to measure depression, a participant with a high score on the scale presumably is in fact truly depressed. Nevertheless, as we will see, some of the variance in most scores obtained from instruments is due to factors other than differences in the true scores.

Typically, the reliability coefficient of scores for variable X is denoted by the symbol r_{xx}. A coefficient of r_{xx} that equals 0.80 indicates that 80% of the variance in the scores is due to true differences, and that 20% is due to other factors. (Note that this coefficient is not squared to obtained variance accounted for, as is the case for a Pearson correlation coefficient.)

With regard to reliability, we first examine several sources of error in measurements: random response error, specific error, transient error, inter-rater disagreement, and scoring and recording errors. Then we discuss how to interpret reliability estimates and how to estimate reliability (that is, the variance due to true scores). Finally, we discuss how reliability affects the relationship among measured variables.

RANDOM RESPONSE ERROR.   There is often some error in any response that a participant makes. The most obvious example of these errors occurs in response to written items in a paper and pencil instrument, but random response error occurs in measurements of all kinds. One participant may read the word "ever" as "never" and respond accordingly; another participant may be distracted by a noise during testing and mark a response to the wrong item; a third participant might forget which end of the scale is "disagree" and which is "agree"; and so forth.

Although later in the text we discuss ways to calculate error due to random responses, a few important points need to be made here. First, the assessment of almost all meaningful characteristics of individuals and situations contains random response error. Simply asking participants "Are you male or female?" produces a random response error of about 5% (that is, has a reliability of coefficient of 0.95; Campbell, Converse, Miller, & Stokes, 1990). With regard to measuring more ambiguous characteristics than gender or age, performance tests (such as intelligence tests) typically have the lowest random response errors (namely, reliabilities in the neighborhood of 0.90). Measurements of other characteristics, such as personality traits or therapist skill level, generally have larger random response errors.

A second point is that instruments typically contain many items measuring the same trait so that a single random response will not unduly affect the total score. Given items of the same quality, instruments with more items will be more reliable than instruments with fewer items. Consider a 15-item scale with reliability of 0.84. It can be shown mathematically (with the Spearman-Brown formula) that randomly selecting seven items to compose the scale would produce a reliability of 0.70. Extrapolating further, a one-item scale would have a reliability of 0.25, a value that is typical of a single-item scale (see Schmidt & Hunter, 1996, scenario 1, for an elaboration of this example). The point is that whenever anything is measured using a single item, one must assume that the reliability of this measurement is catastrophically low (with some exceptions, such as gender and age). Although researchers are aware of this problem, occasionally they believe some phenomenon to be so straightforward that a single item is sufficient. For example, it is all too common to see global evaluations of satisfaction, such as "On a scale of 1 to 100, how satisfied were you with this experience?" In such cases, researchers pay dearly in terms of low reliabilities.

SPECIFIC ERROR.   Specific error is error produced by something unique to the instrument that is different from what the researcher intended. For example, in an instrument designed to measure depression, the questions may be phrased in such a way that participants are well aware that responses to the questions vary in degree of social desirability; in such cases, participants' responses are determined to some extent by the degree to which they wish to appear socially desirable (a legitimate construct in itself), as well as to the degree to which they are depressed. Specific error is a confound because scores on this instrument measure both depression and social desirability.

TRANSIENT ERROR.   Transient errors occur when a researcher is measuring a stable trait at a single point in time or in response to a single stimulus in such a way that the conditions at that time or with the particular stimulus affect the measurement of the trait. Consider the measurement of depression, the manifestation of which can be affected by transient mood states: A depressed college student's responses to a depression inventory, for example, would be affected by receiving a failing grade on an examination in the hour preceding the assessment; other participants' responses would be similarly affected by moods created by recent events. Transient errors can be induced by administering tests in a particular order. For example, an instrument used to assess anxiety may in fact create in participants an anxious mood, which in turn would affect scores on a subsequent instrument, producing artifactual scores on the second instrument. These transient effects create error that is unrelated to true scores.

A related problem is particularly problematic in counseling research. Suppose that one were interested in the assessment of a therapeutic skill level of a beginning counselor, and such a determination is made by the novice counselor's responses to only one client. Idiosyncrasies of the client and of the novice's relationship with this client will affect the assessed level of skill, creating unreliability in the assessment of general counseling competence.

INTER-RATER DISAGREEMENT.   In counseling research, raters are often used to obtain assessments. Consider a study of the antisocial behavior of school children involving naturalistic observations of the children's conduct in the school setting. Although raters would be trained to adhere to some coding system, some of the variance in the observer's rating may be due to the observer rather than the behavior. If ratings reflect the actual behavior and not idiosyncrasies of the observer, then we would expect the observers' ratings to agree. In any observational study, adequate agreement among raters is required.

It should be noted that inter-rater agreement is necessary, but not sufficient, for reliable assessments. If the observers rate an individual's behavior at a single time, then transient error remains problematic. Schmidt and Hunter (1996) described a study (McDaniel, Whetzel, Schmidt, & Maurer, 1994) that found that the correlation between raters of a common job interview was 0.81, but the correlation between raters of the same applicant in different interviews was only 0.52, demonstrating the magnitude of transient error. Specific error may also occur because the rating system is sensitive to some construct other than the targeted construct. For example, raters in the antisocial behavior example who are sensitive to personal appearance may rate unkempt participants as more antisocial, regardless of behavior, which would then add error variance to antisocial ratings. Moreover, observers can agree and still be off the mark. Continuing the antisocial behavior example, several observers may initially be sensitive to every antisocial behavior (as when a student bumps into another student intentionally), but as they are exposed to more egregious behavior (students striking other students or threatening others with weapons) they may become desensitized to and consequently ignore less egregious behavior, all the while maintaining rater agreement. This is called *observer drift*.

SCORING AND RECORDING ERRORS.   Errors in assessment can be created by researchers through scoring and recording errors, which are any errors created in any way by manipulating the data in the process from scoring a protocol to preparing the data for statistical analysis. These errors, which function as random response error (and technically could be classified as such), obscure true score variance. Outliers in data may result from such errors. Researchers are encouraged to treat their data carefully to minimize such errors, although scoring and recording errors are usually minor in comparison to the previously discussed errors.

COMPOUNDING ERRORS.   The errors we have mentioned can be compounded to form an assessment with abysmal reliability. Consider the worst-case scenario: Several observers, each observing one participant, rate some characteristic only a single time in response to a single stimulus using a one-item, pencil-and-paper rating instrument, and then record the response, which later will be entered into the computer. This is exactly the case when a practicum instructor is asked to rate, on a scale of 1 to 100, the skill level of a practicum student with a particular client in a particular session. This operationalization of counseling skill introduces many sources of error. First, there is unknown variance among the practicum instructors. They likely have very different implicit criteria that underlie their judgment of skill; inter-rater reliability is unknown and indeterminate because multiple raters of the same participant were not used. Second, only a single, ambiguous item was used to assess the construct. Third, the skill level displayed in a single session is subject to transient errors due to the characteristics of the client, to the presence of particular factors that affect the success of the session (for example, the mood of student and client), and to other factors. Finally, opportunities for scoring and recording errors were not minimized. Although we are unlikely to encounter a case this extreme, awareness of the various sources of error can help researchers avoid the problems discussed here. In this example, it would have been much better to have more than one rater rate all of the students, over several sessions with several clients, using an instrument that contained multiple items related to skill and was scored via computer.

INTERPRETING RELIABILITY ESTIMATES.   Determining the reliability of a research instrument involves many considerations. First, any reliability coefficient is an estimate of the true reliability, in the same way that a mean of a sample is an estimate of the population mean. Later in this section we describe various methods for calculating reliability coefficients, but it should be kept in mind that these coefficients are estimates that vary across samples.

Second, reliability reflects variance due to true scores, but it does not indicate what the true scores are measuring. A set of scores that are reliable may be measuring something quite different than what was postulated; for example, a personality measure may be measuring social desirability rather than the targeted construct. Developers of scales often attach names to them that indicate some construct (for example, the ABC Scale of Social Skills), but adequate reliability does not establish that the instrument actually measures that construct (in this instance, social skills). It is validity, which will be discussed later in this chapter, that is concerned with whether or the not the construct being measured is the construct of interest.

A third point is that reliability is based on the scores and not on the instrument from which they were derived. The scores have certain properties that are derived from the characteristics of the instrument. A vital consequence of this distinction is that reliability estimates are restricted to the types of participants on whom, and the conditions under which, the psychometric study was conducted. An instrument may perform adequately for one type of participant but not for another type, or under one set of conditions but not under others. For example, an anxiety measure that yields adequate reliability estimates with undergraduates when administered in a classroom may be completely useless for measuring anxiety of agoraphobics in a laboratory setting. Put another way, the instrument may be very sensitive to midrange differences in anxiety but insensitive at the upper range. This is called a *ceiling effect;* all the agoraphobics may have scored at or near the maximum, and thus their scores were not reflective of true differences in anxiety. Of course, this problem may also be manifest at the bottom of the range, creating a *floor effect.* Reliability is also dependent on characteristics of the participants, such as reading ability and age. An instrument may yield adequate reliability for college students but not for high school dropouts because of random error created by the latter's difficulty in reading the items. Moreover, instruments may contain items that have different meanings to different cultures, and it should not be assumed that reliability estimates are transferrable; Ponterotto and Casas found that only 25% of counseling instruments used in multicultural counseling research were developed psychometrically for ethnic minority populations. The implication of this discussion is that researchers should choose instruments that are sensitive in the range of scores anticipated and the type of participants used in the study. Such a choice requires a careful reading of the psychometric studies conducted on various instruments. Alternatively, the reliability of the scores actually obtained in a study could be estimated; typically this is impractical because large numbers of participants are needed for such studies (typically in excess of 300; Nunnally, 1978) and because reliability estimates are affected by mean differences obtained for the various conditions of the independent variable.

How high should reliability be? Some sources indicate that reliability estimates in excess of 0.80 are sufficient. Certainly, all things being equal, the instrument that yielded the highest reliability in the desired range should be chosen over other instruments. However, all things are rarely equal, and choices must be made. Other factors need to be considered, including validity, time required to complete the instrument, and costs (topics to be discussed later in this chapter). Thus, in instances when a construct is elusive, reliability of 0.70 may be adequate. Keep in mind, however, that reliability of 0.70 means that 30% of the variance of the scores on the dependent variable is due to error. Certainly, reliability indexes below 0.50 contain serious psychometric problems that limit the utility of the instrument.

CALCULATING ESTIMATES OF RELIABILITY.   There are many ways to estimate the reliability of scores, each of which is sensitive to one or more of the errors previously discussed. The various coefficients will be briefly discussed here; the reader is referred to psychometric texts.

If the various items of an instrument are measuring the same construct, then scores on the items will tend to covary; that is, someone who has a high level of the construct (for example, is anxious) will tend to answer all the items in one direction (assuming the items are all keyed in the same direction), whereas someone who has a low level of the construct (for example, is not anxious) will tend to answer all the items in the other direction. *Internal consistency* refers to the homogeneity of the items. When scores for the various items are highly intercorrelated, internal consistency is high. Consequently, if the test is internally consistent, then the score derived from one half of the items will be highly correlated with the score derived from the other half of the items. This correlation (corrected for the fact that it is derived from tests half as long) is called the split-half reliability coefficient. Because this coefficient is dependent on the particular split, a better estimate is derived using the formula for the coefficient alpha, which is equal to the mean of the all possible split-half coefficients. One occasionally sees reliability estimated with the Kuder-Richardson 20 formula, which is a special case of coefficient alpha used when items are scored dichotomously (that is, when each item has two possible outcomes, such as correct and incorrect). Although measures of internal consistency are widely used, they are not sensitive to specific and transient errors. For example, a measure of extroversion may reflect (to some degree) transient mood states, or a measure of counseling skill may be specific to a particular client. Scores on extroversion or counseling skill may be internally consistent but contain variance due to extraneous specific or transitory sources.

Indexes that take into account measurements taken at different times or made in response to different stimuli are sensitive to transient effects. The most common such index is the test-retest correlation. If a construct is expected to remain stable over a period of time, and if the instrument is not subject to transient or random response errors, then test-retest correlations should be high. If internally consistency is high but the test-retest coefficient is relatively low and the construct is expected to be stable over that period of time, then the scores reflect transient effects. A similar index can be used to assess transient effects due to different stimuli. If a measure of counseling skill is internally consistent with one client, but the correlation of the skill measure with two different clients is low, then one can conclude that the skill measure is not adequate to measure general counseling competence because it is measuring something related to specific clients. Of course, test-retest coefficients are inappropriate if the construct being measured is not expected to remain constant.

One problem with the test-retest coefficient is that it overestimates reliability because it is not sensitive to specific error. If something unique is measured by an instrument, then this unique characteristic would be measured on the second administration of this instrument as well. One way to address this problem is to use parallel forms at the two times. Correlations between parallel forms of an instrument at two different times (or in response to two different stimuli) help identify random response, specific, and transient errors.

If ratings are used, indexes of inter-rater agreement are necessary. Essentially, multiple raters are needed so that their level of agreement can be calculated. Although there are many ways to measure inter-rater agreement, most methods simply index agreement between the raters and do not take into account random response, specific, or transient errors, as discussed previously. Even if raters are responding randomly, they will agree occasionally merely by chance, and consequently any measure of inter-rater agreement should be corrected for chance agreements.

EFFECTS OF UNRELIABILITY ON RELATIONSHIPS AMONG VARIABLES.   We have made much of the fact that instruments should yield reliable measures in order to be useful in counseling research. We now illustrate, through some examples, the pernicious effects of unreliability. Consider two constructs, A and B, and two measures of the constructs, X and Y, respectively. Suppose that all of the sources of error (internal inconsistency, transient errors, and so forth) for these two constructs is equal to about 30%; that is, $r_{xx} = 0.70$ and $r_{yy} = 0.70$. Now suppose that the researcher claims that the two constructs are distinct because X and Y are highly, but not perfectly correlated—say, $r_{xy} = 0.70$. In this example, the researcher is claiming that two constructs exist, and that interpretations can be made about those constructs from the variables X and Y. But it should be kept in mind that the correlation of 0.70 is the correlation of the measures X and Y, not the correlation of the constructs A and B. Because the error in each of the measures cannot be systematically related (that is, it is random error), then the obtained correlation of the measures is less than the correlation of the constructs, and we say that the correlation of the constructs has been attenuated by the unreliability of the measures. Classical test theory provides a formula for correcting for the attenuation:

$$r_{AB} = r_{xy} / \sqrt{r_{xx} r_{yy}}$$

Put into words, the correlation between the constructs is equal to the obtained correlation between the measures divided by the square root of the product of the reliabilities of the measures. In our present example, the correlation between the constructs would be

$$r_{AB} = .70 / \sqrt{(.70)(.70)} = 1.00$$

That is, the correlation between the constructs is perfect, and the only differences between the scores on X and Y are due to random error—any interpretations involving two distinct constructs would be in error.

The point of this example is that even if two constructs are perfectly correlated, the obtained correlation will be dramatically attenuated by unreliability. (Note that we have not discussed the effect of sampling error, which could also dramatically affect the obtained correlation.) This is not an artificial example; many subscales of instruments are correlated in the neighborhood of 0.70, with reliabilities in the neighborhood of 0.70, suggesting that these subscales are measuring the same construct, rather than distinct constructs (see, for example, Atkinson & Wampold, 1982).

Now consider the following example, which illustrates how unreliability can make it almost impossible to obtain expected results in a study. Suppose that a researcher is interested in the relation between the skills of counselors-in-training and counseling outcome. The generic skill of the beginning counselors is rated by the practicum instructor on a single-item scale anchored by "Very skilled—top 5% of all practicum students" and "Very unskilled—lowest 5% of all practicum students." Suppose further that a single measure of outcome was used—for example, a measure of depression. Now suppose further that the researcher is very fortunate to sample all of the students in a large program, say, about $n = 30$. What are the chances that the researcher will detect a true relationship between skill and outcome? As we will see, the probability is low. As we discussed earlier, the reliability of skill ratings, especially on a single-item instrument, is probably extremely low; for this example, suppose that the reliability of such ratings is generously assigned a value of 0.50. Suppose also that the measure of depression is fairly reliable—say, $r_{yy} = 0.80$. Furthermore, suppose that about 20% of the variance in outcome is due to the skill of the counselor (a reasonable estimate, given that variance in outcome is also due to initial severity, treatment administered, motivation for therapy, social support of client, and so forth). If 20% of the variance in outcome is due to skill, then the population correlation between the constructs of skill and outcome would be 0.45 (that is, variance accounted for is the square of the correlation coefficient). However, this correlation is attenuated by the unreliability of the measures of the constructs; using the attenuation formula, the correlation is reduced to 0.28. The power to detect a population correlation of 0.28 with 30 participants is about 0.35; that is, the probability of rejecting the null hypothesis of no relationship between skills and outcome is 0.35 when the true correlation is 0.28. Said another way, about 65% of the times this study would be executed, the researcher would conclude that there was no relationship between therapist skill and outcome, despite the fact that the true relationship between skill and outcome is strong! This is obviously a disturbing result, because it will likely be concluded that the skills of practicum students are unrelated to outcome, when this is not the case. In Chapter 4 we discussed threats to the statistical conclusion validity of a study due to unreliability of measures and low power; this is a graphic illustration of these effects. The central point here is that the obtained relation between measures of constructs may be very different than the true relationship between constructs, due to the unreliability of measures. When any statistical relation is represented, one must be very clear about whether one is discussing variables (measures of constructs) or constructs.

Although the preceding example involved correlations, the same principles apply to experimental designs. The reliability of the dependent variable, and the degree to which the independent variable faithfully and saliently represents the intended differences between conditions, attenuates the size of the effect and reduces the power of the statistical test of differences among groups. Any conclusion that a treatment resulted in no differences in outcome may be due to the low power resulting from unreliability.

Validity

Of the many types of validity, the most important type for research purposes is construct validity—the degree to which the scores reflect the desired construct rather than some other construct. Clearly, unreliable scores cannot have construct validity because they are due mostly to random error. Nevertheless, as mentioned previously, reliable scores may reflect one or more constructs other than the one specified. Determining construct validity, although complicated and indirect, is vital to the integrity of a study.

One way to establish construct validity is to examine the relation between scores on the instrument and scores on other instruments intended to measure the same and other constructs. Clearly, there should be a high correlation between instruments that measure the same construct. If these expected correlations are found, then *convergent validity* is said to exist. Measures of different constructs should not be highly correlated, although a moderate correlation can be tolerated and may even be expected. It is reasonable to expect that certain constructs,

T A B L E 12-1
Multitrait-Multimethod Matrix with Expected Correlations
for Convergent and Discriminant Validity

	Trait A		Trait B		Trait C	
	Method 1	Method 2	Method 1	Method 2	Method 1	Method 2
Trait A						
Method 1						
Method 2	high					
Trait B						
Method 1	low	low				
Method 2	low	low	high			
Trait C						
Method 1	low	low	low	low		
Method 2	low	low	low	low	high	

although distinct, will be related. Nevertheless, correlation of measures of differ-ent constructs should be smaller than correlations of measures of the same con-struct; if this pattern is found, *discriminant validity* is said to exist.

Convergent and discriminant validity can be examined by constructing a multitrait-multimethod matrix (Campbell & Fiske, 1959). *Multimethod* refers to various means to measure the same trait (for example, behavioral observations, self-reports, and reports of significant others). *Multitrait* indicates that various characteristics (traits) of people are being studied. Correlations of measures of the same trait using different methods should be higher than correlations of measures of different traits using the same or different methods. A multitrait-multimethod matrix, with the expected pattern of correlations, is presented in Table 12-1.

The pattern of correlations displayed in Table 12-1 demonstrates the ideal convergent and discriminant validity to establish the existence of two distinct con-structs; rarely is the measurement of constructs established by such a beautiful demonstration of their construct validity. A perusal of several statistical proce-dures used to examine construct validity demonstrates the difficulty, but the absolute necessity, of establishing the validity of instruments.

With regard to validity, we first discuss using exploratory factor analysis as a means of establishing construct validity. Then we show how the use of multiple measures of a construct improves the validity of conclusions, paying close atten-tion to how multiple measures can alleviate the problems created by unreliability and can remove method variance.

EXPLORATORY FACTOR ANALYSIS AND THE USE OF SUBSCALES OF AN INSTRUMENT.   One way to establish construct validity is through a statistical procedure called factor analy-sis (Tinsley & Tinsley, 1987), a data reduction procedure that examines the factors that underlie a set of variables. If the set of variables are the scores on a variety of tests, then factor analysis can be used to detect a small number of factors that account for the variance in the scores. Variables that measure the same construct will be grouped together in the sense that they will correlate highly (load on) a

T A B L E 12-2
Fictitious Factor Analysis of Six Tests

	Factor 1	Factor 2
ABC Test of Vocabulary	.58	.11
Peter Test of Problem Solving	.65	.09
NBA Test of Eye-Hand Coordination	.14	.49
Amazing Mazes Test	.51	.08
Walter Weight Lifting Test	.02	.62
100-Meter Running Speed	.09	.67

NOTE: Factor 1 is interpreted as a mental-abilities factor because the tests involving mental abilities load on this factor; Factor 2 is interpreted as a physical-abilities factor because the tests involving physical abilities load on this factor.

single factor. The factors are then interpreted as constructs. The results of a fictitious factor analysis of a set of six tests are presented in Table 12-2. In this analysis, two factors underlie the six tests; from the loadings, interpretation of the factors is straightforward. The first factor is mental ability (or intelligence), because the tests that load on this factor clearly are measures of mental abilities; the second factor is physical ability, because the tests that load on this factor clearly are measures of physical abilities.

Sometimes factor analysis is used to develop scales. This strategy involves factor-analyzing items rather than variables. A set of items is subjected to a factor analysis, items are segregated by their loadings on factors, descriptors are assigned to factors, and subscale scores are calculated based on the segregation (for example, to form the score for the subscale that corresponds to Factor 1 is formed by summing the scores for those items that load on Factor 1). Generally, this is not a procedure that produces satisfactory results. There are three problems: (a) The method is atheoretical and may lead to factors that have little psychological basis and are driven by the data; (b) even if the factor analysis uses a method that produces independent factors, the subscale scores likely will be highly correlated, because items load to some degree on all factors; and (c) the reliability of single items is low, and thus the results of factor analyses are often unstable, in which case cross-validations are necessary.

An improvement on the exploratory factor analytic strategy is to develop items specifically to measure factors of a construct. This strategy was used to develop one of the most widely used counseling instruments, the Counselor Rating Form (CRF; Barak & LaCrosse, 1975). The CRF is a 36-item scale designed to measure three characteristics of the counselor related to the social influence the counselor possesses vis-à-vis the client: trustworthiness, attractiveness, and expertness. Each item contains an adjective and its opposite (for example, logical/illogical), and respondents rate their perception of the counselor on a 7-point scale with regard to these adjectives (1 = logical, 7 = illogical). Subscale scores for trustworthiness, attractiveness, and expertness are determined by summing the scores for the items within each subscale. There are 12 items for trustworthiness, 12 items for attractiveness, and 12 items for expertness.

Although factor analyses of the CRF (see Heppner & Claiborn, 1989) have verified the existence of three factors (that is, the 12 items loaded on the expected factor in each case), the correlations among the factors were high (generally in the range of 0.60 to 0.80), suggesting that one general factor may be operating. This general factor, labeled the "good guy" factor (Ponterotto & Furlong, 1985), suggests that responses to the CRF are due primarily to a general opinion about the counselor. Based on a revision of the CRF called the Counseling Rating Form-Short (CRF-S; Corrigan & Schmidt, 1983), Tracey, Glidden, and Kokotovic (1988) showed the pervasiveness of the general evaluation factor using a variation of confirmatory factor analysis. Moreover, in a study of premature termination, Kokotovic and Tracey (1987) found that continuers and dropouts differed in the degree to which they rated their counselors as trustworthy and expert, but when the effects of general satisfaction (measured on a different instrument) were controlled, the three CRF scales poorly discriminated continuers from dropouts.

The preceding discussion of the CRF and its subscales raises an issue: whether one should use the total score of an instrument or its subscale scores. The choice is exclusive; that is, one should never use both the total score and one or more of the subscale scores in the same analysis, as they are linearly dependent and will result in nonexistent or meaningless solutions in statistical analyses. The decision to use subscale scores or total scores is primarily related to the hypotheses of the study, but it is partially related to psychometrics as well. If the hypotheses of the study references the general construct (for example, global evaluation of the counselor), then one should either use the total score or combine the subscale scores, rather than performing analyses on each separate subscale. Trying to interpret results for the subscales in the absence of hypotheses about the subscales will result in ambiguity when some of the subscales lead to statistically significant results but others do not (see Wampold, Davis, & Good, 1990). However, if the hypotheses specify relationships for the constructs of the various subscales, then one should analyze the subscales separately (Huberty & Morris, 1989). For example, Wampold et al. (1995) hypothesized that social-coping skills would vary as a function of Holland type, whereas problem-focused social skills would not; consequently they analyzed the social-coping skills subscales of the Social Skills Inventory (Riggio, 1989) separately from the problem-focused social skills subscales, rather than using a total social skills score. Finally, subscale scores should never be used if there is not persuasive evidence that they are measuring distinct constructs, a point on which we will elaborate subsequently.

MULTIPLE MEASURES OF A CONSTRUCT TO IMPROVE CONSTRUCT VALIDITY.   The use of multiple dependent variables is often recommended (Cook & Campbell, 1979; Kazdin, 1980). No one variable can adequately operationalize a construct because, as was discussed previously, some of the variance in this variable is due to other constructs (specific variance), and some is due to error. Using several variables can more adequately represent the construct because one variable will be sensitive to aspects of the construct absent in other variables. The overlap of these variables reflects the essence of the construct, as represented in Figure 12-1.

The range of potential dependent variables is vast. For example, in treatment studies, outcome may be assessed by behavioral observations, self-reports, reports of others, and therapist ratings (the advantages and disadvantages of which will be

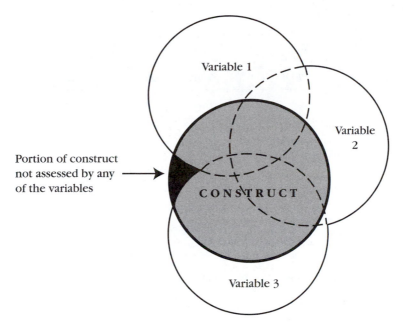

FIGURE 12-1
Use of multiple variables to operationalize a construct.

discussed later in this chapter). Within each method of assessment there are many alternatives. One might ask clients either to judge their progress phenomenologically (for example, how happy are you?) or to report specific cognitions. Moreover, the situation becomes important; a specific behavior may be exhibited in one situation but not in another. Alternatively, one can customize variables for individual participants, such as is the case with goal attainment scaling (Kiresuk & Sherman, 1968). Time further complicates the situation: Is the anticipated effect expected immediately after treatment, a short time thereafter, or at long-term follow-up?

Another reason for including multiple measures is the expectation that different constructs produce different outcomes. For example, McNamara and Horan (1986) investigated how behavioral and cognitive treatments affected behavioral and cognitive manifestations of depression. The cognitive battery contained the Automatic Thoughts Questionnaire, the Cognitive Scale, and the Recalled Cognitions exercises. The behavioral battery included the Pleasant Events Schedule, the Behavioral Scale, and Observer-Evaluated Social Skills ratings. They found that the cognitive treatments clearly reduced cognitive manifestations of depression with some generalization to behavior measures, whereas the behavioral treatments appeared to have little effect on either the cognitive or the behavioral measures.

Multiple measures of constructs can also be used to avoid the attenuation of correlations between constructs and can account for method variance. The next two sections discuss the intricacies involved in using multiple measures to form latent variables, which represent constructs better than any single variable can.

T A B L E 12-3
Correlations of Depression and Anxiety Measures*

	Depression			Anxiety					
	ZungD	BDI	DACL	ZungA	SAI	TAI	MAS	EHE	EHS
ZungD	1.00								
BDI	0.68	1.00							
DACL	0.54	0.60	1.00						
ZungA	0.71	0.67	0.48	1.00					
SAI	0.61	0.60	0.66	0.60	1.00				
TAI	0.74	0.73	0.61	0.69	0.66	1.00			
MAS	0.67	0.71	0.50	0.72	0.53	0.79	1.00		
EHE	0.39	0.42	0.33	0.47	0.37	0.48	0.49	1.00	
EHS	0.40	0.40	0.36	0.41	0.32	0.53	0.52	0.60	1.00

*ZungD = Zung Self-Rating Depression Scale; BDI = Beck Depression Inventory; DACL = Depression Adjective Checklist; ZungA = Zung State Anxiety Measure; SAI = State Anxiety Inventory; TAI = Trait Anxiety Inventory; MAS = Manifest Anxiety Scale; EHE = Endler-Hunt Examination Anxiety; EHS = Endler Hunt Speech Anxiety.
SOURCE: Tanaka-Matsumi, J., & Kameoka, V. A., (1986). Reliabilities and concurrent validities of popular self-report measures of depression, anxiety, and social desirability. *Journal of Consulting and Clinical Psychology, 54,* 328–333.

CALCULATING CORRELATIONS BETWEEN CONSTRUCTS UNATTENUATED BY UNRELIABILITY.   We have discussed how unreliability attenuates measures of association, such as correlations. Multiple measures of a construct can be used to detect relationships among constructs that are untainted by unreliability. We now show how structural equation modeling can be used to detect the true relationships among constructs.

Structural equation modeling is a statistical method that examines the relationship among constructs (sometimes called latent variables or traits) by using several observed measures to operationalize the construct (see Bollen, 1989; Fassinger, 1987; Hoyle, 1995; Loehlin, 1992; Mueller, 1996). The statistical method is complex, and only a conceptual presentation is included here.

The example we consider here is provided by Cole (1987) from data collected on two important constructs—depression and anxiety—by Tanaka-Matsumi and Kameoka (1986). Tanaka-Matsumi and Kameoka administered three commonly used measures of depression and six commonly used measures of anxiety; the correlations among these measures are presented in Table 12-3. Several observations can be made from this table. First, it appears that the measures of the same construct are moderately high, showing some convergent validity (correlations for depression measures ranged from 0.54 to 0.68, and correlations for the anxiety measures ranged from 0.32 to 0.79). The constructs of anxiety and depression seem to be related, but distinct, as the obtained correlations among measures of depression and anxiety ranged from 0.33 to 0.74. However, we must keep in mind that all the correlations in this table are attenuated by unreliability. Structural equation modeling provides a means of estimating the correlation of the constructs of depression and anxiety, taking this unreliability into account.

The results of the structural equation modeling is presented in Figure 12-2. First note the arrows from the ellipse "Depression" to ZungD, BDI, and DACL (observed variables in rectangles), which indicate that the construct (or latent vari-

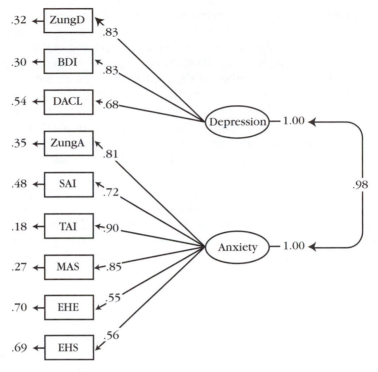

F I G U R E 12-2
Multiple measures of depression and anxiety.

able) of depression loads on these three instruments. This is akin to factor loadings in exploratory factor analysis; here the loadings are 0.83, 0.83, and 0.68, respectively. The latent variable "Depression" is a statistical entity representing the construct operationalized by the three measures of depression. This latent variable represents the construct depression measured without error, because in a sense it is the variance that the three measures have in common, excluding specific or error variance. This procedure statistically accomplished what is pictured in Figure 12-1 (that is, it uses the common variance among measures to produce a variable that represents the construct). Similarly, the construct of anxiety (the ellipse "Anxiety") is the statistically developed measurement of the construct of anxiety from the six observed measures, with factor loadings ranging from 0.55 to 0.90.

The correlation of the constructs of depression and anxiety is then estimated from the latent variables of anxiety and depression. The curved double arrow between "Depression" and "Anxiety" represents this correlation, which was calculated to be 0.98. This says that the estimate of the correlation of the constructs of depression and anxiety, as measured by the three measures of depression and the six measures of anxiety, is 0.98. This correlation is not attenuated by unreliability. The conclusion here is that, at least as measured by these commonly used instruments, the constructs of depression and anxiety are not distinct. If these nine measures were used in an outcome study, it would only make sense to talk about the effect of treatment on the aggregate of the measures because it has been shown that the constructs operationalized are not distinct. It would not make sense to talk about the relative effectiveness of one treatment on one of the constructs but not the other (for example, to say that Treatment A is more appropriate for the treatment of depression) regardless of the pattern of results on the individual measures, a pattern that is surely random (that is, is due to error). It would even be more problematic to perform individual tests on the nine measures and make conclusions about individual measures, as this example has shown that they are measuring the same construct. Moreover, conducting nine statistical tests dramatically increases the probability of obtaining a statistically significant result by chance alone (that is, inflates the alpha level). With nine variables, the probability of obtaining at least one significant result by chance is approximately 0.40, dramatically higher than is desired to make valid conclusions (see Hays, 1988).

Although it has been shown that latent variables can be used to calculate correlations that are not attenuated by unreliability, these correlations may inflated by the fact that measures use the same method of data collection. In the next section we show how this method variance can be removed.

REMOVING METHOD VARIANCE.   In the previous example, all of the measures of anxiety and depression were pencil-and-paper measures. As discussed in Chapter 4, construct validity is dependent on assessments using different methods. It may well be that something in these instruments affects participants' responses but is unrelated to either depression or anxiety. Let's look at some possibilities. One is a construct called social desirability; respondents who are high on this trait tend to answer questions for all instruments in a way that makes them look good, regardless of their level of depression or anxiety—that is, they would appear to be less depressed and less anxious because they respond in a way they perceived to be socially desirable. Another possibility is trait negativity, a general tendency to evaluate self negatively on all dimensions; these respondents would appear to be more depressed and more anxious than is truly the case. Still another possibility are transient mood states that might affect responses to the instruments. Students attending the testing session just after receiving grades on their mid-term may experience transient feelings induced by the results of the exam. Because only one method was used, these possibilities are likely to affect responses to all instruments similarly, increasing the correlations among them. Variance common to all measures using the same method is called method variance. Method variance inflates relationships among variables; that is, obtained correlations between measures using the same method exaggerate the true relationship between constructs. Whereas unreliability attenuates correlations, method variance inflates correlations, as the following example demonstrates.

Table 12-4 displays a multitrait-multimethod correlation matrix in which two traits, A and B, are measured with three methods, forming six measured variables, A1, A2, and A3 (Trait A measured using the three methods) and B1, B2, and B3 (Trait B measured using the three methods). In this fabricated example, the correlations correspond to the desired convergent and discriminant validity presented in Table 12-1. The correlations of the same trait with different methods are relatively high

T A B L E 12-4
Correlations of Two Traits Measured Using Three Methods

	Trait A			Trait B		
	Method 1	Method 2	Method 3	Method 1	Method 2	Method 3
	A1	A2	A3	B1	B2	B3
A1	1.00					
A2	0.64	1.00				
A3	0.57	0.60	1.00			
B1	0.72	0.54	0.46	1.00		
B2	0.39	0.78	0.46	0.56	1.00	
B3	0.35	0.43	0.75	0.54	0.55	1.00

(0.57 to 0.64 for Trait A and 0.54 to 0.56 for Trait B), and the correlations between different traits using different methods are relatively low (0.35 to 0.54). However, the correlations of different traits using the same method are inflated by method variance and are high (0.72 to 0.78). Furthermore, all the correlations are attenuated by unreliability. From this matrix, we want to estimate the correlation between traits A and B to determine whether they are independent, related but distinct, or essentially the same. To this end, we again use structural equation modeling.

The first structural equation model, shown in Figure 12-3, examines the correlation of the latent traits in the same manner as we did for depression and anxiety. It appears that both Trait A and Trait B are measured well because the loadings on the observed variables are high. (Structural equation modeling provides model fit indexes that assess the adequacy of measurement. Although not discussed here, these fit indexes should be examined to determine whether the constructs are being measured well.) Moreover, the two traits are highly correlated (namely, 0.95), indicating that Trait A and Trait B likely are not distinct.

It should be kept in mind, however, that three of the correlations that assessed the relationship between different traits with the same method were inflated by method variance. Structural equation modeling can reflect this method variance by calculating correlations of the same method across traits, shown by the two-headed arrows in Figure 12-4. Essentially, paths have been added to the model to take method variance into account. The correlations 0.25, 0.32, and 0.37 in the figure reflect the method variance for methods 1, 2, and 3, respectively. As expected, the correlation between the traits dropped from 0.95 to 0.76 when the method variance was modeled, indicating that the traits are distinct, although not independent.

Method variance appears often in counseling research when counseling process and outcome are assessed from the same rating perspective. For example, if the counselor rates both quality of counseling sessions (a process variable) and therapeutic progress (for example, symptomatology, an outcome variable), then the correlation between the process and outcome variables is influenced by the rating perspective (the counselor). If the counselor has a generally favorable attitude toward the client, then that counselor will tend to rate all aspects of the counseling and the client as positive. This general tendency for the rater to rate all

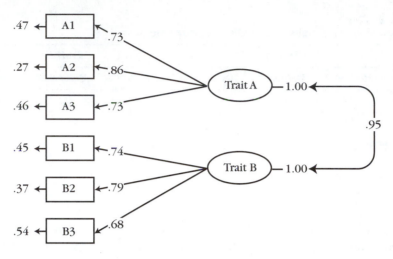

FIGURE 12-3
Multiple measures of Trait A and Trait B.

aspects of an endeavor similarly is method variance, and it tends to inflate correlations. Consequently, correlations between process and outcome, when process
and outcome variables are derived from the same perspective, overestimate the
true relationship between process and outcome (see Chapter 17).

MULTIPLE MEASURES—FINAL CONSIDERATIONS.   The previous sections can be summarized by the following six points:

1. A single operation (that is, a single scale or instrument) will almost always
    poorly represent a construct.
2. The correlation between two constructs is attenuated by unreliability.
3. Unreliability always makes it more difficult to detect true effects (should
    any be present) because of reduced statistical power.
4. The correlation between two measures using the same method is inflated
    by method variance.
5. If possible, multiple measures using multiple methods should be used to
    operationalize a construct.
6. Typically, interpretations of relationships should be made at the construct
    level, for seldom are we interested in the measures per se. Cognizance of
    the effects of unreliability and method variance is critical for drawing
    proper conclusions.

Use of multiple dependent variables raises many concerns for the researcher,
the most obvious of which relates to the selection of specific variables. Clearly, the
researcher must know the area and make informed choices. For example, in a study
of anxiety, the researcher needs to know whether anxiety in a particular context
would be measured best observationally, physiologically, or by self-report, or by
some combination of all three. An understanding of the mechanisms of anxiety is
needed to make this determination.

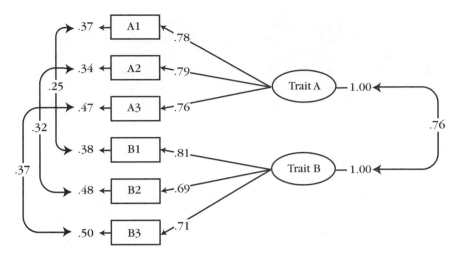

FIGURE 12-4
Multiple measures of Trait A and Trait B accounting for method variance (correlated errors).

Multiple dependent measures also complicates the analysis of the data obtained in a study. As we have discussed, treating each variable distinctly (that is, using a univariate analysis for each variable) ignores the interrelationships among the variables, creates inferential ambiguity, and inflates the probability of Type I errors (see Leary & Altmaier, 1980). In this chapter, several measures were used to create latent variables that indexed constructs without error. In group designs, multivariate analyses of variance are often used to perform one statistical test with multiple measures, although this method does not account for unreliability. Another way to handle multiple measures is simply to aggregate the measures by summing the raw scores if the measures have the same scales (for example, sub-scales of the Weshcler scales of intelligence) or by summing standardized scores if the scales are different. It should be noted that multivariate procedures are com-plex and are often misused, so, to select the proper statistical methods, one must be knowledgeable of the interrelationships among the variables and be willing to make predictions about the pattern of the results (Wampold, Davis, & Good, 1990). Statistical analysis is beyond the scope of this text, but the reader is referred to a special issue of the *Journal of Counseling Psychology* (1987) devoted to the sta-tistical analysis of counseling research.

GENERALIZABILITY.   In our discussion of construct validity, we noted that, as is the case for reliability, validity is a property of the scores and not of the instruments. The degree to which variables produce scores that adequately reflect a construct depends on the type of participants used in the study. The relationships demon-strated by structural equation modeling, such as those shown in Figures 12-2 through 12-4, are generalizable only to persons similar to those used to collect the data. Ponterotto and Casas (1991) analyzed the multicultural research in counsel-ing journals and found that only 25% of the instruments used in those studies were developed using racial and ethnic minority populations. The construct validity of the 75% developed with other groups (primarily middle-class European Americans) is questionable (see Ponterotto, 1988a). Ponterotto and Casas (1991) concluded that the lack of minority-based instrumentation was one of the greatest limitations of the multicultural research they reviewed. Although more minority-based instruments are now available, the assumption of generalizability across groups continues to be a major issue in this area (see Chapter 13).

Reactivity

The dependent variable should be sensitive to some characteristic of the participant, but the assessment process itself should not affect the characteristic directly; that is, the dependent measure should indicate how the participant functions normally. Sometimes, something about obtaining scores on the dependent measure alters the situation so that "false" readings are obtained. Variables that affect the characteristics of the participants they are intended to measure are said to be *reactive*. For example, a test-anxious participant may report increased anxiety on a self-report instrument because completing the instrument is like taking a test; an aggressive child may display less aggressive behavior when being observed by an adult than at other times; a person may smoke less when asked to record the number of cigarettes smoked. Clearly, the reactive nature of dependent variables must be considered in designing research; again, knowledge of the substantive area is vital. Later in this chapter we discuss unobtrusive measures, which are designed to be nonreactive.

Procedural Considerations

A number of procedural issues must be considered when selecting or designing the dependent variable. Often, the time involved with the assessment is critical to the success of the study. Participants will be reluctant to volunteer for studies that demand a long time to complete forms and instruments, or if they do volunteer they may respond carelessly to items (increasing error variance), especially toward the end of a long assessment period. Most psychometric studies assess reliability of scores only after the targeted scale has been administered; the researcher must realize that reliability may be considerably reduced when the scale is administered at the end of a long battery of tests.

   As mentioned previously, the readability of instruments is critical to their psychometric performance. Any instrument administered should be checked to ensure that participants can adequately read the materials. Often the manuals of published tests contain references to the reading level required. Alternatively, the researcher can use one of the relatively easy-to-use methods for determining readability (see Klare, 1974–1975).

   The order of the administration of instruments can have an effect on responses; one instrument may sensitize or otherwise influence responses on another instrument. An instrument that draws attention to a participant's own pathology (for example, the Minnesota Multiphasic Personality Inventory) may well affect how the participant rates others (for example, the counselor on the CRF). Order is also important when the same instrument is administered repeatedly. Performance at a given time may be due to previous responding (a testing effect) rather than to the amount of the characteristic. For instance, on an intelligence test, participants may acquire knowledge about specific questions or tasks (such as picture completion) that improves performance, even though intelligence remains unchanged.

When repeated measures are used in a study, use of alternative forms is desirable if testing effects are anticipated. Alternative forms enable the researcher to give a pretest and a posttest without having to use the identical instrument.

METHODS OF DATA COLLECTION

Given that the basic purpose of the dependent variable is to measure the effect or outcome of the independent variable, an essential aspect of any discussion of dependent variables involves collecting data vis-à-vis the dependent variable. To this point we have emphasized the use of instruments in data collection. Nevertheless, there are a number of other methods to collect data relevant to the dependent variable. For the purposes of this text, we discuss seven nonexclusive methods of data collection that are relevant in counseling: (a) self-reports, (b) ratings of other persons and events, (c) behavioral observations, (d) physiological indexes, (e) interviews, (f) projective techniques, and (g) unobtrusive measures. There are other ways to categorize methods; for instance, measures can be divided into objective versus subjective methods. Whenever relevant, these other methods of classification are discussed. Note also that these seven data collection methods may sometimes overlap; the interview method also is a form of self-report, and ratings of other people are sometimes behavioral measures. The main point is that there is a broad range of data collection methods, each of which has its respective advantages and disadvantages. Finally, each method of data collection should be evaluated in terms of its congruence with the research question, psychometric properties, relation to other methods used in the study, reactivity, and so forth.

Self-Reports

In self-report measures, the participant assesses the degree to which some characteristic is present or to which some behavior has occurred. The self-report may be accomplished by responding to items in an inventory, completing a log, or keeping a journal. In any case, the sine qua non of self-reports is that participants themselves make the observation or report. Generally, the assumption is made that the report accurately reflects the true state of affairs—that participants respond honestly and accurately. In this section we discuss advantages, disadvantages, types of inventories, and scoring formats for self-report inventories.

Advantages of Self-Reports

Although they take many forms, self-reports have some general advantages that make them the most popular assessment device in counseling research. First, they are relatively easy to administer. Most self-report inventories, tests, or question-naires used in counseling research can be administered to a group of participants, providing economy of time. Even when administered individually, self-report mea-sures typically do not require special expertise on the part of the administrator; for example, receptionists can give clients inventories to be completed at the end of a session (see, for example, Kokotovic & Tracey, 1987). Similarly, most self-report inventories are relatively simple to use and require little training of the participant.

Another advantage of self-reports is that they can be used to access phe-nomena that otherwise would be extremely difficult or impossible to measure. Self-reports can assess private cognitions and feelings, behavior in private settings (for example, sexual behavior), and future plans. In addition, participants can be asked to report about cognitions, feelings, and behaviors in hypothetical situa-tions. For instance, counselors could be asked to report how they would respond to a sexual advance by a client, a situation that would be unethical to arrange experimentally.

Self-reports also are advantageous because they are compatible with phe-nomenological views of counseling and psychotherapy. According to the phe-nomenological perspective, the thoughts and feelings of a client are of paramount importance, and self-reports of such constructs as happiness, marital satisfaction, and anxiety are more important than other indicants of these constructs, such as therapist ratings of client change, behavioral observations, physiological measures, or other measures that use a locus other than the self. For example, even though anxiety can be assessed physiologically, the distress caused by anxiety states is the debilitating factor for clients, and their self-reports of anxiety are essential to understanding this phenomenon.

Disadvantages of Self-Reports

The most obvious, and the most troublesome, disadvantage of self-reports is that they are vulnerable to distortions by the participant. For a variety of reasons, the participant may consciously or unconsciously respond in a way that yields a score that reflects a response bias rather than the construct being measured. For exam-ple, participants may guess the hypothesis of the study and respond (a) in a way that they think will confirm the researcher's conjecture, (b) in a manner that makes them look good, (c) in a way that makes them appear more distressed than is truly the case in order to receive promised services, or (d) in a socially desirable way. Some inventories are constructed to minimize such distortions. For example, the Minnesota Multiphasic Personality Inventory-2 (MMPI-2) contains four scales to assess the attitude of the participant. Two scales (L and K) measure whether the participant is trying to look better than is actually the case; one scale (F) mea-sures deviate response sets; and one scale (the "?" scale) indicates the number of questions unanswered, which may indicate the participant's resistance to the test, confusion, or insufficient time to complete the test (Graham, 1990). To avoid participant bias, the Edwards Personality Preference Schedule is constructed so that the two choices for each item are equivalent with regard to social desirability (Sax, 1989).

Another disadvantage of self-report measures is that the participant may not be aware of the characteristic being measured. For example, a test-anxious participant may deny that he or she is anxious and attribute poor performance to inadequate preparation. In such cases, self-report can be used if the characteristic is measured indirectly. For example, participants may be asked to self-report the signs of anxiety (such as cold fingers, difficulty concentrating, or dizziness). However, the case can be made that participants are not aware of some mental processes and that self-reports reflect only the products of cognitive processes (see, for example, Nisbett & Wilson, 1977).

A final disadvantage of self-report measures is the flip side of the advantage related to the congruence between a phenomenological perspective and self-reports: Self-reports are less valued by some other theoretical perspectives. For example, self-reports tend to be of minimal importance to staunch behaviorists. In spite of the disadvantages of self-reports, a listing of the dependent variables used in counseling research clearly indicates that the self-report is the most frequently used dependent measure.

Types of Inventories

There are many different ways to classify self-reports; here we classify them into inventories published by professional publishing companies, those published in the professional literature, and author-generated inventories tailored to a particular study. Clearly, different types of inventories present various advantages and disadvantages when choosing or designing the dependent variable. In addition to briefly discussing these advantages and disadvantages, we indicate how to obtain copies of the various inventories.

Many studies in counseling use tests or inventories published by professional publishing companies. Well-known examples of published self-report inventories include the Minnesota Multiphasic Personality Inventory (MMPI), the Strong Interest Inventory (SII), and the Wechsler scales of intelligence (for example, WAIS-R). Published inventories can be obtained from the publisher; often there is a discount if the test or inventory is used in a research context.

The advantage of published inventories is that generally a substantial amount of research has been conducted on them. Typically, the manual reports the outcome of reliability and validity studies, as well as normative data. Moreover, often many other published studies also report psychometric information about the inventory or have used the inventory in research contexts. For example, thousands of studies have used the MMPI, the SII, and the Wechsler scales. Information obtained from manuals and other studies is invaluable in assessing the appropriateness of the inventory for a particular study. However, publication in and of itself does not ensure the usefulness of an inventory; that determination needs to be made for each inventory.

Most published inventories fall into one of the following classes: personality measures, intelligence and aptitude tests, attitude and value scales, achievement tests, and interest inventories. Although many sources provide information about published tests, the most comprehensive is the series of yearbooks published by the Buros Institute. The most recent, *The Twelfth Mental Measurements Yearbook* (Conoley, Impara, & Murphy, 1995), contains reviews of tests published since the previous yearbook, an index of test titles, a list of acronyms, a subject index, a publisher directory and index, an index of names of authors and reviewers, and an index of the construct or properties measured. To facilitate locating tests in previous yearbooks, the Buros Institute also publishes *Tests in Print,* the most recent of which is *Tests in Print IV* (Murphy, Conoley, & Impara, 1994). Although these sources can be helpful, they are not a substitute for knowledge about the research in an area, including instruments used for measuring constructs central to the topic and their respective psychometric properties. Moreover, these sources often do not include many commonly used counseling-related instruments.

A number of inventories have been developed by researchers and have appeared in various journal articles and books. One of the most widely used inventories in counseling research is the Counselor Rating Form (CRF; Barak & LaCrosse, 1975). As previously mentioned, the CRF was developed to measure a client's perceptions of a counselor in the areas of attractiveness, expertness, and trustworthiness. Although this inventory has never been professionally published, it has been widely researched, used, and revised (see, for example, Barak & LaCrosse, 1975; Corrigan & Schmidt, 1983; Epperson & Pecnik, 1985; Heesacker & Heppner, 1983; Tracey, Glidden, & Kokotovic, 1988).

As was the case with professionally published instruments, researchers are advised to carefully consider the psychometric data on instruments that have appeared in the literature. In the case of the CRF and the CRF-S (short form of the CRF), extensive information is available. Other instruments may have appeared in the literature only once or twice, and their psychometric properties may be uncertain. It is also advisable to read carefully how these instruments have been or are supposed to be used. Often, the items themselves do not appear in the articles but can be inferred from tables or other information in the article. For example, the stems of items and their means may be presented in tables, and the type of scaling used (for instance, a seven-point bipolar scale) may be described in the text. Because inventories can perform differently depending on how the items are arranged on the page, the order in which they are presented, and so forth, care must be taken. When inventories from the literature are used, these aspects may vary from one study to another. It is generally advisable to contact the developer of such inventories to obtain a copy of the instrument and permission to use it.

In some instances, researchers cannot find published or previously researched inventories that meet their needs; in such instances they may develop new scales. Adequately developing items for a questionnaire can be a long and drawn-out process involving writing and rewriting questions, pretesting on a small sample, and still more rewriting. Because participants often complete these instruments in the absence of the experimenter, the instructions and questions must be crystal clear. The format of the questions must also facilitate easy identification of all of the items. Because even the length of the questionnaire and size of type can influence participants' response rate, these matters are additional considerations. Again, this process merits very careful planning and thinking; far too many dissertations have produced ambiguous findings because of a hastily developed questionnaire. In short, developing an inventory is a complex process, and well beyond the scope of this chapter; interested readers should consult various test construction sources (for more details, see Babbie, 1979; Dawis, 1987).

These ad hoc scales can be particularly useful because they can be tailored to measure just what the researcher has in mind. For example, Palmer and Cochran (1988) developed a scale to measure adolescents' relations with their parents with regard to career planning and decision making. One very difficult problem arises when using ad hoc inventories: They have unknown psychometric properties. Although the reliability of an ad hoc inventory can be assessed by analyzing the scores in the particular study, this option is often unsatisfying. First, it may well be that the reliability of the scores obtained is not sufficiently high to conduct any further analysis using the scores. Second, most studies are not designed to enable the researcher to conduct such incidental psychometric analyses; typically there are too few participants for psychometric purposes. Finally, most inventories must be tested, revised, and retested in a number of contexts before confidence in their performance is obtained. It is not uncommon for a researcher to spend ten years developing an inventory (for example, polishing items, confirming factor structure across sample populations, making multiple estimates of reliability and validity). Although the advantage of tailoring a measure to a particular study is a strong one, the total lack of psychometric information on that measure considerably lessens its utility.

Scoring Formats

Self-report measures can also be classified by whether they are scored objectively or subjectively. If there is little ambiguity about the scores assigned to a participant—if the participant, say, circles a number from 1 to 7 for each item, and the circled numbers are summed to form a total score—then the inventory is objectively scored. If participants are asked to record their food intake, and scores are determined by estimating the caloric content ingested, then the ambiguity due to estimation of size of portions, content of food, and so forth means that the inventory is subjectively scored. Clearly, objectivity and subjectivity are not absolutes. It should be noted that the terms *objective* and *subjective* refer to how the scores are determined, not to the format of the inventory. If the food intake report were scored by counting the number of adjectives used to describe the food, then the report would be scored relatively objectively. Objectively scored self-reports are advantageous because little error variance is introduced by the scoring procedure. Nevertheless, subjectively scored self-reports can sometimes be richer in that they may better reflect the construct being measured.

Items that can be objectively scored can be classified into several types. One type involves having the participant select one of several choices. The choices may be "agree/disagree," "yes/no," "approve/no opinion/disapprove," or "approve strongly/approve/neutral/disapprove/disapprove strongly." Alternatively, there may be a point scale with anchors; for example, a seven-point scale with the anchors "agree" and "disagree" might appear as

Agree 1 2 3 4 5 6 7 Disagree

In all these cases, the response to each item is assigned a numeral (for example, yes = 0, no = 1), and typically the sum of the responses for several items is used as a dependent variable. For example, the CRF-S consists of 12 items, and scores on each of the three subscales are derived by summing the responses for each of four items. The use of multiple items to form a scale or subscale score is desirable because it usually enhances the reliability of the scores (assuming that the items relate to the construct being measured). Dependent variables that rely on a single item of this type should be considered carefully, as the reliability will inevitably be low, as discussed previously in this chapter.

Another means of constructing objectively scored measures is to have participants rank-order a set of stimuli according to some criterion. Rank ordering forces respondents to make discriminations that they might not otherwise make. For example, rather than being asked to rate the effectiveness of a set of possible counselor responses, participants might be asked to rank-order the counselor responses from least effective to most effective. This could be a good strategy if respondents otherwise tend to rate all counselor responses as equally effective.

Forced-choice methods require that participants select one of two alternatives. Often the alternatives appear to be equally favorable or unfavorable. For example, the Edwards Personality Preference Schedule contains alternatives that are matched on social desirability, and participants are required to select one of the alternatives that best describes themselves. A variation of the forced-choice method with great potential for counseling research asks participants to identify dimensions within a series of ratings. For instance, participants might be presented descriptions of pairs of counselors that vary on certain dimensions (for example, empathy or unconditional positive regard) and asked to indicate which of the pair they prefer (all possible pairs need to be presented). These data can then be analyzed to indicate the dimensions to which the participants are attending. Multidimensional scaling is one such method (see Fitzgerald & Hubert, 1987).

We have very briefly discussed a few formats for objectively scored scales. It should be recognized that developing instruments to measure constructs is difficult; in fact, many articles appearing in professional journals in counseling, such as the *Journal of Counseling Psychology,* are related to the development and validation of such instruments. Dawis (1987) provides an introduction to this topic for counseling researchers. Furthermore, various formats yield data with particular properties that effect the validity of the statistical tests used. For example, a broader range of statistical analyses are typically available for Likert (1–6) responses than true/false or yes/no responses. Likewise, questions that ask respondents to "*check all items below that apply*" also restrict the range of statistical analyses possible. Care must be used to select statistical tests that are appropriate for the types of data obtained; refer to measurement and statistical sources for discussion of this complicated issue.

Ratings of Other Persons and Events

Counseling research often relies on ratings made of other persons or of events. The procedures here are similar to those for self-reports, except that respondents rate characteristics of the participant or the event. Often the respondents are experts, and their judgment is assumed to reflect accurately characteristics of the person or event. For example, in treatment studies, the therapist or a significant other could rate the degree of dysfunction or improvement of a client. A perusal of the literature in counseling reveals that direct rating of participants is seldom used. However, many studies derive variables from ratings of events, particularly counseling sessions. For example, the Session Evaluation Questionnaire (SEQ; Stiles, 1980) is designed to measure the depth and smoothness of counseling sessions (see, for example, Stiles, Shapiro, & FirthCozens, 1988).

Ratings of other persons and events share many of the advantages of self-reports, particularly their ease of administration and flexibility. When raters are experts, their judgments are particularly valuable because they are made with a rich background and deep understanding. Experienced counselors' judgments take into account years of experience with many types of clients. Another advantage is that many rating scales (for example, the SEQ) have proven psychometric properties under various conditions.

The primary problem with ratings of other persons and events is that the ratings may be systematically biased. This is especially a problem when the raters are aware of the hypotheses and cognizant of the conditions to which participants belong. If counselors are raters who also are involved in the experimental treatment, they may rate the progress of clients higher because they have an interest in the outcome of the study. If at all possible, raters should be blind to as many factors of the experiment as possible.

When raters are used to make judgments about events, the ratings can reflect characteristics of the rater as well as those of the event. When the participants (counselors and clients) judge the depth and smoothness of interviews on the SEQ, they are actually reporting their perceptions of the interview, and in that respect their ratings are self-reports. Thus, when interpreting ratings of events (or of other persons, for that matter), researchers must be careful to separate the variance due to differences in the event from the variance due to the raters themselves. One strategy to examine the variance due to raters is to use neutral or multiple observers, and then test for differences across raters. For example, Hill, Carter, and O'Farrell (1983) compared observers' ratings as well as the counselor's and the client's ratings of counseling sessions.

Another problem with ratings is that because they often are relatively general, it is not possible to determine what led to them. In the SEQ, raters respond to the stem "The session was" on 7-point scales anchored by adjectives such as "bad/good," "dangerous/safe," and "difficult/easy." However, it is unknown which aspects of a session lead to a rater's responding with "difficult" as opposed to "easy."

An imaginative way to use ratings of events is to have participants respond to a stimulus and rate their responses in some way. Tracey, Hays, Malone, and

Herman (1988) used the Therapist Response Questionnaire to obtain counselors' reactions to various client statements. The counselors indicated how they would normally respond, and then these responses were rated on eight dimensions: dominance versus submission, approach versus avoidance, focus on cognition versus affect, immediacy, breadth versus specificity, the extent to which the counselor met the client's demand, verbosity, and confrontation. In this way, Tracey et al. were able to obtain a set of counselor responses to various client statements and then obtain additional dimensional ratings on those counselor responses, which allowed for greater precision and interpretability of the ratings.

Behavioral Observations

Behavioral measures are derived from observations of overt behavior, most typically by a trained observer. Behavioral psychology has emphasized the importance of overt behavior and deemphasized intrapsychic phenomena. Accordingly, observing and recording behavior is the key component of applied behavior analyses (see the *Journal of Applied Behavior Analysis* for examples of this type of research). Essentially, behavioral observations are the same as ratings of other persons or events, except that behavioral measures focus on overt, observable behavior and presumably do not rely on inferences by raters.

As is the case with other modalities of assessment, behavioral assessment encompasses a wide variety of methods (Barlow, 1981; Mash & Terdal, 1988). Generally, behavioral assessment requires an operational definition of the behaviors of interest, direct observation of participants' behavior, recording of occurrences of the targeted behavior, and some presentation or summarization of the data.

The general advantages of behavioral observations are that they are direct and objective measures. Although there can be systematic biases in the observation and recording of overt behavior, behavioral measurements are not typically subject to the personal biases inherent in self-reports. Another advantage of behavioral measures is that participants can be assessed in various environments. Studies have repeatedly shown that behavior is situation-specific; behavioral measures can be used to assess functioning in several situations. Finally, for many dysfunctions the behavior itself is problematic (for example, stuttering, social skills deficits, sexual dysfunction, physical avoidance, substance abuse) and thus warrants specific attention.

Among the disadvantages of behavioral observations is the fact that problems and concerns of clients frequently do not center around behavior. Marital satisfaction is a construct that is difficult to operationalize behaviorally (although there are many behavioral correlates of marital satisfaction). The central question, as with any operationalization, is whether the behavior chosen reflects the construct of interest.

Another disadvantage of behavioral observations is related to representativeness. A presumption of behavioral assessment is that the behavior sampled is representative of behavior at other times. However, for a number of reasons, this may not be the case. For instance, nonrepresentativeness can occur when behavior is recorded at fixed but unusual times (for example, classroom behavior on Friday afternoons). In addition, the reactivity that results when participants are aware that they are being observed leads to observations that may not be representative.

Issues related to reliability are problematic for behavioral assessment. An observer's decision that a particular behavior occurred may be idiosyncratic to that observer. In the context of behavioral assessment, these reliability issues are judged by calculating indexes of agreement; that is, how well do observers agree about the occurrence of targeted behavior? As was the case for traditional assessment, inter-observer agreement is a complex topic (see Suen, 1988).

Even if overt behavior is of paramount importance, it may not be possible or practicable to observe the behavior. Observation of sexual behavior, for instance, is typically precluded. Other behaviors are difficult to observe and are sometimes assessed in contrived situations. In counseling research, the behavior of a counselor often is assessed using confederate clients who appear to manifest some type of problem. Of course, the representativeness of behavior in contrived situations must be considered.

Behavioral observations have been used successfully in counseling and supervision process research. In the usual paradigm, the interactions between counselor and client (or supervisor and trainee) are recorded and coded as a stream of behaviors. A number of coding systems have been developed or adapted for this use (see, for example, Friedlander, Siegel, & Brenock, 1989; Hill et al., 1983; Hill & O'Grady, 1985; Holloway, Freund, Gardner, Nelson, & Walker, 1989; see also Chapter 17). The sequence of behaviors is used to derive measures that can be used to characterize the nature of the counseling or supervision interaction. The simplest measure is the frequency of behaviors. For example, Hill et al. (1983) used the frequency of counselor behaviors to discriminate the best from the worst sessions in a case study of 11 sessions. Simple frequencies, however, are not sensitive to the probabilistic relation between behaviors. More sophisticated methods can be used to ascertain whether the frequency of a behavior of one participant (for example, the client) increases the likelihood of some behavior in another participant (for example, the counselor). Using such methods, Wampold and Kim (1989) showed that the counselor in the Hill et al. study was reinforcing the storytelling behavior of the client. However, methods that look at sequential dependencies are not without their problems or their critics (for example, compare the results of Hill et al., 1983, with Wampold & Kim, 1989; see also Howard, 1983; Lichtenberg & Heck, 1983, 1986; Wampold, 1986a).

Physiological Indexes

Biological responses of participants can often be used to infer psychological states. Many psychological phenomena have physiological correlates that can be used as dependent variables. In fact, physiological responses often can be thought of as direct measures of a construct. For example, whereas self-reports of anxiety can be biased by a number of factors, measures of physiological arousal can be made directly and can be presumed to be free of bias. However, although physiological arousal is a focus in the theoretical conceptualization of anxiety, the relation

between physiological states and psychological phenomena is not as straightforward as was anticipated in the early years of this research. Moreover, physiological
measures are expensive, require special expertise, may be reactive, and may be subject to error due to a number of mechanical and electronic factors (such as electrical interference). As a result, physiological measures are infrequently used in
counseling research.

Interviews

Interviews are straightforward means of obtaining information from participants.
In Chapter 10 we discussed using interviews in qualitative research. Essentially, the
process of using interviews to obtain data on a dependent variable is similar,
except that the goal is to quantify some construct. In everyday life, interviewing is
a pervasive activity; we simply ask people to supply information. Interviews typically involve an interpersonal interaction between the interviewer and the interviewee or participant.

Kerlinger (1986) advocated using personal interviews because of the greater
control and depth of information that can be obtained. The depth of information
most often results from carefully planning and developing the interview schedule.
Personal interviews allow flexibility in questionnaire design; the interviewer can
provide explanations (and thus reduce participant confusion), make decisions during the interview about the adequacy of a particular response (and probe if necessary), and evaluate the motivation of the participant. The flexibility of the
personal interview can be a real advantage if the topic is complex and if participants are unaware of their psychological processes; interviewer probing can then
be extremely beneficial and add considerable depth to the information obtained.
Babbie (1979) also observed that personal interviews that are properly executed
typically achieve a completion rate of at least 80–85% of the participants targeted.
Even though interviews rely on the self-report of the participant, the human interaction with the interviewer provides another facet to the self-report. In short, the
interviewer can also make observations about the participant, which is an additional data source (Babbie, 1979).

Interviews, however, are costly in terms of money and time. If the topics are
sensitive (for instance, sexual behavior), then participants may be more reluctant
to divulge information than if they were allowed to respond to an anonymous
questionnaire. Interviewers must be recruited and trained. It is also important in
quantitative research to standardize procedures across interviews to avoid introducing confounding variables due to different interviewer behavior or biases.
Often considerable training is needed to standardize procedures (general greeting,
introduction of the interview schedule, methods of recording exact responses,
manner of asking questions, responses to participants' questions, handling of
unusual participant behavior, and termination of the interview). Thus, interviewer
training is another task for the experimenter (see Babbie, 1979, for more details
regarding interviewer behavior and training).

The telephone interview consists of a trained interviewer asking a participant a series of questions over the telephone. This method is usually quick and inexpensive (financially), unless long-distance calls are involved. Babbie (1979) recommends that the interview be kept short—10–15 minutes. Such brevity, however, often limits the depth of information obtained. Moreover, the telephone method reduces the amount of evaluative information that the interviewer can observe about the participant. As with other personal interviews, an interview schedule must be developed, but an additional consideration is the generally lower responsiveness of telephone participants.

Although interviews are most often used in qualitative research, interviews have been used to assess the dependent variable. McLaughlin, Cromier, and Cromier (1988) used a structured interview to assess the coping strategies used by participants. In response to questions, participants indicated how often (daily, three times per week, less than three times per week, every other week, infrequently, or never) they used certain behavioral strategies. The researchers in this study chose an interview format because they wanted participants to develop a personal relationship with the research assistants, who were responsible for providing referrals for those participants who needed assistance after completion of the study.

Projective Techniques

The rationale behind projective techniques is that participants' responses to ambiguous stimuli will reveal some facet of their personality. The Thematic Apperception Test (which uses ambiguous drawings) and the Rorschach (which uses inkblots) are probably the two most well-known projective tests. However, a wide variety of possibilities exist, including drawing pictures, writing essays, completing sentences, playing with dolls, associating words, and so forth. The assumption is that because the method is indirect, participants will not censor themselves. In turn, their responses are indirect measures and need to be interpreted in some way. Scoring of projective tests is typically subjective, although there are some very objective systems for scoring them, such as the Exner system for scoring Rorschach responses (Exner, 1974).

Historically, projective techniques have been associated with psychodynamic approaches to understanding human behavior. As the popularity of psychodynamic approaches has decreased, however, so has the use of projective techniques. One of the most troublesome aspects of these techniques is that their scoring is subject to systematic biases that tend to confirm preconceived (but incorrect) conceptions about people (see, for example, Chapman & Chapman, 1969). Furthermore, the connection between underlying personality characteristics and overt behavior is tenuous.

In spite of their disadvantages, some forms of projective techniques have made useful contributions to several areas of counseling research. For instance, one of the conspicuous themes in counseling research involves the matching of environmental structure with conceptual level (Holloway & Wampold, 1986). The conceptual level theory states that high-conceptual thinkers will perform best in low-structured environments, whereas low-conceptual thinkers will perform best in high-structured environments. Studies in this area typically have used the Paragraph Completion Method (PCM; Hunt, Butler, Noy, & Rosser, 1978) to measure conceptual level. The PCM asks participants to respond to six sentence stems; scores are based on the cognitive complexity of the responses.

Unobtrusive Measures

To eliminate reactivity, it is often possible to collect data on participants without their awareness of this process. Measures used in such a way that participants are unaware of the assessment procedure, known as unobtrusive measures, have been described in some detail by Webb, Campbell, Schwartz, Sechrest, and Grove (1981). It may be possible to observe participants without their knowledge in naturalistic settings, to observe participants in contrived situations (for example, with a confederate), to collect data from archives or other sources (such as school records), or to examine physical traces (such as garbage or graffiti). Most psychologists are extremely interested in sources of unobtrusive data. How often do people observe others in public and make interpretations of their behavior?

Of course, the most conspicuous advantage of unobtrusive measures is that they are by definition nonreactive. Because participants are not aware that data are being collected, they do not alter their responses. Furthermore, unobtrusive measures are often very accurate. Grade point averages obtained from the registrar will be more accurate than those obtained from participants' self-reports. Still, there are a number of limitations to unobtrusive measures. Certain types of unobtrusive measures are unethical. For instance, disclosure of personal information by public agencies without the participant's permission is forbidden. Another limitation is that unobtrusive measures are often difficult and/or expensive to obtain. In addition, once the data are obtained, interpretation or classification is often needed; a study of graffiti might involve classifying the graffiti as sexual, drug related, violent, and so forth.

Although use of unobtrusive measures is not widespread in counseling research, the literature contains a number of studies that have used such measures. Heesacker, Elliott, and Howe (1988), in a study relating Holland code to job satisfaction and productivity, assessed a number of variables unobtrusively. Productivity data were obtained through the payroll office by multiplying the units produced by the value of the unit; absenteeism rates were obtained from the payroll office; data on injuries on the job were obtained from examining health insurance claims; and demographic information was gleaned from employment applications. Zane (1989) observed participants in a contrived situation; in a study of placebo procedures, male participants interacted in a waiting room with a person they thought was another participant but who actually was a female confederate. The interaction between the participant and the confederate was surreptitiously videotaped, and subsequently rated and coded for indicators of social skills and social anxiety (such as talk time, facial gaze, and smiles).

SUMMARY AND CONCLUSIONS

The basic purpose of the dependent variable is to measure the effect or outcome of the manipulation of the independent variable. We discussed several issues that relate to operationalizing the construct that represents the effect of some cause. Once the construct has been defined, the psychometric properties of the dependent variable vis-à-vis the construct should be established. Reliability and validity are the primary psychometric considerations. *Reliability* refers to the proportion of variance in the dependent variable that is due to true differences among participants. The remaining variance is error. To be useful, a dependent variable must have adequate reliability. Although there are several types of validity, the one most germane to research design is *construct validity,* the degree to which scores reflect the desired construct rather than some other construct. Establishing construct validity is complicated and indirect, but nevertheless vital to the integrity of a study. Construct validity can be investigated in a number of ways, including recent applications of structural equation modeling. Commonly, a single dependent variable is unable to adequately operationalize a construct; multiple dependent variables are often recommended. The hope is that each variable reflects some aspect of the construct of interest, and that together they measure the essence of the construct. In any study, the researcher must be cognizant of both the attenuation of true relationships due to unreliability and the inflation of true relationships due to method variance. However, the dependent variables are designed or chosen such that they do not react with the treatment.

There are many methods of collecting data related to dependent variables, each of which has its advantages and disadvantages. The most widely used measure in counseling research is the self-report. The sine qua non of the self-report is that participant makes his or her own observations or reports. The advantages of self-reports are that they are relatively easy to administer, can access areas that otherwise would be impossible or difficult to measure (such as sexual behavior), and are compatible with phenomenological views of counseling. The most conspicuous problem with self-reports is that they are vulnerable to distortions by the participant. However, participants may not be consciously aware of the construct being measured, and self-reports are incompatible with several theoretical approaches to counseling (for example, behavioral approaches). Self-report instruments may either be published, either by professional publishers or in the literature, or tailor-made for a specific study, and they can be written in a number of formats.

Less frequently used dependent measures include ratings of other persons and events, behavioral measures, physiological indexes, interviews, projective techniques, and unobtrusive measures. Ratings of other persons and events are useful because experts or participants can be used to judge important aspects of counseling, such as the counseling interview itself. Behavioral measures reflect overt behavior and thus are not subject to the distortions that can plague self-reports and ratings of other persons and events; furthermore, they are compatible with behavioral approaches to counseling, even though they may be incompatible with other approaches (such as psychodynamic approaches). Physiological responses can be used to infer psychological states because many psychological phenomena (for example, anxiety) have physiological correlates; however, due to lack of reliability, significant expense, and other problems, physiological indexes are infrequently used in counseling research. Interviews are advantageous because much information can be obtained quickly and because the interviewer can pose follow-up questions, but they are relatively expensive, depend on the skill of the interviewer, and can be biased. Projective techniques, which use ambiguous stimuli to reveal some facet of personality, can be useful to uncover unconscious aspects of the personality. Unobtrusive measures are designed to eliminate reactivity because the participant is unaware that any measurement is being conducted. Given the multitude of data collection methods, the task of the informed researcher is to collect data with a method that provides the type of information that is most relevant to the research question.

Obviously, the selection of the dependent variable and the method of data collection require considerable forethought and examination of the research literature. Moreover, these tasks often require creative thinking to tailor measurements to the constructs of interest. Unfortunately, sometimes researchers spend very little time in selecting dependent variables, and weak and disappointing findings often result. We firmly believe that careful deliberation and consultation with colleagues can greatly facilitate the selection of dependent variables and enhance the overall quality of research in counseling.

CHAPTER 13

POPULATION ISSUES

The processes involved in selecting participants and generalizing the results based on the data collected from those participants constitute what we call *population issues.* Perhaps the one question we are most frequently asked by student researchers is, "How many participants do I need?" Less frequently asked but perhaps more crucial are questions related to how applicable the results of a study are to other contexts. For example, do the results of a treatment study apply to the types of clients seen in mental health agencies? Does a study of marital satisfaction provide information that is valid for various ethnic/racial groups? Is the use of undergraduates appropriate for a particular study? These and many related questions can be answered only when we understand population issues. But population issues are some of the most perplexing issues involved in research design.

This chapter focuses on the way in which population issues impinge on the design and interpretation of research in counseling. Key population issues for successful research in counseling include (a) what types of participants to use, (b) how many participants to study, (c) how to treat different types of participants in the design and analysis, and (d) to what extent the results are generalizable. Selecting participants for a study typically involves selecting samples from a population of interest. Because the rationale for using samples from a population is based on sampling theory, we discuss this subject first. Then we address practical issues in selecting participants including (a) defining the target population, (b) creating a participant pool, (c) selecting participants, (d) establishing the validity of research in the absence of random selection, and (e) determining the number of participants. Finally, we examine the relationship of external validity to population issues by considering factorial designs involving factors related to person or status variables.

SAMPLING THEORY

Selecting participants for a study typically involves selecting samples from a population of interest. For example, it would be too cumbersome for an investigator interested in homophobia to interview all Americans about homophobia, so instead the investigator selects a sample of participants that presumably reflects American population as a whole. *Sampling theory* provides the foundation for understanding the process and the implications of selecting participants for a particular study. We briefly discuss sampling theory and elucidate some of the real-life restrictions and subsequent problems that investigators encounter.

The essence of sampling theory involves selecting samples that reflect larger or total populations. We typically think of a population as a well-defined set of people, such as college students seeking help at a counseling center, depressed adolescents, or counselors-in-training, but technically a population is a set of observations. Put another way, it is the observations (or scores) of the people, rather than the people themselves, that constitute the population. The important aspect of populations, whether viewed as people or observations, is that conclusions reached from the research sample should apply to the population. By necessity, counseling research is conducted with a limited number of participants; the results for these particular participants alone are rarely of primary interest. The object of most research is to generalize from the observations of these study participants to some larger population; that is, some inference is made about the population based on a small number of observations.

The concept of population, however, is elusive. Some populations are quite real. For example, consider the population that includes the cumulative grade point averages of all college students enrolled as of January 3, 1998, and who have completed at least one term of college. The grade point averages (that is, the observations) exist and can be obtained from student records. The size of the population in this instance is fixed and finite, although quite large. Other populations are more ambiguous. For example, examination of depression in college students might involve a population that includes scores on the Beck Depression Inventory (BDI; Beck, Ward, Mendelson, Mock, & Erbaugh, 1961) for all college students enrolled as of January 3, 1998. Clearly, not every college student has taken the BDI, so in some sense this is a hypothetical population. Nevertheless, there is little difficulty imagining having each student take the BDI; the population would consist of all these scores. However, it probably would be unwise to limit the population to students enrolled as of January 3, 1998, because to be useful the results of the study should be applicable to students enrolled at different times. A truly hypothetical population might involve college students enrolled both currently (at the time of the research) and in the future. This hypothetical population is infinite. Clearly, some problems arise when generalizing to infinite hypothetical populations, some of whose scores exist in the future; however, it is just as clear that limiting conclusions to populations in existence only at a given time restricts the generalizability of the results.

Inferences about populations are made on the basis of samples selected from populations. Technically, a sample is a subset of the population; that is, the observations in the sample are taken from the set of observations that constitute the population. This process is called sampling. Again, inferences about the population of observations are made from the observations of the sample; the validity of the inferences about the population depend on how well the sample in fact represents the population. Representativeness is a complex concept that requires further explanation.

Certainly, selecting 20 males at an Ivy League college and recording their scores on the BDI would poorly represent the population of BDI scores for all college students nationally. Samples that systematically differ from the population in some way are said to be *biased.* More technically, a biased sample is a sample selected in such a way that all observations in the population do not have an equal chance of being selected. In the example of male Ivy Leaguers, the sample is biased because female students do not have the same chance of being selected as males (that is, the probability of selecting a female is zero), and students in non-Ivy League colleges do not have the same chance of being selected as students in the Ivy League.

Samples that are not biased are random samples—that is, samples in which each observation in the population has an equal chance of being selected. Logistically, random samples can be selected by assigning each observation a consecutive number (1, 2, 3, . . .) and then choosing the observations by selecting numbers from a random numbers table or by using a computer-assisted random numbers generator. To randomly select a sample of size 20 from all college students, each student could be assigned an eight-digit number, a computer could be used to generate 20 eight-digit random numbers, and the BDI scores for the students whose numbers were generated would compose the sample. Clearly, this would be a laborious process (and could never realistically be accomplished), but it illustrates how random selection is achieved.

Although random selection eliminates systematic bias, there is no guarantee that a random sample will be representative of the population. For example, even though it is highly unlikely, the random selection process just described *could* yield a sample of 20 male Ivy League students! To understand representativeness, and to comprehend how inferences from samples to populations are made, we now discuss some basic principles of sampling theory. Consider a population that has a mean of 100 (that is, the mean of the observations in the population is 100). Typically, this is denoted by writing $\mu = 100$; the Greek symbol μ (mu) indicates a population parameter. A researcher selects a random sample of 25; if the obtained mean M of the 25 observations is close to 100 (say $M = 103.04$), then in one sense the sample is representative. If the mean of the 25 observations is far from 100 (say $M = 91.64$), then it could be said that the sample is not representative. This all seems logical; however, the situation in the real world is that the population parameter is unknown to the researcher, and the researcher selects only one sample. Therefore, it is unclear how representative any given sample in fact is. Fortunately, statistical theory helps us here by allowing calculation of the probability that an obtained mean is some arbitrary (but acceptable) distance from a specified population value. (More about this later.) It should be noted that larger samples are likely to be more representative of the population than smaller samples. (More about this later as well.)

We now integrate our previous discussion of random assignment from Chapters 4 and 6 with random selection in the context of a particular design (see Wampold & Drew, 1990, for a similar but more technical discussion of these issues). Consider the case of a posttest-only control-group design (as discussed in Chapter 6); let's say the researcher is testing the efficacy of an innovative treatment. Two populations are of interest here: the population of individuals who have received the innovative treatment, and the population of individuals who have received no treatment. Suppose that 30 participants are randomly selected from a well-defined population; the researcher does not know how well the sample represents the population, only that there are no systematic biases in the sample because the participants were selected randomly. The next step is to randomly assign the 30 participants to the two groups (15 in each). Participants in the treatment group are administered the treatment, and at some subsequent time both treatment and the control participants are tested. At this point something crucial should be noticed: The 15 observations for the treated group are considered to be randomly selected from a hypothetical population of observations of individuals in the population *who have received the treatment.* Think of it this way: All people in the well-defined population are eligible to be treated; hypothetically, all of these people could receive the treatment and subsequently be tested. The 15 observations (that is, the posttest scores) in the treatment group are considered to be randomly selected from the hypothetical population of posttest scores for all persons as if they had been treated. The 15 observations in the control group are considered to be randomly selected from the hypothetical population of posttest scores for persons who have not been treated. These concepts are illustrated in Figure 13-1.

Next, we discuss a crucial point about experimental design and the tests of statistical hypotheses. The null hypothesis in this case is that the population mean for all individuals who hypothetically could be treated is equal to the population mean for all individuals who are untreated, symbolically expressed as $\mu_T - \mu_C = 0$. An appropriate alternative hypothesis (assuming higher scores indicate a higher level of functioning) is that the population mean for all individuals who hypothetically could be treated is greater than the population mean for all individuals who are untreated: $\mu_T > \mu_C$. If the statistical test (here a two-group independent t test) is statistically significant, then the null hypothesis is rejected in favor of the alternative. Because statistical hypotheses are written in terms of population parameters, the researcher—by deciding to reject the null hypothesis and accept the alternative—is making an inference about the *population of observations* based on the sample scores. In this example, if the null hypothesis is rejected in favor of the alternative hypothesis (based on, say, a statistically significant t test), then the researcher concludes that the mean of scores of treated persons is in general higher than the mean of scores of untreated persons. However, this conclusion could be incorrect because the samples might not have been representative. Perhaps the 15 participants assigned to the treatment condition were initially superior in some way(s) to the other persons in the population. (Of course, this

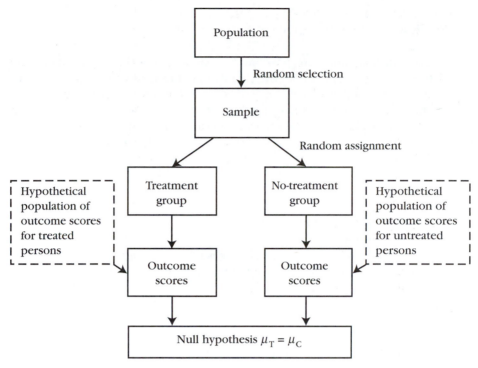

FIGURE 13-1
How sampling is conceptualized for a hypothetical posttest-only control-group design.

cannot be determined with this design.) Nevertheless, protection against this possibility is expressed as the alpha level, the probability of falsely rejecting the null hypothesis. When alpha is set at, say, 0.05, the probability that the null hypothesis is rejected when it really is true is less than or equal to 0.05. Because alpha conventionally is set at low levels (for example, 0.05 or 0.01), the probability that significant results is due to unrepresentative samples is small. Remember this central point: Rejection of a null hypothesis does not mean that the null hypothesis is false; it means that the obtained results would be very unusual if the null had been true, and thus the decision is made to reject the null. However, there is still the small possibility that the null is true, and that sampling error (that is, Type I error) was responsible for the obtained results.

Even though we have just emphasized the importance of random selection from a population, we must point out that random selection is almost always an impossibility in applied research. A perusal of journals in counseling convincingly demonstrates that random selection is seldom used. For all practical purposes, it is not possible to select participants for a treatment study from across the country; researchers are fortunate to be able to afford to select clients locally. Even when random selection is pragmatically feasible (for example, a survey of members of Division 17 of the APA), not all persons selected will choose to participate, creating a bias. In the next section we discuss procedures for conducting research without random selection, and the attendant problems involved.

PRACTICAL CONSIDERATIONS IN SELECTING PARTICIPANTS

If true random sampling were possible, the researcher would define the target population, identify all people in the population, and randomly select from that group of people. But as we have noted, this process is not practical except in the most contrived contexts. In this section we explore the practical issues in participant selection by discussing the following topics: (a) defining the target population, (b) creating a participant pool, (c) selecting participants, (d) establishing validity in the absence of random selection, and (e) determining the number of participants.

Defining the Target Population

The first step in the selection of participants is to define the target population, or the population to which the investigator wants to generalize. Although technically *population* refers to a set of observations, the population is typically defined in terms of the characteristics of people. Researchers must carefully consider many different characteristics in this definition, because ultimately these characteristics define the group to which the study's results will be generalized. Defining characteristics may include diagnostic category, gender, ethnicity, age, presenting problem, marital status, and socioeconomic status, among others. For example, Mahalik and Kivlighan (1988) limited participants in a study of self-help procedures for depression to undergraduates who were mildly depressed (had a score of 10 or greater on the Beck Depression Inventory), had indicated an interest in participating in a self-help program for mood control, and were not receiving psychotherapy.

One important issue in defining the target population is deciding how heterogeneous the population should be. Heterogeneous populations are desirable because they contain a wide variety of characteristics to which the results of the study may be generalizable; conversely, homogeneous populations limit the degree to which the results are generalizable. By limiting the population to undergraduates, Mahalik and Kivlighan restricted the degree to which the results are generalizable; the study does not shed light on the efficacy of self-help procedures with other groups, such as unemployed laborers. Nevertheless, there are problems with heterogeneous populations as well. For one thing, it is unclear how the results of a study apply to various subgroups of a heterogeneous population (a topic that we revisit in a later section); furthermore, by their very nature, heterogeneous populations show much variability in responding, such that the error variance is greater than it would be for homogeneous populations, creating less-powerful statistical tests. Again, as is the case with most decisions in research design, determining a study's optimal degree of population heterogeneity depends on the nature of the problem being investigated. In terms of Kerlinger's "MAXMINCON" principle, this is a trade-off between minimizing within-group variance and controlling extraneous variables.

Creating a Participant Pool

After defining the target population, the researcher needs to identify a group of people who both fit this definition and are accessible; this group is called the participant pool. Suppose that the target population is defined as university counseling center clients. Clearly it is impossible to identify all such clients, so the participant pool is often limited to possible participants in the researcher's vicinity. The participant pool might consist of counseling center clients at the researcher's university, a not uncommon practice (see, for example, Tracey, Glidden, & Kokotovic, 1988). However, restricting the participant pool to a subset of all possible participants introduces various kinds of bias—in this case, those related to geography, including socioeconomic factors, ethnicity, and values. In the Tracey et al. (1988) study, the participants were clients at a "large midwestern university counseling center." Are the results of this study applicable to clients at counseling centers at a small midwestern college, an Ivy League university, or a university in Southern California? Restricting the participant pool restricts the population, and so technically the results of the Tracey et al. study are generalizable only to clients at that particular midwestern university counseling center.

There is no empirical way to determine whether restricting a particular participant pool limits the generalizability of a study, other than by investigating the potential participants excluded from the participant pool. Clearly, this is not a feasible solution, because if those participants were accessible to the researcher, they would have been included in the study in the first place. Therefore, the researcher needs evidence to support the contention that restricting the participant pool does not affect the results. Background knowledge and prior research are crucial in making the decision to restrict the participant pool. For example, the physiological responses to physical stress would not be expected to vary from one area of the country to another, whereas attitudes toward abortion very well might. Of course, restriction of participant pools is not based on geographical criteria alone; often participants are recruited from local mental health agencies, undergraduate participant pools, school districts, and so forth.

In one sense, all participant pools are restricted. Because it is required that research participants take part voluntarily, all participant pools are restricted to participants who satisfy the definition of the target population and volunteer to participate. A bias is introduced here because volunteer participants have been found to be quite different from nonvolunteers; for example, volunteers are better educated, have a higher need for social approval, are more intelligent, are less authoritarian, appear to be better adjusted, and seek more stimulation than nonvolunteers (Rosenthal & Rosnow, 1969).

Another complicating factor in composing participant pools is that because the presence or magnitude of characteristics contained in the definition of the target population may not be readily apparent, testing may be required. For example, in Mahalik and Kivlighan's (1988) study of depressed undergraduates, it was necessary to assess the level of depression of every potential participant. Over 800 students were given the Beck Depression Inventory to identify those who were at least mildly depressed.

Selecting Participants

The next step is to determine those participants in the participant pool who will participate in the study. Ideally, participants are randomly selected from the participant pool. For example, if the participant pool comprised students seeking help at a counseling center at a particular university, then the researcher could assign each such student a number and, with the aid of a random numbers table or a computer-assisted random numbers generator, randomly select the participants for the experiment. However, even this process can be pragmatically troublesome. Often the researcher needs all participants to be at the same stage of counseling, but if there are not enough qualified clients, the researcher may solicit participants as they become available. For example, Tracey et al. (1988) had university counseling center clients evaluate their counselor immediately after the intake session. To obtain a sufficient sample, the researchers asked all clients who presented themselves at the center to participate in the study; in all, 192 of 430 clients agreed to participate and completed the study. Thus in this study, random selection from a participant pool did not occur because all available participants were used.

Establishing Validity in the Absence of Random Selection

Even though random selection has historically been considered a critical element in proper generalization from the results of a study of a sample to a larger population (Serlin, 1987), random selection does not typify research in counseling. Nevertheless, available samples may be "good enough for our purpose" (Kruskal & Mosteller, 1979, p. 259). The "good enough" principle stipulates that nonrandom samples can have characteristics such that generalization to a certain population is reasonable. Accordingly, when samples are obtained by some means other than random sampling, "valid inference can be made to a hypothetical population resembling the sample" (Serlin, 1987, p. 300). In this way, generalization is made rationally rather than statistically.

However, making rationally based generalizations requires care. As Serlin (1987) indicated, generalizations of this type should be theory driven; he cited two areas of counseling research to illustrate this point. The social influence model of change in counseling (Strong, 1968) relies on a credible counselor and an involved client, and thus research with undergraduate psychology majors who are not involved clients has theoretical shortcomings. By contrast, in other areas of counseling research, undergraduates may constitute a sufficient sample from which to make valid inferences. The conceptual-level matching model (Holloway & Wampold, 1986) has implications for the training of beginning counselors; accordingly, participants who are relatively naive with regard to counseling skills are necessary, and thus psychology undergraduates, given their interest in behavior and lack of training in counseling, are perfectly appropriate, even desirable participants. In this case, undergraduates are "good enough," but they are not "good enough" for studies of the social influence model.

Thus, in the absence of random sampling, researchers must take great care in identifying the characteristics of study participants. The burden of proof is on the researcher to establish that the characteristics of participants is such that generalizations to a relevant hypothetical population are valid. The current vogue in counseling research is to eschew studies with limited generalizability in lieu of field studies with actual clients. Accordingly, for studies investigating anxiety (including treatment studies), clients seeking treatment for anxiety are favored over mildly anxious undergraduates who had not presented themselves for counseling. Of course, recruiting clients seeking treatment is more difficult than recruiting undergraduates.

Researchers must take special care when making generalizations about differences between groups defined by categorical status variables. To understand the difficulties, consider first a true experimental design in which a treatment is compared to a control group. In such a design, questions about the cause of any differences found between the treatment and control groups are internal validity questions; if the study is well designed (specifically, if the subjects are randomly assigned), then the effects are relatively unambiguously attributed to the treatment. The generalizability of the results is an external validity issue. Consider, for example, a study in which Kiselica, Baker, Thomas, and Reedy (1994) compared stress-inoculation training to a control group to test the efficacy of this treatment on anxiety, stress, and academic performance of adolescents. Using "48 White students from a public high school in a rural community with a population of approximately 7,000," they found that the stress-inoculation training reduced anxiety and stress vis-à-vis the control group. Because this was a well-designed study, the effects could be attributed to the treatment. However, because the participant characteristics were narrowly defined, the efficacy of stress-innoculation for adolescents with other characteristics (for example, minority populations in urban schools) is unknown. Nevertheless, this study makes an important contribution because it demonstrates, at least in one context, that the treatment works; future researchers could examine generalizability, if they deemed it important.

Now consider a hypothetical status study whose purpose is to compare the anxiety, stress, and academic performance in two samples—European-American and African-American adolescents. Suppose that samples of European-American and African-American students were obtained from a school to which the European-American students were transported from suburban areas, and that significant differences were found between the groups in levels of anxiety, stress, and achievement. Because there was no random assignment, the two populations might well have differed on many characteristics other than ethnicity, such as socioeconomic status (SES), family status, parental involvement and supervision, community crime rates, and so forth. Consequently, it would be difficult to attribute the differences in dependent variables to ethnicity, and therefore the sampling method causes a problem for both internal and external validity. It might well be that the differences between the two groups of students were due to the characteristics mentioned, and had the researchers selected samples that held these factors constant (which would be extremely difficult), the differences would not have been present. The point here is that when status variables are used, internal as well as external validity problems arise, whereas if a study involves a true independent variable, only external validity is problematic.

Because the generalizability of results relies on the characteristics of the participants, researchers must carefully document the important characteristics of the sample. Given that race and ethnicity are always important considerations in generalizability for studies in the United States, Ponterotto and Casas (1991) made the following recommendation:

> Knowing simply the ethnic make-up and mean ages of one's sample is insufficient in assessing result generalizability. Describe the sample fully: mean and median age; educational level (and in immigrant groups, where the education was received); socioeconomic status; gender; preferred language and level of acculturation in immigrant samples; the level of racial identity development; geographic region of the study, and any other sample characteristics you believe your reader would consider when interpreting the results. As a rule of thumb, the more accurately you can describe your sample, the more accurate you can be in determining the generalizability of your results. (p. 107)

The National Institutes of Health's (NIH) guidelines on inclusion of subpopulations recognizes the importance of gender and race/ethnicity as critical status variables in research:

> It is the policy of NIH that women and members of minority groups and their subpopulations must be included in all NIH-supported biomedical and behavioral research projects involving human subjects, unless a clear and compelling rationale and justification establishes to the satisfaction of the relevant Institute/Center Director that inclusion is inappropriate with respect to the health of the subjects or the purpose of the research. Exclusion under other circumstances may be made by the Director, NIH, on the recommendation of an Institute/Center Director based on a compelling rationale and justification. Cost is not an acceptable reason for exclusion except when the study would duplicate data from other sources. . . . Under this statute, when a . . . clinical trial is proposed, evidence must be reviewed to show whether or not clinically important gender or race/ethnicity differences in the intervention effects are to be expected. (NIH Guidelines, 1994, p. 14509)

Recruiting appropriate samples of racial and ethnic groups can often be difficult. Suggestions have been given for the recruitment and retention of American Indians and Alaska Natives (Norton & Manson, 1996), African Americans (Thompson, Neighbors, Munday, & Jackson, 1996), Latinos (Miranda, Azocar, Organista, Muñoz, & Lieberman, 1996), and other ethnic minorities (Areán & Gallagher-Thompson, 1996).

Determining the Number of Participants

The number of participants used in a study is important because as the number of participants increases, so does the probability that the sample is representative of the population. The question "How many participants?" is intimately involved with the concept of statistical power. Recall that power is the probability of rejecting the null hypothesis when the alternative is true, or the likelihood of detecting an effect when the effect is truly present. Even given a treatment that is effective, a study comparing the treatment group to a control group will not necessarily result in a statistically significant finding—it is entirely possible that even though an effect exists (the alternative hypothesis is true), the obtained test statistic is not sufficiently large to reach significance (that is, the null hypothesis is not rejected). Generally, the greater the power, the better the study (although after we discuss factors that lead to increased power, we will present a caveat to this general rule).

Power is dependent on (a) the particular statistical test used, (b) the alpha level, (c) the directionality of statistical test, (d) the size of the effect, and (e) the number of participants. Even though an in-depth discussion of these factors involves statistics more than design, an elementary understanding of statistics is required before the important question "How many participants?" can be answered (see Cohen, 1988; Kraemer & Thiemann, 1987; and Wampold & Drew, 1990, for more complete discussions).

Before power can be determined, the researcher must select a statistical test. For a given situation, often a variety of statistical tests will do the job. For example, for a design with two treatment groups and a control group, the most frequently used test is an analysis of variance. However, nonparametric alternatives exist; in this case, the Kruskall-Wallis test would be appropriate. The relative power of different alternative tests varies, and this topic is beyond the scope of this book (see, for example, Bradley, 1968). The point is that power must be calculated for each specific statistical test.

Another factor that affects power is the alpha level. If a researcher sets alpha conservatively, say at 0.01, then it is more difficult to reject the null hypothesis, and power is decreased. So in being careful not to falsely reject the null hypothesis (in setting alpha small), the researcher sacrifices power.

The directionality of the test also affects power. If a two-tailed (that is, nondirectional) test is used, the researcher reserves the option of rejecting the null hypothesis in either direction. This is helpful when a researcher is interested in results in both directions and/or is unclear about the direction. For instance, when comparing two treatments, knowing whether Treatment A or Treatment B is superior is important; however, keeping options open in both directions costs the researcher power because it is more difficult to detect effects in this case than when one direction or the other is specified. One-tailed (directional) tests are more powerful when the effect is in the expected direction. For example, when testing the efficacy of a treatment vis-à-vis a control group, it makes sense to test only whether the treatment is more effective than no treatment (one is rarely interested in knowing whether the treatment is less effective than no treatment). By specifying the direction (that the treatment is superior to no treatment), the researcher increases the power of the statistical test.

The most difficult factor to specify in any determination of power is the size of the true effect. When a treatment is extraordinarily effective, the effect of the treatment is relatively easy to detect, and thus power is high. For example, if a treatment of depression reduces self-deprecating statements from an average of 20 per hour to zero, achieving a statistically significant finding will be easy. However, if the reduction is from an average of 20 self-deprecating statements to 18, then detecting this small change will be difficult. Of the many ways to quantify effect size (see Rosenthal, 1984), all share an index of the strength of the relationship between variables.

Specifying the size of the effect before the study is conducted is problematic—if one knew the effect size for any experiment beforehand, there would be no need to conduct the study. Nevertheless, the effect size must be stipulated before the number of participants can be determined. The effect size can be stipulated in a number of ways. First, prior research in relevant areas often provides clues about the size of effects. For instance, if the effect of cognitive-behavioral treatments of test anxiety is known to be a certain size, it is reasonable to expect that the effect of a cognitive-behavioral treatment of performance anxiety would be approximately the same size. Haase, Waechter, and Solomon (1982) surveyed the effect sizes obtained in the counseling psychology research in general, although it is unclear how applicable these results are to specific areas within the field. A second way to stipulate effect size is to specify the effect size considered to have practical or clinical significance. For example, in a treatment study involving a treatment group and a control group, the researcher might want to stipulate the percentage of those treated that exceeds the mean of those untreated. Using normal distributions, it can be shown that an effect size of 1.00 indicates that at the end of treatment, 84% of the treatment group functioned better than the mean of the control group (assuming normality); an effect size of 1.5 indicates that 93% functioned better than the mean of the control group; an effect size of 2.0 indicates that 98% functioned better than the mean of the control group. Translation of effect size into indexes of clinical improvement allows the researcher to gauge how large the effect must be to have clinical significance. Finally, based on a number of considerations, Cohen (1988) classified effects into three categories: small, medium, and large. This scheme makes it possible for a researcher to determine the number of participants needed to detect each of these three effect sizes. Of course, the researcher must still stipulate which of three sizes of effects the study should detect. Furthermore, Cohen's determination of effect size is arbitrary and cannot apply equally well to all areas of social and behavioral research. Nevertheless, in the absence of other guiding lights, stipulation of a "medium"-sized effect has guided many a researcher.

The last determination needed before deciding how many participants to use in an experiment is the level of power desired. Power of 0.80 has become the accepted standard (although again this level is arbitrary). A level of power of 0.80 refers to a probability level; that is, 80% of the time the stipulated effect size will be detected (that is, the test will be statistically significant). It also means that there is a 20% chance that no statistically significant results will be found when the effect in fact exists!

Once the researcher has selected the statistical test to be used, chosen whether to use a one-tailed or two-tailed test, set alpha, stipulated a desirable level of power, and determined the effect size to be detected, he or she can ascertain

TABLE 13-1
Number of Participants Needed to Achieve Various Levels of Power ($\alpha = .05$)

	Number of independent variables							
	K = 3				K = 6			
R^2	Power = .30	.50	.70	.90	.30	.50	.70	.90
.10	34	56	83	132	47	74	107	164
.30	11	17	25	37	17	24	33	45
.50	7	10	13	18	11	14	18	24

NOTE: R^2 is the minimum value of the proportion of variance accounted for.
SOURCE: "Use of multiple regression in counseling psychology research: A flexible data-analytic strategy" by B. E. Wampold and R. D. Freund in *Journal of Counseling Psychology, 34,* p. 378. Copyright 1987 by the American Psychological Association. Reprinted by permission.

the number of participants needed to obtain the stipulated level of power. Typically this is accomplished by using tables, such as those provided by Cohen (1988) or Kraemer and Thiemann (1987). Cohen provided extensive examples, but his format uses different tables for different tests. By using approximations, Kraemer and Thiemann were able to reduce the complexity of the process of determining the number of participants needed. Perhaps the simplest way to make this important determination is to use computer programs designed for this purpose (see, for example, Borenstein & Cohen, 1988).

Some caveats are needed about determining sample size. First, all of the procedures presume that the assumptions of the chosen statistical test are met. When assumptions are violated, power is typically decreased, so beware. Second, even though one often hears rules of thumb about sample sizes—10 participants for each variable in a multiple regression, 15 participants to a cell in a factorial design, and so forth—be warned that such rules are almost always misleading, as Table 13-1, an abbreviated power table for multiple regression, shows. In some instances fewer than 10 participants per variable are needed, and in other instances many more than 10 are needed. Third, the general rule that the more participants for an experiment, the better, also is misleading. Certainly, the researcher wants to have a sufficient number of participants to have a reasonable opportunity (say 80%) to detect an effect of a specified size. However, using too many participants raises the possibility that a very small effect size can be detected (see Meehl, 1978, for an excellent discussion of this issue). Although small effects can be interesting, they often mislead the researcher into believing that something important has occurred when in fact only a trivial finding has been obtained. For example, in a regression problem, a statistically significant finding with a large number of participants that accounts for only 2% of the variance in the dependent variable will likely add little to our understanding of psychological processes. Because statistical significance can be obtained for trivial effects, it is often recommended that researchers report effect size and power in addition to significance levels (Cook & Campbell, 1979; Fagley, 1985; Folger, 1989).

EXTERNAL VALIDITY AND POPULATION ISSUES

Recall that external validity refers to the generalizability of findings across persons (for example, adolescents, college students, African Americans, gay men), settings (for example, university counseling center, in-patient hospital setting, mental health center), or times (for example, 1960s, 1990s). The most direct way to increase the external validity of findings is to build into the design variables that represent persons, settings, or times. Because issues related to the generalizability of findings across persons are the most relevant to counseling researchers, we next illustrate these issues and indicate how they might also extend to settings or times. We first describe how population issues can be incorporated into factorial designs, and then we discuss several general considerations of studying external validity in factorial designs. It is important to note that even though factorial designs are discussed here, they are not the only designs that can examine population issues.

Use of Factorial Designs to Study External Validity

To determine how results apply to various groups of persons, a status variable related to persons can be added to the design to create a factorial design (discussed in Chapter 6). Consider a factorial design with one independent variable (with three levels) and a status variable related to persons (with two levels):

Independent variable

	I	II	III
Persons I			
Persons II			

To make this strategy more salient, consider the three levels of the independent variable to be three treatments, and the two levels of the status variable related to persons to be gender. Now the factorial design can be diagramed as follows:

Treatments

	Treatment A	Treatment B	Treatment C
Gender Males			
Gender Females			

Interpretation of the main effects and the interaction effects of this factorial design will illustrate how it establishes the generality of the results across persons. Suppose that it was found that there was no treatment effect; that is, there was insufficient evidence to establish that one treatment was more effective than any other. External validity involves answering the question of whether or not this result applies equally to males and females. It may well be that there was no main effect for gender as well. However, the interaction effect speaks most clearly to external validity. For example, Treatment A may have been most effective with males, whereas Treatment C may have been most effective with females, indicating that the results are not generalizable across gender. This prototypic interaction is illustrated in Panel 1 of Figure 13-2. As can be seen at the right in Panel 1, had the results been analyzed without considering gender, one would have concluded that the treatment variable was not important (that is, that there were no differences in treatment). However, were gender included as a factor, a very different conclusion would have been reached. (Incidentally, had only males been included in the study, one would have concluded that Treatment A was most effective, the opposite of the conclusion that would have been reached had only females been included.) Clearly, considerations of person variables can be vital to the proper understanding of research results. Parenthetically, gender is receiving increased attention in the counseling literature (interested readers could examine Betz & Fitzgerald, 1993; Cook, 1990; Courneyer & Mahalik, 1995; Good, Gilbert, & Scher, 1990; Good et al., 1995; Heppner, 1995; Mintz & O'Neil, 1990; Richardson & Johnson, 1984; Scher & Good, 1990).

Other patterns can result from including a person factor in a factorial design. Panel 2 of Figure 13-2 shows main effects for treatment (Treatment A > Treatment B > Treatment C) and for gender (females > males). Clearly, considering gender adds information because treatments were more effective for females than for males. However, the pattern of results is the same for males and females (that is, Treatment A > Treatment B > Treatment C), and therefore the conclusions reached for males, for females, and for persons in general (both genders) are the same. In this case, one would not be misled if one ignored gender in the design. Thus, in this case, external validity is not increased by including gender, although information about males and females is gained.

In Panel 3 of Figure 13-2, a main effect for treatment is apparent, but neither a gender effect nor interaction effect is observed. In this case, the addition of gender does not affect the results in any way. Of course, the absence of gender effect may be interesting, although the usual caveats about interpreting null effects must be recognized. In Panel 4, there are no main effects for either treatment or interactions; however, effects for gender are present because the treatments are more effective in females than in males. Even though inclusion of gender informs the researcher of some gender effect, the conclusion that participants performed equally well over the three treatments would not change by including gender as a factor in the study.

The general principle to be gleaned from this discussion is that when external validity is examined within a design (by including person as a status variable), it is the interaction effect that is most interesting. An interaction effect indicates that the levels of the independent variable interact with the person variable to produce different outcomes. Researchers with a background in educational research will recognize this phenomenon as essentially that of aptitude-treatment

Results analyzed with gender Results analyzed without gender

Panel 1

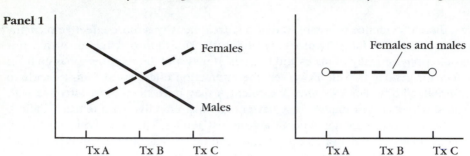

No treatment effect, no gender effect, interaction effect

Panel 2

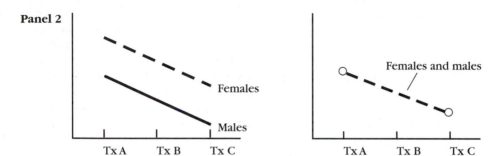

Treatment effect, gender effect, no interaction effect

Panel 3

Treatment effect, no gender effect, no interaction effect

Panel 4

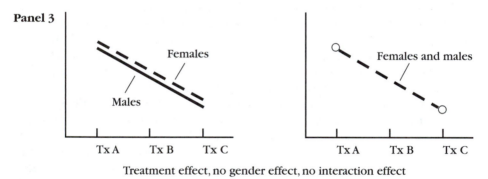

No treatment effect

FIGURE 13-2
Comparison of patterns that can result from including a person factor in a factorial design.

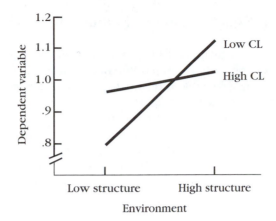

FIGURE 13-3
Means for 12 studies derived from the results of a meta-analysis. Units for y-axis are arbitrary; CL = conceptual level. From "Relation Between Conceptual Level and Counseling-Related Tasks: A Meta-Analysis" by E. L. Holloway and B. E. Wampold in *Journal of Counseling Psychology, 33,* p. 316. Copyright 1987 by the American Psychological Association. Reprinted by permission.

interactions (Cronbach & Snow, 1976); likewise, in career counseling, Fretz (1981) has referred to attribute-treatment interactions.

Some theories in counseling are expressed in terms of interactions between independent variables and person variables, as illustrated by the cognitive complexity model (Miller, 1981). According to this model, low conceptual level thinkers benefit from a more structured environment, whereas high conceptual level thinkers benefit from a less structured environment. In this model, conceptual level is a person variable, and structure of the environment is an independent variable that is manipulated by the researcher. Holloway and Wampold (1986) conducted a meta-analysis of studies investigating this hypothesis and found that the expected interaction effect appears to be operating. The effects found based on 12 studies are represented in Figure 13-3. There is a main effect for environmental structure (participants generally performed better in structured environments) and a (small) main effect for conceptual level (high conceptual level participants generally performed better). However, these conclusions were mitigated by the interaction between environmental structure and conceptual level. According to these results, one should provide more-structured environments to low conceptual level thinkers, whereas high conceptual level thinkers appeared to do about equally well regardless of structure.

Thus far we have discussed external validity in terms of a factorial design, with emphasis on the interaction effect. However, examination of interaction effects is not limited to factorial designs (and concomitant analyses of variance). For example, regression analysis also accommodates interaction effects nicely, and thus, external validity is related to the interaction of independent and person variables, regardless of the analysis.

Considerations in Examining Generalizability Across Populations

Although the factorial design approach to external validity seems straightforward, there are some issues concerning group differences that need consideration. One important, difficult to resolve issue is related to choice of the variables related to persons, settings, or times. Panel 1 of Figure 13-2 illustrates a case in which including gender is crucial to understanding the phenomenon under investigation. However, the researcher cannot know before the study whether this pattern or some other pattern (those portrayed in Panels 2 through 4) will occur. Furthermore, the researcher cannot know whether an interaction effect crucial to external validity would occur with other person, setting, or time variables. Selecting variables related to external validity is tricky business.

The problem is exacerbated by the fact that literally hundreds of such variables might be included in the design, including gender, ethnicity, race, age, level of dysfunction, intelligence, personality types, and type of clinic. Most of these variables are status variables, for which, as we have seen, sampling becomes intimately involved in both internal and external validity. Moreover, some of the most important status variables are not clearly defined. For example, although race is an important aspect of American society, psychologists cannot agree on a definition of this construct (Yee, Fairchild, Weizmann, & Wyatt, 1993). Finally, even if the variables can be well defined and measured, related constructs may be more important. For example, gender and ethnicity appear often in counseling research, but it is possible that sex-role orientation is more critical than biological gender, or that level of acculturation and/or racial identity is more critical than ethnicity. At this juncture, we invoke the usual refrain: Knowledge of the substantive area should inform the choice of variables related to external validity. If prior research or theory—or for that matter, common sense—indicates that gender is an important variable, add it to the design. Nevertheless, it is unwise to include variables when there is no compelling reason for their inclusion.

The field of counseling has placed much emphasis on understanding the role of race/ethnicity/culture on counseling and psychological functioning; researchers are encouraged to investigate this area, for race/ethnicity/culture factors are ubiquitous. Whether or not a given study is directly focused on race/ethnicity/culture, the influence of these factors on behavior and on the research endeavor should be understood (see Alvidrez, Azocar, & Miranda, 1996; Areán & Gallagher-Thompson, 1996; Atkinson & Lowe, 1995; Beutler et al., 1996; Coleman, Wampold, & Casali, 1995; Hohmann & Parron, 1996; Leong, Wagner, & Tata, 1995; Miranda et al., 1996; Norton & Manson, 1996; Ponterotto & Casas, 1991; Rowe, Vazsonyi, & Flannery, 1994; Thompson et al., 1994; Yee et al., 1993).

We have alluded to the problems inherent in comparing two groups formed from differences on a categorical status variable (for example, African-American and European-American groups). Because the issues involved in examining group differences are so important, we explore them again, in a slightly different way. A previous example involved differences between African-American and European-American adolescents in terms of stress, anxiety, and achievement. The goal of such a study was to identify mean differences between the two populations (for example, are the mean levels of anxiety for the two groups different). One of the most persistent but controversial findings in psychology involves just such a comparison—namely, the group differences found on traditional tests of intelligence. The research design point that we want to make is that simply identifying group differences on some variable is of limited usefulness; the goal of re-search is understanding, and research could be profitably used to explore observed differences among groups.

When differences between groups are found, a vital question arises: Are the processes that lead to these differences the same for both groups? Suppose there are two groups, A and B, that reliably show differences in some construct, say antisocial behavior (Group A > Group B). A critical piece of the puzzle is to determine whether the factors that lead to antisocial behavior in the two groups are the same. Given that we know inadequate parental supervision to be a key causal construct in antisocial behavior, the question could be expressed as follows: "Is the rate of antisocial behavior in Group A higher because there is less adequate supervision, or because there is some other variable that uniquely influences behavior in Group A but not Group B?" In a comprehensive reanalysis of several large data sets, Rowe, Vazsonyi, and Flannery (1994) found racial similarity in developmental processes related to achievement and behavior; that is, they found that the variables that predicted achievement and behavior were common across groups, and that no variables were uniquely important to specific racial groups.

Clearly, then, if a researcher is going to examine group differences, then an understanding of the processes that lead to those differences is paramount to making sense of the results. Basically, if an examination across populations reveals that the causal factors are similar, then the efficacy of interventions would be similar; if causal factors are not similar, then group-specific interventions would be needed. As is becoming clear, such research is needed to establish the efficacy of culture-specific educational and psychological interventions.

As an example of unique processes in different groups, Eugster and Wampold (1996) found that the factors that predicted global evaluation of a counseling session were different for the counselor and the client. Although clients and therapists had some factors in common, the researchers found that clients' global evaluation of a session was positively related to their perceptions of therapist interpersonal style and of the real relationship, whereas therapists' evaluations were positively related to their perceived expertness and negatively related to perceptions of the real relationship. These differences were verified by statistically testing the differences in regression equations. The goal of this research was not to determine whether there were mean differences between client and therapist evaluation of sessions, but to determine whether the factors that form the bases of these evaluations were different.

The statistical and methodological issues involved in testing common versus unique processes are complex. Essentially, unique processes involve mediating and moderating influences. In the gender example illustrated in Panel 1 of Figure 13-2, an interaction between treatment and gender showed that the processes were different (that is, treatments worked differentially across gender). Eugster and Wampold (1996) examined the equivalence of regressions to test for unique processes. Rowe, Vazsonyi, and Flannery (1994) present a particularly cogent explanation of research issues related to testing models involving the hypothesis that psychological processes differ among groups.

Another, although subtle, issue related to group differences involves the proportions of participants assigned when status variables are included in a factorial design. It is desirable in a factorial design to have equal numbers of participants in each cell; in this way, main and interaction effects are independent (provided the assumptions of the analysis of variance are met; see Wampold & Drew, 1990). Accordingly, equal numbers of participants of each type should be selected (recruited). For instance, in the example that examined types of treatment (depicted in Figure 13-2), equal numbers of males and females should be selected and then randomly assigned to the three treatments. For research on gender, this presents no problems; however, when the base rates of various person variables are different, conceptual (as well as statistical) problems occur. For example, selecting equal numbers of Native Americans and European Americans for a study results in a sample that is not representative of the general population (that is, it is biased toward inclusion of Native Americans). This is problematic because the results are peculiar to the manner in which the sample was obtained. For example, correlations are affected by the proportions of types of participants included (see Cohen & Cohen, 1983). This is a complex issue and is beyond the scope of this text, but a simple example will illustrate the problem. If one were conducting a study to examine how various types of political television commercials affected voting preferences of European Americans and Native Americans, equal numbers of these persons would be selected. The design of the experiment might involve exposing participants to various types of commercials and then measuring their attitudes. The results of this study might be theoretically interesting and applicable to real political campaigns. However, if one were polling to determine the expected outcome of an election, one would not want to bias the sample by having equal numbers of Native Americans and European Americans in the sample. Generally, experimental studies that examine theoretical phenomena or treatment efficacy should have equal numbers of participants. However, for studies that examine relations between variables in society, participants should be selected so that the proportions of the various person variables reflect the proportions in the population.

The factorial design approach to external validity also has philosophical implications for various classes of persons. Typically, studies are either conducted on predominantly majority samples (for example, European Americans) or include person variables that contrast a majority sample with a minority sample (for example, European Americans versus African Americans). The latter design includes the assumption that European Americans are somehow the norm, and that all other groups are to be contrasted with them (Ponterotto, 1988a). It is also assumed that each of these groups is homogeneous. African Americans comprise a diverse population, and typically such diversity (in, for example, level of acculturation, racial identity, and generational status; again, see Ponterotto, 1988a) must be considered in research designs. Furthermore, there are phenomena that may be culture-specific and for which it is not optimal or even sensible to use a design that contrasts various groups. For instance, the reasons for the underutilization of mental health clinics by ethnic minorities, which is a major concern to providers of service, may best be understood by examining intra-ethnic processes rather than interethnic differences.

External validity is often established using multiple studies. For example, single-participant designs preclude the inclusion of person variables because only one or a few participants are used. Therefore, researchers use a strategy called systematic replication (Barlow & Hersen, 1984), which involves replicating an experiment while varying a single element. By systematically varying the one element over time, the researcher can identify its effects. For example, a single-participant design that establishes the efficacy of social reinforcement in the attenuation of off-task behavior with students in a primarily European-American urban school might be replicated in a rural school with a European-American student body, in an urban school with a Hispanic student body, and so forth.

The idea of systematic replication can apply to group studies as well. For example, the interaction effect shown in Panel 1 of Figure 13-2 might have been identified by two studies that differed only insofar that one had female participants and the other had male participants. However, there are disadvantages of such a strategy. True replication is difficult to accomplish, and thus the differences between two studies may be due to factors other than different types of participants. Furthermore, examination of external validity in one study allows direct estimation of the size of the interaction effect, a procedure that is precluded in the systematic replication strategy.

SUMMARY AND CONCLUSIONS

Population issues affect the design and interpretation of research in counseling. A critical issue in the development of a study is the selection of a sample of participants from a broader target population. Considerable care is needed to (a) define the target population (or the population to which the investigator wishes to generalize), and (b) select participants that fit the definition of the target population. Theoretically, the generalizability of the results is established by randomly selecting a sample from a population. Because of the practical constraints on most counseling research, sampling is rarely achieved through true random selection. Instead, researchers often use nonrandom samples that have similar relevant characteristics to a target population, and then rationally argue that the results apply to a population with the same characteristics. Finally, a critical issue in selecting participants is determining how many participants are needed to adequately test the relationships among the study's constructs of interest. The number of participants needed for any study pertains to statistical power, or the probability of rejecting the null hypothesis when the alternative hypothesis is actually true. With regard to estimating statistical power (and thus the number of participants needed), we discussed (a) the particular statistical test used, (b) alpha level, (c) directionality of the statistical test, and (d) effect size. Thus, investigators must make a number of decisions in selecting participants for a study.

Typically, researchers are interested in generalizing the results of a particular study to a larger population of individuals, which is the essence of external validity. External validity also relates to the generalizability of findings across persons, settings, or times. We suggested that the most direct means to increase the external validity of findings is to build into the design factors that represent relevant persons, settings, or times. In this way, external validity can be investigated by examining the interaction of the independent variable and a variable related to persons, settings, or times.

Because counseling is an applied profession designed to help a broad array of individuals in various settings across different times, external validity is very important. Far too often, convenience samples consisting of predominantly white undergraduate participants are used in counseling research. We strongly encourage efforts to broaden the external validity of research in counseling in order to develop the more extensive databases that are needed in the counseling profession.

CHAPTER 14

INVESTIGATOR, EXPERIMENTER, AND PARTICIPANT BIAS

When a researcher designs a study, he or she seeks to examine the relationships among specified variables. One of the most crucial tasks that confronts the researcher is to control the extraneous variables or reduce the error variance (serious threats to Kerlinger's "MAXMINCON" principle) that may influence the relationships among the study's experimental variables of interest. Most often, when the extraneous variables or sources of measurement error are known, they are relatively easy to control; the problem is that in designing most studies, it is difficult, if not impossible, to identify all of the possible extraneous variables and error variance.

The purpose of this chapter is to identify potential sources of bias in participants, investigators, and experimenters of particular relevance to researchers in counseling. By the term *bias,* we mean the systematic introduction of extraneous variables that may distort or disguise the relationships among the experimental variables. Whereas *error variance* (or "noise" or "static") refers to variance due to random events, *bias* refers to creation of differential effects between groups or subgroups of participants due to some systematic kinds of errors.

In this chapter, *investigator* refers to the person who designs the study, and *experimenter* refers to the person who executes the investigation. The first section of this chapter examines investigator and experimenter bias, particularly with regard to (a) experimenter attributes, (b) investigator and experimenter expectancies, and (c) experimental procedures. The second section of this chapter examines participant bias, particularly with regard to (a) demand characteristics, (b) participant characteristics, and (c) introspective abilities. Throughout both sections we use examples from previous research efforts to clarify different types of bias. Moreover, in discussing the various sources of bias, we also discuss some strategies for controlling or minimizing these variables.

INVESTIGATOR AND EXPERIMENTER BIAS

In an ideal world, an investigator is an objective, unbiased seeker of truth who engages in a systematic, scientific enterprise and is able to remain an impartial, passive observer throughout. In this way, the researcher does not contaminate the research in any way, but rather is an unbiased observer of some phenomenon, and subsequently a reporter of the truth. We might even assume that

> All experimenters [investigators] are created equal; that they have been endowed by their graduate training with certain interchangeable properties; that among these properties are the anonymity and impersonality which allow them to elicit from the same participant identical data which they then identically observe and record. Just as inches were once supposed to adhere in tables regardless of the identity of the measuring instrument, so needs, motives, traits, IQs, anxieties, and attitudes were supposed to adhere in patients and participants and to emerge uncontaminated by the identity and attitude of the examiner or experimenter. (Friedman, 1967, pp. 3–4)

We know, however, that investigators do not conduct research in such an unbiased manner. Moreover, we know that experimenters who execute investigations may consciously or unconsciously affect the results of their studies. Instead, researchers sometimes have opinions, beliefs, and values that unconsciously (or even consciously) compromise their objectivity, sometimes in very subtle ways. Likewise, researchers' values and cultural biases are inherent in their assumptions concerning participants, research hypotheses, data analysis strategies, and conclusions. Thus, culturally encapsulated researchers may unknowingly make a number of decisions that might introduce a number of systematic biases in their research.

The story of Clever Hans nicely illustrates the effects of subtle experimental bias. Hans was a horse around the turn of the twentieth century that reliably computed various arithmetic problems, identified musical intervals, and had a working knowledge of German. His owner, Herr Wilhelm von Osten, would ask Hans all kinds of questions; Hans would tap numbers out with his hoof or gesture with his head toward objects. Hans passed a number of tests with various local citizens and professionals, much to everyone's amazement—until, that is, a young psychologist, Oskar Pfungst, came along. Pfungst discovered that Hans could reliably answer questions (that is, nine times out of ten) only when the interrogator knew the correct answers, but his performance dropped to one out of ten if the interrogator was ignorant of the answer. As it turned out, Hans had not learned math, or music, or the German language, but rather had learned to read subtle cues in the interrogator's posture, breathing, and facial expressions (Pfungst, 1911). Research in the 1980s revealed that laboratory animals can learn to read a wide variety of subtle behavioral cues in trainers that give away the intended answer.

In short, investigators and experimenters can be the source of extraneous variables and error variance that may very well bias the results of a study. We next discuss three major types of bias: experimenter attributes, investigator and experimenter expectancies, and experimental procedures. In addition, we offer some strategies for reducing such biases.

Experimenter Attributes

Experimenter attributes are primarily biological and interpersonal characteristics of the experimenter that may cause differential responses in participants. Examples include the experimenter's age, gender, race/ethnicity, physical appearance, and interpersonal style. For example, some participants might respond more honestly to a female researcher investigating sexual harassment than to a male. Likewise, an experimenter of age 50 might inhibit younger participants but facilitate disclosure for older participants. In another case, the experimenter's interpersonal style (say, unfriendly and dominant) might interact with the independent variable (for example, expertness cues) such that some participants feel uncomfortable or even threatened during the experiment. Another potential biasing characteristic pertains to previous contact between the experimenter and participants. Some participants may feel that having some prior knowledge about an experimenter would make it easier for them to respond, whereas others may feel much less likely to disclose personal information.

In short, a wide range of experimenter characteristics might influence some or all participants to respond differentially in a particular experiment, thereby confounding its results. In fact, several writers (see, for example, Christensen, 1980; Kazdin, 1980) have reported empirical investigations that document that experimenter characteristics can affect responses given by participants on various tasks, such as self-report inventories, projective tests, laboratory tasks, and measures of intelligence (see, for example, Barber, 1976; Johnson, 1976; Masling, 1966; Rumenik, Capasso, & Hendrick, 1977).

In short, experimenter attributes create threats to validity. Consider the following example, which raises questions about construct validity. Imagine an investigator (Professor Kay Tharsis) who has reason to believe that a psychodynamic, insight-oriented therapy group would be more effective in treating bulimic clients than a cognitive-behavioral therapy group. The good professor designs a study in which two bright, advanced graduate students act as experimenters to conduct the group therapies, each lasting ten weeks. Each student conducts one of the treatment groups. Suppose a broad array of extraneous participant variables are controlled (for example, age, sex, and personality dynamics), the treatments are carefully matched, and random assignment of clients is used. Imagine further that the results clearly favor the psychodynamic treatment group on a broad array of dependent variables (such as self-report, behavioral indexes, and therapist observations). Nonetheless, in this example the results of the treatment groups cannot be separated from the different experimenter attributes and their potential biases. In reality, it may be that the two therapists' attributes did not affect clients differentially, but we have no way of determining whether or not this is the case. Thus, if different experimenters are used to administer different treatments, it may be difficult to determine whether the results are due to the different treatments, the different experimenters, or an interaction between the two.

Experimenter attributes can also threaten the external validity or generalizability of a study by interacting in some way with the independent variable. For example, it could be that the results of a study would generalize only to therapists with certain characteristics, such as androgynous men, feminist therapists, or African-American therapists. Imagine the following modifications to the fictitious example just mentioned. Suppose that Professor Kay Tharsis seeks out and uses two female therapists in their thirties with excellent interpersonal skills to co-lead both groups. Within the psychodynamic, insight-oriented treatment, a major therapeutic intervention involves the use of the therapeutic relationship to provide interpersonal feedback and promote awareness of each client's interpersonal style and intrapersonal dynamics (see Yalom, 1985, for such a therapeutic orientation). Again imagine that the insight-oriented therapy clearly results in the more favorable outcomes. Would these obtained results generalize to other female therapists who may not have excellent interpersonal skills, or to male therapists? Even though this is obviously an empirical question, it is useful because it highlights how experimenter attributes might interact with independent variables and possibly limit the generalizability of specific findings.

Among the many strategies that investigators can use to reduce the possible effects of experimenter attributes are the following:

• *Avoid using a single experimenter* for different levels of the independent variable if at all possible, as this clearly confounds the study's construct validity with experimenter attributes. Whenever possible, use two or more experimenters for each level of the independent variable.

• If two or more experimenters are used for each level of the independent variable, statistically *analyze the data for differences across experimenters* to determine whether any differences could be related to experimenter attributes such as gender. Often this is done as a preliminary data analysis to rule out possible confounding variables related to experimenter attributes. For example, McCarthy, Shaw, and Schmeck (1986) were interested in studying whether stylistic differences in client information processing (shallow versus deep processors) would be related to their verbal behaviors during counseling sessions. They used two counselors, each of whom saw half of the participants across all of the conditions. Before doing their main data analysis, they did a preliminary analysis to determine whether there were any main effects or interactions due to the counselors on the dependent variables. No differences were found, suggesting that the counselors did not differentially affect the dependent variables. Thus, the authors were able to rule out differences due to different experimenters and to proceed with their main statistical analyses.

• Because there are currently so many unknowns concerning the effects of experimenter attributes, it would be useful for investigators to *specify the characteristics of therapists used in treatment interventions.* Perhaps over time patterns pertaining to certain therapist characteristics might emerge. Kazdin (1980) suggested that investigators analyze their data for experimenter characteristics (gender), which might provide a useful knowledge base over time. One review of two major counseling journals revealed that at the time, more authors analyzed their results for gender differences than they did a decade earlier (Lee, Heppner, Gagliardi, & Lee, 1987).

• Authors should explicitly *examine the generalizability of their data in terms of experimenter attributes,* and qualify the conclusions in their discussions accordingly. For example, if researchers used only male therapists, then the discussion of the results should focus on male therapists, and not on therapists in general. Gender is a particularly important variable in counseling research. For now, suffice it to note that Lee et al. (1987) found that authors still tended to overgeneralize their results in terms of gender, although less than they did a decade earlier.

Investigator and Experimenter Expectancies

Investigator and experimenter expectancies are beliefs and desires about either how the participant should perform or how the study should turn out. Kazdin (1980) noted that the effect of these expectancies has been referred to as an "unintentional expectancy effect," because even though the investigator and experimenter may not intentionally try to influence the participant, they actually do so unconsciously through a range of verbal and nonverbal behaviors (such as head nods, smiles, glances, or subtle comments). Such bias obviously introduces confounding variables, as illustrated in the Clever Hans story.

Robert Rosenthal, one of the first to investigate this topic in the early 1960s, found that investigator and experimenter expectancies directly influenced how participants performed (see Rosenthal, 1966). Subsequent research indicated that investigator and experimenter bias can influence participants in a wide variety of contexts, such as learning studies, ability studies, psychophysical studies, reaction time studies, inkblot test studies, structured laboratory studies, and person perception studies (see Rosenthal, 1966). Although some writers have argued that the effect of experimenter bias has been overstated (Barber, 1976; Barber & Silver, 1968), it is generally concluded that investigators and experimenters can and do influence participant responses (Barber, 1976; Christensen, 1980).

Expectancies can be positive or negative and occur in many different ways. Investigator and experimenter bias can affect participants or clients at any stage of an investigation, such as during participant recruitment, during data collection, or after treatment interventions. For example, an exuberant experimenter (serving as a therapist) may subtly or not-so-subtly promote the effectiveness of one intervention over others. This form of bias is operative when an investigator's enthusiasm for a new treatment intervention (that perhaps he or she has developed) gets communicated to the experimenter, who then might consciously or unconsciously be too enthusiastic in conducting the therapeutic role within a study. Sometimes the desire to be effective even leads experimenters serving as therapists to break protocol and engage in activities outside of normal therapeutic or experimental procedures. For example, in one study that examined the counseling process, a relatively inexperienced therapist was found engaging in a friendly conversation with the client immediately after the counseling session, during which time the client was completing forms evaluating the counseling session and the counselor!

Investigator and experimenter bias also can influence clients in a negative way. For example, if an experimenter is not very motivated or interested in conducting a study, the lack of enthusiasm can very well affect client recruitment and willingness to participate. Halfhearted efforts by experimenters can result in halfhearted responses by clients. Biases resulting from lack of experimenter motivation can be a particular problem with doctoral dissertations, notably when the author asks a friend to assume total responsibility for certain aspects of a study (such as recruitment, data collection, or monitoring data flow); even most "good friends" will not be as motivated as the researcher, especially as problems arise and frustrations mount. Sometimes inexperienced investigators feel shy or guilty about asking clients to participate in a study, but telling clients three or four times in an apologetic tone that they do not have to participate is not especially persuasive. Another probable source of bias can arise during the administration of inventories to participants or clients; a busy counseling center receptionist, for example, might be tired at the end of each working day, given the added demands of the research, and verbally or nonverbally convey impatience to the final clients.

In summary, there are many opportunities for investigator and experimenter bias to contaminate the results of a study. Experimenter and investigator expectancies can bias participants whenever anyone involved in conducting the study interacts with participants, can bias the results to favor one treatment over another, or can affect the generalizability of findings. Thus, experimenter and investigator expectancies can affect both construct and external validity in similar ways to the those discussed with respect to experimenter attributes.

Some strategies to lessen the effects of investigator and experimenter expectancies include the following:

• Perhaps the most common strategy to offset experimenter biases is to *keep experimenters "blind"* as to the purpose of the study. Thus, for example, an investigator who is comparing the effectiveness of two treatment approaches would not communicate to the experimenters serving as therapists the specific purposes and hypotheses of the study, thereby reducing the probability that the therapists will unintentionally influence participants in the hypothesized direction. In fact, the investigator may want to keep anyone involved in the study who has contact with participants (for example, receptionists, therapists, or assistants who collect data from participants) blind as to the specific purpose of the study.

• Because keeping various personnel blind is more difficult in some studies than others, the investigator may need to *resort to a partial-blind strategy.* For example, it would be very difficult to keep therapists blind as they administer a cognitive-behavioral group treatment for bulimics that will be compared with a placebo nondirective discussion group. In such cases, the investigator might try to keep the therapists as blind as possible, and especially with regard to the specific hypotheses and variables involved in the study. Another strategy is to restrict the amount of contact the partial-blind therapists have with participants; therapists might administer the treatments only and not be involved in participant selection, data collection, and debriefing. In short, even when one can only achieve a partial-blind situation, the goal is to keep the experimental personnel as blind as possible to the purpose of the study.

• Because experimenter expectancies can affect participant responses, another strategy is for investigators to *assess the accuracy of experimenter expectancies.* For instance, an investigator may assess whether experimenters correctly surmise the purpose of the study, or even the general hypotheses. If experimenters have accurately pieced together the purpose of the investigation, the potential bias from experimenter expectancies is generally much higher than if the experimenters have not adequately discerned the nature of the study. Even though experimenters might still bias participants in subtle ways even when kept blind about the purpose of a study, the probability that participants will be biased toward the hypotheses is reduced. In short, assessing experimenter expectancies allows for both an evaluation of the degree to which experimenters have been kept blind and an assessment of the accuracy of their expectancies.

• *Use strategies for decreasing negative experimenter bias due to half-hearted efforts.* Investigators should be wary of recruiting "friends" to assume total responsibility for various aspects of a study, especially if the investigator is physically removed from the location of the study. Given our experience, which suggests that no one will do the same quality of work as the researcher most directly affected, investigators should try to avoid conducting a study in absentia; if it is absolutely impossible to avoid such a predicament, researchers should regularly converse with their collaborators and make repeated on-site visits.

Experimental Procedures

Once investigators have carefully developed a study, operationalized constructs, identified variables, and controlled as many extraneous variables as possible, they usually attempt to conduct the experimental procedure in a constant and consistent manner. A typical study involves a wide range of experimental procedures—recruiting participants, greeting participants, obtaining informed consent, administering instructions, providing a rationale, administering interventions, recording observations, reminding participants about returning questionnaires, interviewing participants, administering questionnaires, and debriefing; and imprecision or inconsistencies in the manner in which the experimental procedures are conducted can therefore be a major source of bias and contamination. Procedural imprecision occurs when the activities, tasks, and instructions of an experiment are not specifically defined. As a result, experimenters might treat participants differently because they are unclear exactly how to conduct the experiment in specific situations. Thus, experimenters introduce bias (or error variance, if it occurs randomly) into an experiment due to variability in experimental procedures.

If, for example, an investigator wants to study the effects of training residence hall staff to be career resource specialists, then the training given to the staff should be clearly specified, and the specific ways the staff are to interact with students on their hall floors should be clearly delineated as well. Are the staff supposed to actually dispense career information? If so, what kind of information? Should they make referrals to the career center? If so, to anyone in particular? Should they administer career assessment inventories? If so, which ones? Should they engage in actual counseling sessions with students? If so, are there any guidelines for top-ics and number of sessions? Should they promote information-gathering activities? If so, what kind? This example indicates only some of the ways residence hall staff acting as career resource specialists might behave. If the investigator does not specifically delineate what the staff should and should not do, it is very likely that a wide variability in activities will occur across the different residence hall staff members. Moreover, the lack of delineation of staff responsibilities increases the probability of systematic staff biases, such as preferential treatment for brighter students, for same-gender or opposite-gender students, or students who come from families of higher socioeconomic status.

Likewise, investigator and experimenter biases pertaining to biological sex, race, ethnicity, sexual preference, age, and physical disability might inadvertently affect participants' responses, either negatively and positively. For example, a male investigator who is insensitive to gender issues and makes sexist comments might systematically bias the recruitment of participants. In short, any of a num-ber of culturally insensitive behaviors, comments, instructions, or procedures by investigators and experimenters might bias participants responses.

Even if an investigator has carefully specified the procedures for a particular study, variability across experimenters can occur for a number of reasons, of which we discuss three: fatigue, experimenter drift, and noncompliance. An experi-menter who becomes fatigued over time, resulting in different performances across participants, can be a particular problem if experimenters engage in an intensive activity, such as interviewing several participants or clients in a short period of time. An experimenter may also gradually and unconsciously alter his or her performance over time (experimenter drift); this is of special concern if an experimenter is involved in repetitive tasks over time. Or an experimenter may fail to comply with the exact experimental procedures over time, perhaps because of a lack of awareness of the importance of some procedures. For example, toward the end of a data collection process in one study, an experimenter began to esti-mate a timed task to "about the nearest minute," obviously an imprecise proce-dure! In another study designed to compare the effects of two therapists, a researcher was chagrined to find one counselor complying with the normal 50-minute sessions while the other counselor, trying very hard to do well, conducted therapy sessions for as long as 70 minutes each! In short, even when procedures are carefully specified, experimenter variability can still occur.

At least three problems are associated with procedural imprecision. First, as suggested in the preceding example, experimenters most likely vary among them-selves in addition to introducing systematic biases over time. Thus, not only is there a good chance that each residence hall staff would engage in quite different activities in the role of career resource specialist, it also is likely that they would act differently from one student to another, thereby adding a confounding variable to the study.

Second, if the procedures are unclear, the investigator does not know what actually occurred. It may be unclear whether the independent variable was admin-istered consistently, or whether other variables might have intervened (recall the discussions of construct validity in Chapter 4 and independent variables in

Chapter 11). If significant results are found, it is not clear whether they are to be attributed to the independent variable or to other variables. In short, if investigators do not know what was done in an experiment, their conclusions are confounded, and it is difficult, if not impossible, to discuss the study's results with much precision.

A third problem of procedural imprecision pertains to the statistical issue of introducing error variance or "noise" into the data due to experimenter variability. Statistically speaking, the variability due to the experimenter increases the within-group variability, making it more difficult to find an effect due to the independent variable (assuming such an effect actually exists). Thus, the independent variable must be more potent to offset the increased within-group variability due to experimenter differences.

Given the applied nature of much of our research, procedural imprecision is a particular problem in counseling. For many experiments, the procedural details of a study can be specified and followed. For example, Feldman, Strong, and Danser (1982) were interested in comparing the effects of paradoxical and non-paradoxical interpretation and directives on depressed clients. The authors trained master's-level counselors over the course of ten hours to integrate a series of paradoxical and nonparadoxical interpretations and directives into a basic counseling interview. In this case, the interpretations and directives were uniform within different treatment conditions. At the end of training, counselors were able to integrate the interpretative and directive statements verbatim at certain points within the counseling interview. However, because other counseling interventions that entail several individuals or therapy sessions are more difficult to control, the amount of consistency that can be achieved across counselors depends a great deal on the type of experimental manipulations involved in the study.

The following strategies can be useful in reducing bias due to experimental procedures:

• Perhaps the most basic strategy is to *carefully describe and make explicit the experimental procedures* involved in a particular study. Putting the procedures in writing both organizes the investigator's thoughts and communicates precise procedures for personnel involved in conducting the study. If experimenters are to make specific statements, it is important that they be delivered verbatim and smoothly. Especially for complex or extended therapeutic interventions, it is often useful to write detailed training manuals that identify and document the specific interventions of treatment; for example, see O'Neil and Roberts Carroll (1987) for a detailed description of a six-day gender-role conflict workshop (cited in O'Neil & Roberts Carroll, 1988). Such manuals are helpful both in training experimenters and for communicating to other investigators the content of a particular intervention.

• In another common strategy, investigators *attempt to standardize the procedures* through some type of structure or even automation. For example, an investigator interested in studying the effects of counselor self-disclosure might encounter some difficulties in examining similar types of self-disclosures from different therapists across different clients. However, video or audio recordings portraying counselor self-disclosures can be developed and shown to participants, so that each participant sees or hears identical counselor self-disclosures (see Dowd & Boroto, 1982, for such an example). Another common example of standardization is to develop a structured interview so that experimenters ask the same questions in the same order using exactly the same words. For example, Josephson and Fong-Beyette (1987) developed a structured interview to identify specific behaviors and characteristics of counselors that were correlated with adult female clients' disclosure of incest during counseling. The structured interview consisted of a list of questions, asked in a particular sequence, in four general areas: demographic questions, questions pertaining to the incest experience and its perceived effects on the participants, questions about counseling experiences during childhood, and questions about all counseling experiences since age 18. Other examples of standardization include formulating verbatim statements for experimenters or receptionists, providing participants written instructions for completing tasks or inventories, developing a specific order for participants to complete instruments, and using structured forms to facilitate the observation and recording of data. The intent of all these examples is to enhance consistency throughout various aspects of a study by standardizing or providing structure for various procedures.

• Given that misunderstandings and different assumptions can lead to important differences in experimenter procedures (for example, duration of counseling sessions), it can be useful to *reiterate basic experimental procedures with all personnel,* before a study begins and at various times throughout the study.

• Investigators can often improve standardization if they *train experimenters.* Such training includes specific instructions to experimenters about their experimental tasks and interventions, as well as role-playing, feedback, and skill-acquisition exercises. One way to standardize experimenter behavior is to carefully train experimenters to behave exactly in the manner desired. If at all possible, all experimenters should be trained simultaneously to ensure they will receive identical information. Training typically involves attention to and suggested guidelines for anticipated procedural problems or participants' reactions. Ideally, experimenters will have consistent responses to difficult questions (for example, "How did you get my name?") or ways of responding to infrequent but difficult situations (such as strong negative emotional reactions of clients, including crying or pleas for additional help).

• Another strategy for reducing problems related to experimenter procedures is to *maintain close contact with all the personnel involved with the study.* Close monitoring of experimenters' experiences with their assigned tasks, especially when the research is just getting under way, often reveals unexpected problems that may require small changes in the protocol or procedures. In addition, actively encouraging experimenters to report problems, ask questions, and identify errors leads to useful feedback and opens lines of communication. It is particularly important that the investigator be present to closely monitor all stages of a study, so that, for example, all standardized instructions for completing instruments be conducted in the way the investigator intended. Whereas novice investigators may erroneously believe that they can sit back and relax once the experiment starts, veteran researchers spend a considerable amount of time vigilantly monitoring and troubleshooting to ascertain whether the study is proceeding as planned.

• Investigators have developed various strategies that *check experimenters' performance and combat experimental fatigue.* Most of these strategies are in essence manipulation checks (discussed in Chapter 11). For example, Kazdin (1980) reported on the use of confederate participants to check on the experimenter. The confederates were randomly assigned to the various experimental conditions and provided feedback to the investigator about the adequacy of the experimenter's performance. Sometimes merely informing experimenters that confederate participants will be used is enough incentive to maintain performance standards. Likewise, researchers can use audio recordings or direct observations of structured interviews or counseling sessions to evaluate experimenters' performance. For example, when Hogg and Deffenbacher (1988) compared cognitive and interpersonal-process group therapy in the treatment of depression, as a check on the adequacy of the experimental manipulation they trained undergraduates to identify components of cognitive or behavioral treatments. After the undergraduates listened to the therapy sessions, they were highly proficient (96%) in correctly identifying the type of treatment. Hogg and Deffenbacher concluded that because raters who did not know the details of the experiment were able to discriminate audiotapes of different types of treatment with accuracy and certainty, the therapists were reliably following treatment guidelines. Another strategy is to discuss the potential problem of experimenter fatigue with the experimenters and then enlist their help in finding solutions to this problem.

• As a general strategy, it is a good idea to *have researchers participate in a wide range of diversity training activities* to enhance their awareness, sensitivity, and skills pertaining to a wide range of diverse issues, such as racism, sexism, homophobia (see Fassinger & Richie, 1997; Pedersen, 1994; Pedersen, Draguns, Lonner, & Trimble, 1996; Ponterotto & Pedersen, 1993; Ridley, 1995; Ridley, Mendoza, & Kanitz, 1994).

PARTICIPANT BIAS

Returning again to our ideal world, the perfect participant is an honest, naive person who comes to an experiment without any preconceived notions, willingly accepts instructions, and is motivated to respond in as truthful and helpful a way as possible (Christensen, 1980). Such participants would not be afraid to be seen in a negative light and would be willing to disclose personal information concerning their innermost secrets. Likewise, within counseling, ideal clients would openly discuss their experiences in counseling, the problems they have been unable to solve on their own, the reasons they chose to enter counseling, their perceptions of their counselor, and the ways in which they have changed. Moreover, ideal participants would be aware of both their subjective experiences and the world around them, and thus they could reliably describe their internal and external worlds.

Unfortunately, we know that participants often come to psychological experiments with preconceived notions, sometimes even resenting their participation in a research study (Argyris, 1968; Gustav, 1962). As Christensen (1980) observed, participants entering a psychological experiment are not passive organisms just waiting to respond to the independent variable; instead they bring with them a host of opinions, preferences, fears, motivations, abilities, and psychological defenses that may or may not affect how they respond in different experiments. We discuss three major sources of participant bias—demand characteristics, participant characteristics, and participants' abilities to report their experiences— and again we offer some strategies for guarding against such confounding variables.

Demand Characteristics

One major source of participant bias pertains to what is commonly referred to as demand characteristics, which are cues within an experiment that may influence participants to respond in a particular way apart from the independent variable. Demand characteristics may or may not be consistent with an experimenter's expectancies; they often include events other than the experimenter's expectancies. Examples of demand characteristics include instructions on a personal problems questionnaire that give the impression that most college students do not have personal problems, a receptionist's nonverbal behaviors that seem intended to make potential participants feel guilty if they do not complete a questionnaire, or an experimenter's apologetic nonverbal cues toward participants in the control group.

Demand characteristics are typically subtle influences or pressures, although sometimes they are not so subtle. For example, in one study of client preferences, clients coming to a counseling center were asked very leading questions, such as "What kind of counselor do you expect to see, expert or inexpert?" Not surprisingly, the results of this study revealed most clients preferred expert counselors, although it is unlikely that counselor expertness would have been consistently cited by clients if a more general question were used. Demand characteristics can occur at any point during an experiment, such as in recruiting participants, during interactions with any personnel involved with the experiment, during the completion of inventories or experimental tasks, and in debriefing.

Demand characteristics operating within a particular study are often difficult to identify. Even though investigators' intentions are to be objective and conduct a rigorous study, they may be unaware that the specific instructions on an inventory might influence some participants to withhold personal information. Likewise, very minor comments in recruiting participants may mask the effects of the independent variable. For example, consider the story of a group of researchers interested in the effects of breaches of confidentiality on participants' perceptions of counselor trustworthiness. In the pilot study, the researchers were shocked to find that blatant breaches of confidentiality within a counseling analogue did not seem to affect how participants rated the counselor on trustworthiness. For example, even if the counselor began an interview by commenting on the previous participant, saying something like, "Did you see that person who just left? Boy, he has some serious problems!" the second participant still rated the counselor as quite trustworthy. Close examination of all of the experimental procedures revealed that when participants were initially contacted, they were asked if they would be willing to participate in a counseling study in which they would talk with a "highly competent professional counselor, a person who is well liked and has a very positive reputation with students on campus." Additional piloting of participants revealed that omitting this emphasis on prestige in the introduction resulted in more accurate perceptions of the counselor's behaviors. In sum, demand characteristics operating on participants are often subtle and unintentional.

Participant Characteristics

Not all participants respond in the same way to different experimental tasks and procedures. Some participants may respond more than others to subtle cues or pressures. A broad range of participant characteristics may affect how particpants respond not only to demand characteristics, but on a broader level to the experimental situation as well. We now briefly discuss four participant characteristics that may bias participants' responses: self-presentation style, motivation level, intellectual abilities, and psychological defenses.

Self-Presentation Style

Christensen (1980) has suggested that a consistent theme among participant motives in psychological experiments is positive self-presentation, a desire to present themselves in a positive light. Some participants may begin to feel threatened if they believe their performance is inadequate or their responses are "wrong"; other participants may be reluctant to disclose negative information about themselves or others, especially if they feel that the investigator will be able to connect their responses to their name in some way (see Kelly & Achter, 1995; Kelly, Kahn, & Coulter, 1996; Kelly, McKillap & Neimeyer, 1991). For example, a young researcher debriefing doctoral trainees in a supervision study was shocked when one of the participants acknowledged that he did not dare report his true perceptions because he "just was not sure" who would see his responses.

Likewise, participants may feel compelled to respond in socially desirable ways, such as reporting positive outcomes from counseling or liking their therapist. Social desirability is sometimes a difficult issue when investigating topics that require socially undesirable responses, such as premature termination of counseling. Former clients may feel reticent to report negative perceptions of the counselor, particularly if they believe that their comments will be disclosed to or cause trouble for the counselor.

Participants with a strong desire to present themselves in a positive manner may be more susceptible to being influenced by demand characteristics. Christensen (1980) has argued that such participants use available demand characteristics to identify the types of responses that make them appear most positively. In short, participants who want to present themselves well may try, either consciously or unconsciously, to be the "good participant" and respond in a way they believe is consistent with the experimenter's desires or wishes. Interested readers might examine Friedlander and Schwartz (1985) for a theory of self-presentation in counseling.

Motivation Level

The participant's motivation level can also be a source of bias. Sometimes participants in psychological experiments really do not want at some level to put forth much energy in the study. For a variety of reasons, participants might feel apprehensive about the experimental conditions, apathetic about the experimental tasks, angry about being in a control group, or simply tired. As a result, participants may fail to appear for a scheduled appointment, give halfhearted responses, or, worse yet, give random responses.

Some clients in counseling research may be motivated to "help" their counselor. Thus, in studies that evaluate some aspect of the counselor, clients who feel very grateful or even indebted to the therapist may be motivated to give glowing responses to "help" their counselor.

Intellectual Skills

Sometimes bias is introduced into a study because participants do not have adequate intellectual skills, such as reading or writing ability. One investigator at a midwestern college was surprised to learn from interviews that some of the participants had difficulty reading the assessment inventories; this was after she had collected data on three self-report inventories! Another investigator gave four self-report inventories, commonly used with college students, to rural midwestern farmers and learned that such intellectual activities constituted a very demanding task to this group, who required considerably more time to complete the forms. Yet another investigator found that a group of inpatient alcoholics experienced a great deal of difficulty in completing a commonly used instrument on college campuses; after defining many words in the items, he learned that the average reading level for this group was below the sixth grade. In short, the intellectual skills of the participants can bias the results of a study and thus require some consideration.

Psychological Defenses

Sometimes bias is introduced into a study because of some participants' psychological defenses. For example, even though some men feel sexually aroused when viewing a violent rape film, it is difficult for most of them to admit such sexual arousal even to themselves, much less to others. Thus, some participants may feel threatened by their responses to certain material and may deny or repress their true feelings.

At other times some participants may feel defensive or paranoid about revealing their feelings or thoughts about sensitive topics (for example, sexual orientation, race relations, or feelings of inadequacy or embarrassment). Likewise, participants such as prison inmates may be suspicious of any experimenter and withhold or temper their responses because of perceived danger. In short, bias may be introduced into a study because participants perceive some real or imaginary threat, which consciously or unconsciously tempers their responses.

Participants' Ability to Report Their Experiences

A topic with a great deal of relevance for counselors is clients' ability to accurately report their internal experiences. (This discussion extends the previous discussion in Chapter 12 on self-report inventories.) Nisbett and Wilson (1977) examined a broad array of data to determine participants' ability to reliably report their cognitive processes. In general, their analyses suggested that participants provide more accurate reports when causal stimuli and plausible causes for responses are salient. In addition, participants more accurately report (a) historical facts, (b) the focus of their attention, (c) current sensations, and (d) knowledge of their plans, evaluations, and emotions. However, a considerable amount of data suggest that participants have greater difficulty describing their mental processes when the situation is ambiguous, such as when participants are unaware of the stimuli that trigger their cognitive responses.

An experiment conducted by Maier (1931) aptly depicts participants' inability to connect causal elements in ambiguous situations. Maier used the "string-problem," in which participants were given the goal of holding two cords (one in each hand) hanging some ten feet apart from the ceiling of a room that also contained various objects. Some of the participants, after some trial and error, would tie an object onto one of the cords, swing it like a pendulum, walk over and grab the other cord with one hand, and catch the swinging cord with the other hand. Voilà, the solution! If participants were unsuccessful in finding a solution, Maier, who had been wandering around the room, would walk by the cords and swing one of them into motion. Some of these participants then would subsequently pick up some object, tie it to the end of the cord, swing the cord like a pendulum, and shortly thereafter solve the problem. But when Maier asked these participants how they had arrived at the solution, he got answers such as "It just dawned on me" or "I just realized the cord would swing if I fastened a weight to it." In short, most of Maier's participants could not accurately report the causal events involved in their cognitive and affective processing. More recent research in experimental information processing also suggests that participants have difficulty explaining the causal chain of events in their cognitive processes, particularly with the passage of time (Ericsson & Simon, 1984).

Even though Nisbett and Wilson's (1977) work has been the subject of some debate, their observations should be carefully considered when counseling researchers attempt to examine clients' cognitive processes, especially within the often-ambiguous situation we call counseling. For example, why clients changed or what influenced them to change in the course of counseling may be a very difficult question for them to answer accurately and reliably. Likewise, as one researcher learned, asking clients how they decided to seek help at a counseling center resulted in a very broad range of responses—some of them incomprehensible! In short, counseling researchers in particular must carefully consider the type of information that can be accurately and reliably obtained about clients' mental processes, particularly retrospectively. Researchers may well ask clients to tell them more than the clients can know, and thus clients may provide misleading self-reports.

Strategies for Reducing Participant Bias

Investigators can use several strategies to reduce participant bias:

• Perhaps the most commonly used strategy to reduce participant bias due to the "good participant" role is to *keep participants blind or naive to the real purpose of the study,* which makes it more difficult for participants to consciously or unconsciously conform in ways similar to the predicted hypotheses. Participants are kept blind by withholding information not only about the hypotheses of the study, but sometimes even about the purpose of the study as well. Thus, participants involved in a study might be asked in some unspecified manner to complete an inventory about their perceptions of a college career center. When both participants and the experimenter are kept blind, as discussed in the previous section, the study is called "double blind." Because the double-blind procedure tends to reduce both experimenter and participant bias, it is often recommended in counseling research.

• To reduce bias due to participants' desire to present themselves in a positive light, a general strategy is to *reduce the threat associated with the experiment.* Thus, instructions on a questionnaire may explicitly state that "there are no right or wrong answers" and that "this inventory is not a test." The actual title of an inventory might also be altered if it is found to arouse anxiety or introduce demand characteristics. In addition, some researchers attempt to reduce threat by explicitly normalizing typical participant fears. For example, in a study of the coping process, participants might be told that it is normal to have unresolved personal problems, and that in fact "everyone has them."

• Several procedures can be used to *increase participants' honesty and reduce participants' fears about confidentiality.* First and foremost, researchers often make honest and direct statements about their desire or need to obtain honest responses to increase the profession's understanding of a phenomenon. In addition, researchers typically communicate to participants that their responses will be strictly confidential, and then they explain the mechanisms for safeguarding confidentiality (for example, coding). Moreover, in research using groups of participants, it is often helpful for participants to know that the researcher is interested in how whole groups of participants respond to the items, rather than specific individuals. Sometimes participants are asked to omit their name from their questionnaires, thereby maintaining anonymity. To ensure confidentiality when a researcher needs to collect data on several occasions and then compare a given participant's responses over time, participants can be asked to supply a code name in lieu of their actual name, or to generate an alias or develop a code based on some combination of numbers related to their birthdate, age, social security number, or the like (see Kandel, 1973).

• Often researchers will *make appeals to participants to increase their motivation level.* For example, participants can be briefly told the importance of the research and its possible outcomes (for example, honest responses to the questionnaires will clarify changes or growth within supervision). In exchange, researchers sometimes promise to mail participants the results of the study, particularly if the study is of a survey nature.

• Sometimes researchers concerned about demand characteristics and participant bias *conduct a postexperimental inquiry.* As per our discussion in Chapter 14, after the experiment the experimenter assesses potential participant bias by asking participants questions about their understanding of the purpose of the experiment, about their beliefs concerning how the experimenter wanted them to respond, and about any problems they encountered. Such a postexperimental inquiry might consist of a brief questionnaire (with perhaps follow-up inquiries of those participants who identified the true purpose of a study or those who felt pressured in some way) or be conducted via direct interviewing. Because direct interviewing can introduce demand characteristics in and of itself, it may best be done by someone who has not previously interacted with the participants. Even though there is considerable value in postexperimental inquiries, they have their limits: If participants have been biased by some demand characteristic but are totally unaware of any such influence, postexperimental inquiry will not reveal such participant bias.

• In addition to withholding information about the purpose of a study, a researcher can *reduce participant bias through disguise or deception.* The purpose of a study can be disguised by giving participants information that leads them to believe that a particular study is investigating some other research topic. Such strategies, however, carry important ethical considerations (see Chapter 5). For example, participants about to take part in an attitude-change study might be told that they are being asked to evaluate whether the university should institute final oral exams for all undergraduates. Likewise, a study involving client perceptions of counselors might be framed in terms of evaluating the adequacy of the counseling center's service delivery. In short, another strategy to reduce participant bias is to provide information that disguises a study's true purpose.

• In counseling research that uses undergraduate students who participate fulfill a class requirement, lack of student motivation or apathy can be a serious source of bias. One strategy to counter this bias is to *perform "spot checks" on participants' performance.* For example, a question can be inserted in the middle of a questionnaire asking participants to "Leave this item blank" or "Mark 'strongly agree'"; participants who do not follow such simple instructions are eliminated from the study.

• With regard to intellectual skills, researchers can and should *evaluate the reading level of all instruments* used in a study and match them to the sample. Typically, such information about the sample can be obtained from personnel in the corresponding agencies or from colleagues familiar with the participants of interest.

• Researchers in counseling must *be attentive to participants' ability to report their cognitive and affective processes.* One strategy is to develop questionnaires based on cognitive processes that are most readily accessible to participants.

Another is providing participants additional information to facilitate accurate reporting of the more ambiguous cognitive and affective processes, such as by enabling video or audio replay or by using Interpersonal Process Recall (Kagan, 1975).

SUMMARY AND CONCLUSIONS

This chapter identified potential sources of bias in participants, experimenters, and investigators that might disguise or cloud the relationships between the experimental variables of interest; such biases are major threata to Kerlinger's "MAXMINCON" principle. The more uncontrolled are the conditions of an experiment, the more various biases are likely to create more error variance or extraneous variables. More error variance makes it more difficult to identify systematic variance due to the independent variables in question; the introduction of extraneous variables makes it difficult to isolate the variables responsible for change. Thus, participant, experimenter, and investigator biases introduce extraneous variables that may distort or disguise the relationships among the experimental variables.

This chapter discussed investigator and experimenter biases that may well affect the results of a study. We discussed three major types of experimenter bias: experimenter attributes, investigator and experimenter expectancies, and experimental procedures. We also discussed three major sources of participant bias—demand characteristics, participant characteristics, and participants' abilities to report their experiences—and described several strategies for controlling or minimizing such biases.

Participant, investigator, and experimenter biases represent serious problems for the counseling researcher. These sources of bias can quickly reduce the results of many long hours spent developing and conducting a study into a pile of meaningless information. The veteran researcher remains vigilant of various sources of bias and constantly monitors the study to detect any biases that might have crept in. Bias is a particularly important issue for counseling researchers because much of our research is conducted in applied settings, where fewer experimental controls are available and thus more sources of bias are potentially operative.

Because minimizing and eliminating bias is a matter of degree, and because the researcher is often uncertain whether various sources of bias are operative, it is useful to qualify the results of one's research (typically done in the discussion section) concerning the possible sources of bias that might have been operative. An increasingly commonplace research strategy is for investigators to statistically test for the existence of various biases and confounds in a series of preliminary analyses. Hogg and Deffenbacher (1988) provide a good example of using such preliminary analyses. Such statistical procedures are recommended, as are frank discussions of other possible sources of bias that were untested.

CHAPTER 15

ANALOGUE RESEARCH

This chapter focuses on analogue research in counseling, which is defined as research that is conducted under conditions that resemble or approximate the therapeutic situation. In an effort to follow Kerlinger's "MAXMINCON" principle, some investigators have sought to reduce bias and extraneous variables by creating tightly controlled conditions that approximate the counseling context. Not surprisingly, analogue research has historically been at the heart of the debate on naturalistic versus experimental approaches to research. Bordin aptly depicted the debate in 1965:

> A . . . decision in research strategy is whether to choose the naturalistic or experimental path. This is a familiar controversy with established clichés, e.g., "Only when we bring phenomena under precise control as in the laboratory can true knowledge be gained," versus "Of what use is precision when it is obtained by reduction to the trivial?" A frozen posture is not helpful to psychology or any other scientific discipline. (p. 493)

The first section of this chapter provides a brief historical overview of the use of analogue methodology in counseling; the second and third sections discuss the advantages and disadvantages of this particular methodology. The fourth section proposes that the external validity of analogue research be evaluated by examining variables relevant to real-life counseling, most notably those related to the counselor, the client, and the counseling process. The fifth section maintains that the ultimate utility of analogue methodology must be evaluated within the context of current knowledge bases and existing research methodologies used in a particular topic area. The use of analogue methodology in social influence research in counseling is analyzed to demonstrate this point.

HISTORICAL OVERVIEW

Real-life counseling is a tremendously complex process. Clients differ, therapists differ, and counseling is such a highly interactive, emotionally charged, and complex communication process that it is difficult to describe, much less investigate. About 20 years ago such complexity led Heller (1971) to conclude that the counseling interview, "while an excellent source of research hypotheses, is a poor context for isolating factors responsible for behavior change. The varied complexity of the therapeutic interaction and the inability to specify and control therapeutic operations make it difficult to obtain reliable information concerning exact agents of change" (p. 127). Heller, a strong believer in the scientific method and its use of experimental control, contended that part of the solution to investigating and understanding the complexity within counseling was to exercise the experimental control offered in what he called laboratory research: "The purpose of clinical laboratory research is to determine what factors produce change, under what conditions they operate best, and how they should be combined to produce an effective therapeutic package" (Heller, 1971, p. 127).

Basically, a counseling analogue is an experimental simulation of some aspect of the counseling process involving manipulation of some aspects of the counselor, the client, and/or the counseling process. In the past, analogues have been referred to as "miniature therapy" (Goldstein, Heller, & Sechrest, 1966) or as a "simplification strategy" (Bordin, 1965).

Keet (1948) has been credited with one of the first uses of the analogue methodology in psychotherapy research (see, for example, Bordin, 1965; Heller, 1971; Kushner, 1978). Keet used volunteer participants and examined the efficacy of expressive (reflective) versus interpretative therapeutic statements in overcoming previously identified memory blocks on word association tasks. Interpretative statements were found to be more effective. It is interesting to note that even though subsequent research did not replicate Keet's findings (Grummon & Butler, 1953; Merrill, 1952), Bordin (1965) observed that "so great is the attractiveness of control and simplification as a research strategy that this failure [to replicate] only spurred further efforts in this direction" (p. 494). In general, however, the use of analogue research has been a relatively recent development within counseling research, a phenomenon Heller (1971) attributed to the fact that analogues are rather foreign to psychotherapy because knowledge in the clinical fields has normally been accumulated in the more naturalistic tradition (as, for example, in the case studies of Freud). Munley (1974) attributed the slow emergence of the analogue to the reluctance of counselors to accept a contrived and highly controlled methodology that might well be too artificial and unrealistic.

Bordin (1965) wrote one of the earliest theoretical critiques of "simplification" (analogue methodology) in counseling research. He appears to have been keenly aware of the strengths and limitations of this methodology. Although the experimental control afforded by the analogue was quickly recognized, some researchers expressed concern about the generalizability or external validity of the results (see, for example, Lewin, 1951; Rappaport, 1960). Bordin acknowledged that the criticisms of "simplification" research related primarily to its oversimplification of the phenomenon of interest; to counteract such problems, he proposed three rules for achieving "acceptable simplifications":

1. Start from and keep in central focus the natural phenomenon that aroused the researcher's curiosity.
2. The degree to which a researcher can safely depart from the relevant naturalistic setting is proportional to the amount already known about the phenomenon in question.
3. If not based on prior knowledge, simplification should be accompanied by empirical investigations of the naturalistic phenomenon it simulates.

Researchers initially used analogue methodology in two general lines of research (Heller, 1971). One line of research involved an analysis of therapies to "find their most potent ingredients and the conditions under which each is optimized" (Heller, 1971, pp. 148–149); this approach included analogue studies of systematic desensitization, Rogerian facilitative conditions, and free association.

The second major approach examined the communication process, particularly in terms of the social influence process. This line of research was sparked by the applications of social psychology to counseling, particularly the work of Goldstein, Heller, and Sechrest (1966) and Strong (1968). The late 1960s and early 1970s saw a flurry of analogue studies, primarily examining the effects of counselors' behavior on client perceptions of the counselors' expertness, attractiveness, and trustworthiness. Social influence research "continued unabated" (Borgen, 1984a) until the mid-1980s and has been the focus of most of the analogue research in counseling.

There are several different types of analogue studies. In reviewing the counseling analogue research methods used in the *Journal of Counseling Psychology*, Munley (1974) categorized the analogue studies into five categories: (a) audiovisual counseling studies, with counselor behavior as the dependent variable; (b) audiovisual counseling studies, with client behavior as the dependent variable; (c) quasi-counseling interview studies, with client behavior as the dependent variable; (d) quasi-counseling interview studies, with counselor behavior as the dependent variable; and (e) experimental tasks not directly resembling a counseling interview. To date, the types of analogues that investigators have used are quite broad, ranging from highly artificial recorded simulations to very realistic live simulations involving multiple sessions.

Despite Bordin's (1965) earlier proposal for "acceptable simplifications," debate over the utility of analogue methodology has persisted. A number of theoretical critiques have addressed the utility of the analogue methodology (see, for example, Gelso, 1979; Heller, 1971; Kazdin, 1978, 1980; Strong, 1971). At the center of the controversy is the questionable generalizability of analogue findings. Goldman (1978) summed up the criticisms best by claiming that the "venerated laboratory experiment has been highly overrated as a way to gain understanding of human behavior as it exists in real life. . . . [T]he laboratory has become so 'pure' that it has little or nothing to say about how people function in real life" (p. 8).

Before entering into this debate ourselves, we first discuss in greater detail the advantages and disadvantages of analogue methodology.

ADVANTAGES OF ANALOGUE RESEARCH

The hallmark of analogue research is control of the experimental situation, primarily by eliminating extraneous variables, controlling confounding variables, and manipulating specified levels of an independent variable. In a counseling situation, the many variables present pertain to the client and counselor (for example, personality variables, coping skills, manner of processing information, expectations, and demographic variables), to the counseling process (for example, counselor interventions and client reactions and disclosures), and to the particular situation (for example, room decor and arrangement, cost of therapy, and reasons for seeking help). In analogue designs, variables extraneous to the particular research problem can be eliminated or controlled. For example, participants easily can be randomly assigned to treatment conditions, thereby reducing confounds from participant variability. Participants also can be selected based on a particular variable (such as locus of control or level of depression), which can be either held constant across treatment conditions or varied to create levels of an independent variable. Therapists' theoretical orientation and interview behaviors can be controlled or even standardized across conditions. In short, analogue research allows for a great deal of situational control by enabling the researcher to manipulate one or more independent variables, to eliminate or hold extraneous variables constant, and to use random assignment.

Along with providing situational control, analogue methodology has the advantage of enabling the experimenter to achieve a high degree of specificity in the operational definitions of a variable. For example, level of counselor self-disclosure could be manipulated to enable examination of, say, three distinct levels of self-disclosure (no self-disclosure, five self-disclosures per session, ten self-disclosures per session). In this sense, analogue methodology often offers greater precision—not only in terms of the variables under examination but also in terms of experimental procedures.

Such increased specificity is a major advantage in isolating specific events or processes in the complex activity that is counseling. Thus, within a laboratory analogue it is possible to isolate and examine the effects of rather small events, including self-involving counselor disclosures, specific counselor introductions, the counselor's professional titles, and the client's perceptions of the counselor (see Andersen & Anderson, 1985; Strong & Dixon, 1971).

Another advantage of analogue methodology is often the reduction of practical and ethical obstacles in experimentally examining some aspect of the counseling process. Many times, real-world constraints such as financial limits and unavailability of participants can be substantially reduced by using client surrogates in an analogue design (see, for example, Dixon & Claiborn, 1981). Given that real-life counseling involves clients with real-life problems, stresses, and anxieties, experimental procedures such as randomly assigning clients to placebo groups or to waiting-list control groups can cause problems. Or certain experimental manipulations, such as varying the type of counselor feedback or type of counselor self-disclosure, may pose serious ethical dilemmas when clients with real problems are involved. Creating a situation analogous to counseling or using transcripts, audiotapes, or videotapes of counseling interactions sidesteps ethical problems with manipulations, especially with clients under some kind of duress.

DISADVANTAGES OF ANALOGUE RESEARCH

The major concern about or disadvantage of analogue research pertains to the generalizability of the research findings, or external validity. External validity is of special importance to members of the counseling profession because the primary focus of our work is on real-life, applied counseling with actual clients.

Sometimes the strengths of analogue methodology—experimental control and internal validity—result in rather artificial circumstances. The investigation may be very high in experimental precision but examine events under such artificial and contrived conditions that they no longer resemble actual counseling situations. It can even become unclear whether the research is in fact investigating the counseling process, or instead variables that are so abstract and removed from actual practice that they are irrelevant to real-life counseling. Thus, the most serious concern pertains to whether the results of a particular study can be generalized to actual counseling practice. The power of the experimental controls may result in the loss of external validity, or as Bordin (1965) stated, "oversimplification."

The limitations of analogue methodology often lead to discussions about the relative importance of internal versus external validity. The inexperienced student wants to know which is more important, or which should be the focus of initial research in an area. Although there are reasons to emphasize either internal validity or external validity in undeveloped research areas (see, for example, Gelso, 1979; Kerlinger, 1986), we contend that both internal and external validity are needed in all research areas, and that the knowledge accumulated on any one topic should result from research that balances internal and external validity. Given that knowledge on any topic will accrue over time, the issue of which type of validity to examine first is often less important than the larger issue of overall balance.

VARIABLES TO CONSIDER IN EVALUATING THE GENERALIZABILITY OF ANALOGUE STUDIES

The basic question concerning analogue research is: To what extent does a particular laboratory experiment resemble actual counseling circumstances? One way to evaluate the external validity of analogue methodology is to consider some of the variables that describe the situation of interest—namely, real-life counseling. Several writers have attempted to provide some criteria for evaluating the relevance of analogue methodologies to the practice of counseling (for example, Kazdin, 1980; Strong & Matross, 1973). We propose that the external validity of analogue research can be evaluated in part by examining the resemblance of the analogue variables to those in real-life counseling. Any given study might vary on these variables and resemble the actual counseling situation to various degrees.

Table 15-1 depicts several variables pertaining to the client, the counselor, and the counseling process; each of these variables can be evaluated as having either relatively high, moderate, or low degrees of resemblance to real-life counseling. Rarely are all of the variables relevant for a given study. If, for example, a study focuses primarily on counselor behavior, then evaluating counselor variables would likely be more important to consider than, say, client variables. For research purposes, it may be useful to increase the specificity of these evaluations by developing Likert-type items to assess each variable. Here we use three rather general categories (low, moderate, and high) for each variable primarily to illustrate varying degrees of resemblance on each dimension. Moreover, variables listed in the table were developed through rational means; empirical research may well identify new variables or rule out some of the variables in this table.

TABLE 15-1
Evaluating the Generalizability of Analogue Methodologies to Real-Life Counseling

Variables	Relatively high degree of resemblance	Moderate degree of resemblance	Relatively low degree of resemblance
Client			
Expectations of change	Client expects treatment and change	Person expects experimental treatment	Participant expects course credit or to learn about psychology
Motivation and distress level	Client is distressed enough to seek help at a treatment center	Person is distressed enough to seek relevant academic experiences and psychological experiments	Participant is not distressed and does not seek help; participant has ulterior motivation (such as course credit) other than seeking psychological help and change
Selection of treatment	Client often chooses therapists or type of treatment	Person selects relevant psychological experiments providing treatment	Participant is assigned to treatments and therapists/interviewers
Presenting problem	Real-life problem typically seen in counseling	Hypothetical problems	None, or some experimental task(s)
Knowledge of problem	Relevant and current concern; high level of information processing and knowledge	Relevant but not pressing concern; moderate level of information processing and knowledge	Irrelevant or new issue; low level of information processing and knowledge
Counselor			
Counselor expectations	Client change	Moderate expectation of client change	Successful role play or interview

TABLE 15-1 *(Continued)*

Variables	Relatively high degree of resemblance	Moderate degree of resemblance	Relatively low degree of resemblance
Role credibility	High status; appearance is role congruent	Moderate level of status	Absence of status cues; role incongruent
Knowledge bases	Broad range of knowledge about assessments, personality and counseling theories, and the counseling process	Moderate levels of knowledge about assessments, personality and counseling theories, and the counseling process	Low level of knowledge about assessments, personality and counseling theories, and the counseling process
Counseling skill	High levels of procedural skills within the counseling process	Moderate levels of procedural skills within the counseling process	Low levels of procedural skills within the counseling process
Motivation level	Highly motivated to provide therapeutic relationship and facilitate change	Moderately motivated to provide therapy; possibly some motivation for experimental change	Not motivated to provide therapy; primary goal is to conduct an interview
Experience level	10 years +	3rd-year doctoral student	1st-year M.A. student
Counseling process and setting			
Assessment	Client is carefully diagnosed and goals established	Person may be assessed to determine congruence with treatment goals	Participant is not assessed; goals for specific individual lacking
Interventions	Specifically targeted to client's presenting problems	Relevant to person's problem	Not relevant to participant's concerns or problems
Duration	Several normal-length therapy sessions over time	A few normal-length sessions	A single brief (10 minutes or so) session
Interpersonal interchange	Counselor and client interact and exchange information	Counselor and client/participant interact on restricted topic or in some defined manner	Participant views counseling scenario but does not interact with a counselor
Client reactions	Client processes the counseling experience and reacts in some way to the relevant information	Person reacts to restricted topic or semirelevant topic	Participant views counseling scenario and responds hypothetically

TABLE 15-1 *(Continued)*

Variables	Relatively high degree of resemblance	Moderate degree of resemblance	Relatively low degree of resemblance
Client change or outcome	Client changes or is different in some way because of the counseling interchange	Person may change in some way, providing the treatment is successful	Participant does not change in any way because the counseling scenario was not personally relevant
Environment	Professional treatment center	Facility that may not offer regular treatment services	Laboratory setting or classroom

Client Variables

A number of variables pertaining to clients or participants directly relate to the generalizability of research findings to actual counseling practice. We now discuss several client variables that illustrate important aspects of clients seeking counseling and then relate these variables to evaluating the generalizability of a particular study.

In most actual counseling situations, clients experience personal problems that they have been unable to resolve (Fretz, 1982). These personal problems typically cause anxiety and distress of some sort, as people find themselves "failing" where they want to "succeed" in some way. As people cope with their "current concerns" (Klinger, 1971), they typically engage in a wide range of cognitive, affective, and behavioral trial-and-error processes (Heppner & Krauskopf, 1987). Because these clients typically have thought about their problem and tried a number of possible solutions, they have compiled some kind of knowledge base (whether accurate or inaccurate) pertaining to this problem. After unsuccessful problem solving and the accompanying distress, a person might seek a wide variety of resources for assistance (see Wills, 1987, for a review of client help-seeking) and may even end up at a counseling center or some kind of treatment facility. Most important, people seeking psychological help have expectations about being treated. They often choose a certain therapist based on a recommendation or reputation, and they are motivated to change in some way. In short, typically clients seeking psychological help enter therapy (a) with expectations about change; (b) with expectations about the therapist and treatment; (c) under distress, and thus in a motivated state; (d) with the intention of discussing specific problematic situations; and (e) with a range of information or knowledge about their particular problems. Although there may well be other variables that depict other aspects of clients seeking help, we recommend that researchers evaluating the relevance of analogue methodology begin by considering client variables.

Table 15-1 lists these five client variables and what might constitute relatively high, moderate, and low degrees of resemblance of each to real-life counseling. A relatively high degree of resemblance for client expectations might, for example, entail a client expecting treatment and change, as opposed to a participant simply expecting course credit (low degree of resemblance). Also related to client expectations is the way in which treatment is selected. Clients often choose a type of treatment or therapist based on their presenting problem or a counselor's reputation (high resemblance), rather than being assigned to particular treatments and therapists/interviewers (low resemblance). Distress and motivation levels may also be polarized; a client is distressed enough to seek help at a treatment center (high resemblance), whereas a participant is part of a convenient or captive participant pool and merely seeks course credit (low resemblance) rather than seeking psychological help and change. Perhaps most important, actual clients have both "current concerns" or real problems as well as a high level of information processing and knowledge about that problem (high resemblance); conversely, participants assigned to a potentially irrelevant task have relatively low knowledge levels about the task and thus represent low resemblance to real-life counseling.

The main point is that several client variables might be considered in evaluating the generalizability of particular analogue methodologies within counseling. Strong (1973) facetiously referred to typical participants in social influence investigations as "client surrogates." This rather good phrase underscores participant substitution and its many implications, all of which commonly occur in most analogue studies. If an experimenter designs a study in which the participants do not closely resemble actual clients, then the generalizability of the findings to actual clients comes under question.

Counselor Variables

A number of variables pertaining to counselors or interviewers also directly relate to the generalizability of analogue research findings to actual counseling practice. In the ideal therapeutic counseling relationship, the counselor is experienced and has a broad range of knowledge about assessments, personality and counseling theories, and the counseling process in general. In addition, the therapist has high levels of procedural skill—the interpersonal and counseling skills required to in fact be therapeutic with a client. The therapist also is highly motivated to provide a therapeutic relationship, as reflected in establishing Rogerian conditions such as empathy and unconditional positive regard, or perhaps through other ways of establishing a strong working alliance. Thus, the therapist approaches counseling with the expectation that the therapy will be successful, and that the client will change in some desired way(s). Finally, the therapist appears to be a credible professional, an expert and trustworthy person who can provide therapeutic assistance.

Table 15-1 suggests relatively high, moderate, and low degrees of resemblance of six counselor variables to actual counselors. For example, high degrees of resemblance characterize therapists possessing a broad range of relevant knowledge about counseling and high levels of procedural skill. Such counselors have a considerable amount of counseling experience. By contrast, relatively low resemblance to actual therapists characterizes interviewers or inexperienced counselors who lack both essential knowledge about counseling and the skills to actually do counseling. The other variables can also be polarized, so that people resemble actual therapists when they (a) are highly motivated to provide a therapeutic relationship and facilitate change, (b) expect counseling to be successful and the client to change, and (c) appear credible and congruent within a therapeutic role. Conversely, a person having a relatively low resemblance to actual therapists may be characterized as not intending to provide a therapeutic and caring relationship, but rather being motivated solely to conduct an interview. Moreover, often the interviewer reflects an absence of status and credibility cues.

In some previous research in counseling, the therapist variables under examination did not closely resemble the role or behaviors of a typical therapist; several examples are apparent within what is referred to as the social or interpersonal influence area in counseling (see Corrigan et al., 1980; Heppner & Dixon, 1981; Heppner & Claiborn, 1989). In the past, researchers have manipulated a broad range of cues associated with perceived counselor expertness, attractiveness, and trustworthiness. One goal of much of this research has been to identify behaviors and cues that enhance the counselor's credibility and subsequent ability to affect the client. A common research strategy has been to examine extreme levels of an independent variable to ascertain whether that particular variable has an effect on client perceptions of the counselor, but all too often the therapist variables have not resembled the role of a typical therapist closely enough.

For example, in attempting to lower the perceived expertness of an interviewer, participants have been told, "We had originally scheduled Dr. _____ to talk with you, but unfortunately he notified us that he wouldn't be able to make it today. In his place we have Mr. _____, a student who unfortunately has had no interviewing experience and has been given only a brief explanation of the purpose of this study. We think he should work out all right, though. Now, if you would step this way . . . " (Strong & Schmidt, 1970, p. 82).

Likewise, in some cases the procedural skills of interviewers have been manipulated to produce interviewer behaviors that do not closely resemble those of actual therapists. For example, a counselor portraying an unattractive role "ignored the interviewee when he entered the office, did not smile at him, did not look beyond a few cold glances, leaned away from him, and portrayed disinterest, coldness, and boredom" (Schmidt & Strong, 1971, p. 349). Gelso (1979) referred to such procedures as "experimental deck stacking" and raised questions about the utility of research on such atypical therapist behaviors. In short, although a considerable amount of information was obtained about events contributing to clients' perceptions of counselor credibility, the generalizability of some of this knowledge to actual counseling practice is questionable because of the relatively low resemblance of the events to actual therapist behaviors.

Note that the focus here is on the extent to which a person in a therapeutic role resembles an experienced therapist in terms of knowledge, skill, and expectations. Trainees—perhaps beginning-level practicum students counseling their first actual client—may at best only poorly resemble an actual therapist, and thus, it is important not to confuse a trainee with a therapist just because they both counsel an actual client seeking psychological help at a treatment center. In sum, to evaluate the generalizability of analogue research to actual counseling practice, it is important to consider several variables pertaining to therapists, notably their knowledge bases, skills, expectations, and role credibility.

Counseling Process and Setting

We must also consider a set of variables related to the counseling process when evaluating the external validity of analogue research. In a real-life counseling situation, the counselor and client typically meet for a number of sessions, often once per week, extending over several weeks. Typically, the client and his or her presenting problem are carefully diagnosed, and treatment goals as well as intervention strategies are tailored specifically to this particular client. Most important, the counselor and client freely interact and exchange a wealth of information. The client is not a tabula rasa, but instead assimilates the new information into his or her existing conceptual framework and reacts in some way (see Hill, Helms, Spiegel, & Tichenor, 1988, for a taxonomy of client reactions). In a positive counseling situation, the client changes in some desirable manner, such as learning new behaviors; altering beliefs, attitudes, or feelings; and adapting to environmental demands more effectively. The environmental context for the therapeutic situation is typically a professional treatment center of some sort, a university counseling center, or a community mental health center.

Table 15-1 provides examples of relatively high, moderate, and low degrees of resemblance of seven counseling process variables to actual counseling practice. In terms of assessment and interventions, high resemblance characterizes those situations in which the client is carefully diagnosed and interventions are specifically targeted to the client's problems. Low resemblance involves a lack of assessment, as well as interventions that are not relevant to a participant's concerns or problems. Analogues that resemble the actual therapy process involve multiple 50-minute sessions extended over several weeks (as opposed to one-shot, 10-minute counseling scenarios). In addition, analogues that resemble actual counseling include rather extended interactions between the counselor and client during which a broad range of information is exchanged, as distinct from analogues that do not include live interactions between counselor and client. The analogue also can be evaluated in terms of how much and what kind of information the client processes; high resemblance entails the client's processing the counseling experience repeatedly over time, whereas low resemblance entails the participant's responding to counseling scenarios in a hypothetical and often irrelevant manner. The analogue might also be evaluated in terms of therapeutic outcomes: Did the client change in some desired way? High resemblance involves change of personally relevant behaviors, thoughts, or feelings, whereas low resemblance entails a lack of change on the part of the participant, most likely because the counseling scenario was not personally relevant. Finally, the analogue can be evaluated in terms of the environment or context of the counseling situation. Analogues involving a high resemblance to actual practice take place in a professional environment, such as a treatment or counseling center, whereas an experimental laboratory setting or classroom offers relatively low resemblance.

EVALUATING ANALOGUE UTILITY WITHIN
AN EXISTING KNOWLEDGE BASE

A common goal in counseling—to facilitate change in clients—implies that the counselor can favorably affect the client to alter specific thoughts, attitudes, and behaviors. The process of one person influencing the actions, attitudes, or feelings of another has been labeled the interpersonal or social influence process and has been considered by some the "central core of social psychology" (Zimbardo & Ebbesen, 1970, p. iii). Initially, research in social psychology established the importance of several variables in promoting attitude change: source characteristics (such as perceived expertness or trustworthiness), message variables (such as message discrepancy or incongruity), and recipient characteristics (such as locus of control or authoritarianism). Subsequent research has indicated that the attitude change process is more complex, and different persuasion routes have been proposed and empirically substantiated (Petty & Cacioppo, 1981).

Strong (1968) initially conceptualized counseling as an interpersonal or social influence process, as he explicitly integrated social psychological concepts into counseling. Since 1968, considerable research has been conducted on interpersonal influence variables in counseling. Investigators have examined a wide range of variables affecting counselor power, or the counselor's ability to influence a client (see Corrigan et al., 1980; Dorn, 1986; Heppner & Claiborn, 1989; Heppner & Dixon, 1981; Heppner & Frazier, 1992; Hoyt, 1992; Strong et al., 1992).

Analogue methodology has been used in a very high proportion of published studies of interpersonal influence. Aware of the advantages and disadvantages of the analogue methodology, Strong (1971) proposed five criteria or "boundary conditions" that, if met, would increase the external validity or generalizability of analogue methodology: (a) Counseling takes the form of a conversation between or among persons; (b) status differences between or among interactants constrain the conversation; (c) the duration of contact between interactants in counseling varies and at times is extended; (d) many clients are motivated to change; and (e) many clients are psychologically distressed and are heavily invested in the behaviors they seek to change.

Although other criteria could be used, Heppner and Dixon (1981) used these five conditions to assess the external validity of investigations of the interpersonal influence process in counseling. The third condition (extended duration) was operationally defined as two sessions. Heppner and Dixon reviewed 51 studies that examined events associated with perceived expertness, attractiveness, and trustworthiness; 29 (57%) did not meet any of the boundary conditions, 16 met only the first two conditions, 5 fulfilled three conditions, and 1 met four conditions.

Heppner and Claiborn (1989) did a similar analysis of the interpersonal influence literature in counseling between 1981 and 1989; 37 of the 56 studies reviewed (66%) did not meet any of the boundary conditions. These studies presented the counseling situation to participants via written, audiotaped, or videotaped materials, which can be considered noninterview analogues. Moreover, these noninterview studies contained an average of only about 12 minutes of stimulus material, which suggests that this research is based on minimal information and initial impressions. Thus, a majority of the interpersonal influence research examined by Heppner and Claiborn consists of data collected in situations of questionable generalizability (that is, none of Strong's boundary conditions were met). In addition, only 12 minutes of stimulus material constitutes an extremely small sample of counseling. Twenty-nine percent of the studies (16 of 56) met three or more boundary conditions, compared to about 12% in the Heppner and Dixon (1981) review. Further analysis of these investigations revealed that seven studies were conducted with counseling center clients during actual counseling. Thus, there appears to be some progress in examining the social influence process under conditions more similar to actual counseling situations; still, relatively little research has examined the influence process in a real-life counseling context over time.

Clearly, utility of a particular methodology—in this case, analogue methodology—is contingent upon previous research and the accumulated knowledge bases. There is no doubt that the analogue methodology is powerful and useful. However, when it is by far the most frequently used methodology, the resultant body of knowledge becomes unbalanced and tends to emphasize one methodological approach to the exclusion of others. In short, the utility of the knowledge obtained from the analogue methodology diminishes if this methodology far outweighs other methodologies in a particular research area. Gelso (1979) discussed this issue in terms of paradigm fixation. In addition, when the analogues used are very dissimilar to the actual counseling experience, additional questions are raised about the generalizability of the results.

The question then becomes: Can additional research using the analogue method significantly increase our knowledge base about the influence process in counseling? Although the analogue can still play a powerful role in acquiring knowledge about counseling, additional analogue studies of social influence that do not meet any of Strong's boundary conditions are unlikely to add substantially add to our knowledge base at this time, and their value in the area of social influence will remain doubtful given the generalizability issues. (See Heppner & Claiborn, 1989; Heppner & Frazier, 1992; Hoyt, 1992; and Strong et al., 1992 for recommendations regarding future research directions in this area.)

Conversely, Ponterotto and Casas (1991) expressed concern that a majority of multicultural research has used analogue designs. However, when they analyzed several counseling journals over a six-year period in the late 1980s, they found that only 12.5% of the published multicultural research in these journals was analogue research. They concluded that analogue research was not being overutilized in multicultural research.

In sum, the utility of any given methodology in a particular topic area must be evaluated within the context of existing knowledge bases and prior research methodologies. Studies that consistenly use the same methodology create a knowledge base that is vulnerable with regard to the particular disadvantage of that methodology. Moreover, when the overwhelming majority of research in an area derives from the same methodology, the strength and utility of the knowledge base is unclear.

SUMMARY AND CONCLUSIONS

As Munley (1974) has pointed out, there are several different types of analogue research, including audiovisual and quasi-counseling interviews. Without a doubt, the analogue methodology can be and often is powerful and useful. In terms of Kerlinger's MAXMINCON principle, analogue research typically allows for a great deal of experimental control to manipulate one or more independent variables, eliminate or hold extraneous variables constant, and use random assignment. The major question surrounding analogue methodology in counseling research pertains to the external validity of the results; sometimes analogue methodology examines circumstances so far removed from actual counseling practice that the research becomes oversimplified and artificial. We propose that the external validity of analogue research can be evaluated in part by examining variables that depict real-life counseling in three categories: (a) the client, (b) the counselor, and (c) the counseling process and setting.

We suggest that analogues fall on a continuum from low to high resemblance to the counseling situation. Given the sparsity of empirical research, the relationship between analogues with various degrees of resemblance to actual counseling is unclear. Investigations that have examined the comparability of analogue studies and more applied research have produced mixed results (see, for example, Elliott, 1979; Helms, 1976, 1978; Kushner, 1978). Clearly, more research is needed.

Nonetheless, as Kerlinger (1986) has indicated, the temptation to incorrectly interpret the results of analogue (laboratory) research as they apply to real-life phenomena is great. When an investigator obtains highly statistically significant results in the laboratory, it is tempting to assume that these results would also be applicable to actual counseling practice. As a general rule, *it is questionable to generalize beyond the conditions or population used in a given study.* Thus, if an investigator is primarily interested in generalizing about clients, counselors, and/or the counseling process, then the analogue methodology must be evaluated with those particular conditions or populations in mind. Depending on the degree of resemblance to actual counseling practice, the investigator may be able to conclude that the analogue results apply to actual counseling. Again, as a general rule, *relationships found under laboratory conditions must be tested again in the context to which we wish to generalize—typically, actual counseling.*

But does this mean that all analogues should closely resemble the conditions of actual counseling practice? We believe not. In our opinion, a considerable amount of information can be obtained about counseling from tightly controlled analogue studies that do not closely resemble actual counseling. This may well be the case early in a line of research, when relatively little is known about certain variables. For example, researchers have collected a substantial amount of knowledge from tightly controlled analogue studies about events that affect clients' perceptions of counselor expertness, attractiveness, and trustworthiness (see reviews by Corrigan et al., 1980; Heppner & Claiborn, 1989; Heppner & Dixon, 1981).

The extent to which an investigator emphasizes external validity, and perhaps sacrifices internal validity when examining events in counseling, depends on the knowledge base that currently exists in that particular line of research. One argument states that if relatively little is empirically known, the researcher should avoid sacrificing internal validity (see Kerlinger, 1986). This reasoning emphasizes the role of internal validity in making scientific advancement. Another argument holds that the powerful analogue methodology can be used to refine knowledge obtained from less internally valid field situations (see Gelso, 1979). In this way, the strength of the analogue (precision and experimental control) can be taken full advantage of, and the results may be more readily interpreted within the existing base of knowledge collected in the field. Both lines of reasoning have merit and pertain to a central theme of this book—namely, that the strengths or weaknesses of any particular methodology for a specific research area are related to the existing knowledge base and prior research methods used in that area. In line with Bordin's (1965) recommendation, we suggest that analogue research be combined with empirical investigations conducted in a field setting to create knowledge bases that emphasize both internal and external validity.

CHAPTER 16

OUTCOME RESEARCH: STRATEGIES AND METHODOLOGICAL ISSUES

Does counseling really work? Is therapy effective? Can couples assessment and feedback improve relationships? Are cognitive-relaxation coping skills training groups or social skills training groups more effective in reducing anger expression for early adolescents? Can the addition of brief group therapy to an academic assistance program improve the academic and social functioning of low-achieving elementary school students? Does teaching group clients to set realistic, interpersonal, and here-and-now agendas enhance group participation and member outcome? These and many similar research questions are questions about counseling outcome.

Outcome research attempts to address the question of counseling efficacy by comparing a treatment group to a control group or by comparing different types of treatment. Outcome research—which is not a category of research designs per se, but rather a specific focus within counseling research—is predominantly conducted using true experimental or quasi-experimental designs. The counseling researcher must address a number of methodological issues, which constitute the major focus of this chapter.

By way of introduction to outcome research, we initially discuss how outcome questions have captivated counseling researchers since the beginning of the profession. In addition, we briefly examine how methodological critiques of outcome research have occupied a central role in researchers' thinking about evaluating counseling. Next we describe the different types of strategies used to conduct outcome research (Kazdin, 1998) and provide recent examples of each of these strategies. The subsequent sections focus on three methodological issues in outcome research: (a) selecting the appropriate comparison group, (b) assessing treatment integrity, and (c) measuring change. We also address a recent controversy in the outcome literature, the identification of so called empirically validated treatments. Additionally, we summarize literature that questions some of the fundamental assumptions underlying counseling outcome research.

EARLY OUTCOME RESEARCH IN COUNSELING

Several outcome studies appeared in the first volume of the *Journal of Counseling Psychology.* The first article in the first issue (Forgy & Black, 1954) was a three-year follow-up assessment of 100 Stanford students counseled with either "client-centered permissive counseling procedures and materials" or "highly structured counselor-centered procedures" (p. 1). In the original study, the 100 students were counseled by one of three counselors, each of whom used each counseling method; satisfaction data obtained immediately after counseling suggested that the students were more satisfied with the client-centered procedures. For the follow-up, 77 of the 100 clients in the original sample responded to a mailed survey containing eight open-ended questions addressing the counseling experience and 14 "checklist" questions. Three judges used a global "satisfaction with counseling rating" for the eight open-ended questions; a "checklist score" was computed by matching a client's checklist ranking to that of seven experienced counselors. Forgy and Black found no difference in client satisfaction for either the type of counseling (client-centered versus counselor-centered) or the counselor. They did detect, however, a significant interaction between counselor and type of treatment. One of the three counselors had more satisfied clients when he used the counselor-centered methods, whereas the other two counselors had more satisfied clients when they used the client-centered methods.

Rogers (1954) was interested in comparing two different counseling techniques: a "test-centered" and a "self-evaluation" method of test interpretation. The major differences in the two methods were the amount of client participation in the interview and the relative concentration on nontest data. Rogers conducted all the test interpretation interviews, alternating between the two methods of test interpretation. The outcome measure in this study was a "self-understanding score," which represented the match between the student's self-assessment and the counselor's assessment of the student. Rogers used an integrity check to assess whether or not the two types of test interpretation interviews were conducted properly. Specifically, he and a second counselor listened to audiotapes of 20 sessions (10 tapes from each method of test interpretation) and classified each discussion unit (a counselor-client exchange regarding a given topic). Based on these tape ratings, Rogers concluded that the "test-centered" and "self-evaluation" methods had the expected differences in session content and process. An analysis of changes in self-understanding revealed that both methods of test interpretation lead to increases in self-understanding, but no difference in overall counseling effectiveness was detected between the two methods. Rogers did, however, identify an interaction between students' level of intelligence and the type of test interpretation used: More-intelligent students had gains in self-understanding with either method of test interpretation, whereas less intelligent students showed gains in self-understanding only when the "self-evaluation" method of test interpretation was used.

By today's standards, the outcome measures and statistical analyses used in Forgy and Black (1954) and Rogers (1954) are rather primitive. Still, a clear continuity is evident between the questions and research design strategies used in 1954 and today. Researchers remain interested in comparing different approaches to treatment, and clear differences in effectiveness across different treatment types are still elusive. Early outcome researchers were interested in assessing how faithfully the proposed treatments were delivered, and the results of both 1954 studies stimulated interest in some of the important topics that engage today's counseling researchers. The differential counselor effects found by Forgy and Black (1954) have been replicated in a meta-analytic review (Crits-Christoph et al., 1991). In addition, the differential effects of type of test interpretation session for clients with different levels of intelligence is a good counterexample of what Kiesler (1966) referred to as the uniformity myth in treatment research. Rogers's study is a clear example of how different clients respond differently to the same treatment.

Outcome questions have received a tremendous amount of attention in the past 40 years (for a partial listing, see Bergin & Garfield, 1971, 1994; Garfield, 1993; Garfield & Bergin, 1978, 1986; Gurman & Razin, 1977; Hollon, 1996; Howard, Moras, Brill, Martinovich, & Lutz, 1996; Jacobson & Christensen, 1996; Lambert & Bergin, 1993; Lambert, Christensen, & Dejulio, 1983; Rachman & Wilson, 1980; Strupp & Howard, 1993; Vandenbos, 1996). Perhaps one of the most important challenges has come from Eysenck (1952, 1960, 1969), who asserted that little empirical evidence supports the effectiveness of psychotherapy. Eysenck's critique influenced a number of researchers to examine the outcome question; over the years, more and more knowledge has been created using ever more sophisticated research methodologies. It has become increasingly apparent that the outcome question itself (Is counseling effective?) was oversimplified. Paul (1967) suggested that a more appropriate question was: Which treatments are effective with which types of clients in which settings? Other researchers, suggesting that too much valuable information is lost when researchers examine the outcome question from a pre- and post-perspective only, have argued for the need of data that examined important events from session to session and within sessions (see Chapter 17 for more details on counseling process research).

Increasingly, researchers have needed Paul's (1967) reformation of the counseling question, and outcomes have been examined for more specific symptoms (for example, anxiety management; see Deffenbacher, 1992) or in specific populations (see Atkinson & Thompson, 1992). Although there is now more agreement that counseling and psychotherapy are effective (see Luborsky, Singer, & Luborsky, 1975; Smith & Glass, 1977; Smith, Glass, & Miller, 1980; Vandenbos, 1986; Vandenbos & Pino, 1980), many issues still perplex researchers interested in the outcomes of counseling.

STRATEGIES FOR CONDUCTING OUTCOME RESEARCH

Kazdin (1996) identified six questions typically addressed in outcome studies, which in turn have spawned six types of outcome research or treatment strategies: (a) the treatment package strategy, (b) the dismantling strategy, (c) the constructive strategy, (d) the parametric strategy, (e) the comparative outcome strategy, and (f) the client and therapist variation strategy. We now describe each strategy and provide an illustrative example from the counseling literature.

The Treatment Package Strategy

The most fundamental question that outcome research can address is whether or not a treatment or intervention has an effect. One example is: Do students exposed to information about gender bias make less sex-stereotyped career decisions? This type of effectiveness question is addressed by the *treatment package strategy,* in which the researcher compares a treatment condition to a control condition using a quasi-experimental or true experimental design. Although this strategy seems simple and straightforward, a good deal of disagreement exists among researchers as to what constitutes an appropriate control group. (The issue of selecting a control group will be explored later in this chapter.)

Horan (1996) provided an example of a study that used the treatment package strategy. He wanted to see if a computer-assisted cognitive restructuring program would enhance rationality and self-esteem (compared to a relaxation-training control condition) among a group of 11th- and 12th-grade students low in self-esteem. The control in this research can be described as a placebo control rather than a no-treatment control. Placebo control groups are useful because controlling placebo effects such as expectancy (the client's belief in the treatment) allows a more accurate estimation of the effects of active treatment components (in this case, computer-assisted cognitive restructuring).

Horan (1996) used a two-group (treatment versus placebo control) pretest-posttest experimental design to test his hypothesis that the computer-assisted cognitive restructuring program would enhance rationality and self-esteem in students with low self-esteem. Pretest measures of self-esteem—Janis-Field Feelings of Inadequacy Scale (Eagly, 1967), Rosenberg Self-Esteem Scale (Rosenberg, 1965), and Piers-Harris Children's Self-Concept Scale (Piers, 1984)—were used to identify the 28 male and 28 female students with the lowest levels of self-esteem. These 56 adolescents were then randomly assigned to either the treatment or control condition. The dependent variables (pretests and posttests) in this study were the three self-esteem scales and the Irrational Beliefs Test (Jones, 1969).

Both the control and experimental interventions were administered over two consecutive days. The experimental intervention was an interactive computer program designed to provide belief-specific cognitive restructuring for students' irrational beliefs. The program contained 13 specific modules, each of which initially presented a vignette illustrating a specific irrational belief (for example, "Demand for Approval"). If the student indicated that he/she never engaged in the type of thinking associated with the specific irrational belief, then he/she was reinforced for holding a rational belief and not presented with a rational restructuring dialogue. On the other hand, if the student indicated that he/she sometimes or usually engaged in the type of thinking associated with the specific irrational belief, then he/she was presented with a rational restructuring dialogue. In this manner the computer program could target the specific irrational beliefs that an individual student held. The students in the control condition listened to two audiotaped relaxation exercises produced by Arnold Lazarus (1970). In terms of the construct validity of putative causes, the control condition was critical because it involved a credible treatment that produced equivalent (to the experimental treatment) expectations for improvement. The control condition, however, did not provide cognitive rational restructuring, the independent variable in this design.

Using a $2 \times 2 \times 2$—treatment $\times$ gender $\times$ repeated measures (pretest-posttest)—design to analyze the data collected in this study, Horan (1996) found significant treatment $\times$ repeated measures interactions for the Irrational Beliefs Test and the Janis-Field Feelings of Inadequacy Scale. This result showed that the computerized cognitive restructuring treatment (when compared to the relaxation training control group) effected a decrease in irrational beliefs and feelings of inadequacy. In addition, Horan (1996) found a significant treatment $\times$ gender $\times$ repeated measures interaction for the Rosenberg Self-Esteem Scale. Follow-up tests revealed that, as hypothesized, the self-esteem of male students in the experimental treatment condition increased as compared to that of male students in the relaxation-training, control condition. Unexpectedly, however, the self-esteem of female students in the relaxation control condition also increased as compared to that of female students in the experimental treatment.

Horan (1996) interpreted the results as supporting the efficacy of the computerized cognitive restructuring program. Horan also suggested that because the variable targeted by the experimental intervention—in this case, irrational beliefs—showed consistent changes in relation to changes in participants' self-esteem, there was a causal link between changes in irrational beliefs and changes in self-esteem. This study provides an excellent illustration of the treatment package strategy for conducting outcome research. Especially noteworthy was Horan's attention to the construct validity of the putative cause (i.e., irrational beliefs). By linking changes in irrational beliefs to changes in self-esteem and by using an appropriate placebo control, Horan was able to rather unambiguously attribute changes in participant self-esteem to the cognitive restructuring component of the experimental intervention.

The Dismantling Strategy

Given that several research studies have shown that a multicomponent treatment program is effective in addressing a particular issue or problem, a researcher may want to determine which components of the multicomponent intervention are necessary and which are superfluous. In other words, the outcome question is: What are the active/effective components of the treatment? Kazdin (1996) labeled research examining whether a particular component is necessary for treatment effectiveness as the *dismantling strategy*. In a study using the dismantling strategy, the researcher compares two or more treatment groups that systematically vary in the components of treatment provided.

Worthington, McCullough, Shortz, Mindes, Sandage, and Chartrand (1995) conducted a good example of a study that used the dismantling strategy. The treatment literature suggests that relationship enhancement programs have a small but positive effect on couples' relationship satisfaction. According to Worthington et al. (1995), this small effect may be attributed to motivation to examine the relationship that ensues from participating in the assessments involved in the research (that is, from completing questionnaires or engaging in structured videotaped exercises). On the other hand, perhaps the feedback about the assessment results actually leads to the positive effects of relationship enhancement programs by stimulating the couples to improve their relationship. Worthington et al. (1995) wanted to see if couples who received relationship assessment and feedback would have an enhanced relationship as compared to couples who received only relationship assessment.

Worthington et al. (1995) used a two-group pretest-posttest experimental design to examine relative effects of assessment and feedback on couples' relationships. Forty-eight couples who volunteered to participate in this study were randomly assigned to either a written-assessment-only or an assessment-feedback condition. Fourteen counseling psychology graduate students served as couples assessors in this research study. The dependent variables (pretests, postests, and follow-up tests) were designed to measure different aspects of the couples' relationships. The dependent variables were (a) the dyadic consensus, affectional expression, dyadic satisfaction, and dyadic cohesion subscales of the Dyadic Adjustment Scale (Spanier, 1976), and (b) the constraint and dedication scales of the Commitment Inventory (Stanley & Markman, 1992). The couples in the two treatment conditions were yoked, which meant that a couple in the Written-Assessment-Only condition would complete the Dyadic Adjustment Scale and the Commitment Inventory at the same times as a couple in the Assessment-Feedback treatment condition. Thus each couple completed the two inventories at three different times: prior to the assessment and feedback interviews, at the conclusion of the assessment and feedback interviews, and four weeks after the completion of the assessment and feedback interviews. The couples in the assessment-feedback condition also completed the Couples Pre-Counseling Inventory (Stuart, 1983) and the Personal Assessment of Intimacy in Relationships (Schaefer & Olson, 1981). In addition to these paper-and-pencil assessments, the assessors also asked couples in the assessment-feedback condition to engage in several structured activities: (a) a videotaped discussion of a topic about which the couple often disagreed, (b) an analysis of typical communication patterns within the couple, (c) an assessment of the couple's use of time, and (d) a discussion of the couple's sexual relationship. The assessors used the information from the Couples Pre-Counseling Inventory and the Personal Assessment of Intimacy in Relationships questionnaires and information gleaned from an analysis of the couple's participation in the structured activities to formulate an assessment of the couple's relationship strengths and areas of potential change. This assessment was summarized in a written report and given to the couple during the final assessment and feedback session. In addition, the assessor discussed the couple's reaction to the written report. The researchers attempted to standardize the assessment-feedback interviews and the content of the written reports by giving the assessors a treatment manual.

Worthington and colleagues performed several preliminary analyses (validity checks) to rule out possible confounds. These preliminary analyses showed that the scores on the dependent variables were not a function of either the marital status of the couple (married versus not married) or the gender of the participant (males and females in the couples responded similarly). The main analysis was a 2 (written-assessment-only versus assessment-feedback) × 3 (pretest versus posttest versus follow-up) repeated measures multivariate analysis of variance (MANOVA). The authors found a significant multivariate main effect for time of testing and a significant multivariate interaction effect for treatment condition versus time of testing. Each significant multivariate effect was examined with univariate follow-ups and simple main effect comparisons. The levels of dyadic consensus and personal constraint in couples in both treatment conditions increased over the course of the interventions. For dyadic satisfaction and personal dedication, however, only couples in the assessment-feedback condition showed significant changes over time. These results suggest that assessment alone can have a significant effect on some aspects of couple functioning. However, analyses of effect sizes suggested that the addition of feedback made the intervention consistently more helpful. Thus, the Worthington et al. (1995) study suggests that assessment with feedback is an important component of relationship enhancement interventions.

At least two design aspects make the Worthington et al. study a good example of the dismantling strategy. First, the authors paid careful attention to the construct validity of putative effects by using several variables to operationalize the construct of relationship quality/satisfaction. Second, the construct validity of putative causes was addressed by giving the assessors a written manual that concretely operationalized the assessment-feedback intervention.

The Constructive Strategy

A number of more globally described therapies have accumulated a wealth of data. For example, an interactional group therapy similar to that of Yalom (1995) has been shown to be effective in enhancing personal growth in a number of different studies (Fuhriman & Burlingame, 1994). Given this state of affairs, a researcher may wonder if components or adjunctive therapies can be added to Yalom's basic approach to enhance the effectiveness of this type of therapy. In essence, we are again asking: What are the active/effective components of the treatment? Research examining whether a particular component, when added to an established intervention, enhances treatment effectiveness is considered the *constructive strategy* Kazdin (1996). In a study using the constructive strategy, the researcher compares two or more treatment groups that systematically vary in the components of treatment provided. One group represents the standard treatment regime, and in the other group an adjunctive component is added to the treatment.

Kivlighan, Jauquet, Hardie, Francis, and Hershberger (1993) used the constructive strategy to test Yalom's (1985) hypothesis that group members who set realistic, interpersonal, and here-and-now session agendas would participate more effectively in group sessions and have better outcomes. In this study, Kivlighan et al. (1993) used a goal-setting training intervention as an adjunct to Yalom's (1985) empirically proven therapy.

The authors randomly assigned group counseling participants to one of three treatment conditions: (a) agenda-setting group, (b) stabilizing interview group, or (c) no contact control group. All group participants, regardless of treatment condition assignment, filled out prior to each group counseling session a Session Agenda Questionnaire (Kivlighan & Jauquet, 1990), an open-ended form on which the group members responded to the following query: How do you plan on using this group session? The eight participants in the agenda-setting condition met individually with a researcher after either session 4 or 5, and again after session 14 or 15. In these individual meetings, the researchers implemented the following structured protocol: (a) defining realistic, interpersonal, and here-and-now agendas; (b) reviewing all the agendas that the group participants had written to date, and evaluating to what extent the session agenda was realistic, interpersonal, and here-and-now; and (c) helping the group members set a realistic, interpersonal, and here-and-now session agenda for the next group counseling session. The eight participants in the stabilizing interview condition also met individually with a researcher after either session 4 or 5, and again after session 14 or 15. In these individual meetings, the researchers confined themselves to asking about the group member's experience to date in the group and making reflective statements; the researchers neither talked about the characteristics of a good agenda nor reviewed the session agenda statements that the group member had written. The eight participants in the no contact condition had no additional contact with the researchers.

Confounds arising from group composition and leadership differences have plagued group counseling researchers. For example, Kivlighan et al. (1993) could have randomly assigned participants to groups and then randomly assigned groups to the different treatment conditions. Given this scenario, even if a group of participants (say, the group in the agenda-setting condition) had a better outcome than groups in the other two treatment conditions, it is impossible to determine whether this result is due to the treatment intervention (for example, agenda setting), to leader differences (for example, competence), or to group composition differences (for example, cohesion). Kivlighan et al. (1993) used a strategy developed by Corazzini, Heppner, and Young (1980) to control for differences in group composition and leader characteristics among the four counseling groups studied. Basically, Corazzini et al. (1980) assigned members in the same group to different interventions, thereby reducing confounds due to group leaders and different group experiences. Thus, Kivlighan et al. (1993) first formed the counseling groups and then randomly assigned two members from each group to one of the three treatment conditions. As a result, each treatment condition had group members that worked with each of the four group leaders, and group members that experienced each of the four group atmospheres.

In this study, the dependent variables designed to measure group member outcome were derived from the Interpersonal Relations Scale and the Interpersonal Relations Scale Semantic Differential (Shadish, 1984, 1986). The Interpersonal Relations Scale measures how often group members engage in intimate behaviors in their extragroup relationships; the Interpersonal Relations Scale Semantic Differential measures a group member's attitude toward engaging in intimate behaviors along good-bad, strong-weak, and active-passive dimensions. In addition to assessing outcome, Kivlighan et al. also obtained ratings of the quality of agendas set on the Session Agenda Questionnaire, which served as a manipulation check. Trained judges, who were blind to the treatment condition assignments of the group members, rated the Session Agenda Questionnaires in terms of how realistic, interpersonal, and here-and-now the agenda was.

A 3 (treatment condition: agenda setting versus stabilizing interview versus no-contact control) × (time: sessions 5–14 versus sessions 15–26) repeated measures multivariate analysis of co-variance (MANCOVA) was used to check the integrity of the experimental manipulation. The realistic, interpersonal, and here-and-now ratings for sessions 5–14 and sessions 15–26 were the multiple repeated dependent variables in this analysis; the realistic, interpersonal, and here-and-now ratings for sessions 1–4 were the covariates in this analysis. The analysis of covariance was used to control for individual differences in group participants' initial ability to set realistic, interpersonal, and here-and-now goals. Specifically, a covariance analysis uses a regression approach to adjust the dependent variables for the covariates; by adjusting for initial individual differences in goal-setting ability, analysis of covariance allows a more powerful test of the treatment effects. The analysis revealed significant multivariate main effects for treatment condition and time. Follow-up univariate analyses and planned comparisons showed that the group participants in the agenda-setting condition, as compared with the group participants in the other two treatment conditions, set more here-and-now agendas at both time periods. In addition, agenda-setting quality increased from sessions 5–14 to sessions 15–26 for all group participants, regardless of treatment condition. These results show that the experimental manipulation of goal-setting training had the intended effect, but only for the here-and-now dimension of agenda-setting quality. Because there were no differences in session agenda quality between the stabilizing interview and no-contact control conditions, Kivlighan et al. could rule out the alternative explanation that the effects of the goal-setting intervention were due only to contact and attention.

Like the Horan (1996) and Worthington et al. (1995) studies, the Kivlighan et al. (1993) study had several clear strengths. As in the other studies, Kivlighan et al. attended to the construct validity of the putative effect by providing multiple measures of the construct—in this case, intimacy. The authors also attempted to establish the construct validity of the goal-setting intervention by performing the manipulation check. In addition, Kivlighan et al. used a placebo control group in addition to a no-contact control to address internal validity by ruling out several alternative explanation for their results.

The Parametric Strategy

In using the parametric strategy, counseling researchers try to identify changes in *treatment parameters* that increase the effectiveness of a treatment. The term *parameters* refers to the structural as opposed to the content aspects of the treatment situation, as occurs in investigating whether increasing the number of homework assignments enhances the effectiveness of assertiveness training. Conversely, researchers might want to examine whether changing a treatment parameter detracts from a treatment's effectiveness; for example, will limiting the number sessions reduce the effectiveness of a treatment? Thus, a study using the *parametric strategy,* compares two or more treatments that differ in one of the treatment parameters.

Turner, Valtierra, Talken, Miller, and DeAnda (1996) provide an interesting example of a study that used the parametric strategy, in which they hypothesized that 50-minute counseling sessions would be more effective than 30-minute counseling sessions. The authors used a two-group pretest-posttest design to test their hypothesis. They used the L (Lie), F (Infrequency), K (Correction), HS (Hypochondriasis), D (Depression), Hy (Conversion hysteria), Pd (Psychopathic deviate), Mf (Masculinity-femininity), Pa (Paranoia), Pt (Psychasthenia), Sc (Schizophrenia), Ma (Mania), and Si (Social introversion) of the Minnesota Multiphasic Personality Inventory-2 (Butcher, Dahlstrom, Graham, Tellegen, & Kaemmer, 1989) as a pretest to describe the sample. A total adjustment score from the College Adjustment Scales (Anton & Reed, 1991) and the Client Satisfaction Questionnaire (Attkisson & Zwick, 1982) served as dependent variables. The College Adjustment Scales was administered pre- and post-counseling, whereas the Client Satisfaction Questionnaire was administered only upon the completion of counseling. The 94 college students who came to the counseling center and volunteered to participate in the study were randomly assigned to receive either eight 50-minute sessions or eight 30-minute sessions.

Turner et al. (1996) computed a series of chi-square analyses and *t*-tests to examine the pretreatment comparability of the two treatment groups. Because these analyses indicated that the 50-minute-session and 30-minute-session groups were not significantly different in their gender, age, year in school, or ethnic composition, the authors could rule out these variables as differentially affecting the group's composition and potentially confounding the results. In addition, the 50-minute-session and 30-minute-session treatment groups were not significantly different on most of the Minnesota Multiphasic Personality Inventory-2 scales. The 30-minute-session treatment group had more clients with high scores on the Sc and Hy scales than did the 50-minute-session treatment group.

A 2 (treatment group: 50-minute session versus 30-minute session) × 2 (time; pretest versus posttest) repeated measures ANOVA was used to analyze the College Adjustment Scales data. The Client Satisfaction Questionnaire data were analyzed with a two-level (treatment group: 50-minute session versus 30-minute session) ANOVA. The analysis of the College Adjustment Scales data revealed a significant main effect for time, but no significant main effect for treatment and no significant interaction effect for treatment × time. The analysis of the Client Satisfaction Questionnaire data also revealed no significant effect for treatment group. Turner et al. (1996) concluded that their study "found weekly 30-minute sessions to be as effective as 50-minute sessions when using a brief therapy model with young adult, college students" (p. 231).

The Turner et al. (1996) study had a number of strengths. Most impressive was the detailed attention to examining possible pretreatment differences between clients assigned to the two treatment groups. In addition, using two dependent measures helped the authors overcome threats to the construct validity of putative causes resulting from mono-operator bias. The major problem with the Turner et al. (1996) study concerns the conclusion of treatment equivalence. Failing to reject the null hypothesis—that there was no difference in outcome between clients assigned to 50-minute sessions and those assigned to 30-minute sessions—is not equivalent to proving the null hypothesis. In fact, the null hypothesis can never be proven. But if the null hypothesis can never be proven, how can researchers determine whether changes in treatment parameters do in fact affect the quality of treatment (for example, time-limited versus time-unlimited treatment)? By the logic of significance testing, the null hypothesis can only fail to be disproven. This is a critical issue, and later in this chapter we will return to the question of treatment equivalence when we address statistical issues involved in measuring change.

The Comparative Outcome Strategy

Once researchers determine that two or more interventions are effective in addressing a particular issue or problem, a logical next step is to determine whether one of these interventions is more effective than the other. For example, a researcher might ask: Is a cognitive-behavioral group or an interpersonal interactional group more effective for reducing eating disorders? Kazdin (1996) labels research examining the comparative effectiveness of two or more different treatment approaches as a *comparative outcome strategy*. As we discuss later, issues regarding definition and implementation of the different treatment approaches, and verification that the treatments have been rendered faithfully, are major concerns for researchers using the comparative outcome strategy.

Deffenbacher et al. (1996) provide an example of a well-designed comparative outcome study. Previous research had demonstrated that both cognitive-relaxation coping skills training and social skills training were effective in reducing expressions of anger when compared to control conditions (see, for example, Deffenbacher, Story, Stark, Hogg, & Brandon, 1987). However, this research was conducted mainly with adults and older adolescents, and the cognitive-relaxation coping skills training and the social skills training were never directly compared.

Deffenbacher et al. (1996) used a three-group (cognitive-relaxation coping skills training versus social skills training versus control) pretest-posttest experimental design to examine the relative effectiveness of the treatments for middle school students high in trait anger. They used a pretest measure of trait anger (Trait Anger Scale; Spielberger, 1988) to identify 63 male and 57 female students who had trait anger scores in the upper quartile of their schools' trait anger score distribution. These 120 young adolescents were then randomly assigned to either cognitive-relaxation coping skills training, social skills training, or control condition. The dependent variables (pretests and posttests) in this study were designed to measure four aspects of the students' functioning: (a) anger, (b) emotions, (c) deviant behavior, and (d) alcohol use. Anger measures included (a) the Trait Anger Scale (Spielberger, 1988), (b) the Anger Rating Scale (Oetting, Swaim, Edwards, & Beauvais, 1989), (c) the Anger Situation Rating (Deffenbacher, Demm, & Brandon, 1986), and (d) the Anger Expression Inventory (Spielberger, 1988). Emotional measures included (a) the Trait Anxiety Inventory (Spielberger et al., 1979), (b) the Anxiety Rating (Oetting et al., 1989), (c) the Shyness Rating (Oetting et al., 1989), (d) the Depression Rating (Oetting et al., 1989), and (e) the Self-Esteem Rating (Oetting et al., 1989). Deviant behavior was measured with the Deviant Behavior Rating (Swain, Oetting, Edwards, & Beauvais, 1989), and alcohol use was assessed by asking the students how many times during the past month they (a) drank alcohol and (b) got drunk.

Both the cognitive-relaxation coping skills training and the social skills training groups involved nine 45-minute treatment sessions that met weekly during a class period set aside for special programs and activities. Both the cognitive-relaxation coping skills training and the social skills training were standardized in manuals to increase treatment adherence. The cognitive-relaxation coping skills training consisted of (a) identifying anger-provoking situations, (b) teaching three specific relaxation coping skills, (c) restructuring cognition and biases related to anger, and (d) practicing the relaxation and cognitive restructuring skills in behavioral role plays. The social skills training involved (a) identifying anger-provoking situations, (b) identifying effective and ineffective ways of handling anger-provoking situations, (c) teaching specific communication skills, and (d) practicing the communication skills in behavioral role plays. Students in the no-treatment control condition participated in their normal classroom and school activities and completed the pretests and posttests.

Because two leaders conducted groups in both treatment conditions, Deffenbacher et al. (1996) used a manipulation check to determine whether in the course of leading the two treatment conditions these therapists were different in their (a) interest in the group members, (b) clarity of communication, and (c) expressed expectations for treatment. In addition, a second manipulation check asked students to evaluate the training groups in terms of (a) their application of skills for anger management, (b) their application to other dysfunctional emotions, and (c) program helpfulness.

One potential confound in such a design could be any kind of systematic differences between the therapists. Thus, Deffenbacher et al. (1996) used a separate

2 (therapist) × 2 (active treatment: cognitive-relaxation coping skills training versus social skills training) analysis of covariance (ANCOVA) to examine potential therapist effects for each of the 17 outcome variables. In these analyses, the posttest on a particular variable (for example, trait anger) was the dependent variable, and the pretest for this variable was the covariate. The main effects for therapist and active treatment and the therapist × active treatment interactions were nonsignificant for all 17 dependent variables, suggesting no systematic differences due to the therapists (at least on the 17 variables examined in this study). In addition, similar 2 (therapist) × 2 (active treatment) ANCOVAs were examined for the six variables constituting the manipulation checks. In other words, the therapists did not significantly differ in their delivery of treatment, and they were equally effective delivering the different types of treatment. According to Deffenbacher et al. (1996), these results suggested that there were similar levels of quality in treatment implementation, and that the treatment appeared to participants to be equal in potency and value.

Four separate treatment (cognitive-relaxation coping skills training versus social skills training versus control) MANOVAs were used in the main analyses for this study. The results revealed significant multivariate treatment effects for the anger and emotional and deviant behavior dependent variables clusters, but not for the alcohol variables. Univariate follow-up tests and post hoc analyses were used to examine the sources of the effects for the three significant MANOVAs. When compared to the students in the control condition, students in the cognitive-relaxation coping skills training and social skills training conditions had equivalent reductions in trait, general, and personal-situational anger, and outward anger expressions. In addition, both active treatments helped students increase control of their anger expressions. The cognitive-relaxation coping skills training was superior to both the social skills training and the control condition in lowering depression, shyness, school deviance, and general deviance.

The Deffenbacher et al. (1996) study is an exemplar of the comparative outcome strategy in a number of ways. Especially noteworthy is the attention paid to the construct validity of the putative causes and effects, including (a) using multiple measures to define the constructs of anger, emotions, deviant behavior, and alcohol consumption, (b) attempting to ensure treatment fidelity by standardizing the treatments in manuals, and (c) using manipulation checks to rule out therapist effects as an alternative explanation for the study's results.

The manipulation checks are particularly interesting because they illustrate both a strength and a shortcoming in this study's design. The manipulation checks suggest that students considered the cognitive-relaxation coping skills training and the social skills training to be equally credible and helpful. In addition, the two therapists appeared to be equally competent in delivering the two treatments. As the authors indicated, however, the fidelity of the treatment implementation— how closely the actual implementation of the treatments matched the specifications of the treatments as established in the manual—is unclear. In other words, did the treatments, as implemented, differ only in ways prescribed by the manuals? Interestingly, even though the authors had intended to use audiotapes of the treatment sessions to perform an adherence check, audiotaping was proscibed due to difficulties in obtaining parental consent.

The Client and Therapist Variation Strategy

Counseling researchers are often interested in determining both the range of clients to which a treatment is applicable and the ways therapist characteristics affect treatment effectiveness. These types of issues are addressed using the *client and therapist variation strategy,* in which the researcher manipulates or varies some aspect of the client (for example, introversion versus extroversion) or the therapist (for example, experienced versus inexperienced) and then compares treatments that differ along the varied/manipulated dimension.

Mahalik and Kivlighan (1988) provide an example of a study that used this strategy. Using Holland's person-environment congruence theory, the researchers hypothesized that persons with more conventional, realistic, and investigative interests would do better in a self-help depression treatment program than persons with more artistic, social, and enterprising interests. Because persons with conventional, realistic, and investigative interests tend to be less people-oriented and desirous of structure, they would be expected to respond more favorably to a self-help depression treatment program. In addition, the researchers predicted that persons with higher self-efficacy and a more internal locus of control would also derive greater benefit from the self-help depression treatment program.

Mahalik and Kivlighan (1988) used the Beck Depression Inventory (Beck et al., 1961) to screen over 800 introductory psychology students for the presence of mild to moderate depression. Their final sample consisted of 52 students who scored between 10 and 27 on the Beck Depression Inventory. The ten predictor variables were: (a) the Realistic, Investigative, Artistic, Social, Enterprising, and Conventional interest scales from the Self-Directed Search (Holland, 1985b); (b) the Superiority and Goal Instability scales from Robbins and Patton's (1985) Self-Expression Inventory; (c) the Generalized Self-Efficacy Scale (Tipton & Worthington, 1984); and (d) the Nowicki Strickland Internal-External Control Scale (Nowicki & Duke, 1974). In addition to retesting on the Beck Depression Inventory, the multiple criterion variables were (a) pretest-posttest scores on the Automatic Thoughts Questionnaire (Hollon & Kendall, 1980); (b) four questions assessing the participants' satisfaction with treatment; and (c) a measure of treatment completion.

The treatment in this study consisted of the self-help manual for treating depression developed by Katz and Miller (1982), which provides a structured seven-week program of behavioral and cognitive exercises. The behavioral section of the treatment program focuses on increasing pleasant events through goal setting, advanced planning, and reward systems. In the cognitive section of the treatment program, participants are taught how to identify negative thinking, logical errors, and hidden negative assumptions.

The manual also had a behavioral self-monitoring component in which participants are required to keep a daily record of their mood and their engagement in pleasurable activities using the Daily Adjective Checklist and the Pleasant Events Schedule. Participants were asked to maintain a running graph of their daily mood and the number of pleasant activities in which they engaged. The researchers collected the Daily Adjective Checklist and the Pleasant Events Schedule forms on a weekly basis, which served as a manipulation check to verify that participants were following at least some of the activities suggested in the manual.

Mahalik and Kivlighan (1988) created adjusted change scores by subtracting the posttest scores on these instruments from their pretest scores. In the main analyses, the authors then examined the correlations between the ten predictor variables and the adjusted change score, completion of treatment scores, and satisfaction with treatment scores. Only the Enterprising score from the Self-Directed Search was related to treatment completion. Participants with higher Enterprising interests were more likely to discontinue the self-help program. Change in depression was correlated with the Realistic scale from the Self-Directed Search and to generalized self-efficacy. Those participants with more realistic interests and greater general self-efficacy had the most reduction in depression. Finally, the Realistic, Investigative, and Conventional scales from the Self-Directed Search, the generalized self-efficacy scores, and the control scale scores were all related to satisfaction with treatment: Participants who were less people-oriented and who had more internal resources were the most satisfied with the self-help depression treatment program.

The Mahalik and Kivlighan (1988) study has several strengths, including (a) elimination of mono-operator basis through the use of multiple measures of the constructs, and (b) the use of the Daily Adjective Checklist and the Pleasant Events Schedule as manipulation checks.

METHODOLOGICAL ISSUES IN CONDUCTING OUTCOME RESEARCH

In this section we will address three methodological issues that researchers undertaking an outcome study must address: (a) selecting the appropriate comparison group, (b) assessing treatment integrity, and (c) measuring change.

Selecting the Appropriate Comparison Group

A fundamental feature of outcome research is comparing one group of participants that receives an experimental treatment with another group—the comparison group—that does not receive the treatment. Even though the logic of this comparison is elegant and simple, defining the appropriate comparison group has raised many thorny theoretical and practical problems for outcome researchers. We review several of these issues in this section.

The simplest and most obvious choice of control groups is a *no-treatment control group.* One of the problems in using a no-treatment control group is the placebo effect, which was first described in medical research examining the effects of various drugs. Medical researchers explained the improvement in symptoms in patients given "sugar pills" or placebos in terms of the patients' expectancies. It is now standard operating procedure in clinical drug trials to compare the effects of an active drug to those of a placebo; to be considered effective, the active drug must produce effects beyond those produced by the placebo.

Counseling outcome researchers have incorporated the logic of the "sugar pill" in their outcome studies by using *placebo control groups* to try to control for the "nonspecific effects" due to expectation for improvement, hope, and frequency of contacts. The participants in the placebo control condition are involved in a pseudo-treatment (that is, a discussion group) that is supposed to engage the participants' expectations and hope. Despite their appealing logic, the practical utility of placebo control groups has been found wanting. For example, in a review of many studies, Omer and London (1989) and Horvath (1988) found that placebo control groups too infrequently offered any viable control for these nonspecific factors. Too often the placebo control group failed to establish the desired expectancies.

Counseling researchers have sought other types of control groups to use as comparison groups in their outcome studies. Recently, researchers have been using *alternate therapy control groups,* which are quasi-treatments intended to be seen as credible by the participants. For example, Foa, Rothbaum, Riggs, and Murdock (1991) used a "supportive counseling" group as the control group in examining the treatment of posttramatic stress in rape victims. Unfortunately, there are also problems with using alternate therapies as control groups. Meta-analysis of studies that compared two or more active treatments for depression found that the allegiance of the researcher was related to study outcome (Gaffan, Tsaousis, & Kemp-Wheeler, 1995); specifically, cognitive therapy was found to be more effective in studies conducted by researchers committed to a cognitive approach, and interpersonal therapy was found to be more effective in studies conducted by researchers committed to an interpersonal approach. Wampold (1996) suggested that this pattern of results is consistent with the idea that researchers might tend to implement alternate treatments with less integrity; any treatment implemented with less than complete integrity cannot serve as an effective control in an outcome study.

Given the controversy about what constitutes an appropriate control group, what should the counseling researcher planning an outcome study do? Clearly, there is no single "correct" approach when using a control group. Rather, researchers should be aware of the strengths and weaknesses of whatever control group they use and should interpret the results of their studies in light of the limitations. Additionally, given the importance of a credible control condition, we recommend that counseling researchers routinely include credibility checks in their outcome studies. Deffenbacher et al. (1996) did this by asking participants in the two treatments to evaluate their leaders (in terms of interest, clarity of communication, expectations of success) and treatments (in terms of applicability in controlling anger and other feelings, and program helpfulness).

Assessing Treatment Integrity: Adherence, Competence, and Differentiation

In early comparative outcome studies, researchers tended to compare two or more different treatments. But a number of studies that examined the relative effectiveness of insight versus behavioral treatments (see, for example, Snyder & Wills, 1989) have been roundly criticized "because the specific treatments, as tested, did not represent their usual application in practice." (Kazdin, 1996, p. 417). In order for an outcome study to represent a true test of an experimental treatment, the treatment must be sufficiently specified and delivered as intended. The extent to which a treatment is implemented as intended is labeled *treatment integrity* (Kazdin, 1996).

In order to specify the treatment in outcome studies, researchers often develop treatment manuals. According to Luborsky and Barber (1993), treatment manuals must contain three components: (a) a description of the principles and techniques that characterize the particular treatment, (b) detailed examples of how and when to apply these principles and techniques, and (c) a scale to determine how closely a specific session or treatment conforms (adherence measure) to the principles and techniques described in the manual. Luborsky and Barber (1993) traced the advent of treatment manuals to Kelerman and Neu's (1976) unpublished manual describing an interpersonal approach for treating depression. Another early example of treatment descriptions that meet the first two criteria is Drum and Knott's *Structured Groups for Facilitating Development* (1997), a compendium of manuals describing the treatment of several clinical problems. The treatment manuals developed to date involve far more precise specification of the experimental treatment. Still, treatment manuals in and of themselves do not guarantee that the treatment in any particular study is delivered as the researcher intended.

Adherence measures attempt to assess the degree of match between the intended treatment (as described in the manual) and the treatment actually delivered in a study. Although at least rudimentary treatment manuals have existed for some 25 years, only recently have researchers begun to develop adherence measures that are associated with specific treatment manuals. One adherence measure that has been used in several counseling studies is Butler, Henry, and Strupp's (1992) Vanderbilt Therapeutic Strategies Scale. Developed to measure adherence to Strupp and Binder's (1984) treatment manual, *Psychotherapy in a New Key,* the Vanderbilt Therapeutic Strategies Scale consists of two scales, labeled Psychodynamic Interviewing Style (with 12 items) and Time-Limited Dynamic Psychotherapy (TLDP) Specific Strategies (with 9 items). Trained observers typically watch a videotape or listen to an audiotape of a counseling session and then use the Vanderbilt Therapeutic Strategies Scale to indicate the degree to which each of the 21 items was descriptive of what the therapist had observed.

By using scales like the Vanderbilt Therapeutic Strategies Scale, researchers can begin to obtain an assessment of how well the treatment implemented in a study matches the treatment described in the manual. Measuring adherence, however, is not completely straightforward. One incompletely resolved issue concerns who should perform the ratings of adherence. Some authors propose that ratings of adherence are best done by experienced clinicians who are "experts" in the treatment model being rated (see, for example, Luborsky & Barber, 1993); other authors contend that clients can use treatment adherence measures to report on counselor session behavior (see, for example, Iberg, 1991); still others maintain that the counselor's supervisor is in the best position to assess adherence (see, for example, DeRubeis, Hollon, Evans, & Bemis, 1982). Unfortunately, researchers have not determined the relative strengths and weaknesses of different classes of raters. At a minimum, however, outcome studies should have a treatment manual for the experimental interventions and adherence ratings from at least one source. Clearly, obtaining adherence ratings from multiple sources enhances the construct validity of the experimental treatment.

It is probably not sufficient to rate adherence without also examining the quality of treatment implementation. Counselors may follow all of the principles outlined in the manual and perform all of the associated techniques, but they might not apply the principles and techniques skillfully. Barber and Crits-Christoph (1996) use the term *competence* to refer to the skillful application of principles and techniques, to such things as the correctness and appropriate timing of an interpretation or the correct identification of cognitive distortions. Barber and Crits-Christoph (1996) maintain that measures designed to capture counselor adherence have often confounded adherence to the principles and techniques described in the manual with the competent implementation of these techniques. To address the confounding of adherence and competence, Barber and Crits-Christoph (1996) recently developed a measure of both adherence and competence designed to accompany Luborsky's (1984) manualized expressive-supportive approach. Their research showed that adherence and competence were related, but not identical, constructs (adherence and competence had 25% overlapping variance). In a subsequent study using this measure, Barber, Crits-Christoph, and Luborsky (1996) found that competence showed a stronger relationship to treatment outcome than did adherence.

As with adherence, however, it is not absolutely clear who should determine the competence of the counselor. The conventional wisdom is that only experienced clinicians who are experts in a particular treatment can accurately rate how competently that treatment was delivered. Barber and Crits-Christoph (1996) followed this conventional wisdom when rating competence in supportive-expressive counseling. At least one study, however, asked clients to rate their counselor's competence on three dimensions: facilitating interventions, detracting style, and detracting effect (Thompson & Hill, 1993). Moreover, Thompson and Hill found that facilitating interventions was related to session depth and treatment satisfaction, detracting style was related to treatment satisfaction, and detracting effect was related to symptom change and to treatment satisfaction. At present, both expert-judged (Barber, Crits-Christoph, & Luborsky, 1996) and client-judged (Thompson & Hill, 1993) competence have been shown to relate to aspects of counseling outcome. Unfortunately, no studies have compared competence judgments made by experts and clients. Until further research clarifies the relative efficacy of client- or expert-rated competence judgments, counseling researchers lack an empirical basis for deciding how to best rate counselor competence. Nonetheless, it seem clear that competence ratings are an important part in determining treatment integrity and need to be conducted.

When doing a comparative outcome study, the researcher not only must determine that the treatment manuals were adhered to and the treatments delivered competently, but also that the treatments were differentiated. Kazdin (1996) defines *differentiation* as "whether two or more treatments differed from each other along critical dimensions that are central to their execution" (p. 416). If, for example, a researcher wanted to compare the relative effectiveness of Strupp and Binder's (1984) Time-Limited Dynamic Psychotherapy and Beck et al.'s (1979) cognitive therapy for the treatment of depression, she or he must show that the two treatments, as delivered, differed along the critical dimensions that distinguish the two theories. Specifically, the Time-Limited Dynamic Psychotherapy manual and the associated Vanderbilt Therapeutic Strategies Scale specify that the counselor identifying a maladaptive interpersonal cycle is a critical component of the model. Therefore, the researcher should expect the counselors who use the Time-Limited Dynamic Psychotherapy model to rate high on this component of the Vanderbilt Therapeutic Strategies Scale; conversely, the counselors who use the cognitive therapy model would be expected to rate low on this component of the Vanderbilt Therapeutic Strategies Scale.

This example suggests that differentiation can often be assessed by applying the adherence scales from two different approaches to treatments from both approaches. To demonstrate differentiation, a treatment session must rate highly on its own treatment adherence measure and have low ratings on the adherence measure from the other treatment.

To summarize, the assessment of treatment integrity involves a complex and multidimensional process. First the treatment must be explicitly specified in a treatment manual so that counselors can know how to deliver the treatment, and so that future researchers can replicate the treatment. Next the researcher must demonstrate that the treatment as delivered adhered to the specifications of the manual and was delivered in a competent manner. Finally, in comparative outcome, dismantling, constructive, or parametric studies, the researcher must also show that the treatments compared differed along the crucial dimensions studied. As with many areas of counseling research, the assessment of treatment integrity is not without controversy. For example, Wampold (1996) has offered several criticisms of the standardization of treatments through treatment manuals. First, he argued that the quest to standardize treatments may distract researchers' attention away from more important areas of research focus, that the effects of treatment type pale when compared to therapist effects. By attempting to standardize treatments (and, by consequence, therapists), we may be getting rid of the most potent source (therapist differences) of outcome effects. Second, Wampold noted that adherence to treatment manuals is inconsistently related to treatment outcome. In fact, some studies suggest that training counselors to adhere to a treatment manual may inhibit some areas of their functioning (Henry, Strupp, Butler, Schacht, & Binder, 1993). In short, although the assessment of treatment integrity is crucial, many methodological issues remain to be resolved.

Measuring Change

As noted by Francis et al. (1991), measuring and analyzing change plays a central role in many areas of study, but especially when trying to identify counseling outcomes. There is a voluminous literature dealing with the measurement of change (see, for example, Willett, 1988). Although we cannot review this entire literature here, three areas have particular relevance to counseling researchers: (a) clinical versus statistical significance, (b) hypothesis testing, and (c) growth curve analysis. In the following subsections we discuss how each of these issues relates to the conduct of counseling outcome research.

Clinical Versus Statistical Significance

A number of authors have argued that statistical significance is not a good indicator of treatment effectiveness. Lambert and Hill (1995) asserted that a well-designed outcome study can achieve statistically significant differences between treatment groups without producing real-life differences in enhanced functioning. For example, even though a date rape prevention program may result in a small but statistically significant decrease in rape myth acceptance when compared to a no-treatment control group, it is not clear that this small change makes any difference in the likelihood that one of the program's participants will commit a date rape. To address these types of practical issues, Jacobson, Follette, and Revenstorf (1984) and Jacobson and Truax (1991) introduced methods for calculating clinical significance.

As defined by Jacobson and Truax (1991), *clinical significance* is the degree to which an individual client improves after treatment. Two criteria are used to define improvement or recovery for a particular client. First, to be labeled as recovered, a participant's posttest score on a particular measure (for example, Inventory of Interpersonal Problems) must fall within a functional (as opposed to a dysfunctional) distribution of scores, given that the participant's pretest score on the particular measure fell within a dysfunctional distribution of scores. The second criterion for determining improvement is labeled the *reliable change index,* in which the pretest to posttest difference observed for a client is greater than the change that would be expected due to chance alone. The formula used to calculate the reliable change index is: (Pretest − Posttest) ÷ Standard Error of Measurement. A score greater than 1 on this index indicates that there was more change from pretest to posttest than the measurement error in the instrument. Using these criteria, an individual participant in a treatment study is considered to have improved if her/his posttest score is in the functional distribution and her/his reliable change index is greater than 1. In a study calculating clinical significance for a treatment group versus control group design, the researcher would compare the percentage of participants in the treatment group who had improved versus the percentage of participants in the control group who had improved.

Paivio and Greenberg (1995) used the two criteria proposed by Jacobson and Truax (1991) when examining the effects of "the empty chair" on resolving "unfinished business." Thirty-four clients completed either 12 weeks of counseling using the empty-chair technique or an attention-placebo minimal treatment condition. Although several measures in the outcome battery were used in this research, only the SCL-90-R (Derogatis, 1983) and the Inventory of Interpersonal Problems (Horowitz, Rosenberg, Baer, Ureno, & Villasenor, 1988) were used in calculating clinically significant change. Paivio and Greenberg (1995) averaged the SCL-90-R and the Inventory of Interpersonal Problems scores in their calculation of clinically significant change. Using normative information, Paivio and Greenberg determined that before treatment, 44% of their clients in both experimental conditions were in the functional distribution of SCL-90-R and Inventory of Interpersonal Problems scores. After treatment, however, 89% of the clients receiving 12 weeks of counseling using the empty-chair technique were in the functional distribution, whereas only 59% of the clients in the attention-placebo minimal treatment condition were in this distribution. The improvement rate for the counseling using the empty-chair technique was 45% (89% at posttest – 44% at pretest), whereas the improvement rate for the attention-placebo minimal treatment condition was only 15% (59% at posttest – 44% at pretest). In terms of the reliable change index, 73% of the clients in the counseling using the empty-chair technique had a reliable change index greater than 1, but only 10% of the clients in the attention-placebo minimal treatment condition had reliable change indexes greater than 1. These results led Paivio and Greenberg to conclude that the counseling using the empty-chair technique resulted in clinically significant changes in client unfinished business.

Recently, Tingey, Lambert, Burlingame, and Hansen (1996) presented an extension of Jacobson and colleagues' method for calculating clinically significant change. At the heart of this new method is an expanded definition: Tingey et al. (1996) defined clinically significant change as "movement from one socially relevant sample to another based on the impact factor selected, rather than (moving) from a 'dysfunctional' to a 'functional' distribution as proposed by Jacobson and Revenstorf (1988)" (p. 111). Tingey et al. proposed that multiple samples be used to form a continuum, and that a client's pretest-posttest movement (or lack of movement) along this continuum be used to identify clinically significant change.

According to Tingey et al., five steps are involved in establishing such a continuum:

> 1) selecting a specifying factor that is defined by a reliable outcome instrument; 2) identifying an impact factor (a behavior relevant to society that covaries with different levels of the specifying factor); 3) determining the statistical distinctiveness of these socially relevant samples; 4) calculating RCI's (Reliable Change Indices) for all possible sample pairs; and 5) calculating cutoff points between adjacent sample pairs along the continuum. (Tingey et al., 1996, p. 114)

For example, for step 1, Tingey et al. used the SCL-90-R (Derogatis, 1983) as the specifying factor. According to these authors, one important factor that covaries with the SCL-90-R is the type of psychological treatment a person receives. Consequently, for step 2 they identified four samples of people that differed in the intensity of psychological treatment they were receiving: (a) asymptomatic (a specially collected healthy sample), (b) mildly symptomatic (unscreened community

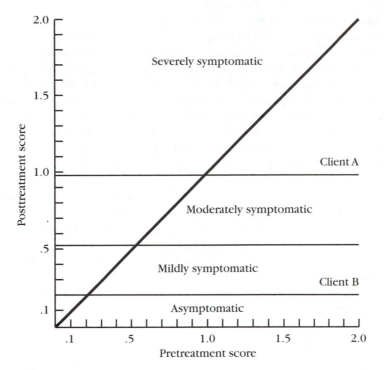

FIGURE 16-1
Cut offs between the normative samples (horizontal lines). Diagonal represents point of no pre- and post-treatment change.

adults), (c) moderately symptomatic (people receiving outpatient counseling), and (d) severely symptomatic (people receiving inpatient counseling). Next, for step 3, Tingey et al. utilized t and "d" tests to ascertain whether or not the four identified samples were in fact distinct. In this example, their tests showed the four samples to be distinct. RCIs were calculated for the ten possible pairs of samples (step 4). Finally, the authors established cutoff points and confidence intervals for each pair of adjacent samples (step 5); these cutoff points represent the point at which a score is more likely to be in one distribution as opposed to the adjacent distribution.

One of the most exciting features of Tingey et al.'s (1996) approach is that any researcher who uses the SCL-90-R as a pretest-posttest measure can use the information provided in the article to calculate the amount of clinically significant change for each individual client in her/his study. In addition, clinicians can use the information to ascertain whether their clients are making clinically significant change. To illustrate the usefulness of Tingey et al.'s calculations, Figure 16-1 both illustrates the cutoff points identified in the article and plots the pretest-posttest changes for two clients involved in the Missouri Psychoanalytic Psychotherapy Research Project (Patton, Kivlighan, & Multon, 1997). In this project, community clients seen for 20 sessions of psychoanalytically oriented counseling were given an extensive battery of tests prior to and upon completion of counseling; one of these measures was the SCL-90-R. As can be seen in the figure, Client A made a substantial and clinically significant improvement, as indicated by movement from the severely symptomatic distribution at pretest to the asymptomatic distribution at posttest. By contrast, Client B, who both began and ended treatment in the moderately symptomatic range, exhibited no clinically significant change.

Lambert and his colleagues (Condon & Lambert, 1994; Grundy & Lambert, 1994a; Seggar & Lambert, 1994) have used this method of defining clinical significance with several other well-validated psychometric instruments (State-Trait Anxiety Inventory, Auchenbach Child Behavior Checklist, and Beck Depression Inventory). However, an attempt to define clinically significant change groups for the Hamilton Rating Scale for Depression was unsuccessful because the authors could not find appropriate samples (Grundy & Lambert, 1994b). Even though the method described by Tingey et al. (1996) is an exciting extension of Jacobson et al.'s (1984) methodology, for the most part the instruments used are not commonly used in counseling outcome research. It would be interesting to examine this method with instruments such as the Career Beliefs Inventory (Krumboltz, 1991) or the Rosenberg Self Esteem Scale (Rosenberg, 1965).

The idea of calculating clinically significant change is very appealing. Clearly, counseling researchers would like to know that their treatment interventions are making a real difference. Even though it would be very useful if the profession had a specified standard for determining the clinical significance of a study's results, the measurement of clinical significance has not been widely embraced by counseling researchers.

Few studies published in counseling-related journals have yet provided calculations of statistically significant change, perhaps in part because this measure is not without psychometric problems. In order to determine if a score is in a functional or a dysfunctional distribution, the researcher must have good psychometric information about a test. At the very least, the test must have been administered to one population clinically defined as dysfunctional, and to another clinically defined as normal. For more sophisticated analyses of clinical change, several different population groups must be identified. For example, Tingey et al. (1996) identified four different samples (asymptomatic, and mildly, moderately, and severely disturbed on the SCL-90-R) in their analysis of clinically significant change. Unfortunately, for many measures used in psychotherapy outcome research, this type of normative data is not readily available. Even when a measure has been used with different samples, the adequacy of the sampling procedure is often questionable. Therefore, a great deal of additional psychometric work must be done before the assessment of clinical significance can become a standard practice in most counseling outcome studies.

Nonetheless, we contend that calculations of the clinical significance of change should be used more widely than currently occurs in counseling research. For example, the population of students that seeks help at a career counseling center is probably more undecided about a career than a population of students in general; although not labeled as dysfunctional, the career center population is one normative group that could be used in a study examining the clinical significance of a career exploration intervention.

Hypothesis Testing

When researchers use the parametric strategy, they often want to show that change in one of the treatment parameters does not affect the quality of the treatment. For example, advocates of time-limited treatment may seek to demonstrate that the effectiveness of time-limited treatment is equivalent to that of time-unlimited treatment. Even though researchers using the comparative outcome strategy often want to show that one treatment is superior to others, Wampold (1996) asserted that it is far more likely that all treatments are equally efficacious. He labeled this situation the *uniform efficacy supposition*. Under the standard hypothesis testing paradigm, it is impossible to show that two treatments are equivalent in their effects because, as we indicated earlier in this chapter, it is impossible to prove the null hypothesis. Even if two treatments are not equally efficacious, the differences between the treatments may be so small as to be of no practical significance. In this case, it would be a waste of resources to pursue elegantly designed studies in attempts to demonstrate these trivial differences in effectiveness.

As Wampold (1996) noted, there is an alternative to the traditional hypothesis testing strategy, which he labeled *equivalence testing*. A researcher can specify, a priori, the smallest difference between treatments that can be considered a nontrivial difference, a difference termed δ. Once δ has been specified, then a null hypothesis can be formulated—that the difference between treatments is greater than δ. If this null hypothesis is rejected, then the researcher can conclude that the two treatments are essentially equivalent. We strongly recommend that researchers conducting parametric or comparative outcome studies use the equivalence testing strategy when conducting statistical tests on their data.

Growth Curve Analysis

In outcome research, counseling researchers are interested in measuring change, typically by using a pretest-posttest design. Many authors have concluded that change is difficult to measure, but this conclusion is based on viewing change as simply an incremental difference between pretest and posttest scores (Willett, Ayoub, & Robinson, 1991). When only a pretest and a posttest are used, the simplest and most straightforward estimate of change for each individual is the observed difference score (pretest – posttest) (Willett et al., 1991). Several authors argue that the observed difference score is not an appropriate measure of change because it is unreliable and correlated with initial status (see, for example, Linn & Slinde, 1977). Willett (1988) has shown, however, that these objections are based on misunderstandings of change. In fact, Willett et al. (1991) concluded that the observed difference score "is unbiased, often valid, and not necessarily unreliable" (p. 39). However, the observed difference score calculated from a pretest-posttest design has a major shortcoming.

The problem with the observed difference score calculated from a pretest-posttest design is that it is a gross estimate of an ongoing process. "Taking a 'snapshot' of status before and after cannot reveal the intricacies of ongoing process of growth" (Willett et al., 1991, p. 39). Using only a pretest and posttest to measure the process of change is like devising a scale with only two items. It is as difficult to get a reliable estimate of change from only two data points (pretest and posttest) as it is to get high internal consistency from a scale that has only two items. Francis et al. (1991) suggested that researchers change their conception of what change entails. Rather than seeing change as "simply . . . taking place between arbitrary time points," researchers should view change as "reflecting a continuous process that underlies performance" (Francis et al., 1991, p. 28).

Viewing change as a continuous process has important implications for both data collection and analysis. In terms of data collection, measuring the process of change involves collecting data at least three times. With more data collection points, the researcher can derive a better estimate of the process of change. In terms of data analysis, counseling researchers can move beyond using repeated measures analyses of variance to using growth modeling, or hierarchical linear modeling (HLM; Bryk, Raudenbush, Seltzer, & Congdon, 1989).

As discussed by Francis et al. (1991), growth modeling allows for "the study of change on interindividual differences in intraindividual change" (p. 30), as opposed to an incremental analysis of growth whereby an index of change is calculated using measures taken only twice. In growth modeling, "behavior is best described by a continuous time-dependent curve that is characterized by a smaller set of parameters" (p. 30). Consequently, change is quantified by a series of growth parameters that measure the "relationship between behavior and time" (p. 30).

Growth modeling differs from trend analysis in ANOVA or MANOVA in that individuals, not group means, are being modeled. Variance in the individual growth parameters (that is, across participants) can then be plotted against correlates of change. Specifically, this type of analysis allows for "a different set of research questions" (Francis et al., 1991, p. 31) than those found in more traditional research (that is, that based on group means only). For a detailed discussion of the statistical aspects of growth models, see Arnold (1992), Bryk and Raudenbush (1992), Francis et al. (1991), and Raudenbush and Chan (1993).

Willett et al. (1991) is one example of a study that used the client and therapist variation strategy, the parametric strategy, and growth modeling to examine change in family functioning. Specifically, they examined the effects of Project Good Start, a program designed to prevent child abuse and neglect. The dependent or outcome variable in their analysis was a rating of family functioning on the Family Function Scale (Ayoub & Jacewitz, 1982). Social workers used the Family Function Scale to rate family functioning on a monthly basis over 3 to 29 months (the average family in the project was rated nine times). Unlike repeated measures analysis of variance, which has problems with missing data, growth modeling can easily accommodate repeated measures that vary in length.

The Family Problem Checklist (Ayoub & Jacewitz, 1982) was used to identify subtypes of families at the onset of treatment. Families were classified as having no or considerable problems with violence/maltreatment, and as having either low, moderate, or high levels of distressed parenting. The treatment parameter examined in this study was time in treatment.

On the seven-point scale used to rate family functioning, the average level of functioning for families entering the program was 4.70. According to Willett et al.

(1991), a rating of 4 meant that the family accepted support but had trouble following through on suggestions, whereas a rating of 5 meant that the family was functioning well but needed continuous outside support. Linear growth rates for family functioning showed a rather large variance for individual families. For some families, functioning increased over time, but in other families functioning decreased. Overall, family functioning tended to increase across the measurement periods; specifically, for every month in treatment, family functioning increased by an estimated 0.028 scale points, resulting in a significant increase in functioning over the entire course of treatment.

Additional analysis examined family functioning using the following five between family variables: (a) level of family functioning on entry into the Project Good Start program, (b) number of violence/maltreatment problems, (c) number of parent distress problems, (d) duration of treatment, and (e) the interaction of parent distress problems and duration of treatment. Willett et al. found that entry-level family functioning and duration of treatment were unrelated to linear change in family functioning, whereas the number of violence/maltreatment problems and the number of parent distress problems in the family were significantly related to linear change in family functioning. In addition, the interaction between the number of parent distress problems and duration of treatment was significantly related to linear growth in family functioning. In general, the families with more severe problems (violence/maltreatment and parent distress) showed less growth (and often a decline) in family functioning. Still, this somewhat pessimistic conclusion is tempered by the significant interaction; when these more distressed families had longer treatment duration (that is, more than 2 years), a significant linear increase in their family functioning occurred.

Willett et al. (1991) conclude that growth modeling had several advantages over traditional approaches for analyzing outcome data. Specifically, they argued that growth modeling allows the researcher to take advantage of the "richness of longitudinal data to estimate changes over time much more precisely than has been possible previously" (Willett et al., 1991, p.46). We agree with this conclusion and urge counseling researchers to use longitudinal data collection and growth modeling when doing outcome research.

EMPIRICALLY VALIDATED TREATMENTS

D. F. Klein, a psychiatrist who advocates the use of psychopharmacological treatments, recently wrote: "The bottom line is that if the Food and Drug Administration (FDA) was responsible for the evaluation of psychotherapy, then no current psychotherapy would be approvable, whereas particular medications are clearly approvable" (Klein, 1996, p. 85). Partially in response to this type of criticism, Division 12 (the Division of Clinical Psychology) of the American Psychological Association appointed a committee to develop criteria for identifying empirically validated treatments (Task Force on Promotion and Dissemination of Psychological Procedures, 1995). This committee attempted to identify treatments shown to be effective with particular psychological disorders by applying a specific list of criteria.

Wampold and colleagues have been critical of the task force's approach because the identified criteria refer to and encourage studies that assess outcome only (Wampold et al., 1997). Specifically, the identified criteria encourage the comparative outcome strategy, often described as "a horse race among treatments." In his critique, Wampold et al. identify a number of problems with the Division 12 criteria for empirically validated treatments (for example, the impossibility of proving a hypothesis of no difference among treatments).

Recently, Wampold et al. (1997) addressed the major argument underlying the "empirically validated treatment" approach by pointing out that Division 12's approach is predicated on identifying differences between or among treatments. Wampold et al. (1997) meta-analyzed outcome studies that compared the effectiveness of two or more bona fide treatments. The results of this analysis supported the Dodo bird hypothesis—that the differences in outcome among treatment is zero. (The Dodo bird hypothesis comes from *Alice in Wonderland,* in which the Dodo bird claims that all have won, so all must have prizes.) The authors concluded that the efficacies of bona fide treatments are essentially equivalent.

The results of the Wampold et al. (1997) study suggest that attempts to identify the unique ingredients of treatment that relate to outcome are probably misguided. Instead, researchers should focus on studies identifying the "process, theory or psychological mechanism of change" (Wampold et al., 1997, p. 203). Some types of outcome research—for example, the client and therapist variation strategy—can be critically important in identifying the mechanisms of change.

SUMMARY AND CONCLUSIONS

Counseling researchers have often addressed questions of counseling outcome. This chapter described six different strategies for addressing outcome questions and provided counseling examples for each. In addition, it addressed a number of methodological issues important for researchers planning a counseling outcome study. Even though counseling practitioners and researchers were among the first to "manualize" treatments for specific problems (that is, produce manuals for structured training groups), with a few notable exceptions counseling researchers have not developed adherence measures to complement the manuals they developed. We strongly encourage counseling researchers to explicitly address issues of treatment adherence, treatment differentiation, and counselor competence in the conduct of counseling outcome studies.

Counseling outcome researchers have also generally failed to address issues of clinical versus statistical significance in their outcome studies; we consider this an important omission. Finally, we encourage counseling researchers to examine some of the new statistical methodologies for assessing change (for example, growth modeling), for these methods could help researchers more powerfully test their outcome hypotheses. It is hoped that the methods and techniques described in this chapter can help counseling researchers to address more critically and powerfully the outcome questions confronting the counseling profession.

C H A P T E R   17

DESIGN ISSUES RELATED TO COUNSELING PROCESS RESEARCH

Every therapist, regardless of level of experience, has reflected on what happens in the course of therapy. Beginning therapists often ask supervisors about ways of establishing a working alliance, how to confront clients, or how to use various counseling interventions, such as the gestalt empty chair technique. Is it OK to touch the client? Does touching a client help or hinder the counseling process? After considerable experience, therapists realize that all clients are not alike, and that it is important to consider, for example, how to establish a working alliance with very different clients. All these counseling topics reflect on aspects of the counseling process in some way and have been the focus of considerable research. This type of counseling research is often considered to be "relevant," "meaningful," and "useful" as the researcher finds "what works" in therapy. Such research can be exciting, as the researcher discovers relationships among variables related to the counseling process.

This chapter provides a general introduction to counseling process research and then discusses issues pertaining to some of the major design issues related to counseling process research. Process research is not a category of research design per se; rather, it is a specific area of focus within counseling research. Moreover, a variety of research designs is used to conduct process research, including descriptive, intensive single-subject, within-subjects, and between-subjects designs.

There are three major sections to this chapter. In the first section we define process research in general terms; then we provide a brief overview of some early and current counseling process research, summarizing some of the major research findings in the counseling process literature. The second section of this chapter focuses on major design issues of particular relevance to counseling process research, such as the types of measurements to use in examining the counseling process or ways of analyzing process data. The third section discusses representative examples of instruments used to assess different aspects of counseling process research. Moreover, we include copies of a wide range of instruments at the end of the chapter.

DEFINING COUNSELING PROCESS RESEARCH

Counseling process research explores the events that occur within the therapeutic encounter, typically examining variables such as therapist behaviors, client behaviors, and therapist-client interactions during treatment (Hill, 1982, 1990). Counseling outcome research typically refers to what therapy does, "the presence and magnitude of both immediate and long-term changes that result from the processes of psychotherapy" (Lambert & Hill, 1994, p. 72). Although these definitions seem straightforward, the conceptualization of the process and the outcome of counseling often overlap. Moreover, beneath the surface lies a number of measurement and methodological issues that introduce considerable complexity to these definitions. For example, research has shown that process variables in a particular counseling session (such as therapist empathy) are experienced quite differently by clients, therapists, and judges (see, for example, Gurman, 1977; Orlinsky & Howard, 1975); thus, important process variables differ depending on whose perspective of the counseling process is examined. Likewise, the term *process* has been used to describe very different units of measurement, from very small units involving micromomentary processes (for example, gaze shifts) to session processes (for example, repair of the working alliance) over the course of an hour or even months (see, for example, Elliott, 1991; Greenberg, 1986a; Orlinsky et al., 1994). For additional reading on this topic, interested readers should consult Elliott (1991), Highlen and Hill (1984), Lambert and Hill (1994), and Orlinsky, Grawe, and Parks (1994).

Almost 50 years of research on the counseling process has identified a very wide range of variables (see, for example, Orlinsky & Howard, 1978; Orlinsky et al., 1994). The large number of variables identified has led numerous researchers to organize the variables into some sort of classification system (see, for example, Hill, 1982, 1992; Kiesler, 1973; Marsden, 1965, 1971; Russell & Stiles, 1979). Although there are disadvantages and advantages to the various classification systems, we present one system here. Hill (1991) listed the following seven types of behaviors that have been examined within the process area, which are enumerated in increasing levels of complexity; the first types are more observable and discrete, whereas the latter tend to involve more abstract behaviors that occur over longer periods of time:

1. Ancillary behaviors such as speech dysfluency, or nonverbal behaviors such as the body-lean of the counselor
2. Verbal behaviors, such as therapist response modes, including therapist self-disclosure, interpretation, and confrontation (see Hill, 1992, for reviews of this literature)
3. Covert behaviors, such as therapist intentions "to support" or "to challenge" (see Hill, 1992, for a partial review)
4. Content, which examines the topics of discussion and typically focuses on client behaviors
5. Strategies, which focus on therapist techniques such as identifying maladaptive cognitions

6. Interpersonal manner, such as therapist involvement, empathy, and congruence
7. The therapeutic relationship, such as the working alliance and control of the topic of discussion

Early Process Research

By way of introduction to process research, we first discuss some of the early process research in counseling. An examination of the first volume of the *Journal of Counseling Psychology (JCP)* attests to the early roots of counseling process research. Not only has process research per se been an important theme within counseling research, but many of the topics and questions studied today have their roots in research published in 1954 in the first volume of *JCP*. Current research, however, is more sophisticated methodologically and conceptually because of technical advances in both of these areas. In this section we compare and contrast the focus of early researchers with those of current process researchers and identify several methodological and conceptual strategies that began in the early counseling research of the 1950s.

Let's consider three studies published in the first volume of *JCP*. Dipboye (1954) was interested in examining differences in counselor style among different content areas of discussion. This researcher used nine mutually exclusive categories to examine counselor style; questions about content, questions about feelings, responses to content, responses to feelings, interpretation of content, interpretation of feelings, suggestions about content, suggestions about feelings, and giving information. These categories bear remarkable similarity to the six categories of response modes (questions, advisements, information, reflection, interpretation, and self-disclosure) that Elliott, Hill, Stiles, Friedlander, Mahrer, and Margison (1987) found to underlie a variety of response mode systems. Dipboye's content categories included test discussion, interpersonal relations, family relations, educational and vocational problems and planning, self-reference, and study skills. Dipboye (1954) found that four of the six counselors he examined changed their style of interaction when different content areas were being addressed. Unfortunately, he did not examine which styles were related to which content areas.

The second process study published in Volume 1 of *JCP* involved an examination of counselor directiveness. Danskin and Robinson (1954) examined counselor directiveness by rating the amount of "lead" in a counselor statement. They defined "lead" as (a) "the extent to which the content of the counselor's remark seems to be ahead of the content of the client's last remark," and (b) "the degree of pressure or definiteness in the counselor's remark that is apparently used to bring about client acceptance of the expressed idea" (p. 79).

Danskin and Robinson's major finding was that counselor lead was related to the type of problem being discussed. They found that the counselor used more leading statements with clients who had a "skills" problem than with clients who had an "adjustment" problem. This focus on counselor lead bears some similarity to Tracey's research, which examined control in individual counseling (see, for example, Tracey & Ray, 1984).

A third study (Berg, 1954) examined differences between two groups of clients (those whose presenting problems either were or were not sexually related) in nonverbal behavior displayed during counseling interviews. Based on psychoanalytic theory, Berg tabulated the following classes of gestures, which were thought to represent sexual symbolism: rotating and sliding, clasping or wrapping, insertion, pressing, and licking and biting. Although the categories of coding nonverbal behavior seem quite different today, there is still a continuity of this line of research (see, for example, Hill & Stephany, 1990). Berg found, contrary to his hypothesis, that both groups of clients made a relatively high number of sexually suggestive gestures. Thus, the content or the presenting concern bore little relationship to the type or number of nonverbal gestures exhibited.

There are important differences between these early studies and more recent process research. Two of the most striking differences involve the emphasis on content in the counseling interview and the link between process and outcome. In two of the studies from Volume 1 of *JCP*, the content of the counseling interview was an important defining variable. As mentioned earlier, Dipboye (1954) categorized segments of counseling interviews as representing one of six content categories. Likewise, Danskin and Robinson (1954) used four categories to classify the content of their counseling interviews. Such emphasis on content is representative of the focus that content received in much of the early research, but content has been almost completely neglected in more recent process research (see reviews by Highlen & Hill, 1984; Hill, 1982, Parloff, Waskow, & Wolfe, 1978).

A second point of discontinuity concerns the process-outcome link. Early counseling research tended to focus solely on either client outcome or counseling process; none of the early studies reviewed attempted to link the process variables with some measure of outcome. For example, Danskin and Robinson (1954) did not know whether more-leading interviews were more productive than less-leading interviews in addressing skill problems. More recently, studies have emphasized linking process to outcome (see Highlen & Hill, 1984; Holloway, Wampold, & Nelson, 1990; Orlinsky & Howard, 1978; Wampold & Kim, 1989). For example, Wampold and Kim (1989) related patterns of client interaction to evaluation of sessions made by counselor, client, and observers.

Two conceptual systems established in early process research remain subjects of current research. F. P. Robinson's book *Principles and Procedures in Student Counseling* (1950) had a seminal influence on early process research. In addition to his emphasis on session content, Robinson also devised a system of classifying counseling behavior based on the concept of counselor roles and subroles. This concept is still the basis for category systems used to classify counselor actions. The second conceptual system that influenced early process research was T. Leary's (1957) system of interpersonal diagnosis. Unlike Robinson's ideas, which led to the classification of counselor behavior in terms of actions or response modes, Leary's system classified counselor behavior in terms of its interpersonal style. W. J. Mueller (1969) used the Leary system to study the manifestation of transference and countertransference in counseling interviews. Researchers continue to apply Leary's system in examining client and counselor interpersonal style (see, for example, Strong, Hills, Kilmartin, De Vries, Lanier, Nelson, Strickland, & Meyer, 1988).

Even though several studies conducted in the 1950s could be classified as counseling process research, Carl Rogers' (1957) formulation of the necessary and sufficient conditions for positive therapeutic change probably served as the major stimulus for much of the process research in the 1960s and 1970s (Toukmanian & Rennie, 1992). Rogers identified what he believed to be the core therapeutic conditions, which in essence were largely process variables, such as therapist empathy and unconditional positive regard. The large volume of process and outcome research that followed empirically tested Rogers's postulations. Although the research initially supported Rogers's ideas, subsequent research revealed that the effective elements of therapeutic change are more complex than he first postulated (see reviews by Parloff et al., 1978; Orlinsky & Howard, 1978; Orlinsky et al., 1994).

Some Current Research Findings

The individual counseling process literature is vast. Orlinsky et al. (1994) counted more than 2300 process and outcome studies from 1950 to 1992. Moreover, over half of these studies appeared in the literature in the past 7 years. Detailed reviews of the counseling process literature can be found in Orlinsky and Howard (1978) and Orlinsky et al. (1994). To date, the research evidence suggests a strong relationship between the following process variables and positive therapeutic outcomes: the overall quality of the therapeutic relationship, therapist skill, client cooperation versus resistance, client openness versus defensiveness, and treatment duration (Orlinsky et al., 1994). The counseling process research has also been expanded to incorporate race and cultural factors, and applied to contexts other than individual counseling.

Even though theorists have suggested for some time that race and cultural factors affect the dynamics of the counseling process (Helms, 1990; Sue & Sue, 1990; Vontress, 1970), relatively few empirical studies have been conducted on racial and cultural factors in the therapy process (Helms, 1994). Some research suggested that black clients report lower levels of rapport with white counselors rather than with black counselors (see Atkinson, 1983), although subsequent research suggested that other variables, such as attention to cultural issues, may be an important variable in affecting client reactions as well (Thompson, Worthington, & Atkinson, 1994). Ridley, Mendoza, Kanitz, Angermeier, and Zenk (1994) recently provided an excellent conceptualization integrating race and cultural factors (particularly cultural sensitivity) into the counseling process by focusing on the cognitive schema of counselors. One of the best resources for beginning process researchers interested in racial and cultural factors in counseling is the *Handbook of Racial/Ethnic Minority Research* (Ponterotto & Casas, 1991). Clearly, race and cultural factors are important topics in process research.

Likewise, process research in career counseling is still "a virtually unexplored territory" (Dorn, 1988, p. 278). Swanson (1995) provided an excellent summary of process research in career counseling. Although there appears to be some overlap in the processes of personal and career counseling (see Bluestein & Spengler, 1995), Swanson (1995) strongly called for the "examination of the process of career counseling, and the linking of process and outcome variables in career counseling research" (p. 252). To date, only two studies have examined process and outcome variables in individual career counseling. Kirshner, Hoffman, and Hill (1994) used the Hill and O'Grady (1985) psychotherapy debriefing model to examine the interplay between counselor intentions and client reactions. The only clear difference between this study and psychotherapy process studies was the greater use of information giving by the counselor. M. Heppner and Hendricks (1995) conducted an in-depth process study of career counseling clients, specifically examining the role of the therapeutic alliance, counselor intentions, and specific counseling events in sessions judged as "best" and "worst" using a modified version of Elliott's Brief Structured Recall. They reported that clients perceived the role of the relationship as critical to their change process; moreover, they found the clients' level of decidedness to be associated with a number of differences in the career counseling process.

DESIGN ISSUES IN PROCESS RESEARCH

It is important to reiterate that process research is not a category of research design. One does not speak of using a counseling process design, because process research is a specific area of focus within counseling research.

Many of the methodological considerations pertaining to the selection of the research topic (see Chapter 2), independent or predictor variables (Chapter 11), dependent or criterion variables (Chapter 12), population issues (Chapter 13), and experimenter/participant bias (Chapter 14) apply to conducting counseling process research. In this section we highlight several methodological and measurement issues of relevance to researchers interested in conducting counseling process research. We start by discussing the initial development of the research question(s) and hypotheses. We then focus on several major methodological issues that typically face the process researcher: What to study and in what context? What to measure? Whose perspective? How much to measure? How to code and analyze the process data?

Although counseling process research can be very exciting, it can also be tedious, and the number of methodological details and the volume of data can be overwhelming. It is not uncommon for beginning students to change research topics after beginning a process study. Beginning researchers may have the misperception that because process research can be relevant and exciting, it will also be easy. The many details and the complexity can translate into more opportunities for problems to arise. Hill (1992) recommended that beginning process researchers become apprentices to an experienced process researcher to facilitate learning the methodological skills needed to conduct process research. Being a part of a research team is another way of both making the demands more manageable while learning about the complexity of the methodological issues.

Getting Started: What to Study and in What Context?

One of the first steps is to choose the general topic or focus of the process research (see Chapter 2). Hill (1982) has underscored the importance of developing a good research question and hypothesis:

> This has been a particularly difficult problem in the process area, perhaps because of the overwhelming nature of the multitude of variables in counseling which can be examined. What seems to have happened in the past is that researchers have responded with a flight into detail, creating an obsessive's nightmare for themselves and their readers. Researchers tend to painstakingly describe, categorize and develop measures but rarely are these put into a context of what they mean for counseling or theory. Further, there has been a tendency to study easy variables that can be measured reliably because of clear operational definitions rather than those which might have more clinical relevance. (Hill, 1982, p. 10)

Thus, given the complexity of the counseling process, it is important to clearly identify a specific research question(s) and subsequent hypotheses. It is common for researchers to develop research ideas as they engage in actual counseling, perhaps by reviewing a tape of a counseling session, or in discussions with a supervisor or supervisee. It is critical to go well beyond the initial identification of the idea and to spend considerable time reviewing relevant literature (see Chapter 2). Hill (1992) recommended "writing a complete proposal of the research project including the data analyses, even if it is not a thesis or dissertation" (p. 90) at this early stage; although such a process may seem tedious, the act of writing typically facilitates the process of identifying the topic, operationalizing variables, and thinking through procedural details.

An equally important issue pertains to the context or setting in which the study is to be conducted; typically, researchers decide to what degree the study will be conducted in a naturalistic setting or in an analogue setting (see Hill, 1982, 1992). This issue basically concerns the levels of internal and external validity that the researcher deems most important to best answer the relevant research questions (see Chapters 10 and 15). If the researcher wants a great deal of internal validity (and typically to be able to manipulate one or more independent variables), an analogue setting might be advisable. However, if external validity (or generalizability) is very important, then a study conducted in more of a naturalistic setting may be advisable. The decision between an analogue/naturalistic setting is not a categorical either/or decision, but rather one that involves a continuum. Some analogue designs emphasize internal validity more than others (see Chapter 15), and some naturalistic designs incorporate analogue methods to create quasi-naturalistic settings (see Chapter 7). In the final analysis, the decision regarding the type of context or setting is thus a matter of the degree to which the research will be conducted in a context that maximizes either internal or external validity.

Another key design issue is whether to use a quantitative or qualitative approach (see Chapters 9 and 10). It is critical to carefully contemplate both the type of research questions of interest and the type of data that will best answer those questions at this time. For example, despite an abundant literature on reducing client resistance, there has been very little research on either willingness to work through interpersonal difficulties in family therapy or a family's level of engagement/disengagement. Because of the lack of empirical data, Friedlander et al. (1994) used a qualitative, discovery-oriented approach to examine events related to successful, sustained engagement in family therapy. Moreover, they were able to develop a conceptual model of successful, sustained engagement based on their qualitative analysis. Researchers are encouraged not to dichotomize their research approach as either quantitative or qualitative, but to integrate these approaches in their research to provide the most informative data possible (see, for example, Cummings, Martin, Halberg, & Slemon, 1992).

What to Measure?

Once a general research topic has been identified, a subsequent issue concerns the aspect of the counseling process to examine. At the most basic level, researchers must decide whether they want to examine aspects of the individual participants' behaviors or aspects of the developing relationship or system. Process research focuses on either a participant (counselor or client), the relationship, or some combination thereof. Indeed, some of the most common activities examined in process research are therapist techniques, client behaviors, and the therapeutic interaction. In group or family counseling, the clients are obviously multiple individuals. In group and family counseling, the counselor dimension often involves a measurement of the activities of co-counselors. In individual counseling, the relationship involves how the client and counselor work together. In group and family process research, this relationship dimension is usually referred to as the group (cohesion, norms) or family (closeness, involvement) process. We will discuss issues pertaining to what to measure specifically with regard to individual participants and the relationship.

Suppose that a researcher, Dr. B. Famous, decides to conduct a process study that examines the counselor's behavior. But there are many counselor behaviors: what the counselor said, how the counselor said it (for example, emphatically or angrily), how often the counselor said it, when the counselor said it, and so on. So the insightful Dr. Famous knows it is necessary to consider specific types of counselor behaviors that might be examined. Elliott's (1991) four focal points of the communication process—content (what is said), action (what is done), style (how it is said or done), and quality (how well it is said or done)—could be used to clarify the focus of the Famous study of "counselor behaviors." Likewise, Hill's (1991) classification scheme (described earlier in this chapter) could be used to think about "what type of behaviors" Dr. Famous might want to examine.

Suppose as well that Dr. Famous was especially keenly interested in counselor intentions; how might she measure that? One strategy might be to make some type of measurement after each counselor statement, but such a measurement would involve many "microscopic" assessments for each interview hour. Another strategy might be to ask counselors to reflect on their overall intentions during a counseling session, which would be a more global type of assessment.

In essence, process researchers must decide at what level they are going to measure the aspects of the process. Greenberg (1986a) suggested that three levels of analysis be used in examining the counseling process: speech acts, episodes, and the relationship. In counseling process research, *speech acts* refers to the microanalysis of statement-by-statement transactions, *episode* refers to a coherent thematic section of counseling, and *relationship* refers to the ongoing counselor-client relationship over multiple sessions. Greenberg (1986a) nicely elucidated the need to examine the notion of different levels of measurement within process research, from the microscopic (statement-by-statement) to the more global or general. He also suggested that process measurements be context-sensitive, such as within a relationship.

Whose Perspective?

Another major question that process researchers must address is: From whose perspective should the counseling process be evaluated? A considerable amount of evidence suggests that client, counselor, and observer perspectives on the counseling process may offer quite diverse views of what happens in counseling (see Eugster & Wampold, 1996; Lambert, DeJulio, & Stein, 1978; Wampold & Poulin, 1992). For example, Dill-Standifond, Stiles, and Rorer (1988) found that clients and counselors had very different views of session impact (in terms of depth, smoothness, positivity, and arousal).

In part, differences and similarities across perspectives may be related to the type of rating used. For example, Lambert et al. (1978) found only minimal relationships among ratings of facilitative conditions across the three perspectives. Likewise, Gurman (1977) found that client ratings of empathy were positively related to therapy outcome, but ratings from outside observers were not related to outcome. Other research reveals little difference between, for example, client and counselor perspectives on the rating of therapist behavior (Carkhuff & Burstein, 1970). Eugster and Wampold (1996) found that regression equations predicting session evaluation from process variables were significantly different for clients and therapists. Likewise, supervisors and supervisees typically differ when asked to rate the frequency of various supervisor behaviors (see, for example, Heppner & Roehlke, 1984).

Different relationships among the three perspectives have been found in research that has examined the working alliance. A study by Tichenor and Hill (1989) suggested that clients, counselors, and observers have different views of the working relationship (correlations among the three perspectives averaged $r = -.02$). Other research, however, found that both client and counselor (Horvath & Greenberg, 1989) and observer (Marmar, Marziali, Horowitz, & Weiss, 1986) ratings of the working alliance are related to client outcome, suggesting that even though different perspectives of the working alliance may measure different constructs, each of them is important.

Less discrepancy among raters from the three perspectives may occur when concrete and observable behaviors are assessed. The more subjective the process variable is (especially if the assessment pertains to the raters' perceptions of conditions), the greater the difference among various raters is likely to be. When researchers want to examine more subjective process variables, they should obtain ratings from multiple perspectives. In this way, researchers can empirically examine the degree of relationship among the perspectives on the particular variable of interest and determine if the different perspectives add useful information. Put another way, the combination of client, counselor, observer perspectives on, say, the working alliance may be a better predictor of counseling outcome than any single perspective.

Clearly, research reveals differences in the ratings obtained from counselors, clients, or outside observers. Moreover, the correlation among the three perspectives on various measures is often minimal (Lambert & Hill, 1994). Thus, the decision from whose perspective to assess the counseling process has major effects on the results of and the conclusions that can be drawn from a study. We encourage researchers to think carefully about the different perspectives when they are developing their research questions. Some research topics might dictate the perspective the researcher decides to examine. For example, a great deal of attention has been focused recently on the nature of client memories of child sexual abuse and the manner in which therapy is related to the retrieval of those memories (see, for example, Enns et al., 1995). Because the research literature provides very little information about either the actual experience of clients in psychotherapy or any factors related to memory retrieval, Phelps, Friedlander, and Enns (1997) conducted a qualitative study from the client's perspective that examined how the psychotherapeutic process was associated with the retrieval of sexual abuse memories.

How Much to Measure?

If you were doing a process study, would it be sufficient to collect data from one session, or should you collect from multiple sessions? If you are using measures that assess statement-by-statement variables (for example, counselor intentions), should you collect data from the whole counseling session, or perhaps from only the first (or last) 15 minutes of the session? Although it seems desirable to collect a lot of data from multiple sessions, which would increase the external validity or generalizability of the findings, such a strategy quickly results in an overwhelming amount of data. Hill et al. (1983) for example, analyzed over 11,000 responses from one intensive single-subject study; another study that examined data from only three group counseling sessions has 5833 adjacent turns in the group communication to categorize (Friedlander, Thibodeau, Nichols, Tucker, & Snyder, 1985). Process researchers must decide how much of a session or how many sessions to use in their analyses. Even though little empirical evidence pertains to this issue, we briefly discuss sampling and its role in counseling process research.

Friedlander, Ellis, Siegel, Raymond, Haase, and Highlen (1988) empirically examined the issue of how much to measure. Specifically, they asked: (a) What fraction of an interview, if any, best represents the entire interview? and (b) At what point in the interview should this "best" sample be drawn? Friedlander et al. decided that the answer to these questions depended on the researcher's purpose. If the researcher was interested in group data, such as the process across several different counseling-client dyads, then fairly small segments of sessions (as little as 10%) were reasonable representations of an entire session. For a group design, the point in the interview at which the researcher drew the sample did not seem to matter. Friedlander et al. did recommend, however, that a "mini-generalizability" study be routinely conducted when using a group design; that is, a subsample of the data should be analyzed to ascertain that the use of small segments is appropriate in that particular case. On the other hand, Friedlander et al. recommended that entire sessions be used when an intensive single-subject strategy is used; their data suggested that sampling of single-subject data leads to enormous differences in the conclusions.

Additional data suggest that clients from different diagnosis groups show different patterns of experiencing the counseling process; for example, one study found that neurotic clients showed an upward trend in experiencing during a counseling session, whereas schizophrenics showed a saw-toothed pattern (Kiesler, Klein, & Mathieu, 1965). Other data suggest that patterns of client responding change over the course of many sessions (see, for example, Kiesler, 1971b). Likewise, some data suggest that counselors change their behavior across counseling sessions (see, for example, Hill & O'Grady, 1985; Mintz & Luborsky, 1971). These studies underscore potential differences across clients and counselors over time.

Thus, the question of whether or not to use sample session segments seems to depend on the type of research question and the nature of the design. Certainly, investigators must be alert to individual differences across clients, particularly across very different diagnostic groups. Moreover, some differences in counselor behavior seem likely over time. Accordingly, researchers might choose to include both individual differences or time intervals in their research questions. If these variables are not desired in the research questions, then the researcher could decide to control these variables to reduce potential confounds. Apart from the individual differences and time intervals, segments of as little as 10% of the session will likely yield acceptable results with group designs, whereas with single-subject designs it is best to use an entire session without sampling. Clearly, the issue of how much to measure is relatively unexplored and needs additional empirical research. Sampling and its effects on external validity merit serious attention in counseling process research.

How to Code and Analyze the Process Data?

Suppose that in carefully designing a process study you have identified specific variables within several focused research questions that interest you. You have also deliberated on what to measure and from whose perspective, and you have decided how much to measure. Now another major issue looms—how to analyze the process data. Although it is tempting to wait until you have collected the data, we strongly recommend that you think carefully about how you will analyze the data before they are collected. As researchers think through various issues related to data analysis, they may realize that more participants are needed, or that the data needs to be collected more frequently. Thus, it is important to think through the issues related to data analysis while designing a process study.

The data analysis might involve a wide range of activities, depending on the nature of the data. Qualitative data might require nonparametric statistics, or perhaps categorizing data in the form of events by independent judges (see Chapter 10). Quantitative data might involve a range of statistical procedures, such as analysis of variance and correlations, or more complex designs such as sequential analysis. Because you typically have a lot of data (maybe even over 11,000 data points!), the data will need to be summarized or reduced in a way that still allows appropriate analysis. Although this book is not a book on data analysis, we will briefly discuss two data analysis issues pertinent to counseling process research: use of nonparticipant judges in rating data, and statistical strategies to analyze quantitative data.

Use of Nonparticipant Judges in Rating Data

It is quite common in process research to have nonparticipant observers "judge the presence, intensity, and frequency of certain events" (Lambert & Hill, 1994, p. 99). However, how can the researcher be sure that a judge's ratings are accurate or reliable? Perhaps a judge's ratings involve personal bias and have little to do with the observed event. Thus, a major issue pertains to the reliability and validity of observers' judgments.

Hill (1992) and Lambert and Hill (1994) have written extensively on issues pertaining to the use of nonparticipant judges. Among the major issues are the number of judges, rater selection, rater bias, rater errors, rater training, assigning judges to data, maintaining morale among judges, rater drift, debriefing of judges, and data aggregation. We now briefly examine some of these issues (see Lambert & Hill, 1994, for more details).

Researchers typically use more than one rater to assure some reliability and validity of the ratings. The recommended number of raters ranges from two (the most common number) to ten (Mahrer, Paterson, Theriault, Roessler, & Quenneville, 1986). Lambert and Hill (1994) recommended that the number of judges be linked to the difficulty of the rating task: The higher the reliability expected, the fewer judges are needed, whereas if lower reliability is expected, pooling ratings from several judges increases the probability of getting closer to the "true" score. Because the skills of the raters can have a major effect on the results of a study (Lambert & Hill, 1994), it behooves the researcher to carefully select skillful raters. But what constitutes a "skillful" rater? Although empirical evidence is lacking, previous researchers have selected raters based on levels of clinical experience, intelligence, theoretical sophistication, interpersonal skills, motivation for the specific project, attentiveness to detail, dependability, trustworthiness, and a sense of ethics (see, for example, Hill, 1982; Lambert & Hill, 1994; Mercer & Loesch, 1979; Moras & Hill, 1991).

Raters are "two-legged meters" (Lambert & Hill, 1994, p. 99) who are asked to interpret and make judgments on observed events. As such, judges bring biases to the rating task and are subject to the broad range of inference errors that humans often make (Gambrill, 1990). Thus, to reduce "error" created by the judges, researchers typically provide raters training concerning description of the rating system, discussion of sample items, rating of sample items, and monitoring of rater drift over the course of the rating task. To ensure that all judges receive exactly the same training, all judges should be trained together in one group. In the first step, the rater must be introduced to the rating system. This step often includes a discussion of the theory base from which the rating system is derived, as well as a description of the specific system. Introduction to the rating system is enhanced by the use of manuals describing examples of expert ratings. Next, the rater uses the rating system on a set of sample items. This aspect of the training is often enhanced if each rater does the ratings independently and if raters are given the whole range of events to be rated so they can become familiar with all points of the ratings scales. Once these ratings are made, the raters discuss the ratings they made and the reasons for them. This step is enhanced if "expert" ratings of the sample items are available so trainees can compare their ratings to those of the experts. Discussion can help judges refine their knowledge of the rating system and make finer distinctions in their ratings. The previous two steps (rating sample items and discussing the ratings) continue until a specified level of agreement exists among the raters. Suppose that after the judges rate the first set of sample items (but before the general discussion of the items) the experimenter calculates the interrater reliability between two raters and finds that the level of agreement is 0.50. (That is, the judges agreed in their ratings only half the time.) Typically, this rate of agreement is considered to be too low. Rather than allowing the judges to proceed to rate all of the responses (and hope their inter-rater reliability goes up!), the experimenter would typically discuss the items and then provide another sample test. Although the "acceptable" level of inter-rater agreement depends on the difficulty of the rating task, 0.80 is generally considered acceptable.

After an acceptable level of inter-rater reliability is obtained, the judges begin the actual rating task. It is essential that judges do their ratings totally independent of each other. If each judge does not rate all of the data, then judges should be ran-domly assigned to various rating tasks to reduce potential error due to any partic-ular judge. Even though judges typically begin the rating task conscientiously, the accuracy of their judgments might decline over time due to fatigue or repetition, or their understanding of the anchor points on rating scales might change. This phenomenon is called rater drift. Marmar (1990) recommended recalibration ses-sions during the rating task to maintain fidelity to the original training standards. Similarly, Elliott (1988) has recommended "the care and feeding of raters"—that is, listening to raters, reinforcing them, and if possible, removing administrative or procedural problems that make the rating task more cumbersome. The "care" of raters is a very important process that requires close monitoring.

At the end of the rating, the experimenter calculates the inter-rater reliability of all ratings. In some ways this is an assessment of the rater training program. Hill (1982) stated that researchers should calculate both inter- and intra-rater reliability. Intra-rater reliability assesses whether or not an individual rater makes consistent ratings over time, whereas inter-rater reliability assesses the amount of agreement among raters. (See Tinsley and Weiss, 1975, for methods of calculating inter- and intra-rater reliability). Once rating has concluded, the experimenter can debrief judges concerning the specific purpose and hypotheses of the study. To ascertain whether the judges were indeed "blind" to the nature of the study (see Chapter 14), the experimenter can first ask judges to relate their ideas about the purpose of the study.

It is appropriate here to introduce the issue of training participants to make certain ratings at the time of data collection. For example, Martin, Martin, and Slemon (1989) found that counselors used different categories of the Hill and O'Grady (1985) Intentions List to record nominally similar descriptions of their intentions. The authors' solution to this problem was to ask therapists to give verbal descriptions of their intentions and then have raters classify these descriptions. This solution is very expensive in terms of time and effort. An alternative approach might be to train the counselors/raters in the use of the intention system. Although providing people training in introspection has a long history in psychology (Wundt, 1904), it is rarely used in modern process research. In this case, counselors could be trained to use the Intentions List by first learning to classify a series of intention statements to a specified level of accuracy. Only after they reached this level on the practice statements would they start to rate their own intentions. Rater drift could be assessed by administering additional series of intention statements to be rated throughout the study.

Statistical Strategies to Analyze Quantitative Data

An important trend in process research has been a move toward studies that explicitly examine the link between counseling process and outcome. This trend has raised important questions about statistically analyzing process data. Traditionally, process has been linked to outcome using a correlational strategy. If, for example, a researcher found a significant positive relationship between counselors' use of interpretation and session depth, then he or she could infer that interpretation was an important process element. Unfortunately, correlational designs cannot enable the researcher to identify causal relationships (whether counselor interpretations caused session depth).

A second example of a correlational design (an ex post facto design) involves comparisons across successfully and unsuccessfully treated cases. In this instance the researcher would examine whether the frequency of a response (for example, open-ended questions) differed across the two kinds of cases. Again, more frequent occurrence of open-ended questions in the successful cases may or may not mean that counselors who use more open-ended questions will be more successful.

Thus, correlational designs in counseling process research, although helpful, have limited utility. In fact, Gottman and Markman (1978) are quite critical of these types of correlational designs in process research. They argued instead for analyses that examine the direct effect of counselor behavior on subsequent client behavior. Stiles (1988) also observed that counselors often use a behavior more frequently not because it is working well, but because it is not working well. For instance, a counselor might offer a lot of interpretations because the client is being "resistant" and is rejecting the interpretations. This situation would cause a higher number of counselor interpretations and likely a low rating for session depth. Thus, the correlation between these two variables alone presents rather misleading information.

An alternative way of examining the relationship between counselor behavior and client response is sequential analysis, a set of statistical techniques that examine the mutual influence of counselor and client behaviors. For example, sequential analysis can be used to examine the likelihood of a client response (for example, self-disclosure) given a prior counselor response (for example, interpretation). At a more sophisticated level, sequential analyses can examine issues such as control and power (that is, is the counselor's response made more predictable by knowing the client's preceding response, or vice versa?). Excellent descriptions of these types of analyses can be found in Bakeman and Gottman (1986), Claiborn and Lichtenberg (1989), Gottman and Roy (1990), and Wampold (1995).

A study by Wampold and Kim (1989) illustrates the power of sequential analysis in examining counseling process. Wampold and Kim reanalyzed data from Hill, Carter, and O'Farrell's (1983) study using an intensive single-subject design across 12 counseling sessions. The process variables used in this study were Hill's counselor and client verbal response category systems. Categories for counselor responses included minimal encouragement, silence, approval-reassurance, information, direct guidance, closed question, open question, restatement, reflection, interpretation, confrontation, nonverbal referent, self-disclosure, and other. Client categories included simple response, requests, description, experiencing, insight, discussion of plans, discussion of client-counselor relationship, silence, and other.

The purpose of the study was to examine the reciprocal influence of counselor and client behaviors. We highlight only a couple of findings here to describe the utility of sequential analysis. First, analyses revealed what Wampold and Kim called two "circuits" between client and counselor behaviors. One circuit was from client description to counselor minimal encouragement back to client description. A second circuit involved client description to counselor confrontation. In addition, Wampold and Kim tested the first circuit for dominance; the dominant member of the dyad was defined as the one with the most influence. For the client description–counselor minimal encouragement–client description circuit, the client was dominant. In other words, the counselor's behavior was more predictable from the client's behavior than the other way around. Wampold and Kim concluded that sequential analysis allowed them to document several important aspects of client and counselor interactions that had been undetected in the correlational and descriptive analysis used by Hill et al. (1983).

Later in this chapter we make a distinction between micro and macro processes. For now, we define micro processes as those that usually occur at the level of the counseling turn (that is, counselor and client statements in a counseling session). The counselor and client verbal response mode categories examined by Wampold and Kim (1989) are examples of micro processes. Macro processes occur over longer periods of time (for example, adherence ratings, or ratings of how closely a particular session conforms to a treatment manual). In counseling process research, the types of sequential analyses recommended by Gottman and Markman (1978) have been used almost exclusively with micro-process data. Only recently have counseling researchers used time-series analyses with macro-process (session level) data.

One example of the recent use of time-series analysis with macro-level data is Patton, Kivlighan, and Multon's (1997) study of time-limited psychoanalytic counseling. Through P-technique factor analysis, Patton et al. (1997) identified four aspects of session-level psychoanalytic counseling process: (a) psychoanalytic technique, (b) client resistance, (c) working alliance, and (d) client transference. These authors were interested in the possible mutual influence of these four aspects of the counseling process across 20 sessions of time-limited treatment.

To examine the possible mutual influence of the four aspects of psychoanalytic counseling process, Patton et al. (1997) used a time-series analysis. According to Gottman and Markman (1978), some questions can be answered only at the intrasubject level; examples include "How does a particular therapist's behavior affect the client?" (p. 28) and the related question, "How does a particular client's behavior affect the therapist?" Although time-series analysis is a sophisticated method for answering this type of within-subjects question, unfortunately few time-series analyses have been applied to counseling/psychotherapy research. According to Jones et al. (1993), in time-series analysis the researcher attempts to infer a causal relationship between observations constituting one series of data points (for example, psychoanalytic techniques) and observations of a second series (for example, client resistance). In other words, the issue is whether series A (psychoanalytic techniques) can predict series B (client resistance).

In the terminology of time-series analysis, the relationship between two series is the cross-correlation function. However, spuriously large cross-correlation coefficients can be found when two time series have large autocorrelations (correlations of a time series with itself). Therefore, time-series analysis involves two steps. In the first step, each individual time-series is examined for the presence on nonstationary trends, which involves plotting and examining the autocorrelation function (ACF) and the partial autocorrelation function (PACF). If the ACF or PACF plots indicate significant or partial autocorrelations for an individual time series, the series is made stationary by transforming it (one method is to use differencing, which controls for trends in the data). Once the identified series are made stationary, these transformed series are then cross-correlated at various lags. The cross-correlation coefficients from this second step are examined for the presence of significant lead/lag relationships. If a significant lead/lag relationship is identified, then the leading variable is considered a potential "cause" of the lagging variable. If the only significant cross-correlation coefficient is for zero lag, then no presumption about the causal direction of the relationships is possible.

The complete results of Patton et al. (1997) are beyond the scope of this discussion. They did find, however, significant cross-correlation functions (CCF) between psychoanalytic technique and client resistance. In examining a cross-correlation analysis, a positive lag means that the counseling process scale indicated first (in this case, psychoanalytic techniques) leads the counseling process scale indicated second (in this case, client resistance). A negative lag means that the counseling process scale indicated second (in this case, client resistance) leads the counseling process scale indicated first (in this case, psychoanalytic techniques). As is the case for a correlation coefficient, the sign of the CCF denotes the direction of the relationship, whereas the absolute value of the CCF indicates the magnitude of the relationship.

In short, Patton et al. found that the CCFs for the psychoanalytic technique–client resistance relationship were significant at lag 1 (-0.57) and at lag 2 (-0.54). This pattern of CCFs suggested that the counselor's relatively higher use of psychoanalytic techniques in a particular session led to lower levels of client resistance during the two subsequent counseling sessions. The Patton et al. (1997) study illustrates the promising results when time-series analysis is applied to session-level data. We hope counseling process researchers will apply these time-series techniques to macro-process data with the same level of enthusiasm that has accompanied their use with micro-process data.

Another critical statistical issue that confronts many counseling process researchers involves the analysis of process variables collected over time. Until recently, there has not been a practical and powerful method for the statistical analysis of repeated measures types of counseling process data. To represent this type of data, process researchers have either (a) used nonstatistical graphical methods coupled with visual inspection, or (b) arbitrarily divided data points into predetermined phases (for example, early, middle, and late periods) and used repeated measures analysis of variance or repeated measures multivariate analysis of variance. As discussed by Willett, Ayoub, and Robinson (1991) and Francis et al. (1991), these methods have proven problematic from both a logical and a statistical perspective. Growth modeling, also known as growth curve analysis, offers a powerful alternative method for analyzing repeated measures types of counseling process data. In the first step of growth curve analysis, a theoretical or heuristic growth model (for example, linear or quadratic curve) is fit both to the data from an individual counseling dyad or a counseling group and to the sample of dyads or groups as a whole. The parameters from these initial models are then used in the second step of the modeling process as outcomes (that is, dependent variables) onto which other variables are regressed. For example, if a linear growth model is used in group counseling research, each group will have (a) an intercept term that represents that group's process score (for example, level of cohesion) at a particular time, and (b) a slope term that represents the linear change in the group's process score (for example, cohesion) over time.

Growth modeling has typically been applied to outcome data. Only Kivlighan and Shaughnessy (1995) and Kivlighan and Lilly (1997) have used growth modeling with counseling process data. In the Kivlighan and Lilly (1997) study, hierarchical linear modeling (HLM) was used to estimate growth curves from group climate data. Based on the theory of hierarchical linear models developed by Bryk and Raudenbush (1992), growth modeling was used in a two-level analysis to estimate growth curves from the within-group, group climate data and to relate the growth parameters from this within-group analysis to the between-group variable of "group success."

Conceptually, HLM involves a two-stage analysis. In the first or unconditional model, the growth trajectory of each individual group is modeled or characterized by a unique set of parameters. This set of parameters, which is assumed to vary randomly, is then used in the second or conditional model as dependent variables in a series of regressions. Arnold (1992) has summarized this analytic technique by describing HLM as "regressions of regressions" (p. 61).

Hierarchical linear modeling differs from trend analysis in ANOVA or MANOVA in that individuals (as opposed to group means) are being modeled; that is, in trend analysis, individual variance is subsumed under the error term. Variance in the individual growth parameters (that is, across groups) can then be plotted against correlates of change. This type of analysis allows for "a different set of research questions" (Francis et al., 1991, p. 31) than is found in more traditional research (that is, based on group means only). For a detailed discussion of the statistical aspects of hierarchical linear models, see Arnold (1992), Bryk & Raudenbush (1992), Francis et al. (1991), and Raudenbush and Chan (1993).

Kivlighan and Lilly investigated how the shape or function of group climate growth patterns were related to the amount of participant-rated benefit from the group experience. HLM analyses were run three times, once for each of the three aspects of group climate (engaged, conflict, and avoiding). Examination of the relationship between group climate ratings and group benefit proceeded through a series of model-building steps.

Several specific findings related group climate to outcome. For example, a quadratic, high-low-high pattern of engaged (cohesion) development was related to increased member benefit. In addition, the pattern of engaged development was more predictive of member benefit than was the absolute level of engaged feeling. In fact, the pattern of group climate development consistently accounted for more of the variance in member benefit than did the absolute level of the group climate dimension. This suggests that pattern over time is an important dimension of counseling process. We believe that growth modeling provides a powerful new methodology for counseling researchers interested in examining repeated measures types of data.

REPRESENTATIVE EXAMPLES OF INSTRUMENTS USED IN COUNSELING PROCESS RESEARCH

A multitude of measures have been used in counseling process research. For a review of some of the most widely used measures, interested readers can consult Greenberg and Pinsof (1986), Kiesler (1973), and Russell (1987). This section provides representative examples of instruments used to assess different aspects of counseling process research. To provide some structure and organization for our discussion, we developed a categorization scheme (see Table 17-1). Basically, we took Hill's (1992) seven aspects of the counseling process and added an evaluative

TABLE 17-1
Instruments Representative of the Counseling Process by Level of Measurement

Counseling process	Level of measurement	
	Micro	Global
Ancillary behaviors	Client Vocal Quality (Rice & Kerr, 1986)	Arousal Scale (Burgoon, Kelly, Newton, & Keeley-Dyreson, 1989)
Verbal behaviors	Hill Counselor Verbal Response Modes Category System (Hill, 1985)	Supervision Questionaire (Worthington & Roehlke, 1979)
Covert behaviors	Thought-Listing Form (Heppner et al., 1992)	Brief Structured Recall (Elliott & Shapiro, 1988); Session Evaluation Questionnaire (Stiles & Snow, 1984)
		Comprehensive Scale of Psychotherapy Session Constructs (Eugster & Wampold, 1996)
Content	Hill Interaction Matrix (Hill, 1965)	Discussion Units (Dipboye, 1954)
Strategies	Counselor Intentions List (Hill & O'Grady, 1985)	Therapist Session Intentions (Stiles et al., 1996)
	Client Reactions System (Hill et al., 1988)	
Interpersonal manner	Interpersonal Communication Rating Scale (Strong et al., 1988)	Check List of Interpersonal Transactions (Kiesler, 1984)
Therapeutic relationship	Categories of Semantic Cohesion Analysis (Friedlander et al., 1985)	Working Alliance Inventory (Horvath & Greenberg, 1989)
Quality	Client Experiencing Scale (Klein, Mathieu-Coughlan, & Kiesler, 1986)	Penn Adherence and Competence Scale for Supportive-Expressive Therapy (Barber & Crits-Christoph, 1996)

dimension (quality) from Elliott's (1991) classification scheme. We then used Greenberg's (1989) notion of different levels of measurement to create two levels of analysis, a micro (statement-by-statement) level and a global (or macro) level. Together, these two dimensions form a 2 × 8 matrix; each of the cells contains one or more appropriate instruments. In the pages to follow we briefly discuss instruments in each of the 16 cells, as well as other representative instruments and research, to provide concrete examples of counseling process measures. Moreover, for each cell we discuss instruments that could be used to assess either the counselor's or client's perspective. To allow a closer look, we present several instruments in the exhibits at the end of the chapter.

Ancillary Behaviors, Micro Level

Ancillary behaviors are the nonverbal behaviors displayed by counseling participants. At the micro level, these ancillary behaviors are nonverbal behaviors connected to particular speech units (for example, sentences or client-counselor turns
at speaking). Ancillary behaviors are important because they carry communicative
value. For example, researchers estimate that as much as 60% of the communication that takes place in groups takes place on the nonverbal level (Kleinke, 1986).
Kiesler (1988) called nonverbal behavior the language of relationship and emotion.

Researchers assess ancillary behaviors because, unlike speech acts, they are
often out of the counseling participants' awareness and therefore out of their conscious control. This lack of conscious control suggests that nonverbal behaviors
may provide a more sensitive indicator of client or counselor emotional state than
self-report measures. In line with this assumption, Mohr, Shoham-Salomon, Engle,
and Beutler (1991) found that nonverbal behaviors provided a more accurate
assessment of client arousal than did verbal reports.

Two classes of nonverbal behaviors have interested counseling process
researchers. Vocalics involve the voice qualities of the interactants; examples are
voice tone or rate of speech. Kinesics are body movements such as facial expressions and gestures. Counseling researchers have measured both kinesics and
vocalics in their process studies.

Rice and Kerr's (1986) Client Vocal Quality (CVQ) measure is probably the
most widely used vocalic index. The CVQ rater uses auditory cues to categorize
client or counselor statements into one of four categories: (a) focused, (b) external, (c) limited, and (d) emotional (see Exhibit A). The focused category describes
an inner-directed exploratory voice quality. An outer-directed, lecturing type of
voice quality is considered external. The emotional category is used when the
voice "breaks its normal platform and expresses emotions." Finally, a low-energy,
wary type of voice is classified as limited. The four CVQ categories are mutually
exclusive, so any individual speech act can only have one vocal quality rating.
Rice and Kerr (1986) have shown that the CVQ has good reliability. In addition,
CVQ ratings have been shown to predict productive engagement in both client-
centered and Gestalt counseling; even though the CVQ system has mainly been
used to rate client speech, it could equally apply to counselor speech.

Greenberg and Foerster (1996) used the CVQ in their task analysis of the
process of resolving unfinished business. Task analysis is a specific approach to
process research that incorporates eight steps, as outlined by Greenberg and Newman (1996): (a) explicating the implicit cognitive map of expert clinicians;
(b) describing the therapeutic task and the context in which this task exists; (c) verifying that the task is therapeutically significant; (d) constructing rational models of
successful task performance; (e) empirically describing cases of actual task performance; (f) revising the rational model by comparing the rationally derived and
empirically derived task performances; (g) validating the task model by comparing
successful and unsuccessful performances; and (h) relating process to outcome.

In the Greenberg and Foerster (1996) study, the CVQ was a critical component of the verification phase of the task analysis paradigm. The focus of this study
was the use of the Gestalt empty-chair dialogue to resolve unfinished business,

defined as lingering bad feelings toward a significant other. Fourteen counselors provided 46 audiotaped counseling sessions containing empty-chair dialogues. Eleven "resolved" and 11 "unresolved" sessions were identified through client, counselor, and judge ratings on a five-point resolution scale. Once these 22 sessions had been identified, clinical judges selected 2-minute sections from each tape for CVQ rating by a second set of judges. Greenberg and Foerster (1996) found that the client dialogue was more focused and emotional in the "resolved" sessions than in the "unresolved" sessions. According to the authors, the CVQ data confirmed that both (a) the intense expression of feelings (that is, higher proportion of emotional responses in the resolved group) and (b) the presence of self-affirmation, self-assertion, or understanding of the other (that is, higher proportion of focused responses in the resolved group) were associated with the successful resolution of unfinished business.

Counseling process researchers have also used micro level ratings of kinesics. Merten, Anstadt, Ullrich, Krause, and Buchheim (1996) studied the affective/emotional exchange between counselors and clients during counseling sessions. According to these authors, emotional exchanges happen at a micromomentary level. Merten et al. (1996) sought to study this process of moment-to-moment emotional exchange by coding the facial expressions of emotion.

Friesen and Ekman's (1984) Emotional Facial Action Coding System (EMFACS) was used to code facial expressions of clients and counselors. The EMFACS is used to measure facial movements potentially associated with affect. In using the EMFACS system, a target facial expression is matched to a dictionary of facial expressions and coded as (a) a primary emotion (happiness, anger, contempt, disgust, fear, sadness, surprise, or social smiles); (b) a blend (two primary emotions occurring simultaneously), (c) a mask (when happiness is used to cover a negative emotion), or (d) nonaffective.

In the Merten et al. (1996) study, 11 severely disturbed clients were treated for 15 sessions by one of 11 experienced therapists. All sessions were videotaped with two cameras, one recording the counselor's facial expressions and the other the client's. Upon completion of the 15 sessions, both clients and counselors completed ratings of success, goal attainment, helpfulness, and contentment with treatment. Based on these outcome ratings, one successful and one unsuccessful client-counselor dyad were selected for further study with the EMFACS.

Both the successful and unsuccessful counseling cases had a similar number of client facial events, 233 for the unsuccessful case and 239 for the successful case. For the unsuccessful case, 73% of the facial events were affective, and 62% of these affective events were primary emotions. By contrast, in the successful case, only 56% of the facial events were affective, and only 46% of these affective events were primary emotions. The counselor in the successful case displayed significantly more facial events ($N = 167$) than did the counselor in the unsuccessful case ($N = 125$). For the counselor in the unsuccessful case, 94% of the detected facial events were affective, with 36% of these affective events being primary emotions. By contrast, in the successful case, only 47% of the counselor's facial events were affective; however, 81% of these affective events were primary emotions.

The vast majority of the primary facial emotions expressed by the counselor in the unsuccessful dyad were happiness or social smiles. Likewise, the unsuccessful client's primary facial expressions were happiness and social smiles. As described by Merten et al. (1996), the facial behavior of the unsuccessful dyad was monotonous, consisting of a series of reciprocal expressions of happiness. The more successful client had a relatively equal balance of happiness, anger, and disgust facial expressions. The facial expressions of this client's counselor were predominantly surprise, disgust, and happiness. There was far less reciprocation of happiness in the successful dyad than in the unsuccessful dyad. It seems clear from this preliminary study that the nonverbal facial behaviors of clients and counselors in successfully and unsuccessfully treated dyads are dramatically different. This suggests that these types of micro-level ancillary behaviors are important topics to address in counseling process research.

Ancillary Behaviors, Global Level

Unlike the micro level, at which the kinesic and vocalic dimensions of ancillary behaviors have usually been measured separately, at the macro level these two dimensions have frequently been combined in a single measure. An example of this type of combined measure is the Arousal Measure developed by Burgoon, Kelly, Newton, and Keeley-Dyreson (1989); see Exhibit B. According to the authors, this scale was intended to measure both the positive and negative aspects of kinesic and vocalic arousal and affect. Trained raters use only the video portion of a videotape when rating the kinesic nonverbal dimensions, whereas vocalic ratings are made from only the audio portion of the tape. One rating, Arousal, is made using both auditory and visual channels.

The Arousal Measure consists of 21 dimensions, with most dimensions containing multiple items. Some items (for example, nodding) are rated on a frequency scale (1 = "none"; 7 = "frequent"). Whereas other items are rated for intensity using bi-polar adjective pairs (for example concern ratings are 1 = "indifferent"; 7 = "concerned"). The 21 nonverbal dimensions (with a representative item in parentheses) are: (a) Arousal (calm), (b) Orientation/Gaze (body orientation), (c) Random Movement (trunk/limb movement), (d) Facial/Head Animation (facial animation), (e) Facial Pleasantness (facial expression), (f) Gestural Animation (gestures), (g) Self-Adaptors (self-adaptors), (h) Object-Adaptors (object-adaptors), (i) Kinesic/Proxemic (involved), (j) Attentiveness (interested), (k) Bodily Coordination (movements), (l) Postural Relaxation (slumped), (m) Body Lean (body lean), (n) Vocal Expressiveness (loudness), (o) Pauses and Laughter (silences), (p) Fluency (nervous vocalizations), (q) Vocal Attentiveness (focused), (r) Vocal Relaxation (rhythm), (s) Vocal Warmth (warm), (t) Loudness (loud), and (u) Pitch (pitch).

Burgoon et al. (1993) compared nonverbal arousal for clients in Cognitive Group Therapy (CT) to clients participating in Focused Expressive Psychotherapy (FEP). As described by the authors, the focus of FEP was emotional arousal, awareness, and resolution of conflict; the focus of CT was identifying and changing dysfunctional cognitions associated with troubling life experiences. As would be expected from a description of the two therapeutic modalities, FEP clients had higher levels of arousal and gesture animation, and lower levels of vocal relaxation and fluency than CT clients. In addition, FEP clients had lower levels of kinesic pleasantness and vocalic pleasantness than CT clients.

Burgoon et al. (1993) also examined the relationship between clients' end of session ratings of resolution (the extent to which the problem worked on was resolved) and the nonverbal arousal measures for clients in the FEP groups. Random movement and vocal relaxation were both associated with client-judged resolution. Specifically, greater amounts of random movement and moderate amounts of vocal relaxation during middle sessions were associated with greater subjective resolution. The results of the Burgoon et al. (1993) study suggest that level of nonverbal arousal is differentially associated with various treatment modalities. In addition, the results suggest that some aspects of nonverbal arousal may be linked to client outcome. The results are encouraging for the continued assessment of macro-level ancillary behaviors in counseling process research.

Verbal Behaviors, Micro Level

Verbal behaviors refer to the communication between counselor and client—not the content of the communication, but rather the grammatical structure (Hill, 1982). Even though various studies have examined linguistic structure (see, for example, Meara, Shannon, & Pepinsky, 1979; Meara & Patton, 1986), most of them have relied on measures of response modes. Response mode refers to the grammatical structure of the response (for example, closed question, open question, or interpretation). Elliott et al. (1987) suggested that for the 20 to 30 systems developed for identifying counselor response modes, the breadth and quality of these systems vary greatly. Accordingly, researchers wanting to measure this level of counselor action are presented with a plethora of choices but little systematic help in choosing a particular response mode system for their studies. Elliott et al. (1987) addressed this problem by comparing six of the more widely used response-mode rating systems.

Elliott et al. (1987) found that a fundamental set of response-mode categories underlie the six systems they examined. These response modes include questions, advisements, information, responses, reflections, interpretations, and self-disclosures. In addition, three other response modes (reassurances, confrontations, acknowledgments) were reliably represented in most of the six systems examined. Unfortunately, Elliott et al. concluded that there was no single best system for rating response modes. Rather, they suggested that researchers examining response modes should at least use systems that contain the six (and probably the three additional) primary response modes to promote comparability across studies. In Exhibit C we present one example of a response mode rating system, the Hill Counselor Verbal Response Modes Category System (Hill, 1985).

One of the strengths of response-mode systems is conceptual clarity. In addition, most of the systems are atheoretical, which enables them to be used across a variety of treatment modalities. In addition, response-mode systems can reliably differentiate among various therapeutic approaches. Research linking therapist response modes to immediate or long-term outcome, however, has revealed only a weak relationship between response-mode use and outcome (Elliott et al., 1987;

Hill et al., 1988). These results suggest that other variables may be more important in accounting for counseling outcomes, and that perhaps the frequency of response mode use in and of itself does not measure a critical ingredient of the change process. After all, the frequency of certain counselor responses tells us little about the myriad of possible client reactions. Given these findings, we recommend that future process researchers not examine response modes in isolation. More useful research could involve examining the interaction between response-mode use and the other aspects (content, style, intention, and quality) of counselor behavior.

An example of this type of research is the study by Hill et al. (1988), which examined the effects of therapist response modes on immediate outcome (client helpfulness ratings, changes in level of client experiencing, client reactions), on session outcome (client and therapist ratings of session depth and smoothness), and on treatment outcome (changes in anxiety, depression, and self-concept). Although certain response modes were significantly correlated with measures of session and treatment outcome, these response modes accounted for only 1% of the variance in immediate outcome. This small relationship between response modes and immediate outcome became more tenuous when other process variables were added to the analysis. In fact, counselor intentions (discussed later) were better predictors of immediate outcome than were response modes. Only when counselor response modes were combined with counselor intentions was an appreciable amount of variance in immediate outcome accounted for in this analysis. The results of this study underscore the need to examine the interaction between therapist response modes and other aspects of counselor behavior in counseling process research.

Unlike counselor verbal behavior, client verbal behavior has received little research attention. Thus, fewer systems have been developed to measure client response modes. Client verbal behavior, like that of the counselor, can be categorized in terms of its grammatical structure. This type of category system results in a measure of client response modes. One such system has been developed by Hill, Greenwald, Reed, Charles, O'Farrell, and Carter (1981). Using this system, client verbal behavior can be classified as simple responses, requests descriptions, experiencing, insight, discussion of plans, discussion of client-counselor relationship, silence, and other. One problem with this system is that verbal behavior (that is, requests) is confused or confounded with content (that is, discussion of plans).

We suspect that client verbal behavior is a research area that deserves more attention. Not only are few ways available for comparing or contrasting different approaches to defining client responses, but few studies have examined the relationship between client response modes and other aspects of client or counselor behavior.

Verbal Behaviors, Global Level

Verbal behaviors have also been examined at a more global level, particularly research examining the supervisory process. Almost all of the studies of counselor supervision (with the exception of those done by Holloway and colleagues; see, for example, Holloway et al., 1989) have relied on supervisor or supervisee ratings of supervision behavior. In this type of research, supervisors and/or supervisees are presented with a list of items describing supervisor behaviors and asked to indicate the general frequency with which the behaviors occurred in the supervision session or during the course of supervision. As an example of an instrument in this area, The Supervision Questionnaire (Worthington & Roehlke, 1979) is presented in Exhibit D.

An example of this type of research is provided by Krause and Allen (1988), who were interested in examining Stoltenberg's (1981) developmental model, which predicted that supervisors would use different behaviors with trainees at different developmental levels. These authors gave a list of 37 items describing supervisor behavior to 87 supervisors and 77 supervisees. The responses of the supervisees and supervisors were factor-analyzed separately. Eight factors accounted for the variance in supervisors' ratings: teacher, counselor, respectful sharing, satisfied colleague, dynamic counselor, perceived impact, laissez-faire, and preparation. A factor analysis of the same items from the supervisees' perspective yielded five factors: supervisor as mentor, supervisor as counselor, directive supervision, supervisor as dynamic counselor, and process supervision.

Krause and Allen used these factors to examine the hypothesis that supervisors would vary their behaviors with supervisees. Using the eight supervisor-derived factors to examine this hypothesis, supervisors rated three of these factors differently depending on the supervisees' training levels. Specifically, structuring and directing behaviors decreased, and collegial and consulting relationships increased, as supervisees advanced in development. An identical analysis using the five supervisee-derived clusters yielded no differences in supervisees' ratings of supervisor behaviors for supervisees at different developmental levels. In sum, the supervisors saw themselves as varying their behaviors with supervisees of different developmental levels, but the supervisees did not.

Did the supervisors actually vary their behaviors with supervisees at different levels? Unfortunately, we cannot provide a complete answer to this question because of the measures used to examine supervisor verbal behavior. Without some outside perspective from which to examine the process at the micro level, it is impossible to determine the reliability of either the supervisors' or supervisees' accounts of the supervisors' behavior.

Covert Behaviors, Micro Level

Covert behavior refers to thoughts, feelings, and perceptions (Highlen & Hill, 1984). One aspect of covert behavior that has received increasing attention is the study of counselor or client self-talk. According to Hines, Stockton, and Morran (1995), counselor self-talk involves the self-reported thoughts that affect the counselor's intention-creation process. Counselor self-talk has been examined in both individual and group therapy. Most of the research on counselor self-talk has attempted to categorize the type of self-talk engaged in by counselors. For example, in individual counseling, Morran, Kurpius, and Brack (1989) found 14 distinct categories of counselor self-talk defined by four dimensions: (a) attending and assessing, (b) information seeking, (c) integrative understanding, and (d) intervention planning.

Counselor self-talk is typically assessed through a thought-listing procedure. Originally developed by social psychologists (for example, Brock, 1967; Greenwald, 1968), thought listing is a means of identifying a person's cognitive responses to a particular stimulus. The stimulus for thought listing can be an entire session, as in Heppner, Rosenberg, and Hedgespeth (1992), or every few minutes within a session, as in Hines et al. (1995). The thought-listing instrument usually consists of some instructions and several "thought-listing" pages containing blanks (see Exhibit E); research participants are instructed to list one thought in each blank. In addition, research participants are encouraged to not worry about spelling or grammar and to be as open and spontaneous as possible. For additional information about constructing a thought-listing form, see Meichenbaum, Henshaw, and Himel (1980) and Petty and Cacioppo (1977).

Hines et al. (1995) used thought-listing to examine the self-talk of novice group leaders (participants who had never led a group), beginning group leaders (participants with one to three group-leadership experiences), and experienced group leaders (participants with six or more group leadership-experiences). The participants watched on videotape a 20-minute staged group counseling session depicting "normal group process occurring around the fourth group counseling session" (Hines et al., 1995, p. 243). Five times during the 20-minute session the tape went blank for 90 seconds, during which research participants were instructed to use the thought-listing forms to record the thoughts they had while viewing the videotape.

As in the Hines et al. (1995) study, thought-listing procedures typically result in a great deal of "qualitative" data that researchers must code or classify. Of the several strategies for dealing with the open-ended data generated by thought-listing procedures, the three most frequently used strategies are: (a) coding statements into a priori categories (positive, negative, and neutral; see, for example, Heppner et al., 1992); (b) developing a classification system based on a reading and analysis of the data collected (see, for example, Heppner et al., 1992); and (c) using a statistical technique such as cluster analysis or multidimensional scaling to empirically group the free sort ratings of several judges (see, for example, Morran et al., 1989).

Hines et al. (1995) used the second method to develop categories of self-talk for the group counselors they studied. The development of categories in this study involved a two-step process. First, two experienced group counselors independently free-sorted into mutually exclusive categories the 1299 thoughts collected in the thought-listing process. These two judges then reached a consensus on the titles and definitions of 17 thought categories. Second, a panel of three judges trained in the definitions of the 17 categories independently coded the 1299 thoughts generated by the research participants into the 17 predefined categories. An agreement level of 94% was achieved by the three judges.

Using this method, Hines et al. (1995) described 17 categories of group counselors' thoughts: (a) observations of group members, (b) observations of group process, (c) observations of co-leader, (d) observations of self, (e) interpretations of members, (f) interpretations of group process, (g) interpretations of co-leader, (h) internal questions regarding members, (i) internal questions regarding group process, (j) internal questions regarding intervention toward members, (k) internal questions regarding intervention toward group process, (l) therapeutic value judgments, (m) personal value judgments, (n) interventions directed toward members, (o) interventions directed toward group process, (p) intervention rehearsals toward members, and (q) intervention rehearsals toward group process. Once the proportion of use for the various thought categories were recorded, Hines et al. correlated these proportions with the number of groups that a participant had led. Four categories of group-leader thought were significantly correlated with group-leading experience. The self-talk of the more experienced group leaders had a relatively higher frequency of interpretations of group process, internal questions regarding members, and interpretations of members, and a relatively lower frequency of therapeutic value judgments, than did the self-talk of less experienced group counselors.

Covert Behaviors, Global Level

On the global level, measures that operationalize counselor intention are not currently available. This is somewhat surprising given the emphasis these actions receive in counselor training and supervision. Among the most common questions addressed to supervisees are things that ask what he or she was trying to accomplish in a given session, or what his or her overall treatment plan involves. Development of this type of measure would be useful in future research and in conceptualizing the counseling process.

Clients also have intentions. In their analysis of the literature, Elliott and James (1989) found eight common themes across the studies that examined client intentions: understanding self and problems, avoiding, getting a personal response from the counselor, feeling relieved or better, changing behavior, getting counselor support, expressing feelings, and following therapeutic directives or procedures. Elliott and Shapiro's (1988) Brief Structured Recall method (see Exhibit F) was designed as a global measure of client intentions. Clients complete a structured assessment that identifies their intentions during a significant event. The intentions include the eight categories described in Elliott and James (1989). Elliot and his colleagues (see, for example, Elliott, James, Reimschuessel, Cislo, & Sack, 1985) have used free recall to study client intentions at a micro level, but these have not been systematized into a more replicable format. Investigating client intentions is a promising area for future research.

One of the most widely used measures of client reactions at the global level is the Session Evaluation Questionnaire (SEQ; Stiles & Snow, 1984), a portion of which is presented in Exhibit G. The SEQ consists of four scales. The Depth and Smoothness scales measure the client's reactions to characteristics of the session. (These scales are discussed in more detail later when we address process measures of the relationship.) The Positivity and Arousal scales measure postsession mood. Positivity, as the name implies, is a measure of how positive or negative the client feels upon completing the session. The Arousal scale is a measure of how much emotional arousal the client feels after completing the session. These SEQ scales have been used to measure consequences (that is, the relationship between therapist response modes and client postsession mood) and antecedents (that is, the relationship between postsession mood and counseling outcome).

Counselor reactions have been measured at a global level with instruments parallel to those used to measure global client reactions. For instance, the Session Evaluation Questionnaire has been used to record the counselor's session-by-session reactions.

A final instrument in this category is the Comprehensive Scale of Psychotherapy Session Constructs (CSPSC; Eugster & Wampold, 1996); see Exhibit H. Basically, the CSPSC measures nine aspects of the session (patient involvement, patient comfort, patient learning, patient real relationship, therapist involvement, therapist comfort, therapist expertness, therapist interpersonal style, and therapist real realationship) from the perspective of both patient and therapist, as well as a global evaluation of the session from both perspectives. Eugster and Wampold (1996) found that therapist session evalution was best predicted by therapist expertness, and patient session evaluation was best predicted by the therapist real relationship. The therapist real relationship negatively predicted therapist session evaluation when all process variables were considered simultaneously. Patient learning and patient involvement significantly and positively predicted both therapist and patient evaluations of the session.

Content, Micro Level

Content refers to the topic or subject of counseling. The Hill Interaction Matrix (HIM; Hill, 1965), which is used in group process research, is an example of a micro-level rating system that focuses on the content of the interaction (see Exhibit I.). The HIM is a statement-by-statement rating system that can be used to rate statements made by either group clients or therapists. The HIM consists of 20 cells formed by combining the dimensions of content style (four types) and work style (five types). The content categories in the HIM system are topic, group, personal, and relationship; and the work-style categories are responsive, conventional, assertive, speculative, and confrontive. The HIM is used by an outside observer who reviews a transcript and places each client or counselor statement into one of the 20 HIM categories. As an example, a researcher could identify how often a group counselor used statements in each of the 20 cells and compare the counselor's rate of use to group members' use of the categories. Research has suggested that the rate of therapist sponsoring is related to the rate of member participation in the different HIM cells (see, for example, Hill, 1965). Hill therefore concluded that the content (and the style) of the counselor's speech is related to (influences) the content (and style) of the client's speech.

Content, Global Level

Research in counseling process would be enhanced by the development of another category system to classify the global content of the counselor's and client's responses. Several early process studies examined the content of discussion, or topical units of discussion. Dipboye (1954) defined a topical unit as the portion of an interview that is devoted to an obvious and clearly recognizable topic of discussion. He defined the following six topical units: (a) test discussion and interpretation, (b) interpersonal relations, (c) family relations, (d) educational and vocational problems and planning, (e) self-reference, and (f) study habits and skills. Dipboye found that the counselors he studied tended to vary their styles or actions as a function of the topical unit of discussion.

This finding was extended in a study by Cummings (1989), who classified problem type or the content of the counseling interaction as either interpersonal or intrapersonal. Like Dipboye (1954), she found that counselors varied their behavior as a function of problem type: Counselors used more information responses with intrapersonal problems and more reflection responses with inter-personal problems.

The research by Dipboye and by Cummings suggests that the content of the material affects the counseling process. Relatively few studies, however, focus on this content dimension, which is quite surprising given that most theories of counseling and therapy specifically advocate the focus on specific content areas, and that counselor training focuses a great deal on content.

One major problem is the lack of any well-developed system for categorizing content material; this lack explains the absence of a global-level content instrument in the exhibits. Diploye's system of classifying content seems biased toward a counselor's definition of "appropriate" content areas, and thus it may be limited. The intrapersonal-interpersonal categorization of Cummings seems useful but perhaps too simple; future research might explore the utility of developing several finer categories rather than the two global categories, and Cummings' distinction might be a starting point. A third major category—impersonal content (weather)—could be added, and each of the three main categories could be divided into subcategories. As an example, Horowitz et al. (1988) identified six types of interpersonal problems: hard to be assertive, hard to be sociable, hard to be submissive, hard to be intimate, too responsible, and too controlling. The categories of intrapersonal and nonpersonal content could be subdivided in a similar manner. Another reason for exploring such a differentiated system is that there is evidence in the coping, problem-solving literature that different problem types lead to different problem-solving activities (see Heppner & Krauskopf, 1987, for a review). In short, additional research is needed to further examine the utility of content and of various classification systems in the counseling relationship.

Strategies, Micro Level

Strategies are defined as interventions or approaches for helping the client (Highen & Hill, 1984). Perhaps the two most frequently used measures in this area are counselor intentions and client reactions, which are the focus of our discussion in this category.

Counselor and client intentions are a relatively new and unexplored area of examination in process research. At present, all of the research has examined intentions at the speech act level, and most of the work has focused on counselor (as opposed to client) intentions. Hill and O'Grady (1985) define a counselor intention as the covert rationale for (or the "why" of) counselor behavior. These authors have developed a list of 19 pantheoretical, nominal, nonmutually exclusive intentions: set limits, get information, give information, support, focus, clarify, hope, cathart, cognitions, behaviors, self-control, feelings, insight, change, reinforce change, resistance, challenge, relationship, and therapist needs; the Counselor's Intention List (Hill & O'Grady, 1985) is presented in Exhibit J. Because intentions are covert, they are available only through counselor introspective reports. To obtain these introspective reports, researchers have counselors review a videotape or audiotape of a recently completed session (Hill and O'Grady recommend that this review take place within 24 hours). For each counselor turn, counselors list up to five intentions that described their goals for that intervention.

This intention measure has been used in numerous studies examining different aspects of counseling process (see, for example, Fuller & Hill, 1985; Kivlighan, 1989; Kivlighan & Angelone, 1991). For instance, Hill and O'Grady (1985) found that counselor theoretical orientation was related to differential intention use, and that intention use changed both within and across sessions. More important was Hill, Helms, Tichenor, Spiegel, O'Grady, and Perry's (1988) finding that counselor intentions were more adequate descriptors of counselor behavior than were response modes. Specifically, intentions either alone or in conjunction with response modes (counselor actions) accounted for significantly more of the variance in immediate outcome ratings than did response mode measures alone. This finding supports the continued use of intention measures for examining counselor behavior.

Some controversy surrounds the measurement of counseling intentions. Hill and colleagues have simply asked counselors to record their intentions while reviewing taped sessions, sometimes with little or no training in the use of the intentions measure. This method of ascertaining intentions makes it virtually impossible to obtain estimates of reliability. Martin, Martin, and Slemon (1989) have contended that counselors often use different intention categories to describe nominally identical reasons for behaving; consequently they have modified Hill and O'Grady's (1985) procedure for collecting intentions. Martin et al. (1989) had counselors review each videotape and for each turn describe their intentions or reasons for the intervention. These descriptions were then transcribed and submitted to judges, who placed the descriptions into the categories in the Hill and O'Grady (1985) intentions list. One advantage of this procedure is that the reliability of category placement can be assessed by examining agreement across judges.

Given the concerns of Martin et al. (1989) about counselors using the intentions list in an idiosyncratic manner, we recommend that researchers use one of two procedures for examining counselor intentions. First, researchers could use a procedure in which counselors orally (Martin et al., 1989) or in writing (Kivlighan, 1990) describe their intentions, and then raters decide on category placement. Second, researchers could develop more extensive training procedures designed to ensure that counselors have a common understanding of the intentions list. A researcher could develop, for example, a list of counselor-stated reasons for intervening and have potential research participants practice placing these reasons into intention categories until an acceptable level of agreement is reached.

Reaction is the internal, subjective response of a client or a counselor to the other's speech act or person. Although counseling process research on the client's and counselor's subjective responses to the session has had a long history (see, for example, Orlinsky & Howard, 1978), examination of the client's or counselor's response to particular speech acts has occurred only recently.

Hill, Helms, Spiegel, and Tichenor (1988) developed a system for categorizing client reactions to counselor interventions; the Client Reactions System is presented in Exhibit K. This system contains 21 categories of reactions, grouped into 14 positive reactions (felt understood, felt supported, felt hopeful, felt relief, became aware of negative thoughts or behaviors, gained better self-understanding, became more clear, became aware of feelings, took responsibility, got unstuck, gained new perspective, got educated, learned new ways to behave, and felt challenged) and 7 negative reactions (felt scared, worse, stuck, lack of direction, confused, misunderstood, and no reaction).

Clients review a videotape of their counseling session, stopping the tape after each therapist response. The clients then use the client reactions list (all 21 reactions) to record their recollected experience. The Client Reactions System has operationalized an important area of counseling process. Even though most counseling theories advocate attempting to alter both clients' external behavior and their internal processing, until the development of the Client Reactions System there was no way of documenting moment-to-moment changes in clients' internal processes. A strength of this system is its ability to differentiate among categories of reactions, which enables the researcher to examine specific effects of counselor interventions (for example, what type of counselor intervention precedes relief in clients, as compared to, say, better self-understanding).

The main concern with this rating system pertains to questions of reliability and validity. We noted that Martin et al. (1989) reported that counselors seemed to use the Counselor's Intentions List in an idiosyncratic manner—that they would record different intentions for nominally similar statements of intent. It is likely that the same problem exists with the Client Reactions System. Researchers may want to consider collecting client reactions in a manner similar to that used by Martin et al. (1989) to collect intentions, which would involve having the client review a tape of a session and describe either orally or in writing his or her response to each counselor intervention. These descriptions could then be given to judges, who would categorize the reactions using the Hill, Helms, Spiegel, and Tichenor (1988) rating system. The researcher would then be able to examine the reliability of the categorizations. Moreover, in terms of validity, the extent to which client reactions are influenced by, for instance, self- or other-deception is presently unknown.

Although counselors certainly have reactions to what their clients do, few systematic investigations have explored this important area. Most researchers seem to view counseling as a one-way interaction, with the counselor influencing the client and the client passively accepting this influence. Heppner and Claiborn (1989) maintained that the client should be considered an active participant in the counseling process who also exerts influence on the counselor. From this perspective, counselors would be expected to have reactions to their clients. Unfortunately, the development of statement-by-statement or micro-level measures of counselor reactions has not kept pace with the theoretical formulations.

Strategies, Global Level

Hill and O'Grady's (1985) Counselor Intentions List was designed to capture the counselor's rationale for selecting a specific behavior, technique, or intervention on a moment-to-moment basis. The rationale of the counselor is clearly an aspect of strategy as defined by Highlen and Hill (1984). Recently, Stiles et al. (1996) argued that the same intentions list can be used to describe typical or principal intentions in a whole session. They used "the term session intention to denote the therapist's rationale for using a class of behaviors, response modes, techniques, or interventions with a client during one or more episodes within a session" (Stiles et al., 1996, p. 403). Stiles et al. called this revised measure the Therapist Session Intentions (TSI), which is presented in Exhibit L.

Like the Counselor Intentions List (Hill & O'Grady, 1985), the TSI consists of 19 items, each of which is rated on a five-point Likert-type scale: 1 = not at all, 2 = slightly, 3 = somewhat, 4 = pretty much, and 5 = very much. The instructions for the TSI are: "Please rate the extent to which you were carrying out or working toward the following activities or goals generally in this session. Rate each item on the basis of the descriptor which fits your intentions best (not every descriptor needs to fit)" (Stiles et al., 1996, p. 405).

Stiles et al. (1996) suggested that counselors use a combination of several different intentions to pursue a treatment goal, referring to this combined use of related session intentions as a focus. "For example, early in therapy, a therapist might seek to gather information from clients, give information about the treatment, and set limits and expectations . . . ; this cluster of session intentions might be called a treatment context focus" (Stiles et al., 1996, p. 403). One of the purposes of the Stiles et al. study was to identify the types of treatment foci that characterized cognitive-behavioral and psychodynamic-interpersonal approaches to counseling.

Stiles et al. (1996) found striking differences in session intention for cognitive-behavioral and psychodynamic-interpersonal sessions. Specifically, cognitive-behavioral sessions had higher levels of the following session-intention categories: reinforce change, cognitions, self-control, behaviors, and change session. Psychodynamic-interpersonal sessions had higher levels of the following session intention categories: feelings-awareness, insight, cathart, and relationship. Factor analysis was used to identify treatment foci in the two types of sessions. Both the cognitive-behavioral and the psychodynamic-interpersonal sessions had seven session foci: (a) treatment context (set limits, get information, give information), (b) session structure (focus, clarify), (c) affect (cathart, feelings-awareness), (d) obstacles (resistance, therapist needs, challenge, relationship), (e) encouraging change (hope, change, reinforce change), (f) behavior (self-control, behaviors), and (g) cognition-insight (insight, cognitions).

Stiles et al. (1996) also examined how the identified foci changed over time in the cognitive-behavioral and psychodynamic-interpersonal treatments. Overall, the cognitive-behavioral treatment sessions had greater focus on treatment context, encouraging change and behavior, whereas the psychodynamic-interpersonal treatment sessions had greater focus on affect and obstacles. In addition, all seven foci showed significant changes in pattern over time. For example, the treatment context and affect foci decreased over time, whereas the encouraging change and cognition-insight foci increased over time.

Interpersonal Manner, Micro level

Interpersonal manner refers to subjective elements of the counseling relationship, such as attitudes, involvement, and communication patterns (Highen & Hill, 1984). Much of the early process literature involved measurement of the necessary and sufficient conditions described by Rogers (1955). The single most widely addressed research topic has been the assessment of counselor empathy (see the review by Parloff, Waskow, & Wolfe, 1978). This assessment has typically involved trained raters listening to or reading transcripts of segments of counseling sessions and rating the empathy of each counselor response. Although the focus of much early research, the examination of counselor empathy (at the micro level) has now slowed to a virtual standstill. (Research on empathy at the global level continues.) More recently, counselor and client interpersonal manner has also been assessed by using some variant of the Leary (1957) system to classify counselor speech along the dimensions of control and affiliation (see, for example, Penman, 1980). A recent version of this system developed by Strong et al. (1988), an inventory called the Interpersonal Communication Rating Scale, is presented in Exhibit M. They used the dimensions of control and affiliation to define eight types or styles of counselor or client communication: leading, self-enhancing, critical, distrustful, self-effacing, docile, cooperative, and nurturant.

Compared to the global level, far less research has examined counselor interpersonal manner at the micro level of speech acts. One study examined differences in counselor interpersonal manner with successfully versus unsuccessfully treated clients (Henry, Schacht, & Strupp, 1986). These authors classified counselor speech acts using Benjamin's (1974) system, which, like the Strong et al. (1988) system, is based on Leary's dimensions of control and affiliation. They found significant differences in counselor interpersonal manner between the successful and unsuccessful cases; specifically, counselors were less likely to reciprocate client hostility in successful cases.

We suspect that additional research addressing counselor interpersonal manner at the microscopic level may be fruitful. It may be especially helpful to conduct research that examines the relations between counselor interpersonal manner at the speech act level and more global ratings of interpersonal manner.

Interpersonal Manner, Global Level

The Barrett-Lennard Relationship Inventory (Barrett-Lennard, 1962) was designed to measure client perceptions of counselor-offered conditions. Clients generally fill out this inventory after interacting with the counselor over a number of sessions. One of the interesting aspects of the research on counselor empathy is the divergence of findings on the connection between counselor empathy and counseling outcome (see Parloff et al., 1978). Research at the micro or speech act level has generally shown no relationship between counselor-offered empathy and client outcome (Gurman, 1977). At the global level, however, research reveals a moderate relationship between client ratings of counselor empathy and client outcome, suggesting that assessments of these global ratings of counselor interpersonal manner are important. In short, empathy at the global level is an important dimension of counselor behavior. Other aspects of counselor interpersonal manner that can be usefully assessed at this relationship level are unclear at this time.

Another widely used global measure of counselor interpersonal manner has been the Counselor Rating Form (Barak & LaCrosse, 1975). Strong (1968) had initially hypothesized that a counselor's power or ability to influence a client (for example, to change an opinion) was related to source characteristics of the counselor—namely, perceived counselor expertness, attractiveness, and trustworthiness. These constructs were operationalized in the Counselor Rating Form as counselor attractiveness, expertness, and trustworthiness. Like the Barrett-Lennard Relationship Inventory, this rating is usually (although not always) made on a session-to-session basis.

Scores from the Counselor Rating Form have been used as both dependent (or criterion) and independent (or predictor) variables in research using the social influence paradigm (see reviews by Corrigan et al., 1980; Heppner & Claiborn, 1989; Heppner & Dixon, 1981; Heppner & Frazier, 1992; Hoyt, 1996). In short, a large body of research has examined the influence of various independent variables (diplomas, communication style) on client ratings of counselor attractiveness, expertness, and trustworthiness. Another group of studies has examined the relationship of client-rated attractiveness, expertness, and trustworthiness to client outcome.

The client's interpersonal manner also has been measured at the global level; the work of Leary (1957) on interpersonal diagnosis has served as a foundation for most of the examination of client style of interacting. Recently, Elliott and James (1989) reviewed the literature on the client's experience in psychotherapy and proposed three dimensions to account for their findings: positive versus negative affiliation, control versus independence, and interpersonal versus task focus. Two instruments developed by Kiesler (1984, 1987) use the control and affiliation dimension to describe client or counselor interpersonal manner. The Impact Message Inventory (IMI; Kiesler, 1987) assesses client interpersonal manner by recording the engagements or pulls that a client has on another interactant or observer (that is, what the person feels, thinks, or wants to do as he or she interacts or observes this client). The Check List of Psychotherapy Transactions (CLOPT) and the Check List of Interpersonal Transactions (CLOIT) define the client's style by describing overt interpersonal actions; the CLOIT is presented in Exhibit N. The IMI, CLOPT, and CLOIT can characterize clients in terms of 16 interpersonal scores: dominant, competitive, mistrusting, cold, hostile, detached, inhibited, unassured, submissive, deferent, trusting, warm, friendly, sociable, exhibitionistic, and assured. These interpersonal scores can be combined to form octant, quadrant, or axes descriptions of client interpersonal style. We believe research in this area is promising. For example, Orlinsky and Howard (1986) noted a positive association between client openness and therapeutic outcome.

Therapeutic Relationship, Micro Level

The relationship in counseling is more than the sum of the interactants. Measuring only what the client and counselor or the group members do individually does not constitute a measure of this relationship. Process measures thus focus on the developing relationship between and among clients and counselors.

The quality of this relationship has received a great deal of theoretical and empirical attention. In individual counseling, the quality of the relationship is usually examined in terms of the therapeutic or working alliance (see, for example, Horvath & Greenberg, 1989). In group research, this dimension is usually examined in terms of cohesion (see the review by Bednar & Kaul, 1978). However, almost all of this work has been at the global level (see next section); indeed, a major issue in assessing the quality of the relationship is the lack of micro-level speech act measures of the working alliance. Bordin's (1979) conceptualizations of the working alliance emphasized the "tear and repair" process, which is best conceptualized at the speech act level. It may be useful to develop speech act measures of the working alliance, so that an examination of the client and therapist behaviors that lead to tearing and repairing the alliance can be concluded.

We are aware of only one measure of cohesion at the speech act level. Friedlander, Thibodeau, Nichols, Tucker, and Snyder (1985) defined cohesion as the semantic relations within a spoken text that make it cohere or coalesce as a unit. They operationalized a cohesive tie as occurring when the interpretation of one speaker's message depends on information contained in the previous speaker's turn. According to these authors, there are five categories or types of cohesive ties: reference, conjunction, substitution, ellipsis, and lexical; these five Categories of Semantic Cohesion Analysis are presented in Exhibit O. Friedlander et al. argued that semantic cohesion is a measure of conversational involvement, an important component of all definitions of cohesion. The results of the Friedlander et al. study indicated that leader style was related to the number of cohesive ties produced in a group, and that groups with more cohesive ties had better client outcomes. These findings suggest that this speech act measure of cohesion may be a useful means of studying this elusive group phenomenon.

Therapeutic Relationship, Global Level

Frank (1974), in summarizing 25 years of research, concluded that "the quality of the therapeutic interaction, to which the patient, therapist, and therapeutic method contribute, is probably the major determinant of short-term therapeutic response" (p. 328). The quality of therapeutic interaction at the global level is the focus of the various measures of the therapeutic or working alliance. Of the four commonly used measures of the working alliance, three were designed for use by trained observers: the California Psychotherapy Alliance Scales (CALPAS; Marmar, Marziali, Horowitz, & Weiss, 1986), the Penn Helping Alliance Rating Scale (Penn, Morgan, Luborsky, Crits-Christoph, Curtis, & Solomon, 1982), and the Vanderbilt Therapeutic Alliance Scale (VTAS; Hartley & Strupp, 1983). The Working Alliance

Inventory (WAI; Horvath & Greenberg, 1989), designed to capture client and therapist perceptions of the working alliance, is presented in Exhibit P.

A study by Tichenor and Hill (1989) compared these various measures of the working alliance. These authors also devised an observer form of the WAI (adopted by altering the pronouns to fit an observer's perspective). All of the working alliance measures had high internal consistency; coefficient alphas ranged from 0.90 for the CALPAS to 0.98 for the WAI-observer form. In addition, the four observer ratings forms had high inter-rater reliability; interclass correlations ranged from 0.71 for the Penn to 0.94 for the CALPAS. Three of the four observer measures (CALPAS, VTAS, and WAI-observer form) also had high intercorrelations, indicating that they were measuring a single working alliance construct. (The Penn was significantly correlated with the WAI-observer form only.) These findings suggest common elements across the four observer measures of the working alliance. In addition, the WAI-observer form was the most economical measure because it did not require any rater training. Replication of the Tichenor and Hill study would provide strong support for using the WAI-observer form to operationalize the working alliance.

Tichenor and Hill (1989) also found the lack of a relationship among observer, client, and counselor perspectives on working alliance ratings. Thus, it is unclear what the measurements of the working alliance from the different perspectives actually assess; further research is needed to address the lack of agreement across the working alliance perspectives.

Fuhriman and Burlingame (1990) described cohesion in groups as analogous to the relationship in individual counseling. Kaul and Bednar (1986) declared that the term *cohesion* has such an endemic use in group treatment that descriptions of what happens in "groups would be practically impossible without reference to cohesion." Despite its clinical utility, the concept of cohesion has been a "spectacular embarrassment" for group researchers (Kaul & Bednar, 1986, p. 707). Most researchers have attempted to measure cohesion at a global level. As implied in Kaul and Bednar's comment, there is no consensus on a definition of or way to operationalize cohesion. Most of the research that examines cohesion has developed idiosyncratic derivatives of the concept, resulting in inconclusive findings and little cumulative knowledge of the construct. It might be a useful step for the group counseling field to examine the relationship between the different measures of cohesion. A study similar in format to Tichenor and Hill (1989) that examines group cohesion measures might well provide both theoretical and operational clarity for this important but messy area.

In summary, the therapeutic relationship is a key ingredient of the counseling process. Additional research is needed to develop a speech act measure of the working alliance. Only with this type of measure can investigators begin to examine Bordin's notion of the "tear and repair" process in the actual formation of the working alliance. Moreover, additional research is needed to examine how the three perspectives (client, counselor, observer) on working alliance formation interact. Are they complementary, unrelated, or just different? Researchers interested in group cohesion research have a promising speech act measure. It appears that research at the global level could be enhanced by a comparative study of the different measures that purport to measure cohesion.

Quality, Micro Level

Quality refers to how well or how completely the counselor carries out a single or a series of interventions, or how well the client enacts his or her role or tasks. Clinically, counselor competence is extremely important, but until recently it has been virtually ignored in process research. For example, even though dynamically oriented counselors speak of the timing and correctness of an interpretation, most research on this topic has simply examined the presence or amount of interpretation (see the review by Claiborn, 1982).

At the speech act level, one of the most commonly used measures of the quality of the counselor's intervention is the Helpfulness Scale (Elliott, 1985). To use this measure, clients review a recently completed counseling session and rate each of their counselor's interventions on a nine-point scale measuring helpfulness. This method assumes that the client is in fact the best arbiter of the usefulness of counseling. At present it is unknown whether such a rating of the helpfulness of specific counselor interventions is related to client outcome. When a client rates therapist interventions as more helpful, for example, will he or she have a better outcome than a client who rates his or her therapist's interventions as less helpful?

A second method for examining quality of counselor interventions at the speech act level has been described by Silberschatz, Fretter, and Curtis (1986). These authors maintained that assessing the quality of counselor behaviors involves two processes: (a) identifying the client's problems and needs, and (b) deciding if a given intervention correctly addresses those problems and needs. Specifically, Silberschatz et al. assessed the quality of therapist interpretations using two steps. The first step involved formulating for each client a plan or conceptualization, a prominent part of which involved identifying insights that would be helpful to the client. Five clinicians independently prepared such a plan for each client using assessment instruments and transcripts from an assessment interview. The second step involved having a second group of judges rate the extent to which each counselor interpretation fit the plan that had been developed. These judges used a seven-point Likert scale ranging from –3 (strongly anti-plan) to +3 (strongly pro-plan) to measure the extent of agreement between the plan and the individual interpretation. Silberschatz et al. found that the compatibility of an interpretation with a plan was a better predictor of immediate outcome (change in client experience) than was type of interpretation (transference versus nontransference).

Silberschatz et al. suggested that their methods or procedures for assessing quality of counselor interventions were transferable to a variety of conceptual frameworks. We agree with this suggestion. To reiterate, this method of assessing quality requires two steps. First, an independent and reliable conceptualization of the client, including a specification of his or her particular learning needs, is needed. Second, an independent and reliable rating of the extent to which particular interventions fit the conceptualization is needed.

As was true for assessing the quality of therapist interventions, there is relatively little consensus concerning measures of client response quality. One obstacle to the development of standardized quality measures is that various theories define the client role differently, and hence the appropriateness or quality of various client responses is viewed in divergent ways. For example, a behavior therapist might construe a client response of questioning or disagreeing with the therapist as a sign of resistance to implementing a treatment protocol, and thus assign it a low quality rating. A dynamic therapist, on the other hand, might construe the same response as a sign of autonomy, and thus assign it a high quality rating. Despite these theoretical differences, there is surprising consistency in usage of two particular speech act ratings of client response quality, which we will now discuss.

One of the most widely used ratings of client response quality is the Client Experiencing Scale (Klein, Mathieu-Coughlin, & Kiesler, 1986); this instrument is presented in Exhibit Q. The Client Experiencing Scale is a seven-point scale used by trained raters to describe a client's level of involvement. Low levels are characterized by client disclosures that are impersonal or superficial. At high levels of experiencing, feelings and exploration are a basis for problem resolution and/or self-understanding. Klein et al. reported high inter-rater reliability and validity, as evidenced by the relationships between client experiencing and self-exploration, insight, working through, the absence of resistances, and high-quality free association.

The second measure that has been used to operationalize the quality of client responding at the speech act level is the Client Vocal Quality Scale (CVQ; Rice, Koke, Greenberg, & Wagstaff, 1979). Like the Client Experiencing Scale, the CVQ is designed to measure the quality of the client's involvement in the counseling process. Vocal quality is a measure of how the energy of a speech act is expressed. According to this system, voice quality can be characterized as limited, externalizing, emotional, or focused (from low to high voice quality). Externalizing vocal quality involves an external or outward movement of energy designed to produce an effect in a listener. In limited vocal quality, there is a lack of energy; the voice has a thinness that seems to suggest a withdrawal of energy. Emotional vocal quality contains an overflow of energy, whereas focused vocal quality involves energy that is concentrated and directed inward. Like the Client Experiencing Scale, the CVQ has good reliability and validity data (Rice et al., 1979).

It is worth noting that the two most widely used measures of client response quality (at the speech act level) were developed by researchers operating within a client-centered perspective, which more than any other theoretical formulation places a premium on the client's involvement in the counseling process. Thus, it is probably not surprising that client-centered researchers have concentrated on developing measures of client process. What is surprising is how widely these client response quality measures have been adopted by researchers from other theoretical perspectives. For example, Silberschatz et al. (1986) used the Client Experiencing Scale to examine the quality of analytic interpretations.

As noted earlier, it seems likely that other theoretical perspectives would define client response quality in terms other than the quality of client involvement. It may be important to develop process measures that offer complementary views of what constitutes client response quality. An example of an alternative perspective for defining client response quality was reported by Martin and Stelmaczonek (1988), who used categories of discourse analysis that were drawn from a theoretical framework of information processing to define the quality of a client's response. Specifically, they rated client speech acts on five information-processing dimensions: (a) deep-shallow, (b) elaborative-nonelaborative, (c) personal-impersonal, (d) clear-vague, and (e) conclusion oriented-description oriented. Martin and Stelmaczonek found that events clients recalled as being important (when compared to events not so recalled) were characterized by client speech acts that involved (a) interpretive, critical, and analytic thinking (deep); (b) thinking that involved unique language, images, or metaphors (elaborative); or (c) interpretations or hypotheses (conclusion-oriented). It would be especially interesting to see how these measures of client response quality, derived from information-processing theory, would relate to the more established measures (experiencing and voice quality) derived from client-centered theory.

Quality, Global Level

There has been far less work measuring counselor quality at a global level. This lack of empirical investigation is probably because the measurement of counselor competence presents a number of thorny problems. Whereas naïve raters can be trained to rate adherence to a treatment model, rating of counselor competence presumes a level of general clinical sophistication and expertise in the particular treatment method being rated. For example, it its easier to train an observer to recognize whether or not a counselor makes an interpretation than it is to train an observer to rate the appropriateness (accuracy, timing) of an interpretation. Several researchers have attempted to measure therapist competence; for example, Barber and Crits-Christoph (1996) developed the Penn Adherence and Competence Scale for Supportive-Expressive Therapy (PACSE) presented in Exhibit R. As the name suggests, the PACSE is designed to rate both the frequency and quality of specific counselor responses associated with Luborky's manualized supportive-expressive treatment. Each item on the PACSE is rated twice: once for adherence (frequency) and once for competence (quality). The competence quality ratings are made on a seven-point scale ranging from 1 (poor quality) to 7 (excellent quality).

In the initial development of the PACSE (Barber & Crits-Christoph, 1996), two Ph.D.-level clinical psychologists rated audiotapes from 33 depressed patients receiving supportive-expressive therapy and seven patients receiving cognitive therapy. The PACSE contains 45 items covering general therapeutic skills (9 items), supportive techniques (9 items), and expressive techniques (27 items). Inter-rater reliabilities for the competence ratings were low when only supportive-expressive sessions were examined; when all sessions were examined, the inter-rater reliabilities were considerably higher. When Barber and Crits-Christoph (1996) examined the correlations between the PACSE adherence and competence ratings, they found that adherence and competence ratings are related but distinct constructs. Presumably, a counselor must have some level of adherence before she/he can demonstrate competence. In a more recent study, Crits-Christoph et al. (1998) used six of the original PACSE expressive items to rate competence in the delivery of a modified form of supportive-expressive counseling. The competence ratings in the Crits-Christoph et al. (1998) study were made by the clinical supervisors of the project counselors. The three very experienced supportive-expressive supervisors made competence ratings for both their own supervisees and the supervisees of the other supervisors. The Barber and Crits-Christoph (1996) and the Crits-Christoph et al. (1998) studies suggest that competence in supportive-expressive counseling can be rated relatively reliably (by experienced supervisors) and that adherence and competence are related but distinct constructs.

The PACSE has now been used in at least three studies (Barber & Crits-Christoph, 1996; Barber, Crits-Christoph, & Luborsky, 1996; Crits-Christoph et al., 1998). These studies show that supportive and expressive competence ratings are related to clients' level of psychopathology, depression, or psychological health and unrelated to current measures of the working alliance (Barber & Crits-Christoph, 1996). In a large-scale training study, expressive competence ratings were shown to change linearly (improve) across counseling sessions for the trainees' first training case (Crits-Christoph et al., 1998). Finally, expressive competence ratings were related to improvement in depression for clients in supportive-expressive treatment for depression. The relationship between expressive competence and improvement remained after controlling for the therapists' use (adherence) of expressive techniques, previous improvement, the therapeutic alliance, and general therapeutic skills (Barber, Crits-Christoph, & Luborsky, 1996).

The results of these studies confirmed the importance of counselor. For our purposes, the most important aspects of the studies by Barber and colleagues are the procedures used to operationalize the global level of therapist competence. To do this, the researcher must first carefully and specifically define the parameters of the treatment. Once the treatment has been specified, then the therapist's behaviors within a session can be examined on the extent to which they match or represent competent expression of the specified behaviors. The critical question for counseling researchers concerns the qualifications of the competence raters/judges. For example, Barber (1998, personal communication) emphasizes that use of the PACSE scale requires training in both the use of the scale and in supportive-expressive therapy. It is likely that only judges who are experts in a particular modality can make accurate competency judgments. The assessment of counselor quality is an exciting and virtually untapped area for process researchers. The methods and procedures developed by Silberschatz et al. (1986) and Barber and Crits-Christoph (1996) to assess counselor quality can serve as models for researchers seeking to measure the quality of counselor behavior from other theoretical perspectives.

The examination of client response quality at the global level has received even more limited attention. One of the most promising dimensions for characterizing client response quality at the global level is formulated in terms of openness versus defensiveness. Orlinsky and Howard (1986) reported that 88% of the studies examining client openness found a positive relationship between this variable and outcome measures. There is, however, little agreement on how this construct should be measured at the global level. In the 16 studies that examined client openness, the same process measure was seldom used to assess this construct. Nor is it known how the different measures that assess client openness relate to one another. Given the positive association between client openness and therapeutic outcome noted by Orlinsky and Howard (1986), development of more standardized ways of assessing this construct at a global level seems important.

Two Postscripts

We have some final comments, concerning two topics: client process measures and assessment strategies. With regard to the former, Hill (1982) observed that counselor process variables have attracted more theoretical and empirical attention than client process variables, perhaps because we as counselors/researchers are most interested in examining what we do, as evidenced by the differential attention focused on counselor and client response modes.

We believe this relative lack of attention to client process variables is a critical omission that hampers our understanding of the counseling process. Moreover, we strongly recommend that the client be conceptualized not as a passive agent to whom interventions are administered, but rather as an active processor of information in the change process (see Heppner & Claiborn, 1989; Heppner & Krauskopf, 1987; Martin, 1984, 1987; McGuire, 1985; Petty & Cacioppo, 1986). The Martin and Stelmaczonek (1988) investigation is an excellent example of conceptualizing the client as an active processor of information. Because human reasoning is a key activity in how people cope with their problems, attention to the active process of human reasoning deserves a central place in counseling process research.

Such a perspective might best be examined in both the content and quality aspects of process research. With regard to content, it may be useful to examine how clients represent their presenting problems to themselves (for example, via schemas), and whether the client's views of the problem change over time in counseling. Are there changes in the client's knowledge of the problem over time, or in the way the client's knowledge is organized? (See Martin, 1985, for an excellent case illustration.) It also may be important to investigate how clients deal with their affective reactions and how they appraise the significance of their problems. In short, we believe it may be very fruitful to examine the internal processes that clients engage in (cognitive, affective, and physiological) as they struggle with their problems before, during, and after counseling. Whereas client satisfaction or perceptions of counselor expertness provide some information about the client, these variables tell us little about how clients process information about the pressing concerns that brought them into counseling (Heppner & Claiborn, 1989; Heppner & Frazier, 1992).

Finally, some comments on assessment strategies are warranted given the multifaceted nature of counseling process and outcome research. Whereas most instruments can be categorized within one of the cells in Table 17-1, some instruments contain items that provide assessments across more than one aspect of the counseling process. Given the need to obtain a broad assessment of the counseling process, and the time-consuming nature of multiple assessments, the advantages of such inventories are clear. For example, consider the Comprehensive

Scale of Psychotherapy Session Constructs (CSPSC: Eugster & Wampold, 1996; see Exhibit H). The CSPSC measures session-level occurrences from either the client's or therapist's perspective of nine counseling process components (patient involvement, client involvement, comfort, learning, real relationship, therapist involvement, expertness, interpersonal style, real relationship) and session evaluation. In short, an 80-item, six-point Likert scale was developed by adapting items from the California Psychotherapy Alliance Scales (Barkham, Andrew, & Culverwell, 1993), the Empathy Scale (Burns, 1981), the Experiencing Scales (Klein, Mathieu, Kiesler, & Gendlin, 1969), the Patient and Therapist Behavior Ratings (Bennum, Hahlweg, Schindler, & Langlotz, 1986), the Patient and Therapist Therapy Session Reports (Orlinsky & Howard, 1978), the Penn Helping Alliance Scales (Luborsky et al., 1983), the Relationship Inventory (Barrett-Lennard, 1962), the Session Evaluation Questionnaire (Stiles & Snow, 1984a), the Session Impacts Scale (Elliott & Wexler, 1994), the Therapist and Patient Action Scales (Hoyt, Marmar, Horowitz, & Alvarez, 1981), the Vanderbilt Psychotherapy Process Scale (Suh et al. 1989), and the Working Alliance Inventory (Horvath & Greenberg, 1986). Eight items were devised for each of the nine constructs and for global session evaluation. Alpha coefficients revealed an average of .73 and .76 for subscales on the therapist and patient forms, respectively. Assessment strategies such as this, and instruments such as the CSPSC in particular, hold a great deal of promise for future research.

SUMMARY AND CONCLUSIONS

This chapter provided a general introduction to counseling process research, or investigations that examine events that occur within the therapeutic encounter. Researchers have examined a very wide range of activities, such as therapist self-disclosure, client reactions, the working alliance, perceived therapist empathy, client openness, and various interventions (for example, interpretations). We discussed Hill's (1991) scheme for classifying the various behaviors within process research, which consists of the following seven types of behaviors: (a) ancillary behaviors, (b) verbal behaviors, (c) covert behaviors, (d) content, (e) strategies, (f) interpersonal manner, and (g) the therapeutic relationship. The discovery of new knowledge pertaining to these categories of counseling process research can be exhilarating.

The research that links counseling process and outcomes is vast; Orlinsky et al. (1994) counted more than 2300 process and outcomes studies from 1950 to 1992. Clearly, process research has been a very important theme within the counseling literature. Perhaps one of the major stimulants for much of the process research in the early 1960s and 1970s was Rogers' (1957) formulation of the necessary and sufficient conditions for therapeutic gain. Most of the counseling process research over the years has focused on individual counseling with European-American participants; relatively few empirical studies have been conducted on racial and cultural factors in the therapy process (Helms, 1994). Moreover, the process of career counseling remains largely unexplored (Dorn, 1988). Although much has been learned about the counseling process in the past

50 years, many basic research questions relative to various ethnic and nonethnic minority populations remain.

Many design considerations for conducting research (for example, selecting variables, experimenter bias) discussed earlier in this book apply to counseling process research. The second part of this chapter highlighted five methodological and measurement issues that are particularly relevant for counseling process researchers: (a) what to study, (b) what to measure, (c) whose perspective, (d) how much to measure, and (e) how to analyze process data. We maintained that it is very important for researchers to be very careful in selecting behaviors to examine in process research; examination of various classification schemes (see, for example, Elliott, 1991; Hill, 1991) might help guide researchers. In addition, it is important to consider at what level the researcher wants to examine the behaviors, from statement-by-statement speech acts to more global levels. Research clearly documents that the counseling process differs across various perspectives, such as from the client, counselor, or observer perspective. We encourage researchers to carefully think about the different perspectives in developing research questions, and if appropriate, to examine the counseling process from multiple perspectives.

We noted that important differences between the first and last session have also been observed in process research. Thus, in determining how much to measure it is critical to think through the research questions very carefully; it may be useful to include individual differences or time intervals in the research questions. With group designs, sampling a part of several sessions will likely yield acceptable results, whereas single-subject designs may need to examine the entire session without sampling. Finally, in terms of analyzing the data, we highlighted the critical issue of using nonparticipatory judges in rating data. The task of rating data from process studies merits careful consideration of a number of issues, including the number of judges, rater selection, rater bias, rater errors, rater training, maintaining morale among judges, and data aggregation. We also briefly discuss statistical strategies to analyze quantitative data, ranging from correlational designs to more powerful sequential analysis.

The final section of the chapter provides representative examples of instruments used to assess different aspects of counseling process research. These examples serve to operationalize some of the constructs that have been examined in the counseling process research.

• • • • • • • • • • • • • • •

EXHIBIT A
The Four Vocal Patterns (Rice & Kerry, 1986)[1]

Aspects	Focused	Externalizing	Limited	Emotional
Production of accents	Achieved with loudness and/or drawl more than pitch rise	Achieved with pitch more than loudness or drawl	Usual balance for English	Not applicable

Continued

E X H I B I T A *(Continued)*

Aspects	Focused	Externalizing	Limited	Emotional
Accentuation	Irregular	Extremely regular	Usual pattern for English	Usually irregular
Regularity of pace	Uneven; usually slowed but may be speeded patches	Even pace	Neither markedly even nor uneven	Usually uneven
Terminal contours	Ragged and unexpected	Highly expected in relation to the structure of what is said	Direction about as usual, but energy tends to peter out, yielding a breathy quality	Unexpected
Perceived energy	Moderate to high; voice may be soft but on platform	Moderate to high; may be a bit above platform but adequate push	Voice not resting on own platform; inadequate push	Not applicable
Disruption of speech pattern	No	No	No	Yes

•   •   •   •   •   •   •   •   •   •   •   •   •   •   •   •

•   •   •   •   •   •   •   •   •   •   •   •   •   •   •   •

E X H I B I T B
Arousal Measure (Burgoon, Kelly, Newton, & Keeley-Dyreson, 1989)[2]

Dimensions	Items	Continuum
Arousal	Cool Calm Still Composed	Cool-Bothered Calm-Anxious Still-Restless Composed-Uncomposed
Orientation/Gaze	Body Orientation Face Orientation Gaze	Direct-Indirect Direct-Indirect Appropriate-Inappropriate
Random Movement	Trunk/Limb Movement Rock/Twist Head Movement	Frequent-None Frequent-None Frequent-None

E X H I B I T B *(Continued)*

Dimensions	Items	Continuum
Facial/Head Animation	Facial Animation	Animated-Impassive
	Concern	Concerned-Indifferent
	Nodding	Frequent-None
Facial Pleasantness	Facial Expression	Pleasant-Unpleasant
	Smiling	Frequent-None
	Smiling	Appropriate-Inappropriate
Gestural Animation	Gestures	Animated-Impassive
	Illustrators	Frequent-None
Self-Adaptors	Self-adaptors	Frequent-None
Object-Adaptors	Object-adaptors	Frequent-None
Kinesic/Proxemic	Involved	Involved-Uninvolved
Attentiveness	Interested	Interested-Bored
	Attentive	Attentive-Inattentive
	Focused	Focused-Distracted
	Alert	Alert-Unalert
	Active	Active-Inactive
Bodily Coordination	Movements	Coordinated-Uncoordinated
Postural Relaxation	Slumped	Slumped-Erect
	Relaxed	Relaxed-Tense
	Loose	Loose-Rigid
Body Lean (proxemics)	Body Lean	Forward-Backward
Vocal Expressiveness	Loudness	Appropriate-Inappropriate
	Rate	Fast-Slow
	Tempo	Varied-No Variation
	Tempo	Appropriate-Inappropriate
	Pitch	Appropriate-Inappropriate
	Pitch	Varied Monotone
	Expression	Expressive-Inexpressive
Pauses and Laughter	Silences	Frequent-None
	Latencies	Appropriate-Inappropriate
	Relaxed Laughter	Frequent-None
Fluency	Fluent	Fluent-Nonfluent
	Nervous Vocalizations	Frequent-None
Vocal Attentiveness	Focused	Focused-Distracted
	Attentive	Attentive-Inattentive
	Alert	Alert-Unalert
	Coordinated	Coordinated-Uncoordinated
Vocal Relaxation	Rhythm	Rhythmic-Jerky
	Clear	Clear-Unclear
	Resonant	Resonant-Flat
	Relaxed	Relaxed-Tense
	Calm	Calm-anxious
	Composed	Composed-Uncomposed
	Cool	

Continued

E X H I B I T B *(Continued)*

Dimensions	Items	Continuum
Vocal Warmth	Warm	Cool-Bothered
	Interested	Warm-Cold
	Involved	Interested-Bored
	Pleasant	Involved-Apathetic
	Friendly	Pleasant-Unpleasant
	Appealing	Friendly-Unfriendly
	Loud	Appealing-Unappealing
Loudness	Pitch	Loud-Soft

• • • • • • • • • • • • • • • •

• • • • • • • • • • • • • • • •

E X H I B I T C
Hill Counselor Verbal Response Modes Category System (Hill, 1985)[3]

1. APPROVAL: Provides emotional support, approval, reassurance, or reinforcement. It may imply sympathy or tend to alleviate anxiety by minimizing the client's problems. These responses can be either very short (e.g., "Good") or long.
2. PROVIDING INFORMATION: Supplies information in the form of data, facts, or resources. It may be information related to the counseling process, the counselor's behavior, or counseling arrangements (time, fee, place, etc.).
3. DIRECT GUIDANCE: Directions or advice that the counselor suggests for the client. DO NOT confuse Providing Information and Direct Guidance: Providing Information gives facts, whereas Direct Guidance requests that the client DO something. Responses in this category are (a) for within the session, and (b) for outside the session.
4. CLOSED QUESTION: Used to gather data. Closed Questions request a one- or two-word answer, a "yes" or "no" or a confirmation. The client responses requested by this type of question are LIMITED and SPECIFIC—the counselor wants some specific information.
5. OPEN QUESTION: Used to request clarification or exploration by the client. When the counselor asks the client to explore, he/she doesn't necessarily want a specific answer but wants to hear the client's thoughts about the topic.
6. PARAPHRASE: Four types of responses fall into this category: restatements, reflections, nonverbal referents, and summaries. They are categorized together because conceptually they seem very similar and they are very hard to differentiate.
   (a) A restatement is a simple repeating or rephrasing of the client's statement(s) and typically contains fewer but similar words and is more concrete and clearer than the client's message. It can be stated either tentatively or as a statement.
   (b) A reflection is a repeating or rephrasing of the client's statements that includes an explicit indication of the client's feelings. The feelings may have been stated by the client (in either exactly the same words or in similar words).
   (c) A nonverbal referent points out or inquires about aspects of the client's nonverbal behavior (e.g., body posture, voice tone or level, facial expression, gestures, etc.).
   (d) A summary restates the major themes the client has been discussing. It may cover the immediate session or the entire course of treatment.

E X H I B I T C *(Continued)*

7. INTERPRETATION: Goes beyond what the client has overtly stated or recognized. An Interpretation usually presents a new meaning or gives a reason or insight for behaviors of feelings. Interpretations usually help clients see things in a new way or:
   (a) Establishes connections between seemingly isolated statements or events
   (b) Points out themes or patterns in client's behavior or feelings
   (c) Interprets defenses, resistance, or transference
   (d) Relates present events to events in the past
   (e) Gives a new framework to feelings, behaviors, or problems

8. CONFRONTATION: Points out a discrepancy or contradiction. Usually a Confrontation contains two parts—the first part states or refers to some aspect of the client's message or behavior (this may be implied by the counselor rather than actually stated). The second part often begins with "But" and presents the discrepancy. There are several types of discrepancies:
   (a) Between words and behaviors (or verbal and nonverbal)
   (b) Between two things the client has stated
   (c) Between the client's and counselor's perceptions (could include disagreements with the client)

9. SELF-DISCLOSURE: The counselor shares something about himself or herself, such as personal experiences or feelings. These statements often start with "I." However, not all counselor statements that start with "I" are Self-Disclosures.

10. OTHER: Includes statements that are unrelated to the client's problems, such as small talk or salutations, and comments about the weather or events; includes any statement that does not fit into any other category or is unclassifiable due to difficulties.

• • • • • • • • • • • • • • • •

• • • • • • • • • • • • • • • •

E X H I B I T D
Supervision Questionnaire (Worthington & Roehlke, 1979)[4]

SUPERVISION QUESTIONNAIRE

Name: _____   Date of Ph.D. Degree _____

Setting: Counseling Center _____

            Academic Department _____

Supervisor's approximate number of years since Ph.D. _____

Supervisor's primary placement: Academic _____

                                   Counseling Center _____

                                   Community Mental Health Center _____

                                   Private Practice _____

Continued

E X H I B I T   D *(Continued)*

Is your supervisor a licensed psychologist (Clinical or Counseling)?
(Circle one)   Yes   No

This questionnaire is designed to evaluate the supervision you received this semester. It has two parts. The first part asks you to rate the effectiveness of the supervision you have received. The second part of the questionnaire is designed to measure more specifically the behaviors of your supervisor. Please consider each item carefully on its own merits. Try to avoid the "halo effect" in which a good supervisor tends to receive "high marks" on everything. Do not mark this second part according to how frequently you think your supervisor "should" have done each behavior; rather, rate the actual frequency of behavior. This form is used at a number of universities and agencies. It is highly likely that your supervisor never did (rating 1) some of the behaviors. Marking a 1 or 2 (or any rating for that matter) is not an indictment of or testimony for your supervisor.

I. Effectiveness of supervision:

1. Satisfaction with supervision.

Totally unsatisfied; it could not have been worse.	Mostly unsatisfied; could have been a little worse.	More unsatisfied than not.	So-so; not really satisfied or unsatisfied.	More satisfied than not.	Mostly satisfied; could have been a little better.	Totally satisfied; it could not have been better.

2. How competent was your supervisor at giving good supervision?

Totally incompetent	Mostly competent	More incompetent	So-so	More competent than not	Mostly competent	Totally competent

3. How much did interactions with your supervisor contribute to improvement in your counseling ability?

Had almost no effect	Had a small effect	Had somewhat of an effect	Had a moderate effect	Had a substantial effect	Had a large effect	Had a very large effect

II. Description of your supervisor's behavior:

Please rate each of the following items as to how descriptive it is of your supervisor's behavior. Use the following 5-point scale to make your ratings.

5—perfectly descriptive of my supervisor's behavior
4—usually descriptive of my supervisor's behavior
3—descriptive of my supervisor's behavior
2—occasionally descriptive of my supervisor's behavior
1—never (or very infrequently) descriptive of my supervisor's behavior

E X H I B I T D *(Continued)*

Behavior (or pseudo behavior) of supervisor	Rating (circle one)
1. Established good rapport with you.	1 2 3 4 5
2. Established clear goals conjointly with you against which progress in supervision was measured.	1 2 3 4 5
3. During the initial sessions the supervisor provided more structure than during later sessions.	1 2 3 4 5
4. Observed you counsel (live observation) at a minimum of one time this semester,	1 2 3 4 5
5. Observed at least three videotapes of your counseling this semester.	1 2 3 4 5
6. Listened to at least three audiotapes of your counseling this semester.	1 2 3 4 5
7. Provided relevant literature or references on specific treatment techniques or assessment techniques.	1 2 3 4 5
8. Gave appropriate feedback to you	
a. About positive counseling behaviors	
b. About nonfacilitative behaviors	
9. Was sensitive to the differences between how you talk about your actions and how you really behave with clients.	1 2 3 4 5
10. Modeled within the supervision session good task-oriented skills.	1 2 3 4 5
11. Gave direct suggestions to you when appropriate.	1 2 3 4 5
12. Supervisor allowed you to observe him or her, do co-counseling with him or her, listen to audiotapes of his or her counseling, or view videotapes of his or her counseling.	1 2 3 4 5
13. Supervisor was available for consulting at times other than regularly scheduled meetings.	1 2 3 4 5
14. Used the relationship between supervisor and supervisee to demonstrate principles of counseling.	1 2 3 4 5
15. Helped you to conceptualize cases. Worked together with you to evolve a joint conceptualization for clients.	1 2 3 4 5
16. Encouraged you to experiment with different assessment and intervention techniques to discover your own unique style.	1 2 3 4 5
17. Suggested specific ways to help you get your client(s) to accept your conceptualization of the client's problems.	1 2 3 4 5
18. Used humor in supervision sessions.	1 2 3 4 5
19. Labeled counselor behavior as effective or ineffective rather than right or wrong.	1 2 3 4 5
20. Helped you develop self-confidence as an emerging counselor.	1 2 3 4 5
21. Helped you realize that trying new skills usually seems awkward at first.	1 2 3 4 5
22. Confronted you when appropriate.	1 2 3 4 5
23. Helped you assess your own:	1 2 3 4 5
a. strengths	
b. weaknesses	
24. Evaluated you at mid-semester.	1 2 3 4 5

Continued

E X H I B I T D *(Continued)*

Behavior (or pseudo behavior) of supervisor	Rating (circle one)
25. Renegotiated goals with you at mid-semester.	1 2 3 4 5
26. Called you by name at least one time per session.	1 2 3 4 5
27. Provided suggestions for alternative ways of conceptualizing clients.	1 2 3 4 5
28. Provided suggestions for alternative ways of intervening with clients.	1 2 3 4 5
29. Discussed with you experiences in the practicus class in addition to clients.	1 2 3 4 5
30. Gave emotional support to you when appropriate.	1 2 3 4 5
31. Supervisor taught you specific counseling behaviors intended to facilitate your style.	1 2 3 4 5
32. Encouraged you to find your own style of counseling.	1 2 3 4 5
33. Helped you with personal problems that may interfere with your counseling.	1 2 3 4 5
34. Supervisor demonstrated, by role playing, techniques of intervention.	1 2 3 4 5
35. Helped you deal with your own defensiveness when it arose in supervision.	1 2 3 4 5
36. Supervisor shared his or her own experiences with clients with you.	1 2 3 4 5
37. Supervisor consulted with you when emergencies arose with your clients.	1 2 3 4 5
38. Supervisor missed no more than one supervisory session per semester. (If a missed session was rescheduled and made up, it is not counted as missed.)	1 2 3 4 5
39. Supervisory sessions lasted at least 50 minutes.	
40. At least 45 minutes of each supervisory session were spent discussing counseling and/or clients.	1 2 3 4 5
41. Focus of most supervision sessions was on the relationship between supervisor and supervisee.	1 2 3 4 5
42. Focus of most supervision sessions was on the content of counseling sessions.	1 2 3 4 5
43. Focus of most supervision sessions was on conceptualizing the dynamics of the client's personality.	1 2 3 4 5
44. Supervisor made it easy to give feedback about the supervision process.	1 2 3 4 5
45. Helped you develop skills at intake interviews.	1 2 3 4 5
46. Helped prepare you for consultation and case disposition after intake interviews.	1 2 3 4 5

•   •   •   •   •   •   •   •   •   •   •   •   •   •   •

• • • • • • • • • • • • • • • •

EXHIBIT E
Thought-Listing Form (Heppner et. al., 1992)[5]

Please provide some idea of the thoughts that crossed your mind during the session that just ended. Simply write down the first thought that comes to mind on the first line, the second thought on the second line, etc., that you were thinking during the session, not the ideas that occur to you now.

My thoughts during the session were:

_____

_____

_____

_____

_____

_____

_____

_____

_____

_____

_____

_____

_____

_____

_____

_____

_____

_____

_____

_____

_____

_____

_____

• • • • • • • • • • • • • • • •

• • • • • • • • • • • • • • • •

EXHIBIT F
Brief Structured Recall (Elliott & Shapiro, 1988)[6]

EVENT RATING FORM—CLIENT

Part D: Client Intentions Ratings

For the following items, please rate what you were doing during the event. Use the following rating scale:

Not at all	Slightly	Somewhat	Pretty much	Very much
1	2	3	4	5

1 2 3 4 5   1. I was wanting or trying to get my therapist to do something for me (e.g., give me information, advice, support, explanation, etc.).

1 2 3 4 5   2. I was agreeing with what my therapist said.

1 2 3 4 5   3. I was disagreeing with what my therapist said.

1 2 3 4 5   4. I was trying to describe something to my therapist; put an experience into words.

1 2 3 4 5   5. I was trying to figure something out about myself; explore an experience or behavior of mine; see if what the therapist said about me fit.

1 2 3 4 5   6. I was trying to figure out what to do about a problem; learn how to do something; see what I thought of a suggestion by my therapist.

1 2 3 4 5   7. I was trying to avoid something I'd rather not deal with or talk about right now.

1 2 3 4 5   8. Other intention(s). (Please describe:)

_____

_____

• • • • • • • • • • • • • • • •

• • • • • • • • • • • • • • • •

EXHIBIT G
Session Evaluation Questionnaire (Stiles & Snow, 1984)[7]

CLIENT POSTSESSION QUESTIONNAIRE

This session was:

Bad	1	2	3	4	5	6	7	Good
Safe	1	2	3	4	5	6	7	Dangerous
Difficult	1	2	3	4	5	6	7	Easy
Valuable	1	2	3	4	5	6	7	Worthless
Shallow	1	2	3	4	5	6	7	Deep
Relaxed	1	2	3	4	5	6	7	Tense

E X H I B I T G *(Continued)*

This session was:

Unpleasant	1	2	3	4	5	6	7	Pleasant
Full	1	2	3	4	5	6	7	Empty
Weak	1	2	3	4	5	6	7	Powerful
Special	1	2	3	4	5	6	7	Ordinary
Rough	1	2	3	4	5	6	7	Smooth
Comfortable	1	2	3	4	5	6	7	Uncomfortable

Right now I feel:

Happy	1	2	3	4	5	6	7	Sad
Angry	1	2	3	4	5	6	7	Pleased
Moving	1	2	3	4	5	6	7	Still
Uncertain	1	2	3	4	5	6	7	Definite
Calm	1	2	3	4	5	6	7	Excited
Confident	1	2	3	4	5	6	7	Afraid
Wakeful	1	2	3	4	5	6	7	Sleepy
Friendly	1	2	3	4	5	6	7	Unfriendly
Slow	1	2	3	4	5	6	7	Fast
Energetic	1	2	3	4	5	6	7	Peaceful
Involved	1	2	3	4	5	6	7	Detached
Quiet	1	2	3	4	5	6	7	Aroused

• • • • • • • • • • • • • • • • •

• • • • • • • • • • • • • • • • •

E X H I B I T H
Comprehensive Scale of Psychotherapy Session Constructs—Revised (Eugster & Wampold, 1996)[8]

Please circle the number that best represents your level of agreement with each statement in terms of your own experience and your perceptions about your patient

THERAPIST FORM	strongly disagree			strongly agree		
1. In this session, my patient was relaxed	1	2	3	4	5	6
2. I took an active role in this session	1	2	3	4	5	6
3. In this session, my patient gained some new understanding	1	2	3	4	5	6
4. In this session, my patient was hostile	1	2	3	4	5	6
5. I explicitly encouraged my patient to express thoughts and feelings in this session	1	2	3	4	5	6
6. In this session, I could not give my patient what s/he needed	1	2	3	4	5	6
7. This session was very helpful	1	2	3	4	5	6
8. My patient did not like me in this session	1	2	3	4	5	6

Continued

E X H I B I T H *(Continued)*

THERAPIST FORM	strongly disagree				strongly agree	
9. My patient was honest and open with me in this session	1	2	3	4	5	6
10. I had a strong personal reaction to something that came up in this session	1	2	3	4	5	6
11. In this session, my patient made a new connection or realized something new about him/herself	1	2	3	4	5	6
12. I was not engaged in this session	1	2	3	4	5	6
13. My patient worked hard in this session	1	2	3	4	5	6
14. This session was rough for my patient	1	2	3	4	5	6
15. I did a good job in this session	1	2	3	4	5	6
16. I expressed thoughts, feelings or ideas in this session	1	2	3	4	5	6
17. This was a good session	1	2	3	4	5	6
18. My patient was tense in this session	1	2	3	4	5	6
19. In this session my patient felt caring toward me as a person	1	2	3	4	5	6
20. My patient was passive in this session	1	2	3	4	5	6
21. I was able to work with everything that came up in this session	1	2	3	4	5	6
22. I used a cooperative approach in this session	1	2	3	4	5	6
23. In this session, my patient gained new insight(s)	1	2	3	4	5	6
24. I lacked expertise in this session	1	2	3	4	5	6
25. I felt comfortable during this session	1	2	3	4	5	6
26. In this session, my patient felt secure	1	2	3	4	5	6
27. This was a valuable session	1	2	3	4	5	6
28. I was indifferent to my patient's feelings in this session	1	2	3	4	5	6
29. My patient did not enjoy seeing me in this session	1	2	3	4	5	6
30. This was a difficult session for my patient	1	2	3	4	5	6
31. I was disturbed by this session						
32. My patient was actively involved in this session	1	2	3	4	5	6
33. My patient brought up issues in this session that made me feel uneasy	1	2	3	4	5	6
34. In this session, I was confident	1	2	3	4	5	6
35. In this session, I was emotionally detached	1	2	3	4	5	6
36. My patient felt uncomfortable in this session	1	2	3	4	5	6
37. In this session, I really cared about my patient as a person	1	2	3	4	5	6
38. In this session my patient explored and expressed thoughts and feelings	1	2	3	4	5	6

E X H I B I T H *(Continued)*

THERAPIST FORM	strongly disagree				strongly agree	
39. This was an insignificant session	1	2	3	4	5	6
40. In this session, I did not disclose any personal information to my patient	1	2	3	4	5	6
41. In this session, my patient learned something important about his/her behavior, assumptions, motivations, or unconscious	1	2	3	4	5	6
42. This session was not worthwhile	1	2	3	4	5	6
43. I was honest and open with my patient in this session	1	2	3	4	5	6
44. In this session, I did not like my patient	1	2	3	4	5	6
45. In this session, I understood what was going on most or all of the time	1	2	3	4	5	6
46. I remained in a formal therapist-role throughout this session	1	2	3	4	5	6
47. Uncomfortable feelings or associations were triggered for me in this session	1	2	3	4	5	6
48. In this session, my patient was detached	1	2	3	4	5	6
49. In this session, I revealed something of what I am really like as a person	1	2	3	4	5	6
50. In this session, I felt I did not care what happens to my patient	1	2	3	4	5	6
51. This was a worthless session	1	2	3	4	5	6
52. In this session, I really knew what was going on with my patient	1	2	3	4	5	6
53. I was silent throughout most of this session	1	2	3	4	5	6
54. In this session, things seemed to my patient to be just the same as they have always been	1	2	3	4	5	6
55. In this session, I was friendly and warm	1	2	3	4	5	6
56. This was an important session	1	2	3	4	5	6
57. I nearly always knew exactly what my patient meant in this session	1	2	3	4	5	6
58. In this session, I disapproved of my patient	1	2	3	4	5	6
59. I interacted with my patient in a casual or spontaneous manner in this session	1	2	3	4	5	6
60. My patient made no progress in this session	1	2	3	4	5	6
61. My patient experienced strong feelings in this session	1	2	3	4	5	6
62. I did not enjoy seeing my patient this session	1	2	3	4	5	6
63. I did not know what I was doing in this session	1	2	3	4	5	6
64. In this session, my patient felt close to me	1	2	3	4	5	6
65. I did not feel anxious in this session	1	2	3	4	5	6
66. Nothing new emerged for my patient in this session	1	2	3	4	5	6
67. I was not very helpful in this session	1	2	3	4	5	6

Continued

E X H I B I T H *(Continued)*

THERAPIST FORM	strongly disagree				strongly agree	
68. In this session, I was not very interested in what my patient had to say	1	2	3	4	5	6
69. My patient felt safe in this session	1	2	3	4	5	6
70. In this session, my patient felt connected to me only as my patient	1	2	3	4	5	6
71. My patient did not move forward on anything in this session	1	2	3	4	5	6
72. My patient felt good in this session	1	2	3	4	5	6
73. This was an awful session	1	2	3	4	5	6
74. I did not offer any guidance or direction in this session	1	2	3	4	5	6
75. In this session, my patient related to me with genuine feeling	1	2	3	4	5	6
76. In this session, I felt I did not see my patient as s/he really is	1	2	3	4	5	6

Please circle the number that best represents your level of agreement with each statement in terms of your own experience and your perceptions about your therapist

PATIENT FORM	strongly disagree				strongly agree	
1. In this session, I was relaxed	1	2	3	4	5	6
2. My therapist took an active role in this session	1	2	3	4	5	6
3. In this session, I gained some new understanding	1	2	3	4	5	6
4. In this session, I was hostile	1	2	3	4	5	6
5. My therapist explicitly encouraged me to express thoughts and feelings in this session	1	2	3	4	5	6
6. In this session, my therapist could not give me what I needed	1	2	3	4	5	6
7. This session was very helpful	1	2	3	4	5	6
8. I did not like my therapist in this session	1	2	3	4	5	6
9. I was honest and open with my therapist in this session	1	2	3	4	5	6
10. My therapist had a strong personal reaction to something that came up in this session	1	2	3	4	5	6
11. In this session, I made a new connection or realized something new about myself	1	2	3	4	5	6
12. My therapist was not engaged in this session	1	2	3	4	5	6
13. I worked hard in this session	1	2	3	4	5	6
14. This session was rough	1	2	3	4	5	6
15. My therapist did a good job in this session	1	2	3	4	5	6
16. My therapist expressed thoughts, feelings or ideas in this session	1	2	3	4	5	6

E X H I B I T H (Continued)

PATIENT FORM	strongly disagree				strongly agree	
17. This was a good session	1	2	3	4	5	6
18. I was tense in this session	1	2	3	4	5	6
19. In this session I felt caring toward my therapist as a person	1	2	3	4	5	6
20. I was passive in this session	1	2	3	4	5	6
21. My therapist was able to work with everything that came up in this session	1	2	3	4	5	6
22. My therapist used a cooperative approach in this session	1	2	3	4	5	6
23. In this session, I gained new insight(s)	1	2	3	4	5	6
24. My therapist lacked expertise in this session	1	2	3	4	5	6
25. My therapist felt comfortable during this session	1	2	3	4	5	6
26. In this session, I felt secure	1	2	3	4	5	6
27. This was a valuable session	1	2	3	4	5	6
28. My therapist was indifferent to my feelings in this session	1	2	3	4	5	6
29. I did not enjoy seeing my therapist in this session	1	2	3	4	5	6
30. This was a difficult session	1	2	3	4	5	6
31. My therapist was disturbed by this session	1	2	3	4	5	6
32. I was actively involved in this session	1	2	3	4	5	6
33. I brought up issues in this session that made my therapist feel uneasy	1	2	3	4	5	6
34. In this session, my therapist was confident	1	2	3	4	5	6
35. In this session, my therapist was emotionally detached	1	2	3	4	5	6
36. I felt uncomfortable in this session	1	2	3	4	5	6
37. In this session, my therapist really cared about me as a person	1	2	3	4	5	6
38. In this session I explored and expressed thoughts and feelings	1	2	3	4	5	6
39. This was an insignificant session	1	2	3	4	5	6
40. In this session, my therapist did not share any personal information with me	1	2	3	4	5	6
41. In this session, I learned something important about my behavior, assumptions, motivations, or unconscious	1	2	3	4	5	6
42. This session was not worthwhile	1	2	3	4	5	6
43. My therapist was honest and open with me in this session	1	2	3	4	5	6
44. In this session, my therapist did not like me	1	2	3	4	5	6
45. In this session, my therapist understood what was going on most or all of the time	1	2	3	4	5	6

(Continued)

EXHIBIT H *(Continued)*

PATIENT FORM	strongly disagree				strongly agree	
46. My therapist remained in a formal therapist-role throughout this session	1	2	3	4	5	6
47. Uncomfortable feelings or associations were triggered for my therapist in this session	1	2	3	4	5	6
48. In this session, I was detached	1	2	3	4	5	6
49. In this session, my therapist revealed something of what s/he is really like as a person	1	2	3	4	5	6
50. In this session, my therapist did not seem to care what happens to me	1	2	3	4	5	6
51. This was a worthless session	1	2	3	4	5	6
52. In this session, my therapist really knew what was going on with me	1	2	3	4	5	6
53. My therapist was silent throughout most of this session	1	2	3	4	5	6
54. In this session, things seemed to be just the same as they have always been	1	2	3	4	5	6
55. In this session, my therapist was friendly and warm	1	2	3	4	5	6
56. This was an important session	1	2	3	4	5	6
57. My therapist nearly always knew exactly what I meant in this session	1	2	3	4	5	6
58. In this session, my therapist disapproved of me	1	2	3	4	5	6
59. My therapist interacted with me in a casual or spontaneous manner in this session	1	2	3	4	5	6
60. I made no progress in this session	1	2	3	4	5	6
61. I experienced strong feelings in this session	1	2	3	4	5	6
62. My therapist did not enjoy seeing me this session	1	2	3	4	5	6
63. My therapist did not know what s/he was doing in this session	1	2	3	4	5	6
64. In this session, I felt close to my therapist	1	2	3	4	5	6
65. My therapist did not feel anxious in this session	1	2	3	4	5	6
66. Nothing new emerged for me in this session	1	2	3	4	5	6
67. My therapist was not very helpful in this session	1	2	3	4	5	6
68. In this session, my therapist was not very interested in what I had to say	1		3	4	5	6
69. I felt safe in this session	1	2	3	4	5	6
70. In this session, I felt connected to my therapist only as his/her patient	1	2	3	4	5	6
71. I did not move forward on anything in this session	1		3	4	5	6

EXHIBIT H *(Continued)*

PATIENT FORM   strongly disagree   strongly agree

72. 1 felt good in this session   1   2   3   4   5   6
73. This was an awful session   1   2   3   4   5   6
74. My therapist did not offer any guidance or   1   2   3   4   5   6
    direction in this session
75. In this session, I related to my therapist with   1   2   3   4   5   6
    genuine feeling
76. In this session, my therapist did not see me   1   2   3   4   5   6
    as I really am

Scoring Key (Note: R = Reversed Scored)

Session Evaluation: 7, 17, 27, 39R, 42R, 51R, 56, 73R	Therapist Involvement: 2, 5, 12R, 16, 22, 35R, 53R, 74R
Patient Involvement: 4R, 13, 20R, 32, 38, 48R, 61	Therapist Comfort: 10R, 25, 31R, 33R, 47R, 65
Patient Comfort: 1, 14R, 18R, 26, 30R, 36R, 69, 72	Therapist Expertness: 6R, 15, 21, 24R, 34, 45, 63R, 67R
Patient Progress: 3, 11, 23, 41, 54R, 60R, 66R, 71R	Therapist Interpersonal Style: 28R, 50R, 52, 55, 57, 58R, 68R
Patient Real Relationship: 8R, 9, 19, 29R, 64, 70, 75, 76R	Therapist Real Relationship: 37, 40R, 43, 44R, 46R, 49, 59, 62R

•   •   •   •   •   •   •   •   •   •   •   •   •   •   •   •

•   •   •   •   •   •   •   •   •   •   •   •   •   •   •   •

EXHIBIT I
Hill Interaction Matrix (Hill, 1965)[9]

Work on the HIM first began in 1954 and has been continuing ever since. A comprehensive account of this work appeared in monograph form in 1961 and was revised in 1965. A scoring manual was also published in 1961 and revised in 1965. The present publication has as its purpose updating HIM developments and especially the dissemination of information on the rating scales associated with the HIM. A brief account of the HIM category system is included to provide a context and point of ready reference, especially for those who have not read the HIM Monograph and Scoring Manual.

INTRODUCTION TO HIM CATEGORY SYSTEM

The categories of this interaction rating system were empirically derived by studying intensively a considerable number of therapy groups. This resulted in deriving two basic dimensions which seemed to be paramount in distinguishing groups. Both dimensions are manifested in 'styles' of operation. One dimension deals with the 'content,' that is, what groups talk about. The Content/Style has four categories—Topic, Group, Personal, and Relationship. A group's style can be characterized by talking about the 'here and now' relationships and reactions of members to each other (Relationship, IV), or talking about the problem of a member in a historical manner (Personal, III), or about the group itself (Group, II), or about all the topics external to the group itself, e.g., current events (Topic, I). These categories can be treated as nominal but in the HIM they are put into an ordinal scale of presumed increasing therapeutic potential from I through IV.

The other dimension deals with the level of Work obtaining in a group. Work has five categories, in order of significance, Responsive, Conventional, Assertive, Speculative, and Confrontive. Work, a term borrowed from Bion, is a meaningful concept but elusive of definition. In HIM terms it is characterized by someone in the group playing the helping or therapist role and someone asking for help or playing the patient or client role in an attempt to get self-understanding. Within the Work/Style dimension there are

(Continued)

E X H I B I T I *(Continued)*

two subdivisions, Work and Pre-Work. In Pre-Work no one is really trying to obtain self-understanding. The lowest level is Responsive (A), which is characterized by the fact that little or nothing is taking place except in response to leader's probes. Next is Conventional (B), which resembles everyday *social* groups that interact about social amenities, gossip, chit chat, etc. Assertive (C) is the highest ranking of the Pre-Work categories and represents social protest behavior, usually the asserting of independence from group pressure. Superficially, Assertive behavior may look like Work—a member presenting his problem—but he is 'acting-out' his problem, not 'acting-on' it. Work categories are two: Speculative (D) and Confrontive (E): the former being the 'conventional' way of transacting therapy, i.e., playing the therapeutic game. Confrontive style is intended to have real involvement and impact, and is characterized by tension and risk taking. The dimensions are arranged in matrix form with Content/Style on the horizontal axis and Work/Style on the vertical axis. The matrix thereby has twenty cells—each characterizes typical behavior to be found in treatment groups. Figure I-1 presents the cells and determinants of the Hill Interaction Matrix (HIM).

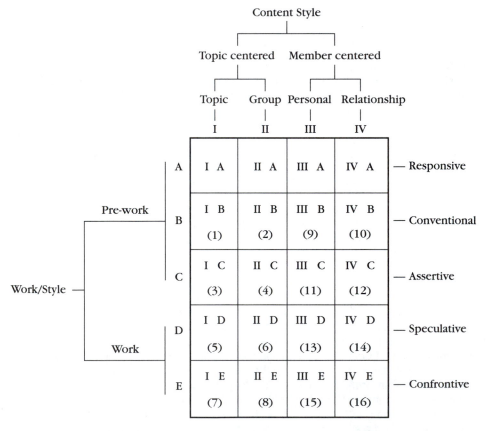

FIGURE I-1
Cells and determinants of the Hill Interaction Matrix.

•　•　•　•　•　•　•　•　•　•　•　•　•　•　•

EXHIBIT J
Intentions List (Hill & O'Grady, 1985)[10]

INSTRUCTIONS

To judge intentions, the therapist should review the tape within 24 hours so that the session is as fresh and vivid in memory as possible. The therapist should stop the tape after each therapist turn (everything the therapist says between two client speech acts, excluding minimal phrases) and indicate as many intentions as applied for that turn. You should strive to remember exactly what was going through your mind right at the time of the intervention *and* be as honest as possible in reporting what you were actually thinking. Remember that there are no right or wrong answers; the purpose is simply to uncover what you planned to do at that moment. Also remember that you should indicate your intentions only for that immediate intervention, rather than report global strategies for the entire session. Note that not every phrase in the definition for each intention needs to fit to judge that the intention applies. In general, the therapist should choose those intentions that best apply, even if all the phrasing is not exactly applicable to the current situations or does not fit the way he or she would say it.

INTENTIONS
1. *Set limits:* To structure, make arrangements, establish goals and objectives of treatment, outline methods to attain goals, correct expectations about treatment, or establish rules or parameters of the relationship (e.g., time, fees, cancellation policies, homework).
2. *Get information:* To find out specific facts about history, client functioning, future plans, and so on.
3. *Give information:* To educate, give facts, correct misperceptions or misinformation, give reasons for therapist's behavior or procedures.
4. *Support:* To provide a warm, supportive, empathic environment; increase trust and rapport and build relationship; help client feel accepted, understood, comfortable, reassured, and less anxious; help establish a person-to-person relationship.
5. *Focus:* To help client get back on the track, change subject, channel or structure the discussion if he or she is unable to begin or has been diffuse or rambling.
6. *Clarify:* To provide or solicit more elaboration, emphasis, or specification when client or therapist has been vague, incomplete, confusing, contradictory, or inaudible.
7. *Hope:* To convey the expectation that change is possible and likely to occur, convey that the therapist will be able to help the client, restore morale, build up the client's confidence to make changes.
8. *Cathart:* To promote relief from tension or unhappy feelings, allow the client a chance to let go or talk through feelings and problems.
9. *Cognitions:* To identify maladaptive, illogical, or irrational thoughts or attitudes (e.g., "I must be perfect").
10. *Behaviors:* To identify and give feedback about the client's inappropriate or maladaptive behaviors and/or their consequences, do a behavioral analysis, point out games.
11. *Self-control:* To encourage client to own or gain a sense of mastery or control over his or her own thoughts, feelings, behaviors, or impulses; help client become more appropriately internal rather than inappropriately external in taking responsibility for his or her role.

(Continued)

E X H I B I T J *(Continued)*

12. *Feelings:* To identify, intensify, and/or enable acceptance of feelings; encourage or provoke the client to become aware of or deepen underlying or hidden feelings or affect or experience feelings at a deeper level.
13. *Insight:* To encourage understanding of the underlying reasons, dynamics, assumptions, or unconscious motivations for cognitions, behaviors, attitudes, or feelings. May include an understanding of client's reactions to others' behaviors.
14. *Change:* To build and develop new and more adaptive skills, behaviors, or cognitions in dealing with self and others. May be to instill new, more adaptive assumptive models, frameworks, explanations, or conceptualizations. May be to give an assessment or option about client functioning that will help client see self in a new way.
15. *Reinforce change:* To give positive reinforcement or feedback about behavioral, cognitive, or affective attempts at change to enhance the probability that the change will be continued or maintained; encourage risk taking and new ways of behaving.
16. *Resistance:* To overcome obstacles to change or progress. May discuss failure to adhere to therapeutic procedures, either in past or to prevent possibility of such failure in future.
17. *Challenge:* To jolt the client out of a present state; shake up current beliefs or feelings; test validity, adequacy, reality, or appropriateness of beliefs, thoughts, feelings, or behaviors; help client question the necessity of maintaining old patterns.
18. *Relationship:* To resolve problems as they arise in the relationship in order to build or maintain a smooth working alliance; heal ruptures in the alliance; deal with dependency issues appropriate to stage in treatment; uncover and resolve distortions in client's thinking about the relationship that are based on past experiences rather than current reality.
19. *Therapist needs:* To protect, relieve, or defend the therapist; alleviate anxiety. May try unduly to persuade, argue, or feel good or superior at the expense of the client.

•   •   •   •   •   •   •   •   •   •   •   •   •   •   •   •   •

•   •   •   •   •   •   •   •   •   •   •   •   •   •   •   •   •

E X H I B I T K
Client Reactions System (Hill, Helms, Spiegel, & Tichenor, 1988)[11]

INSTRUCTIONS

Review the tape immediately after the session. Try to remember what you were experiencing during the session. Stop the tape after each therapist intervention and list the numbers of up to five reactions that you felt when you first heard what the therapist said. Choose those reactions that best describe your experience, even if every part of the definition does not apply or the phrasing is not exactly accurate.

1. *Felt understood:* I felt that my therapist really understood me and knew what I was saying or what was going on with me.
2. *Felt supported:* I felt accepted, reassured, liked, cared for, or safe. I felt like my therapist was on my side or I came to trust, like, respect, or admire my therapist more. This may have involved a change in my relationship with my therapist, such that we resolved a problem between us.
3. *Felt hopeful:* I felt confident, encouraged, optimistic, strong, pleased, or happy, and felt like I could change.

E X H I B I T K *(Continued)*

4. *Felt relief:* I felt less depressed, anxious, tense, guilty, angry, or had fewer uncomfortable or painful feelings.

5. *Became aware of negative thoughts or behaviors: I* became aware of specific thoughts or behaviors which cause problems for me or others.

6. *Gained better self-understanding:* I gained new insight about myself, saw new connections, or began to understand *why* I behaved or felt a certain way. This new understanding helped me accept and like myself better.

7. *Became more clear:* I got more focused about what I was really trying to say, what areas I need to change in my life, what my goals are, or what I want to work on in therapy.

8. *Became aware of feelings:* I felt a greater awareness of or deepening of feelings or could express my emotions better.

9. *Took responsibility:* I felt more responsibility for myself, blamed others less, and realized my part in things.

10. *Got unstuck:* I overcame a block and felt freed up and more involved in what I have to do in therapy.

11. *Gained new perspective:* I gained a new understanding of another person, situation, or the world. I found a new framework for understanding *why* people or things are as they are.

12. *Got educated:* I gained greater knowledge or information. I learned something I had not known.

13. *Learned new ways to behave:* I got specific ideas about what I can do differently to cope with particular situations or problems. I solved a problem, made a choice or decision, or decided to take a risk.

14. *Felt challenged:* I felt shook up, forced to question myself, or to look at issues I had been avoiding.

15. *Felt scared:* I felt overwhelmed or afraid. I wanted to avoid or not admit to having some feeling or problem. Perhaps my therapist was too pushy. I may have felt that my therapist would disapprove of me or would not like me.

16. *Felt worse:* I felt less hopeful, sicker, out of control, dumb, incompetent, ashamed, or like giving up. Perhaps my therapist ignored me, criticized me, hurt me, pitied me, or treated me as weak and helpless. I may have felt jealous of or competitive with my therapist.

17. *Felt stuck:* I felt blocked, impatient or bored. I did not know what to do next or how to get out of the situation. I felt dissatisfied with the progress of therapy or having to go over the same things again.

18. *Felt lack of direction:* I felt angry or upset that my therapist didn't give me enough guidance or direction.

19. *Felt confused:* I did not know how I was feeling or felt distracted from what I wanted to say. I was puzzled or could not understand what my therapist was trying to say. I was not sure I agreed with my therapist.

20. *Felt misunderstood:* I felt that my therapist did not really hear what I was trying to say. Perhaps my therapist misjudged me or made assumptions about me that were incorrect.

21. *No reaction:* I did not have a particular reaction to because my therapist was just gathering information, making social conversation, or the statement was too short or unclear.

•   •   •   •   •   •   •   •   •   •   •   •   •   •   •   •

•   •   •   •   •   •   •   •   •   •   •   •   •   •   •   •

E X H I B I T L
Therapist Session Intentions (Stiles et al., 1996)[12]

Item	Description
1. Set limits	To structure, make arrangements, establish goals and objectives of treatment, outline methods to attain goals, correct expectations about treatment, or establish rules or parameters of relationship (e.g., time, fees, cancellation policies, homework).
2. Get information	To find out specific facts about history, client functioning, future plans, etc.
3. Give information	To educate, give facts, correct misperceptions or misinformation, give reasons for therapist's behavior or procedures.
4. Support	To provide a warm, supportive, empathic environment; to increase trust and rapport and build relationship; to help client feel accepted, understood, comfortable, reassured, and less anxious; to help establish a person-to-person relationship.
5. Focus	To help client get back on the track; to change subject or channel/structure the discussion if he/she was unable to begin or was being diffuse or rambling.
6. Clarify	To provide or solicit more elaboration, emphasis, or specification when client or I was being vague, incomplete, confusing, contradictory, or inaudible.
7. Hope	To convey the expectation that change is possible and likely to occur; that I will be able to help the client; to restore morale; to build up the client's confidence to make changes.
8. Cathart	To promote relief from tension or unhappy feelings, to allow the client a chance to let go or talk through feelings and problems.
9. Cognitions	To identify maladaptive, illogical, or irrational thoughts or attitudes (e.g., "I must be perfect").
10. Behaviors	To identify and give feedback about the client's inappropriate or maladaptive behaviors and/or their consequences; to do a behavioral analysis; to point out games.
11. Self-control	To encourage the client to own or gain a sense of mastery or control over his/her own thoughts, feelings, behaviors, or impulses; to help client become more appropriately responsible for his/her own role.
12. Feelings/awareness	To identify, intensify, and/or enable acceptance of feelings, to encourage or provoke the client to become aware of or deepen underlying or hidden feelings or affect or to experience feelings at a deeper level.
13. Insight	To encourage understanding of the underlying reasons, dynamics, assumptions, or unconscious motivation for cognitions, behaviors, attitudes, or feelings. May include an understanding of client's reactions to others' behaviors.

E X H I B I T L *(Continued)*

14. Change

To build and develop new and more adaptive skills, behaviors, or cognitions in dealing with self and others. May include instilling new, more adaptive assumptive models, frameworks, explanations, or conceptualizations. May include to give an assessment or opinion about client functioning that will help client see self in new way.

15. Reinforce change

To give positive reinforcement or feedback about behavioral, cognitive, or affective attempts at change in order to enhance the probability that the change will be continued or maintained; to encourage risk taking and new ways of behaving.

16. Resistance

To overcome obstacles to change or progress. May include dealing with client's failure to adhere to therapeutic procedures in past or preventing possible relapse in future.

17. Challenge

To jolt the client out of a present state; to shake up current beliefs or feelings; to test validity, adequacy reality, or appropriateness of beliefs, thoughts, feelings, or behaviors; to help client question the necessity of maintaining old patterns.

18. Relationship

To resolve problems as they arise in the relationship in order to build or maintain a smooth working alliance; to heal ruptures in the alliance; to deal with dependency issues appropriate to stage in treatment; to uncover and resolve distortions in client's thinking about the relationship that are based on past experiences rather than current reality.

19. Therapist needs

To protect, relieve, or defend the therapist; to alleviate anxiety. May include unduly attempting to persuade, argue, or feel good or superior at the expense of the client.

• • • • • • • • • • • • • • • •

• • • • • • • • • • • • • • • •

E X H I B I T M
Interpersonal Communication Rating Scale (Strong et al., 1988)[13]

RATING PROCEDURE

The objective of this rating is to place each communication unit in an interaction into one of the eight categories of the model and to indicate the extremity of the unit within the category. *A communication unit is defined as a person's communication uninterrupted by another's verbal utterance.* Units are classified in terms of the behaviors they contain. The behaviors are the combination of the content of a communication unit and the person's manner of being during the communication, the linguistic and non-linguistic (kinesic and paralinguistic) aspects of communication. The linguistic aspects of a communication are the words used and their structure. The kinesic and paralinguistic aspects include facial expression, eye gaze, body posture, speech rate, and voice qualities such as tone, volume, and intonation. Rating involves identifying the behaviors the

(Continued)

E X H I B I T M *(Continued)*

communicator presents in the linguistic *and* non-linguistic aspects of the communication.

Each communication unit is to be rated as an independent entity. It must be classified on the basis of its own characteristics without regard for the context within which it occurs. The overall tone of the interaction or the nature of the communication units that precede or follow a communication are not to be considered. The Interpersonal Communication Rating Scale was developed to classify communications with the aid of videotapes and transcripts of interactions. Using audiotapes or transcripts alone will alter ratings due to the loss of nonlinguistic cues.

Some classification decisions are based primarily on the linguistic characteristics of a communication. Other decisions are based primarily on the non-linguistic characteristics. Still other decisions are based on their combined effects.

The easiest and most reliable way to rate behaviors is to do the judgement task in the following three steps:

1. Concentrate on the linguistic form, structure, and content of the communication unit presented in the transcript. Follow the procedure presented below using the transcript alone and arrive at a preliminary judgement of the best rating for the unit.

2. Concentrate on the non-linguistic aspects of the communication presented in the videotape, noting especially speech rate, voice volume, tone, and intonation, eye gaze, attentiveness to other, body posture, affect, and energy level. Go through the procedure presented below again, this time focusing on the nonlinguistic aspects.

3. Base your final judgement of the best rating for the unit on both the linguistic and nonlinguistic aspects of the communication.

The procedure for classifying each communication unit is as follows:

1. Using both videotape and transcript, determine the communication unit to be rated. A communication unit is defined as a person's communication uninterrupted by another's verbal utterance.

2. Examine the communication unit. Using Figure M-2, identify to which category(s) the behavior(s) may belong.

3. Review the rating conventions and category descriptions. Determine to which category(s) the behavior(s) belongs.

4. If the communication unit contains more than one behavior, determine the predominant behavior in the unit. Assign the unit to the category to which the predominant behavior belongs.

5. Determine the extremity level of the predominant behavior by matching it with the behaviors in the four levels of the chosen category in Figure M-2. Adjust the level assignment as specified in Rating Convention 5, *Softeners.*

6. Finally, record the two-digit rating that identifies the category and level of the unit on the Rating Sheet.

COMMON NONLINGUISTIC ASPECTS OF BEHAVIORS

Common Leading (1) Nonlinguistic Cues

Facial expression is neutral, uplifted, pleasant, and aroused. Holds eyes open, relaxed, and alert; eyes are clear. Maintains direct and personable eye contact with frequent, sustained, and attentive gazes; attention to the other is directive and social. Relaxes eyebrows to a normal (base line) position. Holds mouth in a normal (inexpressive) posi-

E X H I B I T M *(Continued)*

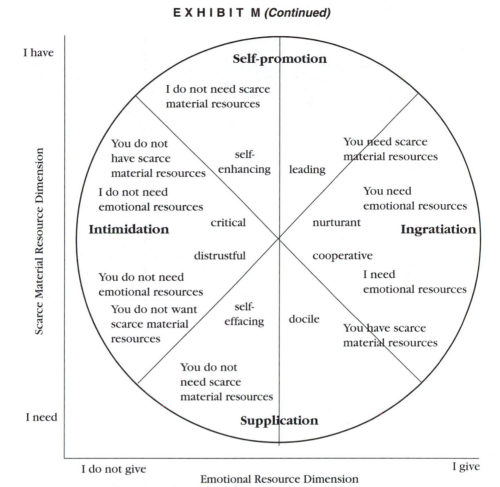

FIGURE M-1
Resource messages of interpersonal behaviors.

tion, shows a slight smile at the corners, or exposes teeth in an open smile. The face is relaxed, open, and interested. Lips are full and moist.

Paralinguistic cues. Speaks with normal to moderately loud voice, smooth and moderately fast verbal flow, and slightly upward, deep, and full intonation. Air movement is excited but controlled. Laughs rather often, and accompanies laughter with increased eye contact.

Body movements. Holds head straight up and facing the other. Nods with assurance. Sits facing the other in an open, comfortable, and erect position with shoulders back and carried high; may sit on the edge of the seat, Leans slightly forward while listening. Holds arms open. Keeps hands relaxed or actively gesturing. Uses controlled, purposeful, and coordinated gestures and confines them to a small space; holds palms up. May actively point to materials. May preen by throwing head back and brushing hair away to expose face. Orients legs toward the other. Places legs in a casual parallel position with feet flat on the floor, or scissors legs comfortably apart at the knee.

(Continued)

E X H I B I T   M *(Continued)*

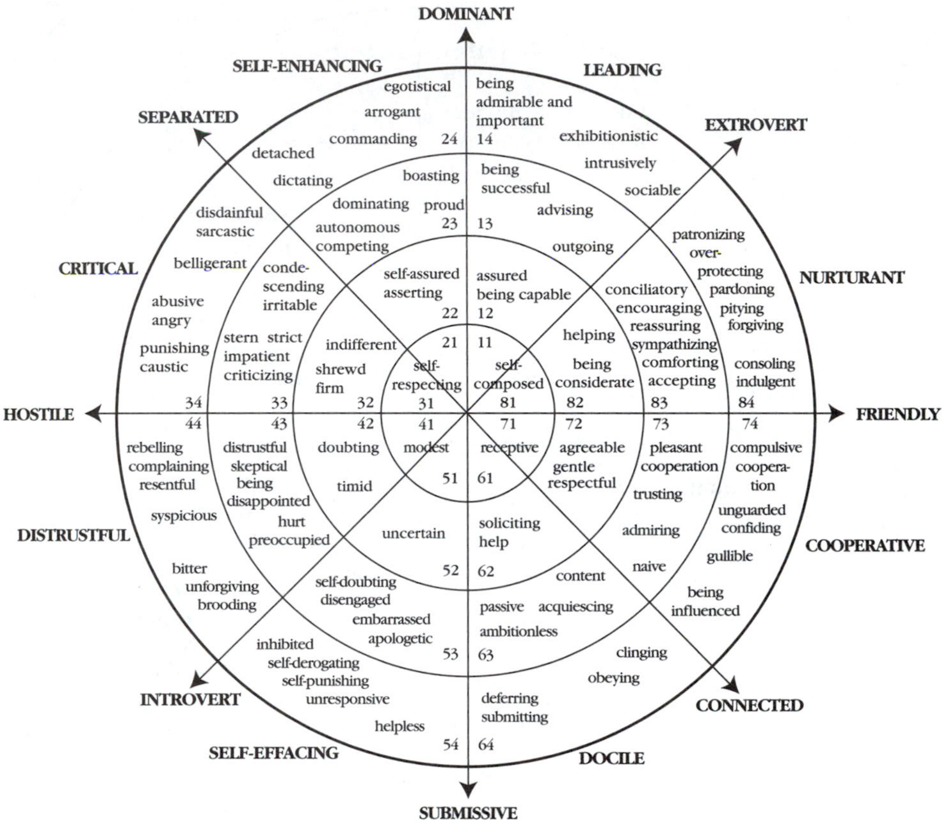

DOMINANT

SELF-ENHANCING

LEADING

SEPARATED

EXTROVERT

egotistical
arrogant
commanding   24 | 14
being admirable and important
exhibitionistic

detached
dictating
boasting
dominating proud
autonomous   23 | 13
competing
being successful
intrusively
sociable
advising
outgoing

CRITICAL

disdainful
sarcastic
belligerant
conde-
scending
irritable
self-assured
asserting   22 | 12
assured
being capable
conciliatory
encouraging
patronizing
over-
protecting
pardoning
pitying
forgiving

NURTURANT

abusive
angry
punishing
caustic
stern strict
impatient
criticizing
indifferent   21 | 11
shrewd
firm
self-
respecting
self-
composed
helping
being considerate
reassuring
sympathizing
comforting
accepting
consoling
indulgent

34 | 33 | 32 | 31 | 81 | 82 | 83 | 84

HOSTILE ◄

► FRIENDLY

44 | 43 | 42 | 41 | 71 | 72 | 73 | 74

rebelling
complaining
resentful
distrustful
skeptical
being
disappointed
doubting
timid
modest   51 | 61
receptive
agreeable
gentle
respectful
pleasant
cooperation
trusting
compulsive
coopera-
tion

syspicious
hurt
preoccupied
uncertain   52 | 62
soliciting
help
admiring
naive
unguarded
confiding
gullible

DISTRUSTFUL

COOPERATIVE

bitter
unforgiving
brooding
self-doubting
disengaged
embarrassed
apologetic
content
being
influenced

inhibited
self-derogating
self-punishing
unresponsive
helpless
passive acquiescing
ambitionless   53 | 63
clinging
obeying

INTROVERT

deferring
submitting
54 | 64

CONNECTED

SELF-EFFACING

DOCILE

SUBMISSIVE

FIGURE M-2
Classification of interpersonal behavior

Common Self-enhancing (2) Nonlinguistic Cues

Facial expression is animated, aroused, decisive, and excited when speaking, and tense, uplifted, determined, unwavering, firm, and controlled when the other speaks. Opens eyes wide with animation. Does not attend closely when the other speaks, and shows mild irritation through short gazes, eye rolls, and stares into space. Often stares straight ahead when speaking, or may maintain steady and unflinching eye contact with little blinking to intimidate the other; dramatic gazes. Raises eyebrows and furrows forehead. Holds mouth in a normal (inexpressive) position and seldom smiles at other. Lips may be tight, set, and dry.

Paralinguistic cues. Speaks with a loud voice, fast and animated verbal flow, and slightly upward, deep, robust, full, and abrupt intonation. Spontaneously clicks tongue, hums, and whistles. Air movement is excited and controlled. May burst into hearty laughter; guffaw.

Body movements. Holds head straight up. May face the other head on during intimidation or short gazes. Nods infrequently; quick, jerky head movements. Body

Rating Sheet: Interpersonal Communication Rating Scale

Person Odd		Person Even		Condition		Part		Rater		Date		Study	
Unit	Rating	Unit	Rating	Unit	Rating	Unit	Rating	Unit	Rating	Unit	Rating	Unit	Rating
1		26		51		76		101				126	
2		27		52		77		102				127	
3		28		53		78		103				128	
4		29		54		79		104				129	
5		30		55		80		105				130	
6		31		56		81		106				131	
7		32		57		82		107				132	
8		33		58		83		108				133	
9		34		59		84		109				134	
10		35		60		85		110				135	
11		36		61		86		111				136	
12		37		62		87		112				137	
13		38		63		88		113				138	
14		39		64		89		114				139	
15		40		65		90		115				140	
16		41		66		91		116				141	
17		42		67		92		117				142	
18		43		68		93		118				143	
19		44		69		94		119				144	
20		45		70		95		120				145	
21		46		71		96		121				146	
22		47		72		97		122				147	
23		48		73		98		123				148	
24		49		74		99		124				149	
25		50		75		100		125				150	

E X H I B I T M *(Continued)*

movements are alert, enthusiastic, and energetic. Faces body straight into the room. Sits proudly and erect, with shoulders back and carried high. Sits straight up on the edge of seat without leaning forward even when shown something. May sprawl with an arm or leg thrown over the edge of the chair. Holds arms and hands open and tense. Holds materials in front. May jam hands together and thrust elbows outward to signal authority. Rests elbows on chair arms and laces fingers together placing index fingers up and touching at collarbone level. Uses gestures that are confident, controlled, and open, and generally confines them to a small space. To emphasize a point, may use wide, intrusive, dominant, and animated gestures with palms out. Raises hand slightly while listening, ready to disagree. Deliberate movements; may drum pencil to communicate disinterest. May hold legs in parallel position with feet flat on the floor.

Common Critical (3) Nonlinguistic Cues

Facial expression is scornful, sneering, disdainful, serious, severe, disgusted, rejecting, displeased, disapproving, annoyed, angry, and frustrated. Avoids eye contact. Attends to external stimuli to show irritation or disinterest, but attends to the other during attacks. Glances away from the other into space or looks out a window to show disinterest, or rolls eyes to signal irritation. Darts eyes furtively away, then quickly glares at the other during attack. May glare at the other with a serious and severe look (pin the other down with the eyes). Uses long, frequent blinking. Stares aggressively with eyebrows moved over eye area. Lifts head and lowers eyelids to cut off communication. May lower upper eyelids and raise lower lids into a narrow, tense, and squared pattern; squints. Lowers eyebrows and pulls them together; knits brows; furrows forehead. Dilates and flares nostrils. Smiles infrequently and does not return smiles. May smile cynically when the other has not said anything funny. Draws lips tightly together, turns down corners, raises upper lip and depresses lower lip. The lips are tight, set, and dry. Clenches jaw and displays taunt jaw and facial muscles. Drops jaw.

Paralinguistic cues. Speaks with a normal to loud voice, moderately fast to fast verbal flow, and irregular, up and down, clipped, harsh, icy, cold, and gruff intonation. Spontaneously coughs, sighs, and hisses. Takes short, repressed, and ingressive breaths; snorts. Laughs infrequently; snickers; snide and partially stifled laughs; sardonic laughs that are bitter, scornful, and cynical. Accompanies laughs with nasal aspiration and controlled movements.

Body movements. May hold head straight, tilted, or down; quick, jerky head movements; may throw head back. May face the other head on. Infrequently nods, but occasionally uses forced nods (three or more nods in quick succession). Places chin in palm with index finger on cheek while leaning back to signal negative evaluation. Positions finger between nose and lip while listening to signal displeasure. Pushes up middle of forehead with fingers to signal disinterest. May raise finger and then drop it in coordination with negative head shakes. Posture is tense, tight, and stiff. May sit straight up or slump back and away from the other. Does not lean toward the other even when shown something. Turns body away when the other is speaking; positions body straight at the other when attacking. Occasionally uses quick and forced movements. Blocks the other with shoulder. May cross arms over chest and make fists with hands (a bulwark); may hold self and rock. May push hands into seat while looking away from the other, or lean forward in seat with palms down on thighs (bellicose position). Makes intrusive and attacking gestures that are overly broad, with sharp movements and palms out. Fidgets while

E X H I B I T M *(Continued)*

the other is speaking to show irritation: taps pencil, drums fingers, looks at watch, picks imaginary lint from clothing, engages in prolonged and agitated self-scratching, rubs eyes, or swings foot. Holds legs tightly together with feet flat on the floor and away from the other, or scissors legs apart at knee away from the other. Shields or masks mouth and face with hands; uses materials and forearms as shields.

Common Distrustful (4) Nonlinguistic Cues

Facial expression is miserable, sad, gloomy, droopy, distressed, hesitant, suffering, doubting, resentful, dejected, serious, and frustrated. Avoids eye contact. Does not attend much to the other or to external stimuli; is self-involved. Darts eyes away from the other; long frequent blinks. Emphasizes disbelief and resentment with furtive and guarded sideways glances followed by downward gazes. Looks up suddenly, then down or to the side. Raises inner corners of the upper eyelids and draws eyebrows up at inner corner. May narrow eyelids. Smiles infrequently; fake smiles. May raise upper lip or protrudes lower lip (pouts). May turn corners of the mouth downward. Lips are thin and dry.

Paralinguistic cues. Speaks with a soft to normal voice, slow verbal flow, and up and down, but overall downward, intonation (whiny, breaking, nasal, choking). Spontaneously coughs and sighs. Takes deep, labored, repressed, and intrusive breaths. Laughs infrequently; laughter is incongruous.

Body movements. May hold head down, tilted or bowed slightly, while glancing suspiciously at the other. Shakes head slowly. May hold chin in palm with index finger on cheek while leaning back to show negative evaluation or doubt. May position index finger on the nose or raise finger and drop it to communicate doubt. Slouches, retracts shoulders, and draws body back; body is tense. Moves body cautiously, occasionally shrugs shoulders or blocks the other with shoulder. Faces the other or turns away. Does not lean forward when shown something. May cross arms over chest or hold self and rock. Closes hands almost into fists. May clasp hands or lace fingers tightly in lap. Uses materials and forearms as shields; shields and masks face and mouth with hands. May cover face with hair. May rub eyes or hands; picks; prolonged and agitated self-scratching. Covers forced cough with hand over mouth. Makes tight, uncomfortable, and stiff gestures. Holds legs tightly together in a parallel position. May wrap one foot over the other and tuck feet toward body.

Common Self-effacing (5) Nonlinguistic Cues

Facial expression is depressed, suffering, distressed, tense, anxious, sad, droopy, shameful, embarrassed, submissive, and uncertain. Passively attends to the other to look for signs of approval; does not attend to external stimuli. Little gazing; averts eyes to signal submission. Blinks excessively; blank stares. Glances downward to show modesty. Frequently looks down at materials on lap. Raises inner corners of the upper eyelids and draws up inner corners of eyebrows to show sadness. Turns the corners of the lips slightly upwards to show modest smiles. Rolls lips inward toward mouth or turns them downward. Bites lips. Lips are dry and thin.

Paralinguistic cues. Speaks with a soft voice that may dwindle to a whisper, slow and hesitant verbal flow with irregular pauses, and downward, shaky, drawling intonation. Spontaneously clears throat, coughs nervously, gasps, and sniffs. Breathes deeply and exhales slowly, or inhales quickly, pauses, then exhales slowly with noise.

(Continued)

E X H I B I T M *(Continued)*

Laughs infrequently; titters (a restrained nervous giggle accompanied by blushing and head lowering).

Body movements. Holds head down and lower than does the other, looks at the other at an angle to the side and up. Tilts, cocks, or bows head toward the other. Shakes head negatively. May support head with one hand. Sits back in the seat, bows shoulders, sinks chest, and droops as if in surrender; body is tense and defensive; assumes a fetal position. Makes guarded, hesitant, and uncertain body movements. Occasionally squirms nervously. May shrug shoulders. Gathers arms tightly toward the body and holds self. May rock. Hands are tense, almost fists. Clasps hands and laces fingers tightly in the lap. May use materials or forearms as shields or obstacles; may hide or mask mouth and face with hands. May position hair over eyes to close off face. Makes infrequent, hesitant, breaking, awkward, and uncertain gestures. May fondle ring, bracelet, etc., chew on pencil, or play with hair. Places finger on chin or holds finger in mouth to signal uncertainty. May rub eyes. May doodle on materials or pick nails. May position legs in parallel, tuck feet close in toward body, cross legs at the ankle, or keep knees in and touching.

Common Docile (6) Nonlinguistic Cues

Facial expression is neutral, a mask, poker-faced, submissive, unresponsive, sleepy, droopy, calm, still, tranquil, tired, serene, placid, even, and steady. Infrequent eye contact; shows lack of involvement with slow, infrequent gazes. Averts eyes to signal submission. Blank stares. Attends to the other passively; unresponsive. Slightly relaxes and lowers upper eyelids. Relaxes eyebrows and mouth to normal (inexpressive) positions. Relaxes jaw. Smiles infrequently.

Paralinguistic cues. Speaks with a soft voice, slow, breaking, and slurred verbal flow with irregular pauses, and flat, monotone, gravelly, dull, and heavy intonation. Breathes deeply and exhales slowly. Occasionally yawns or slowly sighs. Does not laugh.

Body movements. Holds head down, lower than does the other. Looks at the other at an angle; bows head to the side and up. May support head in hands. Nods head slowly and infrequently. Relaxes body into a caved in, slumped, resting, limp, and still position. Moves body passively. Sits back in the chair and positions body slightly toward the other. May stretch out while leaning back. Hangs arms and hands relaxed at sides or in lap with palms up. Places materials in lap. Makes infrequent, faint, and weak gestures. May rub eyes or gently stroke leg with finger. Positions legs in casual parallel with feet on heels or crossed at the ankle; may close legs and tuck feet near body.

Common Cooperative (7) Nonlinguistic Cues

Facial expression is relaxed, friendly, pleasant, calm, content, pleased, submissive, respectful, sympathetic, thoughtful, reverent, and loyal. Holds eyes open, relaxed, and clear. Actively attends to the other; shows involvement with the other with frequent, sustained, and intense gazing. Relaxes eyebrows to a normal (base line) position. Holds mouth in a normal (inexpressive) position, shows a slight smile at the corners, or exposes teeth in an open smile. Smiles frequently and in coordination with generous and cooperative responses to the other. Lips are full and moist.

Paralinguistic cues. Speaks with a normal voice, normal and smooth verbal flow, and slightly upward, smooth, and sweet intonation. Breathes normally. Laughs frequently and happily, and accompanies laughter with increased eye contact.

E X H I B I T   M *(Continued)*

Body movements. Holds head lower than does the other and orients it at an angle (side and up). Shows approval with single and double head nods. May support head with the hands. Centers and keys body position on the other while listening. Relaxes posture with shoulders cupped; sits on the edge of the seat and leans forward to follow the other with interest. Holds arms and hands open and relaxed, positioned at the side or in the lap. Places materials on lap. Makes open, broad and even gestures with the palms up. May preen by slowly patting hair. May tie shoes, take off glasses, or touch hand to chest. Positions legs in casual parallel and places feet flat on the floor, turned in, or crossed at the ankle.

Common Nurturant (8) Nonlinguistic Cues

Facial expression is relaxed, warm, pleasant, happy, affectionate, thoughtful, concerned, pitying, empathic, and commiserating. Holds eyes open, relaxed and clear. Actively attends to the other. Emphasizes involvement with frequent, sustained, and intense gazes that communicate concern and empathy. Relaxes eyebrows to a normal (base line) position. Holds mouth in a normal (inexpressive) position, shows a slight smile at the corners, or exposes teeth in an open smile. Holds mouth open and receptive to the other; smiles frequently. Lips are full and moist.

Paralinguistic cues. Speaks with a normal voice, normal verbal flow, and an overall upward, singing, resonant and full intonation (baby talk). Breathes normally. Laughs frequently and happily, and accompanies laughter with increased eye contact.

Body movements. Holds head straight up or tilts it gently; faces the other. Shows approval with single and double head nods. Sits straight up facing the other in a relaxed posture with shoulders comfortably back. Sits on the edge of the seat with a forward lean and follows the other with interest. Sits close to the other. Centers and keys body and face on the other while listening. Places materials in lap. Holds arms open. Uses hands expressively, relaxes them at the side, or places them in lap. Uses broad, open, and even gestures with palms up. May place hand on the chest or touch the other to emphasize a point. Preens by slowly patting hair. May tie shoes, take off glasses. Positions legs in casual parallel and places feet comfortably on the floor, or scissors legs apart at the knee toward the other.

•   •   •   •   •   •   •   •   •   •   •   •   •   •   •   •

•   •   •   •   •   •   •   •   •   •   •   •   •   •   •   •

E X H I B I T   N
Check List of Interpersonal Transactions (Transaction Rating Form)
(Kiesler, 1984)[14]

DIRECTIONS

The following pages contain lists of actions that can occur in interactions between two persons. Your task is to check each item which accurately describes an action exhibited in your transactions by the person targeted for you.

(Continued)

E X H I B I T N *(Continued)*

Make your judgments about occurrence of this person's actions solely on the basis of your personal encounters with that person. Check only those items which describe actions by that person which occurred "live" in your presence.

In order to receive a check, the action described by a particular item must have occurred in your presence *and* must be judged by you as typical of the way that person acts with you. If an item describes an action that does not typically occur in your interactions with this person, leave that item blank.

WHEN IN MY COMPANY, THIS PERSON . . .

_____ 1. suggests topics or issues to discuss, or directions or actions to pursue

_____ 2. is hesitant to express approval or acceptance of me

_____ 3. is careful to speak or act unemotionally or undemonstratively, or with little variation in tone or manner

_____ 4. finds it difficult to take the initiative; or looks to me for direction or focus; or shows a desire to do "whatever you want"

_____ 5. is receptive and cooperative to my requests, directions, appeals, or wishes; or is quick to assist or work together with me

_____ 6. expresses pleasure in self; or comments on own accomplishments, awards, or successes

_____ 7. scans carefully to detect any of my reactions, evaluations, or motives that might have a harmful intent

_____ 8. shows little attention, interest, curiosity, or inquisitiveness about my personal life, affairs, feelings, or opinions

_____ 9. waits for or follows my lead regarding topics or issues to discuss, directions or actions to pursue

_____ 10. is quick to express approval or acceptance of me

_____ 11. speaks or acts emotionally or melodramatically, or with much variation in tone or manner

_____ 12. shows an intense task focus or desire to "get down to business"; or suggests directions or objectives

_____ 13. is quick to resist, not cooperate, or refuse to comply with my requests, directions or objectives

_____ 14. makes self-critical statements; or expresses low self-worth; or apologizes frequently

_____ 15. gazes at me in an open, receptive, trusting, or nonsearching manner

_____ 16. inquires into or expresses attention, interest, or curiosity about my personal life, affairs, feelings, or opinions

_____ 17. dominates the flow of conversation, or changes topic, or interrupts and "talks down"

_____ 18. avoids at any cost showing affection, warmth, or approval

_____ 19. endlessly prefaces or qualifies statements to the place where points being made get lost, or views or positions are unclear or ambiguous

_____ 20. goes out of way to give me credit for my contributions, or to admire or praise me for my good ideas or suggestions

_____ 21. inconveniences self or sacrifices to contribute, help, assist, or work cooperatively with me

E X H I B I T N *(Continued)*

_____ 22. is cocky about own positions or decisions; or makes it abundantly clear s/he can do things by self; or avoids any hint that I can help

_____ 23. in response to my inquiries or probings acts evasively as if hiding important secrets

_____ 24. refrains at all costs from close visual or physical contact or direct body orientation with me

_____ 25. finds it almost impossible to take the lead, or to initiate or change the topic of discussion

_____ 26. constantly expresses approval, affection, or effusive warmth to me

_____ 27. makes startling or "loaded" comments; or takes liberties with facts to embellish stories

_____ 28. works hard to avoid giving me credit for any contribution; or implies or claims that good ideas or suggestions were his/her own

_____ 29. is openly antagonistic, oppositional, or obstructive to my statements, suggestions, or purposes

_____ 30. urgently solicits my advice, help, or counsel even for everyday troubles or difficulties

_____ 31. responds openly, candidly, or revealingly to the point of "telling all"

_____ 32. continually stands, sits, moves or leans toward me to be physically close

_____ 33. expresses firm, strong personal preferences; or stands up for own opinions or positions

_____ 34. acts in a stiff, formal, unfeeling, or evaluative manner

_____ 35. works at being careful or precise in his/her statements; or searches for precise words to express thoughts

_____ 36. is content, unquestioning, or approving about the focus or direction of a given topic of discussion or course of action; or is quick to follow my lead

_____ 37. expresses appreciation, delight, or satisfaction about me, our situation, or our task

_____ 38. is quick to rely on own resources to make decisions or solve problems

_____ 39. claims that I misunderstand, misinterpret, or misjudge his/her intents or actions

_____ 40. remains aloof, distant, remote, or stand-offish from me

_____ 41. expresses own preferences hesitantly or weakly; or yields easily to my viewpoints; or backs down quickly when I question or disagree

_____ 42. acts in a relaxed, informal, warm, or nonjudgmental manner

_____ 43. makes comments or replies that "pop out" quickly and energetically

_____ 44. questions or expresses reservation or disagreement about the focus or direction of the conversation or course of action

_____ 45. grumbles, gripes, nags, or complains about me, our situation, or our task

_____ 46. readily asks me for advice, help, or counsel

_____ 47. communicates that I am sympathetic or fair in interpreting or judging his/her intents or actions

_____ 48. is absorbed in, attentive to, or concentrates intensely on what I say or do

_____ 49. states preferences, opinions, or positions in a dogmatic or unyielding manner

_____ 50. has absolutely no room for sympathy, compromise, or mercy regarding my mistakes, weaknesses, or misconduct

(Continued)

E X H I B I T N *(Continued)*

_____ 51. understates or hedges on evaluations of me, events, or objects, or constantly minimizes expressions of emotion

_____ 52. makes statements that are deferentially, softly, or carefully presented as if s/he desperately wants to avoid any implication of disapproval, criticism, or disagreement

_____ 53. seems always to agree with or accommodate me; or seems impossible to rile

_____ 54. brags about achievements, successes, or good-fortune; or "puts on airs" as if in complete control of his/her life

_____ 55. expresses harsh judgment, "never forgetting," or no forgiveness for my mistakes, weaknesses, or injurious actions

_____ 56. seems constantly uncomfortable with me as if s/he wants to leave or be by self

_____ 57. claims s/he doesn't have an opinion, preference, or position, or that "it doesn't matter," "whatever you want," "I don't know," etc.

_____ 58. goes out of way to understand or be sympathetic towards me, or to find something about me to approve of, endorse, or support

_____ 59. constantly overstates evaluations of me, events, or objects; or exaggerates expression of his/her feelings

_____ 60. challenges or disputes my ideas or statements; or attempts to get the better of me or put me down

_____ 61. argumentatively challenges or refutes my statements or suggestions; or "tells me off," "lets me have it" when disagrees

_____ 62. claims s/he is a constant failure, or is helpless, witless, or at the mercy of events and circumstances

_____ 63. expresses unbending sympathy, understanding, or forgiveness for my hurtful or injurious actions

_____ 64. finds it difficult to leave me; or goes out of way to secure more and more of my company

_____ 65. seizes opportunities to instruct or explain things, or to give advice

_____ 66. expresses stringent, exacting, rigorous standards or expectations of me

_____ 67. is slow to make decisions; or deliberates carefully before acting

_____ 68. shares credit with me for good happenings or joint accomplishments; or points out ways I have been helpful; or "plays down" own contributions

_____ 69. is attentive to, considerate or solicitous of my feelings, or sensitive to pressures or stresses in my life

_____ 70. speaks or acts in a composed or graceful manner, confident about what s/he wants, remaining calm and unruffled

_____ 71. expresses doubt, mistrust, or disbelief regarding my intentions or motives

_____ 72. is slow to respond or speak to me; or seems distracted by own thoughts

_____ 73. is quick to ask me for information, instruction. explanations, or opinions

_____ 74. expresses lenient, soft-hearted, or compassionate standards or expectations of me

E X H I B I T N *(Continued)*

_____ 75. makes hasty decisions; or jumps into new activities with little premeditation

_____ 76. makes comments that avoid sharing credit with me for good happenings or joint accomplishments; or "plays up" own contributions

_____ 77. ignores, overlooks, or is inconsiderate of my feelings; or disregards pressures or stresses in my life

_____ 78. is unsure or "iffy" about what s/he wants; or acts in an uneasy and inept manner; or is easily embarrassed

_____ 79. expresses belief or trust in, or reliance upon, my claims about good intentions or motives

_____ 80. initiates greetings, chats easily, or shows enjoyment in being with or talking to me

_____ 81. overwhelms or "steamrolls" me by his/her arguments, positions, preferences, or actions

_____ 82. expresses severe, inflexible, or uncompromising expectations for my conduct

_____ 83. endlessly avoids or delays choices, decisions, or actions, or commitment to positions

_____ 84. makes flattering or glowing comments about me, our situation, or our joint task

_____ 85. makes unconditionally supportive, encouraging, endorsing, comforting, or bolstering comments to me

_____ 86. acts as if excessively "full of self," or as feeling special or favored, or as cocksure of his/her future

_____ 87. is bitterly accusatory, suspicious, or disbelieving of me

_____ 88. seems totally unmoved, unaffected, or untouched by my comments or actions

_____ 89. seems unable to assert what s/he wants, or to stand up to me, or to take any opposing position

_____ 90. is unwaveringly tolerant, patient, or lenient in regard to his/her expectations for my conduct

_____ 91. seems compelled to act out feelings with me, or impulsively to jump into new actions or activities

_____ 92. makes critical, demeaning, snide, or derisive statements about me, our situation, or our joint task

_____ 93. swears at me; or makes abusing, disparaging, damaging, or crude comments to me

_____ 94. is constantly dissatisfied with self, guilty or depressed; or feels hopeless about the future

_____ 95. shows blind faith or polyannish trust in me; or believes almost anything I say

_____ 96. seems totally engrossed in me; or is constantly moved, affected, or responsive to my comments or actions

• • • • • • • • • • • • • • • • •

• • • • • • • • • • • • • • • •

E X H I B I T O
Categories of Semantic Cohesion Analysis (Friedlander et al., 1985)[15]

Category	Subtype		Example
Reference	Pronominal	A:	Did *Henry* make you angry?
		B:	<u>He</u> sure did.
	Demonstrative	A:	*I'm not clear on what Jane just said.*
		B:	<u>That's</u> what I wanted to say, too.
	Comparative	A:	I've been involved with *two guys recently.*
		B:	The <u>younger</u> guy is the one you mentioned last week?
Conjunction	Additive	A:	He's far from perfect.
		B:	<u>And</u> that's what you can't stand.
	Adversative	A:	Whatever happens, it'll be my decision.
		B:	<u>But</u> what if you fail?
	Causal	A:	I'm just fed up, I guess.
		B:	<u>So</u> where do you go from here?
	Temporal	A:	So what happened?
		B:	<u>Just then</u> my husband walked in.
	Continuative	A:	I don't suppose I'll go tonight after all.
		B:	<u>Of course</u> you wish you could.
Substitution	Nominal	A:	I much prefer the lighted *dashboard.*
		B:	The <u>one</u> in the blue car over here?
	Verbal	A:	Did Henry *make you angry?*
		B:	He sure <u>did.</u>
	Clausal	A:	*You're being far too hard on me.*
		B:	I don't think <u>so.</u>
Ellipsis	Nominal	A:	I'm fed up with Alice's *insults.*
		B:	Are you putting up with more <u>ɸ</u>?
	Verbal	A:	Were you *laughing*?
		B:	No, I wasn't <u>ɸ.</u>
	Clausal	A:	Did he ever *tell you directly*?
		B:	Yes, <u>ɸ</u> twice.
Lexical	Same Item	A:	My *housemate* is a real pain!
		B:	Have you ever had <u>housemates</u> before?
	Synonym/Hyponym	A:	Our *house* is infested with fleas!
		B:	Who lives at <u>home</u> with you?
	Superordinate	A:	The store is out of that *volume.*
		B:	Is the <u>collection</u> there, though?
	Collocation	A:	I didn't say that as a *joke*!
		B:	I wasn't <u>laughing</u> at you.

NOTE: The presupposed item is in italics, and the cohesive tie is underlined or represented by ɸ in the cases of ellipsis.

E X H I B I T O (Continued)

Category	Subtype	Example
	General Item	A: I shouldn't have climbed the *tree*. B: That old <u>thing</u> is safe enough.

•   •   •   •   •   •   •   •   •   •   •   •   •   •   •   •

•   •   •   •   •   •   •   •   •   •   •   •   •   •   •   •

E X H I B I T P
Working Alliance Inventory
(Horvath & Greenberg, 1989)[16]
Client

On the following pages there are sentences that describe some of the different ways a person might think or feel about his or her therapist (counselor). As you read the sentences, mentally insert the name of your therapist (counselor) in the place of the _____ in the text. If the statement describes the way you *always* feel (or think), mark the circle under number 7; if it *never* applies to you, mark the circle under number 1. Use the numbers in between to describe the variations between these extremes. Work fast; your first impressions are the ones we would like to see. (Please don't forget to respond to every item.)

	Never 1	Rarely 2	Occasionally 3	Sometimes 4	Often 5	Very Often 6	Always 7
I believe the way we are working with my problem is correct.	○	○	○	○	○	○	○
We agree on what is important for me to work on.	○	○	○	○	○	○	○
_____ and I agree about the things I will need to do in therapy to help improve my situation.	○	○	○	○	○	○	○
What I am doing in therapy gives me new ways of looking at my problems.	○	○	○	○	○	○	○
I believe _____ likes me.	○	○	○	○	○	○	○
I am confident in _____'s ability to help me.	○	○	○	○	○	○	○
I feel that _____ appreciates me.	○	○	○	○	○	○	○
_____ and I trust one another.	○	○	○	○	○	○	○
_____ does not understand what I am trying to accomplish in therapy.	○	○	○	○	○	○	○
_____ and I are working toward mutually agreed upon goals.	○	○	○	○	○	○	○

(Continued)

E X H I B I T P *(Continued)*

	Never 1	Rarely 2	Occasionally 3	Sometimes 4	Often 5	Very Often 6	Always 7
_____ and I have different ideas on what my problems are.	○	○	○	○	○	○	○
We have established a good understanding of the kind of changes that would be good for me.	○	○	○	○	○	○	○

Therapist

On the following pages there are sentences that describe some of the different ways a person might think or feel about his or her client. As you read the sentences, mentally insert the name of your client in the place of the _____ in the text. If the statement describes the way you *always* feel (or think), mark the circle under number 7; if it *never* applies to you, mark the circle under number 1. Use the numbers in between to describe the variations between these extremes. Work fast; your first impressions are the ones we would like to see. (Please don't forget to respond to every item.)

	Never 1	Rarely 2	Occasionally 3	Sometimes 4	Often 5	Very Often 6	Always 7
_____ believes the way we are working with her/his problems is correct.	○	○	○	○	○	○	○
We agree on what is important for _____ to work on.	○	○	○	○	○	○	○
_____ and I agree about the steps to be taken to improve his/her situation.	○	○	○	○	○	○	○
My client and I both feel confident about the usefulness of our current activity in therapy.	○	○	○	○	○	○	○
I believe _____ likes me.	○	○	○	○	○	○	○
I am confident in my ability to help _____.	○	○	○	○	○	○	○
I appreciate _____ as a person.	○	○	○	○	○	○	○
_____ and I have built a mutual trust.	○	○	○	○	○	○	○
I have doubts about what we are trying to accomplish in therapy.	○	○	○	○	○	○	○
We are working toward mutually agreed upon goals.	○	○	○	○	○	○	○
_____ and I have different ideas on what his/her real problems are.	○	○	○	○	○	○	○

E X H I B I T P *(Continued)*

	Never 1	Rarely 2	Occasionally 3	Sometimes 4	Often 5	Very Often 6	Always 7
We have established a good understanding between us of the kind of changes that would be good for _____.	○	○	○	○	○	○	○

•   •   •   •   •   •   •   •   •   •   •   •   •   •   •

•   •   •   •   •   •   •   •   •   •   •   •   •   •   •

E X H I B I T Q
Client Experiencing Scale (Klein et al., 1986)[17]

SCALE STAGES

These general descriptions of each of the seven scale stages are amplified considerably in the manual (Klein et al., 1969) and also outlined in Table Q-1.

STAGE 1   The chief characteristic of this stage is that the content or manner of expression is impersonal. In some cases the content is intrinsically impersonal, being a very abstract, general, superficial, or journalistic account of events or ideas with no personal referent established. In other cases, despite the personal nature of the content, the speaker's involvement is impersonal, so that he or she reveals nothing important about the self and the remarks could as well be about a stranger or an object. As a result feelings are avoided and personal involvement is absent from communication.

STAGE 2   The association between the speaker and the content is explicit. Either the speaker is the central character in the narrative or his or her interest is clear. The speaker's involvement, however, does not go beyond the specific situation or content. All comments, associations, reactions, and remarks serve to get the story or idea across but do not refer to or define the speaker's feelings. Thus the personal perspective emerges somewhat to indicate an intellectual interest or general, but superficial, involvement.

STAGE 3   The content is a narrative or a description of the speaker in external or behavioral terms with added comments on feelings or private experiences. These remarks are limited to the events or situations described, giving the narrative a personal touch without describing the speaker more generally.

Self-descriptions restricted to specific situations or roles are also part of Stage 3. Thus feelings and personal reactions come into clear but limited perspective. They are "owned" but bypassed or rooted in external circumstances.

STAGE 4   At Stage 4 the quality of involvement or "set" shifts to the speaker's attention to the subjective felt flow of experience as referent, rather than to events or abstractions. The content is a clear presentation of the speaker's feelings, giving a personal, internal perspective or account of feelings about the self. Feelings or the experience of events, rather than the events themselves, are the subject of the discourse, requiring the speaker to attempt to hold on to inner referents. By attending to and presenting this

(Continued)

E X H I B I T Q *(Continued)*

TABLE Q-1
Short Form of Experiencing Scale (Patient)

Stage	Content	Treatment
1	External events; refusal to participate	Impersonal, detached
2	External events; behavioral or intellectual self-description	Interested, personal, self-participation
3	Personal reactions to external events; limited self-descriptions; behavioral descriptions of feelings	Reactive, emotionally involved
4	Descriptions of feelings and personal experiences	Self-descriptive; associative
5	Problems or propositions about feelings and personal experiences	Exploratory, elaborative, hypothetical
6	Felt sense of an inner referent	Focused on there being more about "it"
7	A series of felt senses connecting the content	Evolving, emergent

SOURCE: Copyright 1970 by The Regents of the University of Wisconsin. Revised, 1983.

experiencing, the speaker communicates what it is like to be him or her. These interior views are presented, listed, or described, but are not the focus for purposeful self-examination or elaboration.

STAGE 5   The content is a purposeful elaboration or exploration of the speaker's feelings and experiencing. There are two necessary components: First, the speaker must pose or define a problem, proposition, or question about the self explicitly in terms of feelings. The problem or proposition may involve the origin, sequence, or implications of feelings or relate feelings to other private processes. Second, the speaker must explore or work with the problem in a personal way. The exploration or elaboration must be clearly related to the initial proposition and must contain inner references that have the potential to expand the speaker's awareness of experiencing. These may also be evidence of and/or references to the process of groping or exploration itself.

STAGE 6   At Stage 6 the way the person senses the inner referent is different. There is a *felt sense* of the there-and-yet-to-be-fully-discovered, that is, of an unclear inner referent that has a life of its own. It is a sense of potentially more than can be immediately thought or named. This felt sense is more than recognizable feelings such as anger, joy, fear, sadness, or "that feeling of helplessness." If familiar or known feelings are present, there is also a sense of "more" that comes along with the identified feelings.

STAGE 7   The content reveals the speaker's steady and expanding awareness of immediately present feelings and internal processes. He or she clearly demonstrates the ability to move from one inner referent to another, linking and integrating each immediately felt nuance as it occurs in the present experiential moment, so that each new sensing functions as a springboard for further exploration and elaboration.

E X H I B I T Q *(Continued)*

T A B L E Q-2
Additional Stage Criteria

Scale Stage	Grammatical	Expressive	Paralinguistic	Content
1	No first-person pronouns; past or present tense	Remote, impersonal	Fluent	Impersonal, others' activities or events
2	Personal pronouns; past or present tense	Interested, intellectual	Usually fluent	Ideas, events, actions
3	Personal pronouns; past or present tense	Limited reactions	Some affect indicators, e.g., laughs, sighs	Parenthetical or limited references to feelings, subjective experiences and associations
4	Present or past tense	Immediate, expressive	Focused voice, expressions of affect	
5	Present tense, but past can be included; Subjunctive, tense questions	Immediate, groping, tense, tentative	Dysfluency	Questions about unclarity in own awareness
6	Present tense or vivid representation of past	Declarative, fresh, real	Exclamation, alternations of dysfluency and fluency, pauses	Directly sensed and emergent feeling
7	Present tense primarily	Affirmative	More fluency than dysfluency	What one "knows" for oneself

• • • • • • • • • • • • • • • •

• • • • • • • • • • • • • • • •

E X H I B I T R
Penn Adherence and Competence Scale for Supportive-Expressive Therapy
(Barber and Crits-Christoph, 1996)[18]

Therapist (Name/#): ⎯⎯⎯⎯⎯⎯   Rater: ⎯⎯⎯⎯⎯⎯

Session Number: ⎯⎯⎯⎯⎯⎯   Date of Rating: ⎯⎯⎯⎯⎯⎯

Session Date: ⎯⎯⎯⎯⎯⎯   Patient Number: ⎯⎯⎯⎯⎯⎯

Site: ⎯⎯⎯⎯⎯⎯

Please rate the therapy session using the following scale:

(Continued)

EXHIBIT R *(Continued)*

A) Rate how much the therapist engaged in the described behavior (amount) on the blank on the left side of the item. After you have rated the **frequency** or **amount** of the therapist behavior, please rate next to it the **quality** of the response.

B) In case a therapist behavior is not present during the session. Its adherence rating (frequency) should be rated as not at all (1).

C) But its competence rating (quality) requires the following judgment: Do you think the therapist should have performed these actions or not? If the therapist should have done something and did not, the quality rating should also be low. But if you think it was appropriate for the therapist to not do what he or she did not do, then your quality rating should be relatively higher for that item.

D) Whenever the behavior described in the item is spontaneously done by the patient without any therapist's intervention, put a cross to the far left of the rating scale.

1	2	3	4	5	6	7
Not at all		Some		Considerably		Very Much

GENERAL THERAPEUTIC BEHAVIORS:

amount/quality

_____|_____   1. The therapist encourages (directly or by a facilitating atmosphere) the patient's expression; that is, to say what he or she thinks or feels.

_____|_____   2. The therapist listens openly (acceptingly and non-critically) to what the patient is saying.

_____|_____   3. The therapist's responses are kept simple and relatively brief

_____|_____   4. The therapist encourages the patient to explore the personal meaning of an event or feeling.

_____|_____   5. Therapist and patient have decided (in this session or in a previous one) what the goals of treatment are.

_____|_____   6. The therapist introduces new topics within the last five minutes of a session.

_____|_____   7. The therapist helps the patient to consider ways to improve or change the patient's interpersonal relationships.

_____|_____   8. The therapist listens to the patient for some time before giving a response.

_____|_____   9. The therapist gives advice to the patient.

_____|_____ 10. The therapist conveys a sense of respect, understanding and acceptance to the patient.

E X H I B I T R *(Continued)*

1 Not at all	2	3 Some	4	5 Considerably	6	7 Very Much

SUPPORTIVE COMPONENT:

amount/quality

_____|_____ 11. The therapist conveys a sense of supporting the patient's wish to achieve the goals of treatment.

_____|_____ 12. The therapist conveys a sense of liking the patient.

_____|_____ 13. Therapist and patient work as a team to help the patient with better self-understanding.

_____|_____ 14. The therapist recognizes the patient's improvement towards the attainment of the therapeutic goals,

_____|_____ 15. The therapist communicates a realistically hopeful attitude that the treatment goals are likely to be achieved.

_____|_____ 16. The therapist conveys a sense of respect for the patient's growing ability to do by her/himself what the therapist is doing during the session and encourages her/him to do so.

_____|_____ 17. The therapist is supportive of the patient (e.g., the therapist recognizes that treatment is sometimes hard for the patient).

_____|_____ 18. The therapist does not analyze qualities, circumstances or defenses that are effectively supporting the patient and/or vital to his mental health and current level of adaptation.

EXPRESSIVE COMPONENT:

amount/quality

A: Focus on the interpersonal theme

_____|_____ 19. The therapist helps the patient to realize the various manifestations of the patient's central relationship difficulty or conflict *across situations.*

_____|_____ 20. The therapist focuses attention on similarities among the patient's past and present relationships.

_____|_____ 21. The therapist helps the patient to realize how the relationship difficulties are reexperienced with the therapist in the here and now.

_____|_____ 22. The therapist's questions are focused on aspects of the central problems or main relationship theme. That is, the therapist gathers data about the patient's interpersonal problems.

_____|_____ 23. The therapist clarifies and interprets to the patient *facets* of the main relationship problem or conflict. That is, the therapist gives feedback to the patient about the patient's interpersonal problems.

(Continued)

E X H I B I T R *(Continued)*

1	2	3	4	5	6	7
Not at all		Some		Considerably		Very Much

_____I_____ 24. The therapist refers to the main relationship problem or conflict often enough to facilitate the patient's "working through."

_____I_____ 25. The therapist relates the way the patient feels about the therapist to the way the patient feels about significant others (e.g., friends, boss, or parent).

_____I_____ 26. The therapist relates improvement in the patient to the patient's increased understanding of the relationship theme.

B: Responses from Others (RO)

_____I_____ 27. The therapist helps the patient to understand other people's reactions to her/him in various interpersonal relationships.

_____I_____ 28. The therapist helps the patient to understand other people's reactions to the patient when s/he experiences specific emotions.

C: Responses from the Self (RS)

_____I_____ 29. The therapist helps the patient to understand how the patient views or responds to her/himself in various interpersonal relationships.

_____I_____ 30. The therapist helps the patient to understand how the patient views or responds to her/himself when s/he experiences specific emotions.

D: Wishes:

_____I_____ 31. The therapist helps the patient to understand what s/he implicitly and explicitly wants or needs from other people.

E: CCRT

_____I_____ 32. The therapist relates the patient's main wish to the patient's anticipated reactions of others and to the patient's responses to others' reactions and to the patient's responses to her/his wishes.

F: Symptoms

_____I_____ 33. The therapist *relates* the appearances of symptoms during the session (including things such as change of affect, slips or other temporary memory problems, etc.) to the various components of the relationship problem or conflict.

_____I_____ 34. The therapist's responses deal with an aspect of the relationship problem and relates it to the patient's presenting symptoms (e.g., depression, anxiety or interpersonal difficulties).

_____I_____ 35. The therapist conveys to the patient how the symptoms are faulty attempts to solve an emotional problem or conflict.

E X H I B I T R *(Continued)*

1	2	3	4	5	6	7
Not at all		Some		Considerably		Very Much

G: Resistance

_____I_____ 36. The therapist helps the patient become aware of the strong disposition to view others including the therapist in a particular pattern.

_____I_____ 37. The therapist helps the patient to realize that the patient does not mention specific topics or people that should have been mentioned.

_____I_____ 38. The therapist helps the patient to understand sudden shifts of mood, topics, attitudes, silence, vagueness, and inappropriate affect.

_____I_____ 39. The therapist addresses the patient's self-defeating behaviors which may include the patient's lack of improvement, etc.

H: Termination

_____I_____ 40. The therapist relates the resurgence of symptoms during termination to the main relationship problem or conflict.

_____I_____ 41. The therapist helps the patient see the implications and the meanings of the termination.

I: Depression

_____I_____ 42. The therapist focuses on various aspects of the depressive syndrome.

_____I_____ 43. The therapist elicits material concerning the context in which depressive mood changes.

_____I_____ 44. The therapist focuses on the aspects of the CCRT that fit best with the depressive mood alteration.

_____I_____ 45. The therapist relates symptoms such as hopelessness and helplessness to depression.

J: Summary of therapist evaluation

_____I_____ 46. Overall judgment of the applicant's skills as a dynamic psychotherapist.

_____I_____ 47. Overall judgment of the applicant's skills as a Supportive-Expressive dynamic psychotherapist.

_____I_____ 48. Overall judgment of the applicant's skills at formulating the patient's central issue or CCRT.

_____I_____ 49. Overall judgment of the level of difficulty presented by the patient (1—not difficult at all to 7—extremely difficult patient).

Notes

1. From "Measures of client and therapist vocal quality," by L. Rice and G. Kerry, in L. Greenberg and W. Pinsof (Eds.), *The Psychotherapy Process: A Research Handbook,* pp. 73–106. Reprinted by permission of Guilford Press.
2. From "The nature of arousal and nonverbal indices," by J. K. Burgoon, D. L. Kelly, D. A. Newton, and M. P. Keeley-Dyreson, *Human Communication Research,* 1993, *16,* 217–255. Reprinted by permission of the authors.
3. From *Manual for the Hill Counselor Verbal Response Modes Category System,* by C. E. Hill, 1993. Reprinted by permission of the author.
4. From "Effective supervision as perceived by beginning counselors-in-training," by E. L. Worthington, Jr. and H. J. Roehlke, *Journal of Counseling Psychology,* 1979, *26,* 64–73. Copyright 1979 by the American Psychological Association. Reprinted by permission of the authors.
5. From "Three methods in measuring the therapeutic process: Clients' and counselors' constructions of the therapeutic process versus actual therapeutic events," by P. P. Heppner, J. I. Rosenberg, and J. Hedgespeth, *Journal of Counseling Psychology,* 1992, *39,* 20–31. Reprinted by permission of the authors.
6. From "Brief structured recall: A more efficient method for studying significant therapy events," by R. Elliott and D. A. Shapiro. In *British Journal of Medical Psychology,* 1988, *61,* 141–153. Reprinted by permission of the author.
7. From "Counseling session impact as viewed by novice counselors and their clients," by W. B. Stiles and J. S. Snow. In *Journal of Counseling Psychology,* 1984, *31,* 3–12. Reprinted by permission of the author.
8. From "Systematic effects of participant role on evaluation of the psychotherapy session," by S. L. Eugster and B. E. Wampold. In *Journal of Consulting and Clinical Psychology,* 1996, *64,* 1020–1028. Revised and reprinted by permission of the authors.
9. From *HIM: Hill Interaction Matrix,* by W. F. Hill. Los Angeles: University of Southern California, Youth Study Center. Reprinted by permission of the author.
10. From "List of therapist intentions illustrated in a case study and with therapists of varying theoretical orientation," by C. E. Hill and K. E. O'Grady. In *Journal of Counseling Psychology,* 1985, *32,* 8. Copyright 1985 by the American Psychological Association. Reprinted by permission.
11. From "Development of a system for categorizing client reactions to therapist interventions," by C. E. Hill, J. E. Helms, S. B. Siegel, and V. Tichenor. In *Journal of Counseling Psychology,* 1988, *35,* 27–36. Copyright 1988 by the American Psychological Association. Reprinted by permission.
12. From "Therapist session intentions in cognitive-behavioral and psychodynamic-interpersonal psychotherapy," by W. B. Stiles, M. Startup, G. E. Hardy, M. Barkham, A. Rees, D. A. Shapiro, and S. Reynolds. In *Journal of Counseling Psychology,* 1996, *43,* 402–414. Copyright 1996 by the American Psychological Association. Reprinted by permission of the authors.
13. From "The dynamic relations among interpersonal behaviors: A test of complementarity and autocomplementarity," by S. R. Strong et al. In *Journal of Personality and Social Psychology,* 1988, *54,* 798–810. Copyright 1988 by the American Psychological Association. Reprinted by permission of the author.
14. From *Check List of Psychotherapy Transactions (CLOPT) and Check List of Interpersonal Transactions (CLOIT),* by Donald J. Kiesler. Richmond: Virginia Commonwealth University. Copyright © 1984 by Donald J. Kiesler. Reprinted by permission of the author.

15. From "Introducing semantic cohesion analysis: A study of group talk," by M. L. Friedlander, J. R. Thibodeau, M. P. Nichols, C. Tucker, and J. Snyder. In *Small Group Behavior, 16*(3), pp. 285–302. Copyright © 1985 by Sage Publications, Inc. Reprinted by permission of Sage Publications, Inc. and the author.
16. From "Development and validation of the Working Alliance Inventory," by A. O. Horvath and L. S. Greenberg. In *Journal of Counseling Psychology,* 1989, *36,* 223–233. Reprinted by permission of the authors.
17. From "The experiencing scales," by M. H. Klein, P. Mathieu-Coughlan, and D. J. Kiesler. In L. Greenberg and W. Pinsof (Eds.), *The Psychotherapeutic Process: A Research Handbook,* pp. 21–72. Reprinted by permission of Guilford Press.
18. From "Development of a therapist adherence competence rating scale for supportive-expressive dynamic psychotherapy," by J. P. Barber and P. Crits-Christoph. In *Psychotherapy Research,* 1996, *6,* 79–92. Reprinted by permission of the author.

CHAPTER 18

PROGRAM EVALUATION

Matrese Benkofski
Clyde C. Heppner

The focus of this book throughout has been on research design, its application in the counseling profession, and the conditions needed to conduct quality research. Turning to a slightly different topic, this chapter describes program evaluation—what it is, how it is similar to and differs from counseling research, and how it is used within counseling settings. The chapter describes in considerable detail the phases of program evaluation to introduce professionals to the field. The first step is to define program evaluation.

PROGRAM EVALUATION DESCRIBED

What is program evaluation, and how is it similar to and different from research? In Chapter 16 we discussed Project Good Start. In this research study, Willett et al. (1991) used a standardized scale (the Family Problem Checklist) to assess potential difficulties faced by several families, and then used the Family Function Scale to measure the progress of each family as treatment progressed. From a research perspective, the use of a repeated measures design to provide a quantifiable measure of a family's functioning over time is far superior to the traditional "before and after" snapshot. We reexamine this study here to illustrate important differences between research endeavors and program evaluation.

Whereas researchers are typically most interested in enhancing the profession's knowledge base, such as comparing the efficacy of two particular treatments, program evaluators are most interested in the effectiveness of a particular program for a particular group of people. Thus, program evaluators would want to be involved while programs such as Project Good Start are being designed. For example, during planning meetings they might learn that the community and neighborhood citizenry wanted the counselors to come from the community so that they would be sensitive to the families' cultural differences and needs. However, this could have both positive and negative effects on the program's outcomes: If counselors are culturally sensitive, program recipients may be more likely to disclose to them so that real progress can occur, but the families may be so familiar with the counselors that they feel uncomfortable talking with a "friend" about their parenting style. By being present during the planning meetings and knowing the community's requirement of selecting only local counselors, an evaluator could be sure to include "level of familiarity between counselor and client" as a variable in the database.

By being involved during the planning stage, evaluators also learn more about how the particular counseling treatment was chosen. Perhaps it was the only counseling treatment considered; perhaps several counseling treatments were identified, and this particular treatment was judged by the community's counseling professionals as most likely to be most effective with dysfunctional families in violent environments; or perhaps part of the program is to create a new counseling treatment not guided by a theoretical perspective. In short, for program evaluators, knowing how a particular counseling treatment was chosen and what outcomes it can be expected to deliver has a direct impact on the choice of outcomes measures. It then becomes an evaluator's responsibility to determine if there is a match among the treatment, the anticipated outcomes, and the outcome measures.

After the program has begun, the evaluator typically carefully monitors the data collection procedures to ensure that the Family Problem Checklist is administered prior to the first counseling session. In addition, the evaluator periodically checks the family's file to record each time a family attends counseling and to ensure that the family completes the Family Function Scale each month. During these visits the evaluator also makes various observations. How are families treated when they enter the center for counseling? Is the receptionist friendly and welcoming, or disinterested and rude? This information may be needed if the evaluator finds a very high or a very low dropout rate at the program's end.

While at the center, the evaluator may also note who the clients are and whether they represent the targeted population. As an example, consider a drug rehabilitation program aimed at people arrested and charged with drug possession. When the program evaluator visited the treatment site, she was surprised to see that the court had not only required drug users, but also drug dealers, to participate in the program. It was a common sight to see drug deals being made in front of the treatment center! So, returning to Project Good Start, if it were designed to address the needs of intact families, are all members of the family present for counseling? Perhaps the program evaluator should bring up in focus group discussions how important it is to have all family members involved in counseling and how the family and the ultimate success of counseling were affected when some family members did not participate in counseling. The evaluator might also raise the same issue with the counselors.

In addition to making periodic visits to the counseling site, the evaluator also includes home visits to observe the families before, during, and after the counseling sessions. Prior to these visits, the evaluator has worked with the counselors and program administrators to create a list of behaviors that would indicate that a family needs counseling in parenting skills and that the counseling has improved the family's interactions. After being pilot-tested and then refined, this list would serve with the Family Function Scale as a measure of change within each family.

By being actively involved in the program from conception to implementation, evaluators are in a position to (a) identify problems with the data collection procedures to minimize the risk of losing valuable data; (b) collect data to evaluate program effectiveness; (c) formulate and then test hypotheses that arise as the program matures; (d) document changes in the program's implementation over time; (e) give possible explanations for unanticipated results; and (f) document unanticipated positive outcomes. For the sake of this example, suppose that no significant difference in family functioning as measured by the Family Function Scale was detected. By being actively involved in the program, the program evaluator might, through a review of his or her field notes, be able to identify reasons for the lack of significant change in family functioning and modify the program before implementing it again at the same or another site.

Or, suppose instead that the evaluator identified significant differences in family functioning over time, but through discussions with the program recipients and observations at the treatment center, the evaluator ascertained that because the program was housed within a community center, the families also availed themselves of social services other than counseling. In that case, to say that the improvement in family functioning was due solely to the counseling program would be erroneous. Without being engaged in many aspects of the program, the program evaluator might incorrectly ascribe the effects to the counseling treatments alone.

By looking at Project Good Start from a program evaluator's perspective, several distinctions between research and program evaluation become evident. Whereas the goals of research are primarily to enhance the profession's knowledge base, the program evaluator's goal is evaluating the effectiveness of a particular program with a defined group of participants. The researcher develops specific hypotheses and emphasizes internal and/or external validity; the program evaluator typically collects a wide range of data to answer whether an intervention was effective, and to formulate other hypotheses about the causes and effects that explain the outcomes. Whereas both researchers and evaluators carefully select assessment measures a priori, the program evaluator also collects a wide range of additional data as the program unfolds. Although program evaluators often use research methodologies standard in psychology, they may also use observational methods developed and refined by anthropologists or cost/benefit analyses used in the business sector.

Unlike counseling psychology, which can trace its roots back to Frank Parsons in the early 1900s, program evaluation is still rather young. Evaluators have a wide range of experiences, preferred data collection methodologies, formal training, and professional viewpoints. Thus, it is often difficult to define program evaluation. It is often described as a process for judging the worth of a program relative to other alternatives, based on defensible, previously defined criteria (Scriven, 1980). Put another way, program evaluation is undertaken when a program's decision makers, recipients, funders, and/or managers want to determine whether a program is effective, to what degree, under what conditions, at what financial or social costs, and with what intentional or unintentional outcomes.

The data collection methodologies used during an evaluation are evolving with the profession. In the previous chapters on outcome and process research, we saw that as the counseling field has matured, the focus of counseling research has shifted—from an almost exclusive emphasis on outcome or process measures, to more integration of both process and outcome measures and recognition of increased complexity in counseling. A similar evolution has occurred in program evaluation. Perhaps because of its roots in education and testing, early program evaluations focused almost exclusively on measures of program recipients' progress after exposure to a program—how many new life skills recipients had mastered after a program designed to build basic skills, or how much self-esteem had increased after attending a youth camp for "at risk" high school students. Yet, as we saw in the Project Good Start example, much more than just the program's outcomes must be measured during an evaluation of a program. The environment, the population, the political climate, the needs of the community where the program is being implemented, the beliefs of program administrators as to the targeted population's needs, and many other factors play an integral role in defining the program and must be measured in the evaluation of the program.

PHASES OF PROGRAM EVALUATION

The steps for conducting a program evaluation do not always follow a routine set of procedures. In essence, what an evaluation looks like—what aspects of a program it examines, what data are collected, and how its results are used—depends largely on what stage in the program the evaluation occurs. Typically we think of doing an evaluation at the end of a program, and often this is when it in fact occurs, but an evaluation can occur at one or a combination of four stages of a program: during conceptualization, design, or implementation, or upon completion (Rossi & Freeman, 1993). Consider the following example:

> A university counseling center wishes to offer a stress-reduction program intended to help students cope with the anxiety, frustration, and potential for self-abusive behaviors (such as excessive drinking and erratic sleeping patterns) common during the final weeks of each semester. As scientist-practitioners, the counseling center staff decide to "evaluate" the program.

An evaluation of this program could take on many different forms, depending on the stage of the program at which the evaluation occurs, the needs of "stakeholders" (that is, individuals and groups of individuals who have a stake in the program), and the time frame and resources available for the evaluation. The specific "stakeholders" who are asked for input can dramatically change the results of the evaluation. For example, in this case, the stakeholders could be the students who enroll in the stress-reduction program, the counseling staff providing the program, university administrators, and even nonparticipating students who feel the program would be beneficial. If an evaluator is called to conduct the evaluation during the program's initial planning meetings, what steps would the evaluator take during the course of the evaluation? Starting with the framework presented by Herman, Morris, and Fitz-Gibbon (1987), an evaluator undertakes four phases of program evaluation, applicable at any stage of a program: (a) setting the boundaries of the evaluation; (b) selecting appropriate evaluation methods; (c) collecting and analyzing information; and (d) reporting the findings. Within each of these four phases are specific steps, which we examine in the following sections.

Setting the Evaluation's Boundaries

This first phase entails (a) determining the purposes of the evaluation, (b) collecting background information about the program, (c) writing a description of the program and then ascertaining whether your understanding matches that of others associated with the program, (d) making a preliminary agreement as to what the evaluation may include, and (e) coming to a final agreement concerning the program evaluator's role, and the specific services and final products the evaluator will provide. This same agreement also describes the resources available to the evaluator and a preliminary estimate of the costs associated with the evaluation.

During this initial phase, it is crucial that the evaluator understands the program, its mission, its scope, and its magnitude. The clearer the evaluator is as to what the program is designed to do, the less likely unforeseen issues will pop up after the evaluation's budget, time line, and methodology have been set. Much of the information about the program can be obtained by meeting with the program manager, but it is also wise to meet with others associated with the program—funders, program advocates, and perhaps even opponents—to get a broad view of the mission and scope of the program. The evaluator might request written summaries of the program to provide an initial understanding before these meetings. Either through the written documents, the initial meetings, or a combination of these sources, the evaluator should obtain at least preliminary answers to the following questions, using the university counseling center's stress-reduction program as an example:

1. What are the stress-reduction program's objectives, and how will this program be implemented to address these objectives? Knowledge of the program objectives are essential in order to link what the program was designed to accomplish and the measurable behaviors observed in the evaluation.
2. What will this stress-reduction program involve? How long will the program last? How many sessions will a participant typically attend? What type of stress-reduction techniques will be used? This information helps the evaluator to shape the evaluation, the time line, and the types of statistics (nonparametric or parametric) used in the analyses.
3. What types of effects do program planners anticipate? When should these effects be measurable? Does the program manager anticipate long-term benefits of the program? What type of evidence would the program manager need to claim that the program's mission has been met? Information

about these questions enables the evaluator to tailor the evaluation methods to the informational needs of stakeholders and program planners alike.

4. Has anyone written a proposal for funding? Are any program requirements tied to program funding (for example, including a segment of a special population as program recipients, paying program providers, or using some specific treatment in the program)? If, for example, the women's center on campus provided a portion of the program's funding, they may require the program to address stress as it relates specifically to raising a family while attending classes. These kinds of stipulations can have dramatic implications on the evaluation design, and it is better to know this before the evaluation has been set in motion.

5. What is the funding level for the program, and how much has been set aside for the evaluation process? A rule of thumb is that the funding for the evaluation should constitute approximately 10% of the cost of the program. This helps to prevent a very small project from having a far too expansive evaluation, and vice versa. Designers of programs often severely underestimate the cost of conducting a program evaluation.

6. What are the program manager's expectations for the evaluation? Does he or she have a preferred data collection strategy? What role will the evaluator play? Some agencies have staff members capable of helping with data collection, which reduces the billing cost of the evaluation. In some cases, the program manager expects the evaluator to be highly visible throughout the program's direction. Knowing what the program manager feels comfortable with in terms of evaluator exposure helps in planning the evaluation.

7. Why is an evaluation of the program being undertaken? Is it required by the funders? Have the outcome measures and the sampling procedures been predetermined? Knowing the reasoning behind the evaluation enables the evaluator to tailor the evaluation to the needs of the program manager and stakeholders. If the funders of the evaluation have clearly stated that objective, measurable, and scientifically rigorous data must be collected in order to be considered for continued funding, the evaluation will be quite different from one designed to help program implementors better serve and understand their clients.

8. What resources are available to the evaluator? Will counseling staff help with data collection? Are interns or clerical help available? What records are available to the evaluator? Given that the stress-reduction program is aimed at improving the physical health of the recipients, will medical records be available to the evaluator? Academic records? Again, knowing what resources are readily available enables the evaluator to select data sources that provide reliable and easily accessible, understandable data.

Among the many purposes of these questions, first and foremost the evaluator seeks to understand what the program is designed to do, what people associated with the program expect it to accomplish, and what outcomes or results are anticipated. The evaluator uses the answers to these questions to begin formulating a strategy for carrying out the evaluation. Moreover, the evaluator is trying to understand what aspects of the evaluation have already been arranged or agreed upon, and what aspects are yet to be determined.

Experienced evaluators also try to ascertain whether a request for an evaluation is sincere, or an attempt to "rubber stamp" a program as being a quality program. Novice evaluators, especially eager ones, often find themselves caught up in these situations. Our advice: Do not get involved. It will come back to haunt you, perhaps by giving you the reputation for taking any work, regardless of its merit. All evaluators wish they had never undertaken certain projects because they did not conduct the type of evaluation they had envisioned. Normal experience gives evaluators enough of these experiences; do not take them on willingly! Evaluators can use the following questions to determine whether they want to agree to an evaluation: Are there sufficient time and resources to conduct the evaluation? Do I have the needed resources, background knowledge, and time to commit to the evaluation? Typically, evaluators need not be a content expert—that is, an expert in stress reduction, in this case—to conduct the evaluation, but some program managers also rely on the evaluator to judge the worthiness of the treatment. If this is the case, and you are not a stress-reduction expert, is there sufficient funding to hire a content expert, or will the program evaluator take on that role, too?

Evaluators cannot expect all of these questions to be answered fully. Not all programs are precisely defined, and many of these questions may not be answerable, especially during the initial planning. Although this leaves a lot of gray area for constant negotiation between the evaluator and the program designers, we prefer that evaluators come to a program during its planning phase because that allows them to integrate the evaluation's data collection procedures into the day-to-day operations of the program, rather than coming in after the program has begun. In the latter case, the data collection procedures become "add-ons" that are often viewed by already overworked staff as optional, as time-fillers, or, worse yet, as mindless paperwork. But by asking these questions, the program evaluator is in a position to make an informed decision about whether or not to agree to conducting the evaluation.

During the initial meetings and throughout the evaluation process, the evaluator must develop the ability to listen to his or her intuition, "gut instincts," or "inner voice." Program evaluation is probably three-quarters science and one-quarter art. The art of program evaluation involves listening to and then coming to trust your intuition. Even though being a competent researcher, possessing above-average written and oral skills, and exhibiting excellent organizational skills will make for an above-average program evaluator, the ability to hear and then trust your intuition is required for entering the ranks of the expert. A good program evaluator often carries a notebook for keeping notes of meetings, interactions, and observations—and to jot down impressions and insights as well. Even though many of these notes and insights are never acted upon, some of them—especially those that keep reappearing—become working hypotheses for further investigation and study. Keeping a log of these impressions, insights, and hunches, and reviewing them from time to time, can take an evaluation from a regurgitation of facts to a more complete understanding of a program, including its benefits and its deficits.

At the end of this first phase, an evaluator should have a good understanding of the program's objectives, how it will be implemented, what outcomes it is intended to accomplish, and a preliminary understanding of what its designers anticipate the evaluation might entail. To help crystallize this understanding, the evaluator writes a description of the program, which has three purposes. First, by setting down on paper what he or she understands about the program, the evaluator can often identify fuzzy thinking or unanswered questions. Second, the evaluator should share this document with others in the program, as a reality check. Discussing points of disagreement often helps program designers identify and clarify fuzzy aspects of the program. Finally, this document can serve as the first section of the program report: the program description. The evaluator should include with the description a short memo stating that he or she has agreed to proceed with the evaluation, assuming that a final agreement can be reached concerning the cost and methodology of the evaluation. This memo can serve as an informal agreement until a more detailed one can be drafted.

Selecting Appropriate Evaluation Methods

During the second phase of the evaluation process, the focus moves from a description of the program and its objectives to the evaluation—how it will measure or provide information about the program's effects. One of the most difficult parts of conducting an evaluation is keeping the evaluation in focus—concentrating on those aspects of the evaluation that are important, and not being sidetracked by interesting but unimportant side issues. Taking specific steps to keep the evaluation in focus is a crucial but sometimes forgotten task. The results of such an omission include wasting valuable time and resources collecting data on unimportant aspects of the program; causing anxiety and frustration, and tension between the evaluator and stakeholders as they sort out what is supposed to be included in the evaluation; missing opportunities to collect important data; and perhaps even entirely missing the aim of the evaluation, such that results are deemed useless. Every evaluator likely has, at one time or another, failed to adequately plan for an evaluation and has suffered the frustration, professional embarrassment, and perhaps even panic associated with scrambling to fill in gaps in the evaluation as the final report comes due. Enough forces and factors—political posturing, incompetent program staff, belligerent program recipients, and funding cuts—potentially lurk around some evaluations to derail the program and its evaluation; this confusion does not need to be intensified by a poorly focused evaluation.

The following seven steps are the key tasks in creating a focused evaluation:

1. Solicit input from stakeholders
2. Design a plan for examining program implementation
3. Design a plan for evaluating program progress
4. Create a consolidated data collection plan
5. Plan the data analyses
6. Estimate the financial and time costs of the evaluation
7. Come to a final agreement about services, costs, and responsibilities

Soliciting Input from Stakeholders

The process of creating the evaluation's focus begins with face-to-face meetings with the program managers, funders, and others who have some special interest in the program. Notice that this list does not include only those people responsible for carrying out the program.

This step is the first one in helping to foster investment and commitment by stakeholders. By believing in the evaluation process and then personally committing time to design the evaluation, periodically review the evaluation process, and perhaps even collect some data, stakeholders see their concerns about the program being addressed. When they become fully involved in the evaluation of the program, stakeholders are more likely to make certain that funds are set aside for the evaluation, that data are faithfully collected, and that the evaluation's results are disseminated and incorporated into the next cycle of the program.

Getting stakeholders actively involved in the evaluation process is one of the most counterintuitive steps of evaluation. Beginning evaluators often approach evaluation like research, setting down a protocol for collecting data, implementing it, and then analyzing the results. Allowing others to help shape the protocol, to suggest data-collection methods, and to help interpret the findings seems to fly in the face of scientific objectivity! Experience with involving stakeholders leads most evaluators to the following observations. First, stakeholders often take a very objective perspective, even when they are deeply committed to the program. They tend to quickly understand that using suspect evaluation methods jeopardizes the evaluation and the implementation of the evaluation's results. Rather than being too lax, stakeholders often favor the most objective methods available. Second, with even minimal guidance from the evaluator, stakeholders often create the type of evaluation the evaluator had originally envisioned. Third, evaluators should remember that they are soliciting input from the stakeholders, not turning the entire evaluation over to them. Ultimately it is the evaluator, not the stakeholders, who makes final decisions about the evaluation protocol. Fourth, choosing to involve stakeholders should not be mere "lip service," but rather a commitment to weigh the opinions of the stakeholders. Anything less can jeopardize the evaluation because it is the stakeholders that ultimately make the final decisions about the utility of the program.

Including stakeholders in the initial planning meetings allows the evaluator to include data collection strategies that meet these stakeholders' need for information when determining a program's worth. Inclusion helps to decrease the temptation of some stakeholders to claim that the evaluation was flawed, especially if the program does not fair well in the final report.

It is important, however, not to be disheartened if stakeholders show a lack of interest in becoming involved in the program evaluation planning process. Some people have a propensity to be silent or even uninvolved, unless a program's continuance is threatened. In these cases it is helpful to actively solicit the opinions and suggestions of stakeholders. The key word here is "actively"; it may take more than one formal invitation of marginal stakeholders, plus a well-placed phone call from the evaluator, during which the importance of the stakeholder's participation is emphasized. Another strategy for garnering stakeholder input is for the same individuals to be involved in both the initial planning of the program and the planning of the evaluation, assuming that this group also includes people who will be using the program.

At the least, the evaluation plan, once prepared in first draft, should be presented publicly through existing meetings typically attended by program recipients and/or the general public. When evaluating the counseling program for stress reduction, for example, the evaluation plan should be presented to governing bodies involved in funding the counseling center. For other programs, this public body may be the PTA of a school program, the city council (for a city-sponsored program), or a steering committee for campus programs. It is very important that the input of such meetings be incorporated into the evaluation plan; this is not the time to force a plan without an adequate discussion or to solicit input only to dismiss it. If evaluators seek input from stakeholders, it is their responsibility to consider their suggestions and input seriously.

During discussions in which the focus of the evaluation is being generated, a few questions should be kept in the forefront: What aspects of the program should be evaluated? Will the whole program be evaluated, or only newly added components? At what point in the program will the evaluation begin, and when will it end? Will it focus on the conceptualization stage, the design stage, or the implementation stage of the program? Is the program sufficiently mature for the evaluator to expect any measurable efficacy? By reflecting on these questions while formulating the evaluation plan, the evaluator is more likely to keep the evaluation on track. Moreover, by keeping the program's time frame and maturity in mind while designing the evaluation, it is more likely that the evaluation will be appropriate for the program.

This is also the time that the evaluator heeds the specific questions to be answered during the evaluation. Conducting an evaluation with only the very general questions, "Is this program worthwhile?" or "Has this program been successful?," is not sufficient and violates the first standard of program evaluation—the need for utility (Joint Committee on Standards for Educational Evaluation, 1994). Put another way, the evaluation must answer the questions of interest to the stakeholders.

These initial meetings are a good time for the evaluator to come to understand the needs and interests of the primary stakeholders, and their relationships with one another. During the meetings the evaluator should pay attention to how people are interacting with one another. Are there factions within various groups? How deep are these divisions, and on what are they based? How large an effect will these factions have on the evaluation process, and on the reception of the evaluation's results? How are differing points of view dealt with? Are viewpoints in opposition to the key stakeholders' allowed to surface and be fully considered, or are they quickly dismissed? If the latter occurs, the evaluator should steer the conversation back to the overlooked viewpoint, perhaps by saying, "I'd like to come back to a point just made. Could you elaborate on . . . ?" It is the evaluator's responsibility to ensure that the concerns raised at meetings represent not just the opinions of the vocal, but also those of potentially disenfranchised, underrepresented, or overlooked stakeholders.

Throughout these initial meetings, The evaluator is typically considered by the program managers and other stakeholders to be an "expert" whose words are taken as fact. Thus, it is important that evaluators allow others to speak and facilitate the process. If the evaluator becomes too vocal, the evaluation can quickly become one devised by the evaluator, not the one envisioned by stakeholders.

Designing a Plan for Examining Program Implementation

After the evaluator has heard what questions stakeholders would like the evaluation to answer, the evaluator creates two plans for data collection, each with a different focus. The first plan, which we cover in this section, addresses collecting evidence of what the program actually did or how it was actually implemented. The second plan (described in the next section) presents the data collection strategy for measuring the progress of the program. Both of these plans require the evaluator to work back and forth among the set of evaluation questions proposed by the stakeholders, the limited resources such as funds and time, and commonly accepted data collection methods. Perhaps the easiest way to begin is to create a matrix like that shown in Table 18-1. For each evaluation question, five categories are examined: (a) sources of information, (b) needed resources, (c) data collection methodology, (d) time line, and (e) data analyses.

Consider again the stress-reduction workshop provided through the campus counseling center. What information is needed to determine whether the program was a success? First, the evaluator would need to know that a stress-reduction workshop occurred, what it involved, who attended it, and how well it matched its attendees' needs. These are measures of program implementation. It may seem obvious to state that only after you knew that the workshop occurred would it make sense to judge its merits. However, it is important not to assume that what is supposed to happen in fact happens, or that the unexpected never occurs.

Every program evaluator has numerous examples of a disparity between what the program was intended to be and what it in fact turned out to be. And although there are numerous examples of a program failing because some of its components were omitted, other programs succeed in unintended ways. One example is a program designed to help physically challenged students attend a large, midwestern university. The student services center's goals were to improve the study skills of these students, both through skill building workshops (for example, test-taking strategies, pneumonics) and by providing them cutting-edge technology to facilitate the access of information (for example, large-print computer monitors for students with poor vision, or a Morse-code word processor for quadriplegic and paraplegic students). These services were made available to students, and some students were quite successful because of the training. However, conversations with the students revealed that the two most important, beneficial aspects of the program were having a place to come between classes, where they could interact with other students with disabilities, and knowing that there were people who could assist them in more mundane activities such as buttoning a coat, fixing eyeglasses, or coming to get them if their wheelchairs became inoperable. It was these services that enabled them to be full-time students on a large college campus.

TABLE 18-1
An Example of an Evaluation Planning Matrix for a Workship

Evaluation Questions	Sources of Information	Needed Resources	Data Collection Methodology	Time Line	Data Analyses
How is the information presented in the workshop?	Workshop; workshop's presenters	Planning documents	Structured observations; workshop planning documents	Throughout the duration of workshop	Descriptive statistics
Did the workshop meet the needs of attendees?	Workshop participants' journals; survey of attendees	Journals for a sample of attendees; possibly some payment for completion; printed surveys	Journals; survey	Journals to be returned at last workshop; survey to be administered at final workshop	Qualitative data

Some form of observational methodology is the most common way to determine whether the program took place and the form it took during implementation. One common form of observation requires the observer to be detached from the activity, and typically the observations sample the program's activities in a structured fashion. Structured observations for the stress-reduction program would require the evaluator to observe the workshops for a specified amount of time—for example, 25 times for 5-minute intervals over the course of a six-hour workshop. In each of the five-minute intervals, the evaluator would mark on a standardized code sheet what is taking place in the workshop. If one of the goals of a counseling program is to use real examples from life as the vehicle for presenting information, rather than relying on a theoretical, lecture-style presentation, then a structured observation would, among other things, monitor how the counselor is providing information during one-minute segments. Potential categories of presenting information might be (a) statements of fact, (b) presentations of examples, (c) questions and answers, (d) other, and (e) no presentation of information. Having more than one observer reliably code human behavior in discrete categories can be tricky, so pilot-testing these forms before formally collecting the data is time well spent. Worthen, Sanders, and Fitzpatrick (1997) is a very good reference for learning how to construct and pilot-test observation forms and analyze structured observation data.

The other commonly used observation methodology is participant observation, which requires the observer to actually become involved in the process, typically as a program participant. Participant observation is much less structured and more qualitative, and it requires the observer to take notes throughout the course of the activity or as soon after the activity as possible. Readers wanting more information about participant observation methodologies are referred to Patton (1980). Whereas structured observations are designed to capture how much of various activities occurred, participant observations are especially useful when descriptions of the mood preceding, during, and following an activity are also desired.

Even though structured observations and participant observations provide two different data sets and typically answer different questions, it is not uncommon to use both observation methods during an evaluation (although not simultaneously!). Assessing program activities through both periods of structured and participant observations provides a rich data set. The program evaluator asked to evaluate the stress-reduction program may begin with participant observations. The evaluator might attend the first few workshops, describing the structure of these workshops, the extent to which the participants actually practice stress-reduction techniques, and how she/he felt during these workshops. During these observations, the evaluator might, in-turn, create some potential hypotheses about the program, such as: "Discussions about stressors are often brought up by participants but not addressed by the counselor" or "These stress-reduction techniques sound easy here in class, but I don't think I would practice them outside of this workshop. My life is just too hectic to take the time." These hypotheses, as well as impressions, observations, and other hypotheses, can then be used to create questions for participant surveys or followed-up through a structured observation.

Although observational methods are especially useful in evaluating a program's implementation, other methods may be useful as well. Program records such as activity logs, sign-in sheets, and individual client records (with permission) can provide a useful paper trail as to what activities occurred during a program. For example, if one component of Project Good Start involved referring families to community support programs providing medical attention, food resources, or child-care classes, then reviewing a random sample of client records should document the extent to which these services were suggested by the program staff. These same records may even indicate whether or not the client sought these sources of assistance, and the extent to which these services were provided to the client. Other times, however, the client may have to be asked directly what services they were referred and what services they actually experienced. There can, of course, be a difference between the number of clients referred to a community resource and the number of clients who ultimately receive services.

This example provides a good illustration of how, as an evaluation process unfolds, an evaluator can easily lose the focus of the evaluation. For example, even though it might be interesting to ask why clients referred to services never follow through with them—is it because they were referred to the wrong service agency, they did not qualify for the particular service, they never went to the initial appointment due to a lack of transportation or child care, or they do not trust social services agencies and refused to go?—the program evaluator must first stick to the evaluation questions, and then determine whether new questions are within the scope of the evaluation. If not, the new questions are set aside, at least for now.

Designing a Plan for Evaluating Program Progress

Not only must the evaluation examine how the program was implemented, it also must ascertain whether the anticipated effects of the program are evident, and (if the program has not reached completion) whether the program is on-track to achieve the stated program goals. As with monitoring program implementation, program documents and observations can be used to measure a program's progress related to the program's anticipated outcomes. In addition, satisfaction surveys, focus groups, self-report logs or journals, and content testing may be useful. We discuss each of these methods next.

Surveys are a fairly easy and inexpensive method to collect information about a program's effects on participants. Traditional surveys have several advantages that often make them the method of choice when soliciting input from program participants, as well as some disadvantages (see Fowler, 1993, and Chapter 9 for more details). Surveys are relatively inexpensive to create and produce, and typically they require only simple descriptive statistics for reporting purposes. Surveys can be used to collect information about the participants before and after a program, so that changes in affect, cognition, and/or behaviors can be measured. Surveys are also quickly and easily administered to a large number of people; most people are familiar with surveys, which makes them easy to administer. On the other hand, the program evaluator needs to assess the population asked to complete the survey. If, for example, illiteracy is an issue for this population, then the evaluator may wish to use an oral interview administered either individually or in a group setting. If a pre-post design is to be used, are the program participants easily located, or would tracking these individuals to collect the post-program information be difficult? Is the information easily conveyed in a singular response, or is further clarification needed before a full understanding is possible? Written surveys should not be the data collection method of choice when detailed written responses are needed; people typically will not complete numerous open-ended questions, and generally the responses are never more than a sentence or two. Other methods, such as focus groups or interviews, are better means for collecting in-depth responses.

Situations that limit the usefulness of survey methodologies are often present in social programs. In one example, an agency hired to conduct evaluations of three independent programs had difficulties with all three surveys of program participants. The data for families in public housing were lost because of major difficulties in collecting the post-program data; in the middle of the year-long program, the public housing units were renovated, thereby scattering the program's families across the city, and very few of the displaced families returned to the public housing units or provided a forwarding address. The evaluation of another program, again located in a public housing facility, required housing residents to respond to a written survey concerning aspects of their community they would like to change. Only after the data were analyzed did the evaluator, unable to see a consistent pattern of responses, realize that the respondents were illiterate and had randomly marked responses on the questionnaire! The third evaluation required the program staff to help program recipients complete a survey after completing a four-week course but before receiving services. The evaluator assumed that this was occurring but learned only after the program had ended that staff seldom had program recipients complete the survey before beginning the program; almost none of the respondents had both pre- and post-program surveys.

Another methodology commonly used to collect data about the effects of a program is focus group methodology, which relies on the interaction of people as they discuss a common experience or viewpoint. Because the data are always qualitative and reflect people's experiences, thoughts, ideas, and impressions, this method is basically a self-report of how the program affected participants. Focus groups need not always involve program participants, however; program staff can also share their concerns and impressions about a program, its benefits, and its worth. Some specific skills are needed for conducting a successful focus group; see Krueger (1994) for an excellent discussion of focus group methodology as it applies to the social sciences.

Self-report logs or journals, which are often overlooked by program evalua-tors, represent an excellent method for capturing participant and staff reactions to a program or recording the frequency of specific behaviors. Self-report logs are typically in a checklist format on which the respondent periodically records the frequency of the behavior under study; journals are narrative descriptions of the behavior. With the stress-reduction program, program participants might carry a small notebook; every time they feel stressed they would jot down the stressor, their initial reaction to it, and a description of how this behavior either increased, decreased, or had no effect on the stress they were feeling. If quantitative data were needed, the program evaluator could generate a mutually exclusive list for each of the categories (stressor, behavior, and consequences) and ask participants to check off one item in each category. A more complex log might involve col-lecting information about the conditions surrounding the stressful event, the dura-tion of the stressful feelings, and the time of day the stressor occurred. Logs and journals can provide specific data about behaviors *as they occur* rather than the broader statements about behaviors and feelings collected in more general surveys.

Content testing, yet another method for collecting data on a program's effect, evaluates program participants' knowledge about a topic, typically using some paper-and-pencil activity. Course exams are a form of content testing. This type of data is useful when distinct facts or information is being conveyed through the program. In the stress-reduction program, respondents might be asked to name the stress-reduction techniques introduced in the workshop, the physiological symptoms associated with stress, the psychological manifestations of stress, and the five most common stressors faced by people in their age group. An even better data set would result from administering the same test before and after the workshop to measure the amount of information respondents acquired from it. Of course, using content testing requires the test to be highly correlated with the material presented in the workshop, and the individual items must be specific and difficult enough that only workshop attendees can answer the ques-tions correctly.

Another use of content testing is to determine respondents' familiarity with a specific topic. One evaluator used a content test to evaluate a city's biking and walking trails. Respondents were asked how familiar they were with the biking and walking trail system (using a 1 to 5 scale to assess the respondent's self-report of familiarity), as well as 20 questions about the trails. Only respondents who had used the trails were able to correctly answer a majority of the questions. These data then were used to subsequently classify the respondents into "high," "medium," and "low" trail users, a categorization that was subsequently used for other statistical analyses.

Creating a Consolidated Data Collection Plan

It is sometimes easy to become lost in the "forest" of data and end up with too much data in one area and no data in another. After considering all data collection options, it is good to make a matrix with the evaluation question in the first column and the various methods that will be used to answer the particular question in the other columns. In evaluation terms, an evaluator often will "triangulate" the data collection process (Denzin, 1978) using multiple methods, multiple data sources, and more than one data collector or observer for data collected over more than one time period. Such a strategy reduces the reliance on any particular source. Just as a medical diagnosis seems more reliable when it comes from several different physicians, so too is the judgment of a program's worth more reliable when based on several sorts of data. Thus, for observations of the stress-reduction workshop, an evaluator who uses triangulation would have more than one observer trained in the observation procedure (to minimize observer bias), and these observations would be distributed over the length of the workshop (to minimize situational bias). If the workshop is repeated within the time frame of the evaluation, the evaluator would collect observational data from the other workshops as well. Finally, if the observations were used to describe the workshop's content, then the evaluator would also examine the written descriptions of the workshop's curriculum or planned activities as yet another source of data.

Planning the Data Analyses

The final column in the matrix of evaluation questions and data collection methods in Table 18-1 is "data analyses." If, for example, a survey is being used, will subscores be calculated, or will frequencies for each item be calculated? Will a respondent's survey data be correlated with workshop attendance, and if so, is there a way to match these two pieces of data, either through a name or a code? What statistical analysis will be performed on the data, and are the data in a form that allows the analysis to occur without extensive manipulation? If the data are qualitative, how will the data be analyzed? Will there be case studies or a summary of findings? Time spent planning for the data analyses, whether the data are qualitative, quantitative, or archival, can save considerable time in conducting the data analyses. Extensive planning can also prevent fatal data collection errors from occurring, such as collecting pre- and post-test data only to find that there is no way to link the data because no identifying names or codes were included on the survey instrument.

Estimating the Financial and Time Costs of the Evaluation

"The cost of an evaluation is difficult to predict accurately" (Herman, Morris, & Fitz-Gibbon, 1987) is an assessment with which almost anyone who has conducted an evaluation will likely agree without hesitation. There are no hard-and-fast rules about how much time a survey, for example, will take to design, print, distribute, analyze, and interpret. Herman et al. suggest first determining the fixed-costs—those over which you have no control, such as postage, consultant time, overhead costs (heat, electricity, phone, and so on), printing, test and instrument purchase, and supplies or equipment needed to complete the project. They also suggest that you then calculate the "per unit" cost for each of these items. Thus, printing costs should be "per page," and overhead costs might be calculated "per month." Similarly, "person-hours" should also be calculated on a monthly or daily basis. Per person costs should include all the expenses associated with individuals, such as benefits, income tax, and social security tax that routinely are charged for a person's employment.

After the per unit costs have been calculated, the evaluator can begin to create the actual budget. The exact level of detail and layout of the budget depend on funders' needs, any forms required by your own organization, and your experience. This process can be quite complex, especially for a large evaluation, but it can be made less daunting by creating a detailed list of specific tasks needed to complete each component of the program evaluation. Thus, for a survey, the evaluator would estimate the costs for each step needed to move the survey from creation to data interpretation. Experience makes this process easier, for knowing some of the areas that can cause problems allows the evaluator to allocate sufficient resources within the budget. It is rare when an evaluator says, "I overestimated the amount of time this project would take" or "I have more resources than I know what to do with!" The more detailed this list of tasks is, the less likely it is that you will underestimate the time associated with each task. Clearly, the more information you can add to this list, the better estimate you will make. Some details result from specific decisions, such as how many surveys will be given out and how they will be distributed and returned; other details come from talking with others. For example, if you learn that the data entry specialist charges by the key stroke rather than by the hour, you might want to know what the survey will look like before moving forward on that line in the budget. Colleagues can be good resources in helping to create realistic time lines and budgets. Each component should be broken into its individual tasks, and then estimates of time to complete each task and the subsequent cost for that task should be made. Even though this procedure creates a budget with a built-in time line, the evaluator may wish to create a time line in calendar form, with target dates for each component's completion highlighted. Several commercially available computer programs can create a master calendar of projects, in addition to monthly calendars. This software can be very helpful for keeping track of target dates in projects, especially if the evaluator is working on several projects simultaneously.

Coming to a Final Agreement About Services, Costs, and Responsibilities

After outlining the data collection procedures and creating a time line and budget to encompass these activities, the program evaluator submits these materials for final approval to the agency commissioning the program evaluation. The documents submitted should contain the following items:

1. A document that provides an overview of what will and will not be covered in the evaluation process, how and to whom the data will be

reported, the cost of the evaluation, and the terms for payment. This document, sometimes known as a letter of agreement, should be short and
succinct. It serves as an overview of the entire evaluation process and
should be signed by both the program evaluator and a representative of
the agency commissioning the program evaluation.
2. A document that identifies the following for each component of the program evaluation: a brief rationale, what data will be collected, the procedures for collecting the data, the person responsible, the roles and responsibilities of assistants, the time line, and the costs.
3. A current vitae or resume of the program evaluator

Modifications to these documents are common, both before the documents
are signed and after the evaluation has begun. All modifications in the data collection procedures need to be documented in writing, and a copy of these written changes must be provided to the client. These documents can be invaluable
should disputes arise concerning any component.

Collecting and Analyzing Information

All the steps we have described up to this point occur *before* one piece of data
has been collected. With proper planning and documentation, collecting and analyzing the information and then reporting the findings are rather straightforward.
With proper planning and good record keeping, the evaluator should know
exactly what data need to be collected; when during the program the data will be
collected, and by whom; and how the data will be analyzed and interpreted. More
important, perhaps, the evaluator will have a framework for judging whether collecting additional data would be beneficial, whether funds allow for following up
on a newly presented data collection opportunity, and how any follow-up data
will fit into the overall evaluation. In essence, up to this point the program evaluator has been creating a road map that will be used to keep the evaluation on track
once data collection is underway. Moreover, this road map will also guide decisions about the format, content, and style of the evaluation report.
    The role the evaluator has negotiated determines how actively involved he
or she is in the day-to-day data collection process. If the program is large and will
be replicated at several sites, or if site employees will collect a majority of the data
to keep the cost of the evaluation down, then the evaluator becomes a data manager. At other times the evaluator serves as the principal data collector. Regardless, *ultimately the evaluator is responsible for the data, their integrity, their
validity, and their timely collection.* Thus, several steps must be undertaken to
ensure that the data are clean, as error-free as possible, unbiased, and collected on
time and within budget.
    First, every data collection procedure should undergo pilot testing. This
requires thoroughly training any data collectors or site personnel concerning how
the data are to be collected. Do not rely simply on written instructions; actual
face-to-face training with several opportunities for role playing and questions can

eliminate many points of confusion. If a questionnaire is to be administered, data collectors should practice administering it; if observations are to be made, practice sessions should occur until all data collectors observe the same situation and collect exactly the same data 90 to 95 percent of the time. If such coding reliability does not happen within a reasonable amount of time, the evaluator should consider simplifying the observation form or replacing some observers.

When the evaluator is not the principal data collector, the second step is to establish a check-and-balance system. All data should be examined. Are the surveys filled out correctly and completely? Are pre-tests being given to clients before the first counseling session? Are files complete enough so that clients can be tracked for a 6-month follow-up interview? The evaluator should never assume that the data are being collected as instructed; periodic monitoring of the data collection process is essential. An inexperienced evaluator once failed to check on a data collector because this particular collector had been working with the evaluation group for a couple of years before working for the evaluator. You can imagine the evaluator's horror, dismay, and embarrassment when, while visiting the program site, she was asked when the data collector was going to observe the program; she had just looked over the data supposedly collected from that site the previous week! The combination of that and similar experiences has led the evaluator to hang above her desk the following sign, which summarizes her philosophy about data collection:

> If you haven't seen it, heard it, touched it, smelled it, rolled in it, felt it, and tasted it, you don't know it.

Periodic checks of the program site, both announced and unannounced, are essential for monitoring the program and helping to keep the data clean.

The task of checking the data does not end once they arrive on the evaluator's desk. Data entry must be checked for accuracy, especially if performed by someone new to the evaluator. Are missing data being coded properly? How many errors are there per 100 data entry keystrokes? A skilled data entry person probably has no more than one or two errors. Are the data being entered using standardized procedures to make data analyses easy and to minimize data transformation or manipulation? The evaluator should never assume that the person entering the data knows how to do so in a format that is usable by a given statistical computer package.

Once all of the data have been collected and readied for analyses (that is, quantitative data have been entered into a spread sheet or statistical analysis package; field notes have been typed into case notes; tapes of focus groups have been transcribed, and either paper copies or computer files are available), then the evaluator is now ready to conduct the data analysis. We divide data analysis into two distinct steps: primary analyses and secondary analyses.

Primary Data Analyses

The first analyses, called primary analyses, are identical to those presented in the results sections of empirical articles. The data from each component of the evaluation are analyzed in isolation from other data. Thus, for example, the results of the survey that measured respondent happiness are analyzed and reported separate from the descriptions of the stress-reduction workshop activities prepared by the participant-observer; each component has its own methods, results, and summary sections, as if each were the only data collected for the evaluation.

There are several advantages to analyzing and interpreting each data component in isolation from the other components. First, these primary data reports are excellent vehicles for periodically presenting data to stakeholders. They give stakeholders some preliminary indication of some of the findings; moreover, they begin to prepare stakeholders for the final report. Second, they prevent the data from becoming backlogged. By analyzing and writing the report for each data set as soon as it is ready, program evaluators are not faced with piles and piles of data as the completion deadline approaches. Third, primary data reports help the evaluator see holes in the data or areas that need additional examination. Programs are fluid entities; despite the best planning, changes in the program, failed data collection procedures, or ambiguous results sometimes require the evaluator to augment planned data sources. By analyzing the data as they come in, the evaluator may have enough time to develop a plan for collecting additional data before the program has ended. Finally, conducting a primary data analysis also expedites the secondary data analyses, as we discuss next.

Secondary Data Analyses

A secondary data analysis ties together the individual, primary analyses to describe a component of the program. Because multiple sources of data are used, the program evaluator must reexamine each of the primary analyses to determine where findings support one another and where there are discrepancies. When answering the question, "Did the stress-reduction program provide program participants with strategies they could implement?" the evaluator would look at all the data collected. The evaluator would look at the survey items (which had been summarized into frequencies and percentages in the primary analyses) that asked respondents how often they used a particular technique, as well as examine journals kept by the respondents and the field notes taken during the participant-observations. If program participants said they used meditation frequently to reduce stress, was this technique emphasized in the workshops? If "effective decision making" was a technique emphasized during training but did not appear in the participants' journals, was this because they did not understand the importance of decision making in stress reduction or because it was not presented clearly enough to be useful?

Although there are several differences between how a researcher and an evaluator conduct the study of a social program, one of the elemental differences comes in the collection and interpretation of several data sources. Multiple data sources that provide insight into the worth of a social program are a hallmark of program evaluation, and the multiplicity of data sources requires some method for weaving together these sources. This method involves secondary data analyses. The evaluator begins with the program's goals and objectives and examines the primary data reports to see how the results of each data collection component supports or refutes the supposition that the program met its goals. What evidence is there that college students who have taken part in the stress-reduction program have learned several new stress-reduction techniques? Did items on the questionnaire given in the workshop address this question? What did respondents say in focus groups when asked if they learned new techniques? According to the field notes of the participant-observer, were workshop attendees introduced to "several" techniques? Perhaps another goal of the stress-reduction workshop was to have respondents feel better able to handle stressful situations. What evidence either supports or refutes this claim of the program? If workshop attendees kept journals, do they contain evidence that attendees improved their stress-coping skills over time?

The secondary analysis moves back and forth from stated program goals and objectives to data sources. The importance of reducing the data via primary data analyses should now be evident: Wading through raw data at this point would be inefficient and cumbersome, if not impossible; relying on the summary statements made in the primary report helps to expedite the writing of the secondary analyses.

The secondary analysis—this moving back and forth from the program's objectives to the evidence, the weaving together of the individual pieces of data into a holistic picture—*is* program evaluation. Combined with recommendations and comparisons to similar programs, the secondary analysis creates the evaluation of the program. A program evaluator should never leave the interpretation of the evaluation to the stakeholders. It is the program evaluator's role to pull the pieces together and to clearly state what they mean in terms of the program's implementation, anticipated outcomes, and implications for the successful conduct of this or future programs.

Reporting the Evaluation's Findings

The evaluation process is not finished with the analysis and interpretation of the data. The last step, writing the final report, includes a few aspects that may be new to researchers. A good evaluation report, according to Worthen, Sanders, and Fitzpatrick (1997), contains the following sections: (a) an executive summary; (b) an introduction to the report stating the evaluation's purpose, the audience for whom the report was intended, any needed disclaimers of limitations, and an overview of the report contents; (c) a section that describes the focus of the evaluation and the program under evaluation; (d) an overview of the evaluation procedures; (e) a presentation of the evaluation results (the primary and secondary analyses); (f) the conclusions and recommendations; (g) responses to the report (if any); and (h) appendices, including the detailed evaluation plan, copies of instruments, and detailed analyses (the primary analyses). Several very good references provide the reader detailed information about each of these sections (see Newman & Brown, 1996; Patton, 1986; Smith, 1982; Worthen, Sanders, & Fitzpatrick, 1997). We next present a few comments on two of these sections: the recommendations and the executive summary.

Writing Recommendations for Improvement

Although writing the recommendations for improvement is perhaps the most important part of the evaluation process, it is daunting, especially for people new to program evaluation. Even experienced evaluators can have doubts, thinking "Who do you think you are, making suggestions about the program? You are not a content expert in counseling, in education, or in whatever area the program functions." The solution is not to write the recommendations in isolation. Just as evaluators should work to establish a rapport and understanding between themselves and the stakeholders when designing the evaluation, and should update stakeholders during the data collection and analyses, the evaluator/stakeholder relationship should continue through the report- and recommendation-writing stage.

An experienced evaluator might write the recommendations and then present them to stakeholders for discussion, but a more inclusive method is to present the final report minus the recommendations. Then, after stakeholders have had an opportunity to digest the contents of the final report—and stakeholders will do this at different levels of intensity—the evaluator schedules a meeting at which the evaluator facilitates the group in the generation of recommendations based on the final report. As recommendations are written by the stakeholders, the evaluator notes the differences from his or her own prewritten recommendations. The evaluator also may need to draw the group's attention to points not yet brought into the discussion. By using this method of including stakeholders in writing the recommendations, two important goals are achieved. First, stakeholders are reminded that program evaluation is not something that happens to them and their program, but instead is a collaborative discussion in which several perspectives shape the final recommendations. Second, the evaluation report and the subsequent recommendations are not viewed as being the sole property of the evaluator but rather as reflecting the thoughts of several professionals closely related to the program.

Utilizing the experience of stakeholders to help formulate the recommendations can be very beneficial, but a successful meeting does not occur without proper planning. First, because it is likely that many stakeholders assembled have not read the report prior to the meeting, the evaluator should provide a 15- to 20-minute presentation that outlines the evaluation findings. Moreover, the evaluator should have a list of recommendations he or she feels are absolutely crucial for inclusion and should ensure their inclusion in the discussion. A block of uninterrupted time must be set aside for this meeting. No one has ever complained if a meeting does not fill the whole block of time, but trying to hurry through the discussion can leave stakeholders feeling that ideas have been thrust upon them. The evaluator should be the keeper of the agenda and move the meeting along at a reasonable pace, allowing for discussion but preventing it from straying from the stated purpose. Finally, it is extremely important to invite the full range of stake-holders to this meeting, *including those with dissenting views,* and everyone invited should be notified as to who else will be in attendance. The evaluator should act as a facilitator, encouraging people to express their opinions within the constraints of the program. This meeting is not the vehicle for settling long-standing disagreements.

Recommendations include both the positive and negative aspects of the program as it was implemented and the subsequent outcomes. The strengths of the program are always listed first, separate from the weaknesses (sometimes called the limitations) of the program. Careful wording of the recommendation section of the report is crucial; the goal is to write a recommendation that adequately describes the strengths and weaknesses of the program without being overly critical or mired in detail. One good perspective addresses the future—either in the next year of the program or the next time the program is replicated: What aspects of the program would be absolutely critical for success next time? What are the key, beneficial features of the program that need to be incorporated into future programs? What parts of the program were not implemented as anticipated, and what does this mean for future replications of the program? What is missing from the current program that, if included in future years, would make it stronger? What can be done to strengthen the program in future replications? Some evaluators simply list recommendations; others include a short rationale that describes the formulation of the conclusions drawn in the report.

Writing the Executive Summary

The other aspect of the evaluation report that may be unfamiliar to researchers is the executive summary. Attention to the style of this section and the recommendations is time well spent, because although few people read a report from cover to cover, the executive summary and the recommendations are read by most people who come in contact with the report. To illustrate this point, Worthen, Sanders, and Fitzpatrick (1997) described an experience in evaluating a statewide, "controversial program" for which three separate reports were prepared for review by stakeholders: (a) the full report containing all of the technical detail of how the evaluation was conducted; (b) a medium-size summary of major interpretations drawn from the data; and (c) a brief executive summary:

> Availability of these three reports was broadly announced in the newspapers and on television. . . . Nearly 400 individuals [requested and] read the executive summary, 40 read the mid-size interpretive report, and only one person ever even requested the complete report (and he was an expert methodologist hired by opponents of the evaluation to see if he could find fault with it). As these results show, shorter reports will often be most widely disseminated. (Worthen, Sanders, & Fitzpatrick, 1997, p. 416)

The executive summary should be no more than three pages, give the reader an overview of the goals of the program, and indicate the services provided, the outcomes anticipated, and the extent to which these objectives were met. An executive summary should stand on its own; it should contain enough detail so that a person can grasp the program, its purpose, and its impact by reading it alone.

Disseminating the Report

Who owns the data and to whom the written findings are disseminated are points negotiated prior to signing a letter of agreement. The evaluator and program administrators should come to an understanding about how many copies of the final report are needed, the number of presentations the evaluator is expected to make, and how the evaluation results should be disseminated. Some agencies are bound by the Public Information Act, which makes the report automatically available to anyone who requests a copy. But who is the spokesperson for the evaluation and its results? What are the limitations for using the evaluation data and the subsequent report? This answer lies in the *Program Evaluation Standards* (Joint Committee on Standards for Educational Evaluation, 1994). Suppose the local newspaper chooses to print only that portion of an evaluation that outlines a controversial program's weaknesses, or suppose the program administrator requests from the evaluator an updated summary but then forwards to a federal funding agency only those portions of the evaluator's report that favor the program. In both cases, the evaluator and the program administrator could have taken steps to prevent or minimize the effect of these actions. In the *Program Evaluation Standards,* the "formal parties [in this case, the evaluator and program administrator] should ensure that the full set of evaluation findings along with pertinent limitations are made accessible to the persons affected by the evaluation, and any others with expressed legal rights to receive the results" (Propriety Standard 6). Both the evaluator and the program administrator are responsible for monitoring the release and use of the evaluation. In the second situation, it was the evaluator's responsibility to require the program administrator to provide a copy of the summary prior to releasing it to the funding agency. An evaluator should *never* give up editing responsibility to others; editing, summarizing, or releasing portions of an evaluation should remain exclusively in the evaluator's direct control.

Concluding the Evaluation

The final two steps in conducting a program evaluation involve creating an evaluation trail and conducting a meta-evaluation. An evaluation trail is a file, either electronic or paper, that outlines the steps taken during the evaluation, beginning with a copy of the letter of agreement. All original data, including completed surveys, field notes, copies of transcribed tapes, and data files, should be organized, labeled, and included in this file. Paper copies of data files used in statistical analyses and the computer command files and output files should also be included and clearly labeled. Also needed are any internal review board documents, signed consent forms, and financial records outlining how money for the evaluation was spent. Finally, a clean copy of the final report, including any appendices, should be placed in this file. This evaluation trail should stand as an archival record of when and how the evaluation was completed, and should contain all original documents associated with the evaluation.

The last step in the evaluation process encourages growth and reflection by the evaluator. After each evaluation, the program evaluator should take some time to reflect on the evaluation process—what went well, and what aspects of the evaluation could have been completed more efficiently, professionally, or rigorously. Some evaluators keep a professional journal in which they keep a record of the pitfalls and triumphs of each evaluation. When completed honestly and reviewed periodically, these journals can help evaluators identify recurring themes that need to be addressed. They also can serve as personal histories of evaluators' growth and accumulating experience.

SUMMARY AND CONCLUSIONS

This chapter introduces program evaluation—how it differs from research and the steps used in conducting it. Although program evaluation uses many of the data collection methods used in empirical research, the scope of a program evaluation is often much broader than that of empirical research. Whereas empirical research often occurs in controlled settings, program evaluation typically occurs without a control group and in settings outside the control of the program evaluator. Rather than following experimental research protocols and methodologies, program evaluation at best adheres to quasi-experimental designs.

Evaluations of social programs examine not only the effects of the program (outcomes), but also the program's implementation (process). An examination of how the program is implemented often reveals the reasons a program met or failed to meet specified outcomes. Documenting the factors that both limit and enhance the program as it was administered can help to strengthen the program or similar programs in the future. A defining feature of program evaluation is the use of and interpretation of *triangulated* data—data collected from more than one source, at more than one setting, using more than one data collection methodology. By using data triangulation, program evaluators increase the validity of the evaluation's findings.

This chapter describes four phases of program evaluation. An evaluator begins the process by setting the boundaries of the evaluation. A crucial step in this phase involves allowing all stakeholders to have a voice in the scope of the evaluation to ensure that the evaluation's findings are fair and unbiased. Utility is also enhanced by linking the program's goals and objectives to specific evaluation questions.

After setting the boundaries of the evaluation, the second phase involves selecting appropriate evaluation methods. The selection of the methodology depends on the information needs of the evaluation audience; the time, personnel, and financial resources available to the evaluator; and the constraints of the program. During this phase the program evaluator also plans how the data will be collected and prepared for analyses, and trains the program staff to ensure reliable collection.

The third phase entails the actual collection and analyses of the data. The evaluator pilot-tests all newly created or modified instruments and observation forms, monitors data collection by program staff or evaluation staff, and ensures that agreements of anonymity and/or confidentiality are upheld. Primary data analyses are conducted and reported in a manner similar to those conducted in empirical research. Secondary analyses examine the various primary data analyses to focus the findings on specific evaluation questions.

The final phase of evaluating a program requires the evaluator to report the findings of the evaluation. Methods of dissemination, report deadlines, and types of reports to be created should be agreed upon by the evaluator and client as part of the evaluation contract. All evaluation reports should contain sections that describe (a) the program, (b) the evaluation process, (c) the data collection procedures, and (d) the results and findings of the evaluation. In addition, all reports should contain an executive summary and a list of recommendations that include the positive aspects of the program as well as the areas that may need improvement. These two sections should not exceed five or six pages.

PART FOUR

PROFESSIONAL
ISSUES

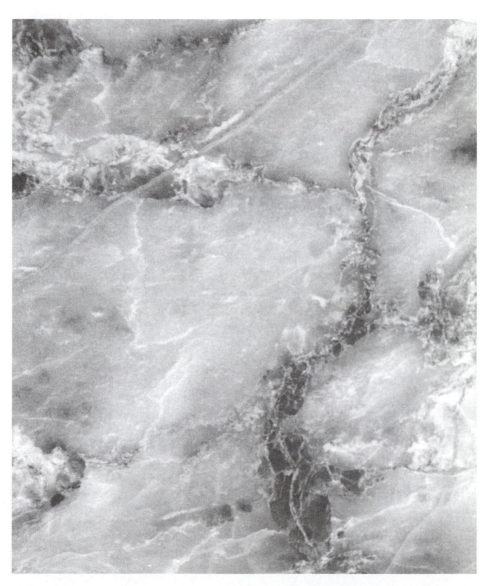

CHAPTER 19

WRITING AND RESEARCH TRAINING

This chapter discusses two important professional issues related to research—writing the research report and training others to be researchers. With regard to writing, it must be realized that a study is not any better than the written report that discusses it. Although it could be argued that results of studies are disseminated in ways other than written reports (such as conference presentations), the research report is critical. Journal articles, books, dissertations, and (to a lesser extent) written summaries of conference presentations are the permanent records of counseling research. Unless a study is discussed in one of these sources, it is unlikely that a researcher interested in the topic will be able to learn about the study. Nevertheless, a poorly written report, even if it is retrieved, will limit the usefulness of the research. It is a shame when the informative results of an elegantly conducted study are obscured by a contorted and confusing report. The preparation of a clear and informative research report is a critical step in the research process.

Few readers are likely to begin conducting research without having had at least some instruction in writing. A critical element in learning to write is practice with feedback. Of all the elements of the research process, writing is the most difficult to teach. Nevertheless, we would be remiss if we did not discuss important aspects of the research report writing process. Others have discussed psychological report writing (see, for example, APA, 1983; Dorn, 1985; Seeman, 1959; Sternberg, 1988); our emphasis here is on the aspects of the report that relate to research design. Several authors have also discussed writing various types of articles, including review articles (Bem, 1995), methodological articles (Maxwell & Cole, 1995), and meta-analytic reviews (Rosenthal, 1995).

Writing style is personal; the opinions of authors, critics, and educators in this matter differ. Furthermore, style varies according to constraints of the publication in which the writing will appear. For example, the American Psychological Association (APA) carefully details the required elements of manuscripts submitted to APA journals in its *Publication Manual of the American Psychological*

Association (APA, 1994). This reference book is indispensable for most authors who publish in counseling and related professional journals. Graduate schools typically have their own requirements for dissertations.

This chapter focuses on generic components of the research report. First, we present the major sections of a report and discuss their relation to the principles of research design previously discussed in this book. Although we could discuss various organizational formats, we focus on the title, abstract, introduction, method, results, and discussion. We also present some general principles for writing research reports: (a) be informative, (b) be forthright, (c) do not overstate or exaggerate, (d) be logical and organized, (e) have some style, (f) write and rewrite, and (g) if all else fails, just write!

It is also important to acknowledge at the beginning that everyone has difficulty in writing at one time or another. It may be due to "writer's block," fatigue, a particularly complex writing task, or a myriad of fears and apprehensions about the product (for example, "I will make a mistake, which will be there for everyone to see"; "What I have to say is really not very important"; "If I can't write it perfectly, I won't write anything"). For inexperienced authors, many of these fears are particularly acute but developmentally normal. However, even the veteran author experiences fears and apprehensions. Writing is just one more skill the researcher needs to acquire, and like any other skill, this skill takes practice, feedback, analysis of successful models of writing (such as published articles), and rewriting.

The second part of this chapter examines what we know about training others to become researchers. Fortunately, counseling researchers have considered research training to be important enough to study, and consequently we can use the results of this research to systematically guide how we train students to conduct research. In this chapter we examine a model of research training proposed and tested by Kahn and Scott (1997) and discuss various recommendations. Throughout this book we have tried to convey a positive and enthusiastic attitude toward research while providing the guiding principles of design, in the hope that the book could assist readers in becoming motivated and competent researchers. In this final section we provide guidance in training others to be motivated and competent researchers.

SECTIONS OF A RESEARCH REPORT

The exact organization of a research report varies, depending on the publication for which it is intended and the nature of the study. Nevertheless, a perusal of counseling journals reveals that articles are typically organized as follows:

Title
Abstract
Introduction
Method

> Participants
> Measures (or Variables or Instruments)
> Materials
> Design (or Design and Analysis)
> Procedure
> Results
> Discussion (or Conclusions)
> References
> Tables
> Figures

The nature of each of these components depends on the publication and its readership. Nevertheless, some aspects of each of these components are crucial to well-written research reports. In this discussion we will focus on those aspects of the components that relate to research design (see APA, 1994; Dorn, 1985; and Sternberg, 1988, for other discussions related to these components). We will not discuss reference lists, tables, and figures, as these are clearly described in the *APA Publication Manual.* As we discuss these components sequentially, keep in mind that they are held together by a common focus—the research hypotheses—which helps the reader comprehend the study as a whole. For this reason, presentation of the results, for example, should mirror presentation of the design used to test the research hypothesis, as discussed in the method section.

Title

The title of a research report does much more than just give it a name; it is used in a variety of ways to make the report accessible to readers. Many services depend on titles to index and abstract publications; users of these services often see only the title. Furthermore, readers perusing journals or other sources (such as *Current Contents* or *PsychLit*) often decide to read a report solely on the basis of its title. Therefore, choose the title carefully.

A title should accurately summarize the research, describing the topic, the independent and dependent variables, the design, and the outcome succinctly (in 12 to 15 words, according to most sources). Given the limitations on the length of titles, redundancies and irrelevancies must be avoided. Omit such phrases as "A Study of" or "The Relation Between." However, even within these constraints, interesting and stylistic titles can be developed.

Alloy and Abramson (1979) provide an example of a seminal article with a title that is both descriptive and attention-getting: "Judgment of Contingency in Depressed and Nondepressed Students: Sadder but Wiser?" The title describes the independent variable (depressed versus nondepressed), the dependent variable (judgment of contingency), the participants (students), and the results (sadder but wiser). The phrase "Sadder but Wiser?" not only adds interest, but has also become a mnemonic; it is often used to refer to this article.

Abstract

The abstract is a summary of the research report. Like the title, the abstract is used for indexing and retrieving articles. After the title, the abstract is the most-often read portion of a research report, and thus it should be succinct, accurate, and comprehensive. It should summarize the content of each of the major sections of the report, including the hypotheses, method (participants, measures, materials, design, and procedure), results, and conclusions. Remember that nonsignificant results are informative; typically, it can be useful to report and discuss all results, not just those that were expected. The length of abstracts depends on the publication; APA journals require abstracts of empirical studies to be between 100 and 120 words. Writing accurate and informative abstracts is a difficult task.

The abstract should be self-contained; the reader should not need to depend on any other section of the report to make sense of the abstract. Therefore, avoid abbreviations and acronyms to the extent possible, or at the very least make sure that they are defined in the abstract. Explain unique and technical terms. Because readers of abstracts often do not have access to the entire research report, do not refer to other articles in an abstract. Exceptions to this rule include abstracts of reaction articles (for instance, an article written in response to a previous article or a reanalysis of data from a published article).

Introduction

The introduction to a research report sets the stage for the study. It should orient the reader to the problem, develop the logic behind the study, and indicate as specifically as possible the hypotheses being tested. Several questions should be answered in the introduction: Why is this an important topic to study? What previous work (empirical and theoretical) bears on the topic? How does this previous work logically lead to the author's research question and hypotheses? How will this question be researched? What predictions can be made? To answer these questions, the introduction of a research report typically contains three elements: (a) introduction to the problem, (b) development of the framework for the study, and (c) statement of the research hypotheses. These three elements often blend together in journal articles; theses and dissertations may require formal separation of these elements into different chapters.

The introduction to the problem should begin by orienting the reader to the topic, including why this is an important area to investigate. This discussion should be achieved with broad strokes. A study of child abuse might begin with some general statistics about the prevalence of child abuse and its implications for society; a study of supervision might begin by discussing difficulties involved in understanding the supervisory process (see, for example, Friedlander, Siegel, & Brenock, 1989); a study of social support vis-à-vis the effectiveness of group therapy might begin with a statement about the widespread finding that social support mediates stressful life changes (see Mallinckrodt, 1989). The introduction to the problem should begin to narrow the topic by identifying important developments relevant to the topic area. With regard to child abuse, the identification of stress as a precursor of abuse could be cited (if that is the direction the researcher will pursue). The introduction to the problem can be concluded with a statement of the problem in general terms.

The second element in an introduction is the development of a rationale for the study. The framework for the rationale is built through the logical interconnectedness of empirical results and theory that leads to a critical, unanswered research question. We quite deliberately avoid the use of the more traditional term *literature review,* for it implies (at least to some) a synopsis of one study after another, along with considerable integration and synthesis of the findings; in contrast, a *framework* consists of elements connected in some logical way. In some ways, the development of a framework is similar to that of a legal brief. When the case is solid, there is one inescapable conclusion; similarly, by the time the readers have completed reading this section, should be saying, "I know exactly what research question should be asked" and then find that the author asked that research question.

The literature cited in the development of the framework should be pertinent to this particular research study. If reviews of the literature exist, cite the review articles rather than the original studies if this is sufficient to build the case. In any discussion of a previous study, discuss only the pertinent aspects of that study—typically those aspects related to the findings of that study, but perhaps methodological issues (such as type of participants), design, and statistical tests as well. For example, reference to a study would not mention the number of participants used in that study unless those data were pertinent, which would be the case if the point being made was related to inadequate power to detect an effect. Discussion of previous findings and theories need to be intertwined logically. When you discuss a particular study or theory, the purpose of the discussion visà-vis the framework should be clear to the reader. Don't hesitate to inform the reader directly: "Left and Write's (1980) application of the Direct Counseling Approach (DCA) is important because it extends previous studies using DCA to children." Furthermore, you should integrate the material reviewed. Often studies result in contradictory findings; you need to speculate about the reasons for the discrepancy and to indicate how these discrepancies (and the reasons behind them) relate to the present study.

A word about completeness is needed. Certainly, the scope of the framework and the literature discussed in it is determined by the publication for which it is intended; more completeness is needed for a dissertation than for a journal article. Nevertheless, the goal is the same: to develop a logical argument that will lead to a research question and/or hypothesis, not to review all the studies ever written on a topic. Generally, this element of the introduction should be complete enough that it touches on issues raised elsewhere in the research report; it should not be necessary to review literature when hypotheses are stated or when dependent variables are operationalized. One exception to this rule is that it is common to report psychometric information under the measures subsection of the method section.

If the framework has been developed properly, the purpose of the present research should be readily apparent. One purpose might be to reconcile discrepancies in previous research; in that case the study will explain why contradictory findings have been obtained. Another purpose might be to apply results from some noncounseling area to problems in counseling (see, for example, the social influence model, Strong, 1968). Still another purpose of the study might be to extend previous results to a different population.

The final element of the introduction is the statement of the research hypotheses. Occasionally writers will also pose their research questions at this time, rather than when they are building their rationale. Again, the research hypotheses should follow logically from the framework built previously. The hypotheses stated at this point should be a critical test of some important theoretical or practical question (Cook & Campbell, 1979; Wampold, Davis, & Good, 1990). A good theory will allow several implications to be drawn from it; a hypothesis is critical to the extent that it tests an implication from a theory and that the implication is unique to that theory (see Wampold, Davis, & Good, 1990). In that way, knowledge progresses because poor theories are winnowed out.

Research hypotheses are written in terms of theoretical constructs; operationalization of the constructs comes later. For example, the research hypothesis might state that a cognitive-behavioral treatment will lower state anxiety but not trait anxiety. Unless there is some particular issue with operationalization that this study addresses directly, operationalization of state and trait anxiety is typically discussed under the measures subsection of the method section. Thus, discussion of particular measures used to operationalize a construct should not be included in the introduction, unless a particular operationalization is related to the research hypothesis (for example, the study differs from previous studies in the manner in which a construct is operationalized).

Research hypotheses should be stated unambiguously. Of course, the degree to which a hypothesis can be specific depends on the specificity of the theory. However, statements such as "the purpose of the present study is to explore the relation between" or "the purpose is to determine the relation between" are insufficient because some relation will always be discovered (even if the relation is null—that is, no relation). Such statements do not make clear how the discovered relation relates to theoretical predictions, and the researcher must create post-hoc explanations.

An example of an unambiguous research hypothesis is provided by Ponce and Atkinson (1989). The purpose of this study was to examine the effects of counselor ethnicity, participant acculturation, and counseling style on Mexican-American participants' perceptions of counselor credibility and influence. It was hypothesized that participant acculturation would interact with both counselor ethnicity and counseling style in such a way that unacculturated participants would prefer a Mexican-American counselor who used a directive style, whereas acculturated clients would have no preference for either counselor ethnicity or counseling style.

Method

The method section describes how the research hypotheses were tested, including how all aspects of how the study was conducted. Enough detail is needed so that a reader can (a) determine the validity of the study and (b) replicate the study.

Of all the sections of a manuscript, the method section has the highest correlation with editorial decisions concerning rejection or acceptance for publication in the *Journal of Counseling Psychology* (Munley, Sharkin, & Gelso, 1988); therefore it is imperative that the method section be well written.

The method section is typically divided into subsections. Research in counseling usually contains subsections on participants, measures (or variables or instruments), materials, design, and procedures, each of which we briefly describe here. Organization of the method section depends, to a great extent, on the nature of the study. The order of the subsections may be altered (for instance, design often appears as either the first or last subsection), but they should fit together like a puzzle, providing at the end a very clear picture of what was done and how it was done. Furthermore, it should explain how the researcher analyzed the data so that the reader is primed for the presentation of the results.

Participants

The subsection on participants should indicate, at a minimum, (a) the total number of participants, (b) how the participants were selected, and (c) characteristics of the participants relevant to the outcome of the study (including, for example, age, educational level, gender, ethnicity, geographical area of residence, pretest level of functioning, depending on the study; see Chapter 13 for a discussion of this issue). Other aspects that may be mentioned in this section include assignment of participants to conditions of the independent variable (including number of participants in each condition), attrition, statistical power, and circumstances under which the participants participated (for instance, financial remuneration or course credit). If a power analysis was conducted to determine the number of participants needed, results of this analysis should be included either here or in the design subsection.

Measures (or Variables or Instruments)

The purpose of the measures subsection is to operationalize the constructs to which the research hypotheses referred. Recall that Ponce and Atkinson (1989) mentioned counselor ethnicity, participant acculturation, counseling style, and perceptions of counselor credibility in their statement of the research hypothesis. Counselor ethnicity was a participant characteristic, and counseling style was a manipulated independent variable; participant acculturation and perceptions of counselor credibility were operationalized using the Acculturation Rating Scale for Mexican-Americans (ARSMA) and the Counselor Effectiveness Rating Scale (CERS), respectively. Therefore, Ponce and Atkinson discussed the ARSMA and the CERS under a subsection called "Instruments."

The measures subsection discusses the operationalization of constructs, including the rationale for choosing particular instruments. Why was a particular instrument chosen? Why were three measures of a construct used rather than one (or two, or four)? Why were commonly used measures omitted? Furthermore, the measures subsection should include a discussion of each instrument chosen, including its title, a citation (manual, article, or other primary source), a description (for example, number and type of items, direction of scoring), factors or sub-scales, and psychometric properties (such as reliability and validity). Statements about reliability and validity estimates should refer to the context in which these estimates were calculated (for example, the population).

Because of the need to justify choice of operationalizations, the measures subsection is one place in the method section where it is not unusual to cite various studies (for instance, studies of psychometric properties). However, if the operationalization of a crucial construct is controversial, then discussion of these issues probably fits best in the introduction (as a part of the development of the framework). This would be the case if the researcher claims that previous attempts to corroborate a theory were unsuccessful because of improper operationalization of the dependent variable and the present study used different instruments to measure the same construct.

In a treatment study, operationalization of the independent variable is vital, usually taking the form of describing the treatments for each condition. Sometimes the amount of detail needed to describe a particular treatment intervention adequately becomes prohibitive; in such cases it often is helpful to develop a detailed treatment manual to which interested readers can be directed via a footnote (see, for example, O'Neil & Roberts Carroll, 1988).

Materials

The materials subsection describes any materials used in the study. Pilot testing of the materials would also be described in this section. Sufficient information should be given to enable an independent researcher to reproduce the materials and replicate the study. If space limitations make this impossible, it is customary to indicate in a footnote that additional information or the materials themselves are available from the author.

Design (or Design and Analysis)

This subsection describes the design of the study. After this section, readers should have a clear understanding of the independent, status, and dependent variables and the manner in which participants were assigned to levels of the independent variables. For example, if a factorial design is used, the factors should be labeled, the number of conditions within a factor should be indicated, and the nature of the factors (such as between versus within, or random versus fixed) should be stated. If the analyses are mentioned (for example, a two-way analysis of variance applied to a factorial design), then the name of the subsection should include "Analysis." A power analysis, if conducted, can also be included in this subsection.

The connection between the design and the research hypotheses should be clear; after reading this subsection, the reader should understand how the hypotheses were tested (see Wampold, Davis, & Good, 1990). Often (especially in a dissertation), the research hypotheses are restated in operationalized form, such as "To test the research hypothesis that [statement of hypothesis], a two-way analysis of variance was conducted. [Explain factors and indicate dependent variable.] It was predicted that a statistically significant F test for the interaction would be obtained."

Procedure

The procedure subsection describes how the research was conducted with the participants. Discuss everything that the researchers did with the participants, from beginning to end, including instructions to the participants, the formation of groups, and experimental manipulations. The procedure subsection is typically organized chronologically. Enough detail should be included so that the study can be replicated. If a separate design subsection is not included, details related to randomization and other features of the design can be included in this subsection.

Results

The purpose of the results section is to summarize the data and the results of the statistical analysis. Generally, two types of results should be reported: (a) summary statistics and results of preliminary analyses and (b) results related to research hypotheses. The summary statistics typically include the means and standard deviations of the dependent variables for each level of the independent variable (or combination of levels, as in a factorial design) and the correlation matrix for all variables, when appropriate (for example, regression analyses, factor analyses, or structural equation modeling). Results of preliminary analyses may be related to manipulation checks, dropouts, verification of stimulus materials, and so forth.

Results related to research hypotheses should be organized so that the reader can tie the results of specific statistical tests to research hypotheses stated earlier in the report. There should be a one-to-one correspondence between the hypotheses and the statistical tests (see Wampold, Davis, & Good, 1990). This organization is facilitated by appropriately titled subsections, such as "Preliminary Analyses," "Summary Statistics," or "Test of Hypothesis 1."

The results section should report the findings, but discussion of the results is saved for the discussion section. Nevertheless, introduce each result so that its purpose is clear. For example, indicate why a preliminary analysis was conducted and what various outcomes mean: "A preliminary analysis on the observers' ratings of the therapy sessions was conducted to determine whether or not the treatments were perceived as different. The [name of statistical test] was statistically significant [give information about test statistic], indicating that the observers did indeed rate the treatments differently."

Some confusion often exists about what information to include concerning statistical tests. The *APA Publication Manual* (1994) gives specifics about reporting statistical tests in the text and in tables. However, these specifications are inadequate because for the most part they indicate *how* to report rather than *what* to report. The trend has been to report less; for example, one rarely sees analysis of variance source tables anymore. More disturbing is the tendency not to report important information (such as size of test statistic and probability levels) when results are nonsignificant. This minimalist point of view puts the emphasis on statistical significance and ignores concepts such as effect size, estimation, and power. Failure to report information other than significance levels makes it difficult or impossible for readers to verify results, calculate other indexes (such as effect size or power), and conduct meta-analyses. A persuasive argument can be made for reporting size of test statistics, exact probability levels (rather than, say, $p < .05$) for significant and nonsignificant findings, some measure of effect size, power, and other indexes as appropriate (Rosnow & Rosenthal, 1988). An article by Ellis, Robbins, Shult, Ladany, and Banker (1990) provides a good example of reporting a variety of indexes other than level of significance.

Results are often presented in tables or figures, which are useful because results can be understood while taking up a minimal amount of space. Locating important results in text is much more difficult than finding them in a well-organized table. Figures are particularly useful for illustrating patterns of results, such as an interaction in an analysis of variance. When tables or figures are used, total recapitulation of the results in the text should be avoided, although sometimes it is useful to summarize key results presented in the tables. The writer must, however, tell the reader what to look for in the tables. For example, one might say, "The main effects of the 3 (treatment) by 2 (gender) analysis of variance were statistically significant, as shown in Table 1"; it is then unnecessary to note, for example, the degrees of freedom, the F statistics, and so forth, because that information is in the table.

Discussion (or Conclusions)

The discussion should include (a) an explanation of whether or not the data support the research hypotheses, (b) a statement of the conclusions, (c) an indication of the study's limitations, and (d) a discussion of the implications. This section allows the author to expand on the findings and to place them in the context of previous research and theory on this topic.

The discussion typically begins with a statement of whether or not the research hypotheses were supported. You may choose at this point to integrate your findings with previous research.

After indicating whether or not the hypotheses were supported, discuss the implications: What conclusions can be reached from the results? Has new knowledge been generated by support of the hypotheses? If the data lead to reformulated hypotheses, state them, but indicate that they have been formulated post hoc (that is, have not been tested directly). If future research is needed, indicate what types of hypotheses should be tested and how future studies should be designed.

Every discussion of results should include a statement of the limitations, which typically are related to low power, the analogue nature of the study, violated assumptions of statistical tests, confounds, and so forth. Remember that no study is perfect; it is best to be forthright about the limitations and discuss how the results are interpretable in spite of the limitations.

Finally, given the support (or nonsupport) for the hypotheses and the limitations, you are free to indicate the implications of the study for theory and for practice. However, because the results of one study are rarely important enough by themselves to revise theory or to change practice, avoid statements such as "Practitioners should refrain from Treatment X and only use Treatment Y."

GENERAL PRINCIPLES FOR WRITING RESEARCH REPORTS

Although it is difficult to identify general principles of writing, we can emphasize seven general rules of thumb: (a) Be informative, (b) be forthright, (c) do not overstate or exaggerate, (d) be logical and organized, (e) have some style, (f) write and rewrite, and (g) if all else fails, just write!

Principle 1: Be Informative

The goal of the research report is to inform the reader about the study. Provide enough detail for the reader to understand what you are explaining, but not so much that the reader becomes bogged down. Of course, the publication format determines the level of detail. Dissertations require the most detail. Some journals are more technical than others and thus require more detail. Are the readers of a particular journal primarily practitioners, other researchers, or statisticians? The best way to include the right amount of detail is to emulate the publication of interest. Most journals periodically present editorials or other information about the materials to be contained in their articles (see the inside covers of most journals for descriptions of appropriate articles).

In any report, discuss the central points and minimize digressions. Obviously, you should not report everything that you did, but only information that readers need to understand the study. For example, preparation of stimulus materials often involves many successive stages of development. It is not necessary to explain each iteration; rather, describe the final product and summarize the development process in a sentence or two. However, do not omit important details, either. Authors frequently refer to a decision that was made but do not discuss the decision rule; if, for example, "three outliers were omitted from the analysis," on what basis were the three data considered outliers? Was this decision rule formulated before the data were analyzed?

Principle 2: Be Forthright

Every study has flaws (Gelso, 1979). It is rare that a researcher would not alter a study, given the chance to do so. Authors should be forthright and discuss the ramifications of a study's limitations, rather than trying to hide flaws in some way. Signs of hidden flaws include obtuse language, esoteric statistical tests (with improper justification), omitted information, and overstated justifications. Reviewers of manuscripts submitted for publication are especially annoyed when they uncover hidden flaws or when they have a vague (intuitive) sense that the author has not been forthright with regard to some limitation.

Such flaws necessitate a fundamental decision: If a flaw is fatal to the study (for example, a confound that cannot be minimized), then it is best to consider the study a time-consuming learning experience. If the flaw is problematic but the results of the study are informative nevertheless, then the author should indicate how the flaw affects the interpretation and why the study remains important. Keep in mind that judgments in this regard typically are made by others—by dissertation committees, editors, and reviewers. Although the author may think that a flaw is not fatal, a journal editor may decide otherwise.

Principle 3: Do Not Overstate or Exaggerate

There is a widely shared tendency to believe that every study will somehow change the course of the field. When expressed in written reports, it appears as unjustified claims about the importance of the results for the field of counseling. Put in the proper perspective, it is highly unusual that any one research study in counseling is sufficient to stand alone; it is only the accumulation of the results from many studies that adds to our knowledge. For example, progress toward the conclusion that a link exists between smoking and health was made inch by inch (P. W. Holland, 1986). The conclusion that smoking is detrimental to health was established by years of research; alternative explanations in one study were ruled out in other studies. Interestingly, it is not unusual for the results of seminal studies to be contradicted by subsequent research. For example, Rosenthal and Jacobson's (1968) conclusion that teacher expectations influence student achievement has not always been supported by subsequent research (Brophy & Good, 1974).

Unsupported statements usually appear in the discussion and conclusions sections of a report. Refrain from stating that, based on the results of your study, practitioners should change their practice or that researchers should abandon some theoretical position. If you feel strongly about a position, state that "the results of this study as well as previous studies [cite those studies] suggest that Theory X should be reconsidered." Let the scientific community decide whether Theory X should be abandoned.

An issue related to overstatement concerns the appraisal of other authors' work. Generally, it is not advisable to be overly critical of others, especially at the beginning of one's career. Again, let the scientific community make judgments about the worth of various schools of thought or of a researcher's contributions. It is acceptable to point out differences of opinion, but do so tactfully. Wampold and Kim (1989) reanalyzed a case study presented by Hill, Carter, and O'Farrell (1983) and came to different conclusions from those reached in the original study. Instead of arguing that their conclusions were justified, Wampold and Kim provided several possible explanations for the differences and made the following conclusion: "Whether Hill et al.'s observations or the patterns revealed by the sequential analysis [conducted by Wampold & Kim] are reflective of the essential nature of the counseling process in this study remains an unanswered epistemo-logical question" (p. 362). Readers are left to draw their own conclusions.

Principle 4: Be Logical and Organized

The written report is not a recitation of facts; it is the presentation of a position. Authors must persuade the reader that their claims are justified. As we indicated previously, the research question should be justified given the literature reviewed, and the logic and organization of the introduction should make the case for the research question. Don't force the reader to guess how the research question fol-lowed logically from the studies reviewed; explain it!

A few general considerations can aid in organization and logic. First, work from an outline that not only lists various parts of the report, but also neatly sum-marizes the logical organization. Second, provide advance organizers and sum-maries of complex materials; that is, tell the reader what is to follow and how it is organized, and, if necessary, summarize at the end of explanations. If the material is lengthy, use headings. Transition statements are particularly helpful when the logic shifts gears.

Writing can be an aid to logic. What may seem perfectly logical in one's own mind may indeed be illogical when expressed in writing. Writing the method sec-tion of a report before the study is conducted often reveals faulty logic. Of course, this is the utility of research proposals.

Principle 5: Have Some Style

Although technical writing is constrained by various parameters, style remains important. Make the research report interesting. Would a reader mildly interested in this topic want to read the entire report? Often, style is the determining factor. Of course, style must be congruent with the publication in which the article will appear. Still, even the most technical writing should be made readable to the fullest extent possible.

Several considerations aid in preparing readable reports. Interest the reader at the outset by choosing good titles, quotations from important sources (ancient Greek sources seem to be the most prestigious), and so forth. Avoid abbreviations; many readers tend to focus on one or two sections of the report, and if they have to flip around to understand abbreviations, they tend to quit reading entirely. Particularly annoying are idiosyncratic abbreviations of variables used in statistical analysis programs that make sense only to the author (for example, NCOCLIN—number of counselor/client interactions). Finally, simpler words and sentence structures are preferable to more complex ones. The corollary of this suggestion is that precision of expression is desirable.

Principle 6: Write and Rewrite

One thing is clear: Except for the extraordinary few, authors need to do some rewriting to prepare a quality research report. Different writers use different methods: Some write as fast as possible and rely heavily on the revision process to create a polished product; others write the first draft carefully and minimize time with revisions. Some like to let the original "age" before revising, while others progress as quickly as possible to the final product.

Often authors become so absorbed with their project that they lose objectivity. Having discussed and thought about a procedure, they are convinced that their explanation of it is clear and concise. However, someone else may have a very different view. We strongly recommend that all authors have a colleague or advisor read and critique research reports as part of the revision process. Unjustified compliments are not helpful, so choose someone who will be properly critical. (Similarly, if asked to review someone else's report, provide direct and helpful comments.) Different types of comments will be provided by different types of readers. Consider readers who are unfamiliar with the area as well as those who are knowledgeable. Someone who disagrees with the author's point of view can often identify problems with the logic. Remember that these critiques are not binding and an author may choose to ignore them. As a courtesy, authors should ask those who provide critiques whether they wish to be credited in the author footnote (for example, "I express my appreciation to Ima Kritiq for her helpful comments").

Principle 7: If All Else Fails, Just Write!

We would be remiss if we did not mention problems related to procrastination. Many of us who enjoy conducting research avoid settling down to write the research report. We venture to say that at one time or another, all researchers have agonized about writing the research report. Rather than stating that "misery loves company," we give this suggestion: Write! Even if you think what you are writing is terrible, write anyway. Drafts can be changed or discarded. In fact, it is usually much easier to revise a draft than to create a first draft. Write a few pages and then decide later whether it is any good. Once started, writing becomes increasingly easy.

RESEARCH TRAINING

In Chapter 1 we discussed the meaning of science as it relates to the roles and development of professionals. We tried to convey an appreciation of the complexity of learning about research, and to put that learning in the context of professional development. For many students in counseling, graduate school is their first introduction to research design, and it evokes the emotional reactions that come with any novel experience. We seek to prepare students to approach the science part of the scientist/practitioner role with enthusiasm for the creativity involved and with a willingness to learn the intricacies of the craft, while making them cognizant of the anxiety that may be created by learning a technical skill that may not be central to one's interest but is required to accomplish a goal (that is, obtaining a graduate degree and becoming a professional in counseling). We conclude the book by conveying ways in which counselors and counseling psychologists can train others to become competent, eager, and productive researchers. In this section we discuss what is known about research training environments, and how environments can be structured to create the opportunity for students to both learn about research and to consume and produce quality research products.

A Structural Equation Model for Research Training

Spurred by discussions of research training (Gelso, 1979; Holland, 1986; Magoon & Holland, 1984; Osipow, 1979), researchers have empirically examined the effects of research environments on such research outcomes as research productivity (see, for example, Brown et al., 1996; Gelso, Mallinckrodt, & Judge, 1996; Gelso et al., 1983; Kahn & Gelso, 1997; Kahn & Scott, 1997; Mallinckrodt, Gelso, & Royalty, 1990; Phillips & Russell, 1994; Royalty et al., 1986; Royalty & Magoon, 1985; Royalty & Reising, 1986). This research has culminated in the development and testing of the complex model (Kahn & Scott, 1997) presented in Figure 19-1. After we discuss this model and the empirical evidence that supports parts of it, we add a few other important aspects of research training not included in the model. The model is a structural equation model (the methods for which we introduced in Chapter 12), and we begin by discussion each of the constructs (that is, latent variables) in the model: personality type, research training environment, research self-efficacy, research interest, research productivity, and career goals in research.

Constructs of the Model

PERSONALITY TYPE.   Most students in counseling and counseling psychology fall into one of three of Holland's (1992) personality types: social, artistic, or investigative. Research has shown that the personality of counseling students is related to interest in research and in research courses (Betz & Taylor, 1982; Mallinckrodt et al., 1990), to choice of graduate research programs with traditions of producing research (Mallinckrodt et al. 1990), and to research productivity (Krebs, Smither, & Hurley, 1991; Tinsley, Tinsley, Boone, & Shim-Li, 1993). Specifically, it appears that students who are investigative types have more interest in research activities and ultimately produce more research. Accordingly, Kahn and Scott predicted that Holland personality type would be directly related to research interest, which in turn would be related to research productivity and career goals related to research (see Figure 19-1). In particular, investigative types are hypothesized to be more

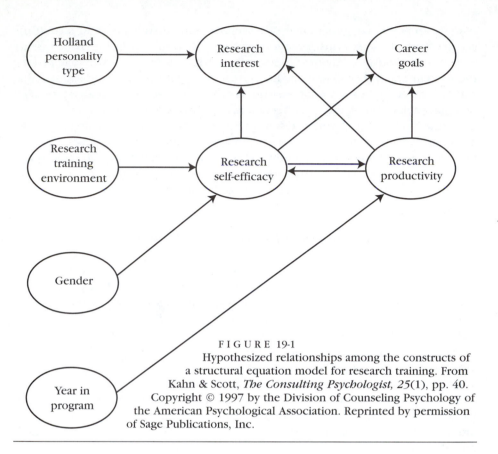

FIGURE 19-1
Hypothesized relationships among the constructs of
a structural equation model for research training. From
Kahn & Scott, *The Consulting Psychologist, 25*(1), pp. 40.
Copyright © 1997 by the Division of Counseling Psychology of
the American Psychological Association. Reprinted by permission
of Sage Publications, Inc.

interested in research, and social types less interested. Later we discuss additional
aspects of personality not included in the model, as proposed by Gelso (1997).

RESEARCH TRAINING ENVIRONMENT. Gelso (1979; 1993) discussed ten components of
graduate training programs hypothesized to foster positive attitudes toward
research. Based on the initial research related to research training, nine of these
components have been identified as important features of the research training environment: (a) modeling appropriate scientific behavior and attitudes, (b) reinforcing
students' research efforts, (c) involving students in research early and in minimally
threatening ways, (d) teaching relevant statistics and the logic of design, (e) teaching that all research is flawed and limited, (f) teaching varied approaches to research,
(g) wedding science and practice in training, (h) facilitating students' introspection
for research ideas, and (i) conducting science as a partly social experience.

Gelso and colleagues (Gelso et al., 1996; Kahn & Gelso, 1997; Royalty et al.,
1986) developed an instrument (Research Training Environment Scale, RTES, and
its revision, RTES-R) that operationalized these nine components of the training
environment. Because it was unlikely that these aspects are independent, Kahn

and Gelso (1997) factor-analyzed the RTES-R and found that two factors underlie the nine aspects operationalized by the RTES-R. The first factor, labeled *instructional factor,* contains aspects of the environment that are present because of curricular components of graduate training, which included teaching statistics and the logic of design, teaching students to look inward, teaching that experiments are flawed, teaching varied approaches, and wedding science and practice. The second factor, labeled *interactional factor* because the components involved interaction of trainer and trainee, included modeling, reinforcing, involving students early, and conducting science as a social experience. In the model, Kahn and Scott (1997) hypothesized that environmental influences affect research self-efficacy, which in turn affect research interest, career goals related to research, and research productivity.

Although the nine components of the research environment can be reduced to two factors statistically, the examination of the individual components that follows reveals how research trainers can construct curricula and experiences to foster the development of skilled and motivated consumers and producers of research. The components have been modified since their original conceptualization; nevertheless, we recommend that professionals involved in research training read Gelso's (1979) seminal article on research in counseling.

Modeling appropriate scientific behavior and attitudes. Clearly, modeling is a potent way to transfer a variety of skills from master to novice. However, Gelso's conceptualization was that the important aspects of modeling went far beyond the transfer of skills and involved having research mentors exhibit healthy attitudes toward research (Gelso, 1979; Gelso et al., 1996). The primary attitude to be modeled is enthusiasm for the research endeavor. Mentors who enjoy their research and express the excitement inherent in a creative and challenging process will reduce the dread that many students have for research. In our view, the pleasure of research derives from two sources. First, the process of research is inherently creative. Although we have presented many principles of research, designing a valid study is never straightforward—applying principles X, Y, and Z according to some recipe will not yield a study that can answer any research question validly and parsimoniously. Rather, one must understand the literature, develop the critical research question, and creatively form a research design that focuses on that question. Students often are drawn to clinical practice because each client presents a unique challenge; effort is needed to understand every client's complex dynamics, behavior, and emotions and to intervene successfully to produce healthy change. Research is similar—each question is unique, and effort is needed to create a successful design. The second, often overlooked source of enjoyment is the inherent excitement in discovering something new. According to legend, Archimedes leapt from the bath and ran through the streets shouting "Heureka!" because he had discovered a means, based on specific gravity, for determining the proportions of gold and silver in a wreath made for Hieron by weighing it in water.

Wampold (1987, 1998) has emphasized that new research methods should be valued not for their own sake but for what they can discover. As this chapter was being written, one of the authors took a break to read the *New York Times* and was skimming Science Watch, a short summary of important research. Contained in that summary was a piece entitled "Doctor Vs. Laptop" (October 21, 1997, page B11), which noted that primary-care physicians have difficulty diagnosing mental disorders and presented research on the development of systematic methods, including computer-assisted inquiry, to aid physicians' diagnoses. This was particularly interesting because the author, who has long been interested in the application of counseling psychology to the delivery of health services in contexts other than psychotherapy, thought it unfortunate that counseling researchers had missed out on opportunities to contribute something important in this area. So you can imagine his excitement when he realized that the research team leader of this study was a counseling psychologist—and a graduate of his counseling psychology program! It is not often that we can discover something important enough to be reported in the *New York Times,* but it should be communicated to students that research is exciting because of the potential to know, to understand, and to discover.

Gelso (1979) was careful to note that modeling also involves expressing the disappointment involved in research—the rejections, the data that do not inform, the low rate of participation by respondents, and so forth. "The process of scientific discovery, including its trials and tribulations as well as its excitement, must be modeled at least as much as its products" (Gelso, 1979, p. 28).

Reinforcing students' research efforts. An unspoken code pervades the academy: Calling attention to one's own accomplishment is a sign of insecurity regarding scholarly worth. The corollary of this code is that noticing and commenting on others' accomplishments is also avoided. Gelso (1979) commented on a student "who published a fine research paper in a well-refereed journal and made three national convention presentations in one year—and received no acknowledgment from any faculty member for her excellence" (p. 28). Because academics are trained to act as if scholarship is its own reward, we expect students to act similarly, but students (as well as academics) need recognition for their accomplishments. However, the reinforcement should not be withheld from students until the paper is published or presented. From day one, research mentors should recognize students' skill in the components of the research process—in scientific thinking, writing, conceptualizing research, and so forth—at every opportunity. Gelso (1979) discussed many ways to encourage and reward student involvement in science, including manuscript preparation services, money for student travel, awards, recognition at meetings. But often a simple statement of recognition by a professor is prized by students and effective in promoting scientific thinking.

It is important that the reinforcement not be a "circus of ingenuine positive pellet giving, . . . but an honest expression to show appreciation to the student who achieves excellence" (Gelso, 1979, p. 28). We know that a critical component of learning is frequent practice with feedback. Positive comments to a student regarding a deficient (or even imperfect) product or idea, even if those comments are genuine, provide no opportunity for the student to progress and create ambivalence toward the process. Because writing is crucial to success in research, writing assignments are common in research design courses (see recommendations regarding writing that follow). To be useful to the student, the strengths of the product should be recognized, but specific comments about ways in which the product could be improved (including development of ideas, clarity of presentation, grammar, sophistication of thought, and so forth) should also be provided. As we discuss later, students should then rewrite with additional feedback to optimize learning.

Involving students in research early and in minimally threatening ways. As early as possible, students should be involved in research in ways that are interesting and involving but consistent with their skill level (Gelso, 1979; Gelso et al., 1996). Asking students early to perform tasks for which they are not trained (for example, running a statistical analysis) most likely will create anxiety; asking students to perform menial and uninteresting tasks (for example, repetitively scoring protocols) will create boredom. We have found that students can be stimulating thinkers at any point in their training and should be involved in the conceptualization of research projects. In research groups, students of various levels can participate to the extent that they feel comfortable and have something to contribute. New students often have ideas not shaped by conventional approaches to a problem and make suggestions that are insightful and critical in designing an innovative study.

Teaching relevant statistics and the logic of design. Many counseling students have little fondness for statistics and are turned off to research because they equate doing research with studying for statistics examinations. Gelso et al. (1996) have suggested that this unfortunate situation be countered by pedagogy in statistics classes that "is sensitive to students' needs" (p. 311) and by emphasizing the logic involved in designing research. The basis of this recommendation is that poorly taught or overly technical statistics classes create unnecessarily negative attitudes toward research.

This recommendation creates some challenges for curriculum designers, as statistics courses typically are taught in other departments. As is the case with all courses, some statistics courses are interesting, relevant, and pedagogically sound, while others are not. In any case, those who train researchers can draw the connection between statistics and research, ensure relevance, and emphasize the logic of research design and the use of statistics as tools to answer important questions. Moreover, giving students rewarding research experiences will sufficiently attract and inoculate them against poorly taught statistics courses. Still, teaching statistics in a way that is sensitive to students' needs and emphasizes the logic of design does not eliminate the importance of mastering statistics or the principles of design to a reasonably sophisticated degree (Gelso, 1997).

Teaching that all research is flawed and limited. Throughout this book we have noted that any one study cannot rule out all threats to validity, and that knowledge accumulates through repeated investigations. Students should not feel pressure to design the perfect study; rather, they should feel motivated to create a study that can address the research question, taking the principles of research design as well as practical constraints into account. Requiring students to meet standards and achieve excellence is appropriate; forcing students to clear unrealistic hurdles is not.

Teaching varied approaches to research. The conventional advice to "Use the appropriate research method to answer the research question" contains wisdom, but it ignores the person of the researcher. By the nature of their personalities and their interests, students will be attracted to some approaches to knowing more than others. Some students will be attracted to quantitative methods and others to qualitative methods, and these preferences should be respected and honored. Not only do students benefit by using a method that they enjoy, but the field benefits from this methodological pluralism (Gelso et al., 1988).

Wedding science and practice in training. Much has been written about the integration of science and practice (see Chapter 1). However, as Gelso (1979) noted, research motivation stemming from clinical experience is often discounted. This component recognizes that a true integration of science and practice will make research more attractive, especially to the majority of students whose primary interest is in practice. Courses that carefully draw the intimate connection between science and practice, taught by instructors who feel comfortable with the connection and have skills in each area, are truly motivating to students. Research mentors should encourage students to pursue ideas that emanate from practice. Moreover, professionals both in training programs and in practice should foster research in applied settings, for this research typically has more direct clinical implications than laboratory research (Gelso, 1979; Magoon & Holland, 1984). Research in applied settings can be modeled for students in collaborations between university researchers and clinical professionals.

Facilitating the students' introspection for research ideas. For many students, looking inward is to rely on clinical experience, so this component clearly overlaps the wedding of science and practice. When research mentors discount ideas generated from the "person," the "person" is discounted. It is not productive for students to get the idea that legitimate research ideas should be generated only from an objective reading of the literature. It is our belief that those students who have a deep interest in their topic finish their dissertations faster than those who are motivated to finish their programs but who pick a convenient topic of study. The excitement of knowing we discussed earlier is fostered by a person's involvement with a topic. Gelso (1979) provides a compelling example:

> I was supervising a very bright student who was trying to formulate a thesis topic. She came to our scheduled interview dismayed that she could not come up with an idea. She had judiciously gone through the customary procedures, scanning journals, talking with students, etc. She claimed that nothing that she had "come across" really grabbed her. Here I asked the student to take a minute to think about things she would like to know about counseling. Within minutes she generated several ideas capable of eventually being translated into practicable projects. The problem was that she was looking "out there" for an idea and consequently failed to look to her own experiencing. (p. 29)

Accordingly, we now ask students to think ahead to the time when they will be mentoring their own students in research or providing clinical supervision to students working on research (for example, to predoctoral interns); such an exercise helps students think of themselves as scientists, so that they approach their work scientifically and consider their own ideas as topics worthy of scientific scrutiny.

Conducting science as a partly social experience. Many aspects of conducting science involve working alone, but because many counseling students are socially oriented, increasing the social aspects of research will increase the attractiveness of the endeavor for them. Gelso (1979) suggested two opportunities for social interactions: advising and research teams. Advising is a supervisory relationship, and as such it involves the complexities inherent in any such relationship (see Holloway, 1995, for a model that could be applied to advising). As Gelso (1979) noted:

> I suggest that ideally the advisor would be able to offer elements of a generally facilitative relationship, e.g., empathy, respect, interest. In addition, the advisor should be a stimulator of ideas, and himself/herself a scientist who is excited about the work. Depending on the student's level of scientific development and the phase of the research, the research advisor must be able to oscillate between the role of thoughtful critic on the one hand (e.g., when the design is being formulated), and consultant-colleague who allows the students to "do their own thing" on the other. (p. 30)

Research teams also provide social interactions. Although they offer opportunities for social interaction, research teams have a task—to conduct meaningful research—consequently the team leader must keep the group focused while accommodating the need for social interaction and facilitating skill development in team members. Clearly, the leader must use group facilitation skills as well as research skills. The research emanating from research groups is often superior to what could be developed otherwise, and thus research groups provide more than opportunities for socially oriented students to interact around research. Still, great care should be taken that (a) good research is conducted, (b) the social interactions are satisfying, (c) that the needs of the individuals are expressed and met, and (d) members are not used as unpaid research assistants (that is, included in the team solely for the purpose of getting work out of them).

RESEARCH SELF-EFFICACY.   Social cognitive models of academic and career interest and choice hypothesize that self-efficacy mediates the relationship between direct and vicarious experiences and attainment of goals (Lent, Brown, & Hackett, 1994). In the present context, research self-efficacy is defined as "one's confidence in being able to successfully complete various aspects of the research process" (Kahn & Scott, 1997, p. 41). Kahn and Scott (1997), based on social cognitive models and past research in this area (see, for example, Brown et al., 1996; Phillips & Russell, 1994), predicted that research training and research productivity (that is, experiences with research) would predict research self-efficacy, which in turn would predict research interest and research career goals (see Figure 19-1).

RESEARCH INTEREST.   Kahn and Scott (1997) hypothesized that research interest mediates the relationship between personality type and career goals and research productivity. Put another way, the established relationship between personality type and research productivity (and presumably career goals) is due to interest. Investigative types have more interest in research and therefore have goals related to research and produce more research products.

RESEARCH PRODUCTIVITY.   One of the outcome constructs in the Kahn and Scott model (1997) is research productivity, which was defined broadly to include journal articles, unpublished empirical manuscripts, manuscript submission and research in process, presentations presented or in process, intensive case studies, program evaluations, informal research, and involvement in the analysis of data. Research productivity has a long history as an outcome variable due to many observations that the research productivity of graduates from counseling programs is low (see, for example, Watkins, Lopez, Campbell, & Himmell, 1986, who found that the modal number of publications of counseling graduates is zero).

It should be noted that research productivity as a goal is somewhat controversial. Increasing research productivity has often been advocated by leaders in the field. For example, Whiteley (1984) stated that "counseling psychologists need to increase their research productivity" (p. 46), and Magoon and Holland (1984) made suggestions that were aimed at "increasing the proportion of graduates who will become producers of research" (p. 63). Others (Whiteley, 1984; Fong & Malone, 1994) have commented on the lack of quality of research in counseling. Wampold (1986b) noted that the focus on quantity rather than on quality would have deleterious effects:

> If the quality of research presently conducted by counseling psychologists is poor [which we are not convinced is the case], then increasing the number of individuals who publish is not likely to increase the quality of the research and may only result in a greater volume of research with questionable value. It is vital that counseling psychology programs develop training models that will produce graduates who can conduct quality research. (p. 38)

Moreover, the number of counseling psychologists who publish research is about equal to that of other fields, including the sciences (Price, 1963, cited in Magoon & Holland, 1984). The point is that we feel that quantity of the research published by students, before and after they graduate, should not be the primary indicator of the quality of a training program. We think students should be skilled researchers who can conduct quality research (and who do so in their dissertations), but who also can intelligently consume research, cogently think about scientific issues, balance research and practice from an informed standpoint, appreciate and value the scientific method, and apply critical thinking skills to a broad range of research and applied contexts. Hill (1997) noted that even though few of her students had taken academic positions or produced much research, she should not as a result be judged as an inadequate research mentor.

CAREER GOALS IN RESEARCH.   In Kahn and Scott's (1997) model, the second outcome construct was goals related to research, which was defined as preferences for postdoctoral positions as researchers rather than as practitioners. Although this is an appropriate construct for their research, we agree with Hill (1997) that training programs should not be judged by the proportion of students going into research-related careers. Instead, programs should graduate students who are trained consistent with the mission of the program, which we believe should include the acquisition of research skills and appropriate attitudes toward research.

Testing the Model

Kahn and Scott (1997) tested their model by randomly sampling doctoral students from 15 of the 63 APA-accredited doctoral programs in counseling psychology. The final sample consisted of 267 participants who were administered various instruments to operationalize the constructs previously discussed, plus gender and year in the program (see Figure 19-1). Kahn and Scott (1997) tested the structural equation in their model (as well as a measurement model) and then modified the model. This modified model fit the data well. The structural part of the modified model is presented in Figure 19-2.

Several aspects of the modified model are informative. The critical mediating construct was research interests rather than research self-efficacy. This is not surprising if one assumes that most students should feel that they *can* conduct research as a result of their training, although they may choose not to (again, see Hill, 1997). Research interests, an important mediating variable, was predicted by both initial personality and the research training environment. It appears that if we want students who are productive and have career goals in research, we should select students who are investigative types (which was the primary Holland type related to research interests) and provide them the environment suggested by Gelso (1979). The goal of programs may vary along the scientist/practitioner continuum, but regardless, the components of the environment we previously discussed should be in place. However, Gelso (1997) clearly believes, based on his research and experience with students, that the characteristics of the person are more important than the training environment: "I would have to say that, given the choice, I would place more weight on person than environment factors in terms of the proportion of variance they account for in research interest, efficacy, and behavior" (p. 309). But Gelso does not find the secondary role of environment to be troublesome: "I am usually delighted if some intervention I've concocted or am part of can account for 5%–10% of the variance in some worthwhile outcome" (p. 309).

Kahn and Scott's (1997) model operationalized person characteristics narrowly. Gelso (1997), in his discussion of the making of a scientist, broadened the personality construct to include cognitive style as well as interests and personality. He indicated that there is tentative evidence that psychotherapy researchers have verbal/analytic styles, whereas psychotherapy practitioners have global/intuitive styles; researchers have a preference for or have the capacity to use "tight, logical, and orderly thinking" (p. 310). But Gelso also recognized the need for creativity in the research process, a point we endorse enthusiastically.

It is not surprising that in the Kahn and Scott model (1997), research career goals predict research productivity because students who want research careers realize that they need to produce research. We will comment later on the effects of year in the program.

Research Competence—The Missing Construct

From our perspective, the missing construct in the Kahn and Scott (1997) model is research competence. As counselors and counseling psychologists we

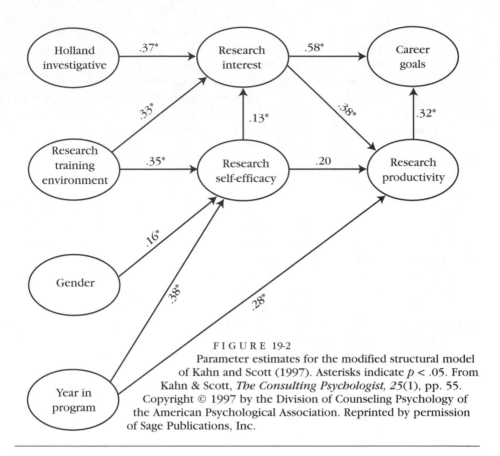

FIGURE 19-2
Parameter estimates for the modified structural model of Kahn and Scott (1997). Asterisks indicate $p < .05$. From Kahn & Scott, *The Consulting Psychologist*, 25(1), pp. 55. Copyright © 1997 by the Division of Counseling Psychology of the American Psychological Association. Reprinted by permission of Sage Publications, Inc.

appropriately attend to how we structure environments to foster positive attitudes and self-efficacy. However, having competencies to conduct and consume research is also critical to producing quality research. Wampold (1986) found that training programs did not teach their students various statistical procedures that were used in typical counseling research. Since that report, numerous other statistical procedures have been introduced in the methodological literature and adopted by counseling researchers. Each of these methods has the potential to reveal discoveries, and the science will not progress unless we understand and appropriately use these methods (Wampold, 1998). Consider the Kahn and Scott (1997) research reviewed here; without a knowledge of structural equation modeling, this research can neither be fully consumed nor extended.

There is additional empirical evidence that the acquisition of research skills in a graduate training program is vital. Royalty and Reising (1986) surveyed professionals and found that respondents felt confident of their research skills, with the exception of statistical and computer skills, two skills that were highly correlated with productivity. Although the respondents indicated that graduate programs adequately contributed to their skill level, they became less confident of their skills later in their careers, and they indicated that it is unlikely that they would augment their research skills after graduation. Further evidence for the importance of skill was provided by Munley, Sharkin, and Gelso's (1988) examination of reviewer ratings of manuscripts submitted to the *Journal of Counseling Psychology*. They found that of the seven scales used by reviewers, two had a pronounced relationship to acceptance for publication: ratings of the overall importance of the manuscript and *the quality of the methodology*.

In the empirical model presented in Figure 19-2, the positive path from year in program to research self-efficacy can be interpreted from a competence perspective. Self-efficacy is due in part to a research environment that fosters positive attitudes toward research, but it is also built upon competencies. We suspect that year in program is most likely a proxy for increased competence because students acquire research skills as a result of experience in the program.

Based on the empirical evidence for competence in statistics and design, Wampold (1986b, p. 44) listed the following design and statistics competencies:

1. Knowledge of designs including, but not limited to, traditional experimental designs, quasi-experimental designs appropriate for field settings, single-subject designs, survey designs, and qualitative designs
2. An understanding of design issues, such as validity, methods of sampling, and power
3. Knowledge of the statistical analyses commonly used in counseling research
4. An understanding of statistical issues, such as the role of assumptions, hypothesis testing strategies, and confirmatory versus exploratory analyses
5. The ability to perform analyses with computer assistance, when appropriate

It is hoped that this book, statistics classes, and other experiences will provide readers these competencies.

One conspicuous competency not listed here is writing, which was discussed in the first half of this chapter. Magoon and Holland (1984) discussed the need for training programs to teach students to write before they find themselves authoring a dissertation. Because systematic training in writing seems to be neglected in research training, we make a few suggestions here. The primary point is that writing instruction should have the same structure as the teaching of other skills: frequent practice of components with feedback. A dissertation is not the time for such instruction; neither is writing a research proposal, a monumental task often left to the end of the term, when it is too late to provide the feedback needed to improve one's skills. Instead, instruction and practice for various parts of writing a research report should be spread throughout classes, feedback should be given as soon as possible, and students should then use that feedback to rewrite.

We endorse the following strategy in teaching students to write introductions. First, the class critiques an introduction to an article; then, as an individual assignment, each student critiques the introduction to an article in their area of interest and receives feedback on their critique from the instructor. The next assignment involves a published article that contains an introduction citing seven other articles (but no books or book chapters). The students are given the published article without the introduction and the seven articles cited. The next assignment is to read the seven cited articles and the published article (without the introduction). At the next class meeting, the class discusses various structures that could be used to conform the introduction to the published article (that is, the logic of the introduction, how the paragraphs would follow each other, how the case would be built for the hypotheses, and so on). In this discussion, it is emphasized that there is no one correct way to write this introduction, but the class agrees on a common structure. The next assignment is for each student to write, in APA style (that is, in accordance with the *Publication Manual of the American Psychological Association,* 1994), an introduction that leads logically to the hypothesis, using only the seven articles as supporting evidence (this assignment is completed in one week). The instructor grades the papers, providing feedback at every level (that is, grammar, sentence construction, paragraph construction, logic, proper citation, and so forth) within one week. The final assignment is to revise the introduction given the instructor's feedback. This revision is again evaluated by the instructor. At the end, the original introduction is critiqued in a class discussion.

A Final Comment on Research Training

Gelso (1997), after years of successfully mentoring graduate students and studying how scientists in counseling psychology develop, made several insightful comments relevant to research training:

> [Effective research training] offers constructive, sensitive and concerned, as well as stimulating and challenging relationships around research and science; [such programs] contain mentors who care about their students' development as scientists and researchers, and probably more generally. Impactful environments are didactically effective. They contain good teachers and good research instruction. . . . Research training environments are most powerful when they contain a consistent message about and value in science and research—when faculty are all on the same ship, so to speak. . . . Finally, . . . the most effective research training environments are those that value and reward sound practice, as well as research. . . . The ideal research training environment—the environment that is most likely to produce graduates who make science an important part of their careers and who do the best research—*is an environment that values both good research and good practice, and appreciates the synergistic relationship between the two* [emphasis added]. (pp. 318-319)

SUMMARY AND CONCLUSIONS

The research report is critical to the research endeavor because it is the vehicle by which the results of studies are typically disseminated. The entire research process is summarized in the research report, from the statement of the problem to the discussion of the results. A coherently organized and well-written report increases the likelihood that the research study will influence the scientific community.

Although organization of the research report varies, most reports contain a title, an abstract, an introduction, a description of the method (participants, measures, materials, design, and procedure), a presentation of the results, and a discussion or conclusion. The content of these sections is determined, to a great extent, by the design of the research.

The style of the written report varies, for each of us has our own style, which we in turn alter depending on the publication for which our writing is intended. Nevertheless, as a rule authors should (a) be informative, (b) be forthright, (c) not overstate or exaggerate, (d) be logical and organized, (e) write in an interesting way, and (f) revise their reports to obtain a polished product.

Professional writing is a complex skill that takes years of practice and feedback. Moreover, it is a skill that involves one's personal style of communicating. Procrastination and other avoidance patterns are common reactions of inexperienced and experienced authors alike. One of the most effective strategies to improve one's professional writing is to work closely with a successful author, writing drafts, receiving feedback, rewriting, and polishing. It is not atypical for graduate students to spend two to three years co-writing with a faculty member to enhance both their professional writing skills and their research skills in general. We strongly urge students to actively solicit feedback on their writing and seek co-writing experiences with established authors.

The trainers of future researchers are the students of today. In this chapter we also have discussed some basic issues related to research training, which we hope will help to create positive attitudes toward research and increase research competence. Nine components of the research environment that have been identified as critical to positive attitudes toward research are: (a) modeling appropriate scientific behavior and attitudes, (b) reinforcing students research efforts, (c) involving students in research early and in minimally threatening ways, (d) teaching relevant statistics and the logic of design, (e) teaching that all research is flawed and limited, (f) teaching varied approaches to research, (g) wedding science and practice in training, (h) facilitating students' introspection for research ideas, and (i) conducting science as a partly social experience.

APPENDIX A

ETHICAL STANDARDS

of the American Counseling Association

PREAMBLE

The Association is an educational, scientific, and professional organization whose members are dedicated to the enhancement of the worth, dignity, potential, and uniqueness of each individual and thus to the service of society.

The Association recognizes that the role of definitions and work settings of its members include a wide variety of academic disciplines, levels of academic preparation, and agency services. This diversity reflects the breadth of the Association's interest and influence. It also poses challenging complexities in efforts to set standards for the performance of members, desired requisite preparation or practice, and supporting social, legal, and ethical controls.

The specification of ethical standards enables the Association to clarify to present and future members and to those served by members the nature of ethical responsibilities held in common by its members.

The existence of such standards serves to stimulate greater concern by members for their own professional functioning and for the conduct of fellow professionals such as counselors, guidance and student personnel workers, and others in the helping professions. As the ethical code of the Association, this document establishes principles that define the ethical behavior of Association members. Additional ethical guidelines developed by the Association's Divisions for their specialty areas may further define a member's ethical behavior.

SECTION A: GENERAL

1. The member influences the development of the profession by continuous efforts to improve professional practices, teaching, services, and research. Professional growth is continuous throughout the member's career and is exemplified by the development of a philosophy that explains why and how a member functions in the helping relationship. Members must gather data on their effectiveness and be guided by the findings. Members recognize the need for continuing education to ensure competent service.

2. The member has a responsibility both to the individual who is served and to the institution within which the service is performed to maintain high standards of professional conduct. The member strives to maintain the highest levels of professional services offered to the individuals to be served. The member also strives to assist the agency, organization, or institution in providing the highest caliber of professional services. The acceptance of employment in an institution implies that the member is in agreement with the general policies and principles of the institution. Therefore the professional activities of the member are also in accord with the objectives of the institution. If, despite concerted efforts, the member cannot reach agreement with the employer as to acceptable standards of conduct that allow for changes in institutional policy conducive to the positive growth and development of clients, then terminating the affiliation should be seriously considered.

3. Ethical behavior among professional associates, both members and nonmembers, must be expected at all times. When information is possessed that raises doubt as to the ethical behavior of professional colleagues, whether Association members or not, the member must take action to attempt to rectify such a condition. Such action shall use the institution's channels first and then use procedures established by the Association.

4. The member neither claims nor implies professional qualifications exceeding those possessed and is responsible for correcting any misrepresentations of these qualifications by others.

5. In establishing fees for professional counseling services, members must consider the financial status of clients and locality. In the event that the established fee structure is inappropriate for a client, assistance must be provided in finding comparable services of acceptable cost.

6. When members provide information to the public or to subordinates, peers, or supervisors, they have a responsibility to ensure that the content is general, unidentified client information that is accurate, unbiased, and consists of objective, factual data.

7. Members recognize their boundaries of competence and provide only those services and use only those techniques for which they are qualified by training or experience. Members should only accept those positions for which they are professionally qualified.

8. In the counseling relationship, the counselor is aware of the intimacy of the relationship and maintains respect for the client and avoids engaging in activities that seek to meet the counselor's personal needs at the expense of that client.

9. Members do not condone or engage in sexual harassment which is defined as deliberate or repeated comments, gestures, or physical contacts of a sexual nature.

10. The member avoids bringing personal issues into the counseling relationship, especially if the potential for harm is present. Through awareness of the negative impact of both racial and sexual stereotyping and discrimination, the counselor guards the individual rights and personal dignity of the client in the counseling relationship.

11. Products or services provided by the member by means of classroom instruction, public lectures, demonstrations, written articles, radio or television programs, or other types of media must meet the criteria cited in these standards.

SECTION B: COUNSELING RELATIONSHIP

This section refers to practices and procedures of individual and/or group counseling relationships.

The member must recognize the need for client freedom of choice. Under those circumstances where this is not possible, the member must apprise clients of restrictions that may limit their freedom of choice.

1. The member's primary obligation is to respect the integrity and promote the welfare of the client(s), whether the client(s) is (are) assisted individually or in a group relationship. In a group setting, the member is also responsible for taking reasonable precautions to protect individuals from physical and/or psychological trauma resulting from interaction within the group.

2. Members make provisions for maintaining confidentiality in the storage and disposal of records and follow an established record retention and disposition policy. The counseling relationship and information resulting therefrom must be kept confidential, consistent with the obligations of the member as a professional person. In a group counseling setting, the counselor must set a norm of confidentiality regarding all group participants' disclosures.

3. If an individual is already in a counseling relationship with another professional person, the member does not enter into a counseling relationship without first contacting and receiving the approval of that other professional. If the member discovers that the client is in another counseling relationship after the counseling relationship begins, the member must gain the consent of the other professional or terminate the relationship, unless the client elects to terminate the other relationship.

4. When the client's condition indicates that there is clear and imminent danger to the client or others, the member must take reasonable personal action or inform responsible authorities. Consultation with other professionals must be used where possible. The assumption of responsibility for the client's(s') behavior must be taken only after careful deliberation. The client must be involved in the resumption of responsibility as quickly as possible.

5. Records of the counseling relationship, including interview notes, test data, correspondence, tape recordings, electronic data storage, and other documents are to be considered professional information for use in counseling, and they should not be considered a part of the records of the institution or agency in which the counselor is employed unless specified by state statute or regulation. Revelation to others of counseling material must occur only upon the expressed consent of the client.

6. In view of the extensive data storage and processing capacities of the computer, the member must ensure that data maintained on a computer is: (a) limited to information that is appropriate and necessary for the services being provided; (b) destroyed after it is determined that the information is no longer of any value in providing services; and (c) restricted in terms of access to appropriate staff members involved in the provision by using the best computer security methods available.

7. Use of data derived from a counseling relationship for purposes of counselor training or research shall be confined to content that can be disguised to ensure full protection of the identity of the subject client.

8. The member must inform the client of the purposes, goals, techniques, rules of procedure, and limitations that may affect the relationship at or before the time that the counseling relationship is entered. When working with minors or persons who are unable to give consent, the member protects these clients' best interests.

9. In view of common misconceptions related to the perceived inherent validity of computer-generated data and narrative reports, the member must ensure that the client is provided with information as part of the counseling relationship that adequately explains the limitations of computer technology.

10. The member must screen prospective group participants, especially when the emphasis is on self-understanding and growth through self-disclosure. The member must maintain an awareness of the group participants' compatibility throughout the life of the group.

11. The member may choose to consult with any other professionally competent person about a client. In choosing a consultant, the member must avoid placing the consultant in a conflict of interest situation that would preclude the consultant's being a proper party to the member's efforts to help the client.

12. If the member determines an inability to be of professional assistance to the client, the member must either avoid initiating the counseling relationship or immediately terminate that relationship. In either event, the member must suggest appropriate alternatives. (The member must be knowledgeable about referral resources so that a satisfactory referral can be initiated.) In the event the client declines the suggested referral, the member is not obligated to continue the relationship.

13. When the member has other relationships, particularly of an administrative, supervisory, and/or evaluative nature with an individual seeking counseling services, the member must not serve as the counselor but should refer the individual to another professional. Only in instances where such an alternative is unavailable and where the individual's situation warrants counseling intervention should the member enter into and/or maintain a counseling relationship. Dual relationships with clients that might impair the member's objectivity and professional judgement (e.g., as with close friends or relatives) must be avoided and/or the counseling relationship terminated through referral to another competent professional.

14. The member will avoid any type of sexual intimacies with clients. Sexual relationships with clients are unethical.

15. All experimental methods of treatment must be clearly indicated to prospective recipients, and safety precautions are to be adhered to by the member.

16. When computer applications are used as a component of counseling services, the member must ensure that: (a) the client is intellectually emotionally, and physically capable of using the computer application; (b) the computer application is appropriate for the needs of the client; (c) the client understands the purpose and operation of the computer application; and (d) a follow-up of client use of a computer application is provided to both correct possible problems (misconceptions or inappropriate use), and assess subsequent needs.

17. When the member is engaged in short-term group treatment/training programs (e.g., marathons and other encounter-type or growth groups), the member ensures that there is professional assistance available during and following the group experience.

18. Should the member be engaged in a work setting that calls for any variation from the above statements, the member is obligated to consult with other professionals whenever possible to consider justifiable alternatives.

19. The member must ensure that members of various ethnic, racial, religious, disability, and socioeconomic groups have equal access to computer applications used to support counseling services and that the content of available computer applications does not discriminate against the groups described above.

20. When computer applications are developed by the member for use by the general public as self-help/stand-alone computer software, the member must ensure that: (a) self-help computer applications are designed from the beginning to function in a stand-alone manner, as opposed to modifying software that was originally designed to require support from a counselor; (b) self-help computer applications will include within the program statements regarding intended user outcomes, suggestions for using the software, a description of the conditions under which self-help computer applications might not be appropriate, and a description of when and how counseling services might be beneficial; and (c) the manual for such applications will include the qualifications of the developer, the development process, validation data, and operating procedures.

SECTION C: MEASUREMENT AND EVALUATION

The primary purpose of educational and psychological testing is to provide descriptive measures that are objective and interpretable in either comparative or absolute terms. The member must recognize the need to interpret the statements that follow as applying to the whole range of appraisal techniques including test and nontest data. Test results constitute only one of a variety of pertinent sources of information for personnel, guidance, and counseling decisions.

1. The member must provide specific orientation or information to the examinee(s) prior to and following the test administration so that the results of testing may be placed in proper perspective with other relevant factors. In so doing, the member must recognize the effects of socioeconomic, ethnic, and cultural factors on test scores. It is the member's professional responsibility to use additional unvalidated information carefully in modifying interpretation of the test results.

2. In selecting tests for use in a given situation or with a particular client, the member must consider carefully the specific validity, reliability, and appropriateness of the test(s). General validity, reliability, and related issues may be questioned legally as well as ethically when tests are used for vocational and educational selection, placement, or counseling.

3. When making any statements to the public about tests and testing, the member must give accurate information and avoid false claims or misconceptions. Special efforts are often required to avoid unwarranted connotations of such terms as IQ and grade equivalent scores.

4. Different tests demand different levels of competence for administration, scoring, and interpretation. Members must recognize the limits of their competence and perform only those functions for which they are prepared. In particular, members using computer-based test interpretations must be trained in the construct being measured and the specific instrument being used prior to using this type of computer application.

5. In situations where a computer is used for test administration and scoring, the member is responsible for ensuring that administration and scoring programs function properly to provide clients with accurate test results.

6. Test must be administered under the same conditions that were established in their standardization. When tests are not administered under standard conditions or when unusual behavior or irregularities occur during the testing session, those conditions must be noted and the results designated as invalid or of questionable validity. Unsupervised or inadequately supervised test-taking, such as the use of tests through the mail, is considered unethical. On the other hand, the use of instruments that are so designed or standardized to be self-administered and self-scored, such as interest inventories, is to be encouraged.

7. The meaningfulness of test results used in personnel, guidance, and counseling functions generally depends on the examinee's unfamiliarity with the specific items on the test. Any prior coaching or dissemination of the test materials can invalidate test results. Therefore, test security is one of the professional obligations of the member. Conditions that produce most favorable test results must be made known to the examinee.

8. The purpose of testing and the explicit use of the results must be made known to the examinee prior to testing. The counselor must ensure that instrument limitations are not exceeded and that periodic review and/or retesting are made to prevent client stereotyping.

9. The examinee's welfare and explicit prior understanding must be the criteria for determining the recipients of the test results. The member must see that specific interpre-

tation accompanies any release of individual or group test data. The interpretation of test data must be related to the examinee's particular concerns.

10. Members responsible for making decisions based on test results have an understanding of educational and psychological measurement, validation criteria, and test research.

11. The member must be cautious when interpreting the results of research instruments possessing insufficient technical data. The specific purposes for the use of such instruments must be stated explicitly to examinees.

12. The member must proceed with caution when attempting to evaluate and interpret the performance of minority group members or other persons who are not represented in the norm group on which the instrument was standardized.

13. When computer-based test interpretations are developed by the member to support the assessment process, the member must ensure that the validity of such interpretation is established prior to the commercial distribution of such a computer application.

14. The member recognizes that test results may become obsolete. The member will avoid and prevent the misuse of obsolete test results.

15. The member must guard against the appropriation, reproduction, or modification of published tests or parts thereof without acknowledgement and permission from the previous publisher.

16. Regarding the preparation, publication, and distribution of tests, reference should be made to:

    a. "Standards for Educational and Psychological Testing," revised edition, 1985, published by the American Psychological Association on behalf of itself, the American Educational Research Association and the National Council of Measurement in Education.

    b. "The Responsible Use of Tests: A Position Paper of AMEG, APGA, and NCME," *Measurement and Evaluation in Guidance,* 1972, 5, 385–388.

    c. "Responsibilities of Users of Standardized Tests," APGA, *Guidepost,* October 5, 1978, pp. 5–8.

SECTION D: RESEARCH AND PUBLICATION

1. Guidelines on research with human subjects shall be adhered to, such as:

    a. *Ethical Principles in the Conduct of Research with Human Participants,* Washington, D.C.: American Psychological Association, Inc., 1982.

    b. Code of Federal Regulation, Title 45, Subtitle A, Part 46, as currently issued.

    c. *Ethical Principles of Psychologists,* American Psychological Association, Principle # 9: Research with Human Participants.

    d. Family Educational Rights and Privacy Act (the Buckley Amendment).

    e. Current federal regulations and various states' rights privacy acts.

2. In planning any research activity dealing with human subjects, the member must be aware of and responsive to all pertinent ethical principles and ensure that the research problem, design, and execution are in full compliance with them.

3. Responsibility for ethical research practice lies with the principal researcher, while others involved in the research activities share ethical obligation and full responsibility for their own actions.

4. In research with human subjects, researchers are responsible for the subjects' welfare throughout the experiment, and they must take all reasonable precautions to avoid causing injurious psychological, physical, or social effects on their subjects.

5. All research subjects must be informed of the purpose of the study except when withholding information or providing misinformation to them is essential to the investigation. In such research the member must be responsible for corrective action as soon as possible following completion of the research.

6. Participation in research must be voluntary. Involuntary participation is appropriate only when it can be demonstrated that participation will have no harmful effects on subjects and is essential to the investigation.

7. When reporting research results, explicit mention must be made of all variables and conditions known to the investigator that might affect the outcome of the investigation or the interpretation of the data.

8. The member must be responsible for conducting and reporting investigations in a manner that minimizes the possibility that results will be misleading.

9. The member has an obligation to make available sufficient original research data to qualified others who may wish to replicate the study.

10. When supplying data, aiding in the research of another person, reporting research results, or making original data available, due care must be taken to disguise the identity of the subjects in the absence of specific authorization from such subjects to do otherwise.

11. When conducting and reporting research, the member must be familiar with and give recognition to previous work on the topic, as well as to observe all copyright laws and follow the principles of giving full credit to all to whom credit is due.

12. The member must give due credit through joint authorship, acknowledgements, footnote statements, or other appropriate means to those who have contributed significantly to the research and/or publication, in accordance with such contributions.

13. The member must communicate to other members the results of any research judged to be of professional or scientific value. Results reflecting unfavorably on institutions, programs, services, or vested interests must not be withheld for such reasons.

14. If members agree to cooperate with another individual in research and/or publication, they incur an obligation to cooperate as promised in terms of punctuality of performance and with full regard to the completeness and accuracy of the information required.

15. Ethical practice requires that authors not submit the same manuscript or one essentially similar in content for simultaneous publication consideration by two or more journals. In addition, manuscripts published in whole or in substantial part in another journal or published work should not be submitted for publication without acknowledgement and permission from the previous publication.

SECTION E: CONSULTING

Consultation refers to a voluntary relationship between a professional helper and help-needing individual, group, or social unit in which the consultant is providing help to the client(s) in defining and solving a work-related problem or potential problem with a client or client system.

1. The member acting as consultant must have a high degree of self-awareness of his/her own values, knowledge, skills, limitations, and needs in entering a helping relationship that involves human and/or organizational change and that the focus of the relationship be on the issues to be resolved and not on the person(s) presenting the problem.

2. There must be understanding and agreement between member and client for the problem definition, change of goals, and prediction of consequences of interventions selected.

3. The member must be reasonably certain that she/he or the organization represented has the necessary competencies and resources for giving the kind of help that is needed now or may be needed later and that appropriate referral resources are available to the consultant.

4. The consulting relationship must be one in which client adaptability and growth toward self-direction are encouraged and cultivated. The member must maintain this role consistently and not become a decision maker for the client or create a future dependency on the consultant.

5. When announcing consultant availability for services, the member conscientiously adheres to the Association's Ethical Standards.

6. The member must refuse a private fee or other remuneration for consultation with persons who are entitled to these services through the member's employing institution or agency. The policies of a particular agency may make explicit provisions for private practice with agency clients by members of its staff. In such instances, the clients must be apprised of other options open to them should they seek private counseling services.

SECTION F: PRIVATE PRACTICE

1. The member should assist the profession by facilitating the availability of counseling services in private as well a public settings.

2. In advertising services as a private practitioner, the member must advertise the services in a manner that accurately informs the public of professional services, expertise, and techniques of counseling available. A member who assumes an executive leadership role in the organization shall not permit his/her name to be used in professional notices during periods when he/she is not actively engaged in the private practice of counseling.

3. The member may list the following: highest relevant degree, type and level of certification and/or license, address, telephone number, office hours, type and/or description of services, and other relevant information. Such information must not contain false, inaccurate, misleading, partial, out-of-context, or deceptive material or statements.

4. Members do not present their affiliation with any organization in such a way that would imply inaccurate sponsorship or certification by that organization.

5. Members may join in partnership/cooperation with other members and/or other professionals provided that each member of the partnership or corporation makes clear the separate specialties by name in compliance with the regulations of the locality.

6. A member has an obligation to withdraw from a counseling relationship if it is believed that employment will result in violation of the Ethical Standards. If the mental or physical condition of the member renders it difficult to carry out an effective professional relationship or if the member is discharged by the client because the counseling relationship is no longer productive for the client, then the member is obligated to terminate the counseling relationship.

7. A member must adhere to the regulations for private practice of the locality where the services are offered.

8. It is unethical to use one's institutional affiliation to recruit clients for one's private practice.

SECTION G: PERSONNEL ADMINISTRATION

It is recognized that most members are employed in public or quasi-public institutions. The functioning of a member within an institution must contribute to the goals of the institution and vice versa if either is to accomplish their respective goals or objectives. It is therefore essential that the member and the institution function in ways to: (a) make the institutional goals specific and public; (b) make the member's contribution to institutional goals specific; and (c) foster mutual accountability for goal achievement.

To accomplish these objectives, it is recognized that the member and the employer must share responsibilities in the formulation and implementation of personnel policies.

1. Members must define and describe the parameters and levels of their professional competency.

2. Members must establish interpersonal relations and working agreements with supervisors and subordinates regarding counseling or clinical relationships, confidentiality, distinction between public and private material, maintenance and dissemination of recorded information, work load, and accountability. Working agreements in each instance must be specified and made known to those concerned.

3. Members must alert their employers to conditions that may be potentially disruptive or damaging.

4. Members must inform employers of conditions that may limit their effectiveness.

5. Members must submit regularly to professional review and evaluation.

6. Members must be responsible for in-service development of self and/or staff.

7. Members must inform their staff of goals and programs.

8. Members must provide personnel practices that guarantee and enhance the rights and welfare of each recipient of their service.

9. Members must select competent persons and assign responsibilities compatible with their skills and experiences.

10. The member, at the onset of a counseling relationship, will inform the client of the member's intended use of supervisors regarding the disclosure of information concerning this case. The member will clearly inform the client of the limits of confidentiality in the relationship.

11. Members, as either employers or employees, do not engage in or condone practices that are inhumane, illegal, or unjustifiable (such as considerations based on sex, handicap, age, race) in hiring, promotion, or training.

SECTION H: PREPARATION STANDARDS

Members who are responsible for training others must be guided by the preparation standards of the Association and relevant Division(s). The member who functions in the capacity of trainer assumes unique ethical responsibilities that frequently go beyond that of the member who does not function in a training capacity. These ethical responsibilities are outlined as follows:

1. Members must orient students to program expectations, basic skills development, and employment prospects prior to admission to the program.

2. Members in charge of learning experiences must establish programs that integrate academic study and supervised practice.

3. Members must establish a program directed toward developing students' skills, knowledge, and self-understanding, stated whenever possible in competency or performance terms.

4. Members must identify the levels of competencies of their students in compliance with relevant Division standards. These competencies must accommodate the paraprofessional as well as the professional.

5. Members, through continual student evaluation and appraisal, must be aware of the personal limitations of the learner that might impede future performance. The instruc-

tor must not only assist the learner in securing remedial assistance but also screen from the program those individuals who are unable to provide competent services.

6. Members must provide a program that includes training in research commensurate with levels of role functioning. Paraprofessional and technician-level personnel must be trained as consumers of research. In addition, personnel must learn how to evaluate their own and their program's effectiveness. Graduate training, especially at the doctoral level, would include preparation for original research by the member.

7. Members must make students aware of the ethical responsibilities and standards of the profession.

8. Preparatory programs must encourage students to value the ideals of service to individuals and to society. In this regard, direct financial remuneration or lack thereof must not be allowed to overshadow professional and humanitarian needs.

9. Members responsible for educational programs must be skilled as teachers and practitioners.

10. Members must present thoroughly varied theoretical positions so that students may make comparisons and have the opportunity to select a position.

11. Members must develop clear policies within their educational institutions regarding field placement and the roles of the student and the instructor in such placement.

12. Members must ensure that forms of learning focusing on self-understanding or growth are voluntary, or if required as part of the educational program, are made known to prospective students prior to entering the program. When the educational program offers a growth experience with an emphasis on self-disclosure or other relatively intimate or personal involvement, the member must have no administrative, supervisory, or evaluating authority regarding the participant.

13. The member will at all times provide students with clear and equally acceptable alternatives for self-understanding or growth experiences. The member will assure students that they have a right to accept these alternatives without prejudice or penalty.

14. Members must conduct an educational program in keeping with the current relevant guidelines of the Association.

APPENDIX B

ETHICAL PRINCIPLES OF PSYCHOLOGISTS AND CODE OF CONDUCT

INTRODUCTION

The American Psychological Association's (APA's) Ethical Principles of Psychologists and Code of Conduct (hereinafter referred to as the Ethics Code) consists of an Introduction, a Preamble, six General Principles (A–F), and specific Ethical Standards. The Introduction discusses the intent, organization, procedural considerations, and scope of application of the Ethics Code. The Preamble and General Principles are *aspirational* goals to guide psychologists toward the highest ideals of psychology. Although the Preamble and General Principles are not themselves enforceable rules, they should be considered by psychologists in arriving at an ethical course of action and may be considered by ethics bodies in interpreting the Ethical Standards. The Ethical Standards set forth *enforceable* rules for conduct as psychologists. Most of the Ethical Standards are written broadly, in order to apply to psychologists in varied roles, although the application of an Ethical Standard may vary depending on the context. The Ethical Standards are not exhaustive. The fact that a given conduct is not specifically addressed by the Ethics Code does not mean that it is necessarily either ethical or unethical.

Membership in the APA commits members to adhere to the APA Ethics Code and to the rules and procedures used to implement it. Psychologists and students, whether or not they are APA members. should be aware that the Ethics Code may be applied to them by state psychology boards, courts, or other public bodies.

This Ethics Code applies only to psychologists' work-related activities, that is, activities that are part of the psychologists' scientific and professional functions or that are psychological in nature. It includes the clinical or counseling practice of psychology, research, teaching, supervision of trainees, development of assessment instruments, conducting assessments, educational counseling, organizational consulting, social intervention, administration, and other activities as well. These work–related activities can be distinguished from the purely private conduct of a psychologist, which ordinarily is not within the purview of the Ethics Code.

The Ethics Code is intended to provide standards of professional conduct that can be applied by the APA and by other bodies that choose to adopt them. Whether or not a psy-

This version of the American Psychological Association Ethics Code was adopted by the American Psychological Association's Council of Representatives during its meeting on August 13 and 16, 1992, and was published in *American Psychologist,* 1992, Vol. 47, 1597-1611. Copyright 1992. Reprinted by permission.

chologist has violated the Ethics Code does not by itself determine whether he or she is legally liable in a court action, whether a contract is enforceable, or whether other legal consequences occur. These results are based on legal rather than ethical rules. However, compliance with or violation of the Ethics Code may be admissible as evidence in some legal proceedings, depending on the circumstances.

In the process of making decisions regarding their professional behavior, psychologists must consider this Ethics Code, in addition to applicable laws and psychology board regulations. If the Ethics Code establishes a higher standard of conduct than is required by law, psychologists must meet the higher ethical standard. If the Ethics Code standard appears to conflict with the requirements of law, then psychologists make known their commitment to the Ethics Code and take steps to resolve the conflict in a responsible manner. If neither law nor the Ethics Code resolves an issue, psychologists should consider other professional materials* and the dictates of their own conscience, as well as seek consultation with others within the field when this is practical.

The procedures for filing, investigating, and resolving complaints of unethical conduct are described in the current Rules and Procedures of the APA Ethics Committee. The actions that APA may take for violations of the Ethics Code include actions such as reprimand, censure, termination of APA membership, and referral of the matter to other bodies. Complainants who seek remedies such as monetary damages in alleging ethical violations by a psychologist must resort to private negotiation, administrative bodies, or the courts. Actions that violate the Ethics Code may lead to the imposition of sanctions on a psychologist by bodies other than APA, including state psychological associations, other professional groups, psychology boards, other state or federal agencies, and payors for health services. In addition to actions for violation of the Ethics Code, the APA Bylaws provide that APA may take action against a member after his or her conviction of a felony, expulsion or suspension from an affiliated state psychological association, or suspension or loss of licensure.

PREAMBLE

Psychologists work to develop a valid and reliable body of scientific knowledge based on research. They may apply that knowledge to human behavior in a variety of contexts. In doing so, they perform many roles, such as researcher, educator, diagnostician, therapist, supervisor, consultant, administrator, social interventionist, and expert witness. Their goal is to broaden knowledge of behavior and, where appropriate, to apply it pragmatically to improve the condition of both the individual and society. Psychologists respect the central

---

*Professional materials that are most helpful in this regard are guidelines and standards that have been adopted or endorsed by professional psychological organizations. Such guidelines and standards, whether adopted by the American Psychological Association (APA) or its Divisions, are not enforceable as such by this Ethics Code, but are of educative value to psychologists, courts, and professional bodies. Such materials include, but are not limited to, the APA's *General Guidelines for Providers of Psychological Services* (1987), *Specialty Guidelines for the Delivery of Services by Clinical Psychologists, Counseling Psychologists, Industrial/Organizational Psychologists, and School Psychologists* (1981), *Guidelines for Computer Based Tests and Interpretations* (1987), *Standards for Educational and Psychological Testing* (1985), *Ethical Principles in the Conduct of Research With Human Participants* (1982), *Guidelines for Ethical Conduct in the Care and Use of Animals* (1986), *Guidelines for Providers of Psychological Services to Ethnic, Linguistic, and Culturally Diverse Populations* (1990), and the *Publication Manual of the American Psychological Association* (3rd ed., 1983). Materials not adopted by APA as a whole include the APA Division 41 (Forensic Psychology)/American Psychology–Law Society's *Specialty Guidelines for Forensic Psychologists* (1991).

importance of freedom of inquiry and expression in research, teaching, and publication. They also strive to help the public in developing informed judgments and choices concerning human behavior. This Ethics Code provides a common set of values upon which psychologists build their professional and scientific work.

This Code is intended to provide both the general principles and the decision rules to cover most situations encountered by psychologists. It has as its primary goal the welfare and protection of the individuals and groups with whom psychologists work. It is the individual responsibility of each psychologist to aspire to the highest possible standards of conduct. Psychologists respect and protect human and civil rights, and do not knowingly participate in or condone unfair discriminatory practices.

The development of a dynamic set of ethical standards for a psychologist's work-related conduct requires a personal commitment to a lifelong effort to act ethically; to encourage ethical behavior by students, supervisees, employees, and colleagues, as appropriate; and to consult with others, as needed, concerning ethical problems. Each psychologist supplements, but does not violate, the Ethics Code's values and rules on the basis of guidance drawn from personal values, culture, and experience.

GENERAL PRINCIPLES

Principle A: Competence

Psychologists strive to maintain high standards of competence in their work. They recognize the boundaries of their particular competencies and the limitations of their expertise. They provide only those services and use only those techniques for which they are qualified by education, training, or experience. Psychologists are cognizant of the fact that the competencies required in serving, teaching, and/or studying groups of people vary with the distinctive characteristics of those groups. In those areas in which recognized professional standards do not yet exist, psychologists exercise careful judgment and take appropriate precautions to protect the welfare of those with whom they work. They maintain knowledge of relevant scientific and professional information related to the services they render, and they recognize the need for ongoing education. Psychologists make appropriate use of scientific, professional, technical, and administrative resources.

Principle B: Integrity

Psychologists seek to promote integrity in the science, teaching, and practice of psychology. In these activities psychologists are honest, fair, and respectful of others. In describing or reporting their qualifications, services, products, fees, research, or teaching, they do not make statements that are false, misleading, or deceptive. Psychologists strive to be aware of their own belief systems, values, needs, and limitations and the effect of these on their work. To the extent feasible, they attempt to clarify for relevant parties the roles they are performing and to function appropriately in accordance with those roles. Psychologists avoid improper and potentially harmful dual relationships.

Principle C: Professional and Scientific Responsibility

Psychologists uphold professional standards of conduct, clarify their professional roles and obligations, accept appropriate responsibility for their behavior, and adapt their methods to the needs of different populations. Psychologists consult with, refer to, or cooperate with other professionals and institutions to the extent needed to serve the best interests of their patients, clients, or other recipients of their services. Psychologists' moral standards and conduct are personal matters to the same degree as is true for any other person, except as psychologists' conduct may compromise their professional responsibilities or reduce the public's trust in psychology and psychologists. Psychologists are concerned about the ethical compliance of their colleagues' scientific and professional conduct. When appropriate, they consult with colleagues in order to prevent or avoid unethical conduct.

Principle D: Respect for People's Rights and Dignity

Psychologists accord appropriate respect to the fundamental rights, dignity, and worth of all people. They respect the rights of individuals to privacy, confidentiality, self-determination, and autonomy, mindful that legal and other obligations may lead to inconsistency and conflict with the exercise of these rights. Psychologists are aware of cultural, individual, and role differences, including those due to age, gender, race, ethnicity, national origin, religion, sexual orientation, disability, language, and socioeconomic status. Psychologists try to eliminate the effect on their work of biases based on those factors, and they do not knowingly participate in or condone unfair discriminatory practices.

Principle E: Concern for Others' Welfare

Psychologists seek to contribute to the welfare of those with whom they interact professionally. In their professional actions, psychologists weigh the welfare and rights of their patients or clients, students, supervisees, human research participants, and other affected persons, and the welfare of animal subjects of research. When conflicts occur among psychologists' obligations or concerns, they attempt to resolve these conflicts and to perform their roles in a responsible fashion that avoids or minimizes harm. Psychologists are sensitive to real and ascribed differences in power between themselves and others, and they do not exploit or mislead other people during or after professional relationships.

Principle F: Social Responsibility

Psychologists are aware of their professional and scientific responsibilities to the community and the society in which they work and live. They apply and make public their knowledge of psychology in order to contribute to human welfare. Psychologists are concerned about and work to mitigate the causes of human suffering. When undertaking research, they strive to advance human welfare and the science of psychology. Psychologists try to avoid misuse of their work. Psychologists comply with the law and encourage the development of law and social policy that serve the interests of their patients and clients and the public. They are encouraged to contribute a portion of their professional time for little or no personal advantage.

ETHICAL STANDARDS

1. General Standards

These General Standards are potentially applicable to the professional and scientific activities of all psychologists.

1.01 Applicability of the Ethics Code

The activity of a psychologist subject to the Ethics Code may be reviewed under these Ethical Standards only if the activity is part of his or her work–related functions or the activity is psychological in nature. Personal activities having no connection to or effect on psychological roles are not subject to the Ethics Code.

1.02 Relationship of Ethics and Law
If psychologists' ethical responsibilities conflict with law, psychologists make known their commitment to the Ethics Code and take steps to resolve the conflict in a responsible manner.

1.03 Professional and Scientific Relationship
Psychologists provide diagnostic, therapeutic, teaching, research, supervisory, consultative, or other psychological services only in the context of a defined professional or scientific relationship or role. (See also Standards 2.01, Evaluation, Diagnosis, and Interventions in Professional Context, and 7.02, Forensic Assessments.)

1.04 Boundaries of Competence
(a) Psychologists provide services, teach, and conduct research only within the boundaries of their competence, based on their education, training, supervised experience, or appropriate professional experience.
(b) Psychologists provide services, teach, or conduct research in new areas or involving new techniques only after first undertaking appropriate study, training, supervision, and/or consultation from persons who are competent in those areas or techniques.
(c) In those emerging areas in which generally recognized standards for preparatory training do not yet exist, psychologists nevertheless take reasonable steps to ensure the competence of their work and to protect patients, clients, students, research participants, and others from harm.

1.05 Maintaining Expertise
Psychologists who engage in assessment, therapy, teaching, research, organizational consulting, or other professional activities maintain a reasonable level of awareness of current scientific and professional information in their fields of activity, and undertake ongoing efforts to maintain competence in the skills they use.

1.06 Basis for Scientific and Professional Judgments
Psychologists rely on scientifically and professionally derived knowledge when making scientific or professional judgments or when engaging in scholarly or professional endeavors.

1.07 Describing the Nature and Results of Psychological Services
(a) When psychologists provide assessment, evaluation, treatment, counseling, supervision, teaching, consultation, research, or other psychological services to an individual, a group, or an organization, they provide, using language that is reasonably understandable to the recipient of those services, appropriate information beforehand about the nature of such services and appropriate information later about results and conclusions. (See also Standard 2.09, Explaining Assessment Results.)
(b) If psychologists will be precluded by law or by organizational roles from providing such information to particular individuals or groups, they so inform those individuals or groups at the outset of the service.

1.08 Human Differences
Where differences of age, gender, race, ethnicity, national origin, religion, sexual orientation, disability, language, or socioeconomic status significantly affect psychologists' work concerning particular individuals or groups, psychologists obtain the training, experience, consultation, or supervision necessary to ensure the competence of their services, or they make appropriate referrals.

1.09 Respecting Others
In their work–related activities, psychologists respect the rights of others to hold values, attitudes, and opinions that differ from their own.

1.10 Nondiscrimination
In their work–related activities, psychologists do not engage in unfair discrimination based on age, gender, race, ethnicity, national origin, religion, sexual orientation, disability, socioeconomic status, or any basis proscribed by law.

1.11 Sexual Harassment
        (a) Psychologists do not engage in sexual harassment. Sexual harassment is sexual solicitation, physical advances, or verbal or nonverbal conduct that is sexual in nature, that occurs in connection with the psychologist's activities or roles as a psychologist, and that either: (1) is unwelcome, is offensive, or creates a hostile workplace environment, and the psychologist knows or is told this, or (2) is sufficiently severe or intense to be abusive to a reasonable person in the context. Sexual harassment can consist of a single intense or severe act or of multiple persistent or pervasive acts.
        (b) Psychologists accord sexual-harassment complainants and respondents dignity and respect. Psychologists do not participate in denying a person academic admittance or advancement, employment, tenure, or promotion, based solely upon their having made, or their being the subject of, sexual harassment charges. This does not preclude taking action based upon the outcome of such proceedings or consideration of other appropriate information.

1.12 Other Harassment
Psychologists do not knowingly engage in behavior that is harassing or demeaning to persons with whom they interact in their work based on factors such as those persons' age, gender, race, ethnicity, national origin, religion, sexual orientation, disability, language, or socioeconomic status.

1.13 Personal Problems and Conflicts
        (a) Psychologists recognize that their personal problems and conflicts may interfere with their effectiveness. Accordingly, they refrain from undertaking an activity when they know or should know that their personal problems are likely to lead to harm to a patient, client, colleague, student, research participant, or other person to whom they may owe a professional or scientific obligation.
        (b) In addition, psychologists have an obligation to be alert to signs of, and to obtain assistance for, their personal problems at an early stage, in order to prevent significantly impaired performance.
        (c) When psychologists become aware of personal problems that may interfere with their performing work-related duties adequately, they take appropriate measures, such as obtaining professional consultation or assistance, and determine whether they should limit, suspend, or terminate their work–related duties.

1.14 Avoiding Harm
Psychologists take reasonable steps to avoid harming their patients or clients, research participants, students, and others with whom they work, and to minimize harm where it is foreseeable and unavoidable.

1.15 Misuse of Psychologists' Influence

Because psychologists' scientific and professional judgments and actions may affect the lives of others, they are alert to and guard against personal, financial, social, organizational, or political factors that might lead to misuse of their influence.

1.16 Misuse of Psychologists' Work

(a) Psychologists do not participate in activities in which it appears likely that their skills or data will be misused by others, unless corrective mechanisms are available. (See also Standard 7.04, Truthfulness and Candor.)

(b) If psychologists learn of misuse or misrepresentation of their work, they take reasonable steps to correct or minimize the misuse or misrepresentation.

1.17 Multiple Relationships

(a) In many communities and situations, it may not be feasible or reasonable for psychologists to avoid social or other nonprofessional contacts with persons such as patients, clients, students, supervisees, or research participants. Psychologists must always be sensitive to the potential harmful effects of other contacts on their work and on those persons with whom they deal. A psychologist refrains from entering into or promising another personal, scientific, professional, financial, or other relationship with such persons if it appears likely that such a relationship reasonably might impair the psychologist's objectivity or otherwise interfere with the psychologist's effectively performing his or her functions as a psychologist, or might harm or exploit the other party.

(b) Likewise, whenever feasible, a psychologist refrains from taking on professional or scientific obligations when preexisting relationships would create a risk of such harm.

(c) If a psychologist finds that, due to unforeseen factors, a potentially harmful multiple relationship has arisen, the psychologist attempts to resolve it with due regard for the best interests of the affected person and maximal compliance with the Ethics Code.

1.18 Barter (with Patients or Clients)

Psychologists ordinarily refrain from accepting goods, services, or other nonmonetary remuneration from patients or clients in return for psychological services because such arrangements create inherent potential for conflicts, exploitation, and distortion of the professional relationship. A psychologist may participate in bartering only if (1) it is not clinically contraindicated, and (2) the relationship is not exploitative. (See also Standards 1.17, Multiple Relationships, and 1.25, Fees and Financial Arrangements.)

1.19 Exploitative Relationships

(a) Psychologists do not exploit persons over whom they have supervisory, evaluative, or other authority such as students, supervisees, employees, research participants, and clients or patients. (See also Standards 4.05–4.07 regarding sexual involvement with clients or patients.)

(b) Psychologists do not engage in sexual relationships with students or supervisees in training over whom the psychologist has evaluative or direct authority, because such relationships are so likely to impair judgment or be exploitative.

1.20 Consultations and Referrals

(a) Psychologists arrange for appropriate consultations and referrals based principally on the best interests of their patients or clients, with appropriate consent, and subject to other relevant considerations, including applicable law and contractual obligations. (See also Standards 5.01, Discussing the Limits of Confidentiality, and 5.06, Consultations.)

(b) When indicated and professionally appropriate, psychologists cooperate with other professionals in order to serve their patients or clients effectively and appropriately.

(c) Psychologists' referral practices are consistent with law.

1.21 Third–Party Requests for Services

(a) When a psychologist agrees to provide services to a person or entity at the request of a third party, the psychologist clarifies to the extent feasible, at the outset of the service, the nature of the relationship with each party. This clarification includes the role of the psychologist (such as therapist, organizational consultant, diagnostician, or expert witness), the probable uses of the services provided or the information obtained, and the fact that there may be limits to confidentiality.

(b) If there is a foreseeable risk of the psychologist's being called upon to perform conflicting roles because of the involvement of a third party, the psychologist clarifies the nature and direction of his or her responsibilities, keeps all parties appropriately informed as matters develop, and resolves the situation in accordance with this Ethics Code.

1.22 Delegation to and Supervision of Subordinates

(a) Psychologists delegate to their employees, supervisees, and research assistants only those responsibilities that such persons can reasonably be expected to perform competently, on the basis of their education, training, or experience, either independently or with the level of supervision being provided.

(b) Psychologists provide proper training and supervision to their employees or supervisees and take reasonable steps to see that such persons perform services responsibly, competently, and ethically.

(c) If institutional policies, procedures, or practices prevent fulfillment of this obligation, psychologists attempt to modify their role or to correct the situation to the extent feasible.

1.23 Documentation of Professional and Scientific Work

(a) Psychologists appropriately document their professional and scientific work in order to facilitate provision of services later by them or by other professionals, to ensure accountability, and to meet other requirements of institutions or the law.

(b) When psychologists have reason to believe that records of their professional services will be used in legal proceedings involving recipients of or participants in their work, they have a responsibility to create and maintain documentation in the kind of detail and quality that would be consistent with reasonable scrutiny in an adjudicative forum. (See also Standard 7.01, Professionalism, under Forensic Activities.)

1.24 Records and Data

Psychologists create, maintain, disseminate, store, retain, and dispose of records and data relating to their research, practice, and other work in accordance with law and in a manner that permits compliance with the requirements of this Ethics Code. (See also Standard 5.04, Maintenance of Records.)

1.25 Fees and Financial Arrangements

(a) As early as is feasible in a professional or scientific relationship, the psychologist and the patient, client, or other appropriate recipient of psychological services reach an agreement specifying the compensation and the billing arrangements.

(b) Psychologists do not exploit recipients of services or payors with respect to fees.

(c) Psychologists' fee practices are consistent with law.

(d) Psychologists do not misrepresent their fees.

(e) If limitations to services can be anticipated because of limitations in financing, this is discussed with the patient, client, or other appropriate recipient of services as early as is feasible. (See also Standard 4.08, Interruption of Services.)

(f) If the patient, client, or other recipient of services does not pay for services as agreed, and if the psychologist wishes to use collection agencies or legal measures to collect the fees, the psychologist first informs the person that such measures will be taken and provides that person an opportunity to make prompt payment. (See also Standard 5.11, Withholding Records for Nonpayment.)

1.26 Accuracy in Reports to Payors and Funding Sources
In their reports to payors for services or sources of research funding, psychologists accurately state the nature of the research or service provided, the fees or charges, and where applicable, the identity of the provider, the findings, and the diagnosis. (See also Standard 5.05, Disclosures.)

1.27 Referrals and Fees
When a psychologist pays, receives payment from, or divides fees with another professional other than in an employer-employee relationship, the payment to each is based on the services (clinical, consultative, administrative, or other) provided and is not based on the referral itself.

2. Evaluation, Assessment, or Intervention

2.01 Evaluation, Diagnosis, and Interventions in Professional Context
(a) Psychologists perform evaluations, diagnostic services, or interventions only within the context of a defined professional relationship. (See also Standard 1.03, Professional and Scientific Relationship.)

(b) Psychologists' assessments, recommendations, reports, and psychological diagnostic or evaluative statements are based on information and techniques (including personal interviews of the individual when appropriate) sufficient to provide appropriate substantiation for their findings. (See also Standard 7.02, Forensic Assessments.)

2.02 Competence and Appropriate Use of Assessments and Interventions
(a) Psychologists who develop, administer, score, interpret, or use psychological assessment techniques, interviews, tests, or instruments do so in a manner and for purposes that are appropriate in light of the research on or evidence of the usefulness and proper application of the techniques.

(b) Psychologists refrain from misuse of assessment techniques, interventions, results, and interpretations and take reasonable steps to prevent others from misusing the information these techniques provide. This includes refraining from releasing raw test results or raw data to persons, other than to patients or clients as appropriate, who are not qualified to use such information. (See also Standards 1.02, Relationship of Ethics and Law, and 1.04, Boundaries of Competence.)

2.03 Test Construction
Psychologists who develop and conduct research with tests and other assessment techniques use scientific procedures and current professional knowledge for test design, standardization, validation, reduction or elimination of bias, and recommendations for use.

2.04 Use of Assessment in General and with Special Populations

(a) Psychologists who perform interventions or administer, score, interpret, or use assessment techniques are familiar with the reliability, validation, and related standardization or outcome studies of, and proper applications and uses of, the techniques they use.

(b) Psychologists recognize limits to the certainty with which diagnoses, judgments, or predictions can be made about individuals.

(c) Psychologists attempt to identify situations in which particular interventions or assessment techniques or norms may not be applicable or may require adjustment in administration or interpretation because of factors such as individuals' gender, age, race, ethnicity, national origin, religion, sexual orientation, disability, language, or socioeconomic status.

2.05 Interpreting Assessment Results

When interpreting assessment results, including automated interpretations, psychologists take into account the various test factors and characteristics of the person being assessed that might affect psychologists' judgments or reduce the accuracy of their interpretations. They indicate any significant reservations they have about the accuracy or limitations of their interpretations.

2.06 Unqualified Persons

Psychologists do not promote the use of psychological assessment techniques by unqualified persons. (See also Standard 1.22, Delegation to and Supervision of Subordinates.)

2.07 Obsolete Tests and Outdated Test Results

(a) Psychologists do not base their assessment or intervention decisions or recommendations on data or test results that are outdated for the current purpose.

(b) Similarly, psychologists do not base such decisions or recommendations on tests and measures that are obsolete and not useful for the current purpose.

2.08 Test Scoring and Interpretation Services

(a) Psychologists who offer assessment or scoring procedures to other professionals accurately describe the purpose, norms, validity, reliability, and applications of the procedures and any special qualifications applicable to their use.

(b) Psychologists select scoring and interpretation services (including automated services) on the basis of evidence of the validity of the program and procedures as well as on other appropriate considerations.

(c) Psychologists retain appropriate responsibility for the appropriate application, interpretation, and use of assessment instruments, whether they score and interpret such tests themselves or use automated or other services.

2.09 Explaining Assessment Results

Unless the nature of the relationship is clearly explained to the person being assessed in advance and precludes provision of an explanation of results (such as in some organizational consulting, preemployment or security screenings, and forensic evaluations), psychologists ensure that an explanation of the results is provided using language that is reasonably understandable to the person assessed or to another legally authorized person on behalf of the client. Regardless of whether the scoring and interpretation are done by the psychologist, by assistants, or by automated or other outside services, psychologists take reasonable steps to ensure that appropriate explanations of results are given.

2.10 Maintaining Test Security

Psychologists make reasonable efforts to maintain the integrity and security of tests and other assessment techniques consistent with law, contractual obligations, and in a manner that permits compliance with the requirements of this Ethics Code. (See also Standard 1.02, Relationship of Ethics and Law.)

3. Advertising and Other Public Statements

3.01 Definition of Public Statements

Psychologists comply with this Ethics Code in public statements relating to their professional services, products, or publications or to the field of psychology. Public statements include but are not limited to paid or unpaid advertising, brochures, printed matter, directory listings, personal resumes or curricula vitae, interviews or comments for use in media, statements in legal proceedings, lectures and public oral presentations, and published materials.

3.02 Statements by Others

(a) Psychologists who engage others to create or place public statements that promote their professional practice, products, or activities retain professional responsibility for such statements.

(b) In addition, psychologists make reasonable efforts to prevent others whom they do not control (such as employers, publishers, sponsors, organizational clients, and representatives of the print or broadcast media) from making deceptive statements concerning psychologists' practice or professional or scientific activities.

(c) If psychologists learn of deceptive statements about their work made by others, psychologists make reasonable efforts to correct such statements.

(d) Psychologists do not compensate employees of press, radio, television, or other communication media in return for publicity in a news item.

(e) A paid advertisement relating to the psychologist's activities must be identified as such, unless it is already apparent from the context.

3.03 Avoidance of False or Deceptive Statements

(a) Psychologists do not make public statements that are false, deceptive, misleading, or fraudulent, either because of what they state, convey, or suggest or because of what they omit, concerning their research, practice, or other work activities or those of persons or organizations with which they are affiliated. As examples (and not in limitation) of this standard, psychologists do not make false or deceptive statements concerning (1) their training, experience, or competence; (2) their academic degrees; (3) their credentials; (4) their institutional or association affiliations; (5) their services; (6) the scientific or clinical basis for, or results or degree of success of, their services; (7) their fees; or (8) their publications or research findings. (See also Standards 6.15, Deception in Research, and 6.18, Providing Participants with Information About the Study.)

(b) Psychologists claim as credentials for their psychological work, only degrees that (1) were carried from a regionally accredited educational institution or (2) were the basis for psychology licensure by the state in which they practice.

3.04 Media Presentations

When psychologists provide advice or comment by means of public lectures, demonstrations, radio or television programs, prerecorded tapes, printed articles, mailed material, or other media, they take reasonable precautions to ensure that (1) the statements are based on appropriate psychological literature and practice, (2) the statements are otherwise consistent with this Ethics Code, and (3) the recipients of the information are not encouraged to infer that a relationship has been established with them personally.

3.05 Testimonials

Psychologists do not solicit testimonials from current psychotherapy clients or patients or other persons who because of their particular circumstances are vulnerable to undue influence.

3.06 In-Person Solicitation

Psychologists do not engage, directly or through agents, in uninvited in-person solicitation of business from actual or potential psychotherapy patients or clients or other persons who because of their particular circumstances are vulnerable to undue influence. However, this does not preclude attempting to implement appropriate collateral contacts with significant others for the purpose of benefiting an already engaged therapy patient.

4. Therapy

4.01 Structuring the Relationship

(a) Psychologists discuss with clients or patients as early as is feasible in the therapeutic relationship appropriate issues, such as the nature and anticipated course of therapy, fees, and confidentiality. (See also Standards 1.25, Fees and Financial Arrangements, and 5.01, Discussing the Limits of Confidentiality.)

(b) When the psychologist's work with clients or patients will be supervised. the above discussion includes that fact, and the name of the supervisor, when the supervisor has legal responsibility for the case.

(c) When the therapist is a student intern, the client or patient is informed of that fact.

(d) Psychologists make reasonable efforts to answer patients' questions and to avoid apparent misunderstandings about therapy. Whenever possible, psychologists provide oral and/or written information, using language that is reasonably understandable to the patient or client.

4.02 Informed Consent to Therapy

(a) Psychologists obtain appropriate informed consent to therapy or related procedures, using language that is reasonably understandable to participants. The content of informed consent will vary depending on many circumstances; however, informed consent generally implies that the person (1) has the capacity to consent, (2) has been informed of significant information concerning the procedure, (3) has freely and without undue influence expressed consent, and (4) consent has been appropriately documented.

(b) When persons are legally incapable of giving informed consent, psychologists obtain informed permission from a legally authorized person, if such substitute consent is permitted by law.

(c) In addition, psychologists (1) inform those persons who are legally incapable of giving informed consent about the proposed interventions in a manner commensurate with the persons' psychological capacities, (2) seek their assent to those interventions, and (3) consider such persons' preferences and best interests.

4.03 Couple and Family Relationships

(a) When a psychologist agrees to provide services to several persons who have a relationship (such as husband and wife or parents and children), the psychologist attempts to clarify at the outset (1) which of the individuals are patients or clients and (2) the relationship the psychologist will have with each person. This clarification includes the role of the psychologist and the probable uses of the services provided or the information obtained. (See also Standard 5.01, Discussing the Limits of Confidentiality.)

(b) As soon as it becomes apparent that the psychologist may be called on to perform potentially conflicting roles (such as marital counselor to husband and wife, and then witness for one party in a divorce proceeding), the psychologist attempts to clarify and adjust, or withdraw from, roles appropriately. (See also Standard 7.03, Clarification of Role, under Forensic Activities.)

4.04 Providing Mental Health Services to Those Served by Others
In deciding whether to offer or provide services to those already receiving mental health services elsewhere, psychologists carefully consider the treatment issues and the potential patient's or client's welfare. The psychologist discusses these issues with the patient or client, or another legally authorized person on behalf of the client, in order to minimize the risk of confusion and conflict, consults with the other service providers when appropriate, and proceeds with caution and sensitivity to the therapeutic issues.

4.05 Sexual Intimacies with Current Patients or Clients
Psychologists do not engage in sexual intimacies with current patients or clients.

4.06 Therapy with Former Sexual Partners
Psychologists do not accept as therapy patients or clients persons with whom they have engaged in sexual intimacies.

4.07 Sexual Intimacies with Former Therapy Patients
(a) Psychologists do not engage in sexual intimacies with a former therapy patient or client for at least two years after cessation or termination of professional services.
(b) Because sexual intimacies with a former therapy patient or client are so frequently harmful to the patient or client, and because such intimacies undermine public confidence in the psychology profession and thereby deter the public's use of needed services, psychologists do not engage in sexual intimacies with former therapy patients and clients even after a two-year interval except in the most unusual circumstances. The psychologist who engages in such activity after the two years following cessation or termination of treatment bears the burden of demonstrating that there has been no exploitation, in light of all relevant factors, including (1) the amount of time that has passed since therapy terminated, (2) the nature and duration of the therapy, (3) the circumstances of termination, (4) the patient's or client's personal history, (5) the patient's or client's current mental status, (6) the likelihood of adverse impact on the patient or client and others, and (7) any statements or actions made by the therapist during the course of therapy suggesting or inviting the possibility of a posttermination sexual or romantic relationship with the patient or client. (See also Standard 1.17, Multiple Relationships.)

4.08 Interruption of Services
(a) Psychologists make reasonable efforts to plan for facilitating care in the event that psychological services are interrupted by factors such as the psychologist's illness, death, unavailability, or relocation or by the client's relocation or financial limitations. (See also Standard 5.09, Preserving Records and Data.)
(b) When entering into employment or contractual relationships, psychologists provide for orderly and appropriate resolution of responsibility for patient or client care in the event that the employment or contractual relationship ends, with paramount consideration given to the welfare of the patient or client.

4.09 Terminating the Professional Relationship
(a) Psychologists do not abandon patients or clients. (See also Standard 1.25e, under Fees and Financial Arrangements.)
(b) Psychologists terminate a professional relationship when it becomes reasonably clear that the patient or client no longer needs the service, is not benefiting, or is being harmed by continued service.

(c) Prior to termination for whatever reason, except where precluded by the patient's or client's conduct, the psychologist discusses the patient's or client's views and needs, provides appropriate pretermination counseling, suggests alternative service providers as appropriate, and takes other reasonable steps to facilitate transfer of responsibility to another provider if the patient or client needs one immediately.

5. Privacy and Confidentiality

These Standards are potentially applicable to the professional and scientific activities of all psychologists.

5.01 Discussing the Limits of Confidentiality

(a) Psychologists discuss with persons and organizations with whom they establish a scientific or professional relationship (including, to the extent feasible, minors and their legal representatives) (1) the relevant limitations on confidentiality, including limitations where applicable in group, marital, and family therapy or in organizational consulting, and (2) the foreseeable uses of the information generated through their services.

(b) Unless it is not feasible or is contraindicated, the discussion of confidentiality occurs at the outset of the relationship and thereafter as new circumstances may warrant.

(c) Permission for electronic recording of interviews is secured from clients and patients.

5.02 Maintaining Confidentiality

Psychologists have a primary obligation and take reasonable precautions to respect the confidentiality rights of those with whom they work or consult, recognizing that confidentiality may be established by law, institutional rules, or professional or scientific relationships. (See also Standard 6.26, Professional Reviewers.)

5.03 Minimizing Intrusions on Privacy

(a) In order to minimize intrusions on privacy, psychologists include in written and oral reports, consultations, and the like, only information germane to the purpose for which the communication is made.

(b) Psychologists discuss confidential information obtained in clinical or consulting relationships, or evaluative data concerning patients, individual or organizational clients, students, research participants, supervisees, and employees, only for appropriate scientific or professional purposes and only with persons clearly concerned with such matters.

5.04 Maintenance of Records

Psychologists maintain appropriate confidentiality in creating, storing, accessing, transferring, and disposing of records under their control, whether these are written, automated, or in any other medium. Psychologists maintain and dispose of records in accordance with law and in a manner that permits compliance with the requirements of this Ethics Code.

5.05 Disclosures

(a) Psychologists disclose confidential information without the consent of the individual only as mandated by law, or where permitted by law for a valid purpose, such as (1) to provide needed professional services to the patient or the individual or organizational client, (2) to obtain appropriate professional consultations, (3) to protect the patient or client or others from harm, or (4) to obtain payment for services, in which instance disclosure is limited to the minimum that is necessary to achieve the purpose.

(b) Psychologists also may disclose confidential information with the appropriate consent of the patient or the individual or organizational client (or of another legally authorized person on behalf of the patient or client), unless prohibited by law.

5.06 Consultations

When consulting with colleagues, (1) psychologists do not share confidential information that reasonably could lead to the identification of a patient, client, research participant, or other person or organization with whom they have a confidential relationship unless they have obtained the prior consent of the person or organization or the disclosure cannot be avoided, and (2) they share information only to the extent necessary to achieve the purposes of the consultation. (See also Standard 5.02, Maintaining Confidentiality.)

5.07 Confidential Information in Databases

(a) If confidential information concerning recipients of psychological services is to be entered into databases or systems of records available to persons whose access has not been consented to by the recipient, then psychologists use coding or other techniques to avoid the inclusion of personal identifiers.

(b) If a research protocol approved by an institutional review board or similar body requires the inclusion of personal identifiers, such identifiers are deleted before the information is made accessible to persons other than those of whom the subject was advised.

(c) If such deletion is not feasible, then before psychologists transfer such data to others or review such data collected by others, they take reasonable steps to determine that appropriate consent of personally identifiable individuals has been obtained.

5.08 Use of Confidential Information for Didactic or Other Purposes

(a) Psychologists do not disclose in their writings, lectures, or other public media, confidential, personally identifiable information concerning their patients, individual or organizational clients, students, research participants, or other recipients of their services that they obtained during the course of their work, unless the person or organization has consented in writing or unless there is other ethical or legal authorization for doing so.

(b) Ordinarily, in such scientific and professional presentations, psychologists disguise confidential information concerning such persons or organizations so that they are not individually identifiable to others and so that discussions do not cause harm to subjects who might identify themselves.

5.09 Preserving Records and Data

A psychologist makes plans in advance so that confidentiality of records and data is protected in the event of the psychologist's death, incapacity, or withdrawal from the position or practice.

5.10 Ownership of Records and Data

Recognizing that ownership of records and data is governed by legal principles, psychologists take reasonable and lawful steps so that records and data remain available to the extent needed to serve the best interests of patients, individual or organizational clients, research participants, or appropriate others.

5.11 Withholding Records for Nonpayment

Psychologists may not withhold records under their control that are requested and imminently needed for a patient's or client's treatment solely because payment has not been received, except as otherwise provided by law.

6. Teaching, Training Supervision, Research, and Publishing

6.01 Design of Education and Training Programs

Psychologists who are responsible for education and training programs seek to ensure that the programs are competently designed, provide the proper experiences, and meet the requirements for licensure, certification, or other goals for which claims are made by the program.

6.02 Descriptions of Education and Training Programs

(a) Psychologists responsible for education and training programs seek to ensure that there is a current and accurate description of the program content, training goals and objectives, and requirements that must be met for satisfactory completion of the program. This information must be made readily available to all interested parties.

(b) Psychologists seek to ensure that statements concerning their course outlines are accurate and not misleading, particularly regarding the subject matter to be covered, bases for evaluating progress, and the nature of course experiences. (See also Standard 3.03, Avoidance of False or Deceptive Statements.)

(c) To the degree to which they exercise control, psychologists responsible for announcements, catalogs, brochures, or advertisements describing workshops, seminars, or other non–degree-granting educational programs ensure that they accurately describe the audience for which the program is intended, the educational objectives, the presenters, and the fees involved.

6.03 Accuracy and Objectivity in Teaching

(a) When engaged in teaching or training, psychologists present psychological information accurately and with a reasonable degree of objectivity.

(b) When engaged in teaching or training, psychologists recognize the power they hold over students or supervisees and therefore make reasonable efforts to avoid engaging in conduct that is personally demeaning to students or supervisees. (See also Standards 1.09, Respecting Others, and 1.12, Other Harassment.)

6.04 Limitation on Teaching

Psychologists do not teach the use of techniques or procedures that require specialized training, licensure, or expertise, including but not limited to hypnosis, biofeedback, and projective techniques, to individuals who lack the prerequisite training, legal scope of practice, or expertise.

6.05 Assessing Student and Supervisee Performance

(a) In academic and supervisory relationships, psychologists establish an appropriate process for providing feedback to students and supervisees.

(b) Psychologists evaluate students and supervisees on the basis of their actual performance on relevant and established program requirements.

6.06 Planning Research

(a) Psychologists design, conduct, and report research in accordance with recognized standards of scientific competence and ethical research.

(b) Psychologists plan their research so as to minimize the possibility that results will be misleading.

(c) In planning research, psychologists consider its ethical acceptability under the Ethics Code. If an ethical issue is unclear, psychologists seek to resolve the issue through consultation with institutional review boards, animal care and use committees, peer consultations, or other proper mechanisms.

(d) Psychologists take reasonable steps to implement appropriate protections for the rights and welfare of human participants, other persons affected by the research, and the welfare of animal subjects.

6.07 Responsibility

(a) Psychologists conduct research competently and with due concern for the dignity and welfare of the participants.

(b) Psychologists are responsible for the ethical conduct of research conducted by them or by others under their supervision or control.

(c) Researchers and assistants are permitted to perform only those tasks for which they are appropriately trained and prepared.

(d) As part of the process of development and implementation of research projects, psychologists consult those with expertise concerning any special population under investigation or most likely to be affected.

6.08 Compliance with Law and Standards

Psychologists plan and conduct research in a manner consistent with federal and state law and regulations, as well as professional standards governing the conduct of research, and particularly those standards governing research with human participants and animal subjects.

6.09 Institutional Approval

Psychologists obtain from host institutions or organizations appropriate approval prior to conducting research, and they provide accurate information about their research proposals. They conduct the research in accordance with the approved research protocol.

6.10 Research Responsibilities

Prior to conducting research (except research involving only anonymous surveys, naturalistic observations, or similar research), psychologists enter into an agreement with participants that clarifies the nature of the research and the responsibilities of each party.

6.11 Informed Consent to Research

(a) Psychologists use language that is reasonably understandable to research participants in obtaining their appropriate informed consent (except as provided in Standard 6.12, Dispensing With Informed Consent). Such informed consent is appropriately documented.

(b) Using language that is reasonably understandable to participants, psychologists inform participants of the nature of the research; they inform participants that they are free to participate or to decline to participate or to withdraw from the research; they explain the foreseeable consequences of declining or withdrawing; they inform participants of significant factors that may be expected to influence their willingness to participate (such as risks, discomfort, adverse effects, or limitations on confidentiality, except as provided in Standard 6.15, Deception in Research); and they explain other aspects about which the prospective participants inquire.

(c) When psychologists conduct research with individuals such as students or subordinates, psychologists take special care to protect the prospective participants from adverse consequences of declining or withdrawing from participation.

(d) When research participation is a course requirement or opportunity for extra credit, the prospective participant is given the choice of equitable alternative activities.

(e) For persons who are legally incapable of giving informed consent, psychologists nevertheless (1) provide an appropriate explanation, (2) obtain the participant's assent, and (3) obtain appropriate permission from a legally authorized person, if such substitute consent is permitted by law.

6.12 Dispensing with Informed Consent

Before determining that planned research (such as research involving only anonymous questionnaires, naturalistic observations, or certain kinds of archival research) does not require the informed consent of research participants, psychologists consider applicable regulations and institutional review board requirements, and they consult with colleagues as appropriate.

6.13 Informed Consent in Research Filming or Recording

Psychologists obtain informed consent from research participants prior to filming or recording them in any form, unless the research involves simply naturalistic observations in public places and it is not anticipated that the recording will be used in a manner that could cause personal identification or harm.

6.14 Offering Inducements for Research Participants

(a) In offering professional services as an inducement to obtain research participants, psychologists make clear the nature of the services, as well as the risks, obligations, and limitations. (See also Standard 1.18, Barter [with Patients or Clients].)

(b) Psychologists do not offer excessive or inappropriate financial or other inducements to obtain research participants, particularly when it might tend to coerce participation.

6.15 Deception in Research

(a) Psychologists do not conduct a study involving deception unless they have determined that the use of deceptive techniques is justified by the study's prospective scientific, educational, or applied value and that equally effective alternative procedures that do not use deception are not feasible.

(b) Psychologists never deceive research participants about significant aspects that would affect their willingness to participate, such as physical risks, discomfort, or unpleasant emotional experiences.

(c) Any other deception that is an integral feature of the design and conduct of an experiment must be explained to participants as early as is feasible, preferably at the conclusion of their participation, but no later than at the conclusion of the research. (See also Standard 6.18, Providing Participants with Information About the Study.)

6.16 Sharing and Utilizing Data

Psychologists inform research participants of their anticipated sharing or further use of personally identifiable research data and of the possibility of unanticipated future uses.

6.17 Minimizing Invasiveness

In conducting research, psychologists interfere with the participants or milieu from which data are collected only in a manner that is warranted by an appropriate research design and that is consistent with psychologists' roles as scientific investigators.

6.18 Providing Participants with Information About the Study

(a) Psychologists provide a prompt opportunity for participants to obtain appropriate information about the nature, results, and conclusions of the research, and psychologists attempt to correct any misconceptions that participants may have.

(b) If scientific or humane values justify delaying or withholding this information, psychologists take reasonable measures to reduce the risk of harm.

6.19 Honoring Commitments

Psychologists take reasonable measures to honor all commitments they have made to research participants.

6.20 Care and Use of Animals in Research

(a) Psychologists who conduct research involving animals treat them humanely.

(b) Psychologists acquire, care for, use, and dispose of animals in compliance with current federal, state, and local laws and regulations, arid with professional standards.

(c) Psychologists trained in research methods and experienced in the care of laboratory animals supervise all procedures involving animals and are responsible for ensuring appropriate consideration of their comfort, health, and humane treatment.

(d) Psychologists ensure that all individuals using animals under their supervision have received instruction in research methods and in the care, maintenance, and handling of the species being used, to the extent appropriate to their role.

(e) Responsibilities and activities of individuals assisting in a research project are consistent with their respective competencies.

(f) Psychologists make reasonable efforts to minimize the discomfort, infection, illness, and pain of animal subjects.

(g) A procedure subjecting animals to pain, stress, or privation is used only when an alternative procedure is unavailable and the goal is justified by its prospective scientific, educational, or applied value.

(h) Surgical procedures are performed under appropriate anesthesia; techniques to avoid infection and minimize pain are followed during and after surgery.

(i) When it is appropriate that the animal's life be terminated, it is done rapidly, with an effort to minimize pain, and in accordance with accepted procedures.

6.21 Reporting of Results

(a) Psychologists do not fabricate data or falsify results in their publications.

(b) If psychologists discover significant errors in their published data, they take reasonable steps to correct such errors in a correction, retraction, erratum, or other appropriate publication means.

6.22 Plagiarism

Psychologists do not present substantial portions or elements of another's work or data as their own, even if the other work or data source is cited occasionally.

6.23 Publication Credit

(a) Psychologists take responsibility and credit, including authorship credit, only for work they have actually performed or to which they have contributed.

(b) Principal authorship and other publication credits accurately reflect the relative scientific or professional contributions of the individuals involved, regardless of their relative status. Mere possession of an institutional position, such as Department Chair, does not justify authorship credit. Minor contributions to the research or to the writing for publications are appropriately acknowledged, such as in footnotes or in an introductory statement.

(c) A student is usually listed as principal author on any multiple–authored article that is substantially based on the student's dissertation or thesis.

6.24 Duplicate Publication of Data

Psychologists do not publish, as original data, data that have been previously published. This does not preclude republishing data when they are accompanied by proper acknowledgment.

6.25 Sharing Data

After research results are published, psychologists do not withhold the data on which their conclusions are based from other competent professionals who seek to verify the substantive claims through reanalysis and who intend to use such data only for that purpose, provided that the confidentiality of the participants can be protected and unless legal rights concerning proprietary data preclude their release.

6.26 Professional Reviewers

Psychologists who review material submitted for publication, grant, or other research proposal review respect the confidentiality of and the proprietary rights in such information of those who submitted it.

7. Forensic Activities

7.01 Professionalism

Psychologists who perform forensic functions, such as assessments, interviews, consultations, reports, or expert testimony must comply with all other provisions of this Ethics Code to the extent that they apply to such activities. In addition, psychologists base their forensic work on appropriate knowledge of and competence in the areas underlying such work, including specialized knowledge concerning special populations. (See also Standards 1.06, Basis for Scientific and Professional Judgments; 1.08, Human Differences; 1.15, Misuse of Psychologists' Influence; and 1.23, Documentation of Professional and Scientific Work.)

7.02 Forensic Assessments

(a) Psychologists' forensic assessments, recommendations. and reports are based on information and techniques (including personal interviews of the individual, when appropriate) sufficient to provide appropriate substantiation for their findings. (See also Standards 1.03, Professional and Scientific Relationship; 1.23, Documentation of Professional and Scientific Work; 2.01, Evaluation, Diagnosis, and Interventions in Professional Context; and 2.05, Interpreting Assessment Results.)

(b) Except as noted in (c), below, psychologists provide written or oral forensic reports or testimony of the psychological characteristics of an individual only after they have conducted an examination of the individual adequate to support their statements or conclusions.

(c) When, despite reasonable efforts, such an examination is not feasible, psychologists clarify the impact of their limited information on the reliability and validity of their reports and testimony, and they appropriately limit the nature and extent of their conclusions or recommendations.

7.03 Clarification of Role

In most circumstances, psychologists avoid performing multiple and potentially conflicting roles in forensic matters. When psychologists may be called on to serve in more than one role in a legal proceeding—for example, as consultant or expert for one party or for the court and as a fact witness—they clarify role expectations and the extent of confidentiality in advance to the extent feasible, and thereafter as changes occur, in order to avoid compromising their professional judgment and objectivity and in order to avoid misleading others regarding their role.

7.04 Truthfulness and Candor

(a) In forensic testimony and reports, psychologists testify truthfully, honestly, and candidly and, consistent with applicable legal procedures, describe fairly the bases for their testimony and conclusions.

(b) Whenever necessary to avoid misleading, psychologists acknowledge the limits of their data or conclusions.

7.05 Prior Relationships

A prior professional relationship with a party does not preclude psychologists from testifying as fact witnesses or from testifying to their services to the extent permitted by applicable law. Psychologists appropriately take into account ways in which the prior relationship might affect their professional objectivity or opinions and disclose the potential conflict to the relevant parties.

7.06 Compliance with Law and Rules

In performing forensic roles, psychologists are reasonably familiar with the rules governing their roles. Psychologists are aware of the occasionally competing demands placed upon them by these principles and the requirements of the court system, and attempt to resolve these conflicts by making known their commitment to this Ethics Code and taking steps to resolve the conflict in a responsible manner. (See also Standard 1.02, Relationship of Ethics and Law.)

8. Resolving Ethical Issues

8.01 Familiarity with Ethics Code
Psychologists have an obligation to be familiar with this Ethics Code, other applicable ethics codes, and their application to psychologists' work. Lack of awareness or misunderstanding of an ethical standard is not itself a defense to a charge of unethical conduct.

8.02 Confronting Ethical Issues
When a psychologist is uncertain whether a particular situation or course of action would violate this Ethics Code, the psychologist ordinarily consults with other psychologists knowledgeable about ethical issues, with state or national psychology ethics committees, or with other appropriate authorities in order to choose a proper response.

8.03 Conflicts Between Ethics and Organizational Demands
If the demands of an organization with which psychologists are affiliated conflict with this Ethics Code, psychologists clarify the nature of the conflict, make known their commitment to the Ethics Code, and to the extent feasible, seek to resolve the conflict in a way that permits the fullest adherence to the Ethics Code.

8.04 Informal Resolution of Ethical Violations
When psychologists believe that there may have been an ethical violation by another psychologist, they attempt to resolve the issue by bringing it to the attention of that individual if an informal resolution appears appropriate and the intervention does not violate any confidentiality rights that may be involved.

8.05 Reporting Ethical Violations
If an apparent ethical violation is not appropriate for informal resolution under Standard 8.04 or is not resolved properly in that fashion, psychologists take further action appropriate to the situation, unless such action conflicts with confidentiality rights in ways that cannot be resolved. Such action might include referral to state or national committees on professional ethics or to state licensing boards.

8.06 Cooperating with Ethics Committees
Psychologists cooperate in ethics investigations, proceedings, and resulting requirements of the APA or any affiliated state psychological association to which they belong. In doing so, they make reasonable efforts to resolve any issues as to confidentiality. Failure to cooperate is itself an ethics violation.

8.07 Improper Complaints
Psychologists do not file or encourage the filing of ethics complaints that are frivolous and are intended to harm the respondent rather than to protect the public.

REFERENCES

Abramson, L. Y. (Ed.). (1988). *Social cognition and clinical psychology: A synthesis.* New York: Guilford Press.

Adler, P. A., & Adler, P. (1991). *Backboards and blackboards.* New York: Columbia University Press.

Adler, P. A., & Adler, P. (1994). Observational techniques. In N. K. Denzin & Y. S. Lincoln (Eds.), *Handbook of qualitative research* (pp. 377–392). Thousand Oaks, CA: Sage.

Albee, G. W. (1970). The uncertain future of clinical psychology. *American Psychologist, 25,* 1071–1080.

Aldenderfer, M. S., & Blashfield, R. K. (1984). *Cluster analysis.* Beverly Hills, CA: Sage.

Alloy, L. B., & Abramson, L. Y. (1979). Judgment of contingency in depressed and nondepressed students: Sadder but wiser? *Journal of Experimental Psychology, 108,* 441–485.

Alvidrez, J., Azocar, F., & Miranda, J. (1996). Demystifying the concept of ethnicity for psychotherapy researchers. *Journal of Consulting and Clinical Psychology, 64,* 903–908.

American Association for Counseling and Development. (1977). Standards for the preparation of counselors and other personnel services specialists. *Personnel and Guidance Journal, 55,* 596–601.

American Association for Counseling and Development. (1988). *Ethical standards.* Alexandria, VA: Author. (Originally published by American Personnel and Guidance Association)

American Psychological Association. (1983). *Publication manual of the American Psychological Association* (3rd ed.). Washington, DC: American Psychological Association.

American Psychological Association. (1990). Ethical principles of psychologists (amended June 1989). *American Psychologist, 45,* 390–395.

American Psychological Association. (1992). Ethical principles of psychologists and code of conduct. *American Psychologist, 47,* 1597–1611.

American Psychological Association. (1994). *Publication manual of the American Psychological Association* (4th ed.). Washington, DC: American Psychological Association.

American Psychological Association Ethics Committee (1983, February 19). *Authorship guidelines for dissertation supervision.*

Andersen, B., & Anderson, W. (1985). Client perceptions of counselors using positive and negative self-involving statements. *Journal of Counseling Psychology, 32,* 462–465.

Anderson, J. R. (1983). *The architecture of cognition.* Cambridge, MA: Harvard University Press.

Anderson, T. R., Hogg, J. A., & Magoon, T. M. (1987). Length of time on a waiting list and attrition after intake. *Journal of Counseling Psychology, 34,* 93-95.

Anderson, W. P., & Heppner, P. P. (1986). Counselor applications of research findings to practice: Learning to stay current. *Journal of Counseling and Development, 65,* 152-155.

Anton, W. D., & Reed, J. R. (1991). *College Adjustment Scales.* Odessa, FL: Psychological Assessment Resources.

Areán, P. A., & Gallagher-Thompson, D. (1996). Issues and recommendations for the recruitment and retention of older ethnicity minority adults into clinical research. *Journal of Consulting and Clinical Psychology, 64,* 875-880.

Argyris, C. (1968). Some unintended consequences of rigorous research. *Psychological Bulletin, 70,* 185-197.

Arnold, C. L. (1992). An introduction to hierarchical linear models. *Measurement and Evaluation in Counseling and Development, 25,* 58-90.

Atkinson, D. R. (1983). Ethnic similarity in counseling psychology: A review of the research. *The Counseling Psychologist, 11,* 79-92.

Atkinson, D. R., & Lowe, S. M. (1995). The role of ethnicity, cultural knowledge, and conventional techniques in counseling and psychotherapy. In J. G. Ponterotto, J. M. Casas, L. A. Suzuki, & C. M. Alexander (Eds.), *Handbook of multicultural counseling* (pp. 387-414). Thousand Oaks, CA: Sage.

Atkinson, D. R., Morten, G., & Sue, D. W. (Eds.). (1989). *Counseling American minorities: A cross-cultural perspective* (3rd ed.). Dubuque, IA: William C. Brown.

Atkinson, D. R., & Thompson, C. E. (1992). Racial, ethnic, and cultural variables in counseling. In S. D. Brown & R. W. Lent (Eds.), *Handbook of counseling psychology* (pp. 349-382). New York: John Wiley & Sons, Inc.

Atkinson, D. R., & Wampold, B. E. (1982). A comparison of the Counselor Rating Form and the Counselor Effectiveness Rating Scale. *Counselor Education and Supervision, 22,* 25-36.

Attkisson, C., & Zwick, R. (1982). The Client Satisfaction Questionnaire. *Evaluation and Program Planning, 5,* 233-237.

Ayoub, C., & Jacewitz, J. (1982). Families at risk of poor parenting: A descriptive study of six at risk families in a model prevention program. *Child Abuse & Neglect, 6,* 413-422.

Babbie, E. R. (1979). *The practice of social research* (2nd ed.). Belmont, CA: Wadsworth.

Baer, D. M., Wolf, M. M., & Risley, T. R. (1968). Some current dimensions of applied behavioral analysis. *Journal of Applied Behavior Analysis, 1,* 91-97.

Bakeman, R., & Gottman, J. M. (1986). *Observing interaction: An introduction to sequential analysis.* Cambridge: Cambridge University Press.

Barak, A., & LaCrosse, M. B. (1975). Multidimensional perception of counselor behavior. *Journal of Counseling Psychology, 22,* 471-476.

Barber, J. P., & Crits-Christoph, P. (1996). Development of a therapist adherence competence rating scale for supportive-expressive dynamic psychotherapy: A preliminary report. *Psychotherapy Research, 6,* 79-92.

Barber, J. P., Crits-Christoph, P., & Luborsky, L. (1996). Effects of therapist adherence and competence on patient outcome in brief dynamic therapy. *Journal of Consulting and Clinical Psychology, 64,* 619-622.

Barber, T. X. (1976). *Pitfalls in human research: Ten pivotal points.* New York: Pergamon Press.

Barber, T. X., & Silver, M. J. (1968). Fact, fiction, and the experimenter bias effect. *Psychological Bulletin Monograph, 70,* 1-29.

Barkham, M., Andrew, R. M., & Culverwell, A. (1993). The California psychotherapy alliance scales: A pilot study of dimensions and elements. *British Journal of Medical Psychology, 66,* 157-165.

Barlow, D. H. (Ed.). (1981). *Behavioral assessment of adult disorders.* New York: Guilford Press.

Barlow, D. H., & Hersen, M. (1984). *Single case experimental designs: Strategies for study-ing behavior change* (2nd ed.). New York: Pergamon Press.

Baron, R. M., & Kenny, D. A. (1986). The moderator-mediator variable distinction in social psychological research: Conceptual, strategic, and statistical considerations. *Journal of Personality and Social Psychology, 51,* 1173–1182.

Barrett-Lennard, G. T. (1962). Dimensions of therapist response as causal factors in thera-peutic change. *Psychological Monographs: General and Applied, 76,* Whole No. 562.

Baumrind, D. (1976). *Nature and definition of informed consent in research involving deception.* Background paper prepared for the National Commission for the Protection of Human Subjects of Biomedical and Behavioral Research. Washington, DC: Department of Health, Education, and Welfare.

Beauchamp, T. L., & Childress, J. F. (1979). *Principles of biomedical ethics.* Oxford, England: Oxford University Press.

Beauchamp, T. L., & Childress, J. F. (1994). *Principles of biomedical ethics* (4th ed.). New York: Oxford University Press.

Beck, A. T., Rush, A. J., Shaw, B. F., & Emery, G. (1979). *Cognitive therapy of depression.* New York: Guilford Press.

Beck, A. T., Ward, C. H., Mendelson, M., Mock, J., & Erbaugh, J. (1961). An inventory for measuring depression. *Archives of General Psychiatry, 4,* 561–571.

Bednar, R. L., & Kaul, T. J. (1978). Experiential group research: Current perspectives. In S. L. Garfield & A. E. Bergin (Eds.), *Handbook of psychotherapy and behavior change,* 2nd ed. (pp. 769–816). New York: Wiley.

Behrens, J. T. (1997). Does the white racial identity attitude scale measure racial identity? *Journal of Counseling Psychology, 44,* 3–12.

Belar, C. D., & Perry, N. W. (1992). National conference on scientist-practitioner education and training for the professional practice of psychology, *American Psychologist, 47,* 71–75.

Bem, D. J. (1995). Writing a review article for *Psychological Bulletin. Psychological Bulletin, 118,* 172–177.

Benjamin, L. S. (1974). Structural analysis of social behavior. *Psychological Review, 81,* 392–425.

Benn, S. I. (1967). Justice. In P. Edwards (Ed.), *The encyclopedia of philosophy* (Vol. 4, pp. 298–302). New York: Macmillan.

Bennum, I., Hahlweg, K., Schindler, L., & Langlotz, M. (1986). Therapist's and client's per-ceptions in behavior therapy: The development and cross-cultural analysis of an assessment instrument. *British Journal of Clinical Psychology, 25,* 275–283.

Berdie, R. F. (1972). The 1980 counselor: Applied behavioral scientist. *Personnel and Guidance Journal, 50,* 451–456.

Berg, I. A. (1954). Ideomotor response set: Symbolic sexual gesture in the counseling inter-view. *Journal of Counseling Psychology, 1,* 180–183.

Bergin, A. E., & Garfield, S. L. (1971). *Handbook of psychotherapy and behavior change.* New York: Wiley.

Bergin, A. E., & Garfield, S. L. (Eds.) (1994). *Handbook of psychotherapy and behavior change.* New York: Wiley.

Bergin, A. E., & Lambert, M. J. (1978). The evaluation of therapeutic outcomes. In S. L. Garfield & A. E. Bergin (Eds.), *Handbook of psychotherapy and behavior change,* 2nd ed. (pp. 139–190). New York: Wiley.

Bergin, A. E., & Strupp, H. H. (1970). New directions in psychotherapy research. *Journal of Abnormal Psychology, 76,* 13–26.

Bernard, J. M., & Goodyear, R. K. (1998). *Fundamentals of clinical supervision* (2nd ed.). Boston: Allyn & Bacon.

Bernstein, B. L., & Kerr, B. (1993). Counseling psychology and the scientist-practitioner model: Implementation and implications. *The Counseling Psychologist, 21,* 136–151.

Bersoff, D. N. (1994). Explicit ambiguity: The 1992 ethics code as an oxymoron. *Professional Psychology: Research and Practice, 25,* 382–387.

Betz, N. E. (1986). Research training in counseling psychology: Have we addressed the real issues? *The Counseling Psychologist, 14,* 107–113.

Betz, N., & Fitzgerald, L. (1987). *The career psychology of women.* New York: Academic Press.

Betz, N. E., & Fitzgerald, L. F. (1993). Individuality and diversity: Theory and research in counseling psychology. *Annual Review of Psychology, 44,* 343–381.

Betz, N. E., & Hackett, G. (1981). The relationship of career-related self-efficacy expectations to perceived career options in college women and men. *Journal of Counseling Psychology, 28,* 399–410.

Betz, N. E., & Hackett, G. (1987). The concept of agency in educational and career development. *Journal of Counseling Psychology, 34,* 299–308.

Betz, N. E., & Taylor, K. M. (1982). Concurrent validity of the Strong-Campbell Interest Inventory for graduate students in counseling. *Journal of Counseling Psychology, 29,* 626–635.

Beutler, L. E., Brown, M. T., Crothers, L., Booker, K., & Seabrook, M. K. (1996). The dilemma of factitious demographic distinctions in psychological research. *Journal of Consulting and Clinical Psychology, 64,* 892–902.

Bhaskar, R. (1975). *A realist theory of science.* Leeds, England: Leeds Books.

Bischoff, M. M., & Tracey, T. J. G. (1995). Client resistance as predicted by therapist behavior: A study of sequential dependence. *Journal of Counseling Psychology, 42,* 487–495.

Blashfield, R. K. (1984). *The classification of psychopathology: Neo-Kraepelinian and quantitative approaches.* New York: Plenum.

Blos, P. (1946). Psychological counseling of college students. *American Journal of Orthopsychiatry, 16,* 571–580.

Bluestein, D. L., & Spengler, P.M. (1995). Personal adjustment: Career counseling and psychotherapy. In W. B. Walsh & S. H. Osigow (Eds.), *Handbook of vocational psychology: Theory, research, and practice* (pp. 295–329). Mahwah, NJ: Erlbaum.

Bollen, K. A. (1989). *Structural equations with latent variables.* New York: John Wiley.

Bordin, E. S. (1965). Simplification as a research strategy in psychotherapy. *Journal of Consulting Psychology, 29,* 493–503.

Bordin, E. S. (1979). The generalizability of the psychoanalytic concept of working alliance. *Psychotherapy: Theory, Research and Practice, 16,* 252–260.

Borenstein, M., & Cohen, J. (1988). *Statistical power analysis: A computer program.* Hillsdale, NJ: Erlbaum.

Borgen, F. H. (1984a). Counseling psychology. *Annual Review of Psychology, 35,* 579–604.

Borgen, F. H. (1984b). Are there necessary linkages between research practices and the philosophy of science? *Journal of Counseling Psychology, 31,* 457–460.

Borgen, F. H.. (1992). Expanding scientific paradigms in counseling psychology. In S. D. Brown and R. W. Lent (Eds.), *Handbook of counseling psychology,* 2nd ed. (pp. 111–139). New York: Wiley.

Borgen, F. H., & Barnett, D. C. (1987). Applying cluster analysis in counseling psychology research. *Journal of Counseling Psychology, 34,* 456–468.

Borgen, F. H., & Weiss, D. J. (1971). Cluster analysis and counseling research. *Journal of Counseling Psychology, 18,* 583–591.

Bowers, B., & Esmond, S. (1996). *Wisconsin partnership program 1996: Report on quality findings for frail elderly consumers.* Technical report, School of Nursing, University of Wisconsin, Madison.

Bracht, G. H., & Glass, V. V. (1968). The external validity of experiments. *American Educational Research Journal, 5,* 437–474.

Bradley, J. V. (1968). *Distribution-free statistical tests.* Englewood Cliffs, NJ: Prentice-Hall.

Breuer, J., & Freud, S. (1955). Studies on hysteria. In J. Strachey (Ed. and Trans.), *The standard edition of the complete psychological works of Sigmund Freud* (Vol. 2). London: Hogarth Press. (Original work published 1893–1895)

Bridgewater, C. A., Bornstein, P. H., & Walkenbach, J. (1981). Ethical issues and the assignment of publication credit. *American Psychologist, 36,* 524–525.

Broad, W., & Wade, N. (1982). *Betrayers of the truth.* New York: Simon & Schuster.

Brock, T. C. (1967). Communication discrepancy and intent to persuade as determinants of counter-argument production. *Journal of Experimental Social Psychology, 3,* 269–309.

Brophy, J. E., & Good, T. L. (1974). *Teacher-student relationships: Causes and consequences.* New York: Holt, Rinehart & Winston.

Brotemarkle, R. A. (1927). College student personnel problems. *Journal of Applied Psychology, 11,* 415–436.

Brown, F. (1982). The ethics of psychodiagnostic assessment. In M. Rosenbaum (Ed.), *Ethics and values in psychotherapy.* New York: Free Press.

Brown, S. D., & Lent, R. W. (Eds.). (1984). *Handbook of counseling psychology.* New York: Wiley.

Brown, S. D., & Lent, R. W. (Eds.) (1992). *Handbook of counseling psychology* (2nd ed.). New York: Wiley.

Brown, S. D., Lent, R. W., Ryan, N. E., & McPartland, E. B. (1996). Self-efficacy as an intervening mechanism between research training environments and scholarly productivity: A theoretical and methological extension. *The Counseling Psychologist, 24,* 535–544.

Brown, W., & Holtzman, W. (1967). *Manual, Survey of study habits and attitudes.* New York: The Psychological Corporation.

Bryk, A. S., & Raudenbush, S. W. (1992). *Hierarchical linear models: Applications and data analysis methods.* Newbury Park, CA: Sage.

Bryk, A. S., Raudenbush, S. W., Seltzer, M., & Congdon, Jr., R. T. (1989). *An introduction to HLM: Computer program and user's guide.* Chicago: Scientific Software.

Buchler, J. (Ed.). (1955). *Philosophical writings of Peirce.* New York: Dover.

Burgoon, J. K., Beutler, L. E., Le Poire, B. A., Engle, D., Bergan, J., Salvio, M., & Mohr, D. C. (1993). Nonverbal indices of arousal in group therapy. *Psychotherapy, 30,* 635–645.

Burgoon, J. K., Kelly, D. L., Newton, D. A., & Keeley-Dyreson, M. P. (1989). The nature of arousal and nonverbal indices. *Human Communication Research, 16,* 217–255.

Burns, B. D. (1981). *Feeling good: The new mood therapy.* New York: The New American Library.

Burt, M. R. (1980). Cultural myths and supports for rape. *Journal of Personality and Social Psychology, 38,* 217–230.

Butcher, J. N., Dahlstrom, W. G., Graham, J. R., Tellegen, A., & Kaemmer B. (1989). *MMPI-2 manual for administration and scoring.* Minneapolis: University of Minnesota Press.

Butler, S. F., Henry, W. P., & Strupp, H. H. (1992). *Measuring adherence and skill in time-limited dynamic psychotherapy.* Unpublished manuscript, Vanderbilt University.

Calvin, A. D. (1954). Some misuses of the experimental method in evaluating the effect of client-centered counseling. *Journal of Counseling Psychology, 1,* 249–251.

Campbell, A., Converse, P. E., Miller, W. E., & Stokes, D. E. (1990). *The American voter.* New York: Wiley.

Campbell, D. T., & Fiske, D. W. (1959). Convergent and discriminant validation by the multitrait-multimethod matrix. *Psychological Bulletin, 56,* 81–105.

Campbell, D. T., & Stanley, J. C. (1963). *Experimental and quasi-experimental designs for research.* Chicago: Rand McNally.

Campbell, L. M., III. (1973). A variation of thought stopping in a twelve-year-old boy: A case report. *Journal of Behavior Therapy and Experimental Psychiatry, 4,* 69–70.

Caple, R. B. (1985). Counseling and the self-organization paradigm. *Journal of Counseling and Development, 64,* 173–178.

Carkhuff, R. R. (1968). A "non-traditional" assessment of graduate education in the helping professions. *Counselor Education and Supervision, 8,* 252–261.

Carkhuff, R. R., & Burstein, J. W. (1970). Objective therapist and client ratings of therapist-offered facilitative conditions of moderate to low functioning therapist. *Journal of Clinical Psychology, 26,* 394-395.

Carney, C. G., & Barak, A. (1976). A survey of student needs and student personnel services. *Journal of College Student Personnel, 17,* 280-284.

Casas, J. M., Ponterotto, J. G., & Gutierrez, J. M. (1986). An ethical indictment of counseling research and training: The cross-cultural perspective. *Journal of Counseling and Development, 64,* 347-349.

Cattell, R. B. (1966). The data box: Its ordering of total resources in terms of possible relational systems. In R. B. Cattell (Ed.), *Handbook of multivariate experimental psychology* (pp. 67-128). Chicago: Rand McNally.

Cattell, R. B., & Luborsky, L. B. (1950). P-technique demonstrated as a new clinical method for determining personality structure. *Journal of General Psychology, 42,* 3-24.

Chapman, L. J., & Chapman, J. P. (1969). Illusory correlations as an obstacle to the use of valid psychodiagnostic tests. *Journal of Abnormal Psychology, 74,* 271-280.

Chickering, A. W. (1969). *Education and identity.* San Francisco: Jossey Bass.

Christensen, L. B. (1980). *Experimental methodology* (2nd ed.). Boston: Allyn & Bacon.

Claiborn, C. D. (1982). Interpretation and change in counseling. *Journal of Counseling Psychology, 29,* 439-453.

Claiborn, C. D. (1984). Training students in research. In R. B. Pipes (Chair), *Basic issues faced by counseling psychology training programs.* Symposium conducted at the annual meeting of the American Psychological Association, Toronto, Canada.

Claiborn, C. D. (1985). Harold B. Pepinsky: A life of science and practice. *Journal of Counseling and Development, 64,* 5-13.

Claiborn, C. D. (1987). Science and practice: Reconsidering the Pepinskys. *Journal of Counseling and Development, 65,* 286-288.

Claiborn, C. D., & Lichtenberg, J. W. (1989). Interactional counseling. *The Counseling Psychologist, 17,* 355-453.

Cohen, J. (1968). Multiple regression as a general data-analytic strategy. *Psychological Bulletin, 70,* 426-443.

Cohen, J. (1988). *Statistical power analysis for the behavioral sciences* (2nd ed.). Hillsdale, NJ: Erlbaum.

Cohen, J., & Cohen, P. (1983). *Applied multiple regression/correlation analysis for the behavioral sciences* (2nd ed.). Hillsdale, NJ: Erlbaum.

Cohen, M. R., & Nagel, E. (1934). *An introduction to logic and scientific method.* New York: Harcourt, Brace & Company.

Cole, D. A. (1987). The utility of confirmatory factor analysis in test validation research. *Journal of Consulting and Clinical Psychology, 55,* 584-594.

Cole, D. A., Lazarick, D. L., & Howard, G. S. (1987). Construct validity and the relation between depression and social skill. *Journal of Counseling Psychology, 34,* 315-321.

Coleman, H. L. K., Wampold, B. E., & Casali, S. L. (1995). Ethnic minorities' ratings of ethnically similar and European American counselors: A meta-analysis. *Journal of Counseling Psychology, 42,* 55-64.

Condon, K. M., & Lambert, M. J. (1994). Assessing clinical significance: Application to the State-Trait Anxiety Inventory. Paper presented at the annual meeting of the Society for Psychotherapy Research, York, England, June 1994.

Conoley, J. C., Impara, J. C., & Murphy, L. L. (1995). *The twelfth mental measurements yearbook.* Lincoln, NE: Buros Institute of Mental Measurements.

Constantine, M. G., Quintana, S. M., Leung, S. A., & Phelps, R. E. (1995). Survey of the professional needs of division 17's ethnic and racial minority psychologists. *The Counseling Psychologist, 23,* 546-561.

Cook, E. P. (1990). Gender and psychological distress. *Journal of Counseling and Development, 68,* 371-375.

Cook, T. D., & Campbell, D. T. (1979). *Quasi-experimentation: Design and analysis issues for field settings.* Boston: Houghton Mifflin.

Cooke, R. A. (1982). The ethics and regulation of research involving children. In B. B. Wolman (Ed.), *Handbook of developmental psychology.* Englewood Cliffs, NJ: Prentice-Hall.

Coopersmith, S. (1981). *SEI, self-esteem inventories.* Palo Alto, CA: Consulting Psychologists Press.

Corazzini, J. (1980). The theory and practice of loss therapy. In B. Mark Schoenberg (Ed.), *Bereavement counseling: A multi-disciplinary handbook* (pp. 71–85). Westport, CT: Greenwood Press.

Corazzini, J., Heppner, P. P., & Young, M. D. (1980). The effects of cognitive information on termination from group counseling. *Journal of College Student Personnel, 21,* 553–557.

Corrigan, J. D., Dell, D. M., Lewis, K. N., & Schmidt, L. D. (1980). Counseling as a social influence process: A review [monograph]. *Journal of Counseling Psychology, 27,* 395–441.

Corrigan, J. D., & Schmidt, L. D. (1983). Development and validation of revisions in the counselor rating form. *Journal of Counseling Psychology, 30,* 64–75.

Cournoyer, R. J., & Mahalik, J. R. (1995). Cross-sectional study of gender role conflict examining college-aged and middle-aged men. *Journal of Counseling Psychology, 42,* 11–19.

Crites, J. O. (1978). *Career Maturity Inventory.* Monterey, CA: McGraw-Hill.

Crits-Christoph, P., Baranackie, K., Kurcias, J. S., Beck, A. T., Carroll, K., Perry, K., Luborsky, L., McLellan, A. T., Woody, G. E., Thompson, L., Gallagher, D., & Zitrin, C. (1991). Meta-analysis of therapist effects in psychotherapy outcome studies. *Psychotherapy Research, 1,* 81–91.

Cronbach, L. J., & Snow, R. E. (1976). *Aptitudes and instructional methods: A handbook for research on interactions.* New York: Irvington.

Crosbie, J. (1993). Interrupted times series analysis with brief single subject data. *Journal of Consulting and Clinical Psychology, 61,* 966–974.

Cross, W. E. (1971). The Negro to black conversion experience: Toward a psychology of black liberation. *Black World, 20* (9), 13–27.

Cross, W. E. (1978). The Cross and Thomas models of psychological nigresence. *Journal of Black Psychology, 5* (1), 13–19.

Cummings, A. L. (1989). Relationship of client problem type to novice counselor response modes. *Journal of Counseling Psychology, 36,* 331–335.

Cummings, A. L., Martin, J., Halberg, E., & Slemon, A. (1992). Memory for therapeutic events, session effectiveness, and working alliance in short-term counseling. *Journal of Counseling Psychology, 39,* 306–312.

Daniels, L. K. (1976). An extension of thought stopping in the treatment of obsessional thinking. *Behavior Therapy, 7,* 131.

Danskin, D. G., & Robinson, F. P. (1954). Differences in "degree of lead" among experienced counselors. *Journal of Counseling Psychology, 1,* 78–83.

Dar, R. (1987). Another look at Meehl, Lakatos, and the scientific practices of psychologists. *American Psychologist, 42,* 145–151.

Daus, J. A. III (1995). *Changes in counseling efficacy across a semester of group supervision: A time series analysis.* Unpublished doctoral dissertation, University of Missouri, Columbia.

Davis, H. T. (1941). *The analysis of economic time series.* Bloomington, IN: Principia Press.

Dawis, R. V. (1984). Of old philosophies and new kids on the block. *Journal of Counseling Psychology, 31,* 467–469.

Dawis, R. V. (1987). Scale construction. *Journal of Counseling Psychology, 34,* 481–489.

Deffenbacher, J. L. (1992). Counseling for anxiety management. In Stephen D. Brown & R. W. Lent (Eds.), *Handbook of counseling psychology* (pp. 719–756). New York: John Wiley & Sons.

Deffenbacher, J. L., Demm, P. M., & Brandon, A. D. (1986). High general anger: Correlates and treatment. *Behavior Research and Therapy, 24,* 481–489.

Deffenbacher, J. L., Lynch, R. S., Oetting, E. R., & Kemper, C. C. (1996). Anger reduction in early adolescents. *Journal of Counseling Psychology, 43,* 149–157.

Deffenbacher, J. L., & Stark, R. S. (1992). Relaxation and cognitive-relaxation treatment of general anger. *Journal of Counseling Psychology, 39,* 158–167.

Deffenbacher, J. L., Story, D. A., Stark, R. S., Hogg, J. A., & Brandon, S. L. (1987). Cognitive-relaxation and social skills interventions in the treatment of general anger. *Journal of Counseling Psychology, 34,* 171–176.

Deffenbacher, J. L., Thwaites, G. A., Wallace, T. L., & Oetting, E. R. (1994). Social skills and cognitive-relaxation approaches to general anger reduction. *Journal of Counseling Psychology, 41,* 386–396.

Denton, D. E. (1980). Understanding the life world of the counselor. *Personnel and Guidance Journal, 59,* 596–599.

Denzin, N. K. (1978). *The research act: A theoretical introduction to sociological methods.* New York: McGraw Hill.

Department of Health and Human Services. (1989). Responsibilities of awardee and applicant institutions for dealing with and reporting possible misconduct in science. *Federal Register, 54* (151), 32446–32451.

DeProspero, A., & Cohen, S. (1979). Inconsistent visual analysis of intrasubject data. *Journal of Applied Behavior Analysis, 12,* 573–579.

Derogatis, L. R. (1983). *SCL-90-R administration, scoring and procedures manual.* Towson, MD: Clinical Psychiatric Research.

Derogatis, L. R. (1992). *The Brief Symptom Inventory (BSI): Administration, scoring, and procedures manual II.* Baltimore, MD: Clinical Psychometric Research.

DeRubeis, R. J., Hollon, S. E., Evans, M. D., & Bemis, K. M. (1982). Can psychotherapies for depression be discriminated? A systematic investigation of cognitive therapy and interpersonal therapy. *Journal of Consulting and Clinical Psychology, 50,* 744–756.

DeSena, P. A. (1966). Problems of consistent over-, under-, and normal-achieving college students as identified by the Mooney Problem Checklist. *Journal of Educational Research, 59,* 351–355.

Diener, E., & Crandall, R. (1978). *Ethics in social and behavioral research.* Chicago: University of Chicago Press.

Diener, E., Emmons, R. A., Larsen, R. J., & Griffen, S. (1985). The Satisfaction with Life Scale. *Journal of Personality Assessment, 49,* 71–75.

Dill-Standifond, T. J., Stiles, W. B., & Rorer, L. G. (1988). Counselor-client agreement on session impact. *Journal of Counseling Psychology, 35,* 47–55.

Dipboye, W. J. (1954). Analysis of counselor style by discussion units. *Journal of Counseling Psychology, 1,* 21–26.

Dixon, D. N., & Claiborn, C. D. (1981). Effects of need and commitment on career exploration behaviors. *Journal of Counseling Psychology, 28,* 411–415.

Dixon, D. N., & Glover, J. A. (1984). *Counseling: A problem-solving approach.* New York: Wiley.

Dixon, D. N., Heppner, P. P., Petersen, C. H., & Ronning, R. R. (1979). Problem-solving workshop training. *Journal of Counseling Psychology, 26,* 133–139.

Dixon, W. A. (1989). *Self-appraised problem solving ability, stress, and suicide ideation in a college population.* Unpublished master's thesis, University of Missouri, Columbia.

Dolliver, R. H. (1969). Strong vocational blank versus expressed vocational interests: A review. *Psychological Bulletin, 72,* 95–107.

Dorn, F. J. (1985). *Publishing for professional development.* Muncie, IN: Accelerated Development.

Dorn, F. J. (Ed.). (1986). *Social influence processes in counseling and psychotherapy.* Springfield, IL: Charles C Thomas.

Dorn, F. J. (1988). Utilizing social influence in career counseling: A case study. *Career Development Quarterly, 36,* 269–280.

Douglas, J. D. (1985). *Creative interviewing.* Thousand Oaks, CA: Sage.

Dowd, E. T., & Boroto, D. R. (1982). Differential effects of counselor self-disclosure, self-involving statements, and interpretation. *Journal of Counseling Psychology, 29,* 8–13.

Drane, J. F. (1982). Ethics and psychotherapy: A philosophical perspective. In M. Rosenbaum (Ed.), *Ethics and values in psychotherapy: A guidebook.* New York: Free Press.

Drew, C. F. (1980). *Introduction to designing and conducting research* (2nd ed.). St. Louis: C. V. Mosby.

Drum, D., & Knott, E. (1977). *Structured groups for facilitating development: Acquiring life skills, resolving life themes, and making life transitions.* New York: Human Sciences Press.

D'Zurilla, T. J. (1986). *Problem-solving therapy: A social competence approach to clinical intervention.* New York: Springer.

Eagly, A. H. (1967). Involvement as a determinant of response to favorable information. *Journal of Personality and Social Psychology, 7,* 1–15.

Edgington, E. S. (1980). *Randomization tests.* New York: Marcel Dekker.

Edgington, E. (1982). Nonparametric tests for single-subject multiple schedule experiments. *Behavioral Assessment, 4,* 83–91.

Edgington, E. S. (1987). Randomized single-subject experiments and statistical tests. *Journal of Counseling Psychology, 34,* 437–442.

Egan, G. (1994). *The skilled helpers: A problem-management approach to helping* (5th ed.). Pacific Grove, CA: Brooks/Cole Publishing.

Elliott, R. (1979). How clients perceive helper behaviors. *Journal of Counseling Psychology, 26,* 285–294.

Elliott, R. (1985). Helpful and nonhelpful events in brief counseling interviews: An empirical taxonomy. *Journal of Counseling Psychology, 32,* 307–322.

Elliott, R. (1988). Issues in the selection, training, and management of raters. In R. Moras & C. E. Hill (Co-Chairs), *Selecting raters for psychotherapy process research.* Workshop conducted at the Society for Psychotherapy Research, Santa Fe, NM, June 1988.

Elliott, R. (1991). Five dimensions of therapy process. *Psychotherapy Research, 1,* 92–103.

Elliott, R., Hill, C. E., Stiles, W. B., Friedlander, M. L., Mahrer, A. R., & Margison, F. R. (1987). Primary therapist response modes: Comparison of six rating systems. *Journal of Consulting and Clinical Psychology, 55,* 218–223.

Elliott, R., & James, E. (1989). Varieties of client experience in psychotherapy: An analysis of the literature. *Clinical Psychology Review, 9,* 443–467.

Elliott, R., James, E., Reimschuessel, C., Cislo, D., & Sack, N. (1985). Significant events and the analysis of immediate therapeutic impacts. *Psychotherapy, 22,* 620–630.

Elliott, R., & Shapiro, D. A. (1988). Brief structured recall: A more efficient method for studying significant therapy events. *British Journal of Medical Psychology, 61,* 141–153.

Elliott, R., Shapiro, D. A., Firth-Cozens, J., Stiles, W. B., Hardy, G. E., Llewelyn, S. P., & Margison, F. R. (1994). Comprehensive process analysis of insight events in cognitive-behavioral and psychodynamic-interpersonal psychotherapies. *Journal of Counseling Psychology, 41,* 449–463.

Elliot, R., & Wexler, M. M. (1994). Measuring the impact of sessions in process-experiential therapy of depression: The session impacts scale. *Journal of Counseling Psychology, 41,* 166–174.

Ellis, A. (1962). *Reason and emotion in psychotherapy.* New York: Lyle Stuart.

Ellis, J. V., Robbins, E. S., Shult, D., Ladany, N., & Banker, J. (1990). Anchoring errors in clinical judgments: Type I error, adjustment, or mitigation. *Journal of Counseling Psychology, 37,* 343–351.

Ellis, M. V., Ladany, N., Krengel, M., & Schult, D. (1996). clinical supervision research from 1981 to 1993: A methological critique. *Journal of Counseling Psychology, 43,* 35–50.

Enns, C. Z., McNeilly, C. L., Corkery, J. M., & Gilbert, M. S. (1995). The debate about delayed memories of child sexual abuse: A feminist perspective. *The Counseling Psychologist, 23,* 181–279.

Epperson, D. L., & Pecnik, J. A. (1985). Counselor Rating Form–short version: Further validation and comparison to the long form. *Journal of Counseling Psychology, 32,* 143–146.

Ericsson, K. A., & Simon, H. A. (1984). *Protocol analysis: Verbal reports as data.* Cambridge, MA: MIT Press.

Eugster, S. L., & Wampold, B. E. (1996). Systematic effects of participant role on evaluation of the psychotherapy session. *Journal of Consulting and Clinical Psychology, 64,* 1020–1028.

Exner, J. E., Jr. (1974). *The Rorschach: A comprehensive system (Vol. 1).* New York: Wiley.

Eysenck, H. J. (1952). The effects of psychotherapy: An evaluation. *Journal of Consulting Psychology, 16,* 319–324.

Eysenck, H. J. (1960). *Behavior therapy and the neuroses.* Oxford: Pergamon Press.

Eysenck, H. J. (1961). The effects of psychotherapy. In H. J. Eysenck (Ed.), *Handbook of abnormal psychology* (pp. 697–725). New York: Basic Books.

Eysenck, H. J. (1965). The effects of psychotherapy. *International Journal of Psychology, 1,* 97–178.

Eysenck, H. J. (1969). *The effects of psychotherapy.* New York: Science House.

Fagley, N. S. (1985). Applied statistical power analysis and the interpretation of non-significant results by research consumers. *Journal of Counseling Psychology, 32,* 391–396.

Farmer, H. (1985). Model of career and achievement motivation for women and men. *Journal of Counseling Psychology, 32,* 363–390.

Farmer, H. S., Wardrop, J. L., Anderson, M. Z., & Risinger, R. (1995). Women's career choices: Focus on science, math, and technology careers. *Journal of Counseling Psychology, 42,* 155–170.

Farrell, A. D., & McCullough, L. (1989). *User's manual for the Computerized Assessment System for Psychotherapy Evaluation and Research, Version 3.1.* Richmond, VA: Virginia Commonwealth University, Department of Psychology.

Fassinger, R. E. (1987). Use of structural equation modeling in counseling psychology research. *Journal of Counseling Psychology, 34,* 425–436.

Fassinger, R. (1990). Causal models of career choice in two samples of college women. *Journal of Vocational Behavior, 36,* 225–248.

Fassinger, R. E., & Richie, B. S. (1997). Sex matters: Gender and sexual orientation in training for multicultural counseling competency. In D. B. Pope-Davis & H. L. K. Coleman (Eds.), *Multicultural counseling competencies: Assessment, education and training, and supervision* (pp. 83–110). Thousand Oaks, CA: Sage.

Feldman, D. A., Strong, S. R., & Danser, D. B. (1982). A comparison of paradoxical and non-paradoxical interpretations and directives. *Journal of Counseling Psychology, 29,* 572–579.

Fiske, S. T., & Taylor, S. E. (1984). *Social cognition.* Reading, MA: Addison-Wesley.

Fitzgerald, L. F., & Hubert, L. J. (1987). Multidimensional scaling: Some possibilities for counseling psychology. *Journal of Counseling Psychology, 34,* 469–480.

Foa, E. B., Rothbaum, B. O., Riggs, D. S., & Murdock, T. B. (1991). Treatment of posttraumatic stress disorder in rape victims: A comparison between cognitive-behavioral procedures and counseling. *Journal of Consulting and Clinical Psychology, 59,* 715–723.

Folger, R. (1989). Significance tests and the duplicity of binary decisions. *Psychological Bulletin, 106,* 155–160.

Folkman, S., & Lazarus, R. S. (1980). An analysis of coping in a middle-aged community sample. *Journal of Health and Social Behavior, 21,* 219–239.

Fong, M. L. (1992). When a survey isn't research. *Counselor Education and Supervision, 31,* 194–195.

Fong, M. L., & Malone, C. M. (1994). Defeating ourselves: Common errors in counseling research. *Counselor Education and Supervision, 33,* 356–362.

Fontana, A., & Frey, J. H. (1994). Interviewing: The art of science. In N. K. Denzin & Y. S. Lincoln (Eds.), *Handbook of qualitative research* (pp. 361–376). Thousand Oaks, CA: Sage.

Ford, D. H. (1984). Reexamining guiding assumptions: Theoretical and methodological implications. *Journal of Counseling Psychology, 31,* 461–466.

Forgy, E. W., & Black, J. D. (1954). A follow-up after three years of clients counseled by two methods. *Journal of Counseling Psychology, 1,* 1–8.

Fouad, N. A., Cudeck, R., & Hansen, J. (1984). Convergent validity of Spanish and English forms of the Strong-Campbell Interest Inventory for bilingual Hispanic high school students. *Journal of Counseling Psychology, 31,* 339–348.

Fowler, F. (1993). *Survey research methods* (2nd ed.). Newbury Park, CA: Sage.

Francis, D. J., Fletcher, J. M., Stuebing, K. K., Davidson, K. C., & Thompson, N. M. (1991). Analysis of change: Modeling individual growth. *Journal of Consulting and Clinical Psychology, 59,* 27–37.

Frank, G. (1984). The Boulder model: History, rationale, and critique. *Professional Psychology: Research and Practice, 15,* 417–435.

Frank, J. D. (1961). *Persuasion and healing: A comparative study of psychotherapy.* Baltimore: Johns Hopkins University Press.

Frank, J. D. (1974). Therapeutic components of psychotherapy. *Journal of Nervous and Mental Disease, 159,* 325–342.

Frankena, W. K. (1963). *Ethics.* Englewood Cliffs, NJ: Prentice-Hall.

Fremont, S., & Anderson, W. P. (1986). What client behaviors make counselors angry? An exploratory study. *Journal of Counseling and Development, 65,* 67–70.

Fretz, B. R. (1981). Evaluating the effectiveness of career interventions. *Journal of Counseling Psychology, 28,* 77–90.

Fretz, B. R. (1982). Perspective and definitions. *The Counseling Psychologist, 101*(2), 15–19.

Friedlander, M. L., Ellis, M. V., Siegel, S. M., Raymond, L., Haase, R. F., & Highlen, P. S. (1988). Generalizing from segments to sessions: Should it be done? *Journal of Counseling Psychology, 35,* 243–250.

Friedlander, M. L., Heatherington, L., Johnson, B., & Showron, E. A. (1994). Sustaining engagement: A change event in family therapy. *Journal of Counseling Psychology, 41,* 438–448.

Friedlander, M. L., & Schwartz, G. S. (1985). Toward a theory of self-presentation in counseling and psychotherapy. *Journal of Counseling Psychology, 32,* 483–501.

Friedlander, M. L., Siegel, S. M., & Brenock, K. (1989). Parallel processes in counseling and supervision: A case study. *Journal of Counseling Psychology, 36,* 149–157.

Friedlander, M. L., Thibodeau, J. R., & Ward, L. G. (1985). Discriminating the "good" from the "bad" therapy hour: A study of dyadic interaction. *Psychotherapy, 22,* 631–642.

Friedlander, M. L., Thibodeau, J. R., Nichols, M. P., Tucker, C., & Snyder, J. (1985). Introducing semantic cohesion analysis: A study of group talk. *Small Group Behavior, 16,* 285–302.

Friedman, N. (1967). *The social nature of psychological research.* New York: Basic Books.

Friesen, W. V., & Ekman, P. (1984). *EMFACS-7: Emotional facial action coding system.* Unpublished manual.

Frontman, K. C., & Kunkel, M. A. (1994). A grounded theory of counselors' construal of success in the initial session. *Journal of Counseling Psychology, 41,* 492–499.

Fuchs, C. Z., & Rehm, L. P. (1977). A self-control behavior therapy program for depression. *Journal of Consulting and Clinical Psychology, 45,* 206–215.

Fuhriman, A., & Burlingame, G. M. (1990). Consistency of matter: A comparative analysis of individual and group process variables. *The Counseling Psychologist, 1*(18), 6–63.

Fuhriman, A., & Burlingame, G. M. (1994). Group psychotherapy: Research and practice. In A. Fuhriman & G. M. Burlingame (Eds.), *Handbook of group psychotherapy* (pp. 3–40). New York: Wiley.

Fuller, F., & Hill, C. E. (1985). Counselor and helpee perceptions of counselor intentions in relation to outcome in a single counseling session. *Journal of Counseling Psychology, 32,* 329–338.

Furlong, M. J., & Wampold, B. E. (1982). Intervention effects and relative variation as dimensions in experts' use of visual inference. *Journal of Applied Behavior Analysis, 15,* 415–421.

Furst, J. B., & Cooper, A. (1970). Combined use of imaginal and interoceptive stimuli in desensitizing fear of heart attacks. *Journal of Behavior Therapy and Experimental Psychiatry, 1,* 87–89.

Gade, E., Fuqua, D., & Hurlburt, G. (1988). The relationship of Holland's personality types to educational satisfaction with a native American high school population. *Journal of Counseling Psychology, 35,* 183–186.

Gadlin, H., & Ingle, G. (1975). Through the one-way mirror, the limits of experimental self-reflection. *American Psychologist, 30,* 1003–1009.

Gaffan, E. A., Tsaousis, I., & Kemp-Wheeler, S. M. (1995). Researcher allegiance and meta-analysis: The case of cognitive therapy for depression. *Journal of Consulting and Clinical Psychology, 63,* 966–980.

Gambrill, E. (1990). *Critical thinking in clinical practice.* San Francisco: Jossey Bass.

Garfield, S. L. (1993). Major issues in psychotherapy research. In D. K. Freedheim (Ed.), *History of psychotherapy* (pp. 335–360). Washington, DC: American Psychological Association.

Garfield, S. L., & Bergin, A. E. (Eds.). (1978). *Handbook of psychotherapy and behavior change* (2nd ed.). New York: Wiley.

Garfield, S. L., & Bergin, A. E. (Eds.). (1986). *Handbook of psychotherapy and behavior change* (3rd ed.). New York: Wiley.

Garfield, S. L., & Bergin, A. E. (Eds.). (1994). *Handbook of psychotherapy and behavior change,* 4th ed. New York: Wiley.

Gelatt, H. B. (1989). Positive uncertainty: A new decision-making framework for counseling. *Journal of Counseling Psychology, 36,* 252–256.

Gelso, C. J. (1979). Research in counseling: Methodological and professional issues. *The Counseling Psychologist, 8*(3), 7–35.

Gelso, C. J. (1982). Editorial. *Journal of Counseling Psychology, 29,* 3–7.

Gelso, C. J. (1985). Rigor, relevance, and counseling research: On the need to maintain our course between Scylla and Charybdis. *Journal of Counseling and Development, 63,* 551–553.

Gelso, C. J. (1993). On the making of a scientist-practitioner: A theory of research training in professional psychology. *Professional Psychology: Research and Practice, 24,* 468–476.

Gelso, C. J. (1997). The making of a scientist in applied psychology: An attribute by treatment conception. *The Counseling Psychologist, 25,* 307–320.

Gelso, C. J., Betz, N. E., Friedlander, M. L., Helms, J. E., Hill, C. E., Patton, M. J., Super, D. E., & Wampold, B. E. (1988). Research in counseling psychology: Prospects and recommendations. *The Counseling Psychologist, 16,* 385–406.

Gelso, C. J., & Carter, J. A. (1994). Components of the psychotherapy relationship: Their interaction and unfolding during treatment. *Journal of Counseling Psychology, 41,* 296–306.

Gelso, C. J., & Fassinger, R. E. (1990). Counseling psychology: Theory and research on interventions. *Annual Review of Psychology, 41,* 355–386.

Gelso, C. J., Mallinckrodt, B., & Judge, A. B. (1996). Research training environment, attitudes toward research, and research self-efficacy: The revised research training environment scale. *The Counseling Psychologist, 24,* 304–322.

Gelso, C. J., Mallinckrodt, B., & Royalty, G. M. (1991). *The Research Training Environment Scale* [test in microfiche]. Princeton, NJ: Educational Testing Service.

Gelso, C. J., Raphael, R., Black, S. M., Rardin, D., & Skalkos, O. (1983). Research training in counseling psychology: Some preliminary data. *Journal of Counseling Psychology, 30,* 611–614.

Gelso, C. J., & Wampold, B. E. (Ed.). (1987). Quantitative foundation of counseling psychology research [special issue]. *Journal of Counseling Psychology, 24.*

Glaser, B. G. (1992). *Emergence vs. forcing: Basics of grounded theory analysis.* Mill Valley, CA: Sociology Press.

Glaser, B., & Strauss, A. (1967). *The discovery of grounded theory: Strategies for qualitative research.* Chicago: Aldine.

Glass, G. V., Willson, V. L., & Gottman, J. M. (1974). *Design and analysis of time-series experiments.* Boulder, CO: Colorado Associated University Press.

Gleitman, H. (1986). *Psychology* (2nd ed.). New York: Norton.

Glock, C. Y. (Ed.). (1967). *Survey research in the social sciences.* New York: Russell Sage Foundation.

Gold, R. L. (1958). Roles in sociological field observations. *Social Forces, 36,* 217–223.

Goldman, L. (1976). A revolution in counseling research. *Journal of Counseling Psychology, 23,* 543–552.

Goldman, L. (1977). Toward more meaningful research. *Personnel and Guidance Journal, 55,* 363–368.

Goldman, L. (Ed.). (1978). *Research methods for counselors: Practical approaches in field settings.* New York: Wiley.

Goldman, L. (1982). Defining non-traditional research. *The Counseling Psychologist, 10*(4), 87–89.

Goldstein, A. P., Heller, K., & Sechrest, L. B. (1966). *Psychotherapy and the psychology of behavior change.* New York: Wiley.

Good, G. E., Gilbert, L. A., & Scher, M. (1990). Gender aware therapy: A synthesis of feminist therapy and knowledge about gender. *Journal of Counseling and Development, 68,* 376–380.

Good, G. E., Robertson, J. M., O'Neil, J. M., Fitzgerald, L. F., Stevens, M., DeBord, K. A., Bartels, K. M., & Braverman, D. G. (1995). Male gender role conflict: Psychometric issues and relations to psychological distress. *Journal of Counseling Psychology, 42,* 3–10.

Good, G. E., Thoreson, R. W., & Shaughnessy, P. (1995). Substance use, confrontation of impaired colleagues, and psychological functioning among counseling psychologists: A national survey. *The Counseling Psychologist, 23,* 703–721.

Goodyear, R. K., & Benton, S. (1986). The roles of science and research in the counselor's work. In A. J. Palmo & W. J. Weikel (Eds.), *Foundations of mental health counseling* (pp. 287–308). Springfield, IL: Charles C Thomas.

Gottfredson, G. D., & Holland, J. L. (1990). A longitudinal test of the influence of congruence: Job satisfaction, competency utilization, and counterproductive behavior. *Journal of Counseling Psychology, 37,* 389–398.

Gottman, J. M. (1973). N-of-one and N-of-two research in psychotherapy. *Psychological Bulletin, 80,* 93–105.

Gottman, J. M. (1979). Detecting cyclicity in social interaction. *Psychological Bulletin, 86,* 338–348.

Gottman, J. M., & Markman, H. J. (1978). Experimental designs in psychotherapy research. In S. L. Garfield & A. E. Bergin (Eds.), *Handbook of psychotherapy and behavior change,* 2nd ed. (pp. 23–62). New York: Wiley.

Gottman, J. M., McFall, R. M., & Barnett, J. T. (1969). Design and analysis of research using time series. *Psychological Bulletin, 72,* 299–306.

Gottman, J. M., & Roy, A. K. (1990). *Sequential analysis.* Cambridge: Cambridge University Press.

Gottschalk, L. A., & Gleser, C. G. (1969). *The measurement of psychological states through the content analysis of verbal behavior.* Berkeley, CA: University of California Press.

Graham, J. R. (1990). *MMPI-2: Assessing personality and psychopathology.* New York: Oxford University Press.

Greenberg, L. S. (1986a). Change process research. *Journal of Consulting and Clinical Psychology, 54,* 4–9.

Greenberg, L. S. (1986). Research strategies. In L. S. Greenberg & W. M. Pinsof (Eds.), *The psychotherapeutic process: A research handbook*. New York: Guilford.

Greenberg, L. S., and Foerster, F. S. (1996). Task analysis exemplified: The process of resolving unfinished business. *Journal of Consulting and Clinical Psychology, 64,* 439–446.

Greenberg, L. S., & Newman, F. L. (1996). An approach to psychotherapy change process research: Introduction to the special section. *Journal of Consulting and Clinical Psychology, 64,* 435–438.

Greenberg, L. S., & Pinsof, W. (Eds.). (1986). *The psychotherapeutic process: A research handbook*. New York: Guilford.

Greenwald, A. G. (1968). Cognitive learning, cognitive response to persuasion, and attitude change. In A. G. Greenwald, T. C. Brock, & T. M. Ostrom (Eds.), *Psychological foundations of attitudes* (pp. 147–190). New York: Academic Press.

Grummon, D. L., & Butler, J. M. (1953). Another failure to replicate Keet's study, two verbal techniques in a miniature counseling situation. *Journal of Abnormal and Social Psychology, 48,* 597.

Grundy, C. T., & Lambert, M. J. (1994a). Assessing clinical significance: Application to the Hamilton Rating Scale for Depression. Paper presented at the annual meeting of the Society for Psychotherapy Research, York, England, June 1994.

Grundy, C. T., & Lambert, M. J. (1994b). Assessing clinical significance: Application to the Child Behavior Checklist. Paper presented at the annual meeting of the Society for Psychotherapy Research, York, England, June 1994.

Gurin, G., Veroff, J., & Feld, S. (1960). *Americans view their mental health*. New York: Basic Books.

Gurman, A. S. (1977). The patient's perception of the therapeutic relationship. In A. S. Gurman & A. M. Razin (Eds.), *Effective psychotherapy: A handbook of research* (pp. 503–543). New York: Pergamon Press.

Gurman, A. S., & Razin, A. M. (Eds.). (1977). *Effective psychotherapy: A handbook of research*. New York: Pergamon Press.

Gustav, A. (1962). Students' attitudes toward compulsory participation in experiments. *Journal of Psychology, 53,* 119–125.

Gysbers, N. C., & Associates. (1984). *Designing careers: Counseling to enhance the quality of education, work, and leisure*. San Francisco: Jossey-Bass.

Gysbers, N. C., & Henderson, P. (1988). *Developing and managing your school guidance program*. Washington, DC: American Association for Counseling and Development.

Gysbers, N. C., Heppner, M. J., & Johnston, J. A. (1998). *Career counseling process, issues, and techniques*. Needham Heights, MA: Allyn & Bacon.

Haase, R. F., Waechter, D. M., & Solomon, G. S. (1982). How significant is a significant-difference? Average effect size of research in counseling psychology. *Journal of Counseling Psychology, 29,* 58–65.

Hackett, G. (1981). Survey research methods. *Personnel and Guidance Journal, 59,* 599–604.

Hair, J. F., Jr., Anderson, R. E., & Tatham, R. L. (1987). *Multivariate data analysis: With readings* (2nd ed.). New York: Macmillan.

Hanfling, O. (1981). *Logical positivism*. Oxford: Blackwell.

Hardin, S. I., Subich, L. M., & Holvey, J. M. (1988). Expectancies for counseling in relation to premature termination. *Journal of Counseling Psychology, 35,* 37–40.

Harmon, L. (1977). Career counseling for women. In E. Rawlings & D. Carter (Eds.), *Psychotherapy for women*. Springfield, IL: Charles C. Thomas.

Harmon, L. W. (1981). The life and career plans of young adult college women: A follow-up study. *Journal of Counseling Psychology, 28,* 416–427.

Harmon, L. (1982). Scientific affairs: The next decade. *The Counseling Psychologist, 10*(2), 31–38.

Harmon, L. W. (1989). Changes in women's career aspirations over time: Developmental or historical. *Journal of Vocational Behavior, 33,* 46–65.

Harre, R. (1950). *Social being: A theory for social psychology.* Totowa, NJ: Littlefield Adams.

Harre, R. (1970). *The principles of scientific thinking.* Chicago: University of Chicago Press.

Harre, R. (1972). *Philosophies of science: An introductory survey.* Oxford, England: Oxford University Press.

Harre, R. (1974). Blueprint for a new science. In A. Nigel (Ed.), *Reconstructing social psychology.* Baltimore: Penguin Books.

Harre, R. (1980). *Social being: A theory of social psychology.* Totowa, NJ: Rowman & Littlefield.

Hartley, D. E., & Strupp, H. H. (1983). The therapeutic alliance: Its relationship to outcome in brief psychotherapy. In J. Masling (Ed.), *Empirical studies of psycho-analytic theories* (Vol. 1, pp. 1–37). Hillsdale, NJ: The Analytic Press.

Harvey, O. J., Hunt, D. E., & Schroder, H. M. (1961). *Conceptual systems and personality organization.* New York: Wiley.

Hathaway, S. R., & McKinley, J. C. (1942). A multiphasic personality schedule (Minnesota): III. The measurement of symptomatic depression. *The Journal of Psychology, 14,* 73–84.

Hathaway, S. R., & McKinley, J. C. (1967). *MMPI manual* (rev. ed.). New York: Psychological Corporation.

Haupt, S. G. (1990). *Client Christian belief issues in psychotherapy.* Unpublished doctoral dissertation, University of Missouri, Columbia.

Hays, W. L. (1988). *Statistics* (4th ed.). New York: Holt, Rinehart & Winston.

Hazaleus, S. L., & Deffenbacher, J. L. (1986). Relaxation and cognitive treatments of anger. *Journal of Consulting and Clinical Psychology, 54,* 222–226.

Heesacker, M., Elliott, T. R., & Howe, L. A. (1988). Does the Holland code predict job satisfaction and productivity in clothing factory workers? *Journal of Counseling Psychology, 35,* 144–148.

Heesacker, M., & Heppner, P. P. (1983). Using real-client perceptions to examine psychometric properties of the Counselor Rating Form. *Journal of Counseling Psychology, 30,* 180–187.

Heller, K. (1971). Laboratory interview research as an analogue to treatment. In A. E. Bergin & S. L. Garfield (Eds.), *Handbook of psychotherapy and behavior change* (pp. 126–153). New York: Wiley.

Helms, J. E. (1976). Comparison of two types of counseling analogue. *Journal of Counseling Psychology, 23,* 422–427.

Helms, J. E. (1978). Counselor reactions to female clients: Generalizing from analogue research to a counseling setting. *Journal of Counseling Psychology, 25,* 193–199.

Helms, J. E. (1990). *Black and white racial identity: Theory, research, and practice.* Westport, CT: Greenwood Press.

Helms, J. E. (1994). How multiculturalism obscures racial factors in the therapy process: Comment on Ridley et al. (1994), Sodowsky et. al. (1994), Ottavi et. al. (1994), and Thompson et al. (1994). *Journal of Counseling Psychology, 41,* 162–165.

Henry, W. P., Schacht, T. E., & Strupp, H. H. (1986). Structural analysis of social behavior: Application to a study of interpersonal processes in differential psychotherapeutic outcome. *Journal of Consulting and Clinical Psychology, 54,* 27–31.

Henry, W. P., Strupp, H. H., Butler, S. F., Schacht, T. E., & Binder, J. L. (1993). Effects of training in time-limited dynamic psychotherapy: Changes in therapist behavior. *Journal of Consulting and Clinical Psychology, 61,* 434–440.

Heppner, M. J., & Hendrichs, F. (1995). A process and outcome study examining career indecision and indecisiveness. *Journal of Counseling and Development, 73,* 426–437.

Heppner, M. J., Multon, K. D., & Johnston, J. A. (1994). Assessing psychological resources during career change: Development of the career transitions inventory. *Journal of Vocational Behavior, 44,* 55–74.

Heppner, P. P. (1978a). A review of the problem-solving literature and its relationship to the counseling process. *Journal of Counseling Psychology, 25,* 366–375.

Heppner, P. P. (1978b). The clinical alteration of covert thoughts: A critical review. *Behavior Therapy, 9,* 717–734.

Heppner, P. P. (1979). The effects of client perceived need and counselor role on clients' behaviors (doctoral dissertation, University of Nebraska, 1979). *Dissertation Abstracts International, 39,* 5950A–5951A. (University Microfilms No. 79-07,542)

Heppner, P. P. (1989). Identifying the complexities within clients' thinking and decision-making. *Journal of Counseling Psychology, 36,* 257–259.

Heppner, P. P. (1995). On gender role conflict in men: Future directions and implications for counseling: Comment on Good et al. (1995) and Cournoyer and Mahalik (1995). *Journal of Counseling Psychology, 42,* 20–23.

Heppner, P. P., & Anderson, W. P. (1985). On the perceived non-utility of research in counseling. *Journal of Counseling and Development, 63,* 545–547.

Heppner, P. P., Baumgardner, A. H., Larson, L. M., & Petty, R. E. (1988). The utility of problem-solving training that emphasizes self-management principles. *Counseling Psychology Quarterly, 1,* 129–143.

Heppner, P. P., Carter, J., Claiborn, C. D., Brooks, L., Gelso, C. J., Fassinger, R. E., Holloway, E. L., Stone, G. L., Wampold, B. E., & Galani, J. P. (1992). A proposal to integrate science and practice in counseling psychology. *The Counseling Psychologist, 20,* 107–122.

Heppner, P. P., & Claiborn, C. D. (1989). Social influence research in counseling: A review and critique [monograph]. *Journal of Counseling Psychology, 36,* 365–387.

Heppner, P. P., & Dixon, D. N. (1981). A review of the interpersonal influence process in counseling. *Personnel and Guidance Journal, 59,* 542–550.

Heppner, P. P, & Frazier, P. A. (1992). Social psychological processes in psychotherapy: Extrapolating basic research to counseling psychology. In S. D. Brown & R. W. Lent (Eds.), *Handbook of Counseling Psychology* (2nd ed.). New York: Wiley.

Heppner, P. P., Gelso, C. J., & Dolliver, R. H. (1987). Three approaches to research training in counseling. *Journal of Counseling and Development, 66,* 45–49.

Heppner, P. P., Kivlighan, D. M., Jr., Good, G., Roehlke, H. J., Hills, H. I., & Ashby, J. S. (1994). Presenting problems of university counseling center clients: A snapshot and a multivariate classification scheme. *Journal of Counseling Psychology, 41,* 315–324.

Heppner, P. P., & Krauskopf, C. J. (1987). An information-processing approach to personal problem solving. *The Counseling Psychologist, 15*(3), 371–447.

Heppner, P. P., & Neal, G. W. (1983). Holding up the mirror: Research on the roles and functions of counseling centers in higher education. *The Counseling Psychologist, 11*(1), 81–89.

Heppner, P. P., & Petersen, C. H. (1982). The development and implications of a personal problem-solving inventory. *Journal of Counseling Psychology, 29,* 66–75.

Heppner, P. P., & Roehlke, H. J. (1984). Differences among supervisees at different levels of training: Implications for a developmental model of supervision. *Journal of Counseling Psychology, 31,* 76–90.

Heppner, P. P., Rogers, M. E., & Lee, L. A. (1984). Carl Rogers: Reflections on his life. *Journal of Counseling and Development, 63,* 14–20.

Heppner, P. P., Rosenberg, J. I., & Hedgespeth J. (1992). Three methods in measuring the therapeutic process: Clients' and counselors' constructions of the therapeutic process versus actual therapeutic events. *Journal of Counseling Psychology, 39,* 20–31.

Herman, J., Morris, L., & Fitz-Gibbon, C. (1987). *Evaluator's handbook.* Newbury Park, CA: Sage Publications.

Hermansson, G. L., Webster, A. C., & McFarland, K. (1988). Counselor deliberate postural lean and communication of facilitative conditions. *Journal of Counseling Psychology, 35,* 149–153.

Hersen, M., & Barlow, D. H. (1976). *Single case experimental designs: Strategies for studying behavior change.* New York: Pergamon Press.

Highlen, P. S., & Finely, H. C. (1996). Doing qualitative analysis. In F. T. L. Leong & J. T. Austine (Eds.), *The psychotherapy research handbook: A guide for graduate students and research assistants* (pp. 177–192). Thousand Oaks, CA: Sage.

Highlen, P. S., & Hill, C. E. (1984). Factors affecting client change in counseling: Current status and theoretical speculations. In S. D. Brown & R. W. Lent (Eds.), *Handbook of counseling psychology* (pp. 334–396). New York: Wiley.

Hill, C. E. (1982). Counseling process researcher: Philosophical and methodological dilemmas. *The Counseling Psychologist, 10*(4), 7–20.

Hill, C. E. (1984). A personal account of the process of becoming a counseling process researcher. *The Counseling Psychologist, 12*(3), 99–109.

Hill, C. E. (1985). *Manual for the Hill Counselor Verbal Response Modes Category System* (rev. ed.). Unpublished manuscript, University of Maryland.

Hill, C. E. (1990). A review of exploratory in-session process research. *Journal of Consulting and Clinical Psychology, 58,* 288–294.

Hill, C. E. (1991). *Almost everything you ever wanted to know about how to do process research on counseling and psychotherapy but didn't know how to ask.* In C. E. Watkins, Jr. & L. J. Scheider (Eds.), *Research in counseling.* Hillsdale, NJ: Lawrence Erlbaum.

Hill, C. E. (1992). Research on therapist techniques in brief individual therapy: Implications for practitioners. *The Counseling Psychologist, 20,* 689–711.

Hill, C. E. (1997). The effects of my research training environment: Where are my students now? *The Counseling Psychologist, 25,* 74–81.

Hill, C. E., Carter, J. A., & O'Farrell, M. K. (1983). A case study of the process and outcome of time-limited counseling. *Journal of Counseling Psychology, 30,* 3–18.

Hill, C. E., Greenwald, C., Reed, K. A., Charles, D., O'Farrell, M. K., & Carter, J. A. (1981). *Manual for the counselor and client verbal response category systems.* Columbus, OH: Marathon Consulting and Press.

Hill, C. E., & Gronsky, B. R. (1984). Researcher: Why and how? In J. M. Whiteley, N. Kagan, L. W. Harmon, B. R. Fretz, & F. Tanney (Eds.), *The coming decade in counseling psychology* (pp. 149–159). Schenectady, NY: Character Researcher Press.

Hill, C. E., Helms, J. E., Spiegel, S. B., & Tichenor, V. (1988). Development of a system for categorizing client reactions to therapist interventions. *Journal of Counseling Psychology, 35,* 27–36.

Hill, C. E., Helms, J. E., Tichenor, V., Spiegel, S. B., O'Grady, K. E., & Perry, E. S. (1988). Effects of therapist response modes in brief psychotherapy. *Journal of Counseling Psychology, 35,* 222–233.

Hill, C. E., & O'Grady, K. E. (1985). List of therapist intentions illustrated in a case study and with therapists of varying theoretical orientations. *Journal of Counseling Psychology, 32,* 3–22.

Hill, C. E., & Stephany, A. (1990). Relation of nonverbal behavior to client reactions. *Journal of Counseling Psychology, 37,* 22–26.

Hill, C. E., Thompson, B. J., & Williams, E. N. (1997). A guide to consensual qualitative research. *The Counseling Psychologist, 25,* 517–572.

Hill, W. F. (1965). *HIM: Hill Interaction Matrix.* Los Angeles: University of Southern California, Youth Study Center.

Hilliard, R. B. (1993). Single-case methodology in psychotherapy process and outcome research. *Journal of Consulting and Clinical Psychology, 61,* 373–380.

Hines, P. L., Stockton, R., & Morran, D. K. (1995). Self-talk of group therapists. *Journal of Counseling Psychology, 42,* 242–248.

Hoch, P. H., & Zubin, J. (Eds.). (1964). *The evaluation of psychiatric treatment.* New York: Grune & Stratton.

Hodder, I. (1994). The interpretation of documents and material culture. In N. K. Denzin & Y. S. Lincoln (Eds.), *Handbook of qualitative research* (pp. 393–402). Thousand Oaks, CA: Sage.

Hoffman, J., & Weiss, B. (1987). Family dynamics and presenting problems in college students. *Journal of Counseling Psychology, 34,* 157–163.

Hogg, J. A., & Deffenbacher, J. L. (1988). A comparison of cognitive and interpersonal-process group therapies in the treatment of depression among college students. *Journal of Counseling Psychology, 35,* 304–310.

Hohmann, A. A., & Parron, D. L. (1996). How the new NIH guidelines on inclusion of women and minorities apply: Efficacy trials, effectiveness trials, and validity. *Journal of Consulting and Clinical Psychology, 64,* 851–855.

Holland, J. L. (1985a). *Making vocational choices: A theory of vocational personalities and work environments.* Englewood Cliffs, NJ: Prentice-Hall.

Holland, J. L. (1985b). *Professional manual for the Self-Directed Search* (3rd ed.). Palo Alto, CA: Consulting Psychologists Press.

Holland, J. L. (1986). Student selection, training, and research performance. *The Counseling Psychologist, 14*(1), 121–125.

Holland, J. L. (1987). *Manual supplement for the Self-Directed Search.* Odessa, FL: Psychological Assessment Resources.

Holland, J. L. (1992). *Making vocational choices: A theory of vocational personalities and work environment* (2nd ed.). Odessa, FL: Psychological Assessment Resources.

Holland, J. L., Daiger, D. C., & Power, P. G. (1980). Some diagnostic scales for research in decision-making and personality: Identity, information, and barriers. *Journal of Personality and Social Psychology, 39,* 1191–1200.

Holland, P. W. (1986). Statistics and causal inference. *Journal of the American Statistical Association, 81,* 945–960.

Hollon, S. D. (1996). The efficacy and effectiveness of psychotherapy relative to medications. *American Psychologist, 51,* 1025–1030.

Hollon, S. D., & Kendall, D. C. (1980). Cognitive self-statements in depression: Development of an Automatic Thoughts Questionnaire. *Cognitive Therapy and Research, 4,* 383–395.

Holloway, E. L. (1987). Developmental models of supervision: Is it development? *Professional Psychology; Research and Practice, 18,* 209–216.

Holloway, E. L. (1992). Supervision: A way of teaching and learning. In. S. D. Brown & R. W. Lent (Eds.), *Handbook of counseling psychology* (2nd ed.) (pp. 177–214). New York: Wiley.

Holloway, E. L. (1995). *Clinical supervision: A systems approach.* Thousand Oaks, CA: Sage.

Holloway, E. L., Freund, R. D., Gardner, S. L., Nelson, M. L., & Walker, B. R. (1989). Relation of power and involvement to theoretical orientation in supervision: An analysis of discourse. *Journal of Counseling Psychology, 36,* 88–102.

Holloway, E. L., & Wampold, B. E. (1986). Relation between conceptual level and counseling-related tasks: A meta-analysis. *Journal of Counseling Psychology, 33,* 310–319.

Holloway, E. L., Wampold, B. E., & Nelson, M. L. (1990). Use of a paradoxical intervention with a couple: An interactional analysis. *Journal of Family Psychology, 3,* 385–402.

Horan, J. J. (1979). *Counseling for effective decision making: A cognitive-behavioral perspective.* North Scituate, MA: Duxbury Press.

Horan, J. J. (1996). Effects of computer-based cognitive restructuring on rationally mediated self-esteem. *Journal of Counseling Psychology, 43,* 371–375.

Horowitz, L. M., Rosenberg, S. E., Baer, B. A., Ureno, G., & Villasenor, V. S. (1988). Inventory of Interpersonal Problems: Psychometric properties and clinical applications. *Journal of Consulting and Clinical Psychology, 56,* 885–892.

Horvath, A. O., & Greenberg, L. S. (1986). The development of the Working Alliance Inventory. In L. S. Greenberg & W. M. Pinsof (Eds.), *The psychotherapeutic process: A research handbook* (pp. 529–556). New York: Guilford Press.

Horvath, A. O., & Greenberg, L. S. (1989). Development and validation of the Working Alliance Inventory. *Journal of Counseling Psychology, 36,* 223–233.

Horvath, P. (1988). Placebos and common factors in two decades of psychotherapy research. *Psychological Bulletin, 104*, 214-225.

Hoshmand, L. L. S. T. (1989). Alternate research paradigms: A review and teaching proposal. *The Counseling Psychologist, 17*, 3-79.

Hoshmand, L. T. (1994). Supervision of predoctoral graduate research: A practice oriented approach. *The Counseling Psychologist, 22*, 147-161.

Howard, G. S. (1982). Improving methodology via research on research methods. *Journal of Counseling Psychology, 29*, 318-326.

Howard, G. S. (1983). Toward methodological pluralism. *Journal of Counseling Psychology, 30*, 19-21.

Howard, G. S. (1984). A modest proposal for a revision of strategies in counseling research. *Journal of Counseling Psychology, 31*, 430-441.

Howard, G. S. (1985). Can research in the human sciences become more relevant to practice? *Journal of Counseling and Development, 63*, 539-544.

Howard, K. I., Moras, K., Brill, P. L., Martinovich, Z., & Lutz, W. (1996). Evaluation of psychotherapy. *American Psychologist, 51*, 1059-1064.

Hoyle, R. H. (1995). The structural equation modeling approach: Basic concepts and fundamental issues. In R. H. Hoyle (Ed.), *Structural equation modeling: Concepts, issues, and applications* (pp. 1-15). Thousand Oaks, CA: Sage.

Hoyt, M. R., Marmar, C. R., Horowitz, M. J., & Alvarez, W. F. (1981). The therapist actions scale and the patient actions scale: Instruments for the assessment of activities during dynamic psychotherapy. *Psychotherapy: Theory, Research and Practice, 18*, 109-116.

Hoyt, W. T. (1996). Antecedents and effects of perceived therapist credibility: A meta-analysis. *Journal of Counseling Psychology, 43*, 430-447.

Huberty, C. J., & Morris, J. D. (1989). Multivariate analysis versus multiple univariate analyses. *Psychological Bulletin, 105*, 302-308.

Huck, S. W., & McLean, R. A. (1975). Using a repeated measures ANOVA to analyze the data from a pretest-posttest design: A potentially confusing task. *Psychological Bulletin, 82*, 511-518.

Hughes, E. C. (1952). Psychology: Science and/or profession. *American Psychologist, 7*, 441-443.

Hunt, D. W., Butler, L. F., Noy, J. E., & Rosser, M. E. (1978). *Assessing conceptual level by the paragraph completion method.* Toronto, Canada: The Ontario Institute for Studies in Education.

Iberg, J. R. (1991). Applying statistical control theory to bring together clinical supervision and psychotherapy research. *Journal of Consulting and Clinical Psychology, 96*, 575-586.

Ingram, R. (Ed.). (1986). *Information processing approaches to clinical psychology.* Orlando, FL: Academic Press.

Jacobson, N. S., & Christensen, A. (1996). Studying the effectiveness of psychotherapy. *American Psychologist, 51*, 1031-1039.

Jacobson, N. S., Follette, W. C., & Revenstorf, D. (1984). Psychotherapy outcome research: Methods for reporting variability and evaluating clinical significance. *Behavior Therapy, 15*, 336-352.

Jacobson, N. S., & Revenstorf, D. (1988). Statistics for assessing the clinical significance of psychotherapy techniques: Issues, problems and new developments. *Behavior Assessment, 10*, 133-145.

Jacobson, N. S., & Truax, P. (1991). Clinical significance: A statistical approach to defining meaningful change in psychotherapy research. *Journal of Consulting and Clinical Psychology, 59*, 12-19.

Jauquet, C. A. (1987). The effects of an agenda setting exercise on process involvement in a counseling training group. Unpublished master's thesis, University of Missouri, Columbia.

Jayaratne, S., & Levy, R. L. (1979). *Empirical clinical practice.* New York: Columbia University Press.

Jensen, A. R. (1969). How much can we boost IQ and scholastic achievement? *Harvard Educational Review, 39,* 1–123.

Jensen, A. R. (1985). The nature of the black-white difference on various psychometric tests: Spearman's hypothesis. *The Behavioral and Brain Sciences, 8,* 193–263.

Johnson, R. F. Q. (1976). The experimenter attributes effect: A methodological analysis. *Psychological Record, 26,* 67–78.

Johnston, J. A., Buescher, K. L., & Heppner, M. J. (1988). Computerized career information and guidance systems: Caveat emptor. *Journal of Counseling and Development, 67,* 39–41.

Joint Committee on Standards for Educational Evaluation. (1994). *The program evaluation standards* (2nd ed.). Thousand Oaks, CA: Sage Publications.

Jones, A. S., & Gelso, C. J. (1988). Differential effects of style of interpretation: Another look. *Journal of Counseling Psychology, 35,* 363–369.

Jones, E. E. (1985). *Manual for the Psychotherapy Process Q-Sort.* Unpublished manuscript, University of California, Berkeley.

Jones, E. E. (1993). Introduction to special section: Single case research in psychotherapy. *Journal of Consulting and Clinical Psychology, 61,* 371–372.

Jones, E. E., Ghannam, J., Nigg, J. T., & Dyer, J. F. P. (1993). A paradigm for single-case research: The time series study of a long-term psychotherapy for depression. *Journal of Consulting and Clinical Psychology, 61,* 381–394.

Jones, H. G. (1956). The application of conditioning and learning techniques to the treatment of a psychiatric patient. *Journal of Abnormal and Social Psychology, 52,* 414–419.

Jones, R. G. (1969). A factored measure of Ellis' irrational belief system, with personality and maladjustment correlates (doctoral dissertation, University of Missouri, Columbia, 1968). *Dissertation Abstracts International, 29*(11b), 4379–4380.

Josephson, G. S., & Fong-Beyette, M. L. (1987). Factors assisting female clients' disclosure of incest during counseling. *Journal of Counseling and Development, 65,* 475–478.

Journal of Counseling Psychology. (1987). Special issue. *34,* 363–489.

Kagan, N. (1975). Influencing human interaction: Eleven years with IPR. *Canadian Counselor, 9,* 44–51.

Kahn, J. H., & Gelso, C. J. (1997). Factor structure of the research training environment scale-revised: Implications for research training in applied psychology. *The Counseling Psychologist, 25,* 22–37.

Kahn, J. H., & Scott, N. A. (1997). Predictors of research productivity and science-related career goals among counseling psychology doctoral students. *The Counseling Psychologist, 25,* 38–67.

Kandel, D. K. (1973). Adolescent marijuana use: Role of parents and peers. *Science, 181,* 1067–1070.

Kanfer, F. H., & Busemeyer, J. R. (1982). The use of problem solving and decision making in behavior therapy. *Clinical Psychological Review, 2,* 239–266.

Katz, N. W., & Miller, W. R. (1982). *A self-help guidebook for improving your mood. Unpublished manuscript,* University of New Mexico, Albuquerque.

Kaul, T., & Bednar, R. L. (1986). Experiential group research. In S. L. Garfield & A. E. Bergin (Eds.), *Handbook of psychotherapy and behavior change,* 3rd ed. (pp. 671–714). New York: Wiley.

Kazdin, A. D., & Kopel, S. A. (1975). On resolving ambiguities of the multiple-baseline design: Problems and recommendations. *Behavior Therapy, 6,* 601–608.

Kazdin, A. E. (1976). Statistical analyses for single-case experimental designs. In M. Hersen & D. H. Barlow (Eds.), *Single-case experimental designs: Strategies for studying behavioral change* (pp. 265–316). New York: Academic Press.

Kazdin, A. E. (1978). Methodology of applied behavior analysis. In A. C. Catania & T. A. Brigham (Eds.), *Handbook of applied behavior analysis: Social and instructional processes* (pp. 61–104). New York: Irvington Press/Halstead Press.

Kazdin, A. E. (1980). *Research design in clinical psychology.* New York: Harper & Row.

Kazdin, A. E. (1982). *Single-case research designs: Methods for clinical and applied settings.* New York: Oxford University Press.

Kazdin, A. E. (1995). Methods of psychotherapy research. In B. M. Bongar & L. E. Beutler (Eds.), *Comprehensive textbook of psychotherapy: Theory and practice.* New York: Oxford Universities Press.

Keet, C. D. (1948). Two verbal techniques in a miniature counseling situation. *Psychological Monographs, 62* (7, Whole No. 294).

Keith-Spiegel, P. (1994). The 1992 ethics code: Boon or bane. *Professional Psychology: Research and Practice, 25,* 315–316.

Keith-Spiegel, P., & Koocher, G. P. (1985). *Ethics in psychology: Professional standards and cases.* New York: Random House.

Kelerman, G., & Neu, C. (1976). *A manual for interpersonal treatment of depression.* Unpublished manuscript, Yale University, New Haven, CT.

Kelly, A. E., & Achter, J. A. (1995). Self-concealment and attitudes toward counseling in university students. *Journal of Counseling Psychology, 42,* 40–46.

Kelly, A. E., Kahn, J. H., & Coulter, R. G. (1996). Client self-presentation at intake. *Journal of Counseling Psychology, 43,* 300–309.

Kelly, A. E., McKillop, K. J., & Neimeyer, G. S. (1991). Effects of counselor as audience on the internalization of depressed and nondepressed self-presentation. *Journal of Counseling Psychology, 38,* 126–132.

Kerlinger, F. N. (1986). *Foundations of behavioral research* (3rd ed.). New York: Holt, Rinehart & Winston.

Kiesler, D. J. (1966). Some myths of psychotherapy research and the search for a paradigm. *Psychological Bulletin, 65,* 110–136.

Kiesler, D. J. (1971). Experimental designs in psychotherapy research. In A. E. Bergin & S. L. Garfield (Eds.), *Handbook of psychotherapy and behavior change* (pp. 36–74). New York: Wiley.

Kiesler, D. J. (1973). *The process of psychotherapy.* Chicago: Aldine.

Kiesler, D. J. (1984). *Check List of Psychotherapy Transactions (CLOPT) and Check List of Interpersonal Transactions (CLOIT).* Richmond: Virginia Commonwealth University.

Kiesler, D. J. (1987). *Research manual for the Impact Message Inventory.* Palo Alto, CA: Consulting Psychologists Press.

Kiesler, D. J. (1988). *Therapeutic metacommunication.* Palo Alto, CA: Consulting Psychologists Press.

Kiesler, D. J., Klein, M. H., & Mathieu, P. L. (1965). Sampling from the recorder therapy interview: The problem of segment location. *Journal of Consulting Psychology, 29,* 337–344.

Kiresuk, T. J., & Sherman, R. E. (1968). Goal attainment scaling: A general method for evaluating comprehensive community mental health programs. *Community Mental Health Journal, 4,* 443–453.

Kirshner, T., Hoffman, M. A., & Hill, C. E. (1994). A case study of the process and outcome of career counseling. *Journal of Counseling Psychology, 41,* 216–226.

Kiselica, M. S., Baker, S. B., Thomas, R. N., & Reedy, S. (1994). Effects of stress inoculation training on anxiety, stress, and academic performance among adolescents. *Journal of Counseling Psychology, 41,* 335–342.

Kitchener, K. S. (1984). Intuition, critical evaluation and ethical principles: The foundation for ethical decision in counseling psychology. *The Counseling Psychologist, 12*(3), 43–55.

Kivlighan, D. M., Jr. (1989). Changes in counselor intentions and response modes and client reactions and session evaluation following training. *Journal of Counseling Psychology, 36,* 471–476.

Kivlighan, D. M., Jr. (1990). Relation between counselors' use of intentions and clients' perception of working alliance. *Journal of Counseling Psychology, 37,* 27–32.

Kivlighan, D. M., Jr., & Angelone, E. O. (1991). Helpee introversion, novice counselor intention use, and counseling session impact. *Journal of Counseling Psychology, 38,* 25–29.

Kivlighan, D. M., Jr., Hageseth, J., Tipton, R., & McGovern, T. M. (1981). The effects of matching treatment approaches and personality types in group vocational counseling. *Journal of Counseling Psychology, 28,* 315–320.

Kivlighan, D. M., Jr., & Jauquet, C. A. (1990). Quality of group member agendas and group session climate. *Small Group Research, 21,* 205–219.

Kivlighan, D. M., Jr., Jauquet, C. A., Hardie, A. W., Francis, A. M., & Hershberger, B. (1993). Training group members to set session agendas: The effects on in-session behavior and member outcome. *Journal of Counseling Psychology, 40,* 182–187.

Kivlighan, D. M., Jr., & Lilly, R. L. (1997). Developmental changes in group climate as they relate to therapeutic gain. *Group Dynamics: Theory, Research, and Practice, 1,* 208–221.

Kivlighan, D. M., Multon, K. M., & Patton, M. J. (1996). Development of the Missouri Addressing Resistance Scale. *Psychotherapy Research 6,* 291–308.

Kivlighan, D. M., Jr., & Shapiro, R. M. (1987). Holland type as a predictor of benefit from self-help career counseling. *Journal of Counseling Psychology, 34,* 326–329.

Kivlighan, D. M., Jr. & Shaughnessy, P. (1995). An analysis of the development of the working alliance using hierachical linear modeling. *Journal of Counseling Psychology, 42,* 338–349.

Klare, G. R. (1974–1975). Assessing readability. *Reading Research Quarterly, 10,* 162–102.

Klein, D. F. (1996). Preventing head injuries about therapy studies. *Journal of Consulting and Clinical Psychology, 64,* 81–87.

Klein, M., Mathieu, P., Kiesler, O., & Gendlin, E. (1969). *The experiencing scale.* Madison: Wisconsin Psychiatric Institute.

Klein, M. H., Mathieu-Coughlan, P., & Kiesler, D. J. (1986). The experiencing scales. In L. Greenberg & W. Pinsof (Eds.), *The psychotherapeutic process* (pp. 21–77). New York: Guilford Press.

Kleinke, C. L. (1986). Gaze and eye contact: A research review. *Psychological Bulletin, 100,* 78–100.

Klingelhofer, E. L. (1954). The relationship of academic advisement to the scholastic performance of failing college students. *Journal of Counseling Psychology, 1,* 125–131.

Klinger, E. (1971). *Structure and functions of fantasy.* New York: Wiley.

Koile, E. A., & Bird, D. J. (1956). Preferences for counselor help on freshman problems. *Journal of Counseling Psychology, 3,* 97–106.

Kokotovic, A. M., & Tracey, T. J. (1987). Premature termination at a university counseling center. *Journal of Counseling Psychology, 34,* 80–82.

Koplik, E. K., & DeVito, A. J. (1986). Problems of freshmen: Comparison of classes of 1976 and 1986. *Journal of College Student Personnel, 27,* 124–131.

Kraemer, H. C., & Thiemann, S. (1987). *How many subjects?: Statistical power analysis in research.* Newbury Park, CA: Sage.

Kratochwill, T. R. (Ed.). (1978). *Single subject research: Strategies for evaluating change.* New York: Academic Press.

Krause, A. A., & Allen, G. J. (1988). Perceptions of counselor supervision: An examination of Stoltenberg's model from the perspectives of supervisor and supervisee. *Journal of Counseling Psychology, 35,* 77–80.

Krebs, P. J., Smither, J. W., & Hurley, R. B. (1991). Relationship of vocational personality and research training environment to the research productivity of counseling psychologists. *Professional Psychology: Research and Practice, 22,* 362–367.

Krivatsky, S. E., & Magoon, T. M. (1976). Differential effects of three vocational counseling treatments. *Journal of Counseling Psychology, 23,* 112–117.

Krop, H., & Krause, S. (1976). The elimination of shark phobia by self-administered systematic desensitization: A case study. *Journal of Behavior Therapy and Experimental Psychiatry, 7,* 293–294.

Krueger, R. (1994). *Focus groups* (2nd ed.). Thousand Oaks, CA: Sage Publications.

Krumboltz, J. D. (1991). *Career Beliefs Inventory.* Palo Alto, CA: Consulting Psychologist Press.

Krumboltz, J. D., & Mitchell, L. K. (1979). Relevant rigorous research. *The Counseling Psychologist, 81*(3), 50–52.

Kruskal, W., & Mosteller, F. (1979). Representative sampling III: The current statistical literature. *International Statistical Review, 47*, 245–265.

Kuhn, T. S. (1970). *The structure of scientific revolutions* (2nd ed.). Chicago: University of Chicago Press.

Kushner, K. (1978). On the external validity of two psychotherapy analogues. *Journal of Consulting and Clinical Psychology, 46*, 1394–1402.

Kvale, S. (1996). *Interviews: An introduction to qualitative research interviewing.* Thousand Oaks, CA: Sage.

Lakatos, I. (1970). Falsification and the methodology of scientific research programmes. In I. Lakatos & A. Musgrave (Eds.), *Criticism and the growth of knowledge* (pp. 91–196). Cambridge, England: Cambridge University Press.

Lambert, M. J., & Bergin, A. E. (1993). Achievements and limitations of psychotherapy research. In D. K. Freedheim (Ed.), *History of psychotherapy* (pp. 360–390). Washington, DC: American Psychological Association.

Lambert, M. J., Bergin, A. E., & Collins, J. L. (1977). Therapist-induced deterioration in psychotherapy. In A. S. Gurman & A. M. Razin (Eds.), *Effective psychotherapy: A handbook of research* (pp. 452–481). New York: Pergamon Press.

Lambert, M. J., Christensen, E. R., & Dejulio, S. (1983). *The assessment of psychotherapy outcome.* New York: Wiley.

Lambert, M. J., DeJulio, S. S., & Stein, D. M. (1978). Therapist interpersonal skills: Process, outcome, methodological considerations, and recommendations for future research. *Psychological Bulletin, 85*, 467–489.

Lambert, M. J., & Hill, C. E. (1994). Assessing psychotherapy outcomes and processes. In A. E. Bergin & S. L. Garfield (Eds.), *Handbook of psychotherapy and behavior change* (4th ed.). New York: Wiley.

Lapan, R. T., Boggs, K. R., & Morrill, W. H. (1989). Self-efficacy as a mediation of investigative and realistic general occupational themes of the Strong-Campbell Interest Inventory. *Journal of Counseling Psychology, 36*, 176–182.

Larson, L. M. (1998). The social cognitive model of counselor training. *The Counseling Psychologist, 26*, 219–273.

Larson, L. M., & Daniels, J. A. (1998). Review of the counseling self-efficacy literature. *The Counseling Psychologist, 26*, 129–218.

Larson, L. M., Heppner, P. P., Ham, T., & Dugan, K. (1988). Investigating multiple subtypes of career indecision through cluster analysis. *Journal of Counseling Psychology, 35*, 439–446.

Larson, L. M., Suzuki, L. A., Gillespie, K. N., Potenza, M. T., Bechtel, M. A., & Toulouse, A. L. (1992). Development and validation of the Counseling Self-Estimate Inventory. *Journal of Counseling Psychology, 39*, 105–210.

Lazarus, A. A. (1970). *Daily living: Coping with tension and anxieties.* Chicago: Instruction Dynamics.

Leary, M. R., & Altmaier, E. M. (1980). Type I error in counseling research: A plea for multivariate analyses. *Journal of Counseling Psychology, 27*, 611–615.

Leary, T. (1957). *Interpersonal diagnosis of personality.* New York: Ronald Press.

Lee, L. A., Heppner, P. P., Gagliardi, J., & Lee, J. S. (1987). Gender bias in subject samples in counseling psychology. *Journal of Counseling Psychology, 34*, 73–76.

Lent, R. W., Brown, S. D., & Hackett, G. (1994). Toward a unifying social cognitive theory of career and academic interest, choice, and performance. *Journal of Vocational Behavior, 45*, 79–122.

Lent, R. W., Brown, S. D., & Lankin, K. C. (1987). Comparison of three theoretically derived variables in predicting career and academic behavior: Self-efficacy, interest-consequence, and consequence thinking. *Journal of Counseling Psychology, 34*, 293–298.

Lent, R. W., Russell, R. K., & Zamostny, K. P. (1981). Comparison of cue-controlled desensitization, rational restructuring, and a credible placebo in the treatment of speech anxiety. *Journal of Consulting and Clinical Psychology, 49*, 608–610.

Leong, F. T. L. (1995). *Career development and vocational behavior of racial and ethnic minorities.* Mahwah, NJ: Erlbaum.

Leong, F. T. L., Wagner, N. S., & Tata, S. P. (1995). Racial and ethnic variations in help seeking attitudes. In J. G. Ponterotto, J. M. Casas, L. A. Suzuki, & C. M. Alexander (Eds.), *Handbook of multicultural counseling* (pp. 415–438). Thousand Oaks, CA: Sage.

Levin, J. R., & Kratochwill, T. (1992). *Single-case research design and analysis: New directions for psychology and education.* Hillsdale, NJ: Lawrence Erlbaum.

Levine, M. (1974). Scientific method and the adversary model, some preliminary thoughts. *American Psychologist, 29,* 661–677.

Lewin, K. (1951). Formalization and progress in psychology. In D. Cartwright (Ed.), *Field theory in social science* (pp. 1–41). New York: Harper.

Lewinsohn, P. M., Mischel, W., Chapel, W., & Barton, R. (1980). Social competence and depression: The role of illusory self-perceptions. *Journal of Abnormal Psychology, 89,* 203–212.

Lichtenberg, J. W. (1984). Believing when the facts don't fit. *Journal of Counseling and Development, 63,* 10–11.

Lichtenberg, J. W., & Heck, E. J. (1983). Use of sequential analysis in counseling process research: A reply to Hill, Carter, and O'Farrell and to Howard. *Journal of Counseling Psychology, 30,* 615–618.

Lichtenberg, J. W., & Heck, E. J. (1986). Analysis of sequence and pattern in process research. *Journal of Counseling Psychology, 33,* 170–181.

Lichtenberg, J. W., & Hummel, T. J. (1976). Counseling as a stochastic process: Fitting a Markov chain model to initial counseling interviews. *Journal of Counseling Psychology, 23,* 310–315.

Liddle, B. J. (1996). Therapist sexual orientation, gender, and counseling practices as they relate to ratings of helpfulness by gay and lesbian clients. *Journal of Counseling Psychology, 43,* 394–401.

Lieberman, M. A., Yalom, I., & Miles, M. (1973). *Encounter groups: First facts.* New York: Basic Books.

Lincoln, Y. S., & Guba, E. G. (1985). *Naturalistic inquiry.* Beverly Hills, CA: Sage.

Lindsey, R. T. (1984). Informed consent and deception in psychotherapy research: An ethical analysis. *The Counseling Psychologist, 12,* 79–86.

Linn, R. L., & Slinde, J. A. (1977). The determination of the significance of change between pre- and posttesting periods. *Review of Educational Research, 47,* 121–150.

Loehlin, J. C. (1992). *Latent variable models: An introduction to factor, path, and structural analysis* (2nd ed.). Hillsdale, NJ: Lawrence Erlbaum Associates.

Lonner, W. J., & Ibrahim, F. A. (1989). Assessment in cross-cultural counseling. In W. J. Lonner & J. E. Trimble (Eds.), *Counseling across cultures,* 3rd ed. (pp. 299–334). Honolulu: University of Hawaii Press.

Lorr, M. (1983). *Cluster analysis for social scientists.* San Francisco: Jossey-Bass.

Luborsky, L. (1984). *Principles of psychoanalytic psychotherapy: A manual for supportive-expressive treatment.* New York: Basic Books.

Luborsky, L., & Barber, J. P. (1993). Benefits of adherence to treatment manuals, and where to get them. In N. Miller, L. Luborsky, J. P. Barber, & J. P. Docherty (Eds.), *Psychodynamic treatment research: A handbook for clinical practice* (pp. 211–226). New York: Basic Books.

Luborsky, L., Crits-Christoph, P., Alexander, L., Margolis, M., & Cohen, M. (1983). Two helping alliance methods for predicting outcomes of psychotherapy. A counting signs vs. a global rating method. *Journal of Nervous and Mental Disease, 171,* 480–491.

Luborsky, L. S., Singer, B., & Luborsky, L. (1975). Comparative studies of psychotherapies. *Archives of General Psychiatry, 32,* 995–1008.

MacKenzie, K. R. (1983). The clinical application of a group climate measure. In R. R. Dies & K. R. MacKenzie (Eds.), *Advances in group psychotherapy: Integrating research and practice* (pp. 159–170). New York: International Universities Press.

Magoon, T. M., & Holland, J. L. (1984). Research training and supervision. In S. D. Brown & R. W. Lent (Eds.), *Handbook of counseling psychology* (pp. 682–715). New York: Wiley.

Mahalik, J. R., & Kivlighan, D. M., Jr. (1988). Self-help treatment for depression: Who succeeds? *Journal of Counseling Psychology, 35,* 237–242.

Mahoney, M. J. (1978). Experimental methods and outcome evaluation. *Journal of Consulting and Clinical Psychology, 46,* 660–672.

Mahrer, A. R., Paterson, W. E., Theriault, A. T., Roessler, C., & Quenneville, A. (1986). How and why to use a large number of clinically sophisticated judges in psychotherapy research. *Voices: The Art and Science of Psychotherapy, 22,* 57–66.

Maier, N. R. F. (1931). Reasoning in humans: II. The solution of a problem and its appearance in consciousness. *Journal of Comparative Psychology, 12,* 181–194.

Malinowski, B. (1922). *Argonauts of the western Pacific.* London: Routledge & Kegan Paul.

Malkiewich, L. E., & Merluzzi, T. V. (1980). Rational restructuring versus desensitization with clients of diverse conceptual levels: A test of client-treatment matching model. *Journal of Counseling Psychology, 27,* 453–461.

Mallinckrodt, B. (1989). Social support and the effectiveness of group therapy. *Journal of Counseling Psychology, 36,* 170–175.

Mallinckrodt, B. (1996). Change in working alliance, social support, and psychological symptoms in brief therapy. *Journal of Counseling Psychology, 43*(4), 448–455.

Mallinckrodt, B., Gelso, C. J., & Royalty, G. M. (1990). Impact of the research training environment and counseling psychology students' Holland personality type on interest in research. *Professional Psychology: Research and Practice, 21,* 26–32.

Mallinckrodt, B., & Helms, J. E. (1986). Effect of disabled counselor's self-disclosures on client perceptions of the counselor. *Journal of Counseling Psychology, 33,* 343–348.

Manicas, P. T., & Secord, P. F. (1983). Implications for psychology of the new philosophy of science. *American Psychologist, 38,* 399–413.

Marmar, C. R. (1990). Psychotherapy process research: Progress, dilemmas, and future directions. *Journal of Consulting and Clinical Psychology, 58,* 265–272.

Marmar, C. R., Marziali, E., Horowitz, M. J., & Weiss, D. S. (1986). The development of the therapeutic alliance rating system. In L. S. Greenberg & W. M. Pinsof (Eds.), *The psychotherapeutic process: A research handbook* (pp. 367–390). New York: Guilford Press.

Marsden, G. (1965). Content-analysis studies of therapeutic interviews: 1954–1964. *Psychological Bulletin, 63,* 298–321.

Marsden, G. (1971). Content analysis studies of psychotherapy: 1954–1968. In A. E. Bergin & S. L. Garfield (Eds.), *Handbook of psychotherapy and behavior change.* New York: Wiley.

Martin, J. (1984). The cognitive mediational paradigm for research on counseling. *Journal of Counseling Psychology, 31,* 558–571.

Martin, J. (1985). Measuring clients' cognitive competence in research on counseling. *Journal of Counseling and Development, 63,* 556–560.

Martin, J. (1987). *Cognitive-instructional counseling.* London, Ontario, Canada: Althouse Press.

Martin, J. S., Goodyear, R. K., & Newton, F. B. (1987). Clinical supervision: An intensive case study. *Professional Psychology: Research and Practice, 18,* 225–235.

Martin, J., Martin, W., & Slemon, A. G. (1989). Cognitive-mediational models of action-act sequences in counseling. *Journal of Counseling Psychology, 36,* 8–16.

Martin, J., & Stelmaczonek, K. (1988). Participants' identification and recall of important events in counseling. *Journal of Counseling Psychology, 35,* 385–390.

Maruyama, M. (1963). The second cybernetics: Deviation-amplifying mutual causal processes. *American Scientist, 51,* 169–179.

Marx, J. A., & Gelso, C. J. (1987). Termination of individual counseling in a university counseling center. *Journal of Counseling Psychology, 34,* 3–9.

Mash, E. J., & Terdal, L. G. (1988). *Behavioral assessment of childhood disorders* (2nd ed.). New York: Guilford Press.

Masling, J. (1966). Role-related behavior of the subject and psychologist and its effect upon psychological data. In D. Levine (Ed.), *Nebraska Symposium on Motivation, 14*, 67–103.

Max, L. W. (1935). Breaking up a homosexual fixation by the conditioned reaction technique: A case study. *Psychological Bulletin, 32*, 734.

Maxwell, S. E., & Cole, D. A. (1995). Tips for writing (and reading) methodological articles. *Psychological Bulletin, 118*, 193–198.

McCarn, S. R., & Fassinger, R. E. (1996). Revisioning sexual minority identity and its implications for counseling and research. *The Counseling Psychologist, 24*, 508–534.

McCarthy, P. R., Shaw, T., & Schmeck, R. R. (1986). Behavioral analysis of client learning style during counseling. *Journal of Counseling Psychology, 33*, 249–254.

McCullough, L., & Farrel, A. D. (1983). The Computerized Assessment for Psychotherapy Evaluation and Research [computer program]. New York: Beth Israel Medical Center, Department of Psychiatry.

McCullough, L., Farrell, A. D., & Longabaugh, R. (1986). The development of a microcomputer-based mental health information system: A potential tool for bridging the scientist-practitioner gap. *American Psychologist, 41*, 207–214.

McDaniel, M. A., Whetzel, D. L., Schmidt, F. L., & Maurer, S. (1994). The validity of employment interview: A comprehensive view and meta-analysis. *Journal of Applied Psychology, 79*, 599–616.

McGuire, W. J. (1985). Attitudes and attitude change. In G. Lindzey & E. Aronson (Eds.), *Handbook of social psychology*, 3rd ed., Vol. 2 (pp. 233–346). New York: Random House.

McKinney, F. (1945). Four years of a college adjustment clinic: I. Organization of clinic and problems of counselors. *Journal of Consulting Psychology, 9*, 203–212.

McLaughlin, M., Cormier, L. S., & Cormier, W. H. (1988). Relation between coping strategies and distress, stress, and marital adjustment of multiple-role women. *Journal of Counseling Psychology, 35*, 187–193.

McNamara, K., & Horan, J. J. (1986). Experimental construct validity in the evaluation of cognitive and behavioral treatments for depression. *Journal of Counseling Psychology, 33*, 23–30.

McNamee, S., & Gergen, K. J. (1992). *Therapy as social construction.* Newbury Park, CA: Sage.

Meara, N. M., & Patton, M. J. (1986). Language use and social influence in counseling. In F. J. Dorn (Ed.), *The social influence process in counseling and psychotherapy* (pp. 85–93). Springfield, IL: Charles C Thomas.

Meara, N. M., Schmidt, L. D., Carrington, C. H., Davis, K. L., Dixon, D. N., Fretz, B. R., Myers, R. A., Ridley, C. R., & Suinn, R. M. (1988). Training and accreditation in counseling psychology. *The Counseling Psychologist, 16*, 366–384.

Meara, N. M., Schmidt, L. D., & Day, J. D. (1996). Principles and virtues: A foundation for ethical decisions, policies, and character. *The Counseling Psychologist, 24*, 4–77.

Meara, N. M., Shannon, J. W., & Pepinsky, H. B. (1979). Comparison of the stylistic complexity of the language of counselor and client across three theoretical orientations. *Journal of Counseling Psychology, 28*, 110–118.

Meehl, P. E. (1971). A scientific, scholarly nonresearch doctorate for clinical practitioners. In R. R. Holt (Ed.), *New horizon for psychotherapy: Autonomy as a profession* (pp. 37–81). New York: International Universities Press.

Meehl, P. E. (1978). Theoretical risks and tabular asterisks: Sir Karl, Sir Ronald, and the slow progress of soft psychology. *Journal of Consulting and Clinical Psychology, 46*, 806–834.

Meehl, P. E. (1987). Why summaries of research on a psychological theory are often uninterpretable. In R. Snow & D. E. Wiley (Eds.), *Strategic thinking: A volume in honor of Lee J. Cronbach.* San Francisco: Jossey-Bass.

Megargee, E. I., & Bohn, M. J. (1979). *Classifying criminal offenders: A new system based on the MMPI.* Beverly Hills, CA: Sage.

Meichenbaum, D., Henshaw, D., & Himel, N. (1980). Coping with stress as a problem-solving process. In W. Krohne & L. Laux (Eds.), *Achievement stress and anxiety* (pp. 127–142). Washington, DC: Hemisphere.

Mercer, R. C., & Loesch, L.C. (1979). Audio tape ratings: Comments and guidelines. *Psychotherapy: Theory, Research, and Practice, 16,* 79–85.

Merrill, R. M. (1952). On Keet's study, "Two verbal techniques in a miniature counseling situation." *Journal of Abnormal and Social Psychology, 47,* 722.

Merten, J., Anstadt, Th., Ullrich, B., Krause, R., & Buchheim, P. (1996). Emotional experience and facial behavior during the psychotherapeutic process and its relation to treatment outcome: A pilot study. *Psychotherapy Research, 6,* 198–212.

Merton, R., Fiske, M., & Kendall, P. L. (1956). *The focused interview.* New York: Free Press

Meyer, V. (1957). The treatment of two phobic patients on the basis of learning principles. *Journal of Abnormal and Social Psychology, 55,* 261–266.

Miles, M. B., & Huberman, A. M. (1994). *Qualitative data analysis* (2nd ed.). Thousand Oaks, CA: Sage.

Mill, J. S. (1953). A system of logic, Book VI; On the logic of the moral sciences. In P. P. Weiner (Ed.), *Readings in philosophy of science* (pp. 255–281). New York: Scribner's. (Original work published 1843)

Miller, A. (1981). Conceptual matching models and interactional research in education. *Review of Educational Research, 51,* 33–84.

Mills, E. A. (1924). *Rocky Mountain National Park.* Garden City, NY: Doubleday, Page, & Co.

Mintz, J., & Luborsky, L. (1971). Segments vs. whole sessions: Which is the better unit for psychotherapy research? *Journal of Abnormal Psychology, 78,* 180–191.

Mintz, L. B., & O'Neil, J. M. (1990). Gender roles, sex, and the process of psychotherapy: Many questions and few answers. *Journal of Counseling and Development, 68,* 381–387.

Miranda, J., Azocar, F., Organista, K. C., Muñoz, R. F., & Lieberman, A. (1996). Recruiting and retaining low-income Latinos in psychotherapy research. *Journal of Consulting and Clinical Psychology, 64,* 868–874.

Mitchell, J. V., Jr. (Ed.). (1983). *Tests in print III.* Lincoln: University of Nebraska Press.

Mitchell, J. V., Jr. (Ed.). (1985). *The ninth mental measurements yearbook.* Lincoln: The Buros Institute of Mental Measurements of the University of Nebraska, Lincoln.

Mitchell, K. M., Bozarth, J. D., & Kraft, C. C. (1977). A reappraisal of the therapeutic effectiveness of accurate empathy, nonpossessive warmth and genuineness. In A. S. Gurman & A. M. Razin (Eds.), *Effective psychotherapy: A handbook of research* (pp. 482–502). New York: Pergamon Press.

Mohr, D. C., Shoham-Salomon, V., Engle, D., & Beutler, L. E. (1991). The expression of anger in psychotherapy for depression: Its role and measurement. *Psychotherapy Research, 1,* 124–134.

Monte, C. F. (1980). *Beneath the mask: An introduction to theories of personality* (2nd ed.). New York: Holt, Rinehart & Winston.

Mooney, R. L., & Gordon, L. V. (1950). *Manual: The Mooney problem checklists.* New York: Psychological Corporation.

Moras, K., & Hill, C. E. (1991). Rater selection in psychotherapy process research: Observation on the state-of-the-art. *Psychotherapy Research, 1,* 113–123.

Morgan, K. S., & Brown, L. S. (1991). Lesbian career development, work behavior, and vocational counseling. *The Counseling Psychologist, 19,* 273–291.

Morgan, R., Luborsky, L., Crits-Christoph, P., Curtis, H., & Solomon, J. (1982). Predicting the outcomes of psychotherapy by the Penn Helping Alliance Rating Method. *Archives of General Psychiatry, 39,* 397–402.

Morran, D. K., Kurpius, D. J., & Brack, G. (1989). Empirical investigation of counselor self-talk categories. *Journal of Counseling Psychology, 36,* 505–510.

Morrison, L. A., & Shapiro, D. A. (1987). Expectancy and outcome in prescription vs. exploratory psychotherapy. *British Journal of Clinical Psychology, 29,* 54–60.

Muehlenhard, C. L., & Linton, M. A. (1987). Date rape and sexual aggression in dating situations: Incidence and risk factors. *Journal of Counseling Psychology, 34,* 186–196.

Mueller, R. O. (1996). *Basic principles of structural equation modeling: An introduction to LISREL and EQS.* New York: Springer.

Mueller, W. J. (1969). Patterns of behavior and their reciprocal impact in the family and in psychotherapy [monograph]. *Journal of Counseling Psychology, 16,* 1–25.

Munley, P. H. (1974). A review of counseling analogue research methods. *Journal of Counseling Psychology, 21,* 320–330.

Munley, P. H., Sharkin, B., & Gelso, C. J. (1988). Reviewer ratings and agreement on manuscripts reviewed for the *Journal of Counseling Psychology. Journal of Counseling Psychology, 35,* 198–202.

Murphy, L. L., Conoley, J. C., & Impara, J. C. (1994). *Tests in print IV: An index to tests, test reviews, and the literature on specific tests* (Vol. 1). Lincoln, NE: Buros Institute of Mental Measurements.

Nagelberg, D. B., Pillsbury, E. C., & Balzor, D. M. (1983). The prevalence of depression as a function of gender and facility usage in college students. *Journal of College Student Personnel, 24,* 525–529.

National Institutes of Health. (1994). *NIH guidelines on the inclusion of women and minorities as subjects in clinical research* (59 FR 14508–14513). Washington, DC: U.S. Department of Health and Human Services.

Neimeyer, G., & Resnikoff, A. (1982). Major contribution: Qualitative strategies in counseling research. *The Counseling Psychologist, 101*(4), 75–85.

Neisser, U. (1976). *Cognition and reality: Principles and implications of cognitive psychology.* San Francisco: Freeman.

Newman, D., & Brown, R. (1996). *Applied ethics for program evaluation.* Beverly Hills, CA: Sage.

Nezu, A. M. (1986). Efficacy of a social problem-solving therapy approach for unipolar depression. *Journal of Consulting and Clinical Psychology, 54,* 196–202.

Nezu, A. M., Nezu, C. M., & Perri, M. G. (1989). *Problem-solving therapy for depression: Theory, research, and clinical guidelines.* New York: Wiley.

Nisbett, R. E., & Ross, L. (1980). *Human inference: Strategies and shortcomings of social judgment.* Englewood Cliffs, NJ: Prentice-Hall.

Nisbett, R. E., & Wilson, T. D. (1977). Telling more than we can know: Verbal reports on mental processes. *Psychological Review, 84,* 231–259.

Nocita, A., & Stiles, W. B. (1986). Client introversion and counseling session impact. *Journal of Counseling Psychology, 33,* 235–241.

Norton, I. M., & Manson, S. M. (1996). Research in American Indian and Alaska Native communities: Navigating the cultural universe of values and process. *Journal of Consulting and Clinical Psychology, 64,* 856–860.

Nowicki, S., & Duke, M. P. (1974). A locus of control scale for noncollege as well as college adults. *Journal of Personality Assessment, 38,* 136–137.

Nunnally, J. C. (1978). *Psychometric theory.* New York: McGraw-Hill.

Oetting, E. R., Swaim, R. C., Edwards, R. W., & Beauvais, F. (1989). Indian and Anglo adolescent alcohol use and emotional distress: Path models. *American Journal of Drug and Alcohol Abuse, 15,* 153–172.

O'Farrell, M. K., Hill, C. E., & Patton, S. M. (1986). A comparison of two cases of counseling with the same counselor. *Journal of Counseling and Development, 65,* 141–145.

O'Malley, S. S., Foley, S. H., Rounsaville, B. J., Watkins, J. T., Sotsky, S. M., Imber, S. D., & Elkin, I. (1988). Therapist competence and patient outcome in interpersonal psychotherapy of depression. *Journal of Consulting and Clinical Psychology, 56,* 496–501.

Omer, H., & London, P. (1989). Signal and noise in psychotherapy: The role of control of nonspecific factors. *British Journal of Psychiatry, 155,* 239–245.

O'Neil, J. M., Helms, B., Gable, R., David, L., & Wrightsman, L. (1986). Gender Role Conflict Scale: College men's fear of femininity. *Sex Roles, 14,* 335-350.

O'Neil, J. M., & Roberts Carroll, M. (1987). *A six-day workshop on gender role conflict and strain: Helping adult men and women take the gender role journey.* Storrs, CT: University of Connecticut, Department of Educational Psychology, Counseling Psychology Program. (ERIC Document Reproduction Service No. ED275963).

O'Neil, J. M., & Roberts Carroll, M. (1988). A gender role workshop focused on sexism, gender role conflict, and the gender role journey. *Journal of Counseling and Development, 67,* 193-197.

Orlinsky, D. E., Grawe, K., & Parks, B. K. (1994). Process and outcome in psychotherapy: Noch einmal. In A. E. Bergin & S. L. Garfield (Eds.), *Handbook of psychotherapy and behavior change,* 4th ed. (pp. 270-376). New York: Wiley.

Orlinsky, D. E., & Howard, K. I. (1975). *Varieties of psychotherapeutic experience: Multivariate analyses of patients' and therapists' reports.* New York: Teachers College Press.

Orlinsky, D. E., & Howard, K. I. (1978). The relation of process to outcome in psychotherapy. In S. L. Garfield & A. E. Bergin (Eds.), *Handbook of psychotherapy and behavior change,* 2nd ed. (pp. 283-330). New York: Wiley.

Orlinsky, D. E., & Howard, K. I. (1986). The relation of process to outcome in psychotherapy. In S. L. Garfield & A. E. Bergin (Eds.), *Handbook of psychotherapy and behavior change,* 3rd ed. (pp. 311-381). New York: Wiley.

Osipow, S. H. (1979). Counseling researchers: Why they perish. *The Counseling Psychologist, 8,* 39-41.

Osipow, S. H., Carney, C. G., Winer, J., Yanico, B., & Koschier, M. (1976). *Career Decision Scale* (3rd rev.). Odessa, FL: Psychological Assessment Resources.

Paivio, S. C., & Greenberg, L. S. (1995). Resolving "unfinished business": Efficacy of experiential therapy using empty-chair dialogue. *Journal of Consulting and Clinical Psychology, 63,* 419-425.

Palmer, S., & Cochran, L. (1988). Parents as agents of career development. *Journal of Counseling Psychology, 35,* 71-76.

Parham, T. A. (1989). Cycles of psychological nigresence. *The Counseling Psychologist, 17,* 187-226.

Parham, T. A., & Helms, J. E. (1981). The influence of black students' racial identity attitudes on preference for counselor's race. *Journal of Counseling Psychology, 28,* 250-257.

Parham, T. A., & Helms, J. E. (1985a). Attitudes of racial identity and self-esteem of black students: An exploratory investigation. *Journal of College Student Personnel, 26,* 143-147.

Parham, T. A., & Helms, J. E. (1985b). The relationship of racial identity attitudes to self-actualization and affective states of black students. *Journal of Counseling Psychology, 32,* 431-440.

Parloff, M. B., Waskow, I. E., & Wolfe, B. E. (1978). Research on therapist variables in relation to process and outcome. In S. L. Garfield & A. E. Bergin (Eds.), *Handbook of psychotherapy and behavior change,* 2nd ed. (pp. 233-282). New York: Wiley.

Parr, J., & Neimeyer, G. J. (1994). Effects of gender, construct type, occupational information, and career relevance on vocational differentiation. *Journal of Counseling Psychology, 41,* 27-33.

Patterson, G. R., & Forgatch, M. S. (1985). Therapist behavior as a determinant for client noncompliance: A paradox for the behavior modifier. *Journal of Consulting and Clinical Psychology, 53,* 846-851.

Patton, M. (1980). *Qualitative evaluation methods.* Beverly Hills, CA: Sage.

Patton, M. (1986). *Utilization-focused evaluation* (2nd ed.). Beverly Hills, CA: Sage.

Patton, M. J. (1984). Managing social interaction in counseling: A contribution from the philosophy of science. *Journal of Counseling Psychology, 31,* 442-456.

Patton, M. J. (1989). Problems with and alternatives to the use of coding schemes in research or counseling. *The Counseling Psychologist, 17,* 490-506.

Patton, M. J. (1991). Qualitative research on college students: Philosophical and method-ological considerations with the quantitative approach. *Journal of College Student Development, 32,* 389–396.

Patton, M. J., Kivlighan, D. M., Jr., & Multon, K. D. (1997). The Missouri psychoanalytic counseling research project: Relation of changes in counseling process to client out-come. *Journal of Counseling Psychology, 44,* 189–208.

Patton, M. Q. (1987). *How to use qualitative methods in evaluation.* Newbury Park, CA: Sage.

Patton, M. Q. (1990). *Qualitative evaluation and research methods* (2nd ed.). Newbury Park, CA: Sage.

Paul, G. L. (1967). Strategy of outcome research in psychotherapy. *Journal of Consulting Psychology, 31,* 109–118.

Payton, C. R. (1994). Implications of the 1992 ethics code for diverse groups. *Professional Psychology: Research and Practice, 25,* 317–320.

Pedersen, P. B. (1994). *A handbook for developing multicultural awareness* (2nd ed.). Alexandria, VA: American Counseling Association.

Pedersen, P. B., Draguns, J. G., Lonner, W. J., & Trimble, J. E. (Eds.). (1996). *Counseling across cultures* (4th ed.). Thousand Oaks, CA: Sage.

Pedhazur, E. (1982). *Multiple regression in behavioral research: Explanation and pre-diction* (2nd ed.). New York: Holt, Rinehart & Winston.

Penman, R. (1980). *Communication processes and relationships.* London: Academic Press.

Pepinsky, H. B. (1984). Language and the production and interpretation of social interac-tions. In H. F. Fisher (Ed.), *Language and logic in personality and society* (pp. 93–129). New York: Columbia University Press.

Pepinsky, H. B., & Pepinsky, P. N. (1954). *Counseling theory and practice.* New York: Ronald Press.

Petty, R. E., & Cacioppo, J. T. (1977). Forewarning, cognitive responding, and resistance to persuasion. *Journal of Personality and a Social Psychology, 35,* 645–655.

Petty, R. E., & Cacioppo, J. T. (1981). *Attitudes and persuasion: Classic and contemporary approaches.* Dubuque, IA: William C. Brown.

Petty, R. E., & Cacioppo, J. T. (1986). *Communication and persuasion: Central and peripheral routes to attitude change.* New York: Springer-Verlag.

Pfungst, O. (1911). *A contribution to experimental, animal, and human psychology.* New York: Holt, Rinehart & Winston.

Phelps, A., Friedlander, M. L., & Enns, C. Z. (1997). Psychotherapy process variables asso-ciated with the retrieval of memories of childhood sexual abuse: A qualitative study. *Journal of Counseling Psychology, 44,* 321–332.

Phillips, J. C., & Russell, R. K. (1994). Research self-efficacy, the research training environ-ment, and research productivity among graduate students in counseling psychology. *The Counseling Psychologist, 22,* 628–641.

Phillips, S. D., Friedlander, M. L., Pazienza, N. J., & Kost, P. P. (1985). A factor analytic inves-tigation of career decision-making styles. *Journal of Vocational Behavior, 26,* 106–115.

Piers, E. V. (1984). *Revised manual for the Piers-Harris Children's Self-Concept Scale.* Los Angeles: Western Psychological Services.

Polkinghorne, D. (1983). *Methodology for the human sciences: Systems of inquiry.* Albany: State University of New York.

Polkinghorne, D. E. (1984). Further extensions of methodological diversity for counseling psychology. *Journal of Counseling Psychology, 31,* 416–429.

Polkinghorne, D. E. (1994). Reaction to special section on qualitative research in counsel-ing process and outcome. *Journal of Counseling Psychology, 41,* 510–512.

Ponce, F. Q., & Atkinson, D. R. (1989). Mexican-American acculturation, counselor ethnic-ity, counseling style, and perceived credibility. *Journal of Counseling Psychology, 36,* 203–208.

Ponterotto, J. G. (1988a). Racial/ethnic minority research in the *Journal of Counseling Psychology:* A content analysis and methodological critique. *Journal of Counseling Psychology, 35,* 410–418.

Ponterotto, J. G. (1988b). Racial consciousness development among white counselor trainees: A stage model. *Journal of Multicultural Counseling and Development, 16,* 146–156.

Ponterotto, J. G., & Casas, J. M. (1991). *Handbook of racial/ethnic minority counseling research.* Springfield, IL: Charles C. Thomas.

Ponterotto, J. G., Casas, J. M., Suzuki, L. A., & Alexander, C. A. (Eds.) (1995). *Handbook of multicultural counseling.* Thousand Oaks, CA: Sage.

Ponterotto, J. G., & Furlong, M. J. (1985). Evaluating counselor effectiveness: A critical review of rating scale instruments. *Journal of Counseling Psychology, 32,* 597–616.

Ponterotto, J. G., & Pedersen, P. B. (1993). *Preventing prejudice: A guide for counselors and educators.* Newbury Park, CA: Sage.

Porter, A. C., & Raudenbush, S. W. (1987). Analysis of covariance: Its model and use in psychological research. *Journal of Counseling Psychology, 34,* 383–392.

Powell, C. J. (1984). Ethical principles and issues of competence in counseling adolescents. *The Counseling Psychologist, 121*(3), 57–68.

Price, D. J. (1963). *Little science, big science.* New York: Columbia University Press.

Putman, H. (1962). What theories are not. In E. P. Nagel, P. Suppes, & A. Tarski (Eds.), *Logic, methodology, and philosophy of science: Proceedings of the 1960 international congress* (pp. 240–251). Stanford, CA: Stanford University Press.

Rabinowitz, F. E., Heppner, P. P., & Roehlke, H. J. (1986). Descriptive study of process and outcome variables of supervision over time. *Journal of Counseling Psychology, 33,* 292–300.

Rachman, S. L., & Wilson, G. T. (1980). *The effects of psychological therapy.* New York: Pergamon Press.

Raimy, V. (Ed.). (1950). *Training in clinical psychology.* New York: Prentice-Hall.

Ramsey, P. (1970). *The patient as person.* New Haven, CT: Yale University.

Rappaport, D. (1960). The structure of psychoanalytic theory. *Psychological Issues,* Monograph 6. New York: International Universities Press.

Raudenbush, S. W., & Chan, W. S. (1993). Application of a hierarchical linear model to the study of adolescent deviance in an overlapping cohort design. *Journal of Consulting and Clinical Psychology, 61,* 941–951.

Raush, H. L. (1974). Research, practice, and accountability. *American Psychologist, 29,* 678–681.

Ravets, P. C. (1993). Group supervision: A multiple case study. *Dissertation Abstracts International, 54,* 2768.

Reising, G. N., & Daniels, M. H. (1983). A study of Hogan's model of counselor development and supervision. *Journal of Counseling Psychology, 30,* 235–244.

Rennie, D. L. (1994). Client's deference in psychotherapy. *Journal of Counseling Psychology, 41,* 427–437.

Rennie, D. L., & Brewer, L. (1987). A grounded theory of thesis blocking. *Teaching of Psychology, 14,* 10–16.

Rennie, D. L., Phillips, J. R., & Quartaro, G. K. (1988). Grounded theory: A promising approach to conceptualization in psychology? *Canadian Psychology/Psychologie Canadienne, 29,* 139–150.

Resnikoff, A. (1978). Scientific affairs committee report, 1975–1977: A discussion of methodology. *The Counseling Psychologist, 71*(4), 67–71.

Revicki, D. A., May, H. J., & Whitley, T. W. (1990). Reliability and validity of the Work Related Strain Inventory among health professionals. *Behavioral Medicine, 17,* 111–120.

Rice, L., & Kerr, G. (1986). Measures of client and therapist vocal quality. In L. Greenberg and W. Pinsof (Eds.), *The psychotherapy process: A research handbook* (pp. 73–106). New York: Guilford Press.

Rice, L. N., Koke, L. J., Greenberg, L. S., & Wagstaff, A. K. (1979). *Manual for client vocal quality, volume 1: Information for the investigation.* Toronto: Counseling and Development Center, York University.

Richardson, M. S., & Johnson, M. (1984). Counseling women. In S. R. Brown & R. W. Lent (Eds.), *Handbook of counseling psychology* (pp. 832–877). New York: Wiley.

Ridley, C. R. (1995). *Overcoming unintentional racism in counseling and therapy: A practitioner's guide to intentional intervention.* Thousand Oaks, CA: Sage.

Ridley, C. R., Mendoza, D. W., & Kanitz, B. E. (1994). Multicultural training: Reexamination, operationalization, and integration. *The Counseling Psychologist, 22,* 227–289.

Ridley, C. R., Mendoza, D. W., Kanitz, B. E., Angermeier, L., & Zenk, R. (1994). Cultural sensitivity in multicultural counseling: A perceptual schema model. *Journal of Counseling Psychology, 41,* 125–136.

Riggio, R. E. (1989). *Social Skills Inventory manual* (research ed.). Palo Alto, CA: Consulting Psychologists Press.

Robbins, S. B., & Patton, M. J. (1985). Self psychology and career development: Construction of the superiority and goal instability scales. *Journal of Counseling Psychology, 32,* 221–231.

Robinson, F. P. (1950). *Principles and procedures in student counseling.* New York: Harper & Brothers.

Rogers, C. R. (1955). Persons or science? A philosophical question. *American Psychologist, 10,* 267–278.

Rogers, C. R. (1957). The necessary and sufficient conditions of therapeutic personality change. *Journal of Consulting Psychology, 21,* 95–103.

Rogers, C. R. (1961). *On becoming a person.* Boston: Houghton Mifflin.

Rogers, L. B. (1954). A comparison of two kinds of test interpretation interview. *Journal of Counseling Psychology, 1,* 224–231.

Rojewski, J. W. (1994). Career indecision types for rural adolescents from disadvantaged and nondisadvantaged backgrounds. *Journal of Counseling Psychology, 41,* 356–363.

Rokeach, M. (1973). *The nature of human values.* New York: Free Press.

Rosenbaum, M. (1982). Ethical problems of group psychotherapy. In M. Rosenbaum (Ed.), *Ethics and values in psychotherapy.* New York: Free Press.

Rosenberg, M. (1965). *Society and the adolescent self-image.* Princeton, NJ: Princeton University Press.

Rosenthal, R. (1966). *Experimenter effects in behavioral research.* New York: Meredith.

Rosenthal, R. (1984). *Meta-analytic procedures for social research.* Beverly Hills, CA: Sage.

Rosenthal, R. (1995). Writing meta-analytic reviews. *Psychological Bulletin, 118,* 183–192.

Rosenthal, R., & Jacobson, L. (1968). *Pygmalion in the classroom: Teacher expectations of the disadvantaged.* New York: Holt, Rinehart & Winston.

Rosenthal, R., & Rosnow, R. L. (1969). The volunteer subject. In R. Rosenthal & R. L. Rosnow (Eds.), *Artifact in behavioral research* (pp. 61–118). New York: Academic Press.

Rosnow, R. L., & Rosenthal, R. (1988). Focused tests of significance and effect size estimation in counseling psychology. *Journal of Counseling Psychology, 35,* 203–208.

Ross, A. O. (1981). Of rigor and relevance. *Professional Psychology, 12,* 318–327.

Ross, R. R., & Altmaier, E. M. (1990). Job analysis of psychology internships in counseling center settings. *Journal of Counseling Psychology, 37,* 459–464.

Ross, W. D. (1930). *The right and the good.* Oxford, England: Clarendon.

Rossi, P., & Freeman, H. (1993). *Evaluation: A systematic approach.* Newbury Park, CA: Sage.

Rotter, J. B. (1966). Generalized expectancies for internal versus external control of reinforcement. *Psychological Monographs: General and Applied, 80*(1, Whole No. 609).

Rowe, D. C., Vazsonyi, A. T., & Flannery, D. J. (1994). No more than skin deep: Ethnic and racial similarity in developmental process. *Psychological Review, 101,* 396–413.

Rowe, W., & Atkinson, D. R. (1995). Misrepresentation and interpretation: Critical evaluation of white racial identity development models. *The Counseling Psychologist, 23,* 364–367.

Rowe, W., Bennett, S. K., & Atkinson, D. R. (1994). White racial identity models: A critique and alternative proposal. *The Counseling Psychologist, 22,* 129–146.

Royalty, G. M., & Magoon, T. M. (1985). Correlates of scholarly productivity among counseling psychologists. *Journal of Counseling Psychology, 32,* 458–461.

Royalty, G. M., Gelso, C. J., Mallinckrodt, B., & Garrett, K. D. (1986). The environment and the student in counseling psychology: Does the research training environment influence graduate students' attitude toward research? *The Counseling Psychologist, 14,* 9–30.

Royalty, G. M., & Reising, G. N. (1986). The research training of counseling psychologists: What the professionals say. *The Counseling Psychologist, 14,* 49–60.

Rubinton, N. (1980). Instruction in career decision making and decision-making styles. *Journal of Counseling Psychology, 27,* 581–588.

Ruch, F. L., & Zimbardo, P. G. (1970). *Psychology and life* (8th ed.). Glenview, IL: Scott, Foresman.

Rumenik, D. K., Capasso, D. R., & Hendrick, C. (1977). Experimenter sex effects in behavioral research. *Psychological Bulletin, 84,* 852–877.

Russell, J. B. (1991). *Inventing the flat earth: Columbus and modern historians.* New York: Praeger.

Russell, R. K., & Lent, R. W. (1982). Cue-controlled relaxation and systematic desensitization versus nonspecific factors in treating test anxiety. *Journal of Counseling Psychology, 29,* 100–103.

Russell, R. K., & Sipich, J. F. (1973). Cue-controlled relaxation in the treatment of test anxiety. *Journal of Behavior Therapy and Experimental Psychiatry, 4,* 47–50.

Russell, R. L. (1987). *Language in psychotherapy: Strategies of discovery.* New York: Plenum.

Russell, R. L. (1995). Introduction to the special section on multivariate psychotherapy process research: Structure and change in the talking cure. *Journal of Consulting and Clinical Psychology, 63,* 3–5.

Russell, R. L., & Stiles, W. B. (1979). Categories for classifying language in psychotherapy. *Psychological Bulletin, 86,* 404–419.

Rust, R. E., & Davie, J. S. (1961). The personal problems of college students. *Mental Hygiene, 45,* 247–257.

Sax, G. (1989). *Principles of educational and psychological measurement and evaluation* (3rd ed.). Belmont, CA: Wadsworth.

Schaefer, M. T., & Olson, D. H. (1981). Assessing intimacy: The PAIR Inventory. *Journal of Marital and Family Therapy, 7,* 47–60.

Schectman, Z., Gilat, I., Fos, L., & Flasher, A. (1996). Brief group therapy with low-achieving elementary school children. *Journal of Counseling Psychology, 43,* 376–382.

Scher, M., & Good, G. E. (1990). Gender and counseling in the twenty-first century: What does the future hold? *Journal of Counseling and Development, 68,* 388–391.

Schmidt, F. L., & Hunter, J. E. (1996). Measurement error in psychological research: Lessons from 26 research scenarios. *Psychological Methods, 1,* 199–223.

Schmidt, L. D., & Meara, N. M. (1984). Ethical, professional, and legal issues in counseling psychology. In S. D. Brown & R. W. Lent (Eds.), *Handbook of counseling psychology* (pp. 56–96). New York: Wiley.

Schmidt, L. D., & Strong, S. R. (1971). Attractiveness and influence in counseling. *Journal of Counseling Psychology, 18,* 348–351.

Schneidler, G. G., & Berdie, R. F. (1942). Representativeness of college students who receive counseling services. *Journal of Educational Psychology, 33,* 545–551.

Schotte, D., & Clum, G. (1982). Suicide ideation in a college population: A test of a model. *Journal of Consulting and Clinical Psychology, 50,* 690–696.

Schuller, R., Crits-Christoph, P., & Connolly, M. B. (1991). The Resistance Scale: Background and psychometric properties. *Psychoanalytic Psychology, 8,* 195–211.

Schutz, A. (1964). *Collected papers II: Studies in social theory* (A. Broderson, Ed.). The Hague, The Netherlands: Martinus-Nijhoff.

Seeman, J. (1959). Organizing a thesis proposal. *American Psychologist, 9,* 794–797.

Seeman, J. (1969). Deception in psychological research. *American Psychologist, 24,* 1025–1028.

Seeman, J. (1973). On supervising student research. *American Psychologist, 28,* 900–906.

Seggar, L., & Lambert, M. J. (1994). Assessing clinical significance: Application to the Beck Depression Inventory. Paper presented at the annual meeting of the Society for Psychotherapy Research, York, England, June 1994.

Serlin, R. C. (1987). Hypothesis testing, theory building, and the philosophy of science. *Journal of Counseling Psychology, 34,* 365–371.

Serlin, R. C., & Lapsley, D. K. (1985). Rationality in psychological research: The good-enough principle. *American Psychologist, 40,* 73–83.

Shadish, W. R. (1984). Intimate behaviors and the assessment of benefits in clinical groups. *Small Group Behaviors, 15,* 204–221.

Shadish, W. R. (1986). The validity of a measure of intimate behavior. *Small Group Behavior, 17,* 113–120.

Sharkin, B. S., Mahalik, J. R., & Claiborn, C. D. (1989). Application of the foot-in-the-door effect in counseling. *Journal of Counseling Psychology, 36,* 248–251.

Shaw, B. F. (1977). Comparison of cognitive therapy and behavior therapy in the treatment of depression. *Journal of Consulting and Clinical Psychology, 45,* 543–551.

Shlien, J. M., Mosak, H. H., & Dreikurs, R. (1962). Effects of time limits: A comparison of two psychotherapies. *Journal of Counseling Psychology, 9,* 31–34.

Silberschatz, G., Fretter, P. B., & Curtis, J. T. (1986). How do interpretations influence the process of therapy? *Journal of Consulting and Clinical Psychology, 54,* 646–652.

Sime, W. E., Ansorge, C. J., Olson, J., Parker, C., & Lukin, M. (1987). Coping with mathematics anxiety: Stress management and academic performance. *Journal of College Student Personnel, 28*(5), 431–437.

Sipich, J. F., Russell, R. K., & Tobias, L. L. (1974). A comparison of covert sensitization and "nonspecific" treatment in the modification of smoking behavior. *Journal of Behavior, Therapy, and Experimental Psychiatry, 5,* 201–203.

Slate, J. R., & Jones, C. H. (1989). Can teaching of the WISC-R be improved? Quasi-experimental exploration. *Professional Psychology Research and Practice, 20,* 408–410.

Slusher, M. P., & Anderson, C. A. (1989). Belief perseverance and self-defeating behavior. In R. Curtis (Ed.), *Self-defeating behaviors: Experimental research, clinical impressions, and practical implications* (pp. 11–40). New York: Plenum.

Smith, M. L. (1981). Naturalistic research. *Personnel and Guidance Journal, 59,* 585–589.

Smith, M. L., & Glass, G. V. (1977). Meta-analysis of psychotherapy outcome studies. *American Psychologist, 32,* 752–760.

Smith, M. L., Glass, G. V., & Miller, T. I. (1980). *The benefits of psychotherapy.* Baltimore: Johns Hopkins University Press.

Smith, N. (Ed.). (1982). *Communication strategies in evaluation.* Beverly Hills, CA: Sage.

Smith, R. E., & Nye, S. L. (1989). Comparison of induced effect and covert rehearsal in the acquisition of stress management coping skills. *Journal of Counseling Psychology, 36,* 17–23.

Snyder, D., & Wills, R. M. (1989). Behavioral versus insight-oriented marital therapy: Effects on individual and interspousal functioning. *Journal of Consulting and Clinical Psychology, 57,* 39–46.

Spanier, G. B. (1976). Measuring dyadic adjustment: New scales for assessing the quality of marriage and similar dyads. *Journal of Marriage and the Family, 38,* 15–28.

Spence, D. P., Dahl, H., & Jones, E. E. (1993). Impact of interpretation on associative freedom. *Journal of Consulting and Clinical Psychology, 61,* 395–402.

Spence, J. T., & Helmreich, R. (1972). The Attitudes Toward Women Scale: An objective instrument to measure attitudes toward the rights and roles of women in contemporary society. *JSAS Catalog of Selected Documents in Psychology, 2,* 1–48.

Spengler, P. M., Strohmer, D. C., Dixon, D. N., & Shivy, V. A. (1995). A scientist-practitioner model of psychological assessment: Implications for training, practice, and research. *The Counseling Psychologist, 23,* 506–534.

Spiegel, D., & Keith-Spiegel, P. (1970). Assignment of publication credits: Ethics and practices of psychologists. *American Psychologist, 25,* 738–747.

Spielberger, C. D. (1988). *State-Trait Anger Expression Inventory.* Orlando, FL: Psychological Assessment Resources.

Spielberger, C. D., Jacobs, G., Crane, R., Russel, S., Westberry, L., Barker, L., Johnson, E., Knight, J., & Marks, E. (1979). *Preliminary manual for the State-Trait Personality Inventory (STPI).* Tampa, FL: Center for Research in Community Psychology, University of South Florida.

Stanley, S. M., & Markman, H. J. (1992). Assessing commitment in personal relationships. *Journal of Marriage and the Family, 54,* 595–608.

Steier, F. (1988). Toward a coherent methodology for the study of family therapy. In L. C. Wynne (Ed.), *The state of the art in family therapy research: Controversies and recommendations* (pp. 227–234). New York: Family Process Press.

Stein, M. L., & Stone, G. L. (1978). Effects of conceptual level and structure on initial interview behavior. *Journal of Counseling Psychology, 25,* 96–102.

Sternberg, R. J. (1988). *The psychologist's companion: A guide to scientific writing for students and researchers* (2nd ed.). New York: Cambridge University Press.

Stewart, G. M., & Gregory, B. C. (1996). Themes of a long-term AIDS support group for gay men. *The Counseling Psychologist, 24,* 285–303.

Stiles, W. B. (1980). Measurement of the impact of psychotherapy sessions. *Journal of Consulting and Clinical Psychology, 48,* 176–185.

Stiles, W. B. (1988). Psychotherapy process-outcome correlations may be misleading. *Psychotherapy, 25,* 27–35.

Stiles, W. B. (1992). *Describing talk: A taxonomy of verbal response modes.* Newbury Park, CA: Sage.

Stiles, W. B. (1993). Quality control in qualitative research. *Clinical Psychology Review, 13,* 593–618.

Stiles, W. B., & Shapiro, D. A. (1995). Verbal exchange structure of brief psychodynamic-interpersonal and cognitive-behavioral psychotherapy. *Journal of Consulting and Clinical Psychology, 63,* 15–27.

Stiles, W. B., Shapiro, D. A., & Firth-Cozens, J. A. (1988). Do sessions of different treatments have different impacts? *Journal of Counseling Psychology, 35,* 391–396.

Stiles, W. B., & Snow, J. S. (1984). Counseling session impact as viewed by novice counselors and their clients. *Journal of Counseling Psychology, 31,* 13–12.

Stiles, W. B., Startup, M., Hardy, G. E., Barkham, M., Rees, A., Shapiro, D. A., & Reynolds, S. (1996). Therapist session intentions in cognitive-behavioral and psychodynamic-interpersonal psychotherapy. *Journal of Counseling Psychology, 43,* 402–414.

Stoltenberg, C. (1981). Approaching supervision from a developmental perspective: The counselor complexity model. *Journal of Counseling Psychology, 28,* 59–65.

Stone, G. L. (1984). Reaction: In defense of the "artificial." *Journal of Counseling Psychology, 31,* 108–110.

Strauss, A., & Corbin, J. (1990). *Basics of qualitative research: Grounded theory procedures and techniques.* Newbury Park, CA: Sage.

Stricker, G. (1982). Ethical issues in psychotherapy research. In M. Rosenbaum (Ed.), *Ethics and values in psychotherapy: A guidebook* (pp. 403–424). New York: Free Press.

Strohmer, D. C., & Blustein, D. L. (1990). The adult problem solver as personal scientist. *Journal of Cognitive Psychotherapy: An International Quarterly, 4,* 281–292.

Strohmer, D. C., & Newman, L. J. (1983). Counselor hypothesis-testing strategies. *Journal of Counseling Psychology, 30,* 557–565.

Strong, S. R. (1968). Counseling: An interpersonal influence process. *Journal of Counseling Psychology, 15,* 215–224.

Strong, S. R. (1971). Experimental laboratory research in counseling. *Journal of Counseling Psychology, 18,* 106–110.

Strong, S. R. (1978). Social psychological approach to psychotherapy research. In J. Garfield & A. Bergin (Eds.), *Handbook of psychotherapy and behavior change,* 2nd ed. (pp. 101–136). New York: Wiley.

Strong, S. R. (1984). Reflections on human nature, science, and progress in counseling psychology. *Journal of Counseling Psychology, 31,* 470–473.

Strong, S. R., & Dixon, D. N. (1971). Expertness, attractiveness, and influence in counseling. *Journal of Counseling Psychology, 18,* 562–570.

Strong, S. R., Hills, H. I., Kilmartin, C. T., De Vries, H., Lanier, K., Nelson, B., Strickland, D., & Meyer, C. W. (1988). The dynamic relations among interpersonal behaviors: A test of complementarity and autocomplementarity. *Journal of Personality and Social Psychology, 54,* 798–810.

Strong, S. R., & Matross, R. P. (1973). Change processes in counseling and psychotherapy. *Journal of Counseling Psychology, 20,* 25–37.

Strong, S. R., & Schmidt, L. D. (1970). Expertness and influence in counseling. *Journal of Counseling Psychology, 17,* 81–87.

Strong, S. R., Welsh, J. A., Corcoran, J. L., & Hoyt, W. T. (1992). Social psychology and counseling psychology: The history, products, and promise of an interface. *Journal of Counseling Psychology, 39,* 139–157.

Strupp, H. H. (1980a). Success and failure in time-limited psychotherapy: A systematic comparison of two cases—Comparison 1. *Archives of General Psychiatry, 37,* 595–603.

Strupp, H. H. (1980b). Success and failure in time-limited psychotherapy: A systematic comparison of two cases—Comparison 2. *Archives of General Psychiatry, 37,* 708–716.

Strupp, H. H. (1980c). Success and failure in time-limited psychotherapy: Further evidence—Comparison 4. *Archives of General Psychiatry, 37,* 947–954.

Strupp, H. H. (1981). Clinical research, practice, and the crisis of confidence. *Journal of Consulting and Clinical Psychology, 49,* 216–219.

Strupp, H. H., & Binder, J. L. (1984). *Psychotherapy in a new key.* New York: Basic Books.

Strupp, H. H., & Howard, K. I. (1993). A brief history of psychotherapy research. In D. K. Freedheim (Ed.), *History of psychotherapy* (pp. 309–334). Washington, DC: American Psychological Association.

Stuart, R. B. (1983). *Couple's pre-counseling inventory: Counselor's guide.* Champaign, IL: Research Press.

Sue, D. W., & Sue, D. (1990). *Counseling the culturally different: Theory and practice.* New York: Wiley.

Sue, D., & Sue, D. (1995). Asian Americans. In N. A. Vacc, S. B. DeVaney, & J. Wittmer (Eds.), *Experiencing and counseling multicultural and diverse populations,* 3rd ed. (pp. 63–90). Bristol, PA: Accelerated Development.

Suen, H. K. (1988). Agreement, reliability, accuracy, and validity: Toward a clarification. *Behavioral Assessment, 10,* 343–366.

Suh, C. S., O'Malley, S. S., Strupp, H. H., & Johnson, M. E. (1989). The Vanderbilt Psychotherapy Process Scale (VPPS). *Journal of Cognitive Psychotherapy, 3,* 123–154.

Super, D. (1957). *The psychology of careers.* New York: McGraw-Hill.

Suppe, F. (1977). *The structure of scientific theories* (2nd ed.). Urbana: University of Illinois Press.

Suzuki, L. A., Meller, P. J., & Ponterotto, J. G. (Eds.). (1996). *Handbook of multicultural assessment: Clinical, psychological, and educational applications.* San Francisco: Jossey-Bass.

Swain, R. C., Oetting, E. R., Edwards, R. W., & Beauvais, F. (1989). Links from emotional distress to adolescent drug use: A path model. *Journal of Consulting and Clinical Psychology, 57,* 227–231.

Swanson, J. L. (1995). The process and outcome of career counseling. In W.B. Walsh & S. H. Osipow (Eds.), *Handbook of vocational psychology: Theory, research, and practice* (pp. 217–255). Mahwah, NJ: Lawrence Erlbaum.

Tanaka-Matsumi, J., & Kameoka, V. A. (1986). Reliabilities and concurrent validities of popular self-report measures of depression, anxiety, and social desirability. *Journal of Consulting and Clinical Psychology, 54,* 328–333.

Task Force on Promotion and Dissemination of Psychological Procedures. (1995). Training in and dissemination of empirically-validated psychological treatment: Report and recommendations. *The Clinical Psychologist, 48,* 2–23.

Taussig, I. M. (1987). Comparative responses of Mexican Americans and Anglo-Americans to early goal setting in a public mental health clinic. *Journal of Counseling Psychology, 34,* 214–217.

Tesch, R. (1990). *Qualitative research: Analysis types and software tools.* New York: Falmer.

Thigpen, C. H., & Cleckley, H. M. (1954). A case of multiple personality. *Journal of Abnormal and Social Psychology, 49,* 135–151.

Thigpen, C. H., & Cleckley, H. M. (1957). *Three faces of Eve.* New York: McGraw-Hill.

Thompson, B. J., & Hill, C. E. (1993). Client perceptions of therapist competence. *Psychotherapy Research, 3,* 124–130.

Thompson, A. S., & Super, D. E. (Eds.) (1964). *The professional preparation of counseling psychologists. Report of the 1964 Greystone Conference.* New York: Bureau of Publications, Teachers College, Columbia University.

Thompson, C. E. (1994). Helms white racial identity development (WRID) theory: Another look. *The Counseling Psychologist, 22,* 645–649.

Thompson, C. E., & Jenal, S. T. (1994). Interracial and intraracial quasi-counseling interactions when counselors avoid discussing race. *Journal of Counseling Psychology, 41,* 484–491.

Thompson, C. E., Worthington, R., & Atkinson, D. R. (1994). Counselor content orientation, counselor race, and black women's cultural mistrust and self-disclosures. *Journal of Counseling Psychology, 41,* 155–161.

Thompson, E. E., Neighbors, H. W., Munday, C., & Jackson, J. S. (1996). Recruitment and retention of African American patients for clinical research: An exploration of response rates in an urban psychiatric hospital. *Journal of Consulting and Clinical Psychology, 64,* 861–867.

Thoreson, R. W., Budd, F. C., & Krauskopf, C. J. (1986). Alcoholism among psychologists: Fac-tors in relapse and recovery. *Professional Psychology: Research and Practice, 17,* 497–503.

Thoreson, R. W., Kardash, K. A., Leuthold, D. A., Morrow, K. A. (1990). Gender differences in the academic career. *Research in Higher Education, 3*(2), 193–209.

Thoreson, R. W., Miller, M., & Krauskopf, C. J. (1989). The distressed psychologist: Prevalence and treatment considerations. *Professional Psychology: Research and Practice, 20,* 153–158.

Tichenor, V., & Hill, C. E. (1989). A comparison of six measures of working alliance. *Psychotherapy, 26,* 195–199.

Tingey, R. C., Lambert, M. J., Burlingame, G. M., & Hansen, N. B. (1996). Assessing clinical significance: Proposed extensions to method. *Psychotherapy Research, 6,* 109–123.

Tinsley, D. J., Tinsley, H. E. A., Boone, S., & Shim-Li, C. (1993). Prediction of scientist-practitioner behavior using personality scores obtained during graduate school. *Journal of Counseling Psychology, 40,* 511–517.

Tinsley, H. E. A. (1992). Psychometric theory and counseling psychology research. In S. D. Brown & R. W. Lent (Eds.), *Handbook of counseling psychology,* 2nd ed. (pp. 37–70). New York: John Wiley & Sons.

Tinsley, H. E. A. (1997). Synergistic analysis of structured essays: A large sample discovery oriented qualitative research approach. *The Counseling Psychologist, 25,* 573–585.

Tinsley, H. E. A., Bowman, S. L., & Ray, S. B. (1988). Manipulation of expectancies about counseling and psychotherapy: Review and analysis of expectancy manipulation strategies and results. *Journal of Counseling Psychology, 35,* 99–108.

Tinsley, H. E. A., Roth, J. A., & Lease, S. H. (1989). Dimensions of leadership and leadership style among group intervention specialists. *Journal of Counseling Psychology, 36,* 48–53.

Tinsley, H. E. A., & Tinsley, D. J. (1987). Use of factor analysis in counseling psychology research. *Journal of Counseling Psychology, 34,* 414–424.

Tinsley, H. E. A., & Weiss, D. J. (1975). Interrater reliability and agreement of subjective judgments. *Journal of Counseling Psychology, 22,* 358–376.

Tinsley, H. E. A., Workman, K. R., & Kass, R. A. (1980). Factor analysis of the domain of client expectancies about counseling. *Journal of Counseling Psychology, 27,* 561–570.

Tipton, R. M., & Worthington, E. L. (1984). The measurement of generalized self-efficacy: A study of construct validity. *Journal of Personality Assessment, 48,* 545–548.

Toukmanian, S. G., & Rennie, D. (1992). *Psychotherapy process research: Paradigmatic and narrative approaches.* Newbury Park, CA: Sage.

Toulmin, S. (1972). *Human understanding: The collecting use and evolution of concepts.* Princeton, NJ: Princeton University Press.

Tracey, T. J. (1983). Single case research: An added tool for counselors and supervisors. *Counselor Education and Supervision, 22,* 185–196.

Tracey, T. J. (1985). The N of 1 Markov chain design as a means of studying the stages of psychotherapy. *Psychiatry, 48,* 196–204.

Tracey, T. J. (1986). Interactional correlates of premature termination. *Journal of Consulting and Clinical Psychology, 54,* 784–788.

Tracey, T. J., Glidden, C. E., & Kokotovic, A. M. (1988). Factor structure of the Counselor Rating Form-Short. *Journal of Counseling Psychology, 35,* 330–335.

Tracey, T. J., Hays, K. A., Malone, J., & Herman, B. (1988). Changes in counselor response as a function of experience. *Journal of Counseling Psychology, 35,* 119–126.

Tracey, T. J., Leong, F. T. L., & Glidden, C. (1986). Help seeking and problem perception among Asian Americans. *Journal of Counseling Psychology, 33,* 331–336.

Tracey, T. J., & Ray, P. B. (1984). Stages of successful time-limited counseling: An interactional examination. *Journal of Counseling Psychology, 31,* 13–27.

Truax, C. B., & Carkhuff, R. R. (1967). *Toward effective counseling and psychotherapy: Training and practice.* Chicago: Aldine.

Truax, C. B., & Wargo, D. G. (1966). Psychotherapeutic encounters that change behavior: For better or for worse. *American Journal of Psychotherapy, 20,* 499–520.

Tschuschke, V., & MacKenzie, K. R. (1989). Empirical analysis of group development: A methodological report. *Small Group Behavior, 20,* 419–427.

Turk, D. C., & Salovey, P. (Ed.). (1988). *Reasoning, inference, and judgment in clinical psychology.* New York: Free Press.

Turnbull, H. R., III (Ed.). (1977). *Consent handbook.* Washington, DC: American Association on Mental Deficiency.

Turner, P. R., Valtierra, M., Talken, T. R., Miller, V. I., & DeAnda J. R. (1996). Effect of treatment on treatment outcome for college students in brief therapy. *Journal of Counseling Psychology, 43,* 228–232.

Tversky, A., & Kahneman, D. (1974). Judgment under uncertainty: Heuristics and biases. *Science, 185,* 1124–1131.

Tversky, A., & Kahneman, D. (1981). The framing of decisions and the psychology of choice. *Science, 211,* 453–458.

Tyler, L. E. (1984). Further implications for counseling research. *Journal of Counseling Psychology, 31,* 474–476.

Underwood, B. J. (1966). *Experimental psychology.* New York: Appleton-Century-Crofts.

Vandenbos, G. R. (1986). Psychotherapy research: A special issue. *American Psychologist, 41,* 111–112.

Vandenbos, G. R. (1996). Outcome assessment of psychotherapy. *American Psychologist, 51,* 1005–1006.

Vandenbos, G. R., & Pino, C. D. (1980). Research in the outcome of psychotherapy. In G. R. Vandenbos (Ed.), *Psychotherapy: Practice, research, policy* (pp. 23–69). Beverly Hills, CA: Sage.

Vasquez, M. J. T. (1994). Implications of the 1992 ethics code for the practice of individual psychotherapy. *Professional Psychology: Research and Practice, 25,* 321–328.

Vontress, C. E. (1970). Counseling blacks. *Personnel and Guidance Journal, 48,* 713–719.

Vredenburg, K., O'Brien, E., & Krames, L. (1988). Depression in college students: Personality and experiential factors. *Journal of Counseling Psychology, 35,* 419–425.

Wade, J. C. (1998). Male reference group identity dependence: A theory of male identity. *The Counseling Psychologist, 26,* 349–383.

Wallenstein, R. S. (1971). The role of researcher training. How much, what kind, how? In R. R. Holt (Ed.), *New horizon for psychotherapy.* New York: International Universities Press.

Wallenstein, R. S. (1989). The psychotherapy research project of the Menninger Foundation: An overview. *Journal of Consulting and Clinical Psychology, 57,* 195–205.

Walsh, W. B., & Osipow, S. H. (Eds.). (1994). *Career counseling for women.* Hillsdale, NJ: Lawrence Erlbaum.

Walsh, W. B., & Osipow, S. H. (1995). *Handbook of vocational psychology: Theory, research, and practice* (2nd ed.). Mahwah, NJ: Lawrence Erlbaum.

Wampold, B. E. (1986a). State of the art in sequential analysis: Comment on Lichtenberg and Heck. *Journal of Counseling Psychology, 33,* 182–185.

Wampold, B. E. (1986b). Toward quality research in counseling psychology: Current recommendations for design and analysis. *The Counseling Psychologist, 14,* 37–48.

Wampold, B. E. (1987). Guest editor's introduction. *Journal of Counseling Psychology, 34,* 364.

Wampold, B. E. (1995). Analysis of behavior sequences in psychotherapy. In J. Siegfried (Ed.), *Therapeutic and everyday discourse as behavior change: Towards a microanalysis in psychotherapy process research.* Norwood, NJ: Ablex.

Wampold, B. E. (1997). Methodological problems in identifying efficacious psychotherapies. *Psychotherapy Research, 7,* 21–43.

Wampold, B. E. (1998). Necessary (but not sufficient) innovation: Comment on Fox and Jones (1998), Koehly and Shivy (1998), and Russell et al. (1998). *Journal of Counseling Psychology, 45,* 46–49.

Wampold, B. E., Ankarlo, G., Mondin, G., Trinidad-Carrillo, M., Baumler, B., & Prater, K. (1995). Social skills of and social environments produced by different Holland types: A social perspective on person-environment fit model. *Journal of Counseling Psychology, 42,* 365–379.

Wampold, B. E., Davis, B., Good, R. H. III (1990). Hypothesis validity of clinical research. *Journal of Consulting and Clinical Psychology, 58,* 360–367.

Wampold, B. E., & Drew, C. J. (1990). *Theory and application of statistics.* New York: McGraw-Hill.

Wampold, B. E., & Freund, R. D. (1987). Use of multiple regression in counseling psychology research: A flexible data-analytic strategy. *Journal of Counseling Psychology, 34,* 372–382.

Wampold, B. E., & Freund, R. D. (1991). Statistical issues in clinical research. In M. Hersen, A. E. Kazdin, & A. S. Bellack (Eds.), *The clinical psychology handbook,* 2nd ed. Elmsford, NY: Pergamon Press.

Wampold, B. E., & Furlong, M. J. (1981a). The heuristics of visual inference. *Behavioral Assessment, 3,* 79–82.

Wampold, B. E., & Furlong, M. J. (1981b). Randomization tests in single-subject designs: Illustrative examples. *Journal of Behavioral Assessment, 3,* 329–341.

Wampold, B. E., & Kim, K. H. (1989). Sequential analysis applied to counseling process and outcomes: A case study revisited. *Journal of Counseling Psychology, 36,* 357-364.

Wampold, B. E., Mondin, G. W., Moody, M., Stich, F., Benson, K., & Ahn, H. (1997). A meta-analysis of outcome studies comparing bonafide psychotherapies: Empirically, "All Must Have Prizes." *Psychological Bulletin, 122,* 203-215.

Wampold, B. E., & Poulin, K. L. (1992). Counseling research methods: Art and artifact. In S. D. Brown & R. W. Lent, *Handbook of counseling psychology,* 2nd ed. (pp. 71-109). New York: Wiley.

Wampold, B. E., & White, T. B. (1985). Research themes in counseling psychology: A cluster analysis of citations in the process and outcomes section of the *Journal of Counseling Psychology. Journal of Counseling Psychology, 32,* 123-126.

Wampold, B. E., & Worsham, N. L. (1986). Randomization tests for multiple-baseline designs. *Behavioral Assessment, 8,* 135-143.

Warchal, P., & Southern, S. (1986). Perceived importance of counseling needs among adult students. *Journal of College Student Personnel, 27,* 43-48.

Watkins, C. E., Jr. (1994). On hope, promise, and possibility in counseling psychology, or some simple, but meaningful observations about our specialty. *The Counseling Psychologist, 22,* 315-334.

Watkins, C. E., Jr. (1997). (Ed.) *Handbook of psychotherapy supervision.* New York: Wiley.

Watkins, C. E., Lopez, F. G., Campbell, V. L., & Himmell, C. D. (1986). Contemporary counseling psychology: Results of a national survey. *Journal of Counseling Psychology, 33,* 301-309.

Watson, J. C., & Rennie, D. L. (1994). Qualitative analysis of clients' subjective experience of significant moments during the exploration of problematic reactions. *Journal of Counseling Psychology, 41,* 500-509.

Webb, E. J., Campbell, D. T., Schwartz, R. C., & Sechrest, L. (1966). *Unobtrusive measures: Nonreactive research in the social sciences.* Chicago: Rand McNally.

Webb, E. T., Campbell, D. T., Schwartz, R. D., Sechrest, L., & Grove, J. B. (1981). *Nonreactive measures in the social sciences.* Boston: Houghton Mifflin.

Webster-Stratton, C. (1988). Mothers' and fathers' perceptions of child deviance: Roles of parent and child behaviors and parent adjustment. *Journal of Consulting and Clinical Psychology, 56,* 909-915.

Wellman, F. (1967). A conceptual framework for the derivation of guidance objectives and outcome criteria: Preliminary statement. In J. M. Whiteley (Ed.), *Research in counseling: Evaluation and refocus* (pp. 153-174). Columbus, OH: Merrill.

White, M., & Epston, D. (1990). An overview of the state of the art: What should be expected in current family therapy research. In L. C. Wynne (Ed.), *The state of the art in family therapy research: Controversies and recommendations* (pp. 249-266). New York: Family Process Press.

White, M. D., & White, C. A. (1981). Involuntarily committed patients' constituted right to refuse treatment. *American Psychologist, 36,* 953-962.

White, O. R. (1974). *The "split middle": A "quickie" method for trend estimation.* Seattle: University of Washington, Experimental Education Unit, Child Development and Mental Retardation Center.

Whiteley, J. M. (1984). A historical perspective on the development of counseling psychology as a profession. In S. D. Brown & R. W. Lent (Eds.), *Handbook of counseling psychology* (pp. 3-55). New York: Wiley.

Wiley, M. O., & Ray, P. B. (1986). Counseling supervision by developmental level. *Journal of Counseling Psychology, 33,* 439-445.

Willett, J. B. (1988). Questions and answers in the measurement of change. In E. Z. Rothkopf (Ed.), *Review of research in education (vol. 15)* (pp. 345-422). Washington, DC: American Educational Research Association.

Willett, J. B., Ayoub, C. C., & Robinson, D. (1991). Using growth modeling to examine systematic differences in growth: An example of change in the functioning of families at risk of maladaptive parenting, child abuse, or neglect. *Journal of Consulting and Clinical Psychology, 59,* 38–47.

Williams, J. E. (1962). Changes in self and other perceptions following brief educational-vocational counseling. *Journal of Counseling Psychology, 9,* 18–30.

Wills, T. A. (1987). Help seeking as a coping mechanism. In C. R. Snyder & C. E. Ford (Eds.), *Coping with negative life events: Clinical and psychological perspectives* (pp. 19–50). New York: Plenum.

Wilson, L. S., & Ranft, V. A. (1993). The state of ethical training for counseling psychology doctoral students. *The Counseling Psychologist, 21,* 445–456.

Winston, Roger B., Jr. (1985). A suggested procedure for determining order of authorship in research publications. *Journal of Counseling and Development, 63,* 515–519.

Wolcott, H. F. (1992). Posturing in qualitative inquiry. In M. D. LeCompte, W. L. Millroy, & J. Preissle (Eds.), *The handbook of qualitative research in education* (pp. 3–52). San Diego: Academic Press.

Wolcott, H. F. (1994). *Transforming qualitative data: Description, analysis, and interpretation.* Thousand Oaks, CA: Sage.

Wolpe, J. (1969). *The practice of behavior therapy.* New York: Pergamon Press.

Worthen, B., Sanders, J., & Fitzpatrick, J. (1997). *Program evaluation: Alternative approaches and practical guidelines* (2nd ed.). White Plains, NY: Longman Publishers.

Worthen, V., & McNeill, B. W. (1996). A phenomenological investigation of good supervision events. *Journal of Counseling Psychology, 43,* 25–34.

Worthington, E. L., Jr. (1984). Empirical investigation of supervision of counselors as they gain experience. *Journal of Counseling Psychology, 31,* 63–75.

Worthington, E. L., McCullough, M. E., Shortz, J. L., Mindes, E. J., Sandage, S. J., & Chartrand, J. M. (1995). Can couples assessment and feedback improve relationships? Assessment as a brief relationship enhancement procedure. *Journal of Counseling Psychology, 42,* 466–475.

Worthington, E. L., Jr., & Roehlke, H. J. (1979). Effective supervision as perceived by beginning counselors-in-training. *Journal of Counseling Psychology, 26,* 64–73.

Worthington, E. L., & Stern, A. (1985). Effects of supervision and supervisor degree level and gender on supervisory relationship. *Journal of Counseling Psychology, 32,* 252–262.

Worthington, R. L., & Atkinson, D. R. (1996). Effects of perceived etiology attribution similarity on client ratings of counselor credibility. *Journal of Counseling Psychology, 43,* 423–429.

Wrenn, R. L. (1985). The evolution of Anne Roe. *Journal of Counseling and Development, 63,* 267–275.

Wundt, W. (1904). *Principles of physiological psychology.* New York: Macmillan.

Wundt, W. (1916). *Elements of folk psychology.* London: Allen & Unwin. (Original work published 1900).

Yalom, I. D. (1985). *The theory and practice of group psychotherapy* (3rd ed.). New York: Basic Books.

Yalom, I. D. (1995). *The theory and practice of group psychotherapy* (4th ed.). New York: Basic Books.

Yates, A. J. (1958). The application of learning theory to the treatment of tics. *Journal of Abnormal and Social Psychology, 56,* 175–182.

Yee, A. H., Fairchild, H. H., Weizmann, F., & Wyatt, G. E. (1993). Addressing psychology's problem with race. *American Psychologist, 48,* 1132–1140.

Zane, N. W. S. (1989). Change mechanisms in placebo procedures: Effects of suggestion, social demand, and contingent success on improvement in treatment. *Journal of Counseling Psychology, 36,* 234–243.

Zimbardo, P. G., & Ebbesen, E. B. (1970). *Influencing attitudes and changing behavior.* Reading, MA: Addison-Wesley.

AUTHOR INDEX

SUBJECT INDEX

TO THE OWNER OF THIS BOOK:

We hope that you have found *Research Design in Counseling,* 2nd Edition, useful. So that this book can be improved in a future edition, would you take the time to complete this sheet and return it? Thank you.

School and address: ————————————————————————————————

Department: ——————————————————————————————————————

Instructor's name: ————————————————————————————————

1. What I like most about this book is: ——————————————————

——

——

2. What I like least about this book is: —————————————————

——

——

3. My general reaction to this book is: —————————————————

——

4. The name of the course in which I used this book is: ———————

——

5. Were all of the chapters of the book assigned for you to read? —————

  If not, which ones weren't? ———————————————————————

6. In the space below, or on a separate sheet of paper, please write specific suggestions for improving this book and anything else you'd care to share about your experience in using the book.

——

——

——

——

Optional:

Your name: _____ Date: _____

May Wadsworth quote you, either in promotion for *Research Design in Counseling,* 2nd Edition, or in future publishing ventures?

Yes: _____ No: _____

Sincerely,

P. Paul Heppner
Dennis Kivlighan
Bruce E. Wampold

FOLD HERE

FOLD HERE